P. B. DOVE

COMBAT READY IT AND PIE

CYBER SECURITY FOR SMALL MEDIUM BUSINESS AND BUSINESS PERPETUALLY IMPROVE EVERYTHING

COMBAT READY IT AND PIE

Cyber Security for Small Medium Business and Perpetual Improvement Everywhere

© P B. Dove 2015

All rights reserved. Apart from any fair dealing for the purposes of research or private study, or criticism, or review, as permitted by the Copyright Designs and Patents Act 1988, no part of this publication may be reproduced, stored or transmitted in any form or by any means, except with the prior permission in writing of the publisher, or in the case of reprographic reproduction, in accordance with the terms of the licences issued by the Copyright Licensing Agency. Enquiries for permission to reproduce material outside those terms should be directed to the publisher.

Combat Ready Girl Soldier Cover Design by Dean Sherriff
Copyright © 2015 Naed Ffirrehs

DISCLAIMER

The book does not seek to dissuade companies from pursuing cyber security best practices, but encourages companies to seek deeper solutions. It makes suggestions on how to deploy people and tools to ready a company against cyber security attacks and reduce the likelihood of infiltration by adversaries. It does not distract from governments initiatives and regulations, which seek to protect National Critical Infrastructures against Nation State adversaries. This book is designed to provide information as the situation stands on 7th July 2015 only. This information is provided and sold with the knowledge that the publisher and author do not offer any legal or other professional advice, it is for guidance only. When a need for any such expertise is required, please consult with a suitable professional. This book does not contain all information available on the subject. Information within has been sourced from government websites, court records, established fraud agencies, national and international press organisations and enforcement actions and website research. The book names some vendors' products purely as examples of available software, services or hardware, and it is impossible to name all the vendors in the world that may offer similar, cheaper or better features or services, companies therefore should satisfy themselves of an appropriate buying decision around infrastructure and cyber security products. The reader should seek proposals and budgetary costs for hardware, software and professional services independently. Budgetary costs referred to in this book are purely indicative for descriptive and entertainment purposes only guide prices that are quoted are subject to change depending on company, market sector, size and location. This book has not been created to be specific to any individuals or organisation's situation or needs. Every effort has been made to make this book as accurate as possible. However, there may be typographical and technical content errors. Therefore, this book should serve only as a general guide and not as the ultimate source of subject information. This book contains information that might be dated, and is intended only to educate and entertain.

The author and publisher shall have no liability or responsibility to any person or entity regarding any loss, or damage incurred, or alleged to have been incurred, directly or indirectly, by the information contained in this book. All parties concerned with this book are not liable for its contents, in printed or digital matter. Each company is different and the advice and strategies contained herein may not be suitable for your situation. While the best efforts have been used in preparing this book, the author and publisher make no representations or warranties of any kind and assume no liabilities of any kind with respect to the accuracy or completeness of the contents, and specifically disclaim any implied warranties of merchantability or fitness of use for a particular purpose. Neither the author nor the publisher shall be held liable or responsible to any person or entity with respect to any loss or incidental or consequential damages caused (or alleged to have been caused), directly, or, indirectly, by the information or programmes of action contained herein. The author shall not be liable for any losses as a result of reliance on information provided. The author assumes no liability for parallel or simultaneous ideas and solutions, attribution and citations have been provided where possible. Any innuendo, which may be attributed to any party mentioned, shall be deemed a comment based on facts truly stated. Derogatory or contentious statements made in error will be swiftly removed upon request and will be accompanied by a posted apology if requested. The information in this book is out of date by the time it is published and will be subject to annual change amendments will be included in the next annual version. You should seek the services of a competent professional before beginning any security improvement programme. Any likeness to actual persons, either living or dead, is strictly coincidental. You hereby agree to be bound by this disclaimer, or you may return this book within the one week time period from date of purchase for a full refund. The authors, owners, and publisher disclaim liability for any errors or omissions. The reader accepts all risks associated with the use of the contents of this book.

The author does not look to distinguish between the individuals, person(s), countries or entities initiating these types of attacks, or the underlying motivation for their actions. These actions may or may not include the legitimate use of information gathering techniques for wider public benefit, or, geopolitical reasons.

TRADEMARKS AND LICENSES

All products mentioned in this book are trademarks of their respective owners. The information in this book is provided on an as-is informational basis. The following trademarks and registered names are under license of the author:

SHAZOPS™, Combat Ready IT©, Perpetual Improvement Everywhere (PIE)®, Piology©, Piosophy©, Auditology©, DocOps®, The Internet Authority™, CRITTERS©. DRIPPS Transition, TIMPY, Licenses for these brands are available via the Combatreadyit.com or www.pie.institute websites.

INVENTIONS

The following words are the inventions of the author; Cyberphobia, Cyberganda Cybrid Wars, Perpetual Improvement Everywhere (PIE), Piology, Piosophy, Auditology, Wraithology, InternetNew, Combat Ready Malware Harm Index, FREXAGON, All Sorts of Things (ASOTS), Via Ferrata Reporting, Omniocular, Emotional Quotient Unification and Intelligence Programming (EQUIP), Risk Ignition Points (RIPS). JAMAICA (Just Action! Make Asks of IT Instantly Chargeable and Available), Roboshoring. Restoration of Essential Data Only (REDO), ADAPT (Admin, Detective, Available, Perpetual, Technical Controls.)

DEDICATION

This book would not have been written without the unwavering love and support from my wife, she gave me the space to craft the book. Without her laughter, leadership, intelligence, deep insights, and daily inspiration, I would not have the motivation to complete this task.

To my eternally loved mother and father, son, sisters and family relatives: thank you for being supportive, for your motivation and kind thoughts. Love, hugs and kisses.

To my mentors, and my students: I warmly thank you for putting up with me. The Old Gang Dixie, Simon, and Reg)

Special thanks go to all those wonderful friends and teams I worked within IT over the last 30 years (Nick and Catherine, Dean, Elenita and Sequoia, Jasmine, Giffin and Alana, Scott, Cath and Richard, Stratton and Carolyn, Patricia and Constantine, Captain Ed, Beau, Bill S, Simon and Lisa M, Marc and Vanessa and Ginerva, Karine, Fliss, Tim, Florent, Randy, Sauro, Bert, Dr. Nick!) thank you for fantastic displays of comradeship, and the memories of many slapstick moments!

To my clients, and the coffee support system team members at Starbucks™: I told you so! Acknowledgements to Scott Ambler, Fergus at OBASHI, Arthur D.Little, McKinseys, Boston Consulting Group, M Quinter at UPC, Michael at First Edit and www.prowriter.com **Finally a massive THANKS to N.Higgins: for technical and sanity checks, and constant friendship.**

BIOGRAPHY

My experience has been grounded in Management Consultancy, IT Operations and Security for thirty plus years. As an engineer, at the age of 22 I developed the Message Waiting Lamp on telephones. I have held various CIO and CTO positions from the age of 24! I have had two strikes at pioneering and still enjoy the cutting edge of technology and still retained as an advisor to several start-ups and enterprise boards. Clients believe my five strengths are: humour, honesty, technical leadership, communicating and strategy. They also say I have uncanny super caster abilities. I travel a great deal and have held operations, project management and process consultant roles in several companies and tenures in forty-four countries. I have spoken at numerous conferences and also educate graduates as a visiting lecturer. I have been engaged by Banks and Venture Capitalists, Credit Card Providers, Military, Government, Telecoms, Cloud Service Providers, Mobile and Technology sectors. My Architecture skills were honed by designing forty-two global reach Internet and VOIP networks. I have project managed billion dollar projects and crafted and managed IT Service outsourced contracts. I turn around ailing companies and as the son of a Scots accountant have saved organisations half a billion dollars in realised cost savings! Pictures on the wall; sixteen IT Certifications for IT Security, ITIL, VOIP, IPTV, Fibre Optic and Cable Networks, Database and Application Design, Systems and Storage, Mobile Coding and Development, ERP and Business Intelligence. Recently I have designed Cloud and Hybrid Data Centres in six countries and become an IOS mobile developer! My mother has no idea what I have been doing for the last quarter of a century!

WHATS IN THE BOOK

This book is in four parts:

- **The first part** reviews the Cyber security Problem and the Root Causes created by an unsafe Internet. Tracing the evolution of cyber-warfare and its migration into Cybrid attacks. There are sections on how hackers attack vectors. A Malware Harm List and Extraordinary and Existential Risks are reviewed.

- **The second part** Security root causes are analysed. An InternetNew solution. Components make up a defensive in depth architecture that can be used in a SMB Hybrid data centre and Public Cloud. Technical components that make up security RIDPOINTS and indicative costs

- **The third part** looks at solutions aimed at executives and team members It describes a Combat Ready IT organisation and how SMBs needs to re-think and re-position operations, security policies and auditing strategies to get ready for the expected catastrophes in the next year - or so.

- **The fourth part** deals with **Perpetual Improvement Everywhere (PIE)**. It deals with a Think Local, Grow Local business approach and how to shore up IT defences in time of conflict. It provides budgetary costs and suggests a "Perpetual Organisation" and Roles and Responsibilities

- **The Appendices** includes a history of malware through the years, security standards, a security policy, and proposes additions to the Internet Big Paper. The acronyms used are fully explained in plain English within the body of the text.

THIS BOOK IS AIMED AT

- **Pioneers and Partnerships** - are prime hacker targets because they are the creative powerhouses of every country's economy. This is in part, due to of the monetary value of data. Data is the new global currency, Intellectual Property is sought after because its data is high in value, small to steal, and relevant to an adversary.

- A **Small and Mid-size Business (SMB)** is a business which, due to its size, has different IT requirements than do large enterprises, and whose IT resources (budget and team members) are often constrained. Gartner defines SMBs by the number of employees and annual revenue attained. The attribute used most often is the number of employees; small businesses are defined as organisations with fewer than 100 employees; midsize enterprises are those organisations with 100 to 999 employees. The second most popular benchmark used to define the SMB market is annual revenue: small business is defined as organisations with less than $50 million in annual revenue; midsize enterprise is defined as organisations that make more than $50 million, but less than $1 billion in annual revenue.[1]

- A **Line of Business (LOB)** is a division of an enterprise with board oversight and builds new products developed by R&D. Unshackled from red tape; they are able to create Shadow IT departments without overarching compliance. Countries and competition employ hackers to steal this valuable Intellectual Property.

CONTENTS

1 ROOT CAUSES - SCOPE OF CYBER ATTACKS — 11
    1.1 IDENTITY THEFT — 12
    1.2 OPERATING SYSTEMS — 13
    1.3 NOT SO SMART PHONES — 16
    1.4 ORGANISED CRIME — 17
    1.5 COUNTRIES HACKED — 19
    1.6 BAITING — 22
    1.7 HEALTH — 23
    1.8 FOOD — 24
    1.9 BANKS — 26
    1.10 TELCOS AND ISPs — 27
    1.11 DDOS — 28
    1.12 INTERNET OF THINGS — 29
    1.13 UTILITIES — 30
    1.14 WEBSITES IMPACTED — 30
    1.15 RETAIL — 32
    1.16 CLOUD SERVICE PROVIDERS (CSP's) — 33
    1.17 COMPONENT ATTACKS — 35
    1.18 GENERAL SKULLDUGGERY — 36
    1.19 HAVING A WHALE OF A TIME — 37
    1.20 A NEW SAVVY GENERATION — 38
    1.21 INFORMATION LEMMINGS — 39
    1.22 STEPCHECK — 41

2 ROOT CAUSE - SYSTEMIC DISINTEGRATION — 42
    2.1 TECHNIQUES — 42
    2.2 BACKDOORS — 44
    2.3 BOTNETS — 45
    2.4 BRICKING — 47
        2.4.1.1 SOFT BRICK — 48
        2.4.1.2 HARD BRICK — 48
    2.5 COOKIES — 48

2.6 CROSS SITE SCRIPTING	51
2.7 DISTRIBUTED DENIAL OF SERVICE (DDOS)	52
2.7.1.1 INCREASING IN STRENGTH	53
2.7.1.2 HTTP FLOODS	54
2.7.1.3 SYN FLOODS	54
2.7.1.4 UDP FLOODS	54
2.7.1.5 REFLECTION DDOS	55
2.7.1.6 MILLIONS OF DEVICES VULNERABLE	56
2.8 DOWNLOADER	56
2.9 DOMAIN NAME SERVICE (DNS)	57
2.9.1.1 ROGUE DNS SERVER	57
2.9.2 DNS CACHE POISONING	58
2.10 INFORMATION STEAL	59
2.11 INSIDER THREATS	60
2.12 MEMORY BASED	62
2.12.1.1 DIRECT ACTION	62
2.12.1.2 MEMORY RESIDENT	62
2.13 MAN IN THE MIDDLE	62
2.13.1.1 MAN IN THE BROWSER	63
2.13.1.2 MAN IN THE PHONE	63
2.13.1.3 FREAKY BEAST HEARTBLEED	63
2.14 MOBILE HACKING	64
2.14.1.1 IPHONE	65
2.14.1.2 ANDROID	66
2.14.1.3 BLACKBERRY	66
2.14.1.4 MICROSOFT	67
2.14.1.5 BLACKPHONE	68
2.14.1.6 SYMBIAN OS	68
2.15 NETWORK ATTACKS	68
2.15.1.1 EAVESDROPPING	69
2.15.1.2 IP SPOOFING	69
2.15.1.3 PASSWORD BASED ATTACKS	69
2.15.1.4 SNIFFER ATTACK	70
2.15.1.5 INSIDER ATTACK	70
2.16 PHISHING	70

2.16.1.1 SPEAR PHISHING	71
2.16.1.2 PHARMING	71
2.17 ROOT KIT	73
2.18 RANSOMEWARE	73
2.19 SPAM -SPAM -SPAM -SPAM	74
2.20 SPYWARE	75
2.20.1.1 UPDATE MUTATION	76
2.20.2 POLYMORPHISM[66]	76
2.20.3 PROGRAMMATIC MUTATION	76
2.21 SQL INJECTION	77
2.22 TARGETED MALWARE	78
2.23 THEY NEVER STOP THEY NEVER DIE	79
2.24 VULNERABILITIES/ZERO DAY EXPLOITS	80
2.24.1.1 HEARTBLEED	81
2.25 WORMS	82
2.25.1.1 HAVE YOU GOT EMAIL WORMS?	82
2.25.2 INTERNET WORMS	83
2.25.3 NETWORK WORMS	83
2.25.4 MESSAGING WORMS	83
2.25.5 MULTIPLE VECTOR WORMS	83
2.26 COMBAT READY MALWARE HARM INDEX	83
2.27 STEPCHECK	85
3 ROOT CAUSE - VENDORS	**86**
3.1 EXECUTIVES FIDUCIARY DUTIES	88
3.2 THE COST OF A DATA BREACH	92
3.3 DATA BREACH COSTS	92
3.4 TIME IS NOT YOUR FRIEND	95
3.5 BREACH = EXPENSIVE	95
3.6 REGULATOR IN ABSENTIA	97
3.7 VENDOR SOFTWARE VULNERABILITIES	100
3.8 ZERO DAY VULNERABILITIES	101
3.9 DOES AUDITING HELP STOP ATTACKS?	104
3.10 THE FUTURE OF AUDITING	107
3.11 LIABILITIES	108

3.12 NEW BUGS MEET OLD BUGS	110
3.13 STEPCHECK	112

4 ROOT CAUSES – IT'S THE USERS FAULT!   114
4.1 EDUCATION	117
4.2 THATS NOT MY NAME	118
4.3 TECHNOLOGY VALUE CENTRES	119
4.4 STEPCHECK	119

5 ROOT CAUSES – RISKY BUSINESS   121
5.1 OUR ANCESTORS WERE SMART	122
5.2 BBC-PR	122
5.3 THE DEFINITION OF CYBRID	126
5.4 COMBAT READY BUSINESS	129
5.5 SAME PROBLEMS DIFFERENT WARS	130
5.6 PRODUCT RE-ENGINEERING	130
5.7 PROCUREMENT	131

6 ROOT CAUSES - EXISTENTIAL RISKS   136
6.1 STEPCHECK	138

7 ROOT CAUSES - AVOID ADVERSARIES   139
7.1 ADVERSARIES AND ADVANCED PERSISTENT THREATS	140
7.2 VERDANT YOUTH	140
7.3 INSIDERS	141
7.4 ORGANISED	142
7.5 DETERMINED	143
7.6 WHITE HATS - ETHICAL HACKERS	143
7.7 CERTIFIED PROFESSIONALS	144
7.8 INFORMATION SECURITY CERTIFICATIONS	145
7.9 TRAINING	146
7.10 STEPCHECK	147

8 INTERNET BASIC TRAINING   148
8.1 ANATOMY OF A COMPUTER	149
8.2 SERVERS AND BLADES	149
8.2.1.1 VMs VERSUS CONTAINERS (DM's)	151
8.3 STORAGE	152

8.4 DESKTOP AS A SERVICE	152
8.5 A ROUTER IS NOT A WOODWORKING TOOL	156
8.5.1.1 SOFTWARE DEFINED NETWORKING	158
8.6 NFV	160
8.7 SWITCHES	161
8.8 CABLE ROUTING OR WIRELESS (CROW) DECISION	163
8.9 WAN CIRCUITS	165
8.10 WI FI	166
8.11 WIFI ENCRYPTION	169
8.12 ANATOMY OF A MOBILE AND TABLET	170
8.13 YOU SAY ISO AND I SAY OSI	171
8.14 FOUR LAYER MODEL	175
8.15 SIP	176
8.15.1.1 SIP TRUNKING	178
8.16 SOFTWARE APPLICATIONS	179
8.17 HARDWARE APPLICATIONS - ROBOTICA	181
8.18 HARD ROBOTS	181
8.19 ROBOSHORING	182
8.20 SMB ADVANTAGE	183
8.21 INDUSTRIAL ROBOTICA	184
8.22 SCADA (aka ICS)	185
8.23 RESHORING, OUTSOURCING ROBOSHORING AND MANUFACTURING	188
8.24 INTERNET COMMUNICATIONS	189
8.25 IP ADDRESSES	189
8.26 IPV6 ADDRESSING	190
8.27 GEOGRAPHIC IPv6	191
8.28 ENUM	192
8.29 QUALITY OF SERVICE (QoS)	193
8.30 MOBILE IPv6	195
8.31 IPSEC	196
9.31.1.1 IPSec TECHY STUFF	197
8.31.1.2 MILITARY IPV6	199
8.31.1.3 IPv6 BUGS	200

8.31.1.4 INTERNET OF THINGS (V6)	200
8.32 CLOUD	202
8.33 EVERY MARKETING IDEA AS A SERVICE	205
8.23.1.1 INFRASTRUCTURE AS A SERVICE (IaaS)	206
8.33.1.2 PLATFORM AS A SERVICE (PaaS):	206
8.33.1.3 SOFTWARE AS A SERVICE (SaaS):	206
8.33.1.4 IDENTITY AS A SERVICE (IDaaS)	207
8.33.1.5 STORAGE AS A SERVICE (STaaS) - vStorage	208
8.33.1.6 DESKTOP AS A SERVICE (DTAAS)	209
8.33.1.7 DATA AS A SERVICE (DaaS)	209
8.33.1.8 SOFTWARE AS A SERVICE BUSINESS INTELLIGENCE (SaaSBI)	210
8.33.1.9 BIG DATA AS A SERVICE (BDaaS)	210
8.33.1.10 vSECURITY AS A SERVICE (SECaaS)	211
8.33.1.11 COMMUNICATIONS AS A SERVICE (CAAS)	212
8.33.1.12 MOBILITY AS A SERVICE (MAAS)	213
8.34 CLOUD PRODUCTS AND BRANDS	214
8.34.1.1 APPLICATIONS	214
8.34.1.2 PLATFORMS	214
8.34.1.3 INFRASTRUCTURE	214
8.34.1.4 VOICE OVER IP AND SIP	215
8.34.1.5 CLOUD SERVICES ORCHESTRATION	215
8.35 STEPCHECK	216
9 VOIP HOW 'Hi' TRAVELS THE INTERNET	**218**
9.1.1.1 MOBILE CALL	218
9.1.1.2 WAN TRANSMISSION	220
9.1.1.3 OSS	220
9.1.1.4 BSS	220
9.1.1.5 CORE INTERNET	222
9.1.1.6 REMOTE TELCO	224
9.1.1.7 HYBRID SMB CLOUD (*ALTERNATIVE*)	224
9.1.1.8 PUBLIC CLOUD (*ALTERNATIVE*)	225
9.1.1.9 SUCCESSFUL CALL COMPLETION	225
10 ROOT CAUSE - INTERNET	**226**
10.1 DOMAIN NAME SERVICE	227

10.2 DNS THREATS	228
10.3 BGP	229
10.4 IP TRANSIT AND IP PEERING	230
10.5 INTERNETNEW - WHAT WOULD IT LOOK LIKE?	237
10.6 HOTHOUSE	240
10.7 INTERNETNEW INITIATIVES FOR SMBs	242
10.8 INTERNETNEW SECURITY	242
10.9 IP FIT FOR PURPOSE	243
10.10 MOBILITY	244
10.11 INTERNETNEW TESTBEDS	244
10.12 TELCOS AND MOBILE SERVICE PROVIDERS	245
10.13 DOMINION INTERNETS	247
10.14 COUNTRY OVERSTRATA	249
10.15 THE LAST MILE RACE	252
10.16 INTERNET GOVERNANCE - LEGITIMACY AND SOVEREIGNTY	253
10.17 THE INTERNET AUTHORITY	255
10.18 AN ECONOMIC MODEL FOR INTERNETNEW	258
10.19 STEPCHECK	262

11 RIDPOINTS

	263
11.1 RIDPOINTS – RISK MANAGEMENT	264
11.2 PROCESS IS DEAD LONG LIVE CRAFTFLOW	265
11.3 VIA FERRATA COMMUNICATION	267
11.4 RISK MANAGEMENT	268
11.5 RIPS	271
11.6 ALE!	272
11.7 SECURITY QUOTIENT	273
11.8 RISK STANDARDS	275
11.9 VERTICAL RISK	276
11.10 GENERIC RISK	276
11.11 APPLYING RISK	277
11.12 SITUATIONAL AWARENESS	278
11.13 MAKING RISK PERPETUAL	279

11.13.1 COST OF SERVICE	279
11.13.1.1 CMdB	280
11.13.1.2 ITAM AND SAM	281
11.13.1.3 OBASHI™	282
11.13.1.4 SHAZOPS™	285
11.13.1.5 SHAZOPS™ ATTACK AND THREAT LOOPS	286
11.14 DISCIPLINED AGILE DEVELOPMENT	287
11.15 VIA FERRATA RISK REGISTER	291
11.16 RIDPOINTS - IDENTITY	293
11.16.1.1 IAM INITIATIVES	294
11.17 AUTHENTICATE	296
11.18 EMAIL USERNAMES & PASSPHRASES	298
11.18.1.1 EMAILS:	298
11.18.1.2 LOGONS:	298
11.19 CREATING A PASSPHRASE	300
12 RIDPOINTS - DEFENCE IN DEPTH (DOMINO)	303
12.1 PHYSICAL SECURITY	304
12.1.1.1 RECEPTIONS	309
12.1.1.2 SHARED OFFICES	309
12.1.1.3 URBAN OFFICES	310
12.1.1.4 FOOD AND WATERING HOLES	311
12.1.1.5 LIGHTING	311
12.1.1.6 ELECTRONIC LOCKS	311
12.1.1.7 SAFE WORDS	311
12.1.1.8 I'VE GOT THE POWER	312
12.1.1.9 LEGITIMATE SURVEILLANCE	312
12.1.1.10 SECURE TRASH	313
12.1.1.11 EXTERNAL DUCTS	313
12.1.1.12 FIRE	313
12.1.1.13 POST ROOMS	314
12.1.1.14 PRODUCTION FACTORY AND DELIVERIES	314
12.2 DOMINO – THE SECURITY POLICY	314
12.3 DOMINO – CLOUD SEPARATION	315
12.4 DOMINO – DATA CENTRE	316

12.5 MIGRATION AND PROJECT TRANSITION	318
12.5.1.1 D.R.I.P.P.S. PROJECT TRANSITION TASKS	319
12.6 DATA CENTRE EVOLUTION	323
12.7 COMBAT READY IT DATA CENTRE DESIGNS	325
12.8 OVERGROUND vs. UNDERGROUND	328
12.9 PRODUCTION BUNKERS	329
12.10 DATA BUNKERS	330
12.11 BRING YOUR OWN BUNKER	330
12.12 DATA CENTRE COSTS	331
12.13 CONTAINER BASED DATA CENTRE	332
12.14 SPARES	333
12.15 DOMINO – BUDGETARY ESTIMATES	333
12. 16 DOMINO– PERIMETER SECURITY	334
12.17 BORDER AND BOUNDARY ROUTERS	334
12.18 FIREWALLS	335
12.18.1.1 SOFTWARE DEFINED FIREWALL	338
12.18.1.2 BITW (Bump in the Wire)	338
12.18.1.3 Web Application Firewalls (WAFs)	338
12.18.1.4 IDS's (INTRUSION DETECTION SYSTEMS)	339
12.18.1.5 IDS Signature based	339
12.18.1.6 IDS Statistical Response based	339
12.18.1.7 IDS Application based	340
12.18.1.8 IPS (Intrusion Prevention System)	343
12.18.1.9 WIRELESS INTRUSION PREVENTION SYSTEMS (WIPS)	343
12.18.1.10 DMZs (Demilitarised Zones)	343
12.18.1.11 DATA LOSS PREVENTION	344
12.18.1.12 WIDE (A) AREA NETWORKS AND CIRCUITS	344
12.18.1.13 DATA CABLING INTEGRITY	344
12.19 DOMINO DEFENCE IN DEPTH – INTERNAL NETWORK	345
12.20 NETWORK ACCESS CONTROL (NAC) AND ENDPOINTS	345
12.21 DOMINO DEFENCE IN DEPTH - HARDENING	346
12.22 DOMINO DEFENCE IN DEPTH – ANTI VIRUS	347
12.23 DOMINO DEFENCE IN DEPTH – INCIDENT RESPONSE	348

12.24 INCIDENT RESPONSE	349
12.24.1.1 SIX STEPS OF INCIDENT RESPONSE	351
12.24.2 PATCH MANAGEMENT	357
12.24.3 DATA SECURITY	357
12.24.4 SECURE STORAGE	358
12.24.5 INFORMATION ASSET AND REDO	358
12.24.6 INFORMATION TAXONOMY	358
12.24.7 DATABASES	359
12.25 RIDPOINTS – PERIMETER DEFENCE	361
12.25.1.1 ENDPOINTS	361
13 THE CLOUD AS THE NEW PERIMETER	**363**
13.1.1 TYPES OF CLOUDS	364
13.1.2 CLOUD SECURITY GOTCHAS	364
13.1.3 CLOUD SLA	365
13.1.4 BULLETPROOF NETWORK	365
13.1.5 VMWARE	366
13.1.6 VIRTUAL SAN	369
13.1.7 TEAM MEMBER RATIOS	370
13.2 HYBRID CLOUD	370
13.2.1 CLOUDIFYING APPLICATIONS	371
13.2.2 HADOOP 2 SPARK	372
13.3 CLOUD SECURITY?	373
14 RIDPOINTS OPERATIONS NERVE CENTRE	**374**
14.1 OMNIOCULAR MONITORING	374
14.2 REAL TIME MONITORING	375
14.3 CLOUD MONITORING	375
14.3.1 FORENSICS	376
14.3.2 VULNERABILITIES	376
14.3.3 PENETRATION TEST	378
15 RIDPOINTS - IT FRAMEWORKS AND REGULATIONS	**379**
15.1 SECURITY BEST PRACTICES	379
15.2 ITIL®	380
15.3 RIDPOINTS - TRAINING	381
15.3.1.1 TEAM MEMBERS	381

15.3.1.2 SECURITY TOOL BOX TALKS	382
15.3.1.3 GAMIFICATION OF APPLICATIONS	382
15.3.1.4 SECURITY APPRENTISHIPS	383

16 RIDPOINTS - SECURITY MANAGEMENT 385

16.1 CONTROLS	385
16.2 SECURITY INFORMATION EVENT MANAGEMENT (SIEM/SIAM)	386
16.3 METRICS	388
16.4 POLICIES	389
16.5 CMMI APPLICATION MATURITY	392
16.6 CMMI SECURITY GUIDES	393
16.7 BUSINESS CONTINUITY AND DISASTER RECOVERY (BCDR)	394
16.8 THE TAI-CHI OF BCDR	395
16.9 SNAPSHOTS	396
16.10 COST OF DOWNTIME	396
16.11 CLOUD OPEX	397
16.12 STEPCHECK	398

17 SLICES OF PIE 400

17.1 GET PERPETUAL	400
17.2 THE CONSUMERISATION OF IT	401

18 PERPETUAL IMPROVEMENT EVERYWHERE 403

18.1 PREDICT THE BLACK MINUTE	404
18.2 THE SEVEN SLICES	406
18.3 GET PROGRESSIVE	406
18.4 THINK PREVENTATIVE	407
18.5 ACT PREDICTIVE	407
18.6 TEAM CULTURE BUILT ON SELF DETERMINATION	408
18.7 HOLACRACY	409
18.8 SOCIOCRACY	409
18.9 HULA HOOP ORGANISATION	410
18.9.1.1 5 x 5 x 5	411
18.9.1.2 THURSDAYS	412
18.9.1.3 DRESS CODE	412

18.9.1.4 ROTATE AND SEPARATE AND SEGREGATE	413
18.10 PIOSOPHY AND PIOLOGISTS	414
18.11 MEASURING PIE	414
18.12 PIE IN THE SKY	415
18.13 STEPCHECK	416

19 PULLING IT ALL TOGETHER 418

19.1 LEADERSHIP	419
19.1.1.1 BATTLE HARDENED LEADERSHIP TRAITS	421
19.1.1.2 INSPIRE THE WORKPLACE AND PIE WILL FOLLOW	423
19.2 HUMAN RESOURCES	424
19.3 GET STRAIGHT A'S	425
19.4 ORGANISATION BUDGETS	427
19.5 SALARIES	429
19.5.1.1 HULA HOOP SCALE OUT	429
19.6 AUTOMATISM IS ESSENTIAL	431
19.6.1.1 PREPARE AND SAVE	432
19.7 ALCHEMY	434
19.7.1.1 GLUEPRINTS AND PATTERNS	435
19.8 FINOPS	437
19.9 DRIVE	439
19.9.1.1 TELL VENDORS HOW TO PERFORM	443
19.9.2 CMdB	444
19.10 RESOLVERS	445
19.11 SecOPS	448
19.11.1.1 SECOPS GREEN TEAM	449
19.12 SecOPS RED TEAM	451
19.12.1.1 BLUE TEAM	453
19.13 SECOPs ORANGE TEAM	454
19.14 SECOPS BLACK TEAM	455
19.14.1.1 SECOPS TOOLKITS	457
19.14.1.2 SECURITY CONTROLS	457
19.15 DISCIPLINED AGILE DELIVERY	458
19.16 MEASURING AGILE	459
19.17 AGILE METRICS	461

19.17.1.1 TECHNICAL DEBT	461
19.17.1.2 EARNED VALUE MANAGEMENT	461
19.18 DEVOPS	463
19.18.1.1 CAMS	465
19.18.1.2 CONTINUOUS INTEGRATION AND DELIVERY	467
19.18.2 THE 6 x Rs OF RUGGED DEVOPS	467
19.18.3 DEVOPS ASSURING CODE	468
19.19 CONTINUOUS DELIVERY	469
19.20 DEVOPS TOOLS	469
19.21 DOCOPS	470
19.22 SINCups	473
19.23 CAMRA - OMNIOCULAR SNAPSHOTS AUDITOLOGY	476
	477
19.23 AUDITOLOGY ROLES AND RESPONSIBILITIES	480
19.24 SERVOPS	482
19.24.1.1 INCIDENTS AND ALARMS	483
19.25 OPEN SOURCE SAUCE	484
19.26 IMPLEMENT COMBAT READY IT	485
19.27 ROLES AND RESPONSIBILITIES	486

20 PARTHIAN SHOT   489

20.1.1 WHAT HAVE YOU LEARNT?	489
20.1.2 KEY TAKEAWAYS FOR SMBs	489
20.1.3 IT TO TVC?	490
20.2 FIN	491

21 FREQUENTLY ASKED QUESTIONS   492

APPENDIX 2 - VIRUS EVOLUTION   495

21.1 A Brief History of Exposures
(Look Back in Angst)   495

APPENDIX 3 - SECURITY CONTROLS   540

APPENDIX 3 – CRIT SECURITY POLICY   543

Endnotes   545

Figure 1 - A FOOL AND HIS DATA IS SOON PARTED	xxx
Figure 3 - BOTNETS AND ZOMBIES	46
Figure 4 - X SITE SCRIPTING	52
Figure 5- NECURS	56
Figure 6- DNS POISONING	58
Figure 7 - PASSTEAL AND PIXSTEAL	59
Figure 8 - MAN IN THE MIDDLE	63
Figure 9 HEARTBLEED	64
Figure 10 MOBILE ATTACKS	65
Figure 11 NETWORK ATTACK	69
Figure 12 SPEAR PHISH	71
Figure 13 SPAM	74
Figure 14 SPAM TO COMPONENT	75
Figure 15 ADWARE AND SPYWARE	76
Figure 16 SQL INJECTIONS	77
Figure 17 TROJAN HORSES	79
Figure 18 VULNERABILITY LIFECYCLE	80
Figure 19 WORM DERIVATIVE STUXNET	82
Figure 20 CYBER ATTACK LIFECYCLE	97
Figure 21 THE VULNERABILITY LIFECYCLE	102
Figure 22 - DISTRIBUTION OF WINDOWS OS ON USERS COMPUTERS 2013 (Kaspersky)	109
Figure 23 THE COCONUTS OF TRANSENDENCE	116
Figure 24 BBC-PR	123
Figure 25 CYBRID WARS WOBBLY LINES	126
Figure 26 THREE CONFLICTS COSTS	134
Figure 27 DISINTEGRATION	135
Figure 28 FREXAGON	142
Figure 29 PC DECOMPOSED	149
Figure 30 VIRTUAL MACHINES AND DOCKER CONTAINERS	151
Figure 31 STORAGE - LOCAL HYBRID AND PUBLIC CLOUD	154

Figure 32 CORE LEAF SPINE AND COMPASS DIRECTIONS	157
Figure 33 ROUTERS AND SDN ANATOMIES	159
Figure 34 CARRIER NFV (ADL, BELL)	161
Figure 34 SWITCH	162
Figure 35 DUAL CABLE ROUTES	163
Figure 36 WAN MULTIPLE LINKS IN DIVERSE ROUTES	166
Figure 37 CLOUD MANAGEMNT OF WIFI (CLOUDESSA)	169
Figure 38 MOBILE TABLET BARE BONES	170
Figure 39 SEVEN LAYER MODEL	172
Figure 40 - BLUE SKY 4 LAYER MODEL	176
Figure 41 SIP CALL FLOW	178
Figure 42 VIRTUALISED CLOUD APPLICATIONS	180
Figure 43 SCADA ICS BASICS	186
Figure 44 IP4 and IPv6 STACKS	189
Figure 45 EXAMPLE TELEPHONE DIRECTORY LISTING	192
Figure 46 IP ENUM (PER SUBSCRIBER)	193
Figure 47 NIST CLOUD COMPUTING STANDARD	203
Figure 48 HOW Hi GETS THROUGH THE INTERNET	217
Figure 49 ORIGINAL INTERNET	226
Figure 50 INTERNET TODAY	231
Figure 51 INTERNETNEW	236
Figure 52 FIXED AND MOBILE CONNECTIONS	238
Figure 53 CONNECTING PSTN, MOBILE and INTERNET	240
Figure 54 - NDN NAMED DATA NETWORKING	243
Figure 55 – COGNET	245
Figure 56 ONOS (OPEN NETWOrK OPERATING SYSTEM)	246
Figure 57 SELF DETERMINED DOMINION INTERNET	247
Figure 58 LAST MILE COSTS PER USER PER 324 SQ KM	253
Figure 59 MULTI STAKEHOLDER GOVERNANCE OF THE INTERNET	254
Figure 60 SIMPLIFIED GEAR STICK INTERNET GOVERNANCE	257

Figure 61 INTERNETNEW POSSIBLE ECONOMIC MODEL	260
Figure 62 RIDPOINTS	264
Figure 63 VIA FERRATA REPORTING LOOPS	267
Figure 64 VIA FERRATA RISK FLOW	269
Figure 65 VIA FERRATA RISK REPORT	270
Figure 66 VIA FERRATA COMPANY SECURITY QUOTIENT	274
Figure 69 COST OF SERVICE	280
Figure 67 OBASHI DATAFLOW EXAMPLES (courtesy of OBASHI)	283
Figure 68 SECOPS ROI VIA FERRATA REPORTING EXAMPLE	284
Figure 69 DISCIPLINED AGILE DEVELOPMENT (courtesy Scott Ambler)	288
Figure 70 VIA FERRATA RISK REGISTER	291
Figure 71 PRIVILEGE MANAGEMENT	293
Figure 72 DOMINO DEFENCE IN DEPTH	302
Figure 73 LOCATION LAYOUT AND BUILDING TYPES	304
Figure 74 WEAPON YIELDS	305
Figure 75 FALLOUT AND BLAST RADIUS	306
Figure 76 MODERN DATA CENTRES	325
Figure 77 OPEN COMPUTE SMB RACK DESIGN	327
Figure 78 PLAN VIEW OF CONTAINER DATA CENTRE SOLUTION	332
Figure 79 DOMINO TRUST BOUNDARIES	335
Figure 80 HYBRID/PUBLIC BOUNDARIES AND PERIMETERS	341
Figure 81 INCIDENT RESPONSE CYCLE	351
Figure 82 DocOPS INFORMATION CLASSIFICATION	360
Figure 83 AUTOMATION AND ORCHESTRATION FOR Devops	371
Figure 84 BCDR DATA CENTRES VM SNAPSHOTS[175]	394
Figure 85 HULA HOOP ORGANISATION	399
Figure 86 PIE CALCULATION	402
Figure 87 ELIMINATE RISK AND RISK APPETITE	406
Figure 88 COMBAT READY METRO MAP	417

Figure 89 LEADERSHIP HANDOFFS   419
Figure 90 TEAM MEMBERS EVALUATION STRAIGHT A's   426
Figure 91 CAREER LAYERS   428
Figure 92 ALCHEMY HANDOFFS   434
Figure 93 FINOPS HANDOFFS   438
Figure 94 DRIVE HANDOFFS   440
Figure 95 RESOLVERS HANDOFFS   446
Figure 96 SECOPS GREEN TEAM HANDOFFS   449
Figure 97 SECOPS RED TEAM HANDOFFS   452
Figure 98 SECOPS ORANGE TEAM HANDOFFS   454
Figure 99 SECOPS BLACK TEAM HANDOFFS   455
Figure 100 DAD HANDOFFS   459
Figure 101 DEVOPS HANDOFFS   465
Figure 102 - 5 x TIERS RESOLUTION WORKFLOW   470
Figure 103 DOCOPS HANDOFFS   471
Figure 104 SINCups HANDOFFS   473
Figure 105 CAMRA HANDOFFS   476
Figure 106 AUDITOLOGY HANDOFFS   478
Figure 107 ALARM RESOLUTION PATH   482
Figure 109 TOOLSETS   484
Figure 110 VIRUS EVOLUTION   495
Figure 111 OWASP TOP 10   541
Figure 112 SANS CONTROL   542
Figure 113 GRAPHICAL SECURITY POLICY   543
Figure 114 PCI PROCESS BASED ON OBASHI   544

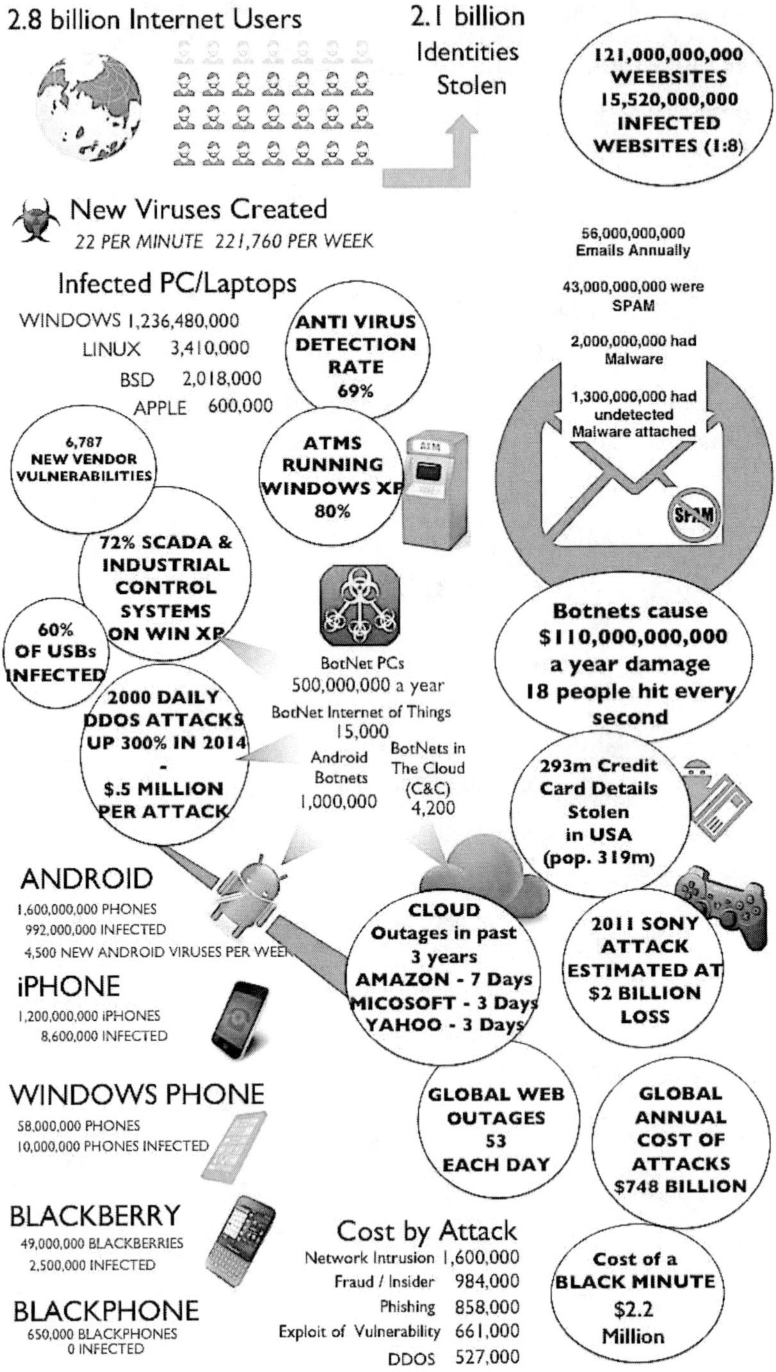

Figure 1 - A FOOL AND HIS DATA IS SOON PARTED

FOREWORD

Information is the new gold, digital bits trade as the new global currency. Information is Knowledge, Knowledge is Power, and Power is Profit, Information is haemorrhaging. We hand adversaries our hard earned information without a fight. Global companies are losing Information, we are not addressing how to stop it and this impacts everybody's bottom line.

THE GOLDEN WAVE OF THE SMB
Like the Industrial Revolution and the Information Technology Age, this year we started a new Wave headlined as the Golden Wave of the SMB - (the age of the Artisan). Enterprises have already commenced reducing their workforces. Craftflows will be handed off out to artisans, specialists, and in particular SMBs. Robotica and automation technology join and the accepted notion of the FTE will disappear. The way we work today will start to change, no job will be safe or long term. Millennial's may never work in the way we perceive work now. The age of the four-man company is here: the Boss, the IT guy, the Specialist, and the Robot. Leisure time will increase and a return to cottage industry and artisans will rise. De-urbanisation will be ignited by the Rich/Poor divide gap widens where only the wealthy can afford city housing and prices. Everyone will rely on the Internet. The Internet cannot cope with this in its current design. Cyber security may degrade the Internet so badly to be unworkable. This book sets out a new way for SMBs to prepare for the change and start Innovating.

- **Cyber Security** is the linking of technologies, risk management, people and business continuity practices that protect networks, computers, programmes and information from perpetual unauthorised attacks, damage or access.

- **Information Security** is the term associated with managing and control of the SMBs' information assets (Intellectual Property, Financial, and Customer Data).

We are in a cyber security war! An SMB needs to be fleet of foot, to be fast you need to travel light, to ease the burden you need automation, if you need automation you need the right tools, to get the right tools you need people to deliver them, if you can't afford the tools use the free ones, and if you can't find the people, buy them in. Reliance on IT will be the key to survival so shore up your security posture. Words, Processes, Regulations, and Frameworks written, drawn, and devised do not prevent you getting hacked - only Technology, Tools and Team Members can do this.

The systemic disintegration of the Internet will continue and is spiral out of control unabated! Governments cannot stop this wave of cyber insecurity. The Internet will not get fixed anytime soon, and our privacy and credentials have already been stolen. Confidence in the Internet is declining and compounded by subscribers paying our Governments to carry out surveillance on us. Its not about our Freedom of Speech anymore – it is the Freedom to Respond.

The Combat Ready IT model describes how to put up the defences, deploying new technology, tools, and team members. Empower the workforce using Perpetual Improvement Everywhere to add quality to the Security culture and stance.

NO EXCUSES: please do not use the tired excuse that you are not "technical" enough to comprehend cyber security - it is not valid anymore. Understanding cyber security is now a basic business skill. As a CxO it is your responsibility to be technical enough to manage your company in a digital age, your backers now demand this as a minimum skillset, and they expect a lucid conversation about it with you - so this book will help you get savvy. Venture Capitalists and Angel backers, banks and boards will gauge your ability to securely protect the business. Consider the start up investment of $1 million dollars into an idea that succumbs to a $3.5 million data breach on day one is why this is of high importance on Business Plan agendas.

According to Entrepreneur.com the average annual revenue of a business is $3.6 million (and those with a website annual revenue of $5.05 million). 42% of all SMBs in the US have a website as its primary marketing tool with 78% connected to the Internet (email only). That's 139 million websites in the US alone fronting SMBs livelihoods. Unfortunately 44% of these websites are already being attacked and 10% having to halt all business activities. I am hoping the remaining 46% will use the wisdom in this book.

The Mission: (should you choose to accept it) is to set up the armoury with up to date technology weapons and tools. Establish a beachhead organisation that allows you to grow low skill team members into trusted, happy, ethical, and engaged team members. You would not continue to employ a salesperson unless they dreamt each night about the product range and pricing margins. You need to understand the root causes of security and why SMBs are vulnerable to attack, you will also need to "walk the talk" of Security Officers. You and your team members need to get addicted to security. It will make your headache a bit, but that will not last long so stick with it.

The Challenge; simply stop your information from being stolen by adversaries. Cyber security has a warehouse stuffed full of multiple standards, frameworks, and regulations that will either help you get organised, or be used to issue fines. For the last decade Security Officers have blamed the business focus for failing at basics. Most cyber security professionals who say that cyber security is the fault of end users, In part that may account for 20% of data breaches, but we are dealing with a technology problem not the effectiveness of a framework. Framework and Regulations do no stop a hacker! At the end of a recent security audit presentation the CEO ended the board discussion in a humorous meeting closing statement. " I had no idea that I didn't know!" The same CEO initially blamed his team members and then the government for negligence, but the root causes are far deeper than that. The Internet, vendors, and a looming global conflict conspire to build a perfect storm that now impacts every business and Internet subscriber on the planet.

The Problem: Major corporations are being hacked (every day news headlines), many are not aware of infections by sleeper malware that still sit on their systems. Many companies wait for external companies, customers, and governments to inform them of a breach. 60% of SMBs don't have cyber security checks and balances in place and will start to be fined for non-reporting. In a statistic from the World Trade Organisation, 330 Million SMBs are online and a further 130 Million about to go online.[2] Commercial survival relies on diversification away from low margin product portfolios. The Speed, Cost and Quality triangle has spawned Shadow IT in Lines of Business, spurred by available Cloud technologies. Traditional IT departments cannot cope with the added security problems of innovative groups and projects pursuing this route. Information is put on Cloud providers without deep thought and security controls resulting in 60% of cloud data is stored unencrypted. Unencrypted data is a smorgasbord for an adversary or insider attack. Insider threats now account for 50% of all known data breaches; a statistic that could be worrisome in two men partnerships?

The Objective: Nobody is going to help you, so, help yourself – it will be cheaper if you do it yourself anyway! Security continuity ceases after external Security Consultants and Auditors have left the building. Recruiting a skilled professional, if you can find and pay one, may not be the solution either. A Security Officers (SO) salary exceeds that of a CIO, but 'one soldier does not an army make'. It will take a year to get a Security policy in place, once you on-board an SO, it may cost $1m plus and in the end still will not help prevent an attack. The selection of infrastructure, individual, and innovation is a pivotal choice here.

On a wider front, global instability risks will impact business - a cold war has re-emerged, global warming is getting hotter, water and food are at a premium and the current depression may triple dip. Existential Risk is your responsibility as it may impact your supply chain. Learn how to spot and manage Risks by understanding cycles and lessons from history. Follow a track that helps highlight risk so everyone in your company has a Risk Angel on their shoulder.

The book suggests systems infrastructure configurations that meet and exceed the most stringent of compliance and regulatory measures. InternetNew is not yet with us and still lingers in abstract. Until InternetNew breathes, companies need to keep information and bank accounts intact. The author suggests how the Internet needs a technical and regulation overhaul and how companies can access further more valuable global markets once it becomes secure. Cyber security attacks on Internet connected SMBs costs $761 billion *every year* in damage. That's like losing the GDP of Thailand every year since 2010.

Company owners and executive officers are now the finger point target for cyber security fines, consumer dissatisfaction, bank manager and shareholder anger. How does your company react to threats and how do you reorganise to maintain reputation? With cyber attacks now happening every 15 seconds, how will your company cope with adversary attacks and how do you build conflict posture in an unstable world?

THE INTERNET IS CLOSED AND COSTLY

Like the Spanish high-speed train that crashed after taking a corner too fast, the Internet is coming off the rails. Cyber attacks are now killing the Internet and should it fail so will companies and billions of jobs will be lost linked to that failure. Governments have already built Internet "kill switches". We need to acknowledge that the Internet has outgrown its current form. Instead of blindly ignoring root causes, we should be finding solutions fast, structural reform must be applied to the Internet. Subscribers are already turning away from the Internet with 15% in 2014 refusing to use the Internet in it's current insecure form, if this trend continues (and if this trend doubles this year) some Internet based companies would cease trading. The Internet is in a "Run to Failure" downward spiral, and hysterical maintenance is the norm.

The Internets original and guiding principles were "to be free and open". People always want something for nothing and the Internet is close to their hearts. Here's the reality: the Internet costs money, needs capital, needs companies and people to run it. Subscribers need to buy computers or smartphones to run browsers — these cost money. Internet users need a subscription to ensure cable; telecoms and ISPs stay in business. Providers need capital to increase network reach and maintain the Internet infrastructure and attract patrons. Vint Cerf [3] has written; "Our protocols were designed to make the networks of the Internet non-proprietary and interoperable. They avoided "lock-in," and allowed for contributions from many sources. This openness is why the Internet creates so much value today. Because it is borderless and belongs to everyone, it has brought unprecedented freedoms to billions of people worldwide: the freedom to create and innovate, to organize and influence, to speak and be heard." Cyber attacks and surveillance are contrary to this laudable intent. The Dark Web is getting darker, and the invisible Deep Web has underground subcultures, cyber anarchists, antisocial media, [4] and a global black market.

THE BLACK MINUTE

It takes only a minute to fall in love, and it takes only a minute to steal data during a hack attack. It takes a year to fall out of love it can be very expensive, and after an attack the legal ramifications will make you question your very existence. Nothing is secure, security defences can be breached, password cracked and 40 Megabytes of data downloaded in a minute (at 8000 bytes per record = 5000 records).[5] I call this the Black Minute, is a disastrous and potentially expensive set of seconds ($36,666 per second). Every piece of Internet traffic needs to be watched every second by team members. Is this possible – maybe during waking hours when operators are watching for anomalies and potential threats, but what happens when everyone goes home – does the last team member switch off the Internet like the office lights when they leave? Companies need to enforce a conscious perpetual improvement approach and implement the right technology to monitor everything non-stop to prevent the Black Minute happening.

BEING OBLIVIOUS TO THE OBVIOUS RESULTS IN OBLIVION

The first step in problem solving is to identify the problem. Then we need to find solutions to the Root Causes of the problems. We are in the midst of a conflict, a Cybrid war (fuelled by cyber security holes in the basic construct of the Internet and the software that runs over it) perverted by adversaries that impacts every person on this planet. Vendors shun accountability and admit no liability; no one is going to help (or compensate) you anytime soon. Governments issue knee jerk cyber laws, based on political points of view rather than solid technical reasons. Regulators will fine you even though a data breach is not your fault. We are fighting a new technology war with our bare hands, and the enemy has automatic weapons. Hackers have become mega sophisticated, and businesses cannot keep up in a technological sense. One cannot help wondering how this mess has started. Have we politically overlooked the obvious and turned a blind eye to the point where we are shooting ourselves in the foot? It's only when Cloud companies accounts held by celebrities get attacked that immediate changes to access Cloud data are imposed. All of these reactionary events are like shutting the stable door when the horse has bolted. We are being oblivious to the obvious.

The modern Internet-driven countries are painfully vulnerable to Cybrid attacks, and the security community is struggling to keep up with the pace of technology. Andrew France, chief executive at cyber-security firm Darktrace (ex GCHQ) states, "The Internet was never designed to be secure, and if you attach your critical national infrastructure to it, then you're asking for trouble. The cost of entry for someone who wishes to damage someone else on the Internet is quite low. You can just download simple tools that can cause a lot of damage."

Developing a cyber-weapon as sophisticated as the devastating Stuxnet or Duqu viruses would previously have cost millions of dollars, but could now be devised for as little as $10,000. These viruses have been reversed engineered and now used against the authors. This causes "serious concerns" for cyber security experts "because it is lowering the barrier to entry to the global cyber arms race", France said. [6]

In fact, you can buy a simple Denial of Service piece of malware for a mere $300 that can knock out an organisation for a day (so don't upset your customers, or sack IT personnel at Christmas). Binary code malware has been quietly sitting (sleeper malware) in nearly all production IT systems for the last decade (and up to 19 years in one example); it's so cleverly programmed and sophisticated it has been missed and left undiscovered by most security defence technologies and undiscovered by penetration and vulnerability tests. We are fighting a high tech war with spears and rocks. **We need to get prepared and organised, get guerrilla, get weapons that are fit for purpose, and get combat ready and be on guard perpetually.**

THE REVERSE PANOPTICON

Jeremy Bentham was an advocate for freedom of expression, women's, and homosexual rights; he also designed a prison in 1787. The purpose was to obtain transparency with surveillance and these are reciprocal. A Panopticon (means Seeing All) is a circular building with an observation tower in the centre of an open space with an outer circumference wall containing cells for occupants. Brick walls divide the cells. The cells are floodlit from the centre so the occupants cannot see they are under surveillance. Occupants are invisible to each other. This makes discipline a passive activity - as there is no privacy.

Information Panopticon's do not need physical arrangements, such as building structures and direct human supervision. A Smartphone or Tablet, can track a team members every move. Programmes assign them specific tasks to perform during their shift. Everything, work breaks, the time to complete tasks is monitored recorded. Workers are given a certain amount of time to complete the task based on its complexity. All this is monitored by supervision from a computer an anonymous public official. Fines for non-compliance are now given to occupants. This is the Internet except every Internet subscribers data ends up at Internet Transit points most of which are in the US. Subscribers pay to have their data taken by a Government agency – this is a prologue to a farce. Mass surveillance now costs each subscriber about $375 a year (the cost of surveillance to monitor a subscriber). Globally subscribers and taxpayers fund overseas governments $21 a year to view their data.

The problem with the Panopticon is that people can only be pushed so far and this in turn creates rebellion. Riots occur, occupants break out, and sub cultures making surveillance a self-fulfilling prophecy foreseeing total collapse. One of these sub cultures (adversaries) has stolen all the details of the guards that watch us. The occupants have now reversed the Panopticon and are studying the guards. There's now a Cloud hovering above the central tower and the occupants are doing rain dances.

In the UK's latest report on the country's security stance, the National Security Strategy[7] on page 14 of that report, I noticed a paragraph that I did a double take on. The words made me sit bolt upright up in my chair. "Organised crime affects our interests and the lives of our people at home and abroad. At present there are around 38,000 individuals involved in organised crime affecting the UK, costing our economy and society between £35 billion and £55 billion per annum". Now, maths may not my strong point by any means but these individuals seem to be making £1,447,368 each and getting away with it. Perhaps I should switch careers! Existing security contingencies cannot cope with this tsunami of attacks[8]. Based on the number of attacks the number of full time adversaries attacking companies has grown to 0.01% of the Internet population (280,000 individuals).

The average long-term period of unemployment has grown from one year to two years during the latest recession. The planet has 200 million unemployed, and that will triple in the next five years as companies implement further Robotica technology, together with the ending of the overseas outsource cycle. Millennial's have been affected by this trend. Over one million in number Millennial's in the UK have never had a job. These are the "digital natives", a group who have grown up in the Internet age and have mentally wrapped their lives around Internet devices. To make money this under 24s and the over 50s are now seeking new revenue streams. This is a greenhouse for the next wave of hackers.

During research it became obvious that we ("we" is a euphemism for 'any country') are doing things wrong and as usual for any potential conflict planning is diabolical. We are already in a series of non-linear attacks, a Cybrid War. Cybrid is a merger of cyber attacks and traditional warfare. On the Cyber side one in three of the world's 2.5 billion Internet-connected users have an existing or hidden virus on their machines; of the world's 1 billion businesses around 75% have already been hacked or are being readied for a data breach. This includes SMB's, which from consensus appears to be the next wave of victims.

It seems though that a truly secure system is as rare as hen's teeth and unicorns. It seems to me we have taken a scattergun stance on security and the root causes. Likewise, we also know what the root causes of viruses are but we refuse to address this by spending the time to make Operating Systems secure. As humans we suppress our addictions, with the notion "it could never possibly happen to me"?

Remaining oblivious to impending threats is a high-risk pastime; the risks being imposed by the Internet wont go away anytime soon. There is a plethora of IT Standards and frameworks but there is no clear plan on how to translate these issues into a formal coherent operations plan that merges with a Defence in Depth infrastructure. There are not enough Security Officers to help guide you so you need to be self-resourcing, self determined, and smart about security. What technologies should be in place to prevent attacks? How would an SMB organisation be composed to prevent incidents, and a potential Black Minute?

Frameworks that have been developed around IT security have multiple commonalities. No matter how good the intentions every country has their own spin on what a secure estate looks like. I deem this the "50 Shades of Grey Spread sheets". There are so many spread sheets available for checklists it makes your head swim. You would think that with so many frameworks malware and attacks would not exist, but it's not so. Frameworks are like the Generals Plan of Attack, which have fallen into enemy hands. Hackers know exactly what to expect.

This book intends to show you a way to grow your business securely and make you competitive and profitable and enforce "Natural Security" through, technology, Perpetual Improvement Everywhere, and common sense, helping you to retain knowledge. Like anything cyclical IT is moving away from distributed hierarchies and Cloud networks to centralisation

STEPCHECK

- A Black Minute can ruin any company
- Hacking has got cheap and profitable and accessible by a Tsunami of IT savvy people
- We are using a media that is unregulated and users are starting to leave
- A combination of unemployment and zero growth global economy will mean a rise in attacks
- Reverse Panopticon attacks are rising
- A cyber war exists - so get ready.

1 ROOT CAUSES - SCOPE OF CYBER ATTACKS

"I think computer viruses should count as life. I think it says something about human nature that the only form of life we have created so far is purely destructive. We've created life in our own image."
—*Stephen Hawking (A Brief History of Time)*
The Daily News, August 4, 1994[9]

Is the Internet safe, trustworthy, and useable for companies? The answer is an emphatic **NO**! Here is a compilation of the latest attacks on companies and people. Here are some of the reasons why:

With an estimated 200 malware attacks a minute this traffic is getting scary. Predictors and bloggers are warning that we are witnessing the beginnings of a Cybergeddon. For a real time view of cyber attacks happening on the Internet readers check out www.digitalattackmap.com to see the volume of attacks in real time if not fully convinced.

By the time you read this page, there is a 15% statistical chance that your machine or mobile device will have been hacked if you are connected to the Internet.

There is a 50% chance that if you are based in a company and using the corporate LAN, someone has viewed your data by an external adversary, or an insider (a cracker). An example of an Insider is Lauri Love, who as a contractor in a US Department had stolen 100,000 identities since 2012.[10]

7 CONTINENTS INTERNET STATISTICS	Population (2015 Est.)	Internet Users 2000	Internet Users Latest Data	Users % Of Table
Africa	1,158,353,014	4,514,400	318,633,889	10.30%
Asia	4,032,654,624	114,304,000	1,405,121,036	45.60%
Europe	827,566,464	105,096,093	582,441,059	18.90%
Middle East	236,137,235	3,284,800	113,609,510	3.70%
America	357,172,209	108,096,800	310,322,257	10.10%
Latin America	615,583,127	18,068,919	322,422,164	10.50%
Oceania	37,157,120	7,620,480	26,789,942	0.90%
7 CONTINENTS TOTAL	7,264,623,793	360,985,492	3,079,339,857	100%

Table 1 INTERNET POPULATION STATISTICS

There are about 21 Billion IP addressable devices (mobiles, PCs, servers, routers etc.,) connected to the Internet; each one accesses a service through fixed or wireless networks. Each device can be compromised in a plethora of different ways. For now assume any IP addressable device is a target.

Seven-year-old Betsy Davies managed to hack a laptop via an open Wi-Fi network in just over ten minutes, having learned how to set up a rogue access point and eavesdrop on traffic in an online tutorial.[11]

1.1 IDENTITY THEFT

Of the 3 billion Internet users worldwide, approximately 1.8 billion identities and passwords have already been stolen (65% loss) due to hacking in the last 10 years due to numerous compromises. In 2014, a Russian gang stole records on a huge scale:

- "The Russian gang, which Hold Security dubbed "CyberVor" ("Vor" means "thief" in Russian), accumulated some 4.5 billion records, mostly stolen 'login' credentials. Of that massive trove, Hold said 1.2 billion of the credentials appear to be unique, and include more than half a billion email addresses. To amass that number of credentials, the company said, the CyberVor group robbed over 420,000 Web and FTP sites. [12]

Cyber crime costs the global economy $731 billion annually.
Software Piracy costs vendors and governments $500 billion annually.
Music and Movie Piracy $35 billion annually
Pirated Goods bought online $200 billion annually

This equates to 39 million jobs and negative tax receipts of $445 billion (around $2 billion for each country) lost annually.

Cyber espionage and stealing individuals' personal information is believed to have affected more than 800 million people during 2013, one billion people in 2014, and 600 million people in 2015. Financial losses from cybercrime and cyber theft has caused as many as 150,000 Europeans to lose their jobs, according to a report conducted by Internet security company McAfee.[13] This threat is decreasing consumers' trust in companies' ability to hold onto personal data properly. As companies are helpless against this onslaught millions of jobs and company reputations are at risk. The onus will fall on company officers to demonstrate Duty of Care regarding the holding of personal data.

1.2 OPERATING SYSTEMS

- Brian Valentine, senior vice-president in charge of Microsoft's Windows development, made a grim admission to the Microsoft Windows Server .Net developer conference in Seattle, USA. [14]

"I'm not proud," he told delegates yesterday (5 September, 2002). "We really haven't done everything we could to protect our customers. Our products just aren't engineered for security," admitted Valentine, who since 1998 has headed Microsoft's Windows division. [15]

- There are 220,000 new viruses and vulnerabilities discovered every day. Viruses can self-replicate and evolve to transform themselves.

- Any Operating System, which includes all variants of Windows (including v8.1), Linux, UNIX, OS X, Mainframes, have been hacked. The only computer system that seems to have avoided this fate is the Tandem Non Stop (now HP Non Stop). Since 2003, Windows XP machines have been susceptible to numerous infected applications and Office templates. Open Source applications are also susceptible; these 'small and useful' applications and templates downloaded from the Web – have backdoor vulnerabilities.

Operating System	Market Share 2013	No of Computers on the Internet 2007	Number of Exposures	Est. Number of Infected Endpoints
Windows	92%	2,576,000,000	2,247,659	1,236,480,000
OSX	3.85%	107,800,000	48	600,000
Linux	2.03%	56,840,000	1898	3,410,400
Free BSD	1.03%	28,840,000	43	2,018,800
Solaris	0.09%	25,956	119	519.12
Unix	1.00%	2,596	212	260
ZOS and Non Stop	0.00%	2,800	1	1

Table 2 TYPE OF MALWARE BY OPERATING SYSTEM

Windows 8 has a backdoor is called "Trusted Computing," and controls a Trusted Platform Module developed and promoted by the Trusted Computing Group, founded a decade ago by the all-American technology companies AMD, Cisco, Hewlett-Packard, IBM, Intel, Microsoft, and Wave Systems. Its presence has caused German Federal Office for Security in Information Technology (BSI) and Chinese Governments to ban the product feature. [16]

- During the first quarter of 2014, AppRiver screened more than 14 billion email messages, nearly 10.9 billion of which were spam and 490 million that contained malware. Users are tricked into opening a "quarterly report" sent via email that is actually malware; running the tool has infected their computers and established connections with an external host. The US was the leading country of origin for spam email messages, and Europe logged the second-highest total with Spain, Germany and Italy making up the top three countries.[17]

- A total of 5.5 million Web pages linked to 560,000 Websites were infected (through Web Redirects, Watering Holes where hackers can infect your browser. Evidence exists that attackers are waging less noticeable exploits in order to remain under the radar.[18]

- October 22, 2014, Neil Ford of IT Governance reported that Microsoft has warned of vulnerability present in Microsoft OLE, which affects all supported releases of Windows except for Windows Server 2003. "At this time, we are aware of limited, targeted attacks that attempt to exploit the vulnerability through Microsoft PowerPoint," the software giant said on 21 October. It is thought that the vulnerability is being used by Sandworm Team, the Russian cyber espionage operators who last week exploited the zero-day vulnerability to conduct attacks on NATO, Ukrainian government organisations, and European energy and telecoms firms. Sandworm Team was identified by iSIGHT Partners.[19] Sandworm appeared in 2009. The team prefers the use of spear-phishing with malicious document attachments to target victims. Many of the lures observed have been specific to the Ukrainian conflict with Russia and to broader geopolitical issues related to Russia." OLE (Object Linking and Embedding) allows applications to create and edit compound data, enabling in-place editing. For example, users can edit Excel spread sheets embedded in Word documents. If a user opens a file containing a malicious OLE object, they open themselves up to attack. All Microsoft Office files, including PowerPoint and Word, could contain malicious

OLE objects. Microsoft continues: "An attacker who successfully exploited this vulnerability could gain the same user rights as the current user. If the current user is logged on with administrative user rights, an attacker who successfully exploited this vulnerability could take complete control of an affected system. An attacker could then: install programs, view, change, or delete data; or create new accounts with full user rights." The exploitation of this vulnerability relies a user to open a malicious file – known as a phishing attack. As ever, IT Governance suggests vigilance. If you don't know a file's origins, don't open it.[20]

1.3 NOT SO SMART PHONES

- There are 4,500 new viruses designed for Android created each week. Android iBanking malware has helped hackers hack Facebook Accounts. There are approximately 1 billion Android phones worldwide and 62% have viruses. One in three Android Apps have malware already built in. The average Android user downloads six applications a year. [21]

Mobile Operating System	Market Share 2014	Shipped since 2007	Shipped in Q2 2014	Est. Number of Infected Phones
Android	79.30%	1,666,000,000	204,000,000	416,500,000
IPhone	13.20%	1,232,400,000	33,800,000	8,626,800
Windows Phone	8.70%	58,200,000	10,200,000	174,600
Blackberry	6.80%	46,700,000	2,500,000	140,100
Linux	1.80%	12,900,000	500,000	2,541,300
IDC 2013 & F-Secure & Kaspersky		5,785,711,351	253,249,980	1,670,492,779

Table 3 MOBILE PHONE INFECTED

- No mobile phone is safe. All smartphones are susceptible to 'ransom-ware' (if a user land on an infected website a malware attack on the device commences and encrypts the devices' data storage) to release the device a payment has to be made to the hacker to obtain a release code. Windows phones now have Trojan infestations as well as the newly released 8.1 Windows version, but these are not as scary as the voluminous attacks seen in the Android world. There are many individuals moving away from the mainstream vendors towards niche security vendors such as Blackphone, which adds robust and encrypted voice traffic (voice conversations between users employing encrypted keys) using PGP (Pretty Good Privacy algorithms) in a reasonably priced smartphone.

- Trojan viruses hidden in downloaded Apps can steal money from digital wallets that secure Digital currencies, such as Facebook Credits, Xbox Points, Zynga Coins and Bitcoins, are now seen by some cyber criminals as just as valuable as cold hard cash. AVG highlighted an incident from June where nearly $500,000 was stolen from a digital wallet on an individual's computer.

- According to Kaspersky, seller of the $10 Kaspersky antivirus app for Android, Android viruses are getting worse. The latest attack vector comes in the form of malicious QR Codes. When you scan a QR code, your phone turns those funky squares into a URL. Just like any other form of URL obfuscation (e.g., shorteners), that URL can be a virus ridden website.

- The Harris Corporation StingRay is an IMSI-catcher with active (cell site simulator) capabilities. It mimics a wireless carrier cell tower to force all nearby mobile phones and other cellular data devices to connect to it. It only costs a $1000

1.4 ORGANISED CRIME

The Internet is so unsafe that even Mexican drug gangs built their own secure network to circumvent surveillance by US Border authorities.

- Rarely is a user informed that their data has been compromised directly by the organisation that got hacked unless you're a celebrity and embarrassing selfies are sprawled across the Web in the aftermath. Usually companies might make a public announcement, but mostly information about these attacks is released only to the industry sector. The privacy and data retention policies of these companies are also dubious. How many Websites have an e-mail address so that you can contact the security department with any security concerns? In 2014, 293 million records (including payment card details, names, addresses, passwords, and email addresses) in the US have been compromised, which is theoretically enough to affect every single US citizen:

  - EBay – Hackers accessed 145 million user records through employee login details.
  - JPMorgan Chase – Names, addresses, phone numbers, and email addresses of 76 million account holders were compromised.
  - Home Depot – 56 million payment cards were stolen from the country's largest home improvement and construction retailer.
  - Staples – 16 million payment cards were compromised in Staples' data breach, which occurred at more than 100 of its stores.

The population of the United States of America is estimated to be 319 million. Therefore, 92% of US citizens have lost their details in 2014 [22]. ContinuityInsights.com reported on the 9th March 2015 that one billion emails were stolen in October 2012.

According to Fox News, 95% of the 450,000 ATMs in the USA alone still run Windows XP. So even if you put your hand over your PIN entry at a cash point, it can still be seen upstream throughout the public and banking network.[23]

HACKED CREDENTIALS PRICE LIST	$
A Persons Identity (Name Date of Birth, Address and Phone Number)	2
Web Dossier (Facebook, LinkedIn, Background Check)	2
Employee Records (Salary Details, Payroll Number)	2
Passport	2
3 Digit (CVV) and Credit Card Details	3
Bank Account Details	5
Old Credit Card Details	5
Bank related email address	5
Mortgage Details	5
Web Based Bank Account Password	8
ATM PIN Code	10
Credit Rating	10
Health Records	20
Web Account (PayPal, EBay, Amazon)	30
New Credit Card Details	45
Covert Relationships	99
Personal Calendar and Vacations	100
Company Dossier	2
HR Records Payroll Number (price per employee)	25
IT Staff Logins and Passwords	45
Server IP Addresses (Login and Firewall)	99
Company Bank Account	150
Customer Detail Records and Financial Transactions	5
Plans and Patents	1000

Table 4 - STREET PRICING [24],[25]

- There are viruses such as Crypto-locker that have been self-replicating since 2008 and have now infected millions of machines, and there is no way to clean the machine if it has been "bricked" – it has to be physically destroyed. This virus is the basis of Ransomware which still in existence and spreading.[26]

1.5 COUNTRIES HACKED

The Pentagon, the White House, EU, governments worldwide - all compromised. If major Governments can be hacked easily, the same can be said for companies. It doesn't matter how big you are there is still no defence.

- REVERSE PANOPTICON ATTACK – On 11th June 2015 the US Office of Personnel Management was hacked in a simple spear phishing attack. 4.2 million personnel records and background checks of every Government employee were hacked. According to federal union boss J.David Cox the "hackers have every affected persons Social Security numbers, military records, status information, address, birth date, job and pay history, health insurance, life insurance, pension information, age, gender, race, union status and more. Worst, we believe that Social Security numbers were not encrypted, a cyber security failure that is totally indefensible and outrageous". Nearly all the millions of security clearance holders, including some CIA, National Security Agency and military special ops personnel, are potentially exposed in the security clearance breach, the officials said.

- Hackers from China penetrated computer networks for months at USIS, the US government's leading security clearance contractor, before the company noticed. The breach, first revealed by the company and government agencies in August, compromised the private records of at least 25,000 employees at the Homeland Security Department and cost the company hundreds of millions of dollars in lost government contracts. The possibility that national security background investigations are vulnerable to cyber-espionage could undermine the integrity of the verification system used to review more than 5 million government workers and contract employees". The information gathered in the security clearance process is a treasure chest for cyber hackers. If the contractors and the agencies that hire them can't safeguard their material, the whole system becomes unreliable," said Alan Paller, head of SANS, a cyber security training school, and former co-chair of DHS' task force on cyber skills. [27]

- Russian hackers have used vulnerability in Microsoft software to spy on targets including NATO and Western European governments. US security firm iSIGHT Partners said a **zero-day vulnerability**, impacting all supported versions of Microsoft Windows and Windows Server 2008 and 2012, was used by hackers in Russia to spy on various targets. NATO, Ukrainian government organisations, Western European government, and energy companies in Poland, European telecommunications firms and academic organisations in the US have been targeted. This could have been operating since 2009.[28]

- The European Commission has spent over a billion Euros researching Cyber Crime and Cyber Warfare for five years finally established EC3 (Europol an equivalent of the US NSA and the UK's GCHQ) in February 2013. However during that period Russian Internet security firm Kaspersky Lab says unknown hackers have been stealing EU and NATO-encrypted files.[29] The operation – dubbed "Red October" – claimed victims in embassies, government and military institutions in nearly every EU country! It also hit Australia, Iran, Israel, Russia and the US, among others. But Belgium, the home of the EU and NATO headquarters, saw 15 breaches. Over the past five years, the hackers pulled material, such as files, as well as keystroke history and Internet browsing history, from desktop and laptop computers, servers and USB sticks. They also stole contact lists; call histories and SMS's from iPhone, Nokia and Windows Mobile smartphones. In some cases, they hunted for classified software which is used by the European Union or NATO", Kaspersky Lab said in its report. They even accessed files that had been deleted by users and used malware that quietly resurrects itself after it has been discovered. The hackers hid behind proxy servers in Austria, Germany and Russia. But Kaspersky Lab's analysis of the malicious code shows traces of Chinese and Russian-speaking authors. "Currently, there is no evidence linking this with a nation-state-sponsored attack. The information stolen by the attackers is obviously of the highest level and includes geopolitical data, which can be used by nation states. Such information could be traded in the underground and sold to the highest bidder, which can be of course, anywhere", it noted. It is good to see the establishment of Europol (EC3)[30]; their 2014 Internet Organised Crime Threat Assessment (iOCTA) uses the term Crime-As-A-Service (amongst others) and espouses the transition to IPv6 quick sharp as a remedial programme of action.

- The plans for the Invisible Jet Fighter at Lockheed are the subject of thousands of attacks per week by Chinese Cyber Spies (Daily Mail 11 May 2013).[31] A source said: "We have recruited a very strong team of young computer engineers who are basically experts in counter-cyber. They are effectively all geeks and spend much of their time war-gaming against the Chinese". They allow the foreign hackers through the first few security levels and then can work out, through a process of reverse engineering, where the attacks are originating.[32]

- The United States has brought cyber-espionage charges against five Chinese military officials accused of hacking into US companies to gain trade secrets. According to the indictment announced Monday, the hackers targeted the US nuclear power, metals and solar products industries and are accused of stealing trade secrets and economic espionage. Their base of operations is People's Liberation Army Unit 61398, an elite cyber-crimes team that operates from a fortified building on the outskirts of Shanghai. That military group, known there as the 'Comment Crew,' was the subject of a ground breaking 2013 report from a US security firm that tracked their activities online to Internet addresses assigned to a specific city block in China's financial capital.[33]

1.6 BAITING

- USBs now have unmatchable malware. Hackers have now been able to tweak the firmware (the embedded software that allows the hardware to connect at operating system level) to perform disturbing attacks: an infected USB can impersonate a keyboard to type any keystrokes the attacker chooses on the victim's machine. The malware affects the firmware of the USB's micro-controller. That attack program would be stored in the rewritable code that controls the USB's basic functions, not in its flash memory—even deleting the entire contents of its storage wouldn't catch the malware (*Wired Magazine*)

- Baiting - The US National Security Agency experimented with distributing viruses on USBs. They left infected USBs outside various commercial offices of various companies' during the lunch break, randomly thrown on the floor and left like litter. It was found that 78% of these USBs were picked up by team members and then inserted into the company's machines during the afternoon. This is called baiting, and usually the USB is labelled with "executive compensation".

Viruses live hidden in picture files, jpegs and gifs and remain undetectable for years. Simply watching a YouTube video can infect your machine. If you have been diligent for the past 20 years and backed up your data to floppy disks, CD ROMs, DVDs and Large USB devices - these are likely to retain (or legacy viruses) sleeper malware that may not have been detected at the time by the virus programme.

1.7 HEALTH

Health records for countries that require in country storage are unwittingly (or knowingly) held in a Cloud offshore data centres. These records are analysed by peoples unknown, but this information is highly attractive to Health Insurance companies. If the records are stored outside a county's jurisdiction then legal frameworks could be ignored. The World Health Organisation was hacked and several hospitals have had patients' records and their credit card details stolen in parallel.

- Modern Medical devices can stray away from its expected behaviour. Security researchers have found significant flaws and pacemakers, XRAY machines, insulin pumps, pregnancy monitors, and anaesthetic pumps.[34]

- "Cyber attackers executed a very sophisticated attack to gain unauthorised access to one of Anthem's (one of the nation's largest health insurance companies) IT systems and have obtained personal information relating to consumers and Anthem employees who are currently covered, or who have received coverage in the past," company spokeswoman, Kristin Binns, said in a statement. The hacked database contains 80 million records but they anticipate the actual number individuals affected will be lower? "Anthem's initial response in promptly notifying the FBI after observing suspicious network activity is a model for other companies and organisations facing similar circumstances. Speed matters when notifying law enforcement of an intrusion, as cyber criminals can quickly destroy critical evidence needed to identify those responsible," said Paul Bresson, an FBI spokesman. The information accessed included names, birthdays, Social Security numbers, street addresses, email addresses and employment information, such as income data, Binns said. "No credit card banking or financial information was compromised, nor is there evidenced at this time that medical information such as claims, test results, or diagnostic codes were targeted or obtained," she said.[35] Why the database was not encrypted is an issue here.

1.8 FOOD

The food industry was subject to around 18% of hacks in 2014.[36] These are partly due to the number of SCADA (and Industrial Control Systems) and Robotica used in food processing plants, which provide simplistic access to a company IP networked infrastructure. Nearly 80% of manufacturing companies has some sort of SCADA management system.

- Over the last few years' hackers have begun to take a larger interest in food, gastronomy and agriculture. Scientists are now making synthetic foods, and so any breakthrough in this area are more valuable than water. Consumers are also demanding sugar replacements that can replace the syrups and chemicals currently laden into nearly every can and packet that may contribute to disease. Studies on human reactions to food and fat content reduction are a particularly competitive environment. The ability to create DIY molecular gastronomy and recipes is an obvious entry point for hackers in countries with exploding population numbers. Intellectual Property surrounding food system redesign particularly relevant to hackers include: utopian cuisines, biotechnologies manipulation and molecular level food design. New techniques and research into new crops to feed burgeoning populations in large countries is especially valuable to emerging nation states.[37]

SCADA technology lingers about ten years behind, are difficult to upgrade and susceptible, attacks often go unreported, as they do not impact personal or payment information. Industrial companies and vendors tend to keep quiet about attacks so there is little information sharing to help stem these attacks.

1.9 BANKS

- In America, the country's biggest bank disclosed that hackers got a hold of names, addresses, phone numbers and e-mail addresses for 76 million households and 7 million small businesses with JPMorgan accounts. While the bank said there is no evidence that thieves obtained customers' passwords, birth dates or Social Security numbers, the thought of criminals running around with your personal information is enough to frighten anyone.

- Adversaries can now circumvent two-step password authorisation systems used by electronic banking Websites.[38]

- Governments are seriously concerned about Bank security. "Federal officials warned companies that hackers have stolen more than 500 million financial records over the past 12 months, essentially breaking into banks without ever entering a building. "We're in a day when a person can commit about 15,000 bank robberies sitting in their basement", said Robert Anderson, executive assistant director of the FBI's Criminal Cyber Response and Services Branch. The US financial sector is one of the most targeted in the world, FBI and Secret Service officials told business leaders at a cyber security event organised by the Financial Services Roundtable. "You're going to be hacked", Joseph Demarest, assistant director of the FBI's cyber division, told business leaders. "Have a plan". Nearly 439 million records were stolen in the past six months, said Supervisory Special Agent Jason Truppi of the FBI. Nearly 519 million records were stolen in the past 12 months, he said. About 35% of the thefts were from Website breaches, 22% were from cyber espionage, 14% occurred at the point of sale when someone bought something at a retail store, and 9% came when someone swiped a credit or debit card, the FBI said. About 80% of hacking victims in the business community didn't even realise they'd been hacked until they were informed by government investigators, vendors or customers, according to a recent study by Verizon cited by Pawlenty[39].

- Russian penetration-testing experts Alexey Osipov and Olga Kochetova described how they tested a new attack method on several ATMs. They say they successfully programmed a credit-card-sized **Raspberry Pi** computer, which can be connected to the inside of an ATM, for use as a "hardware sniffer" as well as a malicious controller. The device can, for example, intercept PIN codes, as well as send directions directly to different components inside the ATM enclosure, telling them to dispense cash or open the safes in which the cash is stored.[40]

1.10 TELCOS AND ISPS

- The entire globes voice communications and data communications now runs over the Internet. The days of leased lines have disappeared and nearly every call made runs on IP. The Telco's and mobile operators are now being hit. Orange lost 1.3 million customers' details. Eircomm closed down their e-mail system due to a data breach. Bell Canada somehow 'lost' 22,000 addresses. As Telco's turn to the Cloud to sell Pay As You Grow managed services to clients, the Telco's have now become high value targets for adversaries.

- Microsoft's Skype has several vulnerabilities and has been used by agencies to record conversations. A user's Webcam can be taken over to take a snapshot of the user (so keep your webcam covered when browsing). I have always wondered what type of person would be employed by agencies to have the mind-numbing task of listening to a billion conversations and watching their faces during the process? Skype retains discussions and videos for 90 days. I am a big fan of cheap calls and Instant Messaging, as you will read later.

- VOIP (Voice over Internet Protocol), which is now the preferred telecoms platform globally by both Telco's and mobile companies can have inserted steganography viruses in company IP phone systems (everyone's) and infect mobiles. 'Steganography', from the Greek steganos, or 'covered', and graphie, or 'writing', is the hiding of a secret message within an ordinary message and the extraction of it at its destination. That means sneaky viruses can hide inside a VOIP conversation.

1.11 DDOS

- A major headache for Telco's is a Distributed Denial of Service. These DDOS attacks use zombie computers called Botnets that flood telecommunication links to the core Internet (including countries), or, Tier 3 downstream companies. The attack can take down routers and telecoms devices and floods Telco's bandwidths with unnecessary bandwidth. According to an Incapsula survey, 45% of the respondents said their organisation suffered a DDoS attack at some point. However, organisations with 500 or more employees are a larger target and more likely to be hit, the attack costs in their case are higher, and they require more employees to mitigate the cyber attack. Survey respondents estimated the cost of a successful DDoS attack at $40,000 per hour. A total of 36% of respondents said the per hour cost of a DDoS attack is between $5,000 and $19,999. Others said the cost of an attack per hour is less than $5,000 (15%), between $20,000 and $59,999 (17%), between $60,000 and $99,999 (17%), and over $100,000 (15%).

- Considering that 49% of attacks last between 6 and 24 hours, the average cost is estimated at roughly $500,000. However, the security company says some attacks can result in much higher costs.

- Organisations that suffered DDoS attacks also had to deal with non-financial consequences, such as loss of customer trust (43%), customer data theft (33%), and loss of intellectual property (19%). Over half of the respondents said they were forced to replace hardware or software following an attack. In some cases, the malicious actors used DDoS to mask other activities — 50% of those who took part in the survey said they had a piece of malware installed or activated.[41]

- According to estimates, botnets have caused over $9 billion in losses to US victims and over $110 billion in losses globally. Approximately 500 million computers are infected globally each year, translating into 18 victims per second.[42]

- Security researchers say they have discovered a huge botnet running on the smartphones of more than a million unsuspecting mobile users in China. The devices had been infected by a Trojan-based attack first discovered in 2011, news agency Xinhua reported. The botnet can allow the smartphones to be hijacked remotely and potentially used for fraudulent purposes.[43]

1.12 INTERNET OF THINGS

All Sorts of Things (ASOTS) is the latest technology craze and comprise intelligent chips which are now embedded in a variety of appliances; car brakes, smart metering, home control devices, fitness bands, coke machines etc.

- Spike botnets have carried out several DDoS attacks not only from Windows and Linux machines, but also from IOT devices, including freezers and Raspberry Pi. Raspberry Pi is the preferred code used by the IOT standards, as it is small and lightweight. The new variant of malware used by Spike botnets is based on an updated version of the Chinese language Spike malware that is targeting poorly configured Internet-of-Things devices. To date this has been found on 15,000 devices.[44]

1.13 UTILITIES

- Although out of scope for this book, SCADA systems in gas, oil, nuclear and electrical utilities have been compromised and mentioned here, as many private companies have still not upgraded their systems. Due to recession and CAPEX restraints the cost of upgrading can run into millions per Programmable Logic Controller (PLC). A SCADA system runs all the critical controls in a process plant and can turn of entire systems within seconds. (Note to self: don't live within 50 miles of a nuclear power plant, gas production, or, propane store). Nuclear sites have already been subject to a SCADA attack. More urgent are the sites that hold used plutonium where it's highly unlikely that a SCADA Command and Control System have ever been upgraded. A lot of these PLC controllers were installed in the 1980s when programming languages were in their infancy. Many programmers today would struggle to understand this code (think Battlestar Galactica) where every communications device is analogue.

- Dell has reported in their 2015 Dell Security Annual Threat Report that 675,186 attacks happened in 2013.

1.14 WEBSITES IMPACTED

- Amazon, eBay (140 million user details), Facebook (including the King of Privacy's own account), AOL, LinkedIn, Twitter, Google and Gmail, PAYPAL, Microsoft and Apple Cloud Services …all hacked in last 5 years (allegedly).

- There are over 121 billion websites in the world, (www.liveinternetstats.com) and growing. The latest Heartbleed virus has compromised two-thirds of them since June 2014. That means there is a one in three chance you will pick up a virus, or one chance for every tenth Web page you visit. A single malicious URL alone accounted for 712 million attacks. The number of offensive webpage attacks launched from web resources located all over the world increased from 1,595,587,670 in 2012 to 1,700,870,654.[45] That means that there has been at least 15 billion infected sites created in the last decade.

- In August 2014, according to DOSarrest Internet Security's findings by its Vulnerability Testing and Optimisation service (VTO) of deep Website scans, 90% of Websites are vulnerable to attack, which really inspires confidence! Further findings include that 95% of the flaws could cause information leakage due to out-dated software versions and installed modules and 71% could allow sensitive information disclosure. More cross-site request forgery (CSRF) flaws (67%) were found in scans of Websites than cross-site scripting (28%) and SQL Injection vulnerabilities (22%). We will review these attacks later.

- There are around 120,000 phishing Websites in the US alone, most of these aimed at dating sites. According to www.statisticbrain.com there are an estimated 42million registered dating users in the US alone, who have inputted their details and credit card particulars in the last three years. Apparently 32% prefer blondes and 30% believe that, 'personality' is a prospective partner's most important trait. I digress so sorry. Hackers' forums on the Internet describe this sector as an 'easy' hack.

- Facial recognition software is used by Facebook to scan any photo that its one billion plus registered subscribers have uploaded. The software could be used to create passport photographs it is so accurate. This can be done without your knowledge. Border guards extensively use Facebook as a tool to check authenticity and background suitability as you attempt to enter certain countries. Facebook does not delete your data when you close your account, for 90 days. This data (perhaps your Intellectual Property) is their

- In one company I discovered that 50% of the 30,000-odd team members spent an average of 3 hours a day on Facebook, a strange statistic because it meant a third of the 50% must have been surfing full time, every day. This group of people are known as cyber loafers.

- URL shorteners, however, can be used to hide the real target of a link. For example, you'd spend 64 characters to point to Wiki's article about URL shorteners: http://en.wikipedia.org/wiki/URL_shortening. With URL shorteners, you can cut that down to 16 characters: http://bit.ly/c1htE.[46] That means a hacked shortener can send you to any of the 15 billion infected websites that languish on the Internet.

1.15 RETAIL

- Mentioned earlier, Home Depot lost 56 million credit card details. Target and Michael Nyman were hit over the 2014 Christmas Holidays. The Sony data breach in 2011 compromised 100 million customer details. Microsoft Xbox got hacked by four hackers aged 18 to 28, one from Canada, one from Australia and two in the USA. They allegedly stole $100m of intellectual property (source code). In the December 2014 repeat of this Sony lost films for release, scripts for new films in production as well as a raft of personal to corporate emails. The Christmas Day Denial of Service also swiftly followed this for Sony and Microsoft games platforms.

- Cyber security suffers from poor execution, former White House cyber security co-ordinator Howard Schmidt has said. "The cyber security strategies we have are all excellent pieces of work, but we are still failing in execution," he told the ISSE 2014 security conference in Brussels. "While we talk about Advanced Persistent Threats (APTs), I agree many are 'persistent' but few are 'advanced' because most exploit known vulnerabilities for which there is a patch, but it has just not been applied," said Schmidt. This is underlined by the fact that many of the recent high-profile data breaches at US retailers can be traced back to something that could have been prevented. Another common reason security fails, he said, is that users of computer systems routinely ignore security warnings because of their desire to get things done. Companies do not check their own applications regularly so a technique is needed to address this flaw.

1.16 CLOUD SERVICE PROVIDERS (CSP'S)

Can the Cloud be hacked? Yes it can – they buy the same server operating systems as everyone else! The easiest way in is via Management Interfaces most admins need to access the Cloud instance via a standard SSH as root when they set up the template. The Cloud is vulnerable to SQL Injection. Clouds have Insiders too that could be bribed or blackmailed. If hackers steal your cloud credentials its 90% certainty that they have your company access too! Encouraging client account compromises is usually carried out through phishing attacks. An average of 100,000 files per customer sit on the Cloud unencrypted – these are usually created by Shadow IT initiatives. That's about 6 billion documents. When two or more CSPs inter-operate (sharing VM's and associated data) these transfers could be infected.

- Besides 7 days downtime in the last 3 years CSPs are getting exploited. During 2014 Data breaches included Google Mail (Gmail) 5 million address and passwords posted to Russian Website, Amazon (Zappos - Credit Cards and Zeus Bot), Microsoft (BPOS). Apple iCloud (celebrity pictures [naked selfies] hacked), AT&T (insider breach affecting 1,600 customers), Community Health Systems (4.5 million health records stolen).

- The Ponemon Institute's recent 2014 study of 613 security professionals revealed:

- Increasing use of cloud services can increase the probability of a $20 million data breach by as much as three times.

- 36 per cent of business-critical applications are housed in the cloud, yet IT isn't aware of nearly half of them, this is called Shadow IT usually caused by business frustration to get things done.

- Approximately 30 per cent of business information is stored in the cloud, 35 per cent of it isn't visible to IT and it isn't encrypted.

- Cloud services are now susceptible to DDOS attacks, a major one from Amazon EC2 after the CIA announced they would be using it in 2013, France-based CloudFlare being the latest. Apple's iCloud was hacked and celebrities' personal and compromising photos put on public display in October 2014.[47] However, this did spur Apple to enable Two Step Authentication.

- The Alert Logic report examines more than 200,000 security incidents at more than 2,000 organisations in North America and Western Europe. The report found that while cloud attacks are on the rise, this only brings them on par with attacks at traditional data centres, and even then only for certain types of attacks, (CIO Reports)

- The most common types of attacks that cloud hosting providers faced were brute force attacks that focused on security credentials and scans for software with known security vulnerabilities. Both of these types of attacks were encountered by 44 per cent of the cloud-based businesses in the study. Alert Logic claims that these numbers are significant because, for the first time, the percentage of cloud-based businesses affected by these types of attacks mirror the percentage of affected businesses with traditional, on-premise data centres.

- Cloud hosting providers are facing an increased threat from malware and botnet attacks although only 11 per cent of these organisations (around 100 CSPs) faced these types of incidents. The report concluded by claiming that neither form of computing is inherently more or less secure and that, over time, the number and types of attacks on cloud hosting providers will probably equal those targeting on-premise data centres.[48]

- In the last five months of 2014, there were 1,413 full Internet outages worldwide, or about nine days, and nearly 8,000 partial outages, or 53 a day, according to figures from the free Internet service tracker. A full outage results when a Web service is unavailable; a partial outage happens when only some of a service's users are affected.[49]

1.17 COMPONENT ATTACKS

- SIM CARDS - Malware code has been discovered on mobile SIM cards produced in Holland …this malware is written into the firmware element of the SIM card allowing National Agencies to steal names passwords and data on an estimated 2 Billion mobile and smartphones.

- HARD DISKS - Kaspersky report that a sophisticated malware agent has been discovered in firmware of popular hard Drives. The malware has been secretly inserted in the hard drives at the manufacturing stage and is only accessible by a custom API. Reformatting the disk does not remove it and it is undetectable by Anti Virus scanning. The hard drives that have been corrupted are from Western Digital, Seagate and Toshiba. Seagate have produced 1.5 billion Hard Drives and have 40% of the market Share. Western

Digital has a 42% and Toshiba have a 13% market share respectively.[50] These Disk Drives are deployed in External Disk Drives (Back Up Storage), Servers, Routers and Storage Arrays. Western Digital has $15.6 billion in assets. Seagate has a $3.7 billion turnover with partners in Server and in Cloud Providers infrastructure. Toshiba is a $60 Billion enterprise making Laptops, Tablets (Like Google Chromebook), TVs, USBs, Wired and Wireless Hard Drives, and Telephone Systems. This product range also extends to Power Systems and Nuclear systems, Printers, Process Control Systems, and Program Logic Controllers (PLC). This may also affect such systems deployed in Agribusiness, Oil and Gas, Mining, Food and Beverage and Pharmaceutical control systems. Kaspersky report that the malware is similar to the STUXNET malware used to attack Iran's nuclear facilities. There is no mention of this on these vendors' websites so it may be hearsay?

1.18 GENERAL SKULLDUGGERY

Although not hacked, the tapes holding the details of US soldiers and their families were stolen from a car in 2011. So physical security is also tightly coupled to cyber security.

Lenovo PCs were shipped with Superfish Malware, which analysed users Internet habits and injects third party advertising into websites on IE and Chrome browsers, this also enabled Man In The Middle attacks by changing certificates. 44,000 laptops apparently infected.

Anyone can openly buy a Trojan (Kronos) for $7,000 on the Dark Web (A shadow Internet based on the TOR network used by criminals, terrorists and anyone who does not want to be part of any Nation State or Government Agency snooping) to hack banking systems – so anyone can do this. Why these Websites remain active on the Web is still an unsettling legal predicament. The Dark Web is now a hacker's playground - as Government Agencies now seek to trace and kill aggressors hackers have hidden their movements and communications so no matter how much monitoring of traffic is listened to there are now parallel webs and shadow Internets and networks that are out of reach to traditional surveillance methods. The TOR network is an example of this; Tor routes Internet traffic through a free, global volunteer network consisting of more than ten thousand relays that conceal a user's location and usage from anyone who conducts network surveillance, traffic analysis, or data capture. Using Tor makes it more difficult for Internet activity to be traced back to the subscriber: this includes "visits to Web sites, online posts, instant messages, and other communication forms". Tor's use is intended to protect the personal privacy of subscribers, as well as their freedom and ability to conduct confidential communication by keeping their Internet activities from being monitored. An extract of a Top Secret appraisal by the National Security Agency (NSA) characterised Tor as "the King of high-secure, low-latency Internet anonymity" with "no contenders for the throne in waiting" [51] The Onion Browser is simply downloaded from the web and anyone can start to use this. The owner of one of the Silk Road servers is now in jail.

Security Officers (SO) and analysts in organisations must be tearing their hair out as the tsunami of malware and exposures makes them seem like they are not doing their jobs. In fact, in 50% of all companies the security officer role is just a sole security practitioner. This is a High Risk path. Security practitioners are not the only ones suffering.

There is an 80% chance that the anti-virus software will not work on your device. Anti-virus cannot keep up with the number of viruses created each day. Anti-Virus companies are overwhelmed and cannot cope with the volume and massively complex number of viruses or malware. It now takes years to analyse threats and release patches.

1.19 HAVING A WHALE OF A TIME

Corporate executives traveling in Asia may need to be extra cautious the next time they connect to a hotel's Wi-Fi network - that is if they haven't already been hacked. Whaling is directed specifically toward senior executives and other high-profile targets within an organisation[52].

Over the last four years, malicious hackers have been stealing data from company executives while they stay in luxury hotels in an attack known as

"Darkhotel," security research firm Kaspersky Lab revealed. Kaspersky Labs explains[53]:

> The hackers wait until, after check-in, the victim connects to the hotel Wi-Fi network, submitting his room number and surname at the login. The attackers see him in the compromised network and trick him into downloading and installing a backdoor that pretends to be an update for legitimate software - Google Toolbar, Adobe Flash or Windows Messenger. The unsuspecting executive downloads this hotel "welcome package," only to infect his machine with a backdoor, Darkhotel's spying software.
>
> Once the hack is over, all trace of the attack is removed and unsuspecting victims go about their lives not knowing that sensitive data on them and their corporations has been stolen, according to Kaspersky. The hackers never go after the same target twice.[54]

1.20 A NEW SAVVY GENERATION

Eleven million digital savvy youngsters have left Facebook since 2011 (a 18.3% reduction in the US alone) according to isstrategylabs.com. As Millennial's get more aware of privacy and surveillance fears together with the knock on effects of cyber bullying, these digital natives are moving away and hiding their tracks. In Germany 15% of adults (10,759,132 users) have now stopped using the Internet in the last year. If we extrapolate the German numbers to meet global penetration that would see a staggering 420 million globally rethinking how they use the Internet or revert back to more traditional methods of social media like talking to people. Social media companies are experiencing difficulty attracting new subscribers. One in Three people are learning not to provide correct details when they sign up for a service, which makes a mockery of sales and marketing campaigns and follow-ups from outbound call centres. Pseudo identities are now the norm; my nephew and nieces now have multiple pseudo identities. One for work, one for banking, and one for personal friends, one for mobiles (et al.), all with varying dates of birth, addresses, email addresses and names. For companies this trend adds high customer acquisition costs in terms of follow-ups and skews targeting market sectors. We now have databases full of nonsense pseudo IDs that could account for 30% of databases integrity. These figures skew every marketing database.

1.21 INFORMATION LEMMINGS

This alarming set of statistics should make you reach for your book of passphrases and change them. It hasn't stopped our love affair with the Internet. Ron Deibart of the Freedom Online Coalition writes; "Cyber security is important to all of us because our lives are now enmeshed with digital information and communication technologies. Our kids, our craft, and our livelihood — everything we do — now depend on instantaneous access to communications and information networks. While everyone can readily agree that cyber security is critical, how to secure cyberspace, to what end, and for whom, are all questions around which there is widespread controversy and disagreement. For some, cyber security means securing the global communication's infrastructure regardless of territorial boundaries, from the code to the satellites and everything in between. For yet others, the security of cyberspace are a function of an overarching concern with the security of human rights.[55]"

Google has 600,000 requests from subscribers to erase digital archaeology from their search engine. This includes companies whose reputation has been tarnished. Governments are hiding awkward policy documents and proceedings that were official judgements from their websites. Nobody wants to share real information anymore. Searches can take an eternity – I find scouring 25 to 30 pages before I find an answer frustrating. So searches that were supposed to help teach the next generation lessons learnt are disappearing.

As we will see, the breaches described so far are just hackers 'test and try' reconnaissance visits from state-sponsored and organised crime teams. We are witnessing the tip of the iceberg from the sinking ship. Criminal adversaries are the organisations who are spearheading the blossoming massive cyber attack that will have global implications and it's visible on the horizon, in fact it's predicted to happen this year. This know how is now being turned against companies In the IT industry we are already discussing *Cybergeddon*-not the *how*, but the *when*. The WEF Global Risk Report 2015 alludes to Cyber Attacks and Critical Information Infrastructure

Breakdown as likely and with the highest of impact this year. [56]We just have not adapted properly to the risk, and our IT departments and IT vendors are clearly at fault. In parallel, executives do not understand the scale of the problem although there is plenty of evidence to support a major Cybrid outbreak. In a recent survey[57] by NTT Com Security of 800 global non-IT executives in large organisations, 63% of globally based executives believed their critical data safe, so the message that it is clearly not safe has not yet resonated with this delusional collective.

We have turned ourselves into Information Lemmings. This is a non-extensive list of Information that most people have left on the Internet during the last twenty years:

- Ex Employers
- Ex employees
- Employees and Contractors
- Schools and Universities
- Government Agencies
- Utilities
- Health Care providers
- Places you have shopped
- On line shopping
- Insurance companies
- Internet Service Providers
- Software Companies
- Hardware PC/Laptop and Tablet manufacturers
- Printer Manufacturers
- Social Networks
- DNS (Domain Name Service)
- Search Engines
- Credit Card providers
- Banks
- Lawyers
- Mortgage brokers

- Scorned lovers
- Everyone else they share it with

1.22 STEPCHECK

- The Internet is not as safe a place as we like to think and has to change for good economic reasons …SMBs can take advantage of this turmoil to find new markets

- Information is a commodity that is worth millions to cyber criminals and hostiles, nothing is stopping this right now so SMBs need a plan to get defensive

- The number of incidents is increasing with the likelihood of a Cybergeddon this year!

- The attack techniques are highly sophisticated, so a company has to be fleet of foot and apply some rigour in the company to minimise the impact

- A new generation is emerging that know their way around computing better than you do, so businesses need to lockdown their IT estates

2 ROOT CAUSE - SYSTEMIC DISINTEGRATION

In this chapter we review some of the known attack techniques that are causing the systemic disintegration of compute platforms and supporting networks.

2.1 TECHNIQUES

Malware is so sophisticated that every technical element of computing is now wide open to attack. If you have had time to read through the Malware timeline in the Appendices you will see the lengths that attackers and snoopers will go to steal Information. In this section we will look at the A to Z of the various techniques used for exposures. This will be used as a baseline for when we discuss RIDPOINTS in a later chapter – how exciting! At the end of each technique description I have placed a remedial action and a basic risk scoring. As we will see later this inputs to the Malware Harm Index. These are firstly practical, and secondly help profile service assurance and assist in basic risk measurement, but it should help add form to the problems that everyone faces - know thy enemy!

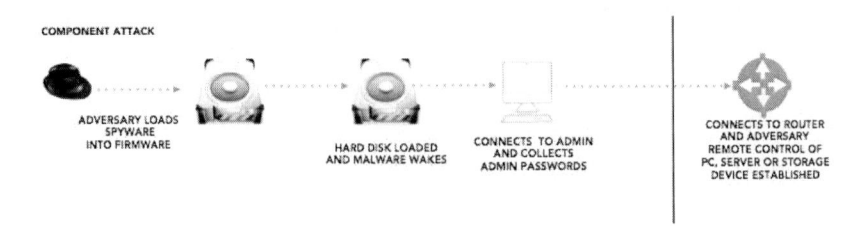

Figure 2 - COMPONENT ATTACK

Malware, when executed, replicates or transforms by inserting copies of itself into other computer applications, data files, or the boot sector of the hard disk (such as a Component Attack) to spread the infection. Malware can hide in a Word document, an Excel spread sheet, a Web script when connecting to a Website via JavaScript and other lightweight code, embedded in a video, or latterly in a pdf or SMS. If you have ever had a virus, you may know from past experience that getting an anti-virus removal tool downloaded from your anti-virus vendor of choice, when running that tool it attempts to disinfect the area on the hard drive, by placing the malicious code in quarantine, known as a sandbox. Operating System vendors build 'sandboxes' into your hard disk so that this code can be kept away from the main kernel. That's OK, except that nowadays these malicious Lines of Code (LOCs) sit there in the sandbox waiting for a future wake-up call, deletion has been engineered out of malware so it will attempt a duplication of itself before it gets moved to the sandbox. Malware now attacks the BIOS (Basic Input Output System firmware) and can wake up when the PC is booted. These concepts may be alien to many readers so we will explore the devices make up and how various viruses can impact components.

Viruses often perform some type of harmful activity on infected hosts, such as stealing hard disk space or Central Processing Unit CPU (the chip) time, accessing private information, corrupting data, displaying political or humorous messages on the user's screen, steal and spam their contacts, or collecting a user's keystrokes, scraping passwords, etc. In the early days of viruses these were visual in nature, i.e., the user would be aware of the infection. After the millennium it all went a bit quiet, so a user would have no idea anything was wrong.

Some viruses were quite funny, replicating the infamous Windows 'Blue Screen of Death' or putting up a V sign on the user's screen. In fact, professional hacking teams ensure that their code does not affect system resources to avoid detection; they quality test their own code to ensure that it remains sleeping and hidden from detection. These adversaries are really very good coders! In the early days it took only about 250 LOC to produce a virus. The Zeus Trojan now has 250,000 odd LOC and can distribute this code on a number of applications. However, not all viruses carry a destructive payload, or attempt to conceal themselves – the defining characteristic of viruses is that they are self-replicating computer programs which install themselves on any component in a PC without the user's consent. Some malware seems to linger on PCs in RAM (Random Access Memory), which makes detection and forensics close to impossible.

2.2 BACKDOORS

Backdoors are a weakness in the authentication process developed in an application. Adversaries use this to secure unauthorised remote access to plaintext. Plaintext (or Cleartext) is information a sender transmits to a receiver as part of a cryptographic message or a file. Operating Systems store plaintext in a file (such as a Web browser that stores a user's password). It is possible to view these browser passwords just by going into the browser security settings options. A backdoor in a login system might take the form of a hard coded user and password combination, which gives access to the system, files; in some custom applications the compiler can be used to reveal these combinations. A programmer can code this functionality in a couple of lines of code and have complete access to the software kernel.

When I used to develop applications I always built in a backdoor to let me support the application remotely. It's the done thing by coders globally. This is generally accepted practice, and fine as long as you are always the one maintaining the code for on-going operations (but remains harmful once the developer has left the company). A backdoor is a means of access to a computer program that bypasses usual security mechanisms. A programmer may sometimes install a backdoor so that the program can be accessed for troubleshooting or other purposes after it is launched into production. However, the problem is exacerbated when revolving around a large deployment, when many disparate coders and companies are building the application under development. These coders and programmers are people dotted around the globe that you have probably never met; they bring a set of tools that they have used in the past, code from other applications and companies, and code downloaded from the Web to help them create bespoke applications. However, attackers often use backdoors that they detect or remotely install themselves, as part of an exploitation project. In some cases, a worm is designed to take advantage of a backdoor created by an earlier attack. A nasty example of this was the Nimda malware that gained entrance through a backdoor left by Code Red. Coders on the open market sell these exploits.

Most application developments are never quality tested or penetration tested before they go into production. They should be tested. Well, that's the theory; 90% of the time applications are thrown over the operations wall under time duress from the business. Methods like Agile and DevOps seek to remedy this by being inclusive of operations, but even these development processes are very rarely inclusive of security, quality, or leaves a documented audit trail.

In January 2014 a backdoor was discovered in Android by a team of hackers. This is a popular attack method since 2005 in Linux machines where the bug voids the SSL authentication process (the 'goto cleanup' backdoor patch was released in March 2014).

Routers have also been caught in this loop when the NSA (allegedly) exploited this exposure and loaded backdoors in new deliveries of Firewalls en route (*sic*) to customers.

REMEDIAL: 6 – Up-to-date patching of all systems, especially servers in the IT Infrastructure Estate. Constant code quality checking during development is essential, as well as security tests on code in production Follow CVMP Cryptographic Module Validation Program. Ensure all storage is encrypted. Regular Cisco IOS updates.

RISK: 7

2.3 BOTNETS

A Botnet resembles a backdoor exploit, but it does this across many computers at the same time (as long as they have the same Botnet commander). A single command and control server, or multiple command and control servers 'wake up' zombie PC's at a prescribed time or date. The ancestry of Botnets goes back to the IRS (Internet Relay Chat) days and chat room administrators devised a script to eject disruptive attendees. This automated script was 'adjusted' in 1999 to become Win32/PrettyPark, a mass-mailing worm that collected IRC users' usernames and passwords and e-mail addresses. The Botnet was controlled in a command and control fashion by the adversary and replicated via IRC channels and infected about 32% of the IRC user base. It evolved to AgoBot and SdBot variants that faded with the popularity of IRC.

The term 'Botnets of Zombies' (or Zombie PCs) is used to describe the PC state once it has been compromised. Botnets can be used to infect the victims PC and data from the victims PC is then sent to a "hop point". A hop point is an intermediary between computers used to attack the victim computer. A Hop Point conceals the true origin of commands being sent to a victim's computer, or the true destination of files and information extracted from a victim's computer. The victims' computer sees only the IP address of the hop point and not the adversaries IP address. This technique conceals the IP address, location and identity of the adversary. The hop point can be a rented server or even a server in an SMB estate. For the SMB this has serious legal implications, as forensics will trace back the data spill link to an unaware company, which would then be liable for fines and damage restitution. So

Botnet variants can be bought off the Web in a commercial malware kits like Reptile and Zeus, so anyone can become a hacker for $200. The Zeus malware kit gave birth to the ZBot family, which is not controlled by an adversary or even a group of adversaries but by self-replicating unrelated Botnets controlled by other unsuspecting people. This allows a high degree of anonymity and acts like a sleeper. It can be spread by social engineering and even attach itself to other forms of malware or even in legitimate code in mail systems.

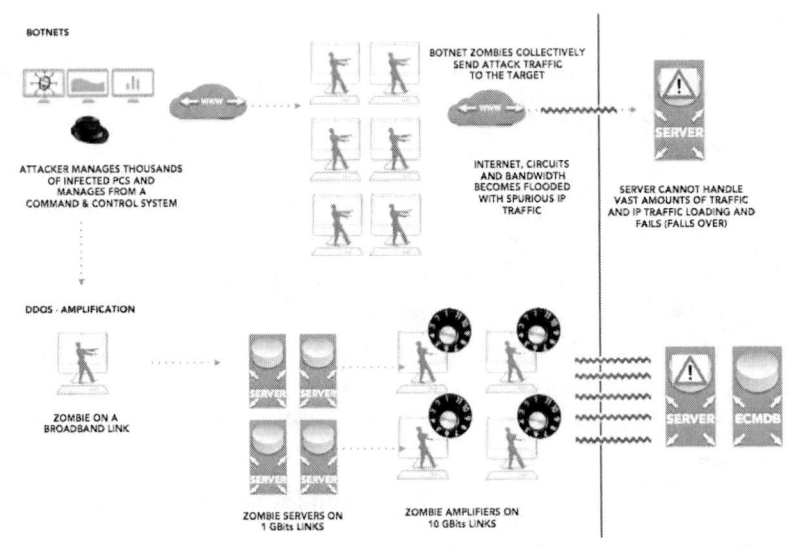

Figure 3 - BOTNETS AND ZOMBIES

Botnets can hide themselves in HTTP, which make them irritatingly difficult to detect. The Win32/Svelta receives instructions from specially decoded entries the adversary puts up on Twitter. They can hide inside TCP or UDP stacks, so cloaking themselves from IPS and IDS tools.

Advertising on the Internet operates on a 'pay-per-click' model; every time a visitor clicks on the ad, the Website operator gets a fee. Google use this model to collect advertising revenues. A click-through can range from .50 cents to $10 for one of those intrusive videos, mostly new car campaigns. Adversaries and organised crime (and perhaps some advertising companies' marketing departments) use Botnets to generate fraudulent clicks on pay-per-click advertisements. A Botnet controller can establish a website with advertisements and negotiate an arrangement with a Web host that pays the controller for clicks on their ads. The controller writes the Bot code that automates the click-through so that the Bots in the Botnet collective (which can number up to 20,000 unique IP's) instantly click on the ads on that Website. It does not take a maths' guru to tell you 20,000 clicks at $10 a time is lucrative. So an advertiser can pay out an estimated $200,000 for zero lead generation. As the Botnets are also unique, the advertiser is liable to pay for this, so a site can claim unique ghost click-thru. This process can be further compromised if the Bot hijacks the start page of a compromised computer so that the click-through are executed each time the owner of the compromised computer opens their browser, victimising both the owner of the system and the Web host. This is why many advertisement campaigns are mostly worthless, and a marketing re-think on the true value of Internet marketing is a beneficial route to market. It's like throwing money over a cliff.

Botnets increase their threat profile by downloading more malware to a user's device to cream traditional profits. Early Botnets often just installed adware, spyware, and other potentially unwanted software in an attempt to earn quick profits. Nowadays they download packet sniffers, keystroke loggers, and additional sophisticated backdoor malware.

REMEDIAL: **5** - weak passwords and/or unprotected file shares, local and domain administrator rights, newer versions of Windows OS or move to another platform.

RISK: **10**

2.4 BRICKING

This is a modern nasty. So many PCs rely on BIOS upgrades and firmware upgrades, usually at the chip level. At one of the largest oil and gas companies in the world they found they couldn't boot up 30,000 PCs one day. A piece of code had lodged itself into the boot up routine and basically stopped each PC starting up.

PCs are not the only devices to experience this now; because the code can be placed at chip level, all sorts of gaming devices such as the ones your teenagers play with all night are experiencing bricking. This means that vendors own security culture is questionable.

2.4.1.1 SOFT BRICK
A soft-bricked device usually boots unsuccessfully and generally gets stuck on the vendor logo or reboots itself endlessly. Some major bugs in smartphones have been discovered that cause the device to crash endlessly.

2.4.1.2 HARD BRICK
Oh dear! The device shows no signs of life and the screen remains blank, resulting in 'the Black Screen of Death'.

REMEDIAL: **10** - If soft bricked, then clear the memory and do a hard reset. Recovering from a hard brick is generally considered difficult and requires the use of JTAG to re-flash firmware or replacing the motherboard of the device. In some cases a JTAG repair isn't possible and replacement of the device's motherboard is required

RISK: **9**

2.5 COOKIES
I wish someone would get rid of these damn things. Originally popularised by Microsoft, AOL, Yahoo and Netscape in their Internet Explorer and Netscape browsers, they have remained around ever since 1994. These cookies are snooping, small, irritating, usually randomly encoded text files that help your browser navigate through a particular Website. The site you're browsing is accepted and processed by your computer's browser software

in turn generates the cookie file. The cookie file is stored in your browser's folder or subfolder. It is a marketing invention that has been around for 20 years and quite frankly is only used by companies (and some governments) to track browsing history, what sites you visited and how often, then tailor directed online advertising in pop-up ads on your screen, even when you're not using a browser.

Vendors should really stamp out the use of cookies once and for all; they skew your computer's performance and suck Internet bandwidth that you ultimately pay for. To be honest, they are nothing but a pain and this was a marketing consultant's wet dream. About 15 years ago the big ISP's came up with the Walled Garden concept. To make money out of Internet users the ISP (or Telco) would keep you in the Garden and monitor your every click. Once you clicked on an advert, the advertiser paid a commission to the portal and then you would be remembered forever. This click-through is how Google created the world's biggest revenue stream (AdSense), which once seemed a cool idea.

Your browser accesses the cookie file again when you visit the Website that created the cookie file. The browser uses the information stored in the cookie file to help ease your navigation of the Website by letting you log in automatically, or remembering settings you selected during your earlier visits to the Website, among many other functions.

They are painful and should have been outlawed years ago. Cookies store usernames and passwords and remember formed content a user has previously entered, such as a credit card number, or, an address. Storing private details should be an encrypted decision provided by a user and not the website. When a user accesses a Website with a cookie function for the first time, a cookie is sent from the server to the browser and stored with the browser in the local computer or mobile. Later, when that user goes back to the same Website, the Website will recognise the user because of the stored cookie with the user's information. These are the credentials that hackers use to steal your passwords and information.

These authentication cookies are the most common method used by Web servers to know whether the user is logged in or not, and which account they are logged in with. Without such a mechanism, the site would not know whether to send a page containing sensitive information, or require the user to authenticate themselves by logging in.

The security of an authentication cookie generally depends on the security of the issuing Website and the user's browser, and on whether the cookie data is encrypted. Security vulnerabilities allow a cookie's data to be read by an attacker and used to gain access to user data, or used to gain access (with the user's own credentials) to the Website to which the cookie belongs. This fuels cross-site scripting and forgery. They are now tied to web beacons, which are transparent image files used to monitor your journey around a single Website or collection of sites. They are also referred to as Web bugs and are commonly used by sites that hire third-party services to monitor traffic. They may be used in association with cookies to understand how visitors interact with the pages and content on a Web site.

Cookie-based ad tracking has also evolved through the years. From simple operations like counting ad impressions, and preserving ad sequence, cookies have evolved to user profiling/Website preference tracking. 'Web-based device fingerprinting' is the process of collecting enough of that information through the browser to perform stateless ad impressions, and preserving ad sequence, cookie's, unique. With the right information, these fingerprints can be collected by private companies who then store and use it to track the device across the Web. This latter group of activities – ad tracking – has attracted controversy among online consumer privacy groups and other concerned parties.

Websites retain your cookie information without your permission. Few Websites actually delete this data, and even Website administrators sell this on to hackers and spammers. This brings me on to a new subject: the selling of personal data to 'third parties'. Years ago, if you wished to target a certain customer type by geography and salary income, then you could approach the company or the internal sys admin to supply the database of names and e-mails pertaining to that collection. This selling on of personal data is rife and should be entirely illegal, but there are no controls to stop this practice. There are very few Websites that actually claim not to sell your information on. There is a Web domain-naming supplier who is actually a marketing company. They are based in Canada but actually keep your information on servers in America so they can do anything with your data. Canada's privacy laws are pretty tight, but America's are not, so the supplier can actually claim it's a legitimate practise.

The problem gets worse when companies and even governments use Cloud services. If you are in a country with stringent privacy laws and you use a Cloud service, your data can be sitting on a server in, say, Romania where these laws are worthless. There is no guarantee from the major Cloud providers that this practice is not employed. This is particularly irksome when dealing with Cloud providers who purvey health records databases. Some sources rumour that health records are kept and maintained offshore in the Middle East (apparently for cleansing); this means most health records are freely accessible by governments and hackers who act outside of country boundaries. This means also that your details could be sold to insurance companies wishing for deep background checks on your insurance viability, and anyone else who is checking credit level. There is no one you should trust your private details with on the Web, a problem we have all been guilty of in the past.

REMEDIAL: Even if there are measures you can take, like enabling 'Do Not Track' on your browser (or if you are desperate not to be tracked switch to Tor), and even with legal protections in place, like those restricting cookies, loading a Webpage requires a personal decision and give and take choice, and what your browser gives away through JavaScript or Flash could be enough for you to be identified and tracked.

RISK: 7

2.6 CROSS SITE SCRIPTING

Scripting languages such as Java can access cookies (see above), which allows the Java (Applet, Java Beans or JavaScript) to capture this information and send it to an adversary's server. This is a constant threat, as there are always ways of crowbarring these into Websites, and Website developers never test or verify these Java applets. It's usually discovered by an external penetration test to reveal this malicious code (sometimes). Forgery can take place if the adversary can still use the cookie during a user's browsing session.

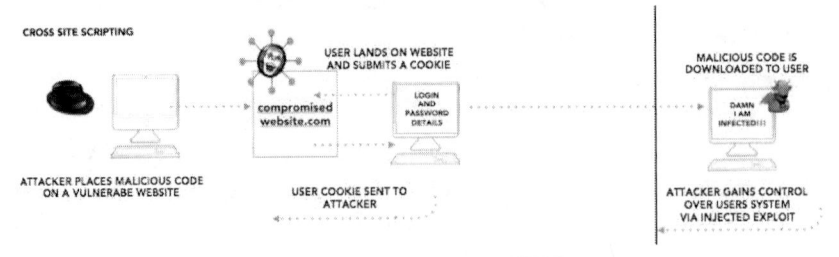

Figure 4 - X SITE SCRIPTING

REMEDIAL: **6** - Use of the CAPTCHA should halt most automated scripts executing. Clear cookies that have not expired, ideally after each Website visit … painful but necessary.

RISK: **8**

2.7 DISTRIBUTED DENIAL OF SERVICE (DDOS)

If you have ever seen panic-stricken network technicians' faces pale beyond white, it's when their network gets a DDOS attack. A DDOS does exactly that: it sends deep panic throughout an organisation because there is little to do about it. Your network is effectively down.

A DDOS overwhelms a server (or servers) in a data centre in an enterprise or in the Cloud. It uses a collective of Botnets to do this, and floods the Wide Area Network (WAN) or broadband communications lines with traffic, blocking out normal network traffic. DDOS attacks target companies or subscribers. An example of this was the attacks on MasterCard, PostFinance.ch, PayPal Blog and the Swedish Prosecutors Website after the WikiLeaks revelations, and these organisations decided to close WikiLeaks accounts. This campaign was called Operation Payback, during December 2010.

Flooding a service/server with legitimate requests starts denials of Service attacks, so that it can no longer reply in a timely fashion. The server cannot cope and ceases functioning. An alternative is to exploit an existing vulnerability in the service that allows deployment of malware to consume resources, or cause the service to crash or become unresponsive. Since flood-based DOS attacks require multiple simultaneous requests/connections to a service, the attacker requires lot of computing power and bandwidth. Most of such attacks make use of a large number of computers, and this often involves hijacking computers, turning them into so called 'zombies', and using them as the source of the attack. In this case, the DOS attack is known as being distributed (DDOS), as it uses multiple, distinct attack sources spread over a large geographical area. The attacker would either need to be in control of a Botnet, or purchase the use of part of a Botnet from the black market for such an attack.

Distributed denials of service attacks are popular with adversaries as it is difficult to protect against them. Simple DOS attacks are detected by firewalls or intrusion detection systems, and the source IP can be automatically blocked, causing the attack to fail. On the other hand, blocking the source of a DDOS is complex, as it is difficult to distinguish between a legitimate connection and one that is part of the DDOS.

2.7.1.1 INCREASING IN STRENGTH

In the US, the incidence of DDOS attacks has increased in 2014 by 18%. Attack parameters such as average attack bandwidth and duration saw a similar consistent increase, a sign that the strength of the attacks is on a similar increasing trend. The most popular targets are vulnerable protocols like Character Generation Protocol (CHARGEN), Network Time Protocol (NTP) and Domain Name System protocol (DNS), these services are often enabled and are all UDP based, allowing attackers hide their identity and source of attack. More than 87% of the attacks take place at infrastructure level, while the rest take place at application level, targeting mostly SSL, HTTP protocols. [58]

A adversarial controller can commence the attack and flood WAN links for days, or schedule attacks at the end of month when they know finance are compiling accounting reports. A collector can make this attack last for a day or for 10 minutes at 20-minute intervals, so carrying out forensics becomes impossible. It has been known for a 10 GB circuit to be completely flooded using this type of attack. The Spamhaus DDOS attack that was aimed at US Banks suffered a 300 GBit/s attack for 30 minutes. There are differing varieties of flood attacks including:

2.7.1.2 HTTP FLOODS

When we review the OSI 7 Layer Model (discussed later), websites are classed as applications in the Application Layer. HTTP uses two programming command lines: GET and POST. GET and POST are the most common commands used in Cloud infrastructures parlance. During SSL sessions this language is used to GET or POST images and information. A Website can be hit with hundreds of thousands of GET requests for data from websites (URLs) from all around the world under the commander's control. The server has to respond to every GET request, which brings about system failures as the server chip and memory becomes overwhelmed by the repeated requests. It's like being the politician at a huge press conference and sequentially answering every question – there is only so much a politician can take before rubbish gets uttered. The overload on the website server is such that server-level caching is unable to stop it. The incoming URLs are dynamic and the application forces a re-load of the content from the database for every new request that is not in cache, which repeatedly creates a new page.

2.7.1.3 SYN FLOODS

There's a protocol flaw in TCP that makes SYN (Synchronise) flood attacks possible – which is addressed in IPv6. This five-step attack sends TCP connections requests faster than a server can process them.

The adversary creates a random source address for each packet (see IPv4 explanation)

The SYN flag set in each packet is a request to open a new connection to the server from the spoofed IP address derived from the Botnet

The attacked server responds to the spoofed IP address, then waits for confirmation, that acknowledgement never arrives (waits about three minutes) and the server connection table fills up waiting for replies

After the table fills up, all new connections and legitimate subscribers are kicked off the service

2.7.1.4 UDP FLOODS

The User Datagram Protocol is part of a TCP/IP stack. A UDP flood is started by a controller to send big UDP packets to random ports on a router or firewall. The router or server will then send out ICMP packets (Internet Control Message Protocol) to say the host is unavailable. The router has to do this repeatedly, blocking normal users. The adversary controller can also spoof their IP address, which could be any other legitimate site. The ICMP attack can lead to a Ping Flood, Smurf and/or Fraggle Attacks.

DDOS represents a dual risk for Security. It results in downtime and lost productivity. It can completely stop e-mail, VOIP, a Website, Cloud processing and data centres. The downtime caused by DDOS can result in significant financial losses. For example, Forrester estimates that the average financial damage from four hours of Website downtime is a loss of $2.1 million dollars, and $27 million for 24-hour outage. Forrester also reports that financial services companies lost an estimated $17 million per DDOS incident in 2012, assume that sum is tripled since that time.[59]

2.7.1.5 REFLECTION DDOS

Reflection and amplification DDOS attacks are launched against protocol stacks such as the Domain Naming Service (DNS), Network Time Protocol (NTP), and Simple Message Transfer Protocol (SMTP Email). Adversaries now abusing Simple Service Discovery Protocol (SSDP) a part of the Universal Plug-and-Play (UPnP) protocol standard – to target home and office. SSDP is a network protocol enabled on millions of networked devices, such as computers, printers, Internet gateways, Router / Wi-Fi access points, mobile devices, Webcams, smart TVs and gaming consoles, to discover each other and automatically establish working configurations that enable services like data sharing, media streaming, media playback control.

The weakness in the Universal Plug-and-Play standard could allow an attacker to compromise millions of devices (including the Internet of Things), and used to launch an effective DDoS attack on a target such as other Internet of Things widgets. Attackers have found that Simple Object Access Protocol (SOAP) used to exchange sensitive information in a decentralised, distributed IT environment – requests "can be crafted to elicit a response that reflects and amplifies a packet, which can be redirected towards a target." An attack can be magnified by a factor of 10, creating a cascade attack known as Amplification (imagine a volume knob control on a guitar amplifier).

2.7.1.6 MILLIONS OF DEVICES VULNERABLE

According to security researchers, about 38 per cent of the 11 million Internet-facing UPnP devices, i.e. over 4.1 million devices, in use today are potentially vulnerable to being used in this type of reflection DDoS attack[60]

REMEDIAL: **7** - Traffic Filtering or External Scrubbing, Cloud Based Proxy, Content Delivery Network (CDN), ISP IP Proxy change, Increase TCP Backlog and SYN Received on the routers. SYN cache and SYN cookies, Firewall spoofing of SYN-ACKS.

RISK: **8**

2.8 DOWNLOADER

When an attacker first exploits a device, the attacker they will cloak the fact that the device has been attacked. As part of a Trojan, this feature/program just exists to download other malicious code (see Botnets). I used to call this the Puppy Dog approach because we all know puppy dogs grow up to become ravenous wolves! This is also known as a Launcher that launches other malicious programs to ensure stealth attacks.

Examples of this attack include NECURS and TidServ: this downloader Trojan spread through spam e-mail, arriving as an attachment. It used root kit techniques to run inside common Windows services (sometimes bundled with fake anti-virus software) or in Windows safe mode, and it hid most of its files and registry entries.

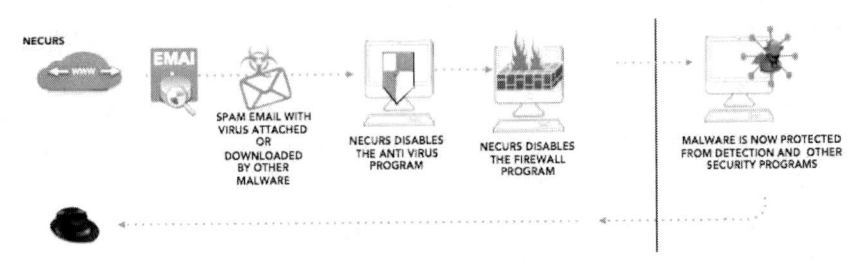

Figure 5- NECURS

REMEDIAL: As this is usually a Windows and Android-based problem, the use of a top of the range Anti Virus program is needed. In enterprises, Deep Scans should be carried out on all devices.

RISK: 7

2.9 DOMAIN NAME SERVICE (DNS)

DNS stands for Domain Name Service. It's a method that resolves names (like web addresses) to TCP/IP numbers like a telephone directory would map names and addresses to telephone numbers. The Internet has Root DNS servers that manage website addresses worldwide (which have been hacked successfully in the past). Internet-connected devices and users attempt to correctly resolve names to the actual addresses that are registered by the owners of an Internet domain implicitly trust DNS servers. Large organisations have their own internal DNS that can be compromised and appear fake.

2.9.1.1 ROGUE DNS SERVER

A rogue DNS server spoofs a domain name of a Website (search engine, bank, doctor, etc.) towards an IP address of a site with dubious content that is usually malware-ridden. When you configure DNS settings to connect to your ISP (or they are automatically configured by your ISP) there are usually two addresses needed (Primary and Secondary). Zombie computers using DNS-changing Trojans can invisibly change these addresses and push infected users to malware soaked websites.

Mass DNS changes are termed Pharming and focussed DNS changes are termed Phishing. ISPs can also manipulate these addresses to their own benefit, but this practice can expose users to cross-site scripting. This can lead to DNS responses skewing Intranet and VPN access from some devices. Google has a public DNS as opposed to a local ISP DNS although Google obviously tracks this lifestyle traffic for informational purposes. Uses should always check the physical location of the DNS server they are attached to. External companies or Systems Integrators engineers can pre-load browsers with fake DNS servers. On one site I found a US based company was resolving to an eastern European site for several years. Also check mobiles and tablets.

2.9.2 DNS CACHE POISONING

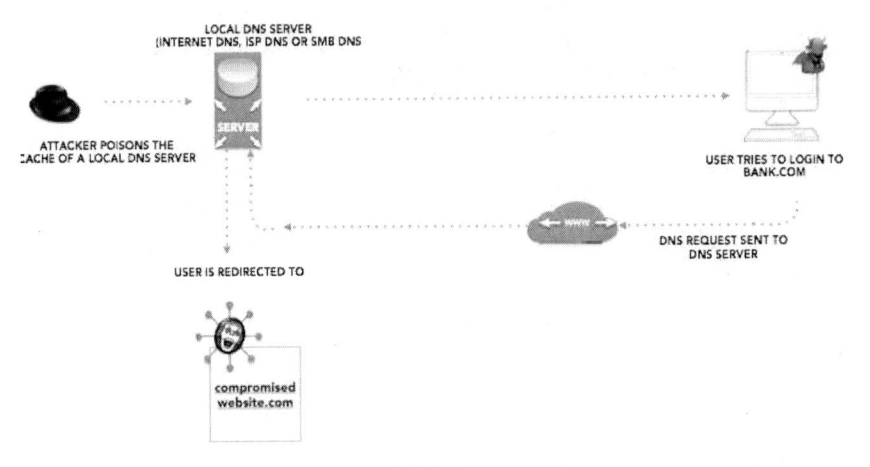

Figure 6- DNS POISONING

This attack happens when an Internet server has its domain name table compromised by malicious code. This table serves as a list of legitimate Internet addresses, but if poisoned, these addresses are replaced with fakes. Instead of being directed to a legitimate Website, requests made through a damaged DNS table send users to spoofed pages. Banking Websites and online retailers are easily spoofed; meaning any password, credit card or personal information will be compromised. It's often found in URLs sent within spam e-mails. These e-mails attempt to scare users into clicking on the URL, which in turn infects their computer. Banner ads and images will take them to fake Websites that are spoofed to look like the real thing, exposing them to risks such as spyware, key-loggers or worms. Clean desktops will get infected immediately if they don't flush their DNS cache as a solution.

REMEDIAL: 7 – Only cache information from Authoritative servers. 'Double Double' checks all IP DNS mappings. Transaction signatures for zone transfer and dynamic updates End User education, DNSSEC (like SSL for DNS it can digitally sign DNS lookups using Public Key Encryption), Endpoint AV, as centrally hosted AV can be compromised, Honeypots and Sinkhole Techniques. SPLIT Caching Nameserver on Internal network and

DNS Authoritative nameserver in DMZ. Firewalls can be used to minimise attacks against the DNS protocol using Transaction ID randomisation, Query and Response verification, DNS Header Flag filtering and DNS message size limitations. Not much you can do about this unless the Internet changes at a Root DNS level.

RISK: 5

2.10 INFORMATION STEAL

This malware usually sits on a device and sniffs for activity on specific applications such as e-mail or online banking. The program can scan password hash-grabbers and send them straight to the attacker. This flavour of malware is particularly difficult to catch; even after a deep scan this cocoons itself and can wait for two-step authentication passwords as a wake-up message. Examples of this attack are Pixsteal and Passteal.

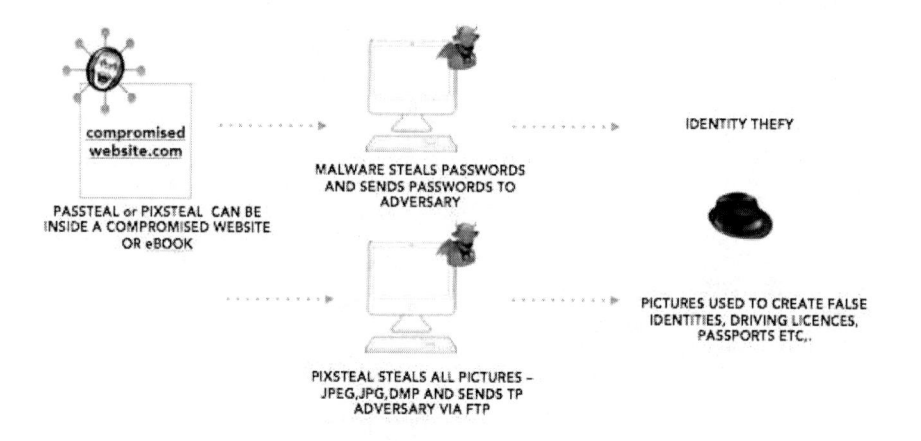

Figure 7 - PASSTEAL AND PIXSTEAL

Many controlled Botnets search a target computer's hard disks for personal information, including computer authentication credentials, bank account numbers and passwords, product keys for popular computer games which are then sold on, and other software products' licences which can then be used on sites pirating illegal applications. Software Piracy costs users and government tax receipts about $500 Billion a year – this could be considered tax fraud and evasion, but it costs emerging countries billions in sales tax receipts.

REMEDIAL: **8** – Prevalent in Torrent type web services where downloads and eBooks are popular. Software Piracy where copies of software are downloaded from the web and license keys is generated. Subscribers should: not use the "save Password " feature in browsers. Clear cookies and cache after each web session. Change passphrases regularly. Endpoint Anti Virus is required as it can affect any device (particularly mobile).

RISK: **8**

2.11 INSIDER THREATS

Any person employed inside an organisation that carries out sabotage, information stealing or fraud. CERT [61] classifies an Insider threat as: "Any information system, network, or data compromise where the suspect has – or used to have – legitimate access to the network/data compromised. The definition includes suspects who are current or former employees of the company whose network was compromised. This includes any efforts to retrieve, change, destroy, or add information to an information system, network or database. These incidents can occur in ANY organisation, public, private, or government, in ANY critical infrastructure sector."[62]

There is a profile for an Insider[63],[64]:

1. 98% were male

2. Majority aged between 19 and 29 (Generation Y)

3. 50% are married

4. Various ethnicity and race

5. 92% of cracks were revenge-based

6. 81% caused significant financial loss

7. A 35% chance that an individual was harmed by the breach

8. 30% had previous arrests

9. 62% were planned in advance

10. 31% of colleagues knew about it

11. **Only 29% were discovered by security team members**

12. 43% had authorised access to the systems

13. 29% were non-technical personnel

14. 59% were discovered after the employee had left the organisation

15. 8% caused vandalism

These studies carried out by RAND in 1990 and Carnegie Mellon in 2005, carried out over a number of industries and government departments (including 62 events in the nuclear industry). This data was based on 86 actual breaches. Insider breaches and resulting fraud costs $652 million a year. About $7.5 million on average per case in 2005. The number of cases increases 35% a year in the US according to CERT, so by my reckoning the todays cost of internal fraud breaches is $13 billion a year. I would also surmise that with the western world's penchant for outsourcing disgruntled technical departments, combined with the recession, a lot of companies would be more susceptible to an insider attack. We have also seen WikiLeaks Diplomatic Cables leak become US government brand affecting. Even if you trust the government spying on you (which may be reasonable for most of us to bear), you might not trust their people, processes or technology.

REMEDIAL: **10** - Check Facebook for signs of disgruntled employees and signs of mental illness. HR should do their job and conduct background checks and consider the results carefully. Actively defend against malicious code. Carry out random Drugs tests on employees. Based on the profile, it seems safer just to employ women, but IT finds it hard to attract the gender. Security and ethical awareness training is required for all employees. Deactivate access following termination – this includes the pseudo names gleaned from dead poets; A.Pope, W.Blake, L.Byron etc., that are usually found in nearly every Active Directory I have audited. Use additional controls for system administrators and privileged users access.

RISK: 8

2.12 MEMORY BASED

2.12.1.1 DIRECT ACTION
Direct Action Infectors simply load their code to Random Access Memory and infect files in whatever locations it is programmed to search, and then immediately exit. Some may infect one file at a time and always in a certain directory, while some try to infect all files on a computer, even on different drives, and, over any networks it can find. These are the simplest viruses, and the easiest to create and the hardest to detect, as they are fleeting in nature. They are the most common in terms of how they have been created, but they do not spread very far or fast

2.12.1.2 MEMORY RESIDENT
Memory Resident Infectors load themselves into the memory and just stay there, continuing to infect files until the computer is shut down. This is spreading to mobile malware and will be prevalent in IOT devices.

REMEDIAL: **5** - Memory Cleaners are only effective during online activities. As Anti Virus products don't usually inspect memory for such code it can become a persistent problem once the organisation is infected.

RISK: **4**

2.13 MAN IN THE MIDDLE
As it suggests, the Man in the Middle (MITM) eavesdrops on end use to host communication's data stream and makes independent transmit and receive connections between two victims. Victims are duped into believing they are communicating directly, but all data is going via the adversary. This form of attack was originally invented in World War 2; the 'Aspidistra Transmitter' did exactly the same operation but on radio. This attack can happen even when the link is encrypted or uses SSL. Allegedly, the NSA impersonated Google at one point. There are several tools that aid this attack: Cain and Abel, Fiddler2, Ettercap, ZeuS, Gozi, URLZone, Sinowal, Limbo and Spyeye

and Interceptor NG, Air Jack and Karma for Wi Fi networks. ATMs are susceptible to this type of attack.

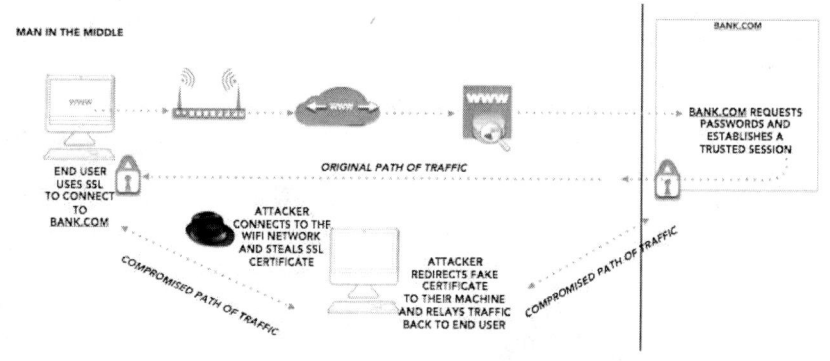

Figure 8 - MAN IN THE MIDDLE

2.13.1.1 MAN IN THE BROWSER
MITB is a Trojan that infects the Web browser and is able to modify Web pages or transactional content and then insert additional transactions (i.e. Web banking). This can happen even if you have SSL/PKI (or two and three factor authentication). An example of this is SilentBanker that records keystrokes; captures screen images from a user's desktop and grabs passwords.

2.13.1.2 MAN IN THE PHONE
MITP is an old-fashioned con trick – the fraudster calls the victim and says their account has been breached, and then proceeds to ask for confirmation of account details. At the same time the fraudster calls the client's bank and relays the information, even passing on Security ID and other personal information.

2.13.1.3 FREAKY BEAST HEARTBLEED
A Zombie resurrected from the 90's. The gist of the FREAK attack is that attackers can intercept traffic between client and server – traffic that is supposed to be encrypted with SSL or TLS. It starts with a man-in-the-middle attack. An attacker intercepts a communication channel between two people and sends both sides a request to use export mode. Now, the encryption key used for the traffic between the two people is significantly weaker, and can

be broken by the attacker. This results in a situation where the attacker can sniff traffic between the two as if SSL wasn't even being used.

Figure 9 HEARTBLEED

REMEDIAL: 7 - Out of Band transaction verification processes can combat MITB. This could be an SMS code from the provider of your mobile. If possible use a separate computer used for online banking with no other applications. Consider a hardened browser on USB (if you can trust a USB that is!).

RISK: Increasing **8**

2.14 MOBILE HACKING

We love our smartphones, but they are powerful computing devices that are scary and intrusive once hacked. We are now in the decade of mobile malware. The world's first smartphone was actually developed by IBM with the SIMON product in 1994. It wasn't until 2007 with the release of the iPhone that sales really took off, and in a three year period sold 73 million phones. Google bought android, and the first Android phone was released in 2008 (HTC Dream). So far the Android has sold 50 Billion apps. The Android is Open Source so Google have only made about half a billion dollars in revenue, whilst the phone makers like Samsung report glowing revenues. Android is also seen as 'Telco-friendly'.

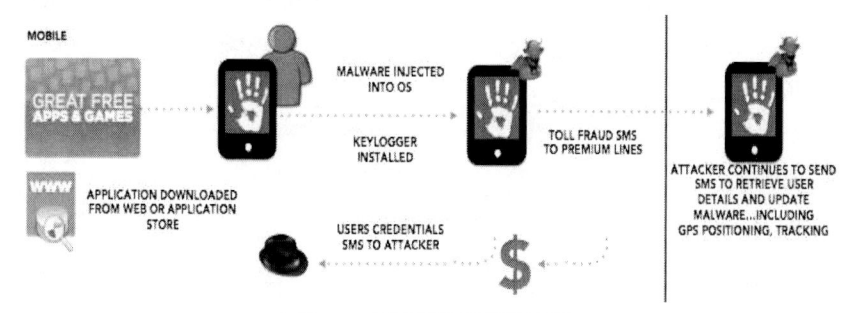

Figure 10 MOBILE ATTACKS

Greater shipments bring greater focus for hackers. Security-focussed operating systems such as Replicant are starting to emerge, in an attempt to harden the Smartphone operating systems. New low cost phones are targeting the remotest parts of the world, including Fairphone, Airtel and the Mozilla Firefox device that retails at $25.

2.14.1.1 IPHONE

Objective C is the key compiler in IOS. The iPhone has seven layers in which (Mach 0) machine application binaries are passed up and down the stack.

- Application
- Framework API
- Objective C Runtime
- IOS
- Processor
- Firmware
- Hardware

In the iPhone, much of the Framework API is hardened by Apple themselves, which allows for little deviation from their secure reviewed world. This is not such a bad thing as vulnerabilities in this field are low on malware and protection of the API is essential whilst still enabling rapid application development. In bespoke Enterprise applications, where an external programmer or development company get involved, it is best to get the application penetration tested before rolling out to production.

To improve security, and much to the annoyance of the USA-based security watchers, Apple decided to encrypt their range of iPhones as part of the IOS 8 release.

2.14.1.2 ANDROID

The Android OS, acquired through acquisition and developed by Google, has not been regulated and closed, so anyone can produce third-party applications that exploit swathes of the Android base code. Base modules include:

- Applications - (Mostly Java) Phone - Browser - Contacts
- Application Framework - Activity Manager - Window Manager - Content Providers
- Libraries - Open GL - SQLite - FreeType - SSL
- Android Runtime - (C or C++) Core Libraries - Dalvik Virtual Machine
- Linux Kernel

It's a playground for adversaries to leverage. There is AV software for Android, but there is no way to remove the malware once it's compromised. In Asia they have their own application stores and this is where the majority of malware resides. The Koler Ransomware has seen a price increase to $300 and is used to blackmail Android users.

2.14.1.3 BLACKBERRY

Blackberry 10 OS still relies on the Blackberry Enterprise Server, which is a highly secure server that usually, links to MS Exchange. The new OS allows for additional custom applications to be developed.

- Applications - JavaScript in QML
- Cascades - UI Framework - Core Controls - Layout - Rendering Engine
- Cascades Platform APIs
- TCP/IP Networking - QT - XML/SQL
- File systems

- Dynamic Linking
- Process Manager
- Multicore Processing
- Interprocess Communication
- QNX Neutrino Microkernel - Core API - Open GL - Crypto/Security

This is still a niche business sector player, but some countries insist on access to the Blackberry Enterprise Server (BES) so that conversation threads can be monitored.

2.14.1.4 MICROSOFT

Windows Mobile OS Windows Phone 8 (+update) is a much more robust environment than its predecessor, but still supports Win32, which has led to the usual hackable suspects. There is now secure boot, and 128-Bit BitLocker encryption.

- Applications - C# / Visual Basic.NET (. NET), C++ (CX) or HTML5, JavaScript
- Windows Runtime - .NET
- Core App Framework
- Text Globalisation and Resources
- Threading and Synchronisation
- Hybrid (NT Kernel)

2.14.1.5 BLACKPHONE

This is a newcomer to the smartphone world and with a million device sales notched up in its first year. It's based on a secure version of the Android system and data is encrypted throughout the system. The project was started by Silent Circle and continues to sell end-to-end encrypted calls. The packages sold are ideal for secure thinking SMBs.

2.14.1.6 SYMBIAN OS

If this is still in circulation, then it is probably not a preferred choice of phone at this time, but I still see the occasional PDA in use today.

REMEDIAL: the SMB, Walled Garden Penetration Tested Applications, and Secure VPN should manage Enforced BYOD device for team members (No public Wi-Fi). For Windows and Android buy AV software that is from AV supplier through subscription. No Jailbreak Phones on site. All devices should be encrypted.

RISK:

IPhone: **6** Android: **10** Blackberry: **6** Microsoft: **8** Blackphone: **1** Symbian: **9**

2.15 NETWORK ATTACKS

Network attacks, can be physical via cable tap or Internet-based. The Internet is nearing capacity (by that I mean there are only a few Border Gateway Protocol BGP links available). Routers only remember 512,000 paths (and there are only 20,000 left on the Internet). IPv4 has some serious flaws and malware, and spurious data can be injected into these packets (see Denial of Server and DDOS) and IPv6, theoretically, should ease some of these problems. Networks are still vulnerable.

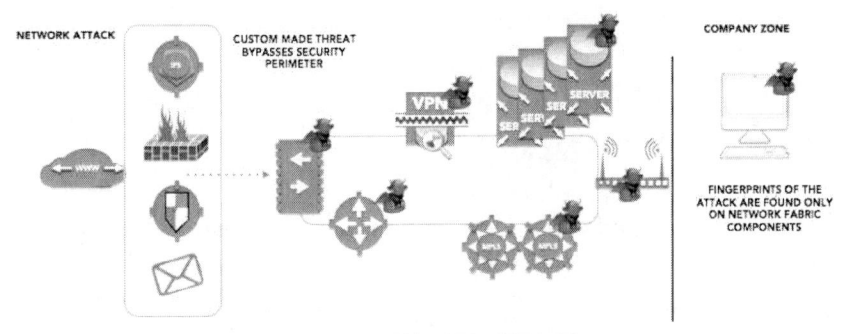

Figure 11 NETWORK ATTACK

2.15.1.1 EAVESDROPPING

Traffic can be intercepted and read by an MITM attack. Wi Fi (if it's not got strong encryption) can be hijacked. This traffic includes cookies, which can be stolen by another computer and entire conversations recorded (see VOIP). Once it's hijacked, the adversary can alter the data in transit. (See Backdoor)

2.15.1.2 IP SPOOFING

An IP address can be spoofed, which hijacks the sender's identity. After gaining access to the network the adversary uses the senders identity and re-routes the data stream. This is a great way to avoid firewalls.

2.15.1.3 PASSWORD BASED ATTACKS

Older applications do not protect username and password logins well. If an adversary manages to sniff the username and password, they can pose as an employee. Usually adversaries change the password and dump a Trojan to catch the new user's password. (Phishing described later). Besides manufacturing passwords are distributed in clear text these are rarely changed on set up. For example Admin Login: **Admin** plus Password: **Password** is extremely common in home routers. Even vendors websites display these default passwords on website support documentation. Password reuse is even more common amongst users. In the white paper from J.Bonneau of Princeton University "The Tangled Web of Password Reuse"[65] 98% of users have only 2 passwords. So the statistical chances of criminals gaining access to multiple sites with a single set of stolen credentials are amazingly high.

2.15.1.4 SNIFFER ATTACK

There are two ways to attach a sniffer to a network. The first is by cable tap (or fibre optic tap) and running a laptop with a sniffer software (such as Wireshark or Ethereal), or the adversary can run these after the user account has been compromised. A sniffer log can reside on a network for years without technical intervention as it's a common Network System Engineer tool so would pass any discovery by internal security. A sniff can send data logs to a remote IP address via FTP, which can hold even encrypted data for further analysis.

2.15.1.5 INSIDER ATTACK

A cracker attack involves an insider attacking the network. Insiders steal and damage on purpose destroying their tracks. Information is used fraudulently and detection rates are poor.

REMEDIAL: 8 - Ensure user to sever connections use Transport Layer Security (at a minimum). A server can specify a secure flag while setting a cookie that forces an encrypted channel such as an SSL link. Running Configuration Management software like Tripwire can detect changes across all an SMB device estate. Ensure physical cabling is checked weekly by wandering around internally and externally (checking manhole covers etc.).

RISK: 7

2.16 PHISHING

These emails are direct from adversaries to a victim and get users to reveal personal information. Similar to the method MITP, the adversary sends messages that appear to come from an institution such as a bank or popular Website. These messages include the company branding and dupe the users to log in. This can catch even seasoned security personnel on the back foot. Mail can come from people you know, as their email credentials have been stolen. About 160,000,000 phishing e-mails are sent each day, and 50% are responded to!

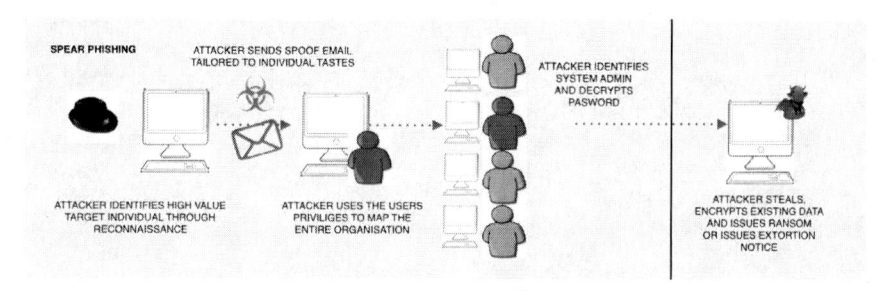

Figure 12 SPEAR PHISH

2.16.1.1 SPEAR PHISHING

Bespoke e-mails are even more difficult; it could come from a compromised internal address and have the hallmarks of familiarity and relevance. Check the e-mail of the sender without opening the e-mail, compare that address to previously sent e-mails from the institution.

2.16.1.2 PHARMING

On a larger scale, Pharmers simply redirect as many users as possible from the legitimate commercial Websites they'd intended to visit and lead them to malicious ones. The bogus sites, to which victims are redirected without their knowledge or consent, will likely look the same as a genuine site. But when users enter their login name and password, criminals capture the information. These Websites look like the real thing, but always check the URL address. About 1 million users click through on one of these a day.

REMEDIAL: 9 - If you are not sure, check the e-mail address of the sender. The sender may have an address like company brand admin@support.com, it should end admin@company.com. Adversaries will also try admin@support.company.com. This means that companies should always check that the company's domain name(s) has not been procured and corrupted by an adversary. Being able to set up websites like this should bring about an instant alerting to the SMB form ICANN but this alerting does not seem to be active. If in doubt – get it out - just delete the offending email. Marilyn Munroe never opened letters. She said that if the matter were important they would write again! Never open or download a file (like a .pdf, or even a .Jpeg) from an unsolicited e-mail, even from someone you know (you can call or e-mail the person to double-check that it really came from them). Delete chain mails that come from friends. Enable two-factor authentication whenever available. Look for HTTPS in the address bar when you enter any sensitive personal information on a Website to make sure your data will be encrypted. Before you buy anything from the web ensure that you have done a separate search for reputation affecting entries regarding the company or product. Be safe and consider every eventuality and ensure you have 'doubledouble' checked your decision with your shoulder angel.

Team Member Education is key…

- Take time reading emails, think carefully and do not give in to pressure.

- Do not trust email attachments

- Some email readers have a bounce feature (like the old Apple Mail) …use it

- Always check the legitimacy and syntax of the senders' email addresses

- Never click on a link you receive by email before checking that it really is what it claims to be.

- Do not willingly provide sensitive personal information such as full PayPal address, logins or passwords, even to people that are supposedly reliable

- Look out for spelling, layout and syntax errors in the emails you receive. In relation with other suspicious elements, they can be most meaningful hints.

- Be extra cautious whenever money is involved in Internet transactions.

RISK: **8**

2.17 ROOT KIT

It's not a garden tool for digging up trees, but similarly does attack the very heart of the computer or mobile operating system. This is malicious code that is designed to conceal the existence of other malicious code. Effectively, it spoofs the Operating System into thinking the code is legitimate and part of the OS itself, so the victim cannot detect it, even some Anti Virus toolkits cannot perceive this change in the operating system configuration. This framework attack is paired with other malware such as backdoor. Windows and Linux systems seem to be popular hits for this malware.

REMEDIAL: **10** - Always keep a copy of your data. Run Anti Virus and then quarantine the root kit code if possible. Re-partition your hard drive or re-install the operating system. As the root kit can change and disguise itself you will need to re-run AV on the new software before you reload your data. Many companies who have had these infections usually rubbish the PCs and donate used PCs to schools and charities, which just exacerbate the spread of the infection, so it is a highly dangerous method of attack.

RISK: **10**

2.18 RANSOMEWARE

Sometimes deemed Blackmail-ware or Scare-ware, it infects and encrypts a device's hard disk and makes the user buy a key from the attacker to unlock the disk. The adversary then has your credit card details. When using anything bought on the Internet use a pre-paid credit card for purchasing. This stops adversaries from stealing rotational credit and can only abuse the remaining balance. Ransomware usually displays a user interface that resembles an anti-virus vendor's site or law enforcement security. It will usually flash up a screen demanding $300 to be sent to an e-mail account. Originally intended as a joke to scare, celebrities and known crooks into parting with ill-gotten gains, it has evolved into a generic global attack.

In a new twist Bloomberg reported that some 20 million usernames and email addresses had been offered for sale after the Russian online dating service Topface was hacked. Atlanta-based fraud detection firm Easy Solutions discovered the breach when a hacker calling himself 'Mastermind' claimed "to be in possession of over 20 million credentials", including "over 7 million credentials from Hotmail, 2.5 million from Yahoo and 2.2 million from Gmail.com."" Topface Chief Executive Dmitry Filatov said the company located the hacker, who had published ads to sell the data but had not actually sold them. 'We have paid him an award for finding a vulnerability and agreed on further cooperation in the field of data security,' Filatov said in an email on Friday, declining to disclose the size of the reward."

REMEDIAL: Use AV software that alerts you in real time of dubious Websites. As half the Websites you visit have some sort of contamination, this is a reasonable tool to run. It can affect any operating system and can be costly.

RISK: **9**

2.19 SPAM -SPAM -SPAM -SPAM

Spam was so christened by Vint Cerf (Grandfather of the Internet and one of the nicest people you will ever meet), the famous Monty Python song. SPAM still accounts for 60% of e-mail traffic, 10% of all spam messages are malicious (about 182 billion a year). I get lots of meaningless spam from my mother, which I have been attempting to get shot of for years. If you get spam from my mother, please ignore it. I am joking of course I refer to tins of corn beef hash!

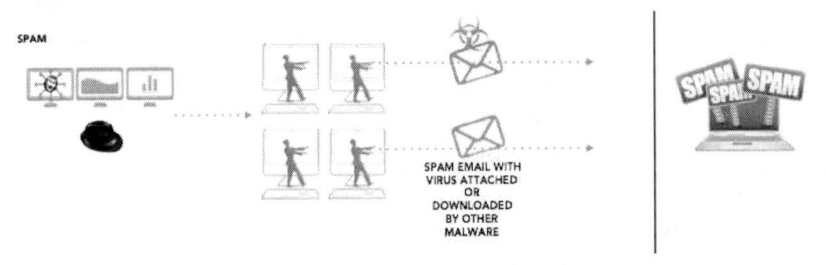

Figure 13 SPAM

About five billion spams are sent daily - three billion are rubbish. The botnet malware takes control of the device and uses it to send out spam e-mails. This is an income generator for the attackers and enhances their portfolio of spam-sending products. Spammers can rent Botnets for paid-for marketing campaigns. The spammers employ millions of these zombie devices so evading ISPs to block them. Company IT system admins can be completely unaware that these could originate from company PCs. This can lead to a serious problem if a company is found hosting this type of service as many spams could be used for a range of purposes beyond that of spam delivery (click fraud and credit card fraud for instance). Several originators of this malware are resting in a prison cell somewhere.

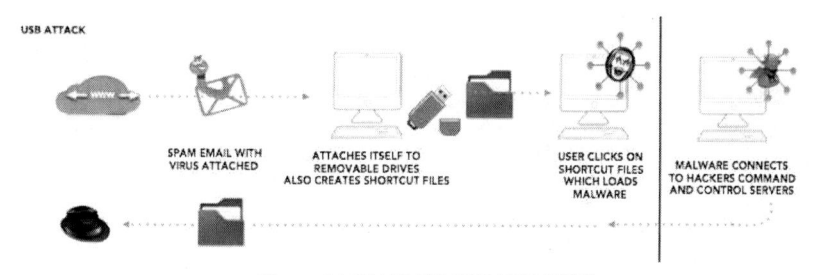

Figure 14 SPAM TO COMPONENT

REMEDIAL: The only government I have seen to take any action on this is the Canadian government, who asked every commercial company to verify that you wish to continue to receive meaningless newsletters, and bargains for unscrupulous or legitimate companies. To get rid of spam, create an alter ego with an address that is not your personal e-mail. Access this address via browser based Webmail only. If you need credentials to access a Website that is not important to you personally, use this address all the time. Talking of e-mail addresses, don't use (standard company practice) your full name nomenclature, like fred.smith@whatever.com. Always use something like fSXXBudgerigar1927@whatever.com, as it stops personalised newsletters starting off with Dear Fred, which I find particularly irritating. Clear out spurious e-mails by unsubscribing to any newsletter once a quarter.

RISK: **8** (purely for the for the irritation factor)

2.20 SPYWARE

Spyware software that is surreptitiously installed on a device sends information about a user's web-surfing habits to an attacker. Some spyware is relatively harmless and written by vendors, designed to generate data about shopping habits. Malicious spyware, however, may be used to hijack web browsers in order to change their home pages, receive waves of pop-up ads or ignore user navigation commands. This code must have been conceived and written by a Macker (Marketing based Hacker). Spyware mutates and can stay ahead of signature-based solutions (see Targeted Malware). Spyware utilises several techniques to help it mutate:

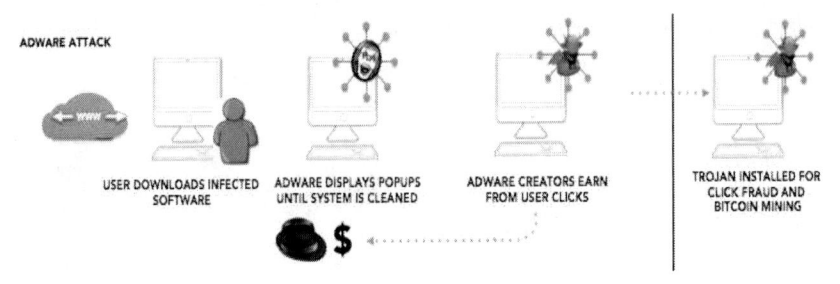

Figure 15 ADWARE AND SPYWARE

2.20.1.1 UPDATE MUTATION

Like Windows, sends users security patches automatically for user installation (always 20 minutes before you need to catch the train to work) this malware is hidden as a fake patch. Once the user clicks the install setup the spyware can 'phone home' and get the latest update and install the updates over the original files. This means the new malware signatures are applied to the old code. Attackers can instantaneously update their code remotely and continue incessant bombardment of the device.

2.20.2 POLYMORPHISM[66]

Malware can morph itself through multiple strains that choose their name and location from a predetermined list, all automatically.

2.20.3 PROGRAMMATIC MUTATION

Spyware can rewrite entire code segments without an attacker's intervention – it is unique and can change every few seconds. It can push code to new parts of the registry, constantly re-inventing itself. This makes IDS (Detection and Prevention systems) look like a three-year-old child trying to catch a bubble they just blew (futile). These are now becoming prolific and self-sustaining chunks of code, so the number of signatures is growing like Moore's Law.

REMEDIAL: **8** - To combat this, IDS employs behaviour-based detection it monitors runtime behaviour at the application layer. Some Email Gateways can also pick this up.

An SMB should run an estate-wide Configuration Manager like Tripwire to ensure estate devices are stable. For example, an application that monitored a Web-based browser and pop-ups started to happen you would deduce from the surveillance that adware had compromised the application (sometimes). In anti-virus, for example, vendors use small abstract code or patterns, to conclude that a file could do something very specific. This works sometimes to catch viruses that have compact, code-level pathologies, but does not scale to complex applications like most other spyware.

RISK: **10**

2.21 SQL INJECTION

This is the adversaries' No 1 tool at the moment. It is capable of trashing a company's brand reputation in minutes, is favoured technique of nation state-based adversaries. SQL injection refers to an adversary inserts a MySQL statement to be run on your database without your knowledge. Injection usually occurs when you ask a user for input, like their name, and instead of a name they give you a MySQL statement that you will unknowingly run on your database. What is amazing is that this attack keeps on working.

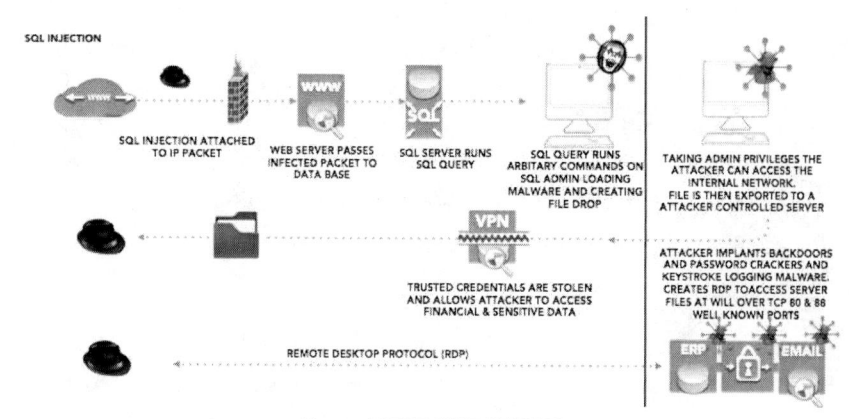

Figure 16 SQL INJECTIONS

REMEDIAL: **10** - With most development platforms, parameterised statements that work with a placeholder instead of embedding user input in the statement. A placeholder can only store a value of a given type and not an arbitrary SQL fragment. Hence the SQL injection would simply be treated as a strange (and probably invalid) parameter value. In many cases, the SQL statement is fixed, and each parameter is scalar, not a table. The user input is then assigned (bound) to a parameter.

RISK: **10**

2.22 TARGETED MALWARE

Targeted malware is bespoke to companies so ideal for espionage or competitive disruption. Usually a large company will have networked-based devices called Intrusion Detection Systems or IDS. The security team, using vendor-supplied lists of known malware, are usually able to capture malware sent through the Internet. The IDS role is to inspect all the network packets coming into the company and assigns a signature to the malware program, so it can be bounced, deleted or quarantined. If the adversary discovers the vendor IDS type and version installed in the SMBs estate they can actually bespoke malware signatures to order.

There are two methods to assign signatures: host-based and network signatures. Signatures allow security teams to fingerprint the program and apply the fix or removal of the offending software. Host-based identifies malware on a compromised PC; it searches for files that have been changed or edited, even after the offensive code has been deleted. In Windows-based PCs, usually malicious code manipulates the Registry. Network signatures monitor network traffic and look for packets that make up the malicious code, and once detected can send them to a 'sandboxed' PC for analysis, away from the company servers. Signature-based solutions are limited, no matter how large the size of the signature database provided by the vendor, as fingerprinting is reactive.

REMEDIAL: Don't tell the world what your network infrastructure is. Don't be a potential vendor use case and ask vendors o remove your logo from their website. These are reconnaissance fodder for adversaries, who will know exactly what to expect on a Beta breach. Do try and mix vendors on the IDS side, as well as AV suppliers. Network diagrams should be encrypted and no IP addresses displayed.

RISK: **8**

2.23 THEY NEVER STOP THEY NEVER DIE

Trojan Horses are destructive programmes that present themselves as a harmless application. Unlike viruses, however, Trojan horses don't replicate themselves. They perform one or more destructive tasks once activated, such as stealing identity or cash data. A Trojan horse also designs itself to make its host more vulnerable to future attacks, or destroy hard-drive applications or data. Trojan horses can be sent by e-mail attachment or even in programs downloaded from the Web. Whenever an unsuspecting person open the e-mail attachment, it would appear as if nothing has happened to the naked eye, but in the background the malicious Trojan horse has installed or executed itself to carry out the havoc. The favourite one at the moment is the 'FTP_v _Trojan' that opens Port 21 on your device so that an adversary can remotely attach via FTP (File Transfer Protocol).

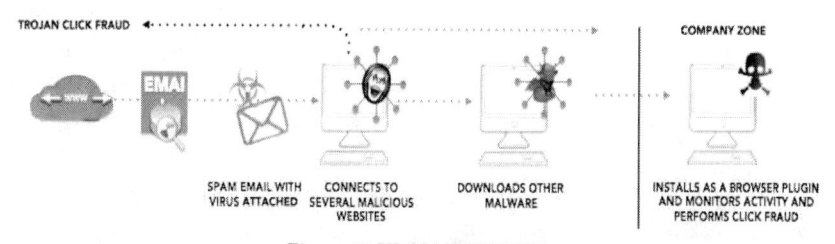

Figure 17 TROJAN HORSES

REMEDIAL: Firstly, shun Greeks bearing gifts (unless they come bearing bail out interest repayments), or never drag huge handmade wooden horses into your citadel after the Greek invading army has departed. Implement gateway virus scanning. Use IPS/IDS to check content at the perimeter of your network for e-mail, HTTP and FTP. It is no good having e-mail anti-virus protection if a user can download a Trojan from a Website and infect your network. Deploy multiple virus engines at the gateway and perimeter edge (and in the Cloud if your CSP delivers Internet Access). Although a good virus engine usually detects all known viruses, it is a fact that multiple virus engines jointly recognise many more known Trojans than a single engine. Quarantine and check any executable file entering your network. You have to analyse what the executable might do by directing that traffic to a Honeypot (more on that later).

RISK: 9

2.24 VULNERABILITIES/ZERO DAY EXPLOITS

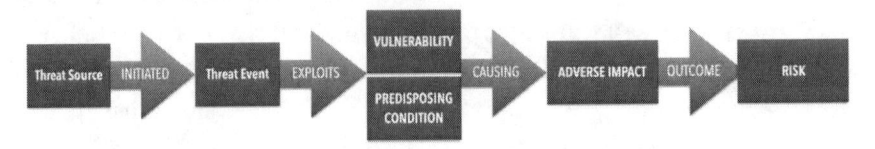

Threat Source → INITIATED → Threat Event → EXPLOITS → VULNERABILITY / PREDISPOSING CONDITION → CAUSING → ADVERSE IMPACT → OUTCOME → RISK

Figure 18 VULNERABILITY LIFECYCLE

These are vulnerabilities (bugs) that are usually found in vendors' software. You should always remember to apply Service Packs and emergency security patches immediately. Patches are vendors' fixes to their software (patchwork); seem to be a daily occurrence nowadays. Have you ever noticed that a huge patch always happens the morning that you are supposed to travel? Anyway, these vendors' wake up calls have been going on for 20 years and it's as though the vendors have been hitting the snooze button – they don't test anything before it's released. Sometimes this could be termed an upgrade – which forces you to buy a whole new set of untested software, and so the cycle starts again as new software is tested on the public at large. It is a philosophy that has to stop – that's why man invented laboratories, so these things can get tested out before consumption. In fact there should be a certificate obtained from a separate and independently funded international organisation that proves a seal of approval for all new software releases. It can take up to a year in some cases to get these holes in the so-called 'solid code' fixed, and in the meantime it's quietly humming on your hard disk.

Hackers are usually able to hack new software in a concerted weekend timeframe, which means that the vendors probably don't have the knowledge to do these test in-house although you expect them to? Oracle Java is a top target for exploits, followed by Adobe Reader, Adobe Flash, Wordpress and Windows Internet Explorer. [67] Qualys reported that, on average, there are 20 vulnerabilities in Internet Explorer that are discovered by Microsoft and other security researchers every single month. It's very tiresome, and there should be a legal and regulatory commission set up akin to the Federal Drug

Administration, where a new drug cannot go on release until it has undergone severe testing to the satisfaction of the commission. Vendors don't care about customers; they care about products and their bottom line.

Many SMB websites use COTS Software (Common, Off-The-Shelf) CMS (Customer Management Systems), ecommerce platforms, software, applications and plugins, which often contain vulnerabilities. Adversaries deploy BOTs to crawl the Internet, sniffing out these vulnerabilities and collecting information.

2.24.1.1 HEARTBLEED

Most of 2014 was headlined by the Heartbleed vulnerability. When you buy online, or, access your bank account via your bank's website, your address bar says "https://" instead of "http://," or you get a pop-up with a closed lock icon? That means your web pages are going through TCP/IP port 443 instead of port 80. HTTPS is just like HTTP, the Internet protocol that serves most web pages, but it goes through an encryption layer, to make your web session more secure. Secure Sockets Layer evolved into Transport Layer Security, and the most widely used open source version of that it OpenSSL. Heartbleed is in the OpenSSL implementation of the TLS/DTLS (transport layer security protocols) heartbeat extension (RFC6520). When it is exploited it leads to the leak of memory contents from the server to the client and from the client to the server. A third of all companies used this client and server combination.

REMEDIAL: Use different vendors flavours of anti-virus, IDS/IPS and Firewalls. Implement heuristic scanning. On your next software license renewal with a vendor, procurement and legal should add a clause to the contract, that they (the vendor) should reimburse the organisation for lost time and revenue caused by the Zero Day Vulnerability (proved by external testers), and my own clause that I invented about ten years ago is that they should bear the cost of upgrades (incremental or forklift) for the next ten years. Most vendors actually sign up to this and often ask me not to tell anyone. Use Patch Management wisely (don't use Patch Adams!): when vendors release patches hackers actually reverse-engineer the patch code and how the vendor repaired their flawed code, increasing the chances of yet further exploits.

RISK: **10**

2.25 WORMS

Worms come in many parasitic forms. Actually named after the tapeworm, as replicated code can break off and regrow, thus maintaining its parasitic cycle. Replication is the name of the game here. The code copies itself and pings other computers (on a company network or Internet) and installs itself on other devices. This is like pyramid selling and an infectious virus lookalike. Worms and viruses are similar, in that they both self-replicate. A worm is designed specifically to spread extremely rapidly and surreptitiously. It can hurt a system by rapid reproduction, sucking up storage and memory resources or network bandwidth. It may also deposit a Trojan horse. The most common method of categorisation is how they spread. Some worms may have multiple methods of spreading.

2.25.1.1 HAVE YOU GOT EMAIL WORMS?

An e-mail message with an attachment gets delivered in a mailbox, and when the user downloads and executes that attachment, the worm creates a new e-mail message with a copy of itself attached and mails itself to one or more other e-mail addresses in the users Contact database. Some e-mail worms such as Nimda can run by themselves without any intervention from the user, and may even infect the computer from the preview pane. Details like the alleged sender, subject, message, attachment name and file type, and method of finding e-mail addresses to send itself to can be radically different

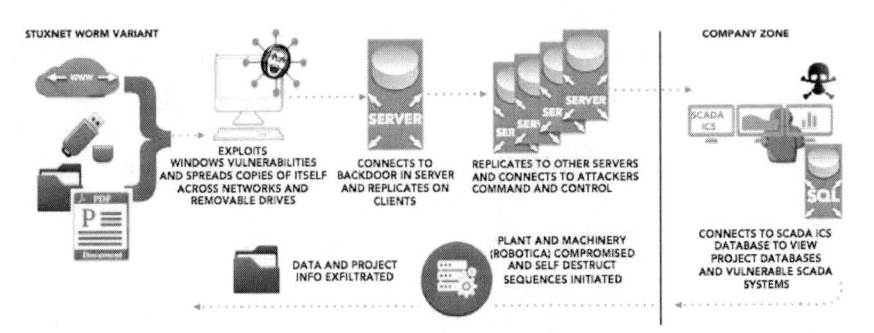

Figure 19 WORM DERIVATIVE STUXNET

2.25.2 INTERNET WORMS

The worm searches for open ports on the Internet and sends itself to other systems. Most of the major worms exploit known vulnerabilities to spread. Consider these worms to be the only 'true' worms, as they require absolutely no user intervention to spread. Morris, Slammer, CodeRed, Blaster and Sasser are a few examples of prominent Internet worms.

2.25.3 NETWORK WORMS

Network worms spread over network file shares (usually configured in the majority of SMBs as the F:> Drive). Network worms are designed to cause chaos on a national scale, and on large-scale networks can spread rapidly over the course of even a few minutes.

2.25.4 MESSAGING WORMS

IRC (Internet Relay Chat), IM (Instant Messenger), P2P (peer-to-peer file-sharing) and other types of worms typically require that one have a client for the particular activity that allows the worm to spread through one's computer.

2.25.5 MULTIPLE VECTOR WORMS

Multiple vector worms have two or more ways of spreading to other computers. Nimda and Swen are examples.

REMEDIAL: There's not much to be done against a worm! Multiple AVs, Windows Malicious Software Removal Tool, Symantec Worm Removal Tool are useful tools.

RISK: **10**

2.26 COMBAT READY MALWARE HARM INDEX

The Malware Harm Index collates the risks reviewed in this chapter. It provides a simple ranking that help contribute toward a risk assessment for the company. This risk assessment should be applied in the Risk Register (and Via Ferrata reporting).

In the case of Situational Awareness the techniques we have covered in this chapter are evolving, even re employing techniques created in the past. The history of virus evolution is included in the appendices. These risks will change over time but the risk ranking that attracts the 10 values are the really nasty types. The top 8 are the leading sources used by adversaries today. It is a new science and liable to change and perspective.

CRIT Harm Index		2013	2014
Malware Risk	Harm	Risk Ranking	Risk Ranking
Botnets	10	10	10
Mobile Hacking	10	7	8
Root Kit	10	8	6
Spyware	10	7	5
SQL Injection	10	10	10
Worms	10	9	8
Zero Day Exploits	10	6	7
Component	10	0	6
Bricking	9	7	2
Ransomware	9	5	9
Trojan Horses	9	9	9
Cross Site Scripting	9	9	9
New Vulnerabilities	9	10	9
SSL/TLS	8	10	9
Macros	8	0	10
DDOS	8	9	10
Information Steal	8	8	9
Insider Threats	8	8	8
Man in the Middle	8	7	8
Phishing	8	9	10
SPAM	8	7	6
Targeted Malware	8	8	9
Backdoors	7	7	7
Cookies	7	7	7
Downloader	7	7	7
Network attacks	6	6	9
DNS	5	1	1
Memory Based	4	2	1
ATM Card	4	0	1
IOT Botnet	3	0	5

TABLE 4 - COMBAT READY IT HARM INDEX

When planning a new application then obtain the employ the SHAZOPS technique that is described later in the book. We will look at a technique to apply these to new applications. Incident Response Teams should create specific and individual plans for each of these virus categories, should your estate get compromised. This is not an easy task and one that cannot be done be external companies, only internal and trusted users working in pairs should do this analysis.

2.27 STEPCHECK

All of these attack techniques are useful to know and understand. These form part of the Risk Register (discussed later) and indicate levels of harm that will affect any business. Adversaries use these as individual weapons or several in unison in an attack on a company. The ingenuity of adversaries is also diversifying. Adversaries are bringing back some of the historic attacks and viruses that were developed in the past to help them circumvent new security defences. A historic view of malware can be found in the appendices.

- The Chapter has described the various types of malware techniques and how they work.

- These techniques can be used individually or as a suite of techniques in a hacker's armoury that leads to a breach and create harm.

- There are millions of variants of the 26 attacks described (An estimated 244 million variants), about a million signed malware are discovered **each week**.

- The Remedial solutions are just as complex and this has cost implications for SMBs. How to stay in front of the exploits and how to minimise the scale of the breach.

- There are no solutions for Component attacks (except to source new components) so a remedy for this has been omitted. We will discuss later how migrating to a virtual estate will help clean Information.

- A Harm Index has been compiled based on the current and known attack techniques

3 ROOT CAUSE - VENDORS

Who is to blame and who pays? Ultimately, you pay the price, through not fault of your own or your company and will continue to pay the price unless we see increased vendor accountability.

Many of the attacks described in the previous chapter are now sickening daily occurrences. I get about 100 e-mails a day reporting on threats, security alerts and data breaches, so the problem is significant and unstoppable. Even I cannot keep up with the number of new malicious attacks and I sympathise with fellow Security Officers trying to keep up with this hourly swathe of alerts and commentary. What does this mean to the reader and any SMB? This chapter looks at the potential of vendors being culpable root cause culprits and the cost of damage that's caused by adversarial attacks. According to Management Consultants Mckinseys; "Looking forward, if the pace and intensity of attacks increase and are not met with improved defences, a backlash against digitization could occur, with large negative economic implications. Using MGI data on the technologies that will truly matter to business strategy during the coming decade, we estimate that over the next five to seven years, $9 trillion to $21 trillion of economic-value creation, worldwide, depends on the robustness of the cyber security environment".[68]

It's difficult to spread the risk. SMBs usually cannot afford the premiums or don't have cyber-insurance at all. Insurance companies who underwrite cyber attacks must be losing increasing sums of money through existing compensation claims. It's like insuring a car without door locks. The key question here is will they pay out? On the other hand the small to medium-sized companies that don't cover themselves with cyber-insurance may not be in business long enough to claim for monetary loss through a breach. Cyber insurance is expensive, and only 60% of companies over 500 employees have coverage, but you wouldn't drive a car without insurance? The company that offers this service to individuals would get my vote immediately, but how you would insure a billion people a year that are already compromised. However, for the companies this book targets it means that your premiums will raise dramatically this year.

In the end, the honest customer ultimately pays with lost time, loss of privacy, inconvenience, and on-going financial loss. There is a one in two chance that your machine is infected by at least two pieces of undetected malware nowadays, and the vendors have been slow to put this right. Vendors are loath to admit liability and government regulators do not take the US based vendors to task, Owning up would cause massive legal ramifications and lawsuits, so it's unlikely to be headline news any time soon. Insurers have not put baseline conditions except to see that SMBs have basic security policies and practices in place.

Losing a customer's private details and credit card information is tantamount to treason – especially if you manage to lose 5000 of these in a Black Minute attack. Based on rules of thumb for start up valuations the cost to acquire a customer is @ $5,000 over 5 years. Customers churn out from company's that have been hacked to around a third of the customer base. Therefore, losing a customer costs any organisation significant revenues. As Data Protection becomes better regulated, potentially a company should also start to be fined by a regulator for not ensuring sufficient data safeguards, in the US new legislation is already passing through the senate to address this. In a cyber-war, accessing records like this can be used to flood the stolen customers with cyberganda and potential cyber blackmail and cyber threats.

3.1 EXECUTIVES FIDUCIARY DUTIES

The aftermath of the Target breach where millions of details were spilt resulted in ten Target board members not getting re-elected.[69] A shareholder sued the Target Corporations directors and officers after what was termed "the worst data breach in retail history". Consumer litigation has also followed the breach.[70] Following a cyber attack a derivative suit could be based on a breach of fiduciary duty:

- The board breached its duty of care by making a decision with regard to cyber security that was "ill advised or negligent"
- The board breached its duty of loyalty by failing to act in the face of a reasonably known threat.

Even though the company had a responsibility to comply with Payment Card Industry (PCI) and Data Security Standard (DSS), there is a technical chasm between Governance and Technology. Written guidance documents such as HIPPA, GLBA, ISO 27032, and NIST and SANS cannot halt a determined adversary (although it may delay them). This will not stop Boards and CIOs losing status after a data breach. An officer of a company has to demonstrate to courts and authorities that the types of precautions were taken by a "reasonable and prudent person". In April 2014, OCIE (SEC Office of Compliance Inspections and Examinations) announced it would examine cyber security within the industry. The recommendations are as follows:

- Create a governance structure and research threats (needs a Security Officer)
- The Full Board Minutes should detail cyber Security minutes at each meeting
- The Audit/Risk and Technical Steering Committees also minute discussions
- Prioritise information assets and analyse risk and shift threats
- Procurement and HR should liaise on Insider and Fraud prevention

- All purchase orders must have four signatures and submitted to the TSC
- Create a security protection plan tied to a technology acquisition strategy
- Encrypt your most precious Information
- Request regular updates and adjust accordingly
- Test the response plan and Public Disclosure plans
- Maintain appropriate insurance coverage
- Provide regular cyber security training

Cyber Security seems to have a western Internet centric availability. This overhead could be seen as a hefty "Cyber Security Tax" a burden seen by many SMBs as welcome as Health and Safety expenditure by some I would guess? Even a Security Officer will not stop you getting hacked. For Small Medium Businesses it could mean a severe margin hit. Premiums for cyber insurance can vary widely[71]. Gartner Inc. who is a technology research and advisory company reported recently that cyber insurance premiums average at $22,500 for $1 million in coverage in the US. Based on the average cost per attack, any organisation will need to budget $135,000 in annual premiums, whilst this pales in the wake of the cost of further lost reputation. While the coverage has become more available, insurers continue to develop their understanding of cyber-risks. Some carriers have underwriters with knowledge and experience regarding cyber-losses while other carriers do not. As a result, insurers have had difficulty pricing this insurance; there are large differences (as much as 25%) between the premiums charged by two different carriers, to insure the same risk.

The limits of liability purchased by US businesses vary widely. Chubb Insurance reports that the average policy limits purchased by its clients are between $1 million and $5 million, while Marsh Insurance reports that its clients purchased an average of $16.8 million in limits across all industries.

Organisations believe they can ride this storm by buying Cyber Insurance. This is a little like slamming the stable shut after the horse has bolted. The trade off here is do you invest in technologies that will act as a deterrent or roll over and pay out annually? This is an era of high and increasing premiums, low coverage and broad exclusions.

In March 2014, a New York trial court ruled that Zurich American Insurance Co. has no duty to defend Sony Corp. of America and Sony Computer Entertainment America in litigation stemming from the April 2011 hacking of Sony Corp.'s PlayStation online services

The Sony PlayStation Network (PSN) was breached in 2011, and the data of millions of users was compromised:

- PSN was offline for several weeks following the breach

- It's estimated by observers that the breach could cost Sony approximately $173m in 2011

- The Information Commissioner's Office (ICO) issued a fine of $250,000 in 2013 to Sony for security failures associated with this breach

- Sony demanded that Zurich American and Zurich Insurance Ltd defend them against lawsuits and possible probes related to hacking of Sony's PlayStation Network.

- Approximately 50 class action complaints have been filed against Sony

- Sony's losses are now estimated at around $2 billion

- In 2014 the courts ruled that Zurich had no duty to defend Sony

- The ruling, which is subject to appeal, highlights the danger of relying on commercial general liability insurance for cybercrime coverage

- The ICO said that its investigation revealed that the attack could have been prevented if the software had been up-to-date while technical developments also meant passwords were not secure [72]

In December 2014 Sony was hacked again:

The attack hits Sony's reputation for a perceived failure to safeguard information, said Jim Lewis, Senior Fellow at the 'Center for Strategic and International Studies'. "Usually, people get over it, but it does have a short-term effect," said Lewis, who estimated costs for Sony could stretch to $US100 million.[73]

If we look at the initial cost estimate of $173 million in 2011 to the NTT estimate of $2billion dollars in 2014 that's a ten fold increase on the original estimate. Could this new breach result in similar costs and escalations?

This also leads to another conundrum, should a company report a data breach or not. If you do not report (only 20% of companies do) and then its reported a clear duty of care would mean your company is liable for all consequential damages. If a data breach is reported from an external source then this can severely harm company's reputation and executives standings. The US Department of Justice issued an instruction (0900.00.01 - August 6, 2013), which details the process for reporting the nature and scope and Incident Response Procedures for Data Breaches. [74] The problem arises of whom to notify… in a data breach response guide from Experian they state, "No single federal law or regulation governs the security of all types of sensitive personal information. As a result, determining which federal law, regulation or guidance is applicable depends in part on the entity or sector that collected the information and the type of information collected and regulated. As a result, data breach notification requirements have largely been left to state legislatures".[75] It may seem a piecemeal approach but compared to global companies and countries this legislation is way ahead. There is no single global responsibility and therefore no accountability and therefore no need to report. This has led to some companies pushing their databases offshore where laws are less restrictive, although this loophole seems to be closing unless the database is maintained by a local branch office.

The last thing to consider and review is the validity of the last Security audit. Security audits merely rubber stamp a SMBs existing processes. An initial deep dive audit is essential but annual audits are not applicable in a real time world. The minute auditors walk out the door there is no liability (unless the company and the auditor has a joint liability contract). So buyers beware, unless there is negligence on the part of the auditor then there is no comeback. We will address audits and their viability later.

3.2 THE COST OF A DATA BREACH

In light of the data breach fallouts, I believe the cost of a company data loss needs revising because ramifications can extend over a protracted period of time. The cost of breaches can have a life of their own and costs can spiral ten fold after an attack. Once an organisation has been hacked, 25% to 30% of customers take their accounts elsewhere. The losses of trust and opportunity costs are rarely reflected in brand and reputation affecting attacks, as the lost business is difficult to quantify. However, the cost of data breaches is always expensive no matter what. If we use the Black Minute and see 5000 records disappear into the ether, which would be a sizeable customer database. I have 5000 contacts in my contacts list as a comparison.

A breach is defined as an event in which an individual's name plus a medical record and/or a financial record or debit card is potentially put at risk—either in electronic or paper format. This record cost changes by country, so I will just benchmark the US - as they experience the most breaches in the world. I extracted the following data based on the Ponemon Institute 2014 Cost of Data Breach Study: Global Analysis [76]:

3.3 DATA BREACH COSTS

The following costs are based on US Financial data.
- The lowest data breach cost was $135.603 and the highest data breach cost $23,143,454

- Average number of breached records per attack was 29,087

- Average cost per record was $201 ($5,846,487 Average Cost per Average number of breached records). Note this has subsequently gone up to the latest indications to $6.5 million

- Average cost of detection and notification (customer contact, IT remediation, experts) $509,237

- Average post data breach costs (legal, help desk, auditing advice services, regulatory fines,) $1,599,996

- Average lost business costs **$3,324,959 (per breach)**

Employing these figures an extrapolated cost for a Black Minute would be:

- 5000 records x $201 = $1,005,000

- Average Cost of IT Detection and Notification at 54.98 per record = $274,905.80

- Average Costs for post data breach at $34.55 per record = $172,757.59

- Average Lost Business at $114.31 per record = 571,554.13

A Black Minute could potentially cost most organisations an average of $2,126,496.

So how much would a data spill of 4 million records cost? Estimated to be around $1.6 billion by current reckoning. The main root causes of data breach on a consolidated basis for all ten countries represented in the Ponemon research were that 41% of incidents involved a malicious or criminal attack, 30% concerned a negligent employee or contractor (human factor), and 29% involved system glitches, which include both IT and business process failures.

CIFAS[77] (A UK based fraud research organisation) also estimates the true cost of insider fraud is up to 15% or more above the initial fraud loss.

Example the average initial fraud loss per incident is $706,600 while the total cost per incident rises to $804,300. These costs include

- The cost of Investigation
- Staff sickness/suspension costs
- Internal disciplinary costs
- External sanction costs (reporting to law enforcement, management time and expenses)
- Permanent team members replacement costs
- Reputation costs
- Months of management time devoted to clean up

We can now adjust the calculation for the cost of a Black Minute fraud would cost an average of $2,930,796.

Think of this as extreme, think again? Herve Falciani (the ex IT worker at HSBC Private Bank in Geneva) borrowed customer transaction data. The Office of the Attorney General of Switzerland said Falciani had transferred this data to his own servers from October 2006 up to the moment he was detained in December 2008. The scandal regarding Tax avoidance surfaced in 2015. Herve allegedly saved names, addresses, account number, and transactions for over 100,000 clients. The ramifications of his actions caused massive global embarrassment to High Net Worth Individuals and Governments. We have had the Snowden revelations, and WikiLeaks that follow the same whistle-blower traits. For an SMB any similar cases and ramifications can be dire.

At these high levels of costs it's easy to see why the majority of data breaches go unreported globally. According to Alien Vault – 20% of companies do not report breaches. Hackers do publish their trophies online though so a company can be blamed and fined even further for any misdemeanour and non-reporting. What would happen to the organisation if we applied the theoretical ten fold (experienced by Sony) increase to the $3m Black Minute? Would a Black Minute that seriously harm your organisations' trading reputation and survivability?

For those companies with a website that could mean an estimated 3% of revenue devoted to Cyber Insurance. I can guarantee that this figure is not in anyone's fiscal budget. With the number of attacks rising by 500% annually you can see the possibility that insurance premiums may rise to meet the demand. The cost of a CISO (Certified Information Security Officer) also needs to be budgeted for if one does not exist already (if you can actually find and recruit one as they are as rare as hens teeth). A CISO is on an equivalent salary to a CIO. CISOs, CISSPs and HISPs are demanding teams to work under them because the workload is extreme. In addition to resourcing and headhunting many CISOs are on 3 months to 6 months notice of termination, so if you are starting from scratch you need to plumb in these on boarding times into a budget. Every business may have to bear these costs. Is this fair to businesses, of course not! It also means you could be 8 months away from establishing a security posture of any significance if you start this mission tomorrow. This gap is critical and needs to be filled.

To get Insurance you need a successful and living Security Policy. To engineer a Security Policy you need help. To get a successful audit you need a successful Security Policy. There are a gaggle of consultants out there to select, but be prepared to pay double the highest rate of normal contractors. You can of course lean on Service Providers to assist you in this endeavour but this will raise your Managed Service premiums.

3.4 TIME IS NOT YOUR FRIEND

In a small sized company it can typically take up to a year to craft and engineer an effective Security Policy and get the basics into the playground. Even engaging external Security Companies to craft a Policy can take a quarter to organise, and Man Day Rates are some of the highest in the industry. So getting from concept to reality will sponge a lot of your Year One CAPEX. Here's the "but", the elapsed time to get through the Plan, Do, Check, Act cycle leaves you exposed by a good 8 months. Plan to remediate the problem.

3.5 BREACH = EXPENSIVE

It takes an adversary about a fortnight to break into a network. Breach detection is invisible and only 25% of attacks are detected in that first week. Most likely your company has never been through an Incident Response drill, a disaster recovery exercise and you are not alone only 36% of SMBs do this globally. Getting external Security Companies to assist in a breach forensics actual attack can take a week to engage. Several events can skew this; most hacks take place during lunch hours, on a Friday, on the last day of the financial month, and prior to, or, during a public holiday. A company's handle on team members' availability is crucial to address this point. In one incident I was involved with the entire management executive team was at an off-site meeting prior to a Christmas holiday. No one was available for a day, during that day a bucket load of data was lost and no external help was available to attend site due to weather and family commitments.

Lets expand the timeline more. Most attacks exploit vulnerability in an existing compute estate. This means a patch may be required, which also means you need your hardware supplier or your software vendor to supply a patch. If your company has invested in 5 years worth of IT that asset value could be in the hundred of thousands or millions of dollars. You are pretty unlikely to replace the whole shebang. Instead you need to wait for a fix - this can take at least a month to solve and the vendor to write a patch and test to shore up your systems. Your estate is still wide open to attack during this period. Another three months can be added to this if your Information is in the Cloud. Lets also consider that malware attacks are getting increasingly malicious and destroy their tracks. During data exfiltration they can delete current and historical records especially customer and financial records. During this exit procedure databases are prone to corruption and this is done to hide logs that track account activity. Once these logs have been lost current versions of data integrity are lost (database keys, dlls, plists etc.). The adversary can also do this over an extended period to the point that IT does not know the best-known backup of data. So a company can restore a database on a clean server only to find they have also restored the infection. If an adversary corrupts the last month of data then a company can lose an entire months revenue and possibly be unable to restore invoices and credit card transactions.

The root cause of cyber security has not yet been addressed or identified yet; we are still dealing with the aftermath. One of these problems is that the Internet is unregulated even though the governments think they control it. There is no global ombudsman to go to judge fair practice when things need arbitration.

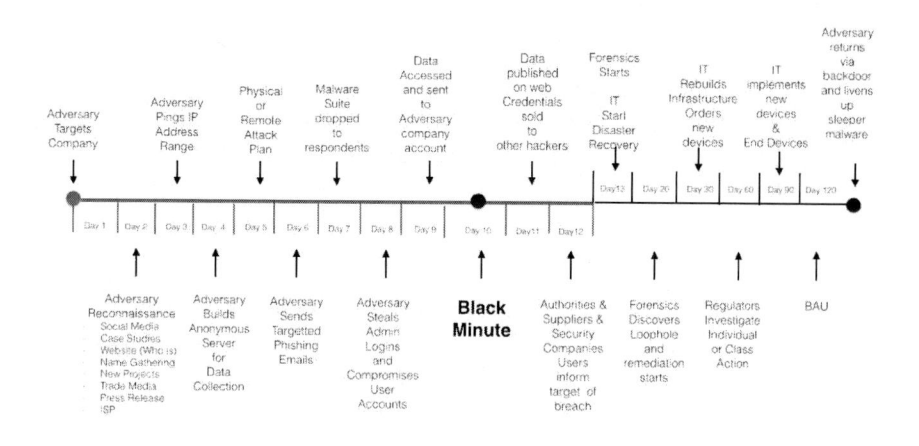

Figure 20 CYBER ATTACK LIFECYCLE

3.6 REGULATOR IN ABSENTIA

Every tenth website you may visit (and through no fault of your own) attempts a malware insert and misuses any data you may have input.[78] There is no comeback on the Website owners or the issuing authorities that allow this to happen as it's incredibly hard to do forensics on and most legitimate website owners do not know of malicious activity. Websites can be bought and established anonymously. This allows adversaries to set up servers and illegal websites based on an email. This practice is ridiculous and allows any adversary to hide. A mechanism is needed where ownership of websites is directly attributable by assigning a website by ground mail and locally administered by a country.

In the US, one in 10 citizens has already been subject to criminal level identity theft (that's around 12 million working people)[79]. There are no studies performed that indicate the scale of monetary and detrimental credit rating loss globally but there are 195 countries in the world besides the US. This is estimated to be in the trillions of dollars. This form of theft is brand affecting; 75% of those who were subject of identity theft moved their funds offshore to safer data and privacy strongholds. This fraud now amounts to $57 Billion a year in the US alone. Globally this figure extrapolated would mean fraud costing $342 billion annually. According to www.privacyrights.org, there were 931,357,921 records breached (stolen) and 4,447 major data breaches since 2005 in the US alone. The recent OPM breach was originally reported to have 4 million details stolen this is now updated to 21 million records.

What's worse is the recovery time that is experienced by citizens who have succumbed to fraud. From personal experience, it takes at least three months to reissue bank accounts and credit cards, and another six months to re-establish your credit status. There is a major push to move credit cards away from plastic and store these on your smartphone, such as Apple's iPhone and its proposal, using an RFID chip (Near Field Communications waving your phone at a checkout to pay[80]) - we have already seen how insecure mobiles are, so this innovation could take these developments beyond reasonable safety.

Product software developers do not, but should, build security into their products from the start, and threats should be tested before release. The vendors are the originators for these lapses in security and relying on consumers to test the bugs in software is a piecemeal approach and could be viewed as irresponsible even with the best of intentions.

Technology companies are amongst the TOP 500 companies in the world, and in the top 1% of the billion-odd companies that exist globally (see Table 4). The Top 50 technology and Telco companies have revenues that compare to medium-sized countries. As most technology companies are geographically located in the US, their contribution to the US Gross Domestic Product (at $16 trillion) is around 10%, and provides for five million jobs. That might explain why the technology companies can influence government thinking with impunity in their sphere of control.

	Company	Employees	($B)		Company	Employees	($B)
1	Apple	96,300	453.03	26	Cisco	79049	101
2	Google	47,756	409.64	27	Vodaphone	91,272	110
3	Samsung	270,000	163.41	28	Huawei	140,000	29.4
4	Microsoft	100,000	370	29	Lenovo	35,026	16.88
5	Foxconn	1,290,000	32.15	30	Oracle	122,458	185
6	AT&T	246,740	166	31	BT	87,800	64
7	Verizon	176,800	197	32	Qualcomm	31,000	45
8	HP	317,500	60.84	33	EMC	63,900	45.84
9	IBM	433,362	187.95	34	TSMC	37,149	6.2
10	Hitachi	326,240	38.46	35	Bell Canada	55,250	3.6
11	China Mobile	181,00	191	36	SAP	66,500	35.5
12	Amazon	117,300	160.49	37	EBay	31,500	68.51
13	Deutsche T	235,132	107	38	Swisscom	19,514	38
14	Sony	146,300	17.6	39	TELUS	43,400	12
15	Panasonic	327,512	22.7	40	Tencent	25,517	65.01
16	Telefonica	272,598	129	41	Facebook	6,337	160.03
17	Softbank	70,336	90	42	Alibaba	28,845	25
18	America Movil	158,694	96	43	Symantec	20,402	14
19	Orange	170,00	39	44	Level 3	11,000	12.87
20	Dell	108,800	22.7	45	Rakuten	10,867	13.06
21	Toshiba	206,087	17.67	46	Priceline.com	8,000	35.58
22	LG Electronics	38,718	17.67	47	VMWare	14,300	41.03
23	Intel	104,000	119.1	48	CA	12,600	11.6
24	Telecom Italia	65,623	90	49	Yahoo	12,200	35.58
25	NTT DoCoMo	22,955	72	50	Adobe	11,144	10.2
							3270.41

Table 5 TOP 50 TECH COMPANIES

Applying sourced country GDP figures from the International Monetary Fund public records I did a little exercise to map out the Annual Revenues of the Top 10 Tech companies to the equivalent entire GDP (Gross Domestic Product) of some countries:

- Apple – *Thailand*
- Google – *Malaysia*
- Samsung – *Ireland*
- Microsoft – *Vietnam*
- Foxconn – *Hungary*
- AT & T – *Angola*

- Verizon – *Morocco*
- HP – *Slovakia*
- IBM – *Ecuador*
- Hitachi – *Oman*

Last on the list is Adobe, but they still manage to be fortuitously twinned with Fiji! In fact, I think it would be nice for all technology companies to twin with a country. When a country stumbles on bad times the technology company could contribute to the said countries GDP to give a helping hand? It's a joke I know but when it comes to extending Internet access to a country there is no reason why the tech giants can contribute (in real terms) on a country basis? Facebook seems to be a leading benefactor in this area. Facebook's' annual revenue ($ 7.87 billion) equates to the country Georgia GDP. Georgia has a population of 4.3 million and 2.2 million Internet users. The problem here is extending the reach of the Internet to rural subscribers. The country is still reeling from the Russo-Georgian War in 2008. This war was deemed the first Cyber War. Russian Military still occupy South Ossetia and Abkhazia. The war displaced 192,000 people, and while many returned to their homes after the war, 20,272 persons remained displaced as of 2014. Russian military occupies Abkhazia and South Ossetia in violation of the ceasefire since August 2008.[81] The recent Ukraine incursion by the Russians mimics the Georgian strategy. So it would be nice to see large companies help war torn countries like Georgia. To roll out Internet to the whole of Georgia would cost $46.3 CAPEX per user, or, $94m to connect 2.1 million users (50% of the population has Internet already).

3.7 VENDOR SOFTWARE VULNERABILITIES

Vendors, Operating Systems, Networks and Applications have inherent security holes that act as the springboard for adversarial threats and associated risks. Vendors are not liable for damage to your companies' platforms and systems, so once you have purchased (or force fed) their solutions you are pushed out to sea in a leaky boat. Are vendors to blame for the vulnerabilities in their products? It would be nice if software were sold the same way as cars are. In the automobile sector if there's a trickle of complaints about a fault in a car it sparks an immediate recall of millions of cars. The US is not regulating Software manufacturing the same way it regulated automobile manufacturing. Perhaps a Ralph Nader evangelist for Technology is needed? Complaints against vendors are usually met with a shrug of the shoulders. Have you ever really read the EULA and Terms and Conditions screens that pop up on software installs? Vendors wrap themselves in this toga of legalise to prevent being served with class actions. It has been this way for decades and so a cavalier manner has proliferated and over time consumers are conditioned and consequently expect to be treated this way.

To meet the desire for new toys and electronics there is a continuous vendor frenzy to have two to three major product releases each year, to remain ahead of the competition. This pressure from the owners and shareholders for constant good news and increased market share means safety and solid coding and testing are secondary to features and without due diligence on customer, or, customer safety. Vendors don't mind instability as long as it is good enough..

3.8 ZERO DAY VULNERABILITIES

For the last decade cyber criminals have operated with privileged vulnerability information from vendors! During the pre-disclosure Discovery phase, groups (Privileged Groups composed of Hackers, Cyber Criminals, Government Intelligence Agencies and Security Researchers) share vulnerabilities. Vulnerabilities can be bought and sold and hackers have access to critical information, which would allow for the compromise of all vulnerable groups systems without the public ever being aware of the threat. Brokers such as Tipping Points' Zero Day Initiative[82] and Versions Defence programmes encourage this dialogue

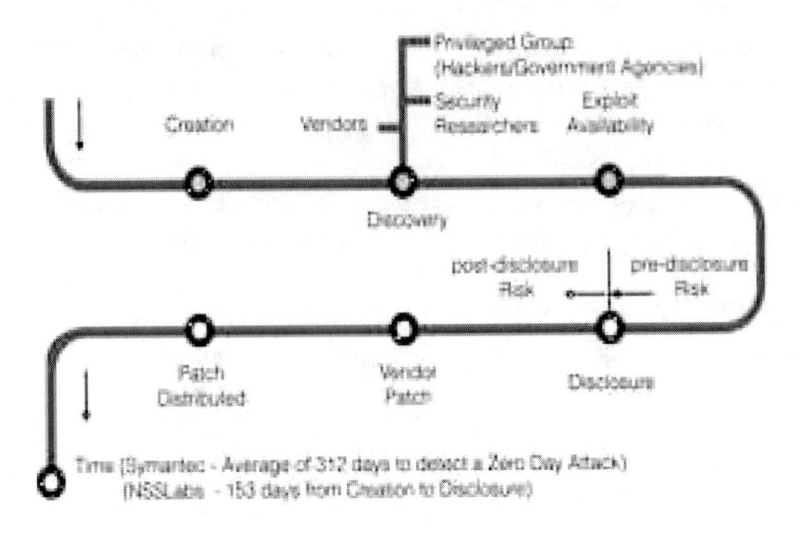

FIGURE 21 THE VULNERABILITY LIFECYCLE

A growing number of software vendors have introduced bug bounty programs, in which finders are compensated for reporting vulnerabilities directly to the software vendors, rather than going public with the information or selling it on the black market. The Mozilla Foundation was one of the first to introduce a bounty program, and since then Google, Facebook, PayPal, and others have followed. In 2013, Microsoft, which had long resisted such a system for 30 years, introduced its bug bounty program

According to NSSLabs most vendors are taking this route seriously:

- Google paid approximately USD $580,000 over three years for 501 vulnerabilities discovered in the Chrome browser (28% of the patched vulnerabilities in same period)

- Mozilla paid approximately USD $570,000 over three years for 190 vulnerabilities discovered in its Firefox browser (24% of the patched vulnerabilities in same period)

- Facebook has paid approximately USD $1 million since the 2011 inception of its program

- Microsoft has paid approximately USD $100,000 since the June 2013 inception of its program for reporting new exploitation techniques

Recent research has found such programs to be economically efficient, comparing favourably to the cost of hiring full-time security researchers to locate bugs internally.[83] This approach apparently reduces the need for vendors to hire internal security team members to test software before public release and availability (why this is such a financial burden for the worlds richest companies is a conundrum). For instance, Applications sold via mobile providers App Stores are outsourced to external companies are security tested but the quality of this approach must always be questioned no matter how stringent the SLA and liability.

In the UK, the Information Commissioners Office (www.ico.org.uk) can now issue non-compliance fines (for lapses in Data Protection) of up to £500,000, but this seems levied at government departments (so one part of the government pays another part of the government). Recently though, things seem to be changing with this being pushed to the commercial sector. The Royal Bank of Scotland learned the cost of an IT systems outage when in 2013 they lost their ATM network for two weeks. The migration resulted in a £56 million fine, as customers were unable to carry out payroll, or do simple bank transfers[84]. If the Internet becomes a public utility these fines could be extended to SMBs in the future.

The closest to a 'vendor' fine is Google, who according to the New York Times entered into a non-prosecution agreement with the government in August 2011, over the use of its AdWords program by Canadian pharmacies, that helped them sell prescription drugs in the United States in violation of a federal law.[85].

In the US Barack Obama has introduced legislation that requires companies to report a data breach within 30 days. [86] This assumes the company knows about the data breach. The individual US states and nationally based regulators fine minimal amounts for transgressions. Fines are never levied at vendors, or their products. We keep overlooking the obvious to coin a phrase I used earlier. If I use an analogy - should an institution such as a bank, and accidentally miss-sold products, I would be expected to pay out large fines as recompense. How many millions of cars are recalled because of defective air bags, seat belts that come undone when you brake hard? Compare this to the number of many major releases of software that have been withdrawn after launch.

Companies should also consider what to do if the data breach was an Insider - they can then be fined for non-compliance over and above an initial fraud breach. We know that Insiders can generate multiple and crippling hacking attacks, they just need to send a Login and a password of an internal company device to a hacking squad and let the chips fall where they may. The team members in outsourced contracts cannot be monitored 24/7 yet they see sensitive information every day.

3.9 DOES AUDITING HELP STOP ATTACKS?

The last 25 years has seen the inexorable rise of IT systems auditing, usually as an end result of a certification requirement to show conformance, or non-conformance, on an annual basis for publicly traded companies. Certifications may go some way to reducing insurance premiums although no one has yet created a Hacker Proof Audit certification? Like most audits of any IT system there are an awful lot of activities, processes and configuration of code and components that production team members can overlook, be ignored and ultimately uncovered by an audit.

Are security audits of any worth (or value) in light of the vast number of data breaches? My answer is you need a starting baseline. It is always useful to do a major audit to help set a baseline to help build a Security Policy and indeed identify crucial fraud loopholes. IT Audits costs start around $30,000, IT Security Audits can easily double that figure. Black Box monthly Audits can cost $3500 a month for business as usual activity and performed after every major code release. These Penetration and Vulnerability audits have to be via alternating suppliers. For secure code and application releases and $10,000 for a pre production application release) is essential (Veracode) and continued until the application is hardened. The scarcity of technically proficient auditors and verified background checked penetration testers adds to these costs.

Financial Audits are priced by a percentage of a company annual revenue and dependent on vertical segment but priced in the range of 0.05% to 0.12%.[87] An audit can take up to two weeks on site to analyse documentation and interviewing key players and a further two weeks desk research to create a report with recommendations.

A Black Box audit should be monthly after a major estate or application change and requires a highly technical auditor. Always have several suppliers capable of doing this and trusted, as they may be required for Incident Response and forensics. Typically a Black Box technician uses several tools to do this: Nessus, SARA (Security Auditors Research Assistant), Whisker, Hping2, ISS Internet Scanner, Foundscan, CORE Security Suite, Bindview, BeyondTrust Powerbroker. There are other hawkish applications that can monitor a companies estate continuously, these are mostly appliance based and can monitor configurations constantly. I recommend Portswiggers Burp which can do a manual penetration test for $300 per user per year. Even Open Source developers can inject code inadvertently so any Open Source application needs a thorough test.

Before a new production system is even started its advisable to get a knowledgeable SHAZOPS Facilitator to give the system a once over. If you are deploying ANY new application (even Open Source Applications) ensure it has undergone a Static Analysis and a Dynamic Analysis Test. This even includes and applies to all the tools used by the auditor. Auditors own tools and equipment are never checked and used on other company's sites before it reaches yours. This second pair of eyes can be useful. If you are bringing on board a cloud provider you should always seek an external audit review of the provider's own security. For a belt and braces approach check the SAAS software application being offered and supported. Look at Veracode as an example of secure testing, their service does a deep dive on a custom application and highlights insecurities. For a 50MB size application they will charge a nominal first pass for $10k. There may be several iterations of the test before go live. I would also recommend getting any Open Source application brought to site going through this process. Never use the same auditor or Audit Company twice and never contract one associated with Financial Auditing Company that audits a companies books. This is because Insider Fraud may be overlooked or delay a Financial Audit.

Pre-audit, there is the month's rush prior to the audit starting to get things done quick time, and everybody works overtime to solve the previous year's audit findings, whilst trying to keep their own house in order. IT operators popularly perceive IT audits as a Complete Waste of Time (CWOT). Not that I am decrying the validity of proper governance, or audits: some can be quite revealing and can help some teams sharpen their minds, pencils and their vitae.

Consider this argument. There is no regulator to say an IT organisation or a vendor has done badly, or should be liable for a fine on audit completion. Besides the usual regulations such as SOX (Sarbanes Oxley), PCI (Payment Card Industry certification) and HIPAA (Health Insurance Portability and Accountability Act 1996) protocols there are few legal tenets to take even 1% of your revenues away. So why bother – what's the point? Let's use the **5 Whys** (an auditor's favourite tool to discover root cause) on why we need an audit:

> *Why* do you want to be IT audited? *Answer:* To make sure our processes are efficient.
>
> *Why* are your processes not efficient? *Answer:* We lose 80% of our workload a year on completing low-value projects to shore up our processes.
>
> *Why* are you doing so many low value projects? *Answer:* Because we have to ensure that we fulfil the conformance findings of the last audit and we don't have time to do the big projects.
>
> *Why* don't you have time to do the big projects? *Answer:* By the time we have completed all the small projects our annual budget is blown.
>
> *Why* so little budget left this year? *Answer:* The only budget we have left is allocated to the cost of the next audit. (And Repeat…)

Typically, audits are driven by the need for discovering fraud, and boards are convinced by accounting auditors that an IT audit is of value, mainly for the benefit of financial auditors' associated consulting companies. Sampling of transactions is now the industry standard for performing audits. It is only when gross errors or fraudulent activities are uncovered that comprehensive audits are performed. As businesses have increased in complexity, 'risk-based' auditing has arisen, to make auditing more efficient and economical? Risk-based auditing starts by assessing whether an audit is even needed, based on a review of information in the financial statements. If the review finds discrepancies, irregularities or suspicious activity, then a full-scale audit will follow. This timing can mean being too late.

These audits are not cheap, and can easily cut down the productivity of an IT department by 20% per annum because the preparation time is intense, and management time to dissect an auditors recommendations. Pointy-finger remediations and endless blame meetings usually suck production time post audit results. The audit findings also kick off knee-jerk projects to satisfy some false gods in the "Pet Project Management Department" or to pursue an unrelated political objective. As several CIOs have commented to me Audits in reality are horizon sales levers to sell more man-days from the audit provider. Usually a team of 20 consultants wearing chinos and sporting goatees for three months, with the end result being a bloated 200 slide PowerPoint presentation recommending an even more bloated ERP system, which is invariably project managed by the company that does the audits in the first instance. Obviously this is an exaggeration and never happens in real life.

The same can be said for most quality audits, even in the manufacturing, environmental and safety worlds. Organisations see little value in the certification process, "how can you do a QA audit on a robot?" has been a statement I have heard before? The ISO 9001 standard, I understand is a process and quality audit standard that helps refine quality management systems, and therefore adds value, but an annual IT audit bears little fruit and can distract team members from genuinely useful preventative measures and solutions. Auditors recognise this as a major problem; the collection and manual direction of sample transactions just does not work. The Public Company Accounting Oversight Board announced that 35% of financial audits are ineffective, could the same be said for IT and Security audits? [88]

3.10 THE FUTURE OF AUDITING
If 50% of public companies have been hacked annually is an annual audit worth the time delay waiting for a seal of "certification"? What happens when an audit happens and then a company decides to go cloud crazy? What

can auditors to cover and limit their liabilities? This is an extract from an AICPA thought-piece, in recognition of the fact that the annual visit route does not work [89]:

"The external audit profession has not yet adopted "close to the event" audit technologies, although they are in the process of advising internal audit departments on how to do so. Pockets of practitioner have developed IT skills. Recently there is growing awareness of the need to increase auditor IT and analytic proficiencies."[90]

Since 2012 there has been little movement on this issue, the problem being that for effective auditing you need to:

- Know what you are talking about

- Understand the 'socio-technical environment' and computing operations

- Realise that being 'close to the event' means being on site and on call (present and available)

- Be able to understand and analyse real time events and data

- Carry out daily forensics on fraud and security breaches

- Understand code and every technical component in a Technology Value Centre estate

- Review and approve production-readiness

- The above bullet list shows traditional auditing is intermittent and annual and should be perpetual.

3.11 LIABILITIES

So should vendors be liable for purveying ready-made compromised systems? In Jeffrey Carr's eye opening book *Inside Cyber Warfare* he describes the root causes as hostages [91]: "A state or non state hacker attacks US critical infrastructure and Department of Defence (DoD) networks at will and without fear of detection or attribution. He is able to do this from behind the protection of two very valuable "hostages", or more precisely, "sacred cows" that US government officials, including the Congress, are loath to change - using Microsoft Windows and regulating a segment of private industry:

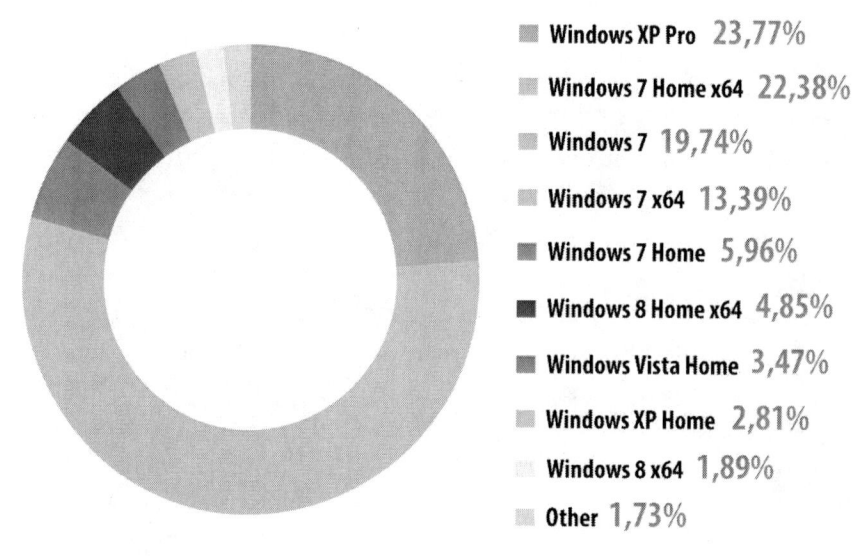

- Windows XP Pro 23,77%
- Windows 7 Home x64 22,38%
- Windows 7 19,74%
- Windows 7 x64 13,39%
- Windows 7 Home 5,96%
- Windows 8 Home x64 4,85%
- Windows Vista Home 3,47%
- Windows XP Home 2,81%
- Windows 8 x64 1,89%
- Other 1,73%

FIGURE 22 *- DISTRIBUTION OF WINDOWS OS ON USERS COMPUTERS 2013 (Kaspersky)*

- **HOSTAGE 1** The pervasive use of Microsoft Windows Operating System (OS) throughout the federal government but particularly within the DoD, the intelligence community, and privately owned critical networks controlling power, water, transportation, and communications networks.

- **HOSTAGE 2** The uninterrupted, sustained economic growth of Internet Service Providers, data centres and domain name registrars who profit by selling services to criminal organisations and nationalistic hackers that prefer the reliability and speed of US networks to the ones found in their own countries."

Now Carr wrote this in 2012, but nothing has changed with this love affair and its risks. I attended a Microsoft XP launch back in 2002 with the key thrust being that selling a raft of consulting round the products fallibilities was more profitable than pursuing traditional unit sales.

This dos not stop other countries outside the US from regulating vendors. The EU has recently badgered Microsoft to unbundle Internet Explorer and Google regarding privacy.

In the EU, the strategy to move away from Windows has actually gone the other way. Strangely, I have seen two companies recently nail their colours to the Microsoft mast, each with over 200,000 end users so perhaps it cannot be all that bad. Microsoft is finally securing their Internet Explorer web browser with the release of Edge Browser. It will take more years for Microsoft to unravel the security flaws in their other product offerings. Given the recent trend return to Macro viruses this may need a fast rethink. Forbes reported that on the 14th May, 2015 "Hackers have always used public resources to store their malicious files, but Chinese digital spies have taken things a step further to hide their tracks. According to FireEye, they used accounts on a Microsoft IT (TechNet) support site to host command and control links to their malware".

So what's really going on here? Is the IT world still driven by company's system administrators who see Windows as the easy option and self-imposed job protection scheme and don't want to know anything that delivers a better solution? Do governments to change from this vendor of any benefit to security services, and possibly global control demonstrate the reluctance? It certainly is not related to ease of use, more like - it's all we know. This is why companies' architectures need a revisit and a complete new approach. 90% of the world's computers are driven by Microsoft's operating system that's around 2 billion devices. Many SMB companies have invested millions on training, so the brand will not go away fast. I am sure the reader may think there is a better choice?

3.12 NEW BUGS MEET OLD BUGS

With any fresh release or software upgrade comes a new wave of bugs and vulnerabilities. Companies like Apple are –becoming the focus of adversaries. Their security alerts seem more populated lately. In Computer Weekly[92] they reported that operator error was the root cause of the catastrophic failure of Microsoft's Azure Cloud computing platform on 19th November 2014, which left many customers unable to access the service.

The outages are an example why some SMB's are reluctant to use Public Clouds.

There are more reasons why throwing your assets up into the Cloud is not a panacea. While Public Cloud operators will argue they experience far less downtime than in-house IT operations. Given the scale of Microsoft and Amazon Web Services (AWS), any hitch impacts *millions* of SMBs. The Azure service was not fully operational for more than 11 hours. Being without a basic utility like gas, electricity or water for 11 hours would be classed as a major incident with possible global ramifications. If an organisation had an e-commerce Website, the cost of downtime amounts to millions of pounds in lost revenue. This equates to a 99.999% uptime Service Level Agreement being missed and the Azure Cloud would therefore report a 99.875% uptime [93]. If you had no back-up facilities or your entire infrastructure was in the Cloud (assuming you had deep pockets and a large risk wallet), you would have potentially lost a day's trading. This is not the last of cloud outages adversaries are already making in-roads to the cloud. Addressing this new set of bugs will test the technical teams to the fullest. Many new technical deployments experience some catastrophe at some point, and these are usually solved in double quick time. AWS attempt to resolve security holes in 90 days across their entire estate, which is very fast. Windows Servers and services are built on many Cloud infrastructures. Sometimes '*old bugs*' get forgotten:

- On November 12th 2014 Microsoft issued a critical fix for a **19-year-old software bug** that affects all existing Windows versions since Windows 95. IBM researchers discovered the bug this past May, and *BBC reports* that they "worked with Microsoft to fix the problem before going public."

The upside here is that some vulnerabilities are being found, and that they are getting fixed after a six month wait. The downside is, what else is out there? And what are the Operating System vendors really doing to fix this as part of a continuous improvement programme. CSPs like Rackspace are the leaders here in terms of transparency. A technical department completely committed to proactive solutions supports Rackspace's exemplary customer service.

This vendor reliance could be termed a predisposing condition by NIST. "A predisposing condition is a condition that exists within an organization, a mission or business process, enterprise architecture, information system, or environment of operation, which affects (i.e., increases or decreases) the likelihood that threat events, once initiated, result in adverse impacts to organizational operations and assets, individuals, other organizations, or the Nation."[94]

3.13 STEPCHECK
SMBs will be forced to take Cyber Security seriously

- Directors need to be fully cognisant of all the legal implications of cyber risk

- Boards need adequate access to cyber security expertise

- Directors, Financiers and Customers need their expectations met that management have an enterprise wide cyber risk management framework in place

- Based on the policy, the company needs to know what to do during and after an incident.

- The cost of a single data breach is around $3million. This would impact any SMB needing to cover the cost, so Insurance is a must have.

- The vendors are still not testing the Operating Systems sufficiently well to stop data breaches

- Auditing IT systems is after the fact and is Sisyphean

- An SMB has no recourse on Vendors and no regulator to complain to

- The Internet as an indicator of the Reverse Panopticon effect is pushing users away?

4 ROOT CAUSES – IT'S THE USERS FAULT!

Subscribers love the Internet but are not educated sufficiently well to understand how their data is used by untrusted entities. This chapter looks at this data love affair and how people regard cyber security as media hooey.

I hear regularly from people when hacking pops up in a conversation is "Oh it won't ever happen to me", to which I reply "well what would you do when it does, and then, how do you know you have not been hacked already"? Conversely, I have organisations tell me "how do you expect us to make an honest profit if we don't collect all this private data?" to which I reply, "what do you do when it's all gone"? I saved all my data to CD so it won't affect me (you probably copied over undetected malware as well)! SMB's believe their data is safe from adversaries (which it's not) and then they retort "we will restore it from the backups" to which I reply "That's good, in part, but how do you know you are not also restoring the malware that forced the attack in the first place?"

Data collection and the limits of privacy is a constant conundrum for all of us. How we select, save, secure, and store and use data costs SMB's big bucks. Subscribers part with their personal information without a second thought, even though they have paid for it to be watched. SMB's are also guilty of pursuing this route, even unavoidably. Everybody's data is held by everyone, provided through consensual means or not. Companies collect and sell this information as if it's his or her property. So Internet subscribers are now avoiding giving it freely.

Western democracy was built on King Johns Magna Carta (Big Paper) and the Rights of Man as described by Thomas Paine. Everything we see our politicians do today suggests our democratic leaders shun the notion of personal freedom. Rand Pauls recent filibuster attempt on the Patriot Act renewal is refreshing. James Madison, the fourth president of the US and 'Father of the Constitution' wrote this:

"Wherever the real power in a Government lies, there is the danger of oppression. In our Governments, the real power lies in the majority of the Community, and the invasion of private rights is chiefly to be apprehended, not from the acts of Government contrary to the sense of its constituents, but from acts in which the Government is the mere instrument of the major number of the constituents." [95]

Benjamin Franklin wrote.

"They who can give up essential liberty to obtain a little temporary safety deserve neither liberty nor safety." [96]

Internet subscribers are now attempting to subvert the system. Terrorists use ground post nowadays because it is virtually unreadable by technology means. So the point of mass data collection is pointless in the eyes of many voters as terrorist activities continue unabated. Subscribers are now adding grey mush data to the fake grey mush. All citizen data is being kept in storage data facilities that require a weekly refresh in new disk space. We are not talking terabytes of data; we are in the region of the Zettabyte galaxy[97].

Zettabytes of data retained information is expensive to maintain and companies have to foot the bill – especially when it is 80% trash data. For each Agency request for data transactions from ISP/CSP and Telco companies there is also a huge cost attached per request in terms of man-days to locate the data. A Customer Detail Record search request costs a Telco around $150,000 to complete, going through several years of back data is time consuming (going through old tapes that may not work when loaded onto new servers). There is no compensation for this by the way costs are bourn by the company. If an average SMB had several requests for CDRs this could cause a hit on revenue. SMBs need a perpetual data tidying and hygiene technique to retain only pertinent data. Information Classification helps your company save money.

Agencies have resorted to using the Cloud for compute and storage as the existing facilities reach capacity - so making the Cloud attractive to adversaries. The contributing reason is that Internet users are using the Internet too much, there just is not enough physical storage available to hold everyone's data transactions, and this traffic will increase, as the Cisco Visual Network Index [98] predicts.

The predicted growth of the consumer Internet directly correlates to future organisations' growth requirements so is a good indication of where data storage investment in SMB estates should go in the coming years. Who in your organisation watches this data and its growth? These figures go against the current curve of global economic growth somewhat and may be optimistic based on the last 6 years of deflationary statistics.

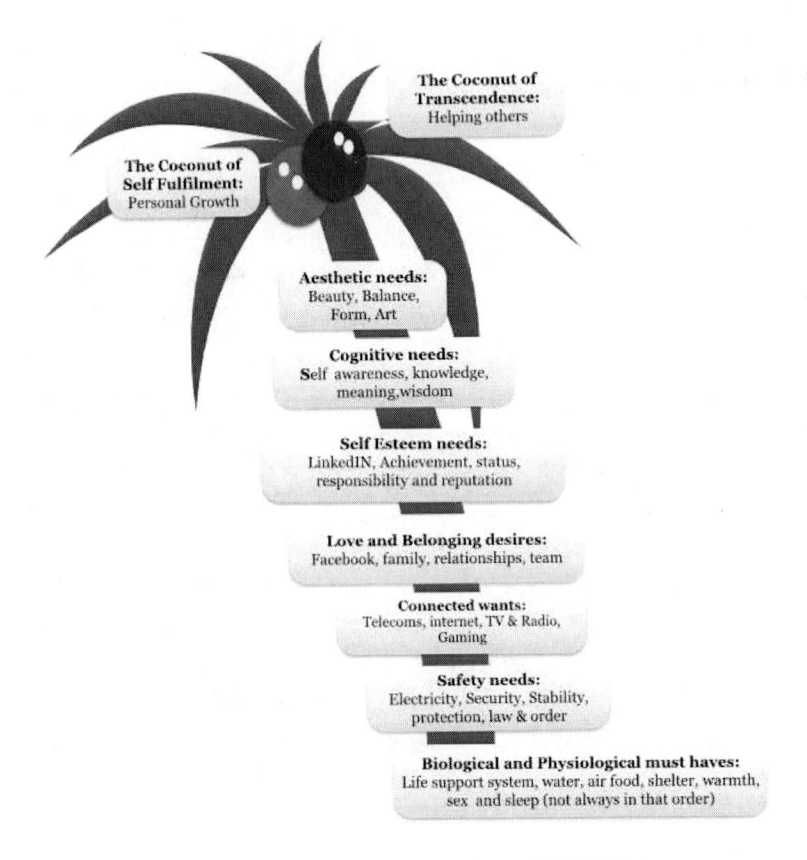

Figure 23 THE COCONUTS OF TRANSENDENCE

4.1 EDUCATION

We still won't let go of the Internet and I had to review how important it is to us by revisiting Maslow's hierarchy of needs. The original Maslow pyramid didn't make much sense since I used it in the eighties - technology has made much more of an impact than I originally perceived, technology has therefore been added to the palm tree graphic. The diagram reflects the strong pull of the Internet and how it now influences daily life.

Maslow's theory is often represented as a pyramid, with the larger, lower levels representing the lower needs, and the upper point representing the need for self-actualisation. Maslow believed that the only reason people do not move upwards towards self-actualisation due to hindrances placed in their way by society. He states that education is one of these hindrances. He recommends ways that education can switch from its usual pigeonhole, person-stunting tactics to person-growing approaches. Maslow states that educators should respond to the potential an individual has for growing into a self-actualising person of his/her own kind. Perhaps the Internet can match this potential over time rather than the self-destruct path it seems to be following at the moment. The heavy reliance on the Internet is changing our socio-economic lookout on life so given all its foibles perhaps we are stuck with it in its current format. Perhaps it does contribute to self-actualisation and possibly self-determination?

The Internet used to be a wondrous thing and in the 90s people were sitting on dial up links all night (blanche nuit) to discover the best websites to go to (all 600 of them), chat with people across the globe, play chess with a senior in another country. Now it is a weapon that attacks basic Safety needs, the puppy has grown up and the evil vet wants to steal it. Millions are currently leaving their countries to find employment elsewhere. Along with this migration go a high percentage of really smart young people. It's a personal ambition of mine to see coding colleges set up for 16 year olds as a vocational diploma. Millennial's would love to get real hands on coding at an early age rather than plod their way through University and its associated debt. Obviously this means adding coding as a middle school qualification. Our world is moving to a completely software bound universe, and great coders are in short supply. I would love to see this developed on a country by country basis where coders can code in their own language and even create country based Operating Systems and Applications. I think maintaining uniqueness on a cultural standpoint will enrich the globe rather than the fascination for speaking American and shopping in the same shops, eating the same burgers and selling the same handbags everywhere.

4.2 THATS NOT MY NAME

Given the palm tree analogy we should question how far it has impacted our every need? For those who are connected and feel the need to check their phones every 6 minutes here are some thought-provoking questions:

- Could you live without your laptop or your mobile for a month? (The Horror!)
- Would your company survive for three months without IT?
- Has your company survived on back-up systems alone for a whole month?
- When was the last time your company held a disaster day?
- Do your IT Systems and Networks have any Single Points of Failure?
- Does your company carry out a penetration test monthly?
- Do you turn tracking off and Location Based services on your smartphone?
- Do you change your passphrases every week?
- Is *all* your data encrypted?
- Would you buy a car without locks or with known safety defects?

As a SMB executive or team member, you answered any of the above questions in the negative you should consider yourself connected - but at risk.

Business also needs to invest in business continuity and disaster preparations. (The auditors collectively shout Yay)! This subject usually meets with a waking/sleeping bird attitude. Birds don't sleep; they switch off one side of their brains and keep one eye open in case of attack. This time we need to get prepared, because the next big bad thing is on the horizon. This is the culmination of joined-up thinking from many leading anti-virus vendors and global business leaders from all around the world. It's not just my viewpoint. However, the caveat is what you back up and whether your stored data is clean from malware.

4.3 TECHNOLOGY VALUE CENTRES

The IT department has been the first place for extreme cost cutting by every corporation for the last decade. This situation needs CIOs to reshape their strategy and turn their cost centre into **Technology Value Centres** that led by innovation and nurtured team members rather than cutting them out. Changing the name helps remarket IT to be a business enabler. Gartner term this a bi-modal approach. This means that IT is now leading innovation and subsequently profit. The latest example of this is some companies are now putting Research and Development and even Finance under the direct management of the CIO. I have seen working examples like Business Transformation (BT), Value Innovation Centre (VIC), Technology Point (TP) and Information Network (IN) (I'm in with the IN Crowd) to avoid the "IT Shop" label. Personally I like the Technology Value Centre tagline as it reflects an ethical connotation as well as an aspiration target. As we will see later SMBs can turn their estates into services for sale internally and externally.

4.4 STEPCHECK

- The Internet needs to demonstrate to net citizens and SMBs executives it is fit for purpose.

- People will not take kindly to SMBs misplacing data

- If the Internet does grow as predicted - SMBs can take advantage of the growth where corporate's cannot. Small companies can deliver quicker where large companies cannot

- CIOs should lead a new budget initiative to lead SMBs into new markets through investment and organisation

- SMBs strategy should reflect the needs of providing businesses with a secure product brokers and become Technology Value Centres in their own right.

5 ROOT CAUSES – RISKY BUSINESS

Understanding Existential, Empirical, Operational and Conflict Risks is essential for any business to manage. Any size SMB can use this relatively new science to help save money and time and build a security culture helping team members become risk adverse. In this chapter we examine how SMBs should prepare for conflict and how to risks are in need of perpetual monitoring.

I am an engineer by trade. I design Cloud data centres and train the team members to operate them. The Cloud is all about patterns: workflow patterns and technical patterns, and these patterns are designed to connect systems across public clouds and private clouds and enable data Craftflows. It is the new language of a Technology Value Centre. We now design workflow cycles that can be technical closed loops, multi level closed processes, or open-ended track handoffs. Like a metro map, or underground map the tracks are useful to understand co-joining branching and station stops and interconnects. You will see this described in the Combat Ready IT handoff diagrams later. This is also how we trace functions, understand risk, and manage security postures.

It is proven that wars (of any scale) usually follow recessions or depressions; wars also follow the peaks and troughs of sunspot activity. Pandemics follow conflict, like the Spanish Flu following World War 1 and even Ebola and MERS following the years of multi-country conflict in West Africa. The latest Ukraine conflict mimics alarms seen prior to World War 2. Likewise Information Technology organisation topology becomes distributed after centralisation, and bull markets follow the seasons and sunspot activity.

Our human spirit is always somehow guided to do certain actions at certain points in time, at some points defensive or attacking, destroying environments or other people. In the last 3500 years some 8000 wars have ensued, so there is a conflict happening (on average) every four months. The Cybrid war we are witnessing now has been in existence since the early 90s when the Chinese came up with the concept of Network Device Warfare, or cyber-war.

5.1 OUR ANCESTORS WERE SMART

The Mayans and Egyptians understood cycles. Around 7000 BC the Egyptians established a 'calendar year' based on a solar cycle 360 days long, divided by 12 lunar cycles of 30 days each. We mimic this is the Gregorian calendar. They built Pyramids that align directly with the Dog Star Sirius to help their Pharaoh's regeneration cycle. We also had the recent Mayan calendar cycle 2012 scare, where the end of the world was predicted. Maybe 4000 years ago the Mayan Calendar was a couple of years out?

Hindus also believed the human spirit is renewed. Around 8000 BC the Hindus built 'Vimanas' [99] based on technologies that took 10000 years to mimic (still unsuccessfully) and built fleets of flying machines, that were fuelled by energy being recycled - a form of massive vortex based engine exerting incredible energy. The Mahabharata and Drona Parva can trace their cyclical history back 48,000 years. The Yuga cycles are well known as birth and rebirth in 6,000-year spans, usually ending in a massive conflagration that resets civilisations knowledge clocks.

5.2 BBC-PR

Not Public Relations for the British Broadcasting Corporation. Our histories are littered with examples of the cyclical rise and fall of empires. Ancient civilisations were fully in touch with natural cycles, birth to death rituals, following solstice events and planetary paths (there was no TV or Web to distract them). But this book doesn't need to preach to intellects that these cyclical events happen, it's the timing of these cycles that is either reduced or elongated. As we become more global, we become more aware of cultural cycles, localised conflicts and global disputes that all have an impact on how we should prepare (sometimes) for disasters.

The history or war and economy seem to follow a five-stage life cycle: Boom – Bust – Conflict – Pandemic – Recovery. (I call this BBC-PR). We know from recent history that a seven to eight year economic peak and trough was experienced during the last century [100]. This Boom/Bust mentality always seems to catch business and commerce on the back foot. Traders use Swing Waves, the Fibonacci ABC patterns and technical rebound measures to match investment cycles. With all this great financial predictability why companies don't set aside 10% of revenue as savings annually to prepare for hard times is always a mind-numbing annoyance to me. However, we still got caught short as the year 2000 saw a peak in global growth up to the tipping point of the 2008 bust. Seven years later, we see only a handful of countries emerging from the recession.

Figure 24 BBC-PR

Since the massive recession from 2008 to 2015 we have witnessed the rise of right wing political parties and the increase of conflict flash points all over the globe. Who would have thought the Cold War would start again, and that it emerged recently that Russia has been preparing its army for nuclear first use capabilities since 2000? There has been a sudden thawing of US Cuba relations to loosen Russia's foothold in the Caribbean. Putin has annexed Crimea. Who would have predicted the Daesh Crusades?

A specific modification of the theory of Kondratieff cycles was developed by Daniel Šmihula. Šmihula identified six long-waves within modern society and the capitalist economy, each of which was initiated by a specific technological revolution:

1. (1600–1780) the wave of the Financial-agricultural revolution
2. (1780–1880) the wave of the Industrial revolution

3. (1880–1940) the wave of the Technical revolution

4. (1940–1985) the wave of the Scientific-technical revolution

5. **(1985–2015) the wave of the Information and telecommunications revolution**

6. (2015–2035?) The hypothetical wave of the post-informational technological revolution (**The SMB Golden Wave**)

Unlike Kondratieff, Šmihula believed that each new cycle is shorter than its predecessor. The main stress is put on technological progress and new technologies as decisive factors of any long-time economic development. Each of these waves have its own **innovation phase**, which is described as a *technological revolution* and an **application phase** in which the number of revolutionary innovations falls and attention focuses on exploiting and extending existing innovations. As soon as an innovation or a series of innovations becomes available, it becomes more efficient to invest in its adoption, extension and use than in creating new innovations.[101]

As we are now in 2015 and at the end of the 5th Šmihula Wave we are at a pivotal year in technology innovation. The earliest signs of this could be the demise of the Internet as a useful medium (unless InternetNew happens), or, even the impact of Quantum Computing and Robotica. Most likely the period from now to 2020 will be conflict bound. Optimistically the 6th Wave will be the re-engineering and rebirth of a safe Internet. I don't want a Half Full cup – I want a cup that runneth over![102]

By 2020, the world's population will grow to 8,000,000,000. Since 1950 (and in the space of 60 years) we have added six billion mouths to feed and water globally. This growth is unprecedented in human history. Even with intensive farming techniques there will be a tipping point where nations are forced into land grab to maintain a nation's food, water and energy needs. Could Artic exploration be a new conflict flash point as the Ice Cap recedes? By 2050 the projected population will be around 10 billion, which will mean around 2 billion unemployed. Also since 1950, the world's economic growth rate has declined from a peak of 2.8% annually to a projected 0.4% in 2020.

Of course, every nation will demand washing machines and fridges and the lifestyle seen on television and the Internet. New manufacturing techniques are needed to meet this dramatic rise in consumer demand. This forces additional consumer demand for clean water supplies, energy, food as population grows exponentially. I remember when tomatoes tasted and smelt like tomatoes. Nowadays, through hydroponics and irradiation, these tastes and smells are rare, due to a dramatic reduction in the quality of the nutrients and minerals in the soil. There are not enough phosphates being mined to maintain the artificial fertilisers that we have relied on for the last 50 years. There are only two mines left in the world capable of mass phosphate production. Of course, in our attempt to heat the world's current population problems we have successfully used all the carbon fossil fuels that took billions of years to form and depleted all those resources during the last 200 years. As fossil fuels are not renewable and the output is sent into the environment, we are successfully heating the planet so that growing food becomes increasingly difficult.

Unfortunately, governments are looking for quick fixes and resorting to nuclear power to at least provide electricity to power our Internet connected devices to the growing and greedy population. In addition, minerals that are required for computer manufacture and chip fabrication are becoming rare and expensive. The scarcity imposes demands on earth resources to maintain the technology high that we have experienced during the last 50 years. Silicon and Copper are in short supply, which are the building blocks of computing and semiconductor manufacture.

We have also become a world that has produced in-built and instant obsolescence in our products. This throwaway attitude means sometimes we buy technology and barely unpack it before we throw it on to the scrapheap. It's only in the last 15 years that we have adopted a recycling and sustainability attitude to hardware devices. Our consumerist lifestyle on which many economies rely is not maintainable. Without constant chip development, even the most innovative of software innovations will come to a grinding halt. There is hope placed in Graphene a hexagonal lattice allotrope of carbon, which is a man evolved silicon type replacement.

The world's reliance on oil and gas reserves has to change. In the 90s, the USA recognised the reliance on imported oil forced conflict. In the last 10 years, the USA has made great strides to increase country-based and local reserves. We have seen Europe and now China are reliant on natural gas being pumped from Russia. With so many customers for the reserves in Siberia, these reserves will also become depleted. Russia will need new fields of exploration to maintain their supplies and routes to market and bolster its economy.

5.3 THE DEFINITION OF CYBRID

This is what's already happened. Cold War alliances and hydra like terror cells are becoming expert at Cybrid war (combining cyber-attacks together with field force numbers to overwhelm the enemy) and this pattern will reoccur regularly in the coming years as these tactics are employed by other conflicts. This increase will only serve one fateful conclusion.

A Cybrid attack is a blended parallel merger of cyber warfare, cyberganda, and traditional espionage, guerrilla military incursions loosely coupled with manoeuvre warfare. It is the unified employment of targeted and destructive digital tools and threats by Internet adversaries to infiltrate Systems and steal government, personal, utility, and commercial data and destroy national assets.

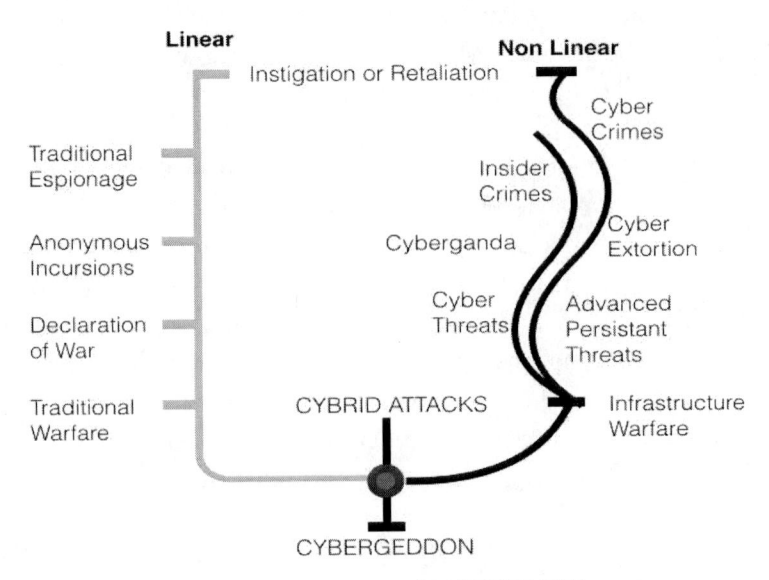

Figure 25 CYBRID WARS WOBBLY LINES

In linear warfare it was possible to extrapolate a timeline of incursions and potential invasions, the ability to next guess attacks on strategic weak points is blurred. Opposing states knew of impending military build-ups and waited for the inevitable declaration of war. In Non Linear war we have no idea of when an attack will take place, a Cybrid attack supports a cloaking ethos. Cloaking involves disguising the army as local activists, having several hydra names for the invading army so no single point of attribution or blame can be asserted to a single state or entity. This mimics cyber security and adversarial attacks.

During this confusion, surprise incursions can grab significant swathes of land. While nation states, armies and diplomats cannot pinpoint the originator, the invasion is near complete and a bridgehead established. Cyber attacks are merged with timing of traditional manoeuvres and can occur out of sequence to enhance deception and confusion.

Manoeuvre warfare advocates that strategic movement can bring about the defeat of an opposing force more efficiently than by simply contacting and destroying enemy forces until they can no longer fight. Instead, in manoeuvre warfare, the destruction of certain enemy targets (command and control centres, logistical basecamps, fire support assets, etc.) is combined with isolation of enemy forces and the exploitation by movement of enemy weaknesses.

The rise of complex adversarial techniques in the last 30 years, in parallel to terrorism, has created hydra-like armies capable of multi-country invasions. The use of cyber-attacks has increased Cold War tensions. Cyber-attacks started in 2007 on Estonia, Georgia in 2008, Middle East IS Social Engineering, and recently the Ukraine. However, it doesn't take several army divisions to demolish a country or even a continent. A lone individual can impose their political will on other individuals, organisations or nation states. [103] A small team of hackers can send an entire country back to the Middle Ages in an incursion lasting minutes. The software giants and the collusion of government policy has produced an unsafe world which is starting to backfire and will inevitably lead to Cybergeddon. We have in effect made a rod for our own backs.

There is now a cyber-arms race in progress. There are new deadly and dangerous cyber-weapons, not like conventional weapons as we know and love them, but both in combination have become lethal. On May 1st 2014 Eugene Kaspersky of Kaspersky Labs warned a major cyber terrorist attack is only a matter of time. In Kaspersky's opinion the world is currently ill prepared for a new wave of cyber-attacks and cyber terrorism, and that is unlikely to change overnight, especially with the global economy still reeling from the financial crisis. One of these (DDOS) attacks is very difficult to defend against, and the solution is usually just to wait them out. "Unfortunately there are zero ideas, zero things to protect the critical internet, mobile and telecoms infrastructure from DDoS attacks – only plans how to recover after an attack," explained Kaspersky. The second type of attack is an assault on critical data. Compromising data crucial to the operation of large companies, industry, infrastructure and government, rather than an individual's personal details. The third type of attack is the most difficult to execute but also potentially the most devastating. It would involve attacking critical infrastructure to cause physical damage to systems, machines and buildings - precisely what Stuxnet was designed to achieve. Cyber weapons (like STUXNET) are like boomerangs, says Eugene Kaspersky: once deployed they can easily be repurposed and sent back to their developers, turning an attacker's weapon against them.[104]

Cyberganda is already a feature being employed by terrorists to attract new recruits, and countries are also using cyberganda to stir dissent among ethnic groups. Countries need to get their heads together on this issue speedily. The US has already identified this as a potential threat and has touted a separate tiering of the Internet to be purely used by the US government with the ability to shut the Internet as a whole down. The Kill Switch is becoming a reality. Governments are creating their own dedicated "privileged Internet" Our reliance on IP devices will increase and as there will be at least one IP addressable device for every single global citizen by 2020 (there are now more mobiles than toilets in the world), the risk of a global Cybrid conflagration becomes increasingly worrying. The problem with Cybrid war is that it is insidious and directly impacts on citizens' morale and finances. There is no tangible enemy to direct anger against, and once citizens are in this confused state it is easy to follow through with an unopposed task force. This morphare has begun and nobody told us. Cybrid attacks are the new way to wage war? [105]

When I present at conferences I like to start my talk with my favourite phrase: "It's not the Elephant in the Room you should be worried about it's the termites that get into every crack and crevice – if your house is built of wood, termites will get in"! Adversaries can infiltrate every element of your life and could use this information against you. Safety on the Internet is a basic tenet and insecurity should not be an obstacle to SMBs seeking new global markets and the ability to establish in other countries.

What would your company do in the next conflict? Are you conflict ready? What is your conflict plan? What would happen to your company if your company data fell into the wrong hands or an invading armies intelligence team. Would your company and your position remain tenable? Have you investigated hat information could an adversary use against you? Is the data in your company of value to a foreign power?

5.4 COMBAT READY BUSINESS

Surprisingly, war can be beneficial to the winning side, whereas losing a war can be economically cleansing and spur a new type of growth. At the end of World War 1 Britain came out economically superior as it made vast profits, and its GDP eclipsed all the other countries. Although Germany had considerable inflation, which didn't recover until 1930, France never really recovered. The rise of fascism in Spain, Germany and Italy was also fuelled by economic downturn. These economic woes are being mirrored today.

The cumulative inflation rate in the UK in World War I was 52% per annum. In World War 2, inflation was around 30% per annum. Overall the global economic wealth in both wars dipped by 16% – as a comparison the overall wealth of the globe during the current recession is 8%, so there are really hard times ahead.

It's very useful for the reader to use their imagination during this chapter. How can you communicate with an overseas outsource when the first target is international fibre optic links? How do I maintain essential data centre components when they are built 8000 miles away? How do I maintain security when all the technical team members are conscripted?

5.5 SAME PROBLEMS DIFFERENT WARS

Labour was obviously at a premium. Men are usually called up to build up armies through volunteering or conscription. Raw materials were also at a premium, which brings about high inflation rates. As many raw materials became in short supply, governments began to ration to control the supply chain. Businesses had to re-think the cost of inventory and sourcing.

5.6 PRODUCT RE-ENGINEERING

Five pressure points:

- Raw Materials (if you can get them locally) rise in price
- Government centralised buying forces some products to be dropped
- Government dictates to its requirements first and the public second
- Loss of skilled workers makes it difficult to continue certain products
- Changes occur in distributing trade in the consuming demand

Products and product lines were dramatically reduced. Many products were so expensive that the governments prohibited making any luxury item above a certain price range. At a single stroke, hundreds of lines representing hundreds of different items were wiped off firm's catalogue and product lists. Six advantageous consequences immediately followed from this evolution, each one making steps toward greater simplification of products.

- The labour that was required per tonne of product was reduced, so solving the general labour shortage. Processes could be highly standardised, reduced to a fool proof routine, and a fixed sequence, making it possible for green unskilled workers to be used and compensating for the loss of skilled men joining the army.

- Standardisation enabled companies to team members smaller by one third, with an average lower-priced product and fewer lines; companies increased their output tonnage and still maintained their volume of turnover.

- The changes in the product also had their effect on buying and stocking policies: reducing the number of lines eliminated the necessity of buying and carrying stocks of a long list of materials.

5.7 PROCUREMENT

Preclusive purchasing (also known as pre-emptive buying) is an economic warfare tactic where one combatant in a conflict purchases materials and operations from neutral countries, not for domestic needs, but to deprive other combatants of their use. The French in World War 1 initiated the tactic.

Preclusive purchasing drives up the price by pushing the demand curve out. It's a lesson that could be adopted now by procurement teams. They should also start to apply the vendor's 50-mile rule. Stocking up is a good thing because Just in Time production won't happen during a conflict.

The British used preclusive purchasing during World War 2 to deny Nazi Germany access to Spanish Wolframite. Similarly, the British and Americans bought chromite ore from Turkey, to reduce Turkey's ability to supply that mineral to Germany, as part of the 'package deal', the Anglo-Americans had to buy Turkish dried fruit and tobacco as well.

In the period prior to the Attack on Pearl Harbour, while the US was officially neutral, the US began to purchase: copper, manganese, rubber, diamonds, quartz crystal, and mica.

If you look at the number of chip manufacturers in the world, it's down to a handful in the West with the majority based in China and Japan. Imagine a state of war where this supply dries up – many of the devices need to travel 8000 miles. This would severely damage normal maintenance capabilities. Access to new products and especially mobiles would dry up, and there would be no way to reignite the supply chain. In the Fukishima event, the semi-conductor industry was severely hampered as most of the factories producing these components were damaged. Alternative supplies needed sourcing as it affected new product rollouts. It has taken many months even in peacetime to get this fabrication resource back to normal.

Procurement had to change:

- Prices of all commodities increased (could your company exist if there was a 50% price hike in the cost price of a product)?

- Markets were dislocated by the difficulty of getting the normal volume of supplies, by the shutting off of some sources, by restrictions on imports of some commodities.

- Shipping difficulties and delays in transportation caused additional problems. You couldn't get anything Just in Time. It was advised by Lord Leverhulme to buy a fleet of delivery trucks that could be serviced by in-house mechanics as most garages closed as most signed up to the war effort. Shipping goods overseas became perilous and so bulk goods were distributed over many ships as contingency. A Green approach was to also share transport so that companies could utilise planned trips by rail. New sources of supply had to be found to replace those shut off entirely, new commodities to replace those that had disappeared from the market or were no longer available.

- All markets were a sellers' market. It was no longer controlled by the buyer

- Commodities had to be bought from anywhere; this obviously affected quality, as consistency was not guaranteed.

- Under war conditions the only safe plan was not to centre on one source of supply. Supplier promiscuity was the order of the day.

- Payments were cash on delivery; cash flow projections therefore had to adjust significantly.

- Contracts based on lowest cost and first-past-the-post bidding were soon dropped; frankness and fair play and the cooperative spirit formed the best basis on which a buyer could do business with a seller.

- What would happen if the Internet was not available at all

General advice given during World War 1 by business owners to meet wartime conditions can still have an impact on today's risk management of systems and procurement. These snippets of wisdom are relevant and increasingly important today given that we could be on the cusp of war. Review your entire list of products; eliminate whatever you can – the hard sellers, the products that are handled in small quantities but have no broad demand, that fills in manufacturing gaps or require exceptional skill and attention but are not trade necessities in your line. Replace these with more staple items. Move the company away from luxury lines, putting your products into the class of war necessities or trade staples. Reduce variations in each line – especially where there is a variation for its own sake. Reduce the assortments, especially as to variety in size and make-up of package. Then simplify and standardise both the lines you make and the process of making them. All this will help you offset increased costs, carry on with fewer workers, release men for war work, carry on with green help, meet the demand for more staple goods.

CONFLICT PROJECTIONS

	WW 1	WW 2	Conflict X
Potential Inflation Rate per Annum	52%	30%	19%
Global Economic Wealth Decrease	16%	16%	16%
Unemployment Rate	0%	5%	6.1% (200 million globally)
Financial Cost of war in Billions	$196	$,2,092	$3,988
Potential Total Casualties	11,016,000	59,028,000	107,040,000
Debt to GDP Ratio	100% (UK)	100% (US)	200% (US & EU)

Figure 26 THREE CONFLICTS COSTS

Local procurement of substitute all-new ingredients marks the second change in the product. Certain materials might be unobtainable, or only attainable in small quantities. Substitutes must be found through local procurement (i.e. within country bounds).

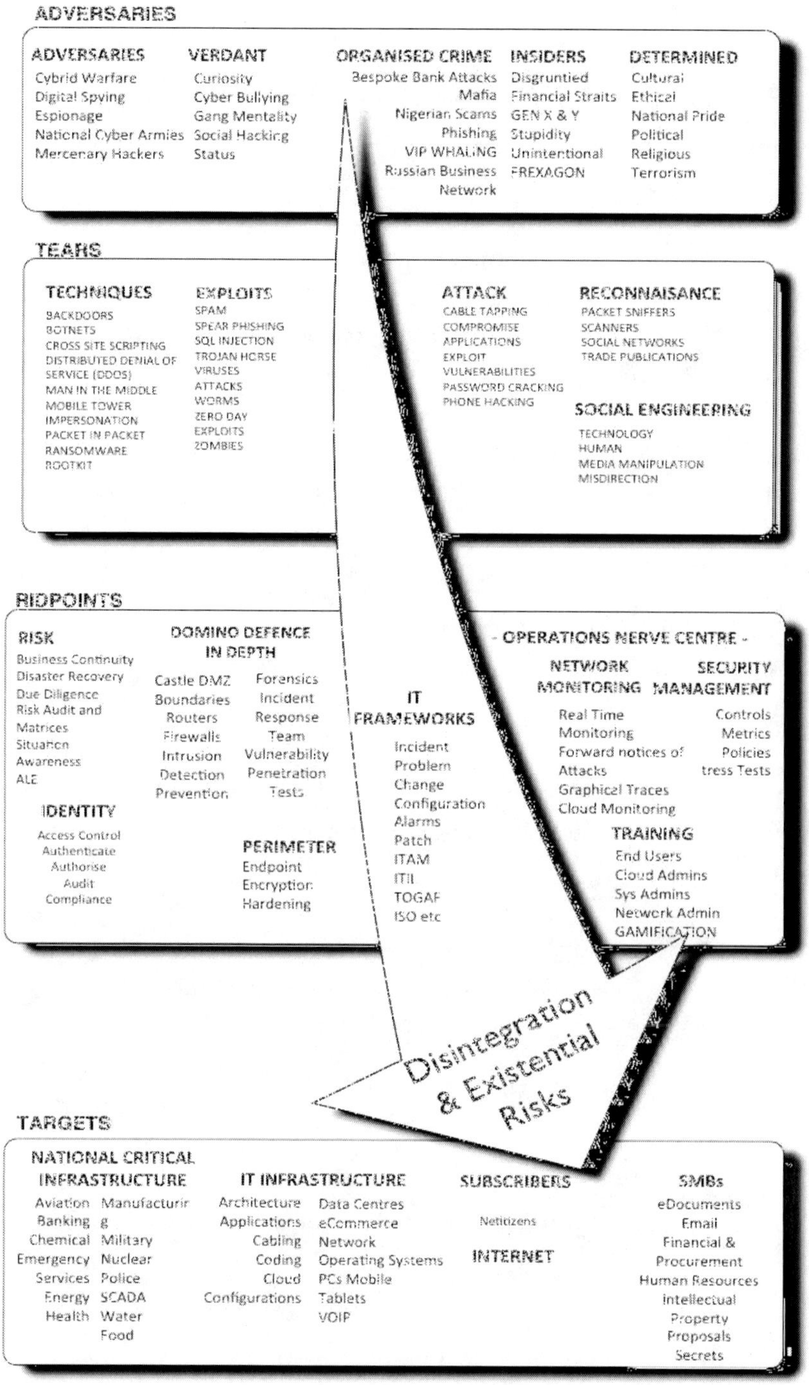

ADVERSARIES

ADVERSARIES
Cybrid Warfare
Digital Spying
Espionage
National Cyber Armies
Mercenary Hackers

VERDANT
Curiosity
Cyber Bullying
Gang Mentality
Social Hacking
Status

ORGANISED CRIME
Bespoke Bank Attacks
Mafia
Nigerian Scams
Phishing
VIP WHALING
Russian Business Network

INSIDERS
Disgruntled
Financial Straits
GEN X & Y
Stupidity
Unintentional
FREXAGON

DETERMINED
Cultural
Ethical
National Pride
Political
Religious
Terrorism

TEAMS

TECHNIQUES
BACKDOORS
BOTNETS
CROSS SITE SCRIPTING
DISTRIBUTED DENIAL OF SERVICE (DDOS)
MAN IN THE MIDDLE
MOBILE TOWER IMPERSONATION
PACKET IN PACKET
RANSOMWARE
ROOTKIT

EXPLOITS
SPAM
SPEAR PHISHING
SQL INJECTION
TROJAN HORSE
VIRUSES
ATTACKS
WORMS
ZERO DAY EXPLOITS
ZOMBIES

ATTACK
CABLE TAPPING
COMPROMISE
APPLICATIONS
EXPLOIT
VULNERABILITIES
PASSWORD CRACKING
PHONE HACKING

RECONNAISANCE
PACKET SNIFFERS
SCANNERS
SOCIAL NETWORKS
TRADE PUBLICATIONS

SOCIAL ENGINEERING
TECHNOLOGY
HUMAN
MEDIA MANIPULATION
MISDIRECTION

BIDPOINTS

RISK
Business Continuity
Disaster Recovery
Due Diligence
Risk Audit and Matrices
Situation Awareness
ALE

IDENTITY
Access Control
Authenticate
Authorise
Audit
Compliance

DOMINO DEFENCE IN DEPTH
Castle DMZ
Boundaries
Routers
Firewalls
Intrusion Detection Prevention

Forensics
Incident Response Team
Vulnerability
Penetration Tests

PERIMETER
Endpoint
Encryption
Hardening

IT FRAMEWORKS
Incident
Problem
Change
Configuration
Alarms
Patch
ITAM
ITIL
TOGAF
ISO etc

- OPERATIONS NERVE CENTRE -

NETWORK MONITORING
Real Time Monitoring
Forward notices of Attacks
Graphical Traces
Cloud Monitoring

SECURITY MANAGEMENT
Controls
Metrics
Policies
tress Tests

TRAINING
End Users
Cloud Admins
Sys Admins
Network Admin
GAMIFICATION

Disintegration & Existential Risks

TARGETS

NATIONAL CRITICAL INFRASTRUCTURE
Aviation
Banking
Chemical
Emergency Services
Energy
Health

Manufacturing
Military
Nuclear
Police
SCADA
Water
Food

IT INFRASTRUCTURE
Architecture
Applications
Cabling
Coding
Cloud
Configurations

Data Centres
eCommerce
Network
Operating Systems
PCs Mobile
Tablets
VOIP

SUBSCRIBERS
Netizens

INTERNET

SMBs
eDocuments
Email
Financial & Procurement
Human Resources
Intellectual Property
Proposals
Secrets

Figure 27 DISINTEGRATION

6 ROOT CAUSES - EXISTENTIAL RISKS

It is essential to have great situational awareness of all geo-political changes and developments in the various attack vectors that now emerge daily. Geopolitics explains the present with an eye on the future. Existential Risks are threats that could cause our extinction or destroy the potential of Earth-originating intelligent life. Some of these threats are relatively well known while others, including some of the gravest, have gone almost unrecognized. Existential risks have a cluster of features that make ordinary risk management ineffective. Cybrid War is one of those features.

Existential Risks Classification
Nick Bostrom Professor of Philosophy at Oxford University classifies Existential Risks as:

- *Bangs* – Earth-originating intelligent life goes extinct in relatively sudden disaster resulting from either an accident or a deliberate act of destruction.

- *Crunches* – The potential of humankind to develop into post humanity is permanently thwarted although human life continues in some form.

- *Shrieks* – Some form of post humanity is attained it is an extremely narrow band of what is possible and desirable.

- *Whimpers* – A post human civilization arises but evolves in a direction that leads gradually but irrevocably to either the complete disappearance of the things we value or to a state where those things are realized to only a minuscule degree of what could have been achieved.

In my youth as a student of history and risk, war-gaming was my hobby. I used to spend most Saturdays in my local reference library researching uniforms I needed to reproduce and paint my 12 mm high lead soldiers, my favourite being the French Zouaves in the American Civil War, the soldiers with the biggest pants in the world. I had 6,000 lead soldiers and even made my own soldiers out of lead. (*Ed*: sounds so sad and geeky!). It was on one of my research trips that I discovered *Pure Logistics: The Science of War Preparation* by George C.Thorpe. This slim tome was written in 1917, and described wars as competitions in mobilisation, covering Roman, Mongol, Napoleonic campaigns. He also wrote:

"War has become a business; therefore, training and preparation for war is a business – vast and comprising many departments. Like commercial activities, it is susceptible of analysis to determine upon proper division of labour, to estimate necessities required to meet the situation, and avoid duplication and waste. The winner of the war will be the nation that has the last 100,000 reserves and has the last one million in credit."

I then understood that supply and logistics and not just the fighting won wars; in fact the First World War personified the last great battlefield of military attrition, and the Second World War was based on the demoralisation of the nation's populace through domestic bombing. The Third World War will be the planned annihilation of the nation's critical infrastructure and systems and by creating confusion, starvation and depravation in the populous to such a point that any army walking into the vicinity would seem heroic. The removal of survival systems will be the main thrust for any adversary, in the Cybrid war this is achieved through digital weapons. Private commercial operator's attention to secure facilities is seen as a costly and unnecessary exercise. This means hacking critical infrastructure is simplistic and viewed as a quick win as a precursor to a Cybrid conflict.

These Existential risks need to be part of the Risk programme, and should include:

- Energy
- Nuclear
- EMP Attacks (Block EMP and Handheld HERF Gun

- Nanobots
- Earthquakes
- Unemployment Levels
- Pandemic,
- Water shortages
- Food shortages
- Diesel
- Snow, Flood, Drought, Tsunami
- Conflicts and Terror Indexes

6.1 STEPCHECK

- The cyclical nature of BBC PR will impact all businesses during conflict

- Conflict is cyclical and will test a companies survivability

- A Cybrid War has started with commentators predicting a Cybergeddon

- Apply a 50 mile rule for the company's supply chain

- Existential risks and Situational Awareness to manage Cyber Security disintegration. These risks are rarely reported as part of an overall risk strategy

7 ROOT CAUSES - AVOID ADVERSARIES

In this Chapter we will review several Adversarial profiles and motivation. We will look at the available education for team members.

AVOID is an acronym that stands for **Adversaries, Verdant, Organised, Insiders and Determined**.

"Who are these adversary chaps anyway?"

I was asked this question recently and realised that society has created a generation of digital whizz kids that started with the Baby Boomers. The hackers I have met in the past are generally highly intelligent and technical, passionate, witty, and geeky. They have infinite patience, research in depth and plan ahead – they are as affable as Frank in the movie *Catch me if you can*. If you have watched the endless repeats of *The Big Bang Theory* in the US or *The IT Crowd* in the UK you probably have an indication of their view of the world. They can be very open and even proud of how they go about their lives. It is heartening to see hackers do great deeds. Generally adversaries just love to push the boundaries of electronics and the digital world and don't do too much harm, in fact if we could get all the hackers into one room they would probably invent the next version of the Internet in a day. The problem has been the hackers tools are now in the hands of Nation States cyber armies, organised crime and Adversaries. These guys may be acting under duress, but have collectively fuelled cyber insecurity.

You often hear that adversaries fall into three types: Black, Grey, and Green, apparently all wearing hats whilst they exploit systems! Black Hats are the bad guys (organised crime, cyber armies, determined), and Grey Hats tend to be inside the organisation. You also hear the term 'Hacktivist'. These guys have a purpose in life, including religious or political goals. You might also see the term 'malicious user'; these are insider, rogue employees or contractors, or part of the collective pay-rolled team members who are either make human errors or are too inquisitive for their own good. Verdant (green) "script kiddies" will obviously wear green hats. White Hats are Ethical Hackers and are certified good guys. The Forensics teams have the most expensive hats — they have dear stalkers (aka Sherlock Holmes)!

7.1 ADVERSARIES AND ADVANCED PERSISTENT THREATS

US government security expert Richard A. Clarke has defined cyber-warfare in his book *Cyber War* (2010). "Cyber warfare" as "actions by a nation-state to penetrate another nation's computers or networks for the purposes of causing damage or disruption." These are generally termed Advanced Persistent Threats (APTs). An adversary behaves like a small autonomous guerrilla task force. It can range from a spy to large teams of remote cyber soldiers always working under central direction. Their role is to expose flaws in the Security defences and then exploit them. These are the major threats that are permanently on the security officer's agenda.

7.2 VERDANT YOUTH

We have all done something stupid in our green youth — it's how we acquire wisdom. If you have never done anything slightly dumb, dishonest, or criminal please submit your sainthood application to the appropriate authority. It's what makes us honest we understand the consequences of being bad and drift to the dark side. The Web is a wonder and endless playground, and a way to hit back at the establishment, ideal for rebels. Acquiring IT skills is encouraged by parents and leaving children alone for half a day to explore the Web and all its temptations can lead some individuals to explore hacking. It's become a form of digital graffiti a totally self-centred and ego-massaging pastime that damages the environment physically, and, morally. A moment of weakness can last a lifetime; however breaking into the school server to get the exam questions is a real motivator!

As the gap between rich and poor gets bigger, MILLENIALS have been burdened by debt caused by student loans that apparently burdens educated people until the age of 32. That means that 71 per cent of students earning a bachelor's degree graduate with an accumulated debt burden, which averages $24,301[106]. This figure doubles to $44,000 for living expenses during study. While most students are able to repay their loans, weighed down by debt, especially as they seek to start a family, buy a home, launch a business, or save for retirement. Based on USA college students' enrolment figures (in isolation), that's about 20 million broke students a year entering commercial companies and government jobs (desperate for a salary). This could mean a generation of resentful and disaffected young people who, if they ever successfully get a job, these broke post teens will look to supplement their income, perhaps from the company that hired them.

Companies are taking seriously this new wave of expectants. How to train, motivate and retain this complement is a major challenge. The Silver Tsunami is making a major return as trusted workers with history and good conduct. As Enterprises turn to Broadsourcing SMBs will also need to follow suit.

Knowledge Worker Traits	Baby Boomers	Gen Y < Millennial's
Ambition	Expects a management role in 10 to 15 years	56% expect a management role in 3 years
Competition	125 for every vacancy	83 for every vacancy
Connected	74% are on LinkedIn	63% are on LinkedIn
Productivity	1 in 5 are working 60 hour weeks	1 in 7 are working 50 hour weeks
Timekeeping	Low sickness and mostly on time	High Sick days and late days
Impress Me	Low expectations of employer	57% expect to leave in two years
Mobility	40% would relocate	90% would relocate within country

Table 6 - CAREER EXPECTATIONS (**Source Gen-Y Firefish Software)

7.3 INSIDERS

Insiders are the hardest adversarial type to track. Sometimes by accident an internal employee can uncover sensitive or secret data. 30% of insider activity is in HR departments, who have full access to employee records, resumes, bank accounts and personal health information and these records are worth good money in the organised world. There are also white-collar information swipes — executives have untold access from the top down and can copy any company secret. These executives can walk out the door with years of research work and set up a competitive company or product within weeks. There are several famous cases where this has happened. I once hired a system engineer who spent all morning working with clients, and in the afternoon would send all the account details to a salesman who worked for the competition. I think everyone has seen some sort of similar corruption. There is no concept of loyalty or trust and a belief the world owes them a living.

There are numerous examples of senior managers and 'C Level' board members either taking bribes or manipulating the procurement of vendors, or even stealing patents and setting up their own companies to further their own personal gains. These merit closer scrutiny by the board and a Technical Steering Committee. Insider attacks have a direct correlation to the level of criminal activity in a country.

About 50% of attacks are started from insiders. Source code stealing of applications might not be seen as taking valuable intellectual property, but to a hacker wishing to carry out espionage this is a simple backdoor. For the purposes of the book I have extended Donald R. Cressey's original Fraud Triangle to a FREXAGON to reflect observable techniques gleaned from interviews, Facebook and team member observations of "out of character behaviour".

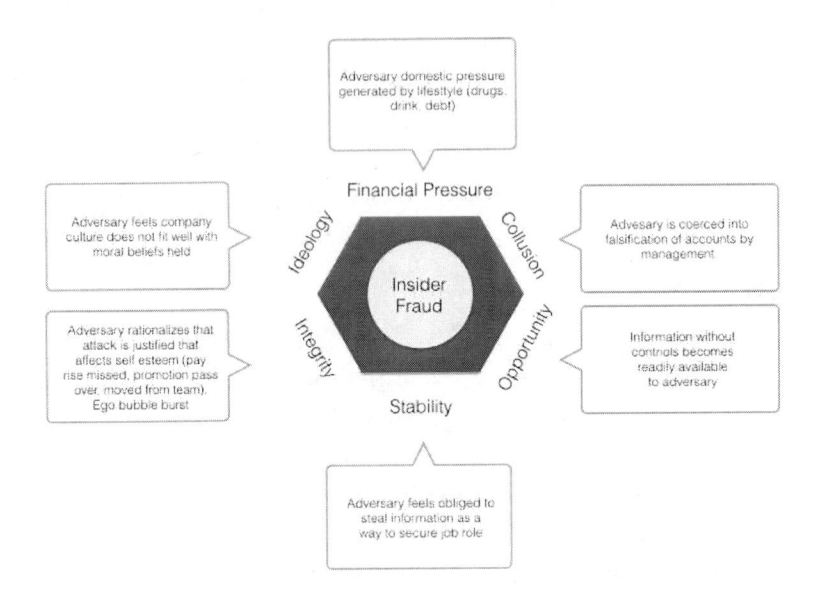

Figure 28 FREXAGON

7.4 ORGANISED

In an interesting development the Mafia (Russia, Eastern Europe, US and Italy) and South American drugs cartels now have full time hackers on their payrolls. Their aim to break into banks, police, legal sites, tax offices and anything else that can build a good identity theft profile is worth doing. This is obviously a successful enterprise given the latest cyber security statistics. The gangs are even paid by enterprises to obtain competitors' data.

7.5 DETERMINED

This is a growing branch of adversaries driven by political, religious or terrorist motivations and causes. The term Advanced Persistent Threats (APTs) has been coined in a plethora of vendor literature. Hacking is now a full-time job and many hackers are now highly experienced and professional. If you delve down into the code of a Botnet there are amazing lines of dense code with hooking techniques that defy conventional methods. Perhaps vendors' developers could learn from these techniques and adjust their Operating Systems accordingly.

7.6 WHITE HATS - ETHICAL HACKERS

Ethical Hackers are security professionals from a technical background sift out and analyse attacks on enterprise systems and applications. They are generally involved in scanning for vulnerabilities internally, Incident response and digital forensics. They also assist in patch management processes and coordinate penetration and vulnerability tests.

Ethical Hackers have attended courses that help recognise system and platform vulnerabilities. For enterprises that have dedicated security and audit teams in their organisations, monitor any incursion into the estate. They are highly technical and really know their stuff and incredibly hard to recruit and retain (churn is about 50%). Anti-virus software vendors' patches and alerts constantly bombard them, but the sheer volume of attacks can swamp even these guys. They have to be aware of all new alerts as well as investigate any penetration into their systems in real time. Also, 80% of their time is spent reviewing suspicious activity from insiders and alerting management that systems require hardening. Churn also increases sharply after an Incident. Many team members take the threat activity personally and they question their own professionalism. It could also mean that they may have contributed to the root cause.

Hardening a system or platform against attack is key. It does not mean coating the device with varnish and leaving it to dry in the sun. It means ensuring all patches and changes on servers and the applications that reside on those servers do not demonstrate vulnerabilities. Change can be the downfall of any established system and can have knock-on effects on multiple applications. So if a new version of Java was installed to a server, there might be several legacy versions built into existing applications. Constant change is where doors are left open, and constant monitoring of alarm logs is key to this.

7.7 CERTIFIED PROFESSIONALS

The CISSP and CISO is an accreditation that stands for Certified Information Systems Security Professional and Chief Information Security Officer respectively. These accreditations have been around since 1994. They have built a significant Common Body of Knowledge and this can be accessed via the Information Systems Audit and Control Association (www.isaca.org). Their framework for Risk Management and Control Audits is called COBIT 5 (latest version at time of writing). ITIL's RESILIA is based on the COBIT lifecycle. The framework has five principles:

- Meeting owner needs
- Covering the enterprise end to end
- Applying an integrated framework
- Enabling a holistic approach
- Separating governance from management

COBIT is primarily used for the governance of IT Systems but is also applied to cover seven enablers for Information Technology:

- Principles, Policies and Frameworks
- Processes
- Organisational Structures
- Culture, Ethics and Behaviour
- Information
- Service Infrastructure and Applications

- People Skills and Competencies

There is also a CISA (Certified Information Systems Auditor) accreditation aimed at the managers of CISSPs, but it covers Security Controls Auditing in depth.

There are also 16 other institutions covering similar certifications:

7.8 INFORMATION SECURITY CERTIFICATIONS

CompTIA	Security+ CASP
Cisco Systems	CCNA Security CCNP Security CCIE-S
EC-Council ECSS ECVP	ENSA CEH CHFI ECSA LPT CNDA ECIH EDRP ECSP ECSO CISO
GIAC (SANS)	GSIF GSEC GCFW GCIA GCIH GCUX GCWN GCED GPEN GWAPT GAWN GISP GLSC GCPM GLEG G7799 GSSP-NET GSSP-JAVA GCFE GCFA GREM GSE GSNA
HISPI	HOLISTIC INFORMATION SECURITY PROFESSIONAL, CAAP
ISACA	**CISA** CISM CGEIT CRISC
(ISC) C	SSCP CAP CSSLP CISSP ISSAP ISSEP ISSMP HCISPP CCFP
ISECOM	OPST OPSA OPSE OWSE CTA
Offensive Security	OSCP OSCE OSWP
Juniper Networks	NCIS Security Specialist JNCIP SP/SE
British Computer Society	**CISMP** Certificate in Business Continuity Management Certificate in Data Protection Certificate in Freedom of Information Certificate in Information Risk Management Certificate in Information Assurance Architecture Chartered IT Professional
The Open Group	Open FAIR Foundation
Cloud Security Alliance	CCSK

CERT	CSIH
ELearnSecurity	eCPPT eWPT
PCI SSC (P2PE) ISA	PCIP QSA PA-QSA QSA (P2PE) PA-QSA QIR ASV
OBASHI	OBASHI FOUNDATION
SHAZOPS	SHAZOPS FACILITATOR

7.9 TRAINING

A typical Boot Camp for any of these certifications can take 3 to 4 weeks out of a team member's productivity. Some tests are held every 6 months why I don't know? Medium-sized companies invest more in IT spending and security technologies than larger companies in the £430m-plus revenue bracket, according to a Computer Economics survey of US IT security managers. Companies of all sizes fail to provide adequate security training in 65% of cases and a similar percentage fail to audit their desktops regularly. My recommendation is to home grow trusted talent into these roles. The cost can be cheaper than headhunting, sourcing and retaining qualified team members.

Traditional security functions role and responsibilities require the Security Operations office (SecOps) to cover the basic three areas:

Area of Speciality:
- Analyse
- Collect and Operate Development Investigate
- Protect and Defend Operate and Maintain Oversight
- Securely Provision

Disciplines:
- Application rigour
- Best Practices
- Security Controls

Depth of Knowledge:
- Cryptography
- IT Governance

- Systems Engineering
- Software Engineering
- Network Engineering
- Penetration Testing
- Vulnerability Assessments

7.10 STEPCHECK

- In this Chapter we looked at the types of adversaries

- We devised a FREXAGON to describe Fraud pressure points

- We briefly looked at the motivations of adversaries and ethical opponents

- We have reviewed the certifications required by various governing bodies for responsible security officers and the expertise levels of security personnel

8 INTERNET BASIC TRAINING

The complexity of the Internet components and the scale of the security problems need to be understood. A potted history might be useful to the majority of readers not familiar with the technologies and components. It's useful at this stage to complement the overview of the dramatic innovations made in the last 30 years with the basic components of the Internet before we visit the Internet as a root cause in the next chapter.

The whole process of selling and supporting PCs was a really challenging affair in the 1980's. Everyone was used to mainframe computers like IBM Z-OS, Cray, DEC, Wang, Sequent, Siemens/Bull, HP and Honeywell. The end users had dumb terminals that were green screen (black letters on a green video), or White on Black if you were lucky. The most popular of the midrange mainframes was an AS400. These mainframes and minis had an uptime of 99.9% and with some exceptions were highly secure. The only problem was that these mainframes and minis had their own communications protocols, which were completely proprietary, so information sharing to other computers and to other companies was a major challenge. IBM had the proprietary IBM Systems Network Architecture (SNA), which gave 3270, and 5250 terminal emulations, so emulating the mainframe output on a PC screen. This was usually a PC add-on card (like EICON) and had to have a separate coax cable connector. Basically, a user would cut and paste between a financial package and a PC based spreadsheet program like LOTUS 123. DEC had VT100 (via a terminal server) that used Ethernet, and so emulation from a PC was much cheaper as long as the LAN was DECNet based. SNA and DECNet were the two major communications protocols, but there were others such as WangNet.

To allow for interconnection of these diverse systems, a seven-layer model was created by the ISO (International Organisation for Standardisation) to guide vendors making communications systems a point of interconnect to exchange data. To fully comprehend how malware proliferates there are the basics to understand on our two most popular devices: the PC (laptop) and the mobile/tablet.

8.1 ANATOMY OF A COMPUTER

Central to the component architecture is the chip (the Central Processing Unit or CPU). The advances in chip technology have been dramatic, and today a 64 Bit chip is commonplace in nearly all devices. Surrounding the chip is the PC bus (8,16,32 and 64) that carries the inputs and outputs (zeroes and ones) to all the peripheral equipment such as keyboard, mouse and video display. It also links the hard disk where the applications and Operating System resides to the firmware memory RAM (Random Access Memory) and BIOS (Basic Input Output System) that boots up the PC when it's switched on. The hard disk holds all the data, and an area called the sandbox is where quarantined viruses are placed. On the hard disk are all the Operating System files where malware usually resides, and this is the prime target for hackers.

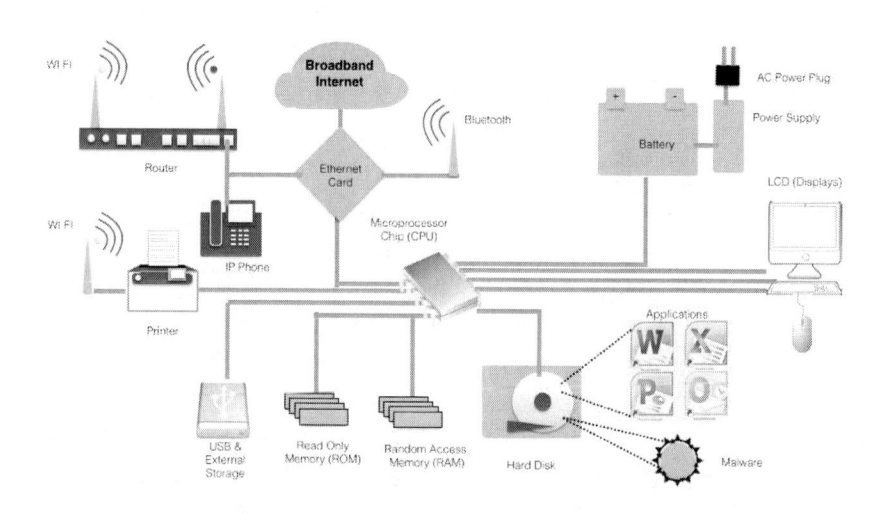

Figure 29 PC DECOMPOSED

8.2 SERVERS AND BLADES

A server which usually sits in a data centre or on a cloud data centre is a beefed up PC, basically has huge hard disks, tons of RAM and multiple CPUs. The size of these servers can be thin (like a blade server - like a razor blade - but physically the size of a paper file folder), or scale up to the size of a mainframe that can be the size of a small van. There is so much memory and hard disk sizes on these servers that the physical server can be logically chunked up to make multiple pseudo servers - these servers are software defined and known as Virtual Machines. A blade server can manage up to 100 VMs – there is a load of variables around this starting point (40 is a Service Provider rule of thumb). This density means that cloud data centres can hold millions of VMs in a data centre. I recommend readers view the Google Container Data Centre Tour video on You Tube (https://www.youtube.com/watch?v=zRwPSFpLX8I) to see what a "cloud like" server farm looks like.[107] The Google data centre is basically cargo ship sized containers mounted in a large warehouse, but the interesting thing is each container holds 10,000 servers. If you think of a Data Centre as a factory you are not far from the truth!

Amazons Elastic Compute estate currently comprises 57 data centres dotted around the globe. Let's extrapolate here if each data centre holds 45,000 "blade servers" and suggest 100 virtual servers per blade then Amazon would be monitoring 256,500,000 server instances. Now also imagine each VM can handle the computing needs of 50 company employees, that would be 6,412,500,000 roughly a virtual machine instances, one for each person on the planet.

Amazon and Google is just two examples of a CSP (Cloud Service Provider) of about 1000 similar companies in the world today and demonstrates the power of cloud computing. Now its obvious that each VM is not used in that equation, servers have different jobs, such as database handling, file serving, web hosting, and email and storage management. VMs can take a snapshot of themselves and save its complete configuration of its parameters and even data to another blade or even another data centre. Security across these blades is also a deep concern, patching an entire blade farm can take up to 90 days (longer in the majority of attacks). This is due to the number of Guest Operating systems the CSP needs to account for in its service catalogue.

In a cloud environment these VMs can be made to work together sharing RAM and Disk space across multiple VMs, so when a VM is idling its resources are moved to a resource pool where additional RAM and Disk is needed on a temporary (elastic) basis. This is called Software Defined Computing and can be self-healing if a catastrophic loss occurs. Much of this is managed automatically and in real time so operator's interventions are not required.

8.2.1.1 VMS VERSUS CONTAINERS (DM'S)

VMs have been around for about 10 years and developed by VMware based on the Microsoft server clustering technologies. This virtualisation allows multiple compute instances to run in volume on a blade chassis. Recently Docker (which is a Linux, based Virtual machine system and primarily Open Source) designed a lightweight Docker Engine. Microsoft, IBM and Red Hat, along with start-ups CoreOS, SaltStack and Mesosphere, are now supporting and contributing to Kubernetes, the open-source container-management project that Google announced in June. Kubernetes is Google's attempt to push its own style of computing into the greater world, something made easier by the exploding popularity of the Docker container technology.

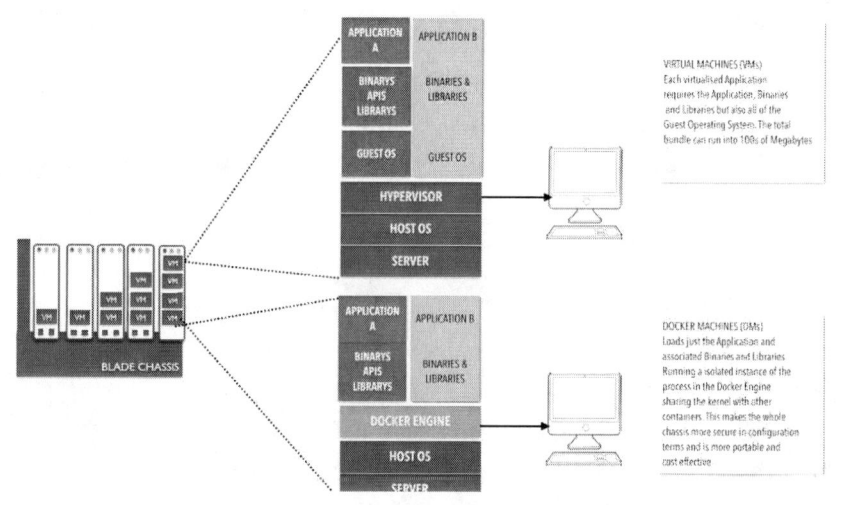

Figure 30 VIRTUAL MACHINES AND DOCKER CONTAINERS

But container-based applications, like all applications, need a little help when it comes to running at scale. Kubernetes is a way of helping users easily launch Docker containers onto a cluster of servers, and then to help those containers communicate with each other. Docker has its own similar project called Libswarm, which it claims, among other things, can let users manage all their containers "across multiple hosts and infrastructure providers, as if they were running on a single host."

Vendors now commoditise these hybrid servers under the Hyper Converged Infrastructure banner (Cisco UCS, VMware, SimpliVity Omnicube).

8.3 STORAGE

Internet users store the files and photos, music etc., on large arrays of Hard Disks. On average a user stores around 20 Gigabytes of data annually. Obviously some users store a lot more and a lot less than this.

In cloud environments this mass storage is a constant capacity battle. The number of items stored grew dramatically in the last decade. A Storage Area Network is basically a huge computer with thousands of hard disks, and I mean thousands. It manages disk space, which the data belongs to and remembers the location of each chunk of data written to the disks. I have seen companies buy JBODs (Just a Bunch of Disks) without considering how DeDupe (Deduplication) can dramatically reduce the cost per GB of data. DeDuplication on a small scale can save deep expenditure. DeDupe allows for the single retention of a PowerPoint, excel file, or email. For instance if you have an email chain that is 10 pages long and the same email went to 50 people with a diagram, not all 50 emails and the 50 diagrams are needed to be saved. Just the original one and a single copy of the original image is all that is required for saving. EMC, NetApp, CommVault, Hitachi and vStorage use this technology extensively.

8.4 DESKTOP AS A SERVICE

Back in 1993 I implemented the first CITRIX WINVIEW installation in the UK. This platform was a remote access application that allowed desktops and applications from the server to be run on a remote PC. Similar to the way terminal servers communicate to a Mainframe or Mini computer, except in a graphical manner. Microsoft adopted CITRIX technology and created Windows Terminal Server. It allows PCs just to use a standard and hardened image created centrally and distributed to many PCs (approximately 30 screens per server). As this is a centrally controlled product, security at the endpoint is guaranteed; you cannot hack what an image.

In 2008 VMware released a ThinApp equivalent, which centred on their Storage capability. The term for these is Virtual Desktop Infrastructure

(VDI) and uses a protocol called PCoIP (a protocol developed by Teradici and adopted by VMware Horizon, Dell, Wyse, and HP). It delivers personalised instances of windows and centralised storage. The server can be on premises or based in the cloud. The ability to scale is impressive with up to 5000 images per connection server so ideal for call centre agents, or even internally. Support is centralised and security is high even across low bandwidth links. It's ideal to provision any device quickly and manage individual users. The ThinApp can be used across PCs, Old PCs that cannot have memory upgrades and can be accessed from remote Laptops, (including Apple Macs), Tablets and even on Smartphones, so a subscribers screen colours and file system remain consistent across different devices. For SMBs this is a godsend and eliminates hand working brand new devices. The other benefit is the number of licences needed per user fall by 60% as licences are pooled and used on demand. Not everyone uses Word all day long usually most users use this only 20% during a workday. This means cost savings as applications are used on a Pay As You Use basis.

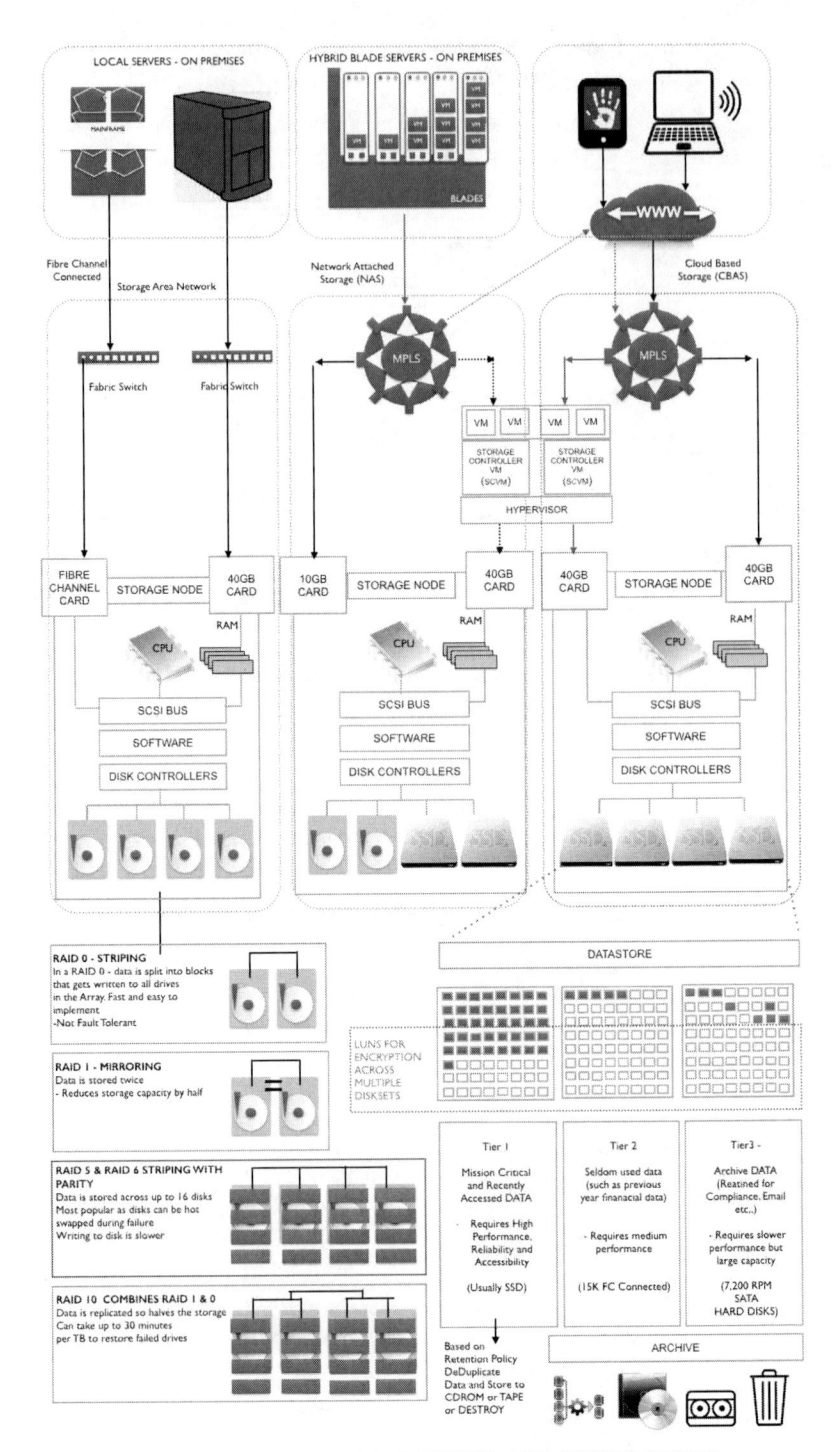

Figure 31 STORAGE - LOCAL HYBRID AND PUBLIC CLOUD

Today, VOIP can be run as well in a remote screen (a browser, or VDI/CITRIX session). This means an SMB with retail outlets does not need a phone system at each branch. Using Counterpath's BRIA client, which uses TLS and SRTP for secure sip instant messages and secure encrypted voice calls. Using a headset means you don't need to run a separate phone system and cabling. If you bought a PABX or key system for a branch the saving would be $450 a user (a BRIA client will cost $35 a user).

The Storage policy closely correlates to the Information Security Policy and should reflect the Top Secret through to Publicly available documents and where and how to store the data given the data retention rules (this is known as tiering). Most companies are required to retain information for several years but are dependent on regulation and vertical sector. The best way to manage data is to select a vendor that has the same hardware as you as well as your Cloud Service Provider. Its much easier to stick to a single vendor as engineers need to restore data as soon as possible and mixing command lines and management systems brings a new set of challenges. Also the data (every part of it) needs to be encrypted, so consistency of key management is also a major consideration. Some of this data is backed up to tape. There are companies such as Iron Mountain that maintain mountain caves full of tapes. If your data is stored in a cloud it's usually replicated to several other data centres geolocated in country, or, located in another country. Some Governments send storage offshore to avoid the Data Privacy and Protection laws of their country so massive Big Data searches can be carried out "legally". For instance, some country's health records are actually stored in data centres in other countries where it is "analysed" by private companies (allegedly).

A LUN is a Logical Unit Number. It can be used to refer to an entire physical disk, or a subset of a larger physical disk or disk volume. The physical disk or disk volume could be an entire single disk drive, a partition (subset) of a single disk drive, or disk volume from a RAID controller comprising multiple disk drives aggregated together for larger capacity and redundancy. LUNs represent a logical abstraction or, if you prefer, virtualisation layer between the physical disk device/volume and the applications.[108] The advantage of storage encryption in a SAN is the fact that it encrypts information! This action hardens the core of the network at relatively low cost. Multiple ciphers can be used for individual files, folders, or data volumes. In addition, two encryption arrangements can be used, one for data in transit and the other for stored and archived data. The ciphers, and the corresponding decryption keys, should be changed frequently. Contrary to edicts issued the United Nations encourages encryption.

Two criteria are said to help support any storage security plan. Firstly, the cost of implementing the plan should be a fraction of the value of the protected data. Secondly, it costs an adversary more, in terms of money and time, to compromise the system than the protected data is worth. In this respect, storage encryption is often seen as a cheap solution. Although not completely fool proof, it is best used with other security measures such as hardware zoning.[109] A zone is the equivalent of a folder or directory. Zoning can be either hard or soft. In hard zoning, each device is assigned to a particular zone, and this assignment never changes. In soft zoning, device assignments can be changed by the administrator to accommodate variations in the demands on different servers. Zoning minimises the risk of data corruption, helps secure data against adversaries, slows the spread of viruses and worms, and minimise the time necessary for servers to reboot. LUN-Level Zoning, which can take place either at the host or target RAID controller level, enables administrators to limit the access zones of users. In addition to the obvious security benefits, the big advantage of LUN-Level Zoning is flexibility. By zoning at the host adapter level, devices on the SAN are pre-configured during system boot, allowing for the seamless change (hot LUN-sparing, or hot-plugging), while allowing for cross-platform support.[110]

8.5 A ROUTER IS NOT A WOODWORKING TOOL

Routers are called "rowtaz" in the US (sounds like political opponents having a row); in the rest of the world we call them "rootaz" (because it rhymes with Hooters)? I have always pitied English sales people in the US who are clearly discombobulated by the choice of phrasing. Routers are the key traffic policemen of the Internet make routing decisions (the path that an IP packet datagram should take). Software configurations are made in the router whether to pass the packets to and internal host, or, send the packet to another router. In a routed architecture routers define how a packet passes from Core to Spine to Leaf.

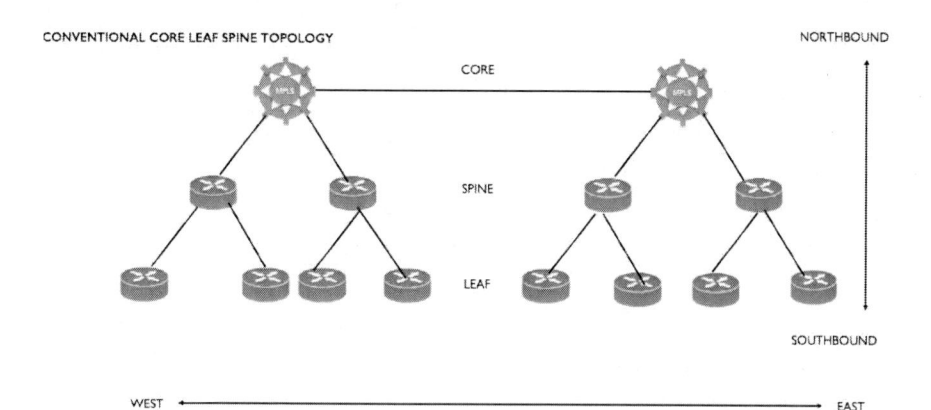

Figure 32 CORE LEAF SPINE AND COMPASS DIRECTIONS

The IP data packets passes over a wide area network (WAN) are addressed in a standard way (this is the IP4 and IP6 schemes that we will discuss later). The Internet basic form of communicating is host to host (a computer sending a IP Packet Datagram to another computer). The host is inside a zone called an Autonomous System (AS), an AS zone could be a country, large company, or city, even a university campus. A router looks up known addresses (AS) and nearest known neighbours, before sending a packet. The IP packet is forwarded to the next known router. Obviously trusted routers are the next connected router in a hop. Each of the many processes of a router or switch can be assigned to one of three conceptual planes of operation:

- **Forwarding Plane** - Moves packets from input to output
- **Control Plane** - Determines how packets should be forwarded
- **Management Plane** - Methods of configuring the control plane (CLI, SNMP, etc.)

For example, you might SSH (**S**ecure **SH**ell is a popular protocol to connect from one computer to another, it establishes an encrypted connection so no one in between can read the traffic, such as passwords, SSH can also establish encrypted data tunnels inside the connection data stream. Everyone should be familiar with the IP VPN service (IP Virtual Private Network). This allows users to forward traffic such as a graphical program's output to a distant server) into the CLI (Command Line Interface) of a router (the management plane) and configure routing information with neighbours (the control plane), which gets installed into its local address table (the forwarding plane). All of these operations occur within the same device, and each node in the network operates autonomously to make its own forwarding decisions based on its local configuration.[111] An IP datagram can take several hops on a path to reach its destination. A router makes a routing decision in milliseconds; on average a router can take 10 milliseconds to make a routing decision this is a contributor to the latency budget. A router looks ahead the path to see if the next known router is available, has sufficient bandwidth to provide a Quality of service (used in video and voice transmission) and whether the packet requires a type of security. A latency budget for VOIP should not exceed 100ms.

A pair of routers should be run in tandem using HSRP (Hot Standby Routing Protocols) to increase resilience and allow failover.

8.5.1.1 SOFTWARE DEFINED NETWORKING
Similar to Software Defined Computing a collection of routers in an Autonomous System can harness the power of multiple routers to redirect traffic to handle peaks and troughs in bandwidth demand, this is known as Software Defined Networking. SDN entails the decoupling of the control plane from the forwarding plane and offloads its functions to a centralised controller.

ROUTER ANATOMY

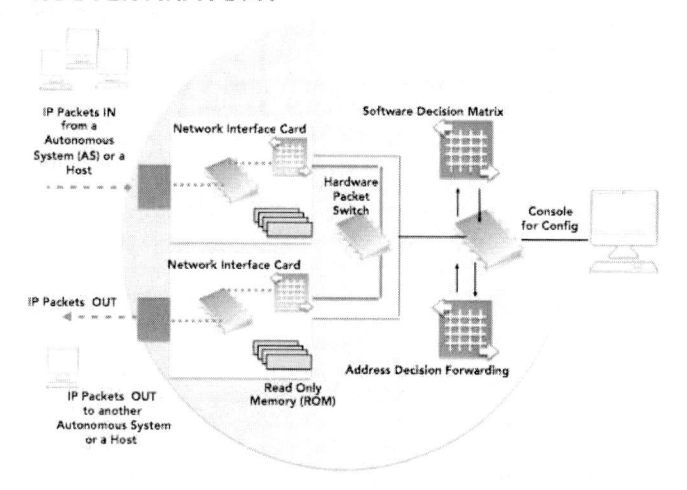

SOFTWARE DEFINED NETWORK

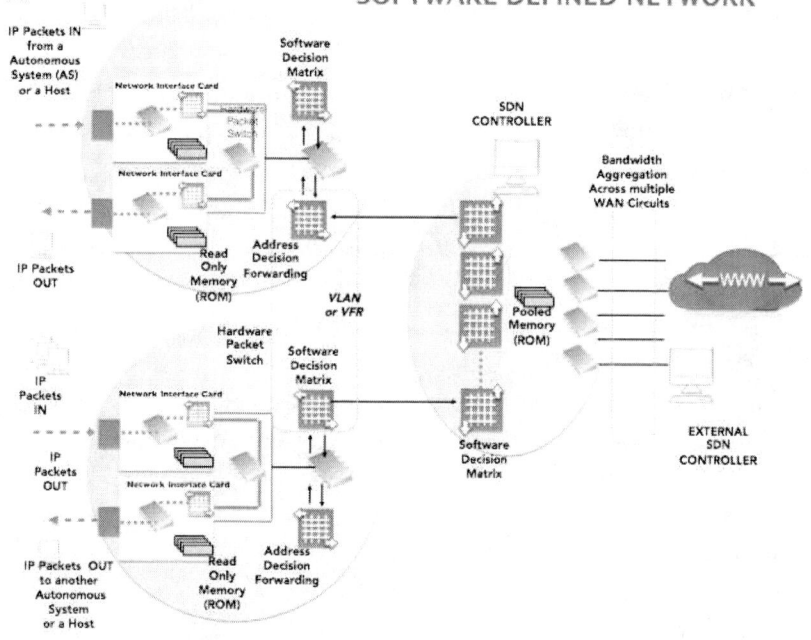

Figure 33 ROUTERS AND SDN ANATOMIES

Rather than each node in the network making its own forwarding decisions, a centralised software-based controller (likely running on commodity server hardware) acts like a Master and Commander. The controller effectively maintains the forwarding tables on all nodes across the network,

SDN-enabled nodes don't need to run control protocols among themselves and instead rely upon the controller to make all forwarding decisions for them. The network, as such, is *defined by software* running on the controller. A packet arrives at a switch in a conventional network, rules built into the switch's proprietary firmware tell the switch where to forward the packet. The switch sends every packet going to the same destination along the same path -- and treats all the packets the exact same way. SDN allows network engineers and administrators respond quickly to changing business requirements. In a software-defined network, a network administrator can shape traffic from a centralised control console without having to touch individual switches. The administrator can change any network switch's rules when necessary -- prioritising or blocking specific types of packets. This is especially helpful in a cloud computing and its multi-tenant architecture because it allows the administrator to manage traffic loads in a flexible and more efficient manner. The most popular specification for creating a software-defined network is an open standard called OpenFlow. OpenFlow let's network administrators remotely control routing tables.[112] An SDN can be considered a series of network objects (such as switches, routers, firewalls) that deploy in a highly automated manner. The automation may be achieved by using commercial or open source tools customised according to the administrator's requirements. A full SDN may only cover relatively straightforward networking requirements, such as VLAN (Virtual Local Area Network) and VRF (Virtual Routing and Forwarding) and interface provisioning. SDN will also be linked to server virtualisation, providing the glue that sticks virtual networks together. SMBs will ultimately benefit as this saves CAPEX. Old routers do not need to be upgraded and can be reused. OPEX is reduced as network management becomes simplistic.

8.6 NFV

This Network Functions Virtualisation (NFV) is designed to reduce network cost and complexity by virtualising network equipment onto switches, servers and storage. NFV (which is a Telco spin on SDN) has the potential to bring service providers savings on capital equipment and network operations costs. It also promises to make real the dream of managing legacy network components and virtual resources as one. NFV is the process of moving services, such as load balancing, firewalls and IPS, away from dedicated hardware into a virtualised environment. This is, of course, part of a wider movement toward the virtualisation of applications and services. NFV is the Telco's OSS and BSS teams imposing the ETSI eTOM (Telecommunications Management Forum) glossary on Software Defined Networking. One core challenge is the operating model schism between network operations (mobile, fixed access and core) and IT operations (back-office systems, collaborations, communications systems and so forth). Currently these teams operate in vertical silos. But introducing NFV and SDN into the network blurs these boundaries. As a result, the operations Craftflows and the management systems at both the business and network layers will need to be integrated in new, better-abstracted, and much more automated ways. [113] This reduces Telco's OPEX and so should be reflected in SMBs service charges.

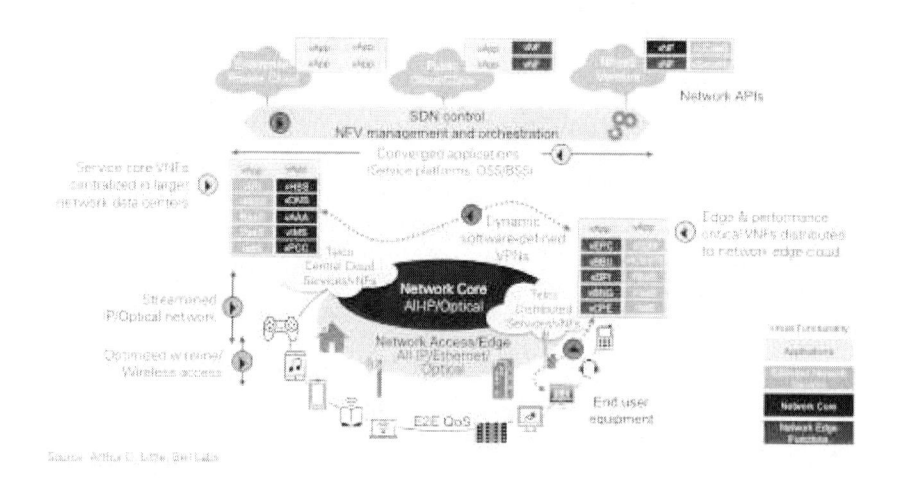

Figure 34 CARRIER NFV (ADL, BELL)

8.7 SWITCHES

A switch (used to be called an Active Cabling Hub) is a device that switches LAN traffic. No intelligence is added – just packet in fast and packet out fast. Multiple cables can be connected to a switch to enable networked devices to communicate with each other, or to extend LAN segments. In the early days of Ethernet these were called Bridges. Switches manage the flow of data across a network by only transmitting a received message to the device for which the message was intended. Each networked device connected to a switch can be identified using a MAC address (Media Access Control), allowing the switch to regulate the flow of traffic. This maximises security and efficiency of the network. These switches use ASICS (Application Specific Integrated Circuits) without software overlay; it takes packets in and throws them out – that is.

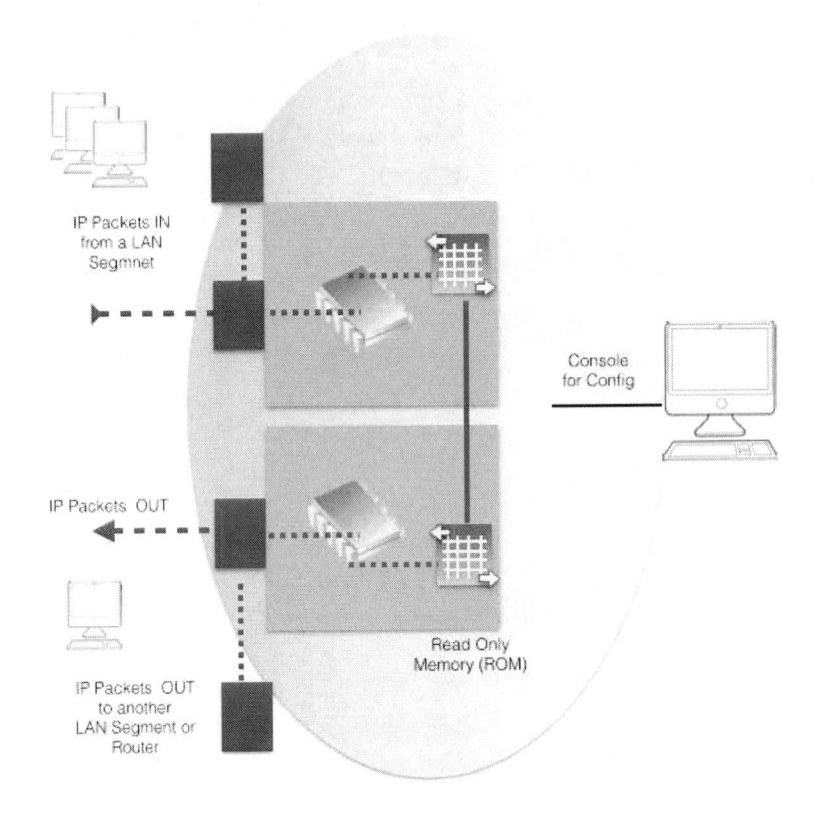

Figure 34 SWITCH

A switch is often considered "active" than a passive network hub, which provides purely cabled connections. Hubs neither provide security, or identification of connected devices. This means that messages have to be transmitted out of every port of the hub, greatly degrading the efficiency of the network. Switches should be wired back to a Network Access Controller. This allows for a high degree of network separation and segregation at a logical and physical level.

8.8 CABLE ROUTING OR WIRELESS (CROW) DECISION

Clients often ask me if they should cable their offices or go to an All Wireless topology. In the past Wi-Fi had a bad time succumbing to War Chalking (where an adversary sits outside a building and captures radio waves then uses a man in the middle attack to load exploits) and this can still happen on unencrypted WIFI sites using passive antennae and hubs. However the same can be said for cable where scanners can break into a fibre optic cable and copper cable infrastructure and Vampire taps used to download LAN traffic to a Sniffer. If deployed correctly a Wireless solution can bring many benefits.

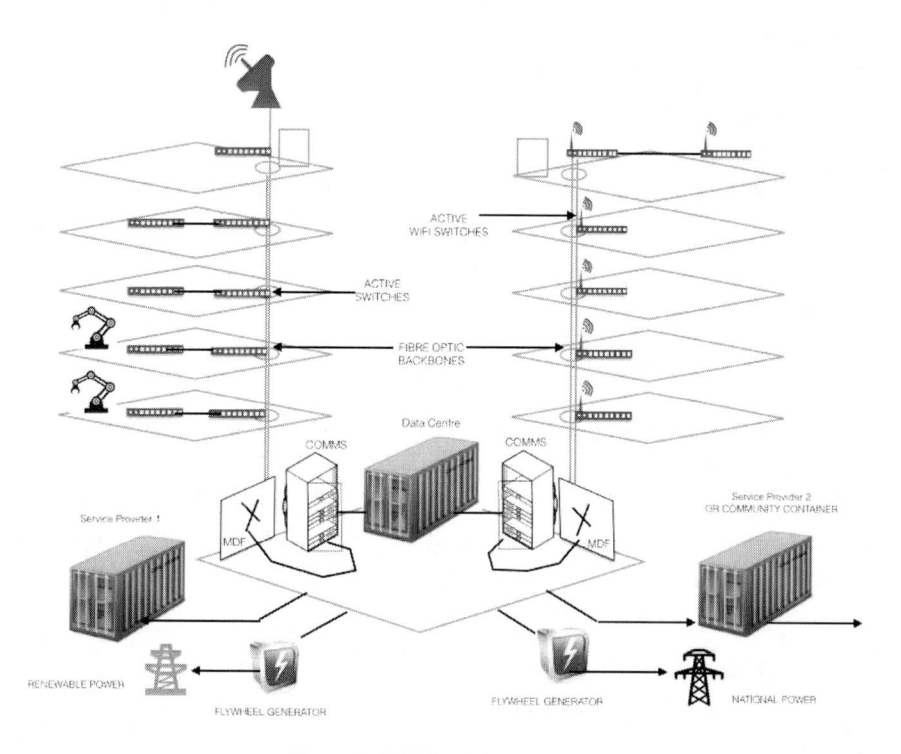

Figure 35 DUAL CABLE ROUTES

In the data centre wireless is not recommended as 40GB <100GB speeds are needed to reduce latency. A company should use an all fibre solution in the Data Centre (www.fibermountain.com), if not then use data centre cabling is covered by ISO/IEC 14763-2:2012. The UTP 6A (Class F) standard incorporates the ability to drive 40GBE and 100GBE in data centres and office plenum. Fibre optics for internal plenum cabling is 62.5/125um and for

WANs (external circuits and links) still employs Single Mode 50/125um. In the Combat Ready Model only 2 rack cabinets for a 1000 users are needed so using a fibre matrix switch for this is economical. An "All Fibre Backbone" lay in the building riser is a "must". To avoid Vampire Taps the Fibre backbone should have a Perspex cover and a visual inspection each week to ensure the cable has not been compromised.[114] Bending is the easiest method. It is undetectable, since there is no interruption to the light signal. Commercially available clip-on couplers cost less than a thousand dollars; these devices place a micro-bend in the cable, leaking a small amount of light through the polymer cladding. Once the light signal has been accessed, the data is captured using a photo detector – a transducer capable of translating an optical signal into an electrical signal. This is then captured into a laptop running a sniffer or packet collector and then transmitted by cellular to a man in a van.

Always ask engineers on the street outside the company building for identification and confirm road works with the local authorities. In some recent instances people physically stealing copper cabling out of ducts. These robbers usually resell the copper for scrap value, however communications can be compromised - I have seen this happen to a hospital with the obvious consequences. This can also happen to power networks, so dual up on electrical suppliers (or build your own) is also required feeding dual flywheel generators. Flywheel UPS generators maintain continuity of supply should a supplier fail and costs around $330 a kilowatt. It also balances power and filters out spikes and brown outs, keeping power supply constant. UPS Batteries will also need to be bought to provide a 20 minute kick in if power is lost (the time to take servers down elegantly).

Rule of Thumb: Two of everything in diverse trunks.
Cabling power, communications, riser cabling, tertiary (horizontal) floor cabling, should be fed to the Data Centres via separated diverse routes (dual risers). Although this is heavy on the CAPEX the downtime is completely minimised. Cabling has a depreciation life span of 15 years so initial costs can be viewed as a company asset in the Profit and Loss summary. Power should be fed from National and Renewable (separate Suppliers) and Cloud communications should also be separate suppliers. Never rely on a single supplier. Ignore the standard practice of patch cabinets in floor risers it's a waste of money. The floor cabling should be shielded (CAT 6e or CAT

7 standard). Industrial Ethernet can be replaced for Robotica should they not require real-time communications. For Ultra Security use Quantum Encryption endpoint devices on cable links between buildings or on the backbone[115].

On the horizontal CAT 6e cables should be used (run POE Power Over Ethernet if you are using telephony and cable powered Wi-Fi antennae (Access Points). Wiring Closets should have Biometric Entry systems enabled and alarmed. Wireless can be used but only in conjunction with a Wireless Controller (Aruba and Cisco) and 802.11n access points. A really useful guide to cabling is the Black Box Cabling Guide [116]

8.9 WAN CIRCUITS

When buying a Wide Area Network circuit always buy them "protected" and diversely routed. For resilience always buy from two suppliers with provisioning from two geographically separate Local Telephone Exchanges or suppliers if possible. Ensure the supplier be it a National Carrier, Cable or a Business ISP provides your company with a graphical display of the link for monitoring. The pricing for fibre optic links has dramatically fallen in the last decade and standardising on 2 x 1GB links (or multiple 10MB or 100MB links) is possibly the best model to opt for. For mega resilience also buy a satellite link. Avoid external companies wishing to sell monitoring services and alarming unless you are pushed into this. A 1GB circuit should provide you with a sub 10 millisecond latency to the nearest cloud infrastructure, this latency should not be any more than this as many database read/writes rely on a deterministic 20 milliseconds. If you moving to the cloud these multiple WAN links are essential for business continuity and storage capabilities. The average price of a 1GB link is around $2,500 a month. If you cannot afford this then consider multiple concatenated broadband links. Some carriers provide this as a service; where up to 4 broadband circuits are bonded together.

Cloud Service Providers if they are within 50 miles of your location may be able to provide dark fibre. You will usually need to commit to a 10-year contract to secure this service so a cost benefit analysis is needed. Dark Fibre is essentially a bundle of 8 fibres you can run any bandwidth over; all you have to do is pay for initial set up (usually means a dig from the nearest

Point of presence - a POP to your data centre). A dig will usually cost you $100 a metre. Includes the cost of an 8 pair fibre - fibre capacity of 40Gbit/s to 100 Gbit/s). An active DWDM box is needed either end. Dense Wave Division Multiplexing creates colours that combine signalling to provide High Speed Bandwidth. Latency is in the microseconds. Fibre Optic costs and dig costs can start from $25 upwards and depends where you want to lay the cable. Cable can be run on National Grid Lines but this requires catenary cable strength capable of handling distances between pylons. About 20 years ago I devised a train laying system that could dig, lay and cover train track cable around entire countries. As Fibre is more available and cheaper so do the CAPEX and OPEX costs. As merged Hybrid and Public Cloud models proliferate this allows companies to reduce the number of high-speed links connecting a company to the outside world to multiple and diverse lower speed WAN links.

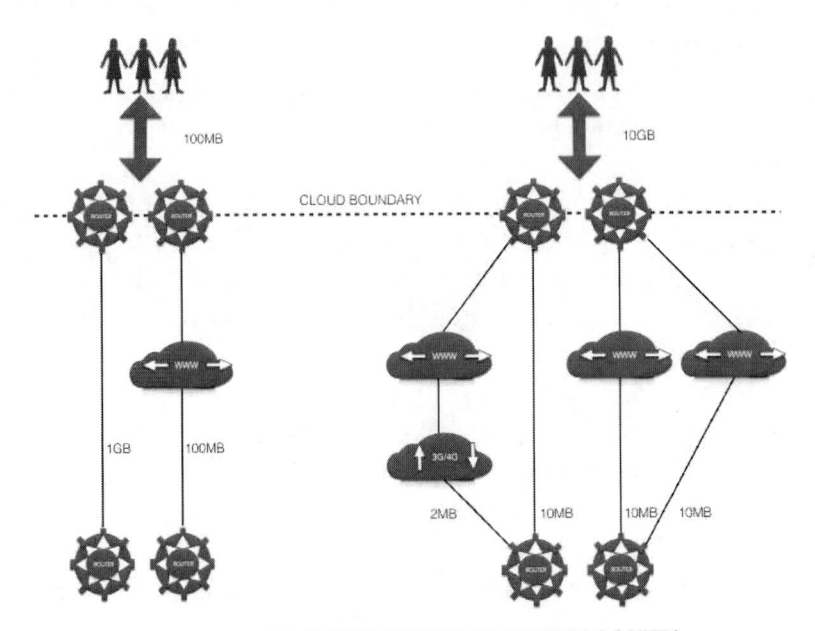

Figure 36 WAN MULTIPLE LINKS IN DIVERSE ROUTES

8.10 WI FI

Wi-Fi only site can dramatically reduce cabling costs on the floor tertiary, it also brings several benefits regarding MAC (Moves, Adds and Changes). Deploying an Active controller that directly links to a RADIUS

Authentication server brings benefits that monitoring a standard cable topology cannot bring. The Active Wi-Fi Controller spots rogue attempts and permanently knocks of these devices permanently, so war chalking is instantly stopped. Also Active Wi-Fi controllers encrypt over the air traffic so anything sniffed is meaningless to an adversary. If your switches are capable of encrypting riser traffic this is even better (between a floor switch and the Data Centre via the riser fibre). Active Controllers can be bought from Cisco, Aruba and others. These controllers could link directly into Intrusion Protection Systems for added security. In addition to this Smartphones and Wi-Fi the Active Controller controls capable phones. This means calls made via the company Wi-Fi can be recorded. These controllers can also manage remote office, branches, retail outlets and teleworker sites (via an IP VPN link) as all authentication data will be back hauled to the central site. If an access point fails on a floor another can take over traffic so zero downtime during moves. Using Wi-Fi does not preclude the ability to record data sessions. Recording of Voice and Data sessions may be regarded as snooping but internal to a company there is no reason why this does not invade team members privacy issues. Knowing that your session at the workplace (and teleworking) may be recorded should curtail many Insider attempts. Wi-Fi also allows for cameras to be deployed in the workplace - I worked at a company where they had a camera in the nose of a wall clock to monitor activity after hours. When team members discovered this pilferage stopped over night, and night cleaners actually cleaned desks.

Wi-Fi standards are managed under the auspices of the IEEE 802 LMSC (LAN / MAN Standards Committee). Of these even 802.11 have a variety of standards, each with a letter suffix attached? These cover everything from the wireless standards themselves, to standards for security aspects, quality of service and the like, for SMBs the prime standard to be concerned with include:

- 802.11a - Wireless network bearer operating in the 5 GHz ISM band with data rate up to 54 Mbps

- 802.11b - Wireless network bearer operating in the 2.4 GHz ISM band with data rates up to 11 Mbps

- 802.11e - Quality of service and prioritisation

- 802.11f - Handover

- 802.11g - Wireless network bearer operating in 2.4 GHz ISM band with data rates up to 54 Mbps

- 802.11h - Power control

- 802.11i - Authentication and encryption

- 802.11j - Interworking

- 802.11k - Measurement reporting

The 802.11ac standard now uses OFDM (Orthogonal Frequency Division Multiplexing) that splits and rebuilds data streams via two antennae, so security is extremely enhanced. Gigabit Wi-Fi also brings several benefits Wireless IP Video Conferencing, Seamless handover of calls and data between floors enabling roaming throughout a building. In a 1000 user building the productivity gains are substantial IDC estimate an[117] annual productivity gain of $1.85 million annual OPEX saving. The Active Controller automates many operational tasks a 75% decrease in Moves Adds and Changes is realised. As Telephones are not needed (headsets and a Wi-Fi enabled PC, Laptop, Tablet and Smartphone), traditional phones are not needed. The desk arrangement only requires power (2 Charging points ((Laptop and Smartphone)), 1 for a large monitor) and so data points are not required. This allows desks to be bought a lot cheaper and they are easier to rearrange. I have seen this deployment in Google offices and in two major Telco's; one in Japan had 20,000 users all on Wi-Fi. This desk flexibility allows for printers to be placed in quiet zones and moved at will.

The average annual cost for a fixed cabling site is $540 per user (this includes HW and SW and Maintenance) but for a WIFI site this falls to $130 per user. A 1000 user site this can save $410k per annum, an annual saving of $2.26 m per annum could be realised. The other benefit to all this is during a conflict, if the company plummets into a disaster recovery situation rebuilding a Wi-Fi network is a lot quicker than laying new cabling systems in another location. Naysayers including "dyed in the wool" cabling consultants will try and discredit this approach but from personal experience I have seen this work effectively and securely so an SMB can save thousands per year.

8.11 WIFI ENCRYPTION

Generally, the use of WPA2-enterprise is preferred in SMB deployments (for obvious reasons); hence, the naming convention. Therefore, the company should generate any key. Voice systems have very high availability requirements, and these may be difficult to achieve in branch and remote environments, when there is a dependency upon a centralised authentication system. This could be addressed by distributing authentication databases to branches through local AAA servers or the embedded AAA services of a Wireless Controller; or by deploying a VoWLAN system that does not rely on centralised authentication. The RADIUS service could be deployed for a hybrid cloud/public cloud configuration.

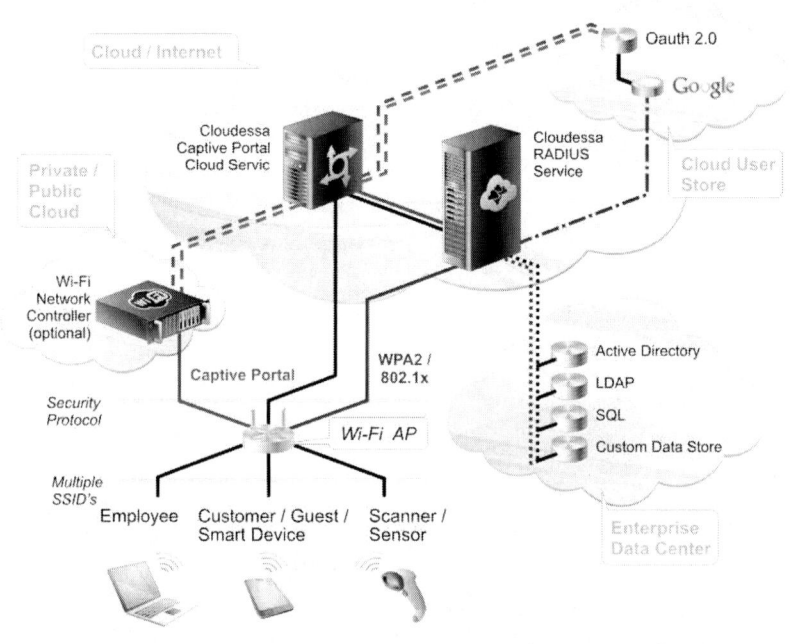

Figure 37 CLOUD MANAGEMNT OF WIFI (CLOUDESSA)

8.12 ANATOMY OF A MOBILE AND TABLET

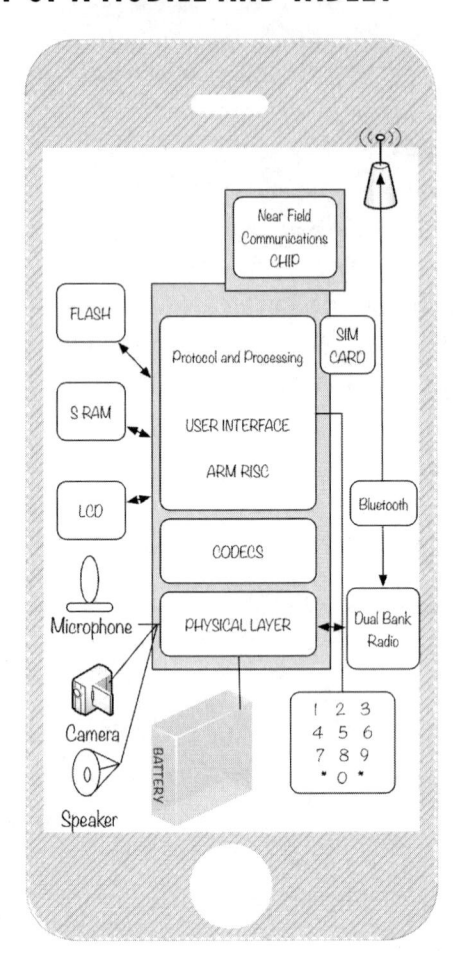

Figure 38 MOBILE TABLET BARE BONES

Like the PC, the mobile also has an Operating System, but this time it is held in RAM. The latest designs place the OS directly on the CPU (chip) including protocols and processing. As the demand for mobile payments increases the use of a technology called Near Field Communications for ATM 'touch' activities at retail Point of Sales cash tills will replace plastic credit cards over time. Once a secure back end platform is proven to be unhackable.

Recently there were reports around the SIM card being infected with a firmware malware affecting 2.5 billion issued SIM Cards. This malware can liven up the phone (or Tablet) and decrypt any communications (Voice and Data) while the phone is in use. Writing applications for the mobile and tablet worlds is easy. Many of the baseline components are pre-written, in IOS and Android; a developer just needs to pull modules together for a bespoke application. Security should be tight; the application portal owners check the application for anomalies. There is usually a rigorous security hardening by Google and Apple. These applications that are checked are usually signed. If you download an app from anywhere other than the vendors' online shops – downloads could be infected. The other point to remember is the power of key loggers these apps listen to your typing as most people have their smartphones next to their computers at work and at home. These logs are sent to an adversary enabling copying of logins and passwords. The GPS locator is also used to track your movements – to avoid kidnapping and your house being broken into its best to turn this off.

8.13 YOU SAY ISO AND I SAY OSI

The Open Systems Interconnection (OSI) reference model describes how the different layers would process information in an IP packet datagram from a software application in one computer and move through a network medium to a software application in another computer host. The seven layers describe the movement of an IP packet within each layer and between each layer.

The OSI reference model still exists today and is a conceptual model composed of seven layers, each specifying particular network functions. The model was developed by the International Standards Organisation in 1980 and released in 1984 (just in time for the Big Brother era), and it is still considered the primary architectural model for inter-computer and Internet communications. It is in dire need of updating. Where is the Eighth layer for security?

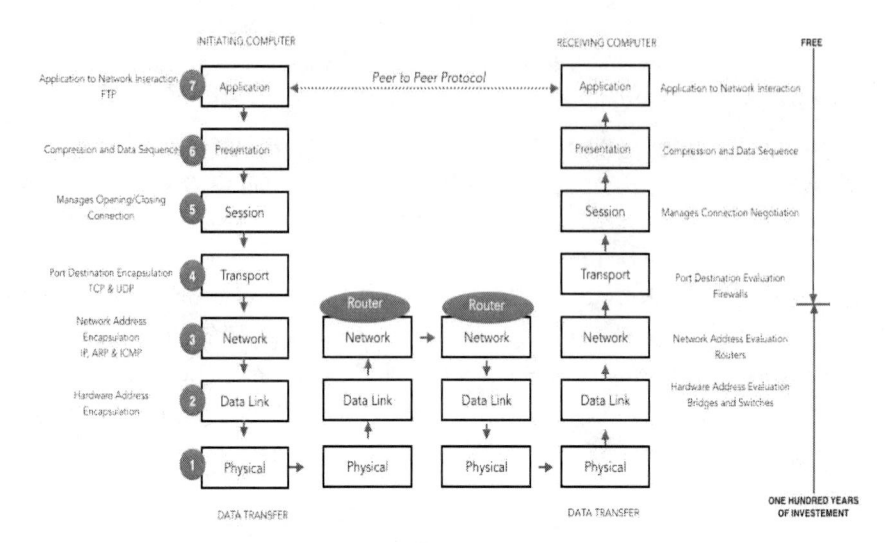

Figure 39 SEVEN LAYER MODEL

The OSI model divides the tasks involved with moving information between networked computers into seven smaller, more manageable task groups. A task or group of tasks is then assigned to each of the seven OSI layers. Each layer is reasonably self-contained so that the tasks assigned to each layer can be implemented independently. This enables the solutions offered by one layer to be updated without adversely affecting the other layers.

When the model was drawn up malware was not a major issue. Therefore focus on a purely Security focussed layer was not included. Most vendors bolted on their security parameters over time. This omission should be rectified given the times we live in, and so an eight-layer model would be more appropriate, if this template would continue, or a four layer model that is proposed later.

1. **Physical Layer** – refers to the electrical hardware interface, cabling, and computer bus.
2. **Data Link Layer** – data transfer method (802x Ethernet). Puts data in frames and ensures error-free transmission. Also controls the timing of the network transmission. Adds frame type, address,

and error control information. IEEE divided this layer into the two following sub layers:

- **Logical Link control (LLC)** – maintains the Link between two computers by establishing Service Access Points (SAPs), which are a series of interface points. IEEE 802.2.

- **Media Access Control (MAC)** – used to coordinate the sending of data between computers. The 802.3, 4, 5, and 12 standards apply to this layer. If you hear someone talking about the MAC address of a network card, they are referring to the hardware address of the card. This number signifies the vendor who manufactured the Network Interface Card in an 8 Bit alphanumeric number.

3. **Network Layer** – IP network protocol. Routes and transmits messages using the best path available.

4. **Transport Layer** – TCP and UDP. Ensures properly sequenced and error free transmission.

5. **Session Layer** – the user's interface to the network. Determines when the session is begun or opened, how long it is used, and when it is closed. Controls the transmission of data during the session. Supports security and name lookup, enabling computers to locate each other.

6. **Presentation Layer** – ASCII or EBCDEC data syntax. Makes the type of data transparent to the layers around it. Used to translate data to computer-specific format such as byte ordering. It may include compression. It prepares the data, either for the network or the application, depending on the direction it is going.

7. **Application Layer** – provides services software applications need. Provides the ability for user applications to interact with the network.

Many protocol stacks overlap the borders of the seven-layer model by operating at multiple layers of the model. File Transport Protocol (FTP) and telnet both work at the application, presentation, and the session layers.

This model still makes sense today and helps explain everything from TCP/IP addresses to the data cable or Wi Fi communications networks that connect your device to the Web. I used to remember the model as **A PSTN** for **Data Processing (*APSTNDP*)**. It's a very helpful tool to explain the PC and mobile worlds. Providers to specify how to move data packets from a source to a destination address in a consistent and standard fashion use the model. It's from this model that Ethernet and Token Ring came into being and high-speed fibre optic networks could carry traffic anywhere in the world. I remember standing in front of a 1000 mainframe owners, presenting a comparison of IBM Token Ring and Ethernet as emerging standards, and how everyone would one day not be constrained by the limitations of COAX star topologies (Coaxial - twisted copper cabling mainly used in Cable TV or Manufacturing deployments). It took about 10 years for cabling to standardise on Ethernet, no matter how much more secure Token Ring was! **Being open means 'not secure'**. The mobile world uses a four-layer model: Physical, Datalink, Network and Application. The mobile and the fixed worlds interface at the Network layer, and this is where TCP/IP comes in. The Transmission Control Protocol/Internet Protocol was soon adopted by the world to provide device and server connectivity. Its ubiquity allowed for businesses to use e-mail systems and link external companies through file sharing or ERP (Enterprise Resource Programmes) such as a SAP platform to integrate supply chain inventories with financial systems.

IBM PCs had a 20MB hard disk, or two 5 and a quarter floppy drives (one to run the program under MS DOS and the other to save files to). These stand-alone PCs fell off the shelves faster than they could be made. Users found that by installing PC cards they could communicate with a mainframe. For accountants this was heaven as they could download mainframe data into Lotus 123 (a DOS-based spread sheet).

There were PC connectivity servers made by Novell, Torus, and Banyan, which allowed PCs to share information across a local area network. IBM realised their market was becoming cannibalised and tried to put their own graphical desktop into the marketplace. They released the OS2 operating system and at one point married up their mainframe data to a GUI-based PC. Enterprises wanted mainframes at a much cheaper price, and IBM released the wonderful AS400, a sort of super-server that could be put into branch offices and connected by 64 Kbit/s leased lines (wow)! Colour terminals were becoming flavour of the day, and DEC released their own colour terminals to counter the rise of the PCs. So very soon we had a central mainframe connected to many AS400s and PCs for the end users running emulation in Windows 386 or OS2.

The model further allowed companies to write applications that were once the constraint of the mainframe and with GUI (Graphical User Interfaces) for Windows users. All of a sudden, databases that were once firmly established in the mainframe and silo of IT became available to anyone who had a penchant for creating a database on their own PC. PCs also became cheaper and faster, and better software evolved speedily. By the end of the 1990s the baseline model for IT was firmly in place and is one we readily associate with today.

The Physical layer describes the electrical characteristics, basically the Morse code needed to move the binary zero and one bits across copper and fibre cable (or over wireless). The Data Link layer describes the network interface and provides a MAC Address. This MAC Address is then associated to an IP Address in the Network Layer. Data packets are then wrapped in the IP protocol (source) and using TCP (Transmission Control Protocol) is sent (routed) to the destination address.

8.14 FOUR LAYER MODEL

As SDN and NFV start their global adoption and customers and vendors produce lower cost software driven devices the OSI 7 Layer Model gets left behind. The schematic below is where I think the model will evolve. At the top will be the Application Layer (no Change there). The exception is that the licencing will be on a pay per use model. This means end users will be forced to input their credentials each time for access. IP ENUM Cost Metrics may take a place here at this point (which we will discuss later) or connect to Identity Management, At the NFV layer IPV6 will address all end nodes at the boundary edge. A security layer needs to be in place here. The ETSI NFV functions do not address the security functions in depth but describes name attributes in micro segmented Virtual Machines. At the CSP layer the Software Defined Data Centre provides VM to hold Content. To improve Content security a Content Label is applied which could be VOIP, Video Streaming Movie downloads etc., This content is then transported over the Software Defined Network which ameliorates and instantiates virtual bandwidth globally dependent on the content QOS requirements on a per session basis. ISO (International Standards Organisation) will adapt ISO/IEC 7498 (and others) to this 4 Layer model. For SMBs the advent of SDN brings the promise of cheap compute, network and storage costs, which will have a dramatic impact on IT capital and operating expenditures. Also as this on the cusp of InternetNew new ventures and start-ups can exploit these new platforms for services and new markets. So following the Šmihula cycle (a Šmihula Hoop).

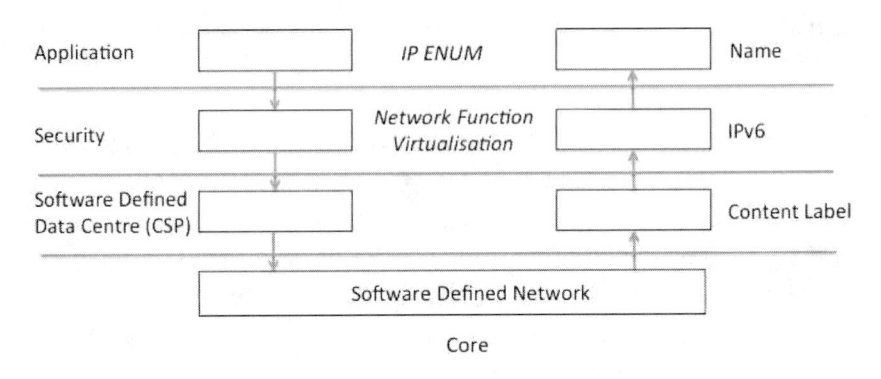

Figure 40 - BLUE SKY 4 LAYER MODEL

8.15 SIP

I had just rolled out the first VOIP network in Europe for AT&T Unisource using Cisco equipment. The whole year was spent working with US based development teams to build interfaces into every PABX you can imagine. Presenting at a Voice on the Net conference in Sweden I explained to the audience that the H323 was a Microsoft designed encoding protocol that was designed around LAN based voice services – a topology that relied on guaranteed bandwidth and latency. Given the immaturity of the Internet of the 1990s the promise of guaranteed bandwidth and latency was impossible. The H323 protocol had 32 ACK/NAKs (Acknowledgement and Negative Acknowledgement) before a call would start. To ensure call integrity ACK/

NACs were the serial fundamental steps to call set up in the PSTN world to enable voice calls, and subsequently data in the IP world. Remember RS232 cables that used to connect your PC to a printer? The ACK NAK flow looks like this:

1. Sender transmits packet, and waits for an ACK or a NAK.

2. If no ACK/NAK is received within some timeout period, or a NAK is received, packet is retransmitted and Sender again waits for ACK/NAK.

3. If ACK is received, next packet is transmitted

After that event Henning Schulzrinne, Mark Hadley, and Jonathan Rosenberg developed SIP. The work was supplemental to Henning's earlier efforts on Real-Time Transport Protocol (defined in RFC2326, RTP is used for transmission of data requiring a high quality of service (QoS) including on-demand media and interactive services). SIP assumes the end user exists and does not expect an ACK. Both protocols were being developed under the auspices of the Internet Engineering Task Force (IETF), the Internet standardization body, and their working group on Multiparty Multimedia Session Control (MMUSIC) who were coordinating development of Internet teleconferencing and multimedia communications. Skype use a form of peer-to-peer SIP architecture in their network. SIP is now used everywhere for voice and video communications. I believe Henning's work on the lightweight SIP protocol coding actually spurred Cloud Application development (GET/PULL/PUSH/REST etc.,).

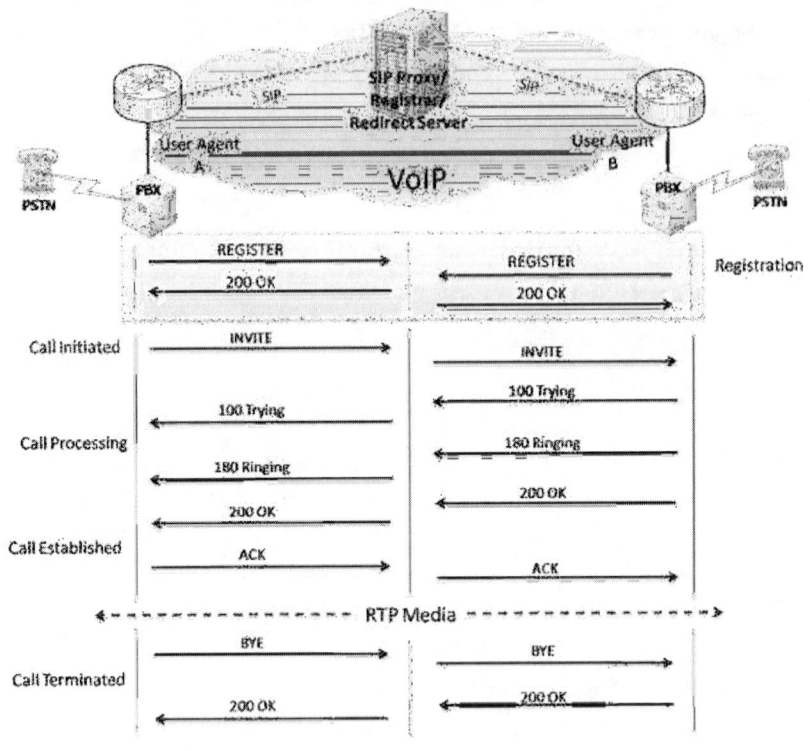

Figure 41 SIP CALL FLOW

8.15.1.1 SIP TRUNKING

This has nothing to do with Elephants it replaces the need for traditional analogue; E1 (or T1) based Public Switched Telephone Network (PSTN) connection. Termination is provided over a company's public or private Internet connection via a SIP provider. For an SMB the cost savings of SIP trunking are substantial. Traditionally high costs may be incurred through a combination of monthly phone bills, which include charges for incoming phone lines, long distance charges, IT and maintenance charges, which can be eliminated by a SIP Trunking provider.

SIP Trunking allows companies to only pay for the number of lines they need it can grow or shrink as required. The savings are realised either by purchasing only the necessary number of channels, or by paying only for minutes used. This allows companies to make more efficient use of communications costs and reduce wasted resources. Use the following simple equation to determine the necessary bandwidth to support your calls:

(Number of concurrent calls at your company's peak) x 85kilobits per second = bandwidth in Megabits per second (Mbps) needed for each users call

SIP Trunking eliminates the physical connection to a phone company. There are no hardware, wiring, or circuit boxes to maintain for connection to the PSTN. Reducing multiple phone lines into dual points of entry drastically reduces charges for incoming lines and the IT cost associated with the maintenance of those lines. SIP Trunking increases reliability of VoIP by providing a level of redundancy if duelled. When system failures and emergencies occur, SIP Trunking providers can reroute services to a redundant data line or forward the PBX to mobile phones to keep your business uptime.

8.16 SOFTWARE APPLICATIONS

The bane of any CIO's life is the need to craft a custom-made application for a company. This also encompasses huge ERP rollouts, which are 'budget-suckers' and take two years to get right, and expensive to maintain. The old way of developing these large deployments was waterfall-based project managed (task after task sequential delivery) and took so long that 60% of the team members that started the project left before go-live, mainly through boredom but also through redundancies (the organisation cutting off its own nose to spite its face). This spurred offshore development, which in turn has caused a loss of localised skills but opened the organisation up to all sorts of security holes.

There are about 170 variants of code generators and compilers in today's market place. This causes problems. The sheer volume of millions of LOC (Lines of Code) make finding internally created malicious code really difficult. Also, demands on coders to deliver thousands of LOCs per day can be a pressure to cookie-cut old code that already has malicious code built in. It's usually the role of the product manager to check this, but in reality this is a task that's usually too much to handle. More should be done around secure coding, and new regulations are starting to emerge. Rugged Coding and Secure Coding methods and testing are examples of these.

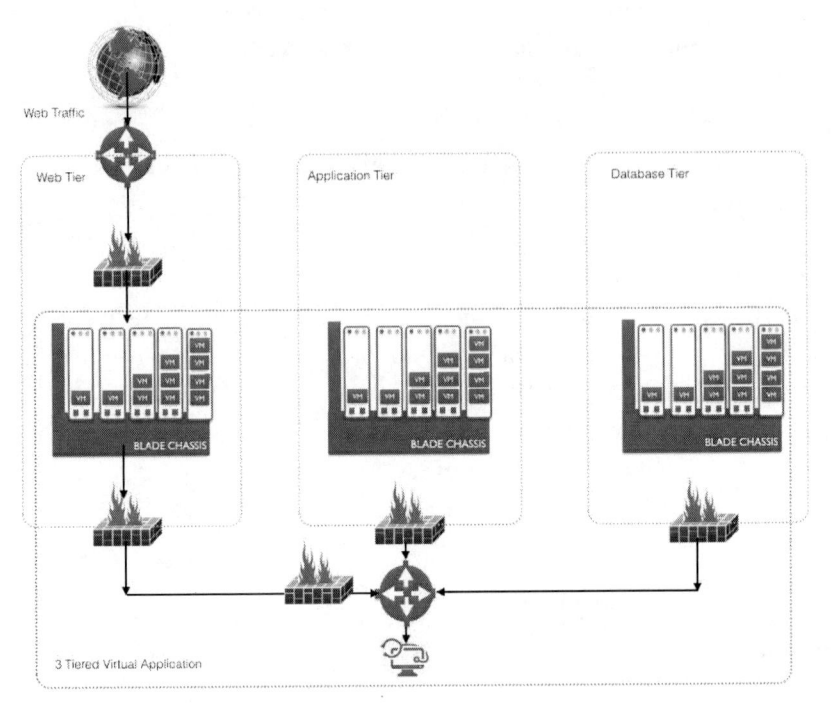

Figure 42 VIRTUALISED CLOUD APPLICATIONS

The way applications are being coded is also changing in line with Internet and Cloud infrastructures. The speed of Wide Area Network circuits has dramatically increased and the intra country latencies are now in microseconds rather than milliseconds. Near Zero latency allows for complete geo-transparency of facilities and how applications communicate. This means a web application may be hosted in the cloud and provide public facing web page access at near real time speeds. An application Tier that handles e-commerce and workflow can be hosted on accompanies premises and a Database tier that could be on supplier's premises in a remote country. This flexibility (theoretically) should provide increased security along the supply chain. Using Cloud patterns and standard APIs and binaries application portability is enabled, so saving company's huge infrastructure holding costs. RESTFUL applications can be developed in Python or Drupal; both provide a high degree of device transparency and features. PHP which retains 72% of website development market will need to adapt.

8.17 HARDWARE APPLICATIONS - ROBOTICA

Robotica will spearhead the next Šmihula cycle. I have named the merging of Hard and Soft robots with Artificial Intelligence – under the banner of Robotica because they are merging. Should we be scared of Robotica - it's not Terminator? I believe that SMBs and Venture Capitalists will plunge huge amounts of funding into this arena in the next few years. Merging 3D printing capabilities (we have seen houses and even cars printed on demand, as well as spanners printed on the Space Station) with advanced applications will fuel the next boom. Concept to Delivery (C2D) will speed the production lifecycle and SMBs will need IT innovation to keep up.

8.18 HARD ROBOTS

A manufacturing robot now costs less than $20,000, and 20 years ago would have cost $1 million! It's reached this price point dramatically in the last few years. Companies realise robots don't need salaries or health care, and a robot mechanism works 24 hours a day without striking.[118] In three years I see the entry point at $2000. Softbank in Japan sells "Pepper" which is an amazing robot developed for retail stores and restaurants. This robotic server (as in waiter) can even empathise with humans' emotions and remember names and faces' using facial recognition costs a mere $1900.

This will spark a massive wave of technology and possibly see the merging of genetics and Artificial Intelligence within a five years timeslot. Each country will jostle for supremacy and need to retain vital ideas within borders. This could severely frustrate emerged markets to the point of a dramatic economic reversal. For instance why would you have a million employees making smartphones when you can produce the same output in container based robotica controlled factories?

8.19 ROBOSHORING

Robotica is being squarely aimed at the services sector through Robotic Process Automation. McKinsey estimate this is a fast growing technology sector and worth more than Cloud, IOT and Mobile Internet technologies. By 2020 McKinsey estimate this Automation of Knowledge work at $2.5 trillion. Knowledge Worker Automation (Autonomics, Augmentation, Intelligent Workflow Automation and Soft Robotica are alternate names) will generate and displace 140 million FTEs. We are already seeing smart factories build TV screens in the US at cheaper operating costs than developing countries. Software robotica have a role to play in the service sector where, even if the cost of automation would not otherwise by economically justified (say for a low volume clerical process), it may be that a particular process is so sensitive (or perhaps that the cost of an error is so high) that it is preferred not to use error-prone – and potentially untrustworthy – people to execute them (insiders). Therefore, robots provide a trustworthy and accurate means of executing key functional processes. Robotica automation follows an established process such as:

- Finance and Accounting (Accounts Payable, Order to Cash, Record to Report),
- Human Resources (Payroll, Employee Data Management, On and Off Boarding, Broadsourcing – Internet Searches for Background checks)
- Procurement (Spend Data Management, Help Desk, Invoice Reconciliation, Asset Management, Supplier Management and Accreditation)
- Supply Chain (Spare Parts, Inventory Optimisation, Load Optimisation)
- Customer Experience Management (Service Support, Technical Support, Billing, and Account Management)
- Legal Services (Litigation Support, Patent Research, Abstraction).

8.20 SMB ADVANTAGE

Locally based (within country boundaries) SMBs can take advantage of this new market sector. It is estimated that Soft Robotica will:

- See Enterprise companies reshore business process outsources in next three years
- HR Broadsourcing will ensure tight personnel security values (HR databases linked by Hadoop and Spark) to centralise Good Conduct Workers true work history and behaviours
- The Silver Tsunami workforce brings back the expertise required by developed countries
- Intelligent tools will support lower skilled workers
- In five years most work will be done by small companies and independent works who subscribe to the Broadsourcing database
- Cottage Industries (Mom and Pop) will see a mass revival

Soft robotica can act as an intermediary plateau between CRM and Help Desk Systems by enabling self-service. A help desk with Self Service Front End can reduce help desk calls by 80%. Password resets down to 10%. By linking Customer Relationship Management Systems (CRM), Help Desk Management Systems, and Instant Messaging/Unified Communications (to escalate to an expert) many Call Centres will become superfluous by 95%. In 2007 it was estimated that there were 475,000 call centre agents in 2500 companies in 17 countries[119]. Extrapolating the 15% annual growth of these companies it's estimated that this number is approximately 1.6 million FTEs. If Soft Robotica is adopted this this figure could drop by 95%!

There are four pioneers already putting this into practice, IPSoft, Ayehu, Arago, and BluePrism[120]. IPSoft have developed Amelia, which is a voice-controlled avatar that interfaces to an Expert System. The soft robot can troubleshoot calls and raise tickets of reviewed user accounts. Blue Prism is the most exciting example of automation I have seen. It already manages a Patient Administration System and a Customer Service department for a mobile company. Companies like Nuance have systems installed in hospitals. A Canadian start up called ROSS have replaced paralegals to look up and analyse (rather than a straight forward *search*) of all legal cases to answer questions,

In terms of security and how to manage repetitive tasks, the Technology Value Centre can set up a user account and load the process into the robot, and that immediately replaces a clerical worker. Again, the cost benefits are enormous and the robots can work 24/7. Some trading floors are already utilising this software. In a financial services context, the opportunity for fraud might be greatly increased by providing a single person with access to multiple banking systems. One option is to segment a process between departments, to the detriment of speed and quality associated with that process. Alternatively, a software robot can be trusted to execute a process as directed, without inappropriate data collection, fraudulent intervention or deviation from the prescribed process. Activities might include performing double data entry, copying and pasting data between computer systems, reconciling and cross-referencing data between different systems and implementing high level decision making at key points along the business process. Such data cleansing and data hygiene activities are frequently performed in many large organisations and these disjointed processes tend to arise out of an organic growth of changing system requirements and the changing needs of the business over time (arising from, for example, changes in consumer demand and regulatory mandates).

The average annual cost of production and clerical workers is around $100,000. Robotica costs around $12,000 per year, and so the economics will drive the technology option. In the next 5 years, robotics could impact half of the human workforce. The Industry 4 initiative takes this initiative further into the realm of 'untouched by human hands'. The only human intervention is programming and maintenance, and Machine Safety elements kick in here. With the advent of self-driving cars companies are already seeking to replace Taxi drivers with a soft robot. For SMBs who recognise this as a route to grow a business speedily – do investigate soon!

8.21 INDUSTRIAL ROBOTICA

A typical robot normally consists of one or more manipulators (arms), end effectors (hands), a controller, a power supply, and possibly an array of sensors to provide information about the environment in which the robot must operate. Robots in the food industry are now the norm. The large food processing plants can produce personal food products just by 3D printing. You can now buy customised Chocolates or Marshmallows with an edible photograph printed on them, and soon you will be able to buy online your own design chocolate boxes made up of your usual favourites. A robotica Pick and Mix if you like.

Robotica has a wide collection of names—such as pick-and-place robot, spray-painting robot, Cartesian robot, laboratory robot, dispensing robot, and so forth. Some of the names are self-evident, others like the Selective Compliance Assembly Robot Arm (SCARA), need a little explaining.

The International Organisation of Standardisation (ISO) came up with a formal, or 'official', definition of industrial robotica. As specified in ISO 8373:1994 the industrial robot is "an automatically controlled, reprogrammable, multipurpose manipulator in three or more axes.[121]"

8.22 SCADA (AKA ICS)

Supervisory Control and Data Acquisition (SCADA) systems, sometimes termed Industrial Control Systems (ICS) are widely used by utilities and industries that are considered critical to the functioning of countries around the world. It is estimated that there are four million ICS systems in use today.

Early in the history of ICS systems the equipment and software were fairly obscure and network exposure to the world was limited. Over time a combination of factors drove vendors to adopting standard IT platforms, and ICS system owners to interconnect their systems to other networks. The rise to adopt Industrial Ethernet was one example of this; the systems also started to embed Microsoft XP. This opening up of systems interconnection has allowed traditional vulnerabilities to be transferred to these control systems via IP, and take advantage of the Microsoft vulnerabilities. In addition, the many bespoke systems that spawn from this means that the cost to upgrade each system can be extremely high (around a million per system)!

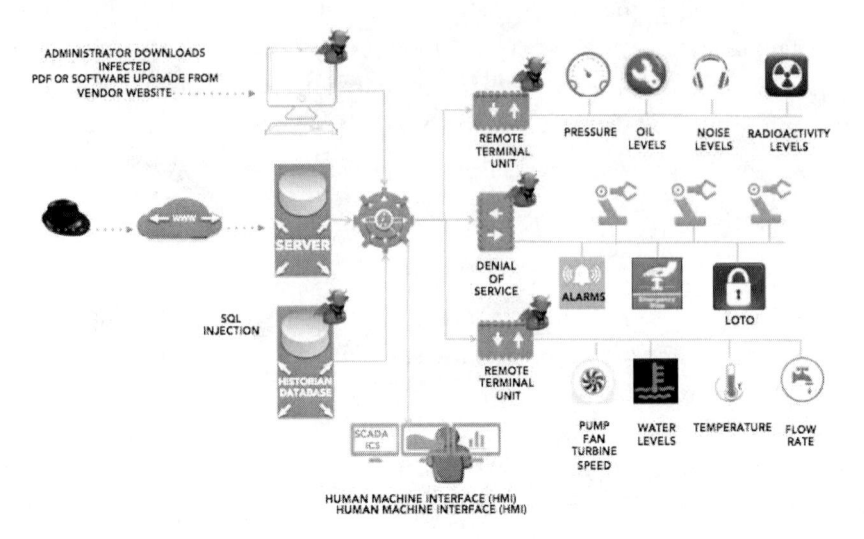

Figure 43 SCADA ICS BASICS

Security threats to ICS systems are similar to office based networked systems and can be grouped as follows:

1. ICS systems are vulnerable to viruses, worms, Trojans and spyware. They corrupt data, overwhelm communications, install back doors and keystroke loggers.

2. Insider – the disgruntled worker who knows the weak points of a system. The insider can disrupt the ICS system subsequently the physical system. An insider may also attempt to gain higher privileges and access to the embedded software. Bored or inquisitive operators (of which there are many) may inadvertently create production problems.

3. Adversaries have the possibility to modifying data related to the manipulation rate creation and restrictions. Most front-end equipment, programmable logic controllers (PLCs), RTUs, and protocol converters lack basic authentication. An intruder could also perform man-in-the-middle (MITM) attacks. By inserting packets into the network, he can issue arbitrary commands throughout the network.

Industrial protocols like MODBUS, wireless HART, and FIELDBUS have poor authentication, no encryption or verification. There is nothing wrong with proprietary systems, as long as they are not surrounded by IP. A method is need to segregate IP from proprietary systems – is a simpler solution. If the system is on a live IP network then never run Penetration Tests on that network! The same can be said for recompiling software, which has led to plant shutdowns in the past.

The IEC have a standard for cyber security to stop attacks on facility systems and networks. IEC 62443 and IEC 61511 standards recommends segregation using firewalls between: Plant Safety Instrumentation System (SIS), Basic Process Control System (BPCS), Control Centre, Plant DMZ (De Militarized Zone) and the Office Environment and onward to the Internet. The problem here is devices like firewall and Anti Virus add latency to the real time needs of plant sensors which impacts the efficiency of the Safety Instrumented System (SIS) and this reduces the scoring of the Safety Integrity Level (SIL). The obvious solution is to not connect to the Internet. As plants must reflect a highly robust security stance (in the US a Presidential edict) and maintain reduced safety risks. It's Safety first every time. Even keeping independent vendors wont help as IP is ubiquitous and once a device or robotica becomes IP addressable it becomes susceptible to network attacks.

The root cause is IP. Eliminate the root cause before adding endless firewall's as this will add latency and weakens the security and safety stance. Firewalls add latency (Bumps in the Wire) and jitter and can cause a new set of safety problems. Every hacker knows how to get around a firewall in a minute! Remote access here is the problem. In the last decade support engineers and PLC developers always want remote access to maintain a facilities plant. If this was not needed the IP devices wouldn't need IP addresses. So why not reintroduce named connections, still using IP stack but a unique addressing schema linked to a local registry. This proposal means local facility can still interlock with local systems (RTUs communicating with ERP systems) but beyond the Office Environment using a named stack. A named stack is similar to an IP software stack that enables numeric IP addressing on an IP device. In the past Operating Systems like IBMs SNA used Alpha addressing (managed by the security module RACF in Mainframe Z-OS). This would allow remote access into the PLC using a dual stack bridge between the outside world and internal world. When IP was introduced IBM and Cisco developed DLSW (Data Link Switching) – a gateway between the two worlds. The need for IP zoning and security trust domains for mission critical systems is not required, so putting safety first.

This is a concept called "verify by called name" which relies on a VPN type pipe requiring point to point named handshakes and a series of authenticated and encrypted Acknowledgements and Authentication locked into an IP ENUM identifier. These principles when combined could provide the secure remote monitoring and support without exposing plant to adversaries. Remote monitoring and support calls from certified sources could take place on a persistent or ad hoc basis. This series of checks and balances handoffs makes MITM attacks impossible. You cannot hack an IP device if IP does not exist. Vendors

8.23 RESHORING, OUTSOURCING ROBOSHORING AND MANUFACTURING

According to the International Labour Organisation Report in 2012, of the 3 billion workers globally more than 197 million people were without a job, or 6% of the world's workforce. In the US since the year 2000 when there were 17.3 million manufacturing jobs, this has decreased by 5.6 million to 11.7 million. The manufacturing sector accounts for 16% of the workforce in the US. The US manufacturing worker is now 38% more effective than 15 years ago, due to technology and robotics.

If we base the number of manufacturing jobs on the prediction that 50% of low skilled jobs will disappear due to robotics by 2024, that will mean a further loss of another five million US based manufacturing and outsourcing jobs. Globally this could have worse ramifications concerning global birth rates. Adding fuel to the fire by 2024 another billion people will be on earth…what will they do?

As conflicts will inevitably arise, then western countries will seek to bring outsource contracts back into secure hands given technology advances. In parallel, the need for technical off shoring and business process will start to collapse. This re-shoring effect will be exacerbated by continued flat growth in the western economies and declining growth in the eastern countries. As Robotica and Roboshoring take hold. This technology change will slow down outsourced demand by 20% per annum. The knock-on effect is that there will be a marked increase of around 750 million jobs lost by 2024 (compounding a billion skilled unemployed workers).

8.24 INTERNET COMMUNICATIONS

Lets look further into the Internet components and see how services get delivered.

8.25 IP ADDRESSES

An IP Address is a unique number assigned to your computer connection by your home or office or employer's Internet Service Provider (ISP).

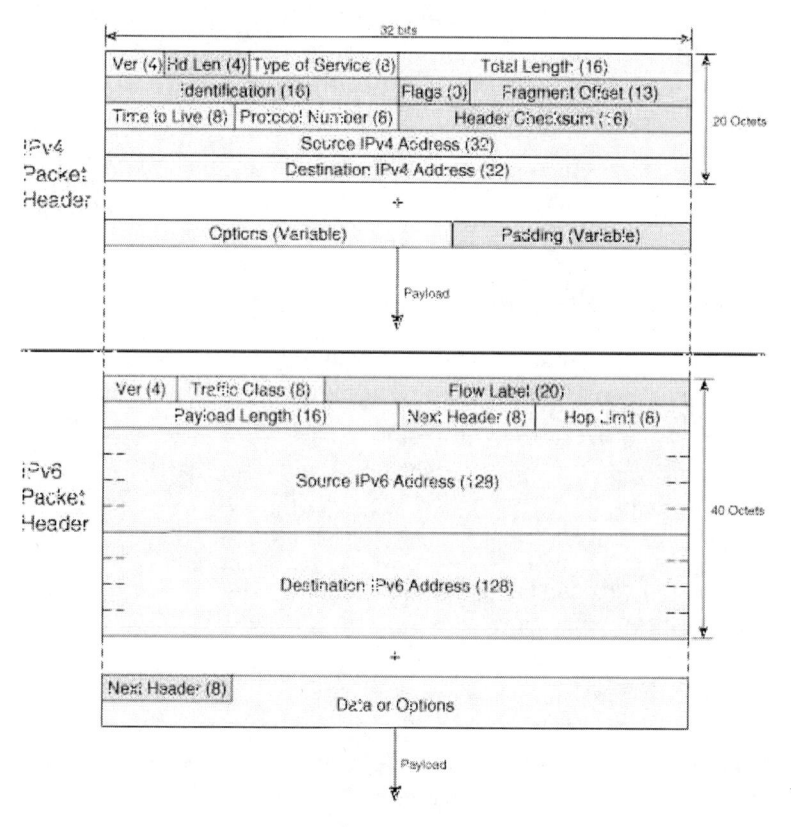

Figure 44 IP4 and IPv6 STACKS

This unique number serves as the ID of your connection when it's accessing the Internet. The way to regard these addresses is that they are like destination telephone numbers in a telephone directory. If you can remember the last time you used a telephone book you are older than you think! There are five classes of Internet addresses: the class indicates the size of the network and host fields. Internet addresses are commonly displayed in dotted decimal notation format: XXX.XXX.XXX.XXX.

The same process applies to your computer. Your IP address is used to route information from the Internet to your computer. IP addresses nowadays come in two flavours: IP v4 (version 4), which has 12 numbers, or IPv6 (you guessed, version 6), which has 128 numbers or letters.

In **IPv6**, the new (but not yet widely deployed) standard protocol for the Internet, addresses are 128 bits wide, which, even with generous assignment of net blocks, should suffice for the foreseeable future. In theory, there would be about 3.403×10^{38} unique host interface addresses. Apparently, if the earth were made entirely out of 1 cubic millimetre grains of sand, then you could give a unique address to each grain in 300 million planets the size of the earth. This large address space will be sparsely populated, which makes it possible to encode more routing information into the addresses themselves.

8.26 IPV6 ADDRESSING

Version 6 addresses are written as an eight 4-digit hexadecimal numbers separated by colons. For readability, addresses may be shortened in two ways. Within each colon-delimited section, leading zeroes may be truncated. Secondly, one string of zeroes (and only one) may be replaced with two colons (::). For example, the following addresses are equivalent:

- 1080:0000:0000:0000:0000:0034:0000:417A
- 1080:0:0:0:0:34:0:417A
- 1080::34:0:417A

Global unicast IPv6 addresses are constructed as two parts: a 64-bit routing part followed by a 64-bit host identifier.

Net blocks are specified as in the modern alternative for IPv4: network number, followed by a slash, and the number of relevant bits of the network number (in decimal). Example:

12AB::CD30:0:0:0:0/60 includes all addresses starting with 12AB00000000CD3.

IPv6 has many improvements over IPv4 other than just bigger address space, including auto-renumbering and mandatory support for IPSec.[122]

The zeros can be dropped to improve notation taking (like *2001:9652*), but they still exist. Everyone used IPv4 (but the allocation of these has just run out) and everyone should be on Version 6 by now. IPv6 is more secure (ahem ... clearing of throat) than v4. Most large organisations, governments and particularly the military, utilities, SCADA devices and mobile phones all still use IPv4. IPv6 is as safe as money in the bank vault (ah!) as it is highly unlikely that you will be able to recall 128 hexadecimal addresses from memory. A Personal Area Network DNS server may be needed.

8.27 GEOGRAPHIC IPV6

Rather than being 32 bit addresses, as with IPv4 (with 4,294,967,296 unique addresses), IPv6 addresses are 128 bit, creating many more addresses. The new system will generate trillions of trillions of addresses.

This means that every square metre in the world could have an address roughly 50 thousand trillion, trillion addresses without any problem. [123] Personally, I don't think this has gone far enough (I jest). It might have solved the number of addresses allocated but it could have been executed with a geographic-based (longitude and latitude) addition that would have solved a lot of forensic questions (i.e., what's the source of the packet so adversaries can be located and therefore liable for damage). Knowing the source and location of the packet's origination would have solved the legal requirement for tracing cyber-attacks (so someone could be blamed at least for Cybrid type campaigns).

8.28 ENUM

ENUM and inclusive Cost Metrics would simplify this IPv6 schema it would help secure the InternetNew. The biggest problem with the Internet is anonymity. Criminals, Child Abusers and Hackers hide behind fake names and addresses. This allows anyone to do as they see fit on the Internet. The concept that the Internet would be self-monitoring, self-policing and adheres to anarchistic principles is no longer and option. If ever you are on a trail of responses on a forum or Twitter there is always a ZBR[124] comment (or Twittertwat) that is shrouded in negativity, or some inane comment about cats. Governments want to introduce blanket Identity Management programmes, which although it would be nice to track these people is overkill and unlikely to be acceptable to existing and new subscribers. It's much easier to revive the Telephone Book! All people want to know is your name, address and telephone number and website.

BANDANA ACCOUNTS Ltd,
   10 Heighton Place, Lancs **0800 111 4225**
   www.banadanaaccounts.ltd.uk

Figure 45 EXAMPLE TELEPHONE DIRECTORY LISTING[125]

IP ENUM is a halfway house, restricting services being bought to a geolocated identity. This would eliminate Dark webs, because your service tag is part of a country ENUM registry and therefore adds legality to a subscriber's connection. Why should countries continue to adopt the Internet if it is to the detriment of their GDP and security? Why would you hand over bank accounts to your fridge monitored by commercial companies? It would make more sense to ease people into responsibility and accountability. IP-ENUM is like a subscribers calling card. ENUM has been around for about 15 years with some registrars adopting the protocol in an ad hoc manner. Telephone Directories still exist so entries would not need to change. The beauty of this is its easy to implement, a single server (OK two for resilience) is needed to manage the service.

Dialling via ENUM in a browser resolves the telephone number to the IP address. However, it's never really penetrated the mainstream because Governments want even more information, although now should be reviewed in light of cyber security demands. This is like an identity card that allows ISPs and Countries to track users to geographic location by session. This single entry point into the Internet allows for non repudiation techniques, we will discuss later how to make this deliver commercial, governmental and cyber security benefits.

ENUM Repudiation

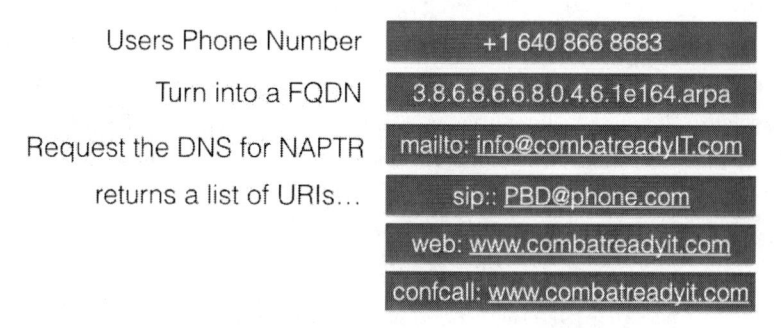

Users Phone Number	+1 640 866 8683
Turn into a FQDN	3.8.6.8.6.6.8.0.4.6.1e164.arpa
Request the DNS for NAPTR	mailto: info@combatreadyIT.com
returns a list of URIs…	sip:: PBD@phone.com
	web: www.combatreadyit.com
	confcall: www.combatreadyit.com

Figure 46 IP ENUM (PER SUBSCRIBER)

8.29 QUALITY OF SERVICE (QOS)

Like anything technical a high degree of quality is always needed. IPV6 brings quality of service that is required for several new applications such as IP telephony, video/audio, interactive games or e-commerce. Whereas IPv4 is a best-effort service, IPv6 ensures QoS, a set of service requirements (Type of Class replaces Type of Service) to deliver performance guarantee while transporting data traffic over the network.

For networking traffic, quality refers to latency (jitter) or available bandwidth to move the packet fast depending on the content (email slow vs video fast). In order to implement QoS marking, IPv6 provides a traffic-class field (8 bits) in the IPv6 header. It also has a 20-bit flow label.

When we look at the arguments for Net Neutrality the roots of this are based on the huge amount of bandwidth that Netflix takes up on the Internet. It is a stunningly popular service is cheap (@ $8 a month) the service is hosted in the Amazon cloud but it does not contribute to the infrastructure needed to carry 70% of the Internets traffic. This is called an Over The Top (OTT) application. The cable companies that have invested billions in cable infrastructure make no money on providing the service to customers. Effectively the cable companies cannot grow or support the demand for the Netflix service. It actually costs the cable companies several times the $8 a month to carry an £8 buck service. The thrust of the cable companies and major US carriers was that there was no way to continue funding free bandwidth to end users without charging for this stream. For instance if n Internet subscriber wanted Netflix then a surcharge of $50 would be made to provide fast downloads for video on demand. This surcharge would have allowed cable companies to continue to rollout cable infrastructure and broadband services. The surcharge would have been applied either to the subscriber or the supplier (in this case Netflix). Core routers need to run QOS (Quality of Service) protocols anyway to run VOIP. QOS is designed to overcome many latency problems associated with Internet Traffic engineering.

- QOS prioritises critical traffic over non-critical traffic (e.g. delivering Real Time Protocol for Voice or Video a higher priority than email or web traffic)

- The Internet is a Best Effort service (fire and forget). Packets may be dropped or discarded by routers in cases of congestion (VOIP conversation sounds like Chicken Talk)

- QOS is patchy …it exists in MPLS Core Routers, Leased Lines and LANS. Real Time Applications such as Netflix work reasonably well when there is sufficient bandwidth available. But during peak hours (Office Hours in the US) the quality of real time applications may be impaired by increased packet loss or delay. (Network Unreachable)

- QOS at Layer 3 can run Differentiated Services codePoint to provide a Type of Service on a per hop basis (PHB) or RSVP (IntServ Integrated Services) for Internet but relies on the fact that all routers in the link support RSVP.

8.30 MOBILE IPV6

This feature ensures transport layer connection survivability and allows a computer or a host to remain reachable regardless of its location in an IPv6 network and, in effect, ensures transport layer connection survivability.

With the help of Mobile IPv6, even though the mobile node changes locations and addresses, the existing connections through which the mobile node is communicating are maintained.

To accomplish this, connections to mobile nodes are made with a specific address that is always assigned to the mobile node, and through which the mobile node is always reachable. Summary of the benefits IPv6:

- Increased address space

- More efficient routing

- Reduced management requirement

- Improved methods to change ISP

- Better mobility support

- Multi-homing

- Security – Extension header type 51 provides integrity and authentication of end to end data

- Scoped address: link-local, site-local and global-address space

- Network-layer security – IPv6 implements network-layer encryption and authentication via IPSec this should make Man in The Middle attacks more difficult

- Stateless auto-reconfiguration of hosts. This feature allows IPv6 hosts to configure automatically when connected to a routed IPv6 network.

- Sequence numbers – prevents replay attacks – does not exceed 232 attempts

- Payload encryption

ENUM translates between PSTN telephone numbers, as specified by the ITU-T in E.164, and Internet Protocol (IP) addresses, as specified for IPv4 in RFC 791 and IPv6 in RFC 2460. ENUM requires that both E.164 and IP addresses be registered with the ENUM Domain Name Service (DNS), which can be consulted by gateways that interconnect the two disparate networks. Thereby, a given call can traverse both the PSTN and the Internet or other IP-based packet network.

8.31 IPSEC

IPSec is a framework of open standards (from IETF) that define policies for secure communication in a network. In addition, these standards also describe how to enforce these policies.

Using IPSec, participating peers (computers or machines) can achieve data confidentiality, data integrity, and data authentication at the network layer (i.e., Layer 3 of the Open Systems Interconnection seven-layer networking model). RFC 2401 specifies the base architecture for IPSec compliant systems.

The main purpose of IPSec is to provide interoperable, high quality, cryptographically based security for IPv4 and IPv6. It offers various security services at the IP layer and therefore, offers protection at this (i.e., IP) and higher layers. These security services are, for example, access control, connectionless integrity, data origin authentication, protection against replays (a form of partial sequence integrity), confidentiality (encryption), and limited traffic flow confidentiality. It does not support QOS in IPSec and Dynamic IP Addresses causes IPSec to fail!

IPSec supports:

- Data Encryption Standard (DES) 56-bit and Triple DES (3DES) 168-bit symmetric key encryption algorithms in IPSec client software.

- Certificate authorities and Internet Key Exchange (IKE) negotiation. IKE is defined in RFC 2409.

- Encryption that can be deployed in standalone environments between clients, routers, and firewalls

- Environments where it's used in conjunction with L2TP tunnelling

From usage point of view, there are three main advantages of IPSec:

- Supported on various operating system platforms

- Right VPN solution, if you want true data confidentiality for your networks. Check with your security company that the VPN you select has not had a history of credential leakage!

- Open standard, so interoperability between different devices is easy to implement

9.31.1.1 IPSEC TECHY STUFF

IPSec has two different modes: transport mode (host-to-host) and tunnel mode (gateway-to-gateway or gateway-to-host). In transport mode, the payload is encapsulated (header is left intact) and the end-host (to which the IP packet is addressed) unwraps the packet. In the tunnel mode, the IP packet is entirely encapsulated (with a new header). The host (or gateway), specified in the new IP header, unencapsulates the packet. In tunnel mode there is no need for client software to run on the gateway and the communication between client systems and gateways are not protected.

IPSec standard supports additional features:
- AH (Authentication Header) that provides authenticity guarantee for transported packets. Check-summing the packages using a cryptographic algorithm does this.

- ESP (Encapsulating Security Payload) that provides encryption of packets.

- IPcomp (IP payload compression) that provides compression before a packet is encrypted.

- IKE (Internet Key Exchange) provides the (optional) means to negotiate keys in secrecy.

It also provides the following components:
- Security Policy Database (SPD) this manages security policy (SP) and selector that correlates SP with actual data traffic.

- Security Association Database (SAD) it contains Security Association (SA), parameters necessary for expressing IPSec connections and applying IPSec.

- IPSec traditionally implements secure remote access connections using virtual private network (VPN) tunnelling protocols such as Layer 2 Tunnelling Protocol (L2TP). Note that IPSec is not really a VPN mechanism. In fact, the use of IPSec is changing in the last few years, since IPSec is moving from the WAN into the LAN to secure internal network traffic against eavesdropping and modification.

- When two computers (peers) want to communicate using IPSec, they mutually authenticate with each other first, and then negotiate how to encrypt and digitally sign traffic they exchange. These IPSec communication sessions are called Security Associations (SAs).

IPSec in IPv6 and why it's important
IPSec is a mandatory component for IPv6, and therefore, the IPSec security model is required to be supported for all IPv6 implementations in near future. In IPv6, IPSec is implemented using the Authentication Header and the ESP extension header. Since at the present moment, IPv4 IPSec is available in nearly all client and server OS platforms, the IPSec IPv6 advanced security can be deployed by IT administrators immediately, without changing applications or networks. The importance of IPSec in IPv6 has grown in recent years as US Department of Defence and federal government have mandates to buy IPv6-capable systems and to transition to IPv6-capable networks within a few years.[126]

8.31.1.2 MILITARY IPV6

The major benefits to be derived from IPv6 are the much larger address space solution it offers, improved routing system, enhanced security (IPSec support is mandatory for all IPv6 compliant devices), and Quality of Service (QoS). New devices being constantly added to the communications arsenal of the military, their interoperability is an imperative aspect. In wartime, there is a visible proliferation of new facilities, personnel, and capabilities all of which have to get quickly connected with the rest of the enterprise. In addition to all these, there is improved support for mobile IP and mobile computing devices, with a much reduced administration need, on an IPv6 platform.

IPv6 makes it possible to implement new NCW (Network-Centric Warfare) concepts and guidelines, and also allows for advanced networking capabilities. The task of implementing IPv6 into a military network is an onerous one, in that due care will have to be taken to ensure that the existing communications capability is by no means affected or impeded in the endeavour to develop a future capability. Secondly, the IPv6 network performance must be equivalent to or better than the existing IPv4 network; the existing capability with regard to auto-configuration, prioritisation, converged voice and video, multicast, mobility and high-speed performance capabilities on the army IPv4 networks is already of a high order. The challenge however, lies in the fact that while most IPv4 vendors are beginning to support IPv6 in the existing devices that run IPv4 networks, the equivalent features and capabilities of IPv6 are years behind IPv4. Vendors are consequently keen to build new IPv4 capabilities rather than to work on improving IPv6 services.

8.31.1.3 IPV6 BUGS

Like everything that's related to the Internet there are bugs. Bugs exist in Network Interface Cards, TCP/UDP and network software libraries. IPv6 security products cannot be expected to be as robust as their IPv4 ancestors. 90% of web filtering tools and business still relies on blacklists. Once the world has finally migrated to IPv6, criminals will rotate IP addresses quickly so nullifying blacklists effectiveness. This is why we need a resolver directory to assign multiple IPv6 addresses to a single geographically based owner. Firewalls will need to operate according to IP stack. Companies that rely on IPv4 (Network Address Translation) NAT will need to migrate each connecting device to IPv6. As NAT is no longer used the IPv6 now exposes the internal network infrastructure! The upshot of all this is that the SMB will be exposed to network attacks more than they are today. Botnet Command and Control systems have already migrated.

8.31.1.4 INTERNET OF THINGS (V6)

To make our lives even more complex and difficult to protect, the IOT swathe of products is now hitting the supermarket shelves. The most popular languages used for IOT are Good old C and C++, Python, Rust that is highly ro*b*ust, and Raspberry Pi (an OS on a chip) due to its lightweight modular composition. Rust seems to be the most popular. The market potential for SMBs wishing to enter this market is lucrative. It is estimated that in 15 years most subscribers will have 100 IOT devices monitoring every part of their digital life. In 30 years time this is expected to boom to 1000 devices per household.

IPv6 has further benefits that the Internet of Things can exploit. IoT6 is a three-year FP7 European Group research project on the future Internet of Things. The EU seems to be ahead of the Americas in architecture definition.

It aims at exploiting the potential of IPv6 and related standards.[127] In particular high focus is being placed upon Smart Cities projects. European and Chinese cities are deploying IOT in new construction projects; to control energy real time energy needs, enable person-to-person communication and electrical appliance collaboration. These are early stage developments providing 32 unique IOT v6 addresses to each household.

6LoWPAN – Low power WPANs are characterised by small packet sizes, support for addresses with different lengths, low bandwidth, star and mesh topologies, battery supplied devices, low cost, large number of devices, unknown node positions, high unreliability, and long idle periods during when communications interfaces are turned off to save energy.

RPL – Routing Protocol for low power and Lossy Networks (LLNs). RPL can support a wide variety of different link layers, including ones that are constrained, potentially lossy, or typically utilised in conjunction with host or router devices with very limited resources, as in building/home automation, industrial environments, and urban applications. It is able to build up network routes, to distribute routing knowledge among nodes, and to adapt the topology in a very efficient way.

CORE – Constrained RESTful Environments and COAP (Constrained Application Protocol) – which easily translates to HTTP for integration with the Web, while meeting specialised requirements, such as multicast support, very low overhead, and simplicity for constrained environments to overcome current shortcomings and fragmentation of the Internet of Things. Its main challenges and objectives are to research, design and develop a highly scalable IPv6-based Service-Oriented Architecture to achieve interoperability, mobility, Cloud computing integration and intelligence distribution among heterogeneous smart things components, applications and services. Its potential will be researched by exploring innovative forms of interactions such as:[128]

- Information and "intelligence" distributed method.
- Multi-protocol interoperability with heterogeneous devices
- Device mobility and mobile phone networks integration
- Cloud computing integration with Software as a Service (SaaS).

- IPv6 - Smart Things Information Services (STIS) innovative interactions

8.32 CLOUD

If the Cloud were totally safe it would be brilliant — but no system is safe and therefore not entirely dependable. As it's not fully robust, the desire of many CIOs is to make this 'somebody else's problem as a service' or seen as an easy alternative to the humdrum of IT. Although it can speed infrastructure development, (speedier under DEVOPS), it skews security controls without proper checks and balances. As we will see later in the Combat Ready Model it is supplemented with a hybrid Cloud that stages data and ensures encrypted data remains close to hand, together with the appropriate checks and balances around it as a complete solution.

Milind Govekar, Managing Vice President at Gartner, shares the benefits and challenges of hybrid cloud computing and examined its critical success factor. Overall, hybrid cloud computing extends the benefits (that an SMB can realise and) that can be gained from cloud computing:

- **Internal private cloud computing helps to maximise asset utilisation.** Hybrid cloud computing maximises this value by balancing the use of internal assets and external services while enabling better scalability.

- **Cloud computing can help with cost-efficiency.** Hybrid cloud computing can maximise cost-efficiency, particularly CAPEX, through competition and automated arbitrage.

- **Private cloud computing ensures isolation.** Hybrid cloud computing enables an enterprise to balance isolation, cost and scaling requirements.

- **Cloud computing can enable high availability and resiliency.** Hybrid cloud computing can improve resiliency and disaster recovery by using multiple providers.

- **Cloud computing can introduce new functionality quickly.** Hybrid cloud computing makes it easier to introduce new functionality quickly and more flexibly.

- **Cloud computing ensures a low barrier to entry.** Hybrid cloud computing can help an SMB build a controllable exit strategy.

- *Addition:* **Cloud Computing can help stabilise a security posture.** Hybrid Clouds can place customer facing services in the cloud while hardening applications on the Hybrid estate.

SMBs and LOBs cannot develop hybrid cloud services without first implementing a private cloud. This allows growth and NEWS (North, East, West South) scale. The ability to grow and shrink the IT estate with business demand is attractive. It has a low CAPEX point of entry and the OPEX is on a par with SMBs compute estates. The Cloud can therefore look cheap but this is short sighted. Security of applications should be tested before release. Many SMBs struggle to implement private clouds and to demonstrate their value because this requires a shift in how IT is delivered, one that involves changes to Knowledge, Individuals, Workflows and Innovation (the KIWI approach).

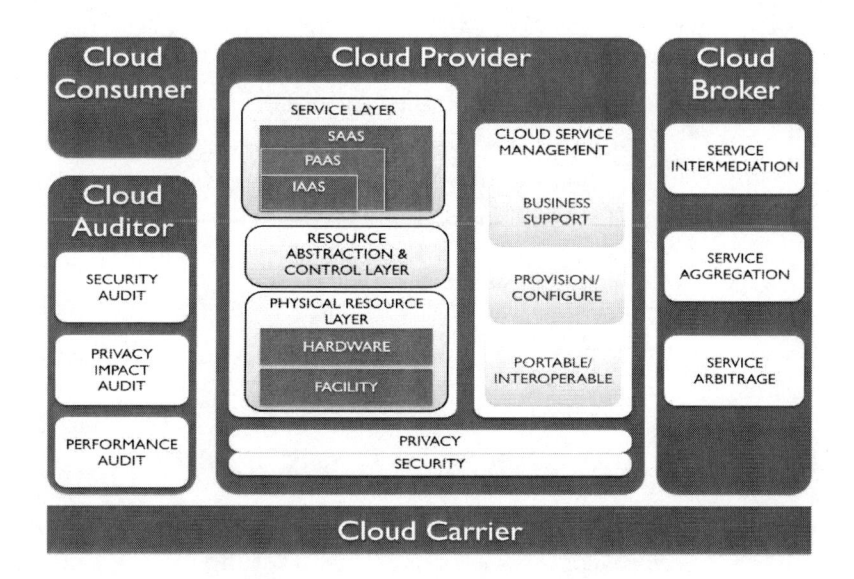

Figure 47 NIST CLOUD COMPUTING STANDARD

Many lines of business buy external cloud services without the initial involvement of, or oversight from, Technology Value Centres leaders: this has an industry tag of **Shadow IT**. To implement hybrid cloud services successfully, CIOs need to introduce an internal cloud services brokerage (CSB) role responsible for the governance, demand management and delivery of cloud services. Those CIOs who do not think and act like an external service provider or evolve into a CSB role will gradually lose the trust of business managers, who will circumvent the TVC organisation to access the IT services they need defined and delivered speedily. **Speed** means high **Cost** over time and low **Quality** (if you think of the triangle). If Quality is low then so is security!

Hybrid clouds also need Cloud Management Platforms (CMPs). SMBs and LOBs buy CMPs to manage and govern the delivery of private cloud services alongside public cloud services. CMPs improve the speed at which services are delivered by enabling self-service requests and automated delivery; they also reduce the overall cost of service delivery. Ensuring consistency of the Hybrid CMP and the Public Cloud CMP delivers incredible cost savings and security. An example of this is the VM Ware Air product, which allows moving VMs between the Public Cloud and the on premises data centre.

There are about 1000 cloud service providers globally. Although adoption rates are staggering the leading supplier (Amazon AWS) manages hundreds of thousands of Virtual Servers in 52 globally based data centres, it has still experienced 7 days of downtime in the last 3 years affecting thousands of SMB users. The SMBs did not appear to complain. Very few companies applied for compensation through class actions. Irrespective of the downtime Cloud growth has been significant since 2012:

- Instances of Amazons Cloud service grew 60% amongst FG500 Companies

- MS Office 365 service is growing at 25% per Qtr. in the US and 50% per Qtr. in the UK[129]

On the flip side of the coin Mckinseys see a 25% slowdown in adoption due to cyber security concerns. Clouds are just blades and bunches of disks its not rocket science but it is numbers science. I have designed and run

Cloud-based data centres in remote locations in the wilds of North America. These were modular-based builds. Taking advantage of the coolness of climate, the modular concept allowed for cheaper expansion. During the mid 1990s and with the advent of faster data bandwidth afforded by the spread of national fibre optic bandwidth, the notion that a company could access data from a remote data centre became viable. As vendors and Managed Service Providers (MSPs) realised this, they spurred on the era of Application Service Providers (ASPs). The uptake of these services was limited to storage and co-location, as many enterprises and governments were loath to part with their infrastructure and data. In the last 10 years, the creation of Cloud-based APIs was spurred on by services such as Amazon's pioneer EC platform (Elastic Compute) allowed companies to create servers on the fly and store ad hoc data on a Pay As You Go basis. Companies in an Industrial Estate can create a Community Cloud sharing and leveraging shared infrastructure. Countries can have a Dominion Cloud, which can be run within territorial boundaries or share Clouds with neighbouring countries in what I call Extra Dominion Clouds that can service regional languages and cultures.

8.33 EVERY MARKETING IDEA AS A SERVICE

Since 'xxx As A Service' applications cannot access a company's internal systems (databases or internal services) Cloud Service Providers (CSPs) predominantly offer integration protocols and application programming interfaces (APIs). These protocols are based on the worklows found in the HTTP languages that operate over a wide area network. Typically, these are protocols based on HTTP, REST (GET/PUT/POST/DELETE), SOAP and JSON. The APIs are familiar to most developers of SIP and HTML5. Web 3.0 promises a new "semantic" web where machines and devices can search metadata in a meaningful way.

The ubiquity of SaaS applications and other Internet services and the standardisation of their API technology has spawned development of mashups, which are lightweight applications that combine data, presentation and functionality from multiple services and across multiple platforms, creating a compound service. Mashups further differentiate SaaS applications from on-premises software, as the latter cannot be easily integrated outside a company's firewall.

For SMBs the following "Services As a Service" are currently explained:

8.23.1.1 INFRASTRUCTURE AS A SERVICE (IAAS)

- The Cloud provider manages and delivers the underlying infrastructure, including storage, network and computing resources.

- You are able to deploy, run and control software, which may include operating systems, and applications, with possibly limited control of select networking components (i.e. firewalls, or, web servers).

This integrates with the Private Cloud on a company premises. It allows companies to expand infrastructure off premises.

8.33.1.2 PLATFORM AS A SERVICE (PAAS):

- The Cloud provider manages and delivers programming languages, frameworks, libraries, services and tools for you to create and deploy applications.

- The service provider also manages and controls the infrastructure, including network, servers, operating systems and storage.

- You have control over the deployed applications and configuration settings for the application-hosting environment.

Agile project teams to scale up and test custom applications can use this service. Applications may be tested on or off premises. Off premises tests should use dummy client details in databases (cleansed and anonymous). In production only partial sets of data should be used to minimise data breach value.

8.33.1.3 SOFTWARE AS A SERVICE (SAAS):

- The Cloud provider manages and controls the underlying Cloud infrastructure, operating systems, application platform and even individual application capabilities, with the possible exception of limited user-specific configuration.

- An SMB has the ability to use the vendor's applications running on a Cloud infrastructure.

- The applications are accessible from various client devices through either a Web browser or an application-programming interface (API).

- Salesforce was the first of these Cloud Based SAAS applications.

- 21% of software used today is SAAS but 70% is purchased by a Business Unit

Data is retained and managed by the SAAS provider. Always check clauses in the SAAS providers Terms and Conditions if the site claims that any data that uses the service and Intellectual Property belongs to the SAAS provider! This is a cut and paste clause invented by a lawyer somewhere and needs to be redacted. Also controls on how the hard earned data is collected is used, accessed, backed up, secured, and located or copied needs to be part of a bespoke contract between the SMB, the Cloud Service Provider and the Software As A Service provider. For instance is the data made available to other companies or agencies for Big Data searches and queries? Is it backed up outside country boundaries? Is the data encrypted and do you retain the key?

8.33.1.4 IDENTITY AS A SERVICE (IDAAS)

- Identity as a Service (IDaaS) is an authentication infrastructure that is built, hosted and managed by a third-party service provider. IDaaS can be thought of as single sign-on (SSO) for the Cloud.

- An IDaaS for the enterprise is typically purchased as a subscription-based managed service. A Cloud service provider may also host applications for a fee and provide subscribers with role-based access to specific applications or even entire virtualized desktops through a secure portal.

Identities could be Cloud based, but only if stringent Data Protection and Data Privacy guarantees are provided by the CSP (example Google) and the commercial company running the ID service (example Facebook). At the moment there is no Security Standard or regulator that has asset of standards to manage this service. Service Level Agreements must be underpinned through monetary fines for downtime (how long can you survive without your email logon?). Should the CSP or ID Service provider succumb to a data breach then costs incurred by the loss of Identity and all other associated costs should be bourn by the CSP and ID Provider. Identity Theft in this area will increase exponentially as services Credit Card credentials are managed on mobiles and subsequently the Cloud. The IDAAS relies on APIs that connect to other ID Providers such as banks and government bodies. These data streams are easy pickings to adversaries. The APIs could be used by Insiders to manipulate and extend subscribers credentials into other ID Providers. (Note: I am starting to think like an adversary now!). So it would be useful to ensure some legal encryption tag around each API service. The APIs need to be opted into by a user employing three steps Authentication (Like Lock Out Tag Out systems). If SMBs use this service for Administrative controls then consider separation (or dual suppliers) for Privileged Access. Controls around ID encryption should be monitored. The CSP and ID Provider should provide clear rules around their internal security practices and not just ISO 27000. Clear definitions and procedures must be proven around destruction of a subscriber's data. So far no provider has given clear guidance on that provision.

8.33.1.5 STORAGE AS A SERVICE (STAAS) - VSTORAGE

The economy of scale in the service provider's infrastructure theoretically allows them to provide storage much more cost effectively than most individuals or corporations can provide their own storage, when total cost of ownership is considered. Beware bandwidth charges, these can escalate quickly based on the volume uploads and downloads which can make the service un-commercial over time. Ensure that the CSP does not charge you for moving your data to another CSP. I have seen a 6-month fee applied to these and similar requests.

- Storage as a Service is often used to solve offsite backup challenges (Space and Disaster Recovery) or extend SANs

- A large amount of network bandwidth is required to move their storage utilising an Internet-based service.

Ensure any data that leaves a SMB premises and stored in a CSP estate is encrypted. The key should be under the SMB management and not copied to data in the Cloud!! Access to storage should have access logs (by user access times) and are checked and alerted in real time. Should data exceed a remote download of XX GB then an alarms should be raised and the service taken offline. (We are trying to avoid a Black Minute here).

8.33.1.6 DESKTOP AS A SERVICE (DTAAS)

Desktop As A Service has been covered earlier in the Storage section. Just to add here that a complete desktop and laptop and tablet image can be managed and run from the cloud.

8.33.1.7 DATA AS A SERVICE (DAAS)

Think of the DaaS model as a new method for accessing data within existing data centres. It often needs new architecture designs, like private Clouds inside a public Cloud. Data is usually located in relational databases inside corporate data centres. Typical business applications include customer relationship management (CRM), enterprise resource planning (ERP), and e-commerce and supply chain systems.

The DaaS approach delivers the following benefits:

- Agility: Because data is easily accessible, customers can take immediate action and do not require in-depth understanding of actual data.

- Affordability: Providers can construct a foundation and outsource the presentation layer, which helps build highly affordable user interfaces and allows more feasible presentation layer change requests.

- Data quality: Data accessibility is controlled through data services, which improves data quality, as there is a single update point.

8.33.1.8 SOFTWARE AS A SERVICE BUSINESS INTELLIGENCE (SAASBI)

A Business Intelligence (BI) delivery model in which applications are implemented outside of a company and usually employed at a hosted location accessed by an end user via protected Internet access. SaaS BI provides a pay-as-you-go or subscription model, versus the conventional software-licensing model with annual maintenance or license fees that may be tied to device, application or names. SaaSBI is also known as Cloud BI or on-demand BI. This allows for data from various sources to be analysed using the compute power of the Cloud. Results from these light queries (NoSQL queries for example) are extremely valuable to hackers. Outputs and results should be closely associated with an individual and not as a shared key within a team.

8.33.1.9 BIG DATA AS A SERVICE (BDAAS)

This allows for huge databases from multiple databases to be "virtually" linked together and queried. This is called a Big Data search. It uses a language called Hadoop and Spark (both from Apache) that can run and query massive databases to find an answer. For instance, you can run a query like how many lettuces were eaten in Romania yesterday, what is the worlds favourite pastime, what's the spread of diabetes look like, how many men does it take to change a light bulb etc., Hadoop is a fantastic tool and patterns of human behaviours can be predicted. The big question here is how this data becomes readily available and where is it stored?

Termed "Bad Ass" (as the acronym hints at) by some database administrators, this is also known as HAAS (Hadoop As A Service) this is the delivery of statistical analysis tools or information by an outside provider that helps organisations understand and use insights gained from large information sets to gain a competitive advantage. Apache Hadoop is open source and Java based, it is not an acronym but named after a yellow toy elephant belonging to the son of Doug Cutting (Chief Architect at Cloudera).

Given the immense amount of unstructured data generated on a regular basis, Big Data as a service is intended to free up organisational resources by taking advantage of the predictive analytics skills of an outside provider to manage and assess large data sets, rather than hiring in-house team members for those functions. Big Data as a service can take the form of software that assists with data processing or a contract for the services of a team of data scientists.

BDaaS is a form of managed services that can run batch or real time Hadoop Queries. Big Data as a service often relies upon Cloud storage to preserve continual data access for the organisation that owns the information as well as the provider working with it. Controls around supplying large volumes of data and whether the data is destroyed and the proof of destruction should be provided. Obviously data is transitory and provided by an SMB on an ad hoc basis so should not be subject to snapshots, replicated or stored at other CSP sites (or anyone else for that matter). The trickiest area here is addressing encrypted databases. Queries cannot run on encrypted databases so a process of de keying the database and loading a copy into the Cloud leaves an SMB exposed.

8.33.1.10 VSECURITY AS A SERVICE (SECAAS)

SECaaS is a managed service in which a large service provider integrates their security services into a corporate infrastructure on a subscription basis, more cost-effectively than most individuals, governments or enterprises can provide in isolation.

In this scenario, security is delivered as a service from the Cloud, without requiring on-premises hardware, avoiding substantial capital outlays. OPEX charges may also be expensive but necessary on a temporary basis; a cost benefit analysis is needed and exhaustive. Extreme SLA, Availability, Data Breach, Incident Response and extraordinary Data Breach expenses need tight contract wording. Check with your cyber insurance provider the risk coverage and increase in premiums. These security services often include authentication, anti-virus, anti-malware/spyware, intrusion detection, and shared security alarm management platforms (SIAM), forensics et al.

Security as a Service offers a number of benefits, including:

- Constant virus definition updates that are not reliant on user compliance.

- Greater security expertise than is typically available within an organisation.

- Speedier end user provisioning (sometimes).

- Outsourcing of administrative tasks, such as log management, to save time and money and allow an organisation to devote more time to its core competencies/inadequacy. It will add latency to detecting cascading alarms.

- A Web interface that allows in-house administration of some tasks as well as a view of the security environment and on-going activities.

If you are an SMB with a TVC team of fewer than ten FTEs (Full Time Employees) this option may make sense until you can establish your own team. Consider the implications of CSP supplier lock in and the cost of migrating the service away and the ability to stagger payments from a monthly to quarterly basis to smooth cash flow. There is no guarantee that this type of service is the right fit. Do due diligence on the CSP and guarantees provided by outsourced operators (transparency of background checks) and limitations on liabilities. An exit strategy is needed and agreed between both parties describing and costing and project plan for service wind down.

8.33.1.11 COMMUNICATIONS AS A SERVICE (CAAS)

VOIP (VAAS) and Unified Communications (UCAAS) can be hosted in the Public Cloud or managed on premise by a Service Provider. Moving your PABX or iPBX to a cloud estate can be beneficial. If you are moving to IPv6 then t selecting a provider with an off premise solution that does not expose your internal infrastructure may be beneficial. Check that Voice and Video Conferencing (Telepresence), Voice Recording features still integrate with your estate. Providers seem to specialise at the moment except for: Microsoft Lync, Cisco's Hosted Call Manager. LiteCloud, XO, VOIP4 Cloud, SecTelco, TitanVOIP, Kryptotel, SecurVox, Versaphon, Secumobi, and Discretio all provide secure VOIP service.

8.33.1.12 MOBILITY AS A SERVICE (MAAS)

Acronym confusion time: possibly due to great minds thinking alike? Not to be confused with Metal As A Service from Ubuntu or Marketing As A Service that is available from MAASPros.com, but Mobile Management (termed by some as Enterprise Mobility Management- EMM). Enterprise mobility management (EMM) platforms help SMBs integrate mobile devices into their security frameworks. It allows SMBs to consume mobile devices, software applications and services as per device, per month fee. SMBs can use EMM tools to perform the following functions for their users:

- Control of BYOD: Contractors can supply their own devices and run MAAS as an IP VPN feature.

- Provisioning: EMM suites configure devices (Smartphones and Tablets) and applications for SMB use.

- Encrypt Information and Email: EMM suites apply technologies to encrypt data, control data flow and remotely revoke user access to mobile applications and information in the event the user or device becomes untrusted (for example, through device loss, unauthorized reconfiguration or employee termination).

- Auditing, tracking and reporting: These products audit mobile devices and applications to track compliance with security policies. They also maintain inventory for cost and asset management purposes and are capable of tracking usage of services and apps.

- Support: EMM suites help TVCs troubleshoot mobile device problems through inventory, analytics and invoking remote actions

MAAS Providers include: IBM, Microsoft, Sophos, Soti, Airwatch (by VMware and Zimbra Email client), MobileIron, Good Technology, and Blackberry.

8.34 CLOUD PRODUCTS AND BRANDS

8.34.1.1 APPLICATIONS

Examples of SAAS include: ContactOffice, Google Apps for Work Drive, HP Converged Cloud, ownCloud, Microsoft Online (Office 365) Azure based, Salesforce.com. Cloud based Finance and ERP packages are especially beneficial for an SMB to rent.

8.34.1.2 PLATFORMS

Amazon EC3, App Engine, GreenQloud, AppScale, Microsoft Azure, Engine Yard, eXo Platform, OutSystems, Force, Heroku, InkTank, Orange Scape, RightScale, Cloud Foundry, Mendip, OpenShift, Elastic, OpenQRM, VMWare vCloud Air and many others

8.34.1.3 INFRASTRUCTURE

Amazon EC2, Abiquo Enterprise Edition, Cloudstack, EMC ATMOS, Eucalyptus, Fujitsu, GoGrid, Luna Cloud, Google Storage, Green Button, GreenQCloud, IBM Cloud Computing, Iland, Joyent, Nimbula, Nimbus, Open Nebula, OpenStack, Orion VM, Backspace Cloud, Zadara Storage, libvirt, libguestfs, OVirt, Virtual Machine Manager, Wakame-vdc, Virtual Private Cloud onDemand.

The wide range of Apps, Platforms and Infrastructure grow daily. SMBs should consider the benefits and drawbacks of Cloud based services. What if your major client did not pay you for several months your cash flow would be shot! Your reserves would be needed just to pay a CSP monthly. They can delete your data for non-payment or withhold service that will force trading to stop.

8.34.1.4 VOICE OVER IP AND SIP

Do you remember the days when a US to UK transatlantic call cost $10 a minute and you had to get connected through an International Operator? The absurdity of the idea of calling the world for free changed when I was designed and developed Voice over X25 networks.

I worked with Cisco developers to deploy the first ever-European wide Voice Over IP network. I also ran the first VOIP test over mobile 3G networks and designed a global Peer-to-Peer VOIP network. I connected old Strowger exchanges in Africa to London over Satellite (E & M Signalling over TCP Sliding Windows for the technocrats out there). Now people can call the world for nothing. When the Internet came into being a Voice packet was hampered by H323, by chance I met Henning Schulzrinne who invented RTP and RTSP he identified the number of ACK NAKS as the problem. Henning Schulzrinne and Mark Handley developed SIP in 1996. The Session Initiation Protocol is ubiquitous nowadays. Most of the Internets VOIP traffic utilises SIP as the preferred Signalling Communications Protocol. Examples of this are Skype (now Microsoft), FaceTime (used by Apple on iPhone, iPAD etc.), and WhatsApp - popular on Android and now owned by Facebook.

8.34.1.5 CLOUD SERVICES ORCHESTRATION

With all these cloud services managing on the Public Cloud available to SMBs how are they tied into the business needs of the company? To manage all the multiple service strands Cloud Orchestration Software is required. Orchestration vendors include Eucalyptus, Flexiant and VMware Realise as examples. These automation products manage all the interlocks between Public Cloud and On-premises (Hybrid) interconnections. This coordinates business service requirements with templates, and glueprints, configurations and patterns (craftflows), and server runtimes. The technical leaps made in the Orchestration arena have resulted in the ability to change, scale and transform the TVC organisation.

Although we are looking at this in depth later in the book its useful for the reader to be aware that the technology is changing rapidly and the organisation has to change as well. IT Shops can remain in silos, vendor handcuffs, blinkered to business needs, resistant to change, rely on broken processes, remain obstinately reactive in break/fix mode around a disjointed infrastructure and generally languish in a downward spiral of mental and technical in fecundity.

A new generation of Millennial's is expecting more, What if the TVC could provide a progressive environment to meet their demanding expectations? Establish the TVC as Millennial centric? Enable tools, agility and automation, able to meet and exceed delivery have time for Innovation. Become self-determined, self-coding and responsible. Above all collaborate.

8.35 STEPCHECK

- We have covered the basics - how end user devices (PC, Laptop, Mobile, Tablet) works

- Reviewed the building blocks of the Internet; routers, switches, blade servers and storage infrastructures

- A Resilient Building Infrastructure has been described

- We have encountered Applications and Robotica, SCADA and ICS systems

- The various Cloud Services have been described

- We have looked at Wi-Fi and VOIP

- The latest IPV6 innovations and impact on the Internet of Things

- Lets learn if we can pull these components together to make a service?

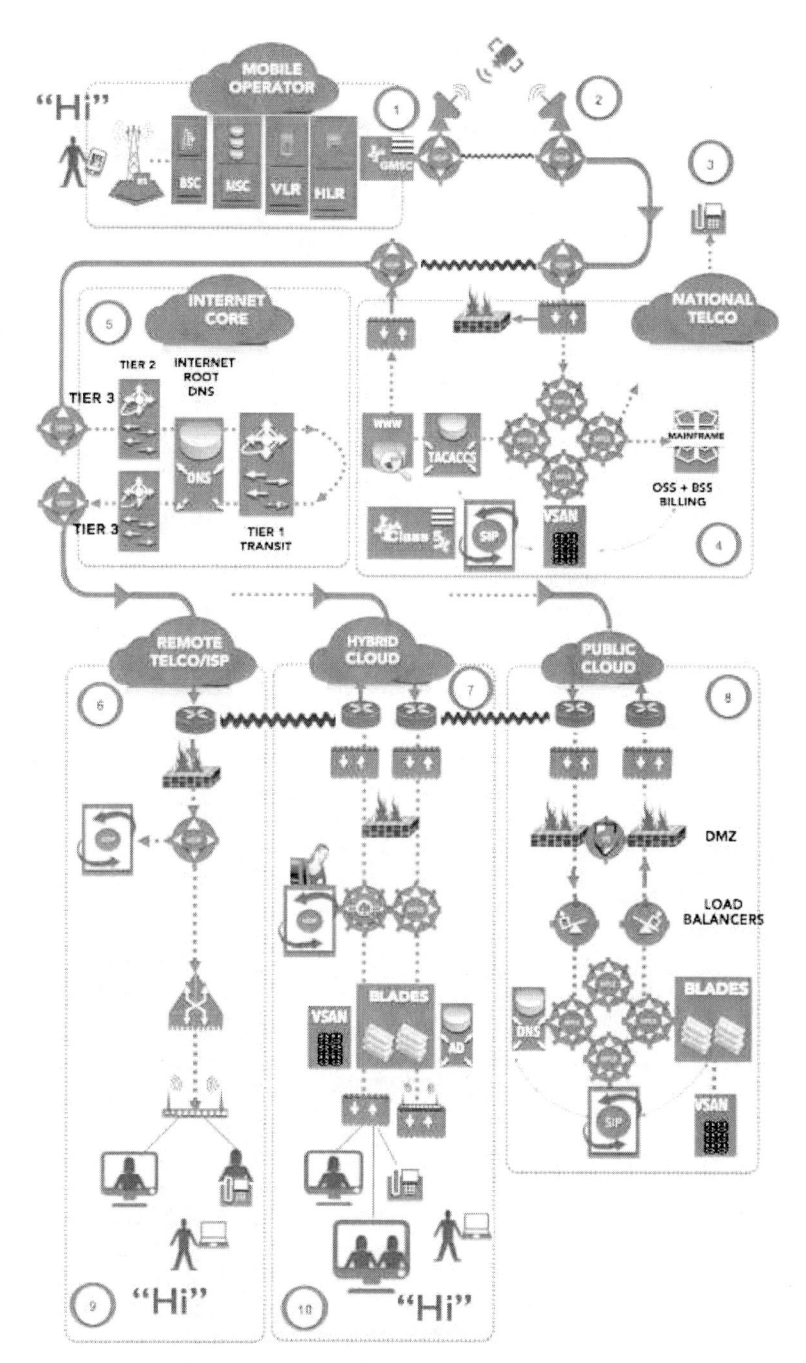

Figure 48 HOW Hi GETS THROUGH THE INTERNET

9 VOIP HOW 'HI' TRAVELS THE INTERNET

It's useful to understand how the Internet allows a packet (IP4 or IP6) through the Internet. As an example of how this happens let's follow a simple greeting "Hi" through the Internet:

9.1.1.1 MOBILE CALL

The caller in the top left of the diagram places a mobile call to two more people (one home-based and people and video conference in the office). Thanks to Alexander Graham Bell we (should) all know that analogue sound waves are converted into electrical signals, a series of binary 0s and 1s. These look like this '01001000 01001001 00001010' [130] which is 'H' and 'I' combined in binary format. We need to stuff these 24 x '0's and '1's into an IP Packet Datagram. Only a single IP Packet is required as there are on 24 Bits that need transporting. A QOS (Quality of Service) and Type of Service (TOS) bits are switched on to indicate to routers that read the packet header it is carrying a VOIP payload. The routers see the QOS and TOS switches are on and look ahead to the next known router to see if the packet can be sent or queued or rejected. These are wrapped up by the voice codec chip (and compared to the language sampling libraries) in the phone and placed into a stream of TCP/IP packets that carries the sender's IP and Mobile telephone number and the destination IP address and mobile telephone numbers of colleagues dwelling in the bottom of the picture (one on a home broadband and the other in an SMB office).

The first leg of the call traverses the Mobile Operators Network (this can be over GSM/4G/5G or even Wi-Fi). To dial a number by name or e-mail address it would probably require an application to be started such as a SIP (Session Initiation Protocol) call to be kicked off on the mobile. The SIP-based application initiates the call and livens up software voice codecs on the phone. The "HI" sounds waves are converted to digital.

The mobile phone user is in a mobile phone cellular network represented by the hexagon with a base station antennae. These are logical hexagons used to track the mobile phone location between mobile phone masts to hand off the signal and the data stream between BTS (Base station Transceiver Stations). These use location-based triangulation to enable roaming calls. A hexagon covers around 10,000 people's calls and the antennas you see on the tops of poles on buildings use orthogonal algorithms to handle thousands of calls per second. The speed of handling got faster, hence GSM, 3G and 4G (Generations) are able to handle voice calls as well as long data streams like Internet browsing sessions. Inside the BTS is a Base Station Controller (BSC) the network element, which provides all the control functions and physical links between the MSC (Mobile Service Centre) and BTS. The BSC provides functions such as handover from one hexagon to another, cell configuration data, and control of radio frequency (RF) power levels in Base Transceiver Stations. The HLR (Home Location Register) manages the handoffs between cells and passes the IP packet to the GMSC, which is similar to a Class 5 Exchanges switch. Designers use capacity and call handling Erlang C calculations to provide sufficient bandwidth across masts and the wide area national or international communication links. In the mobile world this is known as the SS (Switching System). The Switching System contains:

- Home Location Register (HLR) – A database which stores subscriber data, including the Individual Subscriber Authentication Key (Ki) for each Subscriber Identity Module (SIM) the SIM Card which you should all be familiar with.

- Mobile Services Switching Centre (MSC) – The network element which performs the telephony switching functions of the network. The MSC is responsible for toll ticketing, network interfacing, common channel signalling.

- Visitor Location Register (VLR) – A database, which stores temporary information about roaming mobile subscribers.

- Authentication Centre (AUC) – A database, which contains the International Mobile Subscriber Identity (IMSI) the Subscriber

Authentication key (Ki), and the defined algorithms for encryption. If the call needs to be scrambled an encryption key is created here

- Equipment Identity Register (EIR) – A database, which contains information about the identity of mobile equipment in order to prevent calls from stolen, unauthorised, or defective mobile stations.

9.1.1.2 WAN TRANSMISSION

"Hi" is then routed across a fixed Wide Area Network circuit or via a satellite link depending on country topology. The call reaches the National Telco and there are two choices to be made here. The number dialled is looked up on the national routing database and either broken out to a National (in country) number (No.3), or forwarded to the internet if it is an International call after moving through the OSS and BSS processes.

9.1.1.3 OSS

The Operating Support System holds the MXE Message Centre – SMS (Short Message Service), Voice Mail and Fax Mail, the Mobile Service Node which provisions mobile intelligent network (IN) services such as video or audio conferencing, and GMSSC, the Gateway that makes a decision about whether to send the call to another mobile operator or to the Internet via the Interworking Unit. So now we know that at this point the request is to have a three-way call, and the other two callers have either a telephone number (an E164 number, the number you see in printed telephone directories, or ENUM, which reverses the E164 number and resolves it to a e-mail address in SIP format, or simply to a remote IP address).

9.1.1.4 BSS

The Business Billing System is at the area that holds all the subscriber details: credit cards, addresses, calling history and locations you have visited (yes, it's tracked you). The Billing System relies on AAA RADIUS (or DIAMETER for SIP), Authentication, Authorisation, and Accounting (AAA), and manages users that connect and use a network service. RADIUS stands for

Remote Authentication Dial In User Service. RADIUS is used by, telecoms companies, mobile operators (and some large enterprises). RADIUS manages access to the Internet or internal networks, wireless networks, and integrated e-mail services. These networks of devices may incorporate modems, DSL, access points, VPNs, network ports, Web servers, etc.

So now the billing system authorises the call to proceed and starts the MOU (Minutes of Use) counter, or even per second billing, and applies the relevant tariff cost to the length of the call duration. The bill will round up these minutes each month and apply the appropriate tariff. If the call was made by Wi-Fi then the duration is captured in the Call Detail Record (CDR) and the kilobytes used deducted from the monthly data bundle or allocation.

To continue the journey of "Hi", all the service and billing call information and TOS Type of Service is added to the call, and for our purposes is met by the BGP router to the heart of the Internet. The Border Gateway Protocol switches the packet across DWDM (Dense Wave Data Multiplexor) connected fibres traversing cities, countries and continents.

Once the packet reaches the Local Telco (4) the Billing System is checked, Authorisation is given to proceed is given and a CDR is created and saved. Customer Detail Records are the basis of your monthly or quarterly bill. The Packet is then passed to a local Class 5 switch to pass the call out to a local exchange, or, get routed to the Internet.

This information is also wrapped in IP packets and sent with C7 signalling information (the mobile version of SS7) via a router to the mobile operator's world to the Local Telco (2). Now the Wide Area Network links can be leased lines or even a satellite link as shown in the diagram. The satellite link would also carry TCP/IP and probably use a protocol called Erlang C to predict and improve latency. Latency is the Voice over IP killer: the packets must arrive in 100 milliseconds across all the links to maintain voice quality. This is measured by a Mean Opinion Score and MOS of at least 4 out of 5 is necessary and recorded once the call is completed. Obviously getting VOIP packets across the globe in sub-second round trip times is the challenge for the Internet designers. A Rule of Thumb was a Source to Destination series of hops should not exceed 6 hops. If the call exceeds 6 hops these packets can get delayed or even dropped.

9.1.1.5 CORE INTERNET

The Core Internet comprises three Tiers of routers. Tier One is the Transit network and connects all of the global Internet traffic obtained from the worlds Fibre Optic Backbones and undersea cables. Tier Two links the transit networks with Content Delivery Networks and Search Providers like Google and IXQUICK and the Tier 3 routes packets to countries and large Telco's, or, mobile operators. In the Tier 1 network the Internet Root DNS resides, like a master telephone book of Internet and web addresses.

Routers were the brainchild of Ginny Strazisar (like the Marie Curie of the Internet); she developed the first Internet working gateway software for TCP/IP protocols. On August 27th 1976, the first router was used to bridge the gap between the ARPANET and this packet radio set-up. Routers are the cores of the Internet; they are the routing machines that take decisions about where to send packets around the multitude of fibre optics and copper cables that are buried beneath our feet. Think water representing the IP packets and the pumping stations, turbines and pipes as the routers and WAN links. The routers need a raft of protocols to learn where the next router will be, so each router maintains a list of router addresses to understand where the next hop will be. These can be learnt and retained to maintain link persistence or discovered by questioning upstream routers where best to send the packets. Routers can be paired over multiple links and can run in hot standby mode if a link should fail. In an enterprise where there are hundreds of routers, these can be clustered to leverage router spare processing power using virtual technologies like Software Defined Networking (SDN). Most of the BFOR (Big Routers) run a Multi Protocol Label Switching language that speeds up core routing decisions and switches IP Packets based on QOS (Quality of Service). An IXP provides the physical infrastructure by which ISPs and Operators exchange Internet Traffic (Peering) directly rather than wait for latency induced by Tier I DNS (Domain Name Service) requests. The weak points in the Internet are the DNS servers (of which there are about 60 in the world) and the IXPs (of which there are 459 around the globe).

In the early days of the Internet there were four NAPs (Internet Network Access Points) two of them MAE East and Mae West were actually built in underground car parks. In Vancouver the IXP was the largest in the world as it routed network traffic from North America to Asia. The building was deemed so expensive because of the value and importance of the traffic that it became uninsurable. It was probably the first Internet Critical Infrastructure in the world.

The routing protocols are the magic that makes handling of packets by applying Quality of Service, Traffic Monitoring and Inspection, RRSP and VPNs (Virtual Private Networks). These protocols were developed over the last twenty years by vendors, clever inventors and academics using RFCs (Request for Comments) managed by the Internet Engineering Task Force and the Internet Society. There are about 7000 RFCs that describe the various interface features and functionalities of how the Internet technologies should behave. These all revolve around the ISO 7 Layer model.

The routers need to overlay decision-making protocols on the TCP/IP packets. The BTS is connected to the first router, so it needs to know all the addresses in the interior subnet or domain. It uses IGRP (Interior Gateway Routing Protocol) to do this and updates the Access Control List (a list of trusted devices). It then looks up Distance Vectors in the RIP (Routing Information Protocol) and then sends the packet using OSPF (Open Shortest Path First) to the next known (discovered router in the link). The User Datagram Protocol UDP part of the IP packet is used extensively to send message packets to known upstream routers; the UDP carries applications datagrams sockets and is a connectionless protocol. An application binds these sockets to the IP address and a service port. There are 65,535 service ports available to describe the type of application content being sent. As VOIP is a well-known protocol Port 80 is reserved for incoming VOIP traffic.

The CSPs and CDN Providers also have BIG ROUTERS (BFORs) or SPINE Routers that communicate together using a powerfully fast MPLS protocol. These routers communicate over mega high-speed 100 Gigabit per second fibre optics. Petabits capacity routers are capable of forwarding 1000 Terabits (or 1 million Gigabits) of information a second. Latency between these BFORs is measured in nanosecond latencies. The Multi-Protocol Label Switching uses coloured channels and ASICs instead of addresses to fast-switch packets between links to reduce thinking decisions around latency. This technology enables YouTube videos to be watched in Iceland from a server in San Francisco

To forward the packets to the Internet it applies more protocols like the Border Gateway Protocol. The BGP can remember 512,000 upstream and downstream addresses' paths. In August 2014 a Verizon engineer added 15,000 new paths and the Internet basically collapsed, because there are now so many routers on the Internet there is no more capacity left to remember all the paths. In our diagram the decision is to forward the packet to a remote Telco, a company directly or to a Cloud Service Provider (CSP), or and ISP (Internet Service Provider.

9.1.1.6 REMOTE TELCO

Our "Hi" packet reaches the remote Telco network and has to get through a Firewall (note: more about firewalls in RIDPOINTS later). The firewall uses well-known service ports, and filters the inbound and outbound traffic from trusted computers, rejecting unknown computers. The firewall assigns a well-known port and allows the "Hi" into the remote Telco's domain. Behind the firewall is a switch, which reads the header of the TCP/IP packet and sees it's a VOIP packet and switches the packet to a VOIP (SIP) switch. In telecom jargon, this switch was capable of handling 10,000 subscribers.

Let's catch our breath for a minute. We have sent our "Hi" to the Remote Telco infrastructure. In the Switching System the operator needs to know what type of service you want, who you are calling, where to put that call; it authenticates you and makes a billing decision on how much to charge you. So at this point the Switching System sends the information about the data it's collected to the Operation and Support System. It then negotiates the tariff and requests settlement with the Local Telco or the Mobile Operator.

9.1.1.7 HYBRID SMB CLOUD (*ALTERNATIVE*)

If the packet reaches a company location the packet has to traverse all the firewalls and routers and pass the signalling information to the company VOIP (SIP Server), the end users at (No.10) pick up the call and can conference in other subscribers.

9.1.1.8 PUBLIC CLOUD (*ALTERNATIVE*)

Many ISPs host SIP switches and manage outsourced telecoms. Here the call is resolved to a hosted DNS and passed to the Company Cloud (No.7) via a fixed private circuit as a data call. If the Company cloud did not have an on premises based SIP PBX then a direct extension call is created. The ISP cloud is predicated to evolve to IXP (Internet Exchange Points and can also be termed a Community, Country (or Dominion) cloud.

9.1.1.9 SUCCESSFUL CALL COMPLETION

The end-to-end call set up is made and connection initiated, and the colleagues' response is "Hi". The "Hi" now takes the same path back all the way to the originator of the call. Bingo! Call complete! HURRAH!

Today's Challenge: Repeat the same process for 280 million people (10% of the world's population) the number of people making simultaneous VOIP calls every minute. In addition, ensuring delivery and maintain sufficient capacity for the three hours a day average Web browsing for each user in the globe and make the service available for every second of 24 hours a day, all year long

10 ROOT CAUSE - INTERNET

The major Root Cause of Cyber security is the Internet. It relies on ownership and governance by a single country. This chapter looks at the current state of the Internet, new ideas to make its safe. The original architecture is dated and has created its own set of unique problems.

INTERNET ARCHITECTURE (NFSNET US CENTRIC) 1995

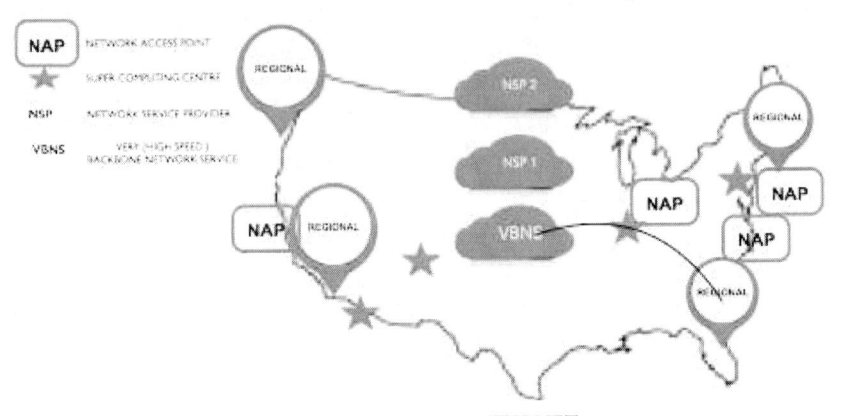

Figure 49 ORIGINAL INTERNET

The Internet was designed with only the US military in mind supporting thousands and not for a global system supporting billions. Despite the Internet's romping success, it has long been known that the Internet architecture has significant deficiencies and security foibles, this is the root cause of cyber network attacks which cost global companies $761 billion a year.[131]

Estimates that hacking causes a trillion dollars a year of cyber damage has been touted by McAfee. The UK alone estimated annual losses at $16.2 billion in a relatively quiet 2011, this is nearing $20 billion a year. Reversing this trend would pay off the National deficit off in a single year. The US would save $72 billion a year in damages. Since the first years of its popularisation, the Internet has been seen as a tool that is capable of removing people's geographic location from the equation of successful collaborative information exchange and has also provided anonymity. To remedy this situation two immediate solutions need to happen – subscriber accountability to accept traceability, and countries legal ability to halt cyber attacks started behind their borders.

Where do we stand today? The protocols used to run the Internet are old. The routers running the globes ISPs are struggling with the vast numbers of addresses. Bandwidth is being drained by DDOS attacks and Over The Top (OTT) services, which makes the Internet a premium service and disjointing the stance of Internet ubiquity. There is a clear disconnect between the hardware driven Internet where connectivity could be charged for versus the software driven Internet where somebody else foots the bill. Organised Crime, adversaries, and anybody who wants it have stolen each Internet subscriber's identity. Perhaps we could start again with something that works. One of the prime contributors to the root cause is a 30-year-old protocol called DNS.

10.1 DOMAIN NAME SERVICE

The DNS protocols are part of the core Internet standards and runs infrastructure in 34 countries. Control of this service should be at the Dominion or Regional level. Web addresses; unique urls (Uniform Resource Locator) are matched to IP addresses are held in cache and distributed databases are updated every 4 minutes. They specify the process by which one computer can find another computer on the basis of its name.

There are 13 Global Root (A to M) Internet DNS Services:

- A. VeriSign Global Registry Services
- B. University of Southern California
- C. Cogent Communications
- D. University of Maryland
- E. NASA Ames Research Center

F. Internet Systems Consortium Inc.

G. US DOD Network Information Center

H. US Army Research Lab

I. Autonomica / NORDUnet

J. VeriSign Global Registry Services

K. RIPE NCC

L. CANN

M. WIDE Project

10.2 DNS THREATS

DNSSEC is used to secure the ageing DNS protocol, but as listed in IETF RFC 3833 there are several exploits that DNS is susceptible to:

- Packet Interception
- ID Guessing and Query Prediction
- Name Chaining
- Betrayal by Trusted Server
- Authenticated Denial of Domain Names
- Wildcards
- Denial of Service

Although there are several patches available adversaries continue to exploit the security weakness of DNS (its easy) to their advantage. By caching address information, name servers don't have to look up the IP address every time a frequently visited site is accessed, and this speeds up the experience for end users. Hackers are able to insert a bogus IP address into a cache; so, all users of that name server will be directed to the wrong site (until the cache expires and is refreshed). Corrupting the operation of DNS in this way can lead to many kinds of fraud and other malicious activity.[132]

10.3 BGP

The Border Gateway Protocol (BGP) is the routing protocol used to exchange routing information between Internet routers. It allows ISPs to connect to each other and for end-users to connect to more than one ISP. BGP is the only protocol that is designed to deal with a network of the Internet's size. BGP supports only the destination-based forwarding paradigm, which assumes that a router forwards a packet based solely on the destination address carried in the IP header of the packet. This matches the set of policy decisions that could be enforced using BGP.

A unique ASN (Autonomous System Number) is allocated to each Autonomous System for use in BGP routing. Autonomous System Numbers are assigned by IANA. The Regional Internet Registries (RIR) provides assignments at regional geographic level. These are the same authorities that allocate IP addresses. There are public numbers, which may be used on the Internet and range from 1 to 64511, and private numbers from 64512 to 65535, which can be used within an organisation.[133] As the Internet grows, so the routing table balloons. Almost half of the IPv4 routing table (45% for IPv4 and 24% for IPv6) contains redundant information. The problems here are highlighted in the Mutually Agreed Norms for Routing Security (MANRS) initiative from the Internet Society:

- Problems related to incorrect routing information;

- Problems related to traffic with spoofed source IP addresses; and

- Problems related to coordination and collaboration between network operators.[134]

As a solution these problems could be moved under the auspices the ITU to provide remediation to adjudicate, audit, and manage. Although this body seems to be at the receiving end of plenty of vociferous discourse lately, they are best placed to independently advise and guide the global amalgam. As an International organisation the experience of managing global communications initiatives has been clearly demonstrated. Countries already contribute to its upkeep and with further technical powers can realign the existing flat architecture that we use today.

10.4 IP TRANSIT AND IP PEERING

Core Internet traffic is moved by 15 independent Internet IP Transit companies (mostly US based) but with global reach, These Tier 1 providers are; AT&T, CenturyLink, Cogent, GTT, Hurricane Electric, KPN, Level3, NTT, Sprint, Tata, Telefonica, TeliaSonera, Verizon, Vodaphone and XO Communications. This Internet Core is a business enabler and provides consumer Voice, Mobile, Data and TV. They make revenue by charging CDNs (Content Delivery Networks) like Netflix, or Mobile providers transit fees. The recent Net Neutrality argument, which would have allowed US, based carriers and Service Providers to rate limit types of data caused a major ruckus in the US. The Netflix Video on Demand product accounts for 70% of all US based Internet traffic but the carriers (like cable companies losing market share to Netflix) wanted to charge customers for this improved level of service while they still had to fund the infrastructure free of charge. The movement of IP traffic between Tiers 1,2 and 3 called IP Transit.

US Monthly rates for IP Transit:

- 10Mbps $7.00
- 50Mbps $4.00
- 150Mbps $2.00
- 300Mbps $1.00
- 600Mbps $0.80
- 1500Mbps — 1.5Gbps $0.65
- 3000Mbps — 3Gbps $0.50[135]

So if you were a CDN and had to push 100 Gbit/s to end-users this would cost $50k a month. This bandwidth cost is then amortised into the subscribers' monthly data package (fixed or mobile). For countries outside the US these prices vary dependent on Service Levels and Latency, so in Japan it could be $25 per Mbps.

INTERNET ARCHITECTURE TODAY

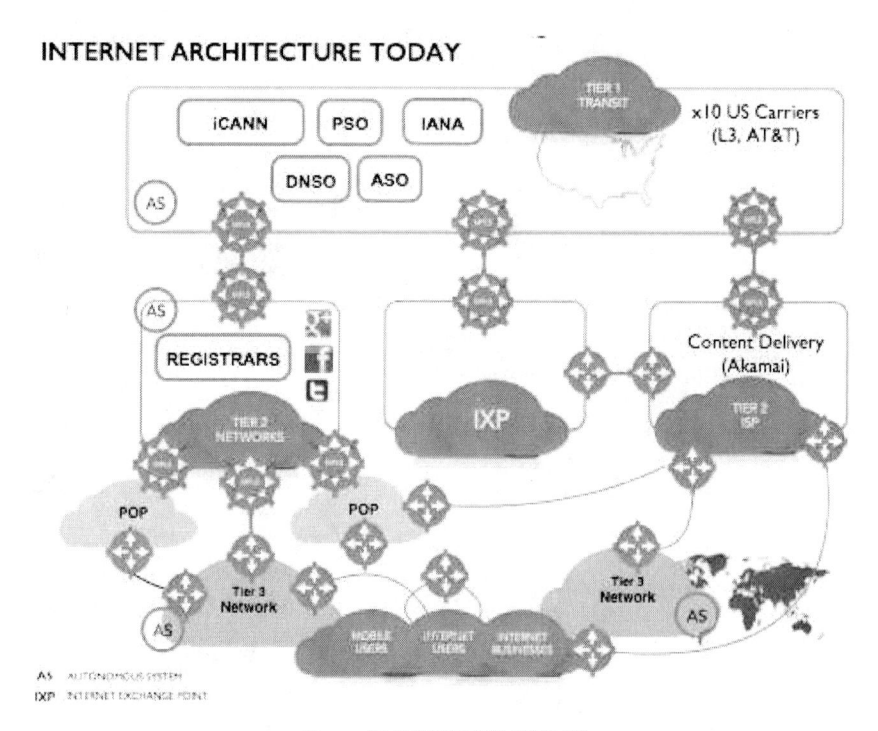

Figure 50 INTERNET TODAY

The FCC (Federal Communication Commission and watchdog) and the Government ruled that the Internet (once free and open) should now be governed as a public utility. In addition, all services should be given equal access without limiting traffic (more of a Canal than a Super Information Highway). This means companies (like OTT type companies) can reserve high-speed last mile highway delivery for their content delivery while other websites are consigned the cycle path.

Although the details and legalise of how this would look have yet to be determined, there are a number of instances we can glean from history that would help us next guess an approach. This ruling means it could allow the FCC the power to micromanage every aspect of how the Internet works. "It's an over reach that will let a Washington bureaucracy and not the American people decide the future of the online world" that was delivered in a statement by Ajit Pai the FCC Commissioner on the 26th February 2015.

The other 219 odd countries in the world are observing these moves:

- To seek investment to build a country controlled Internet within legal borders. Countries will need to establish a Tier 1 Internet peering capability on a regional or global basis.

- Allows for control of Internet activity so accepting responsibility for citizens culture and rights

- Also start self-regulation and regional collaboration

- It will provide for tax revenues to be increased within country borders, so globally operated countries wishing to trade will need to be represented physically in country.

- It will allow for education facilities to be built and train a new generation internally to the country.

- Employment opportunities will increase as inward investment is made

- Provision of the Internet could be tied to trade agreements as each dominion becomes a Tier 1 provider

- Allows for legal interventions on a local basis

- Allows for inter country trading agreements, such as controls on OTT suppliers

- Provides the mechanisms for each country to create innovation

- Encryption standards can be created by each Dominion and encouraged by the recent UN approval

In essence it would be the responsibility of each country to re-invest in its own infrastructure and knowledge base. This can only benefit dominion economies. Think of the Internet like electricity and each country becoming an energy generator or service provider. If you look at the rise of electricity distribution it began by private small companies providing the service on a local country basis (sound familiar?). Each country has its own set of plugs (some safer than others), light switches, Associated appliances ASOTs (All Sorts of Things) and safety standards but it does not stop global business or tourists using electricity or adaptors. In fact it enables countries to invest in its own infrastructure, so, providing citizens with its own utility in a controlled way keeping the train firmly on the tracks. This investment in part has already been made. Some country's infrastructure is superior to others including and western powers (South Korea, Sweden, Switzerland for example) have high penetration of Internet broadband. It also secures country data - a new market would be created for Tier One on a dominion level, countries can therefore provide multiple services for onward sale to other countries - a data market place if you like. Community countries could join and share infrastructure and skills to enable them to provide new high tech collaborations. R & D would benefit in each country and this would spur a new economic era, enabling countries to retain skilled people and stop brain drain and retain culture. For SMBs this new wave of InternetNew self-determination opens up a plethora of new markets. According to Wired magazine Ryan Singel reported in 2010 " Michael McConnell (former director of national intelligence) says we need to re-engineer the Internet. We need to develop an early-warning system to monitor cyberspace, identify intrusions and locate the source of attacks with a trail of evidence that can support diplomatic, military and legal options — and we must be able to do this in milliseconds. More specifically, we need to re-engineer the Internet to make attribution, geo-location, intelligence analysis and impact assessment — who did it, from where, why and what was the result — more manageable. The technologies are already available from public and private sources and can be further developed if we have the will to build them into our systems and to work with our allies and trading partners so they will do the same." Back in 2010 security was not that much of a problem, hacking was an irritation five years on it is now essential. However, the opportunity to develop country citizens is obviously tempting for dominions pursuing self-determination.

The advantages of the Internet are beneficial, businesses can continue to send their goods on a global basis rather than localised markets and contribute dramatically to a country GDP. Education, Health and Food distribution are benefitting nearly everyone on the planet. Indeed the annual 20% growth of the Internet spawns from emerged markets. US companies are trialling new ways to spread the Internet to remote parts of the world, solar powered gliders, helium balloons and satellites. Global spend on the Internet in 2012 was $307 Billion[136] across 168 countries (roughly $4.7 Billon per country). I have estimated a further **$377 billion** is required to provide Internet service to every person on the planet. This analysis is based on a comparison of 65 countries. That's half the cost of the damage to the Internet caused annually by cyber attacks. That's an average of 0.01% of the Global GDP. By the year 2020 I believe the spread of the Internet will have complete geographic coverage. Growth in IP Services was approximately 10% last year (spurred by Smartphone sales). 70% of global IP Services were delivered from US & UK, meaning a drain away from 166 countries with an estimated $3.2 billion taxable revenues from each of these dominions annually.

I have worked in 44 countries around the world. I have seen most countries lose significant revenues by not applying basic controls on the movement of goods and information to the detriment of their citizens. Using effective asset management techniques and a slight capital acquisition and payback regime redesign countries can retain these Internet dollars and pay off national debt. The Global Spend on telecoms comes from emerged markets and BRIC countries. The UK and US will continue to manage 70% of the emerged markets traffic and Transit/Peering growth (up to $1.7 trillion by 2017).[137] Vendors are recognising the importance of emerged markets and the $100 smartphone and a $9 computer is in development, these are is available in developing countries is an example of that.[138] **The new model I have devised (which I address more in depth at the end of this chapter) would generate 3 Trillion dollars of revenue for 166 country participants and an estimated 2 Trillion of new revenues for US tech companies in the next 3 years.**

So it's a question of priorities. Countries should invest in the deployment of further Internet infrastructure to boost the GDP per capita in the next 5 years. The aim here is not to sell off the countries assets to external vendors but create a country community that is advantageous to citizens and country revenues leveraging vendors reach targets. Maintaining country owned assets means keeping citizens identities as part of that valuable Asset base. These are assets and they need a level of control – why would you want to give these away? Giving away country assets is not a good plan; it allows foreign powers to undermine government and commerce. Vendors who claim to have a countries interest at heart are not the people you freely give data to.

COMBAT READY IT 2015 - INTERNET POPULATION AND COSTS BY COUNTRY	ANNUAL GDP	POPULATION	GDP PER CAPITA	INTERNET USERS	POPULATION NEEDING INTERNET CONNECTIVITY	Est. COST TO CONNECT THE UNCONNECTED	% of GDP to extend Internet Access to Population
India	1,875,141,481,991	1,267,401,849	1,480	243,198,922	1,024,202,927	147,075,540,317	7.84%
China	9,240,270,452,047	1,393,783,836	6,630	641,601,070	752,182,766	108,013,445,198	1.17%
Indonesia	868,345,652,475	252,812,245	3,435	42,258,824	210,553,421	30,235,471,256	3.48%
Pakistan	232,286,781,111	185,132,926	1,255	20,073,929	165,058,997	23,702,471,969	10.20%
Bangladesh	149,990,454,542	158,512,570	946	10,867,567	147,645,003	21,201,822,431	14.14%
Nigeria	521,803,314,654	178,516,904	2,923	67,101,452	111,415,452	15,999,258,907	3.07%
Ethiopia	24,880,264,958	96,506,031	258	1,636,099	94,869,932	13,623,322,235	54.76%
Brazil	2,245,673,032,354	202,033,670	11,115	107,822,831	94,210,839	13,528,676,480	0.60%
Republic of Congo	55,731,000,000	77,433,744	720	1,703,542	75,730,202	10,874,857,007	19.51%
Mexico	1,260,914,660,977	123,799,215	10,185	50,923,060	72,876,155	10,465,015,858	0.83%
Philippines	272,066,554,886	100,096,496	2,718	39,470,845	60,625,651	8,705,843,484	3.20%
Russia	2,096,777,030,571	142,467,651	14,718	84,437,793	58,029,858	8,333,087,609	0.40%
Iran	368,904,351,627	78,470,222	4,701	22,200,708	56,269,514	8,080,302,210	2.19%
Myanmar	244,331,000,000	53,718,958	4,548	624,991	53,093,967	7,624,293,661	3.12%
Vietnam	171,390,003,299	92,547,959	1,852	39,772,424	52,775,535	7,578,566,826	4.42%
Thailand	387,252,164,291	67,222,972	5,761	19,386,154	47,836,818	6,869,367,065	1.77%
Tanzania	43,646,747,145	50,757,459	860	7,590,794	43,166,665	6,198,733,094	14.20%
Egypt	271,972,822,883	83,386,739	3,262	40,311,562	43,075,177	6,185,595,417	2.27%
United States	16,768,100,000,000	322,583,006	51,981	279,834,232	42,748,774	6,138,723,946	0.04%
Turkey	822,135,183,160	75,837,020	10,841	35,358,888	40,478,132	5,812,659,755	0.71%
Algeria	210,183,410,526	39,928,947	5,264	6,669,927	33,259,020	4,775,995,272	2.27%
Uganda	24,703,250,651	38,844,624	636	6,523,949	32,320,675	4,641,248,930	18.79%
Iraq	229,327,284,734	34,768,761	6,596	2,707,928	32,060,833	4,603,935,619	2.01%
Malaysia	313,159,097,401	30,187,896	10,374	675,074	29,512,822	4,238,041,239	1.35%
Sudan	66,565,889,417	38,764,090	1,717	9,307,189	29,456,901	4,230,010,984	6.35%
Afganistan	20,309,671,015	31,280,518	649	1,856,781	29,423,737	4,225,248,633	20.80%
Kenya	55,243,056,201	45,545,980	1,213	16,713,319	28,832,661	4,140,370,120	7.49%
South Africa	366,057,913,367	53,139,528	6,889	24,909,854	28,229,674	4,053,781,186	1.11%
Ukraine	177,430,609,756	44,941,303	3,948	16,849,008	28,092,295	4,034,053,562	2.27%
Mozambique	15,630,302,814	26,472,977	590	1,467,687	25,005,290	3,590,759,644	22.97%
North Korea	40,000,000,000	24,895,000	1,607	1,024	24,893,976	3,574,774,954	8.94%
Nepal	19,294,348,174	28,120,740	686	3,411,948	24,708,792	3,548,182,531	18.39%
Italy	2,149,484,516,712	61,070,224	35,197	36,593,969	24,476,255	3,514,790,218	0.16%
Colombia	378,415,326,790	48,929,706	7,734	25,660,725	23,268,981	3,341,425,672	0.88%
Cameroon	29,567,504,656	22,818,632	1,296	1,486,815	21,331,817	3,063,248,921	10.36%
Ghana	48,137,027,487	26,442,178	1,820	5,171,993	21,270,185	3,054,398,566	6.35%
Cote de Ivorie	31,062,026,533	20,804,774	1,493	565,874	20,238,900	2,906,306,040	9.36%
Yemen	35,954,502,304	24,968,508	1,440	4,778,488	20,190,020	2,899,286,872	8.06%
Niger	7,407,418,428	18,534,802	400	298,310	18,236,492	2,618,760,251	35.35%
Peru	202,349,846,974	30,769,077	6,576	12,583,953	18,185,124	2,611,383,806	1.29%
Angola	124,178,241,816	22,137,261	5,609	4,286,821	17,850,440	2,563,323,184	2.06%
Japan	4,919,563,108,373	126,999,808	38,737	109,252,912	17,746,896	2,548,454,266	0.05%
Sri Lanka	67,182,015,336	21,445,775	3,133	4,267,507	17,178,268	2,466,799,285	3.67%
Uzbekistan	56,795,656,325	28,929,716	1,963	11,914,665	17,015,051	2,443,361,324	4.30%
Argentina	609,888,971,036	41,803,125	14,590	24,973,660	16,829,465	2,416,711,174	0.40%
Burkina Faso	12,884,922,231	17,419,615	740	741,888	16,677,727	2,394,921,597	18.59%
Venezuela	438,283,564,815	30,851,343	14,206	14,514,421	16,302,922	2,341,099,599	0.53%
Syria	59,957,000,000	21,986,615	2,727	5,860,788	16,125,827	2,315,668,757	3.86%
Cambodia	15,238,689,686	15,408,270	989	828,317	14,579,953	2,093,681,251	13.74%
Morocco	103,835,702,814	33,492,909	3,100	20,207,154	13,285,755	1,907,834,418	1.84%
Guatemala	53,796,709,475	15,859,714	3,392	2,716,781	13,142,933	1,887,325,179	3.51%
Chad	13,513,552,425	13,211,146	1,023	317,197	12,893,949	1,851,571,076	13.70%
Zambia	26,820,870,559	15,021,002	1,786	2,313,013	12,707,989	1,824,867,220	6.80%
Poland	525,865,974,815	38,220,543	13,759	25,666,238	12,554,305	1,802,798,198	0.34%
Spain	1,393,040,177,014	47,066,402	29,597	35,010,273	12,056,129	1,731,260,124	0.12%
Saudi Arabia	14,791,699,009	29,369,428	504	17,397,179	11,972,249	1,719,214,956	11.62%
Guinea	6,144,131,903	12,043,898	510	205,194	11,838,704	1,700,037,894	27.67%
Zimbabwe	13,490,000,000	14,599,325	924	2,852,757	11,746,568	1,686,807,165	12.50%
Senegal	26,574,000,000	14,548,171	1,827	3,194,190	11,353,981	1,630,431,672	6.14%
Rwanda	7,521,261,791	12,100,049	622	1,110,043	10,990,006	1,578,164,862	20.98%
Germany	3,730,260,571,357	82,652,256	45,132	71,727,551	10,924,705	1,568,787,638	0.04%
Somalia	5,896,000,000	10,805,651	546	163,185	10,642,466	1,528,258,118	25.92%
Romania	189,638,162,013	21,640,168	8,763	11,178,477	10,461,691	1,502,298,828	0.79%
Burundi	2,714,507,031	10,482,752	259	146,219	10,336,533	1,484,326,139	54.68%

*Table 7 - TOP 65 COUNTRY ANALYSIS –
COST TO ACHEIVE COMPLETE INTERNET COVERAGE*

For many, segregating the Internet by country would signal a 'Balkanisation', where the global Internet becomes dis-aggregated into various networks distributed along national lines, producing less communication and cooperation and more competition and conflict. Sascha Meinrath article [139] suggests "the Internet is in danger of becoming like the European train system, where varying voltage and 20 different types of signalling technologies force operators to stop and switch systems or even to another locomotive, resulting in delays, inefficiencies, and higher costs. Netizens would fall under a complex array of different jurisdictions imposing conflicting mandates and conferring conflicting rights. And much as different signalling hampers the movement of people and the trade of physical goods, an Internet within such a complex jurisdictional structure would certainly hamper modern economic activity."

This view could be valid but in light of surveillance misbehaviour, "Balkanisation" looks like a good idea. The trains still run in Europe and has a much better system than other countries (one could argue), it does not stop people travelling (they may need a passport) and they would need a number of electrical adaptors to work electrical devices in each country. The revenues from the Balkanised territories don't end up in a single pot. The different jurisdictions would help retain country identity, culture and ethics.

ICANN is a US incorporated non-profit organisation. ICANN'S continued existence relies on US laws and regulation, regardless of whether or not it has a future contractual relationship with the federal government. Although this existing governance is in process of being pushed to a regional model. If countries adopted this model at a dominion level it would require ENUM registrars in each country. ENUM would allow each country to unify local and global identification efforts.

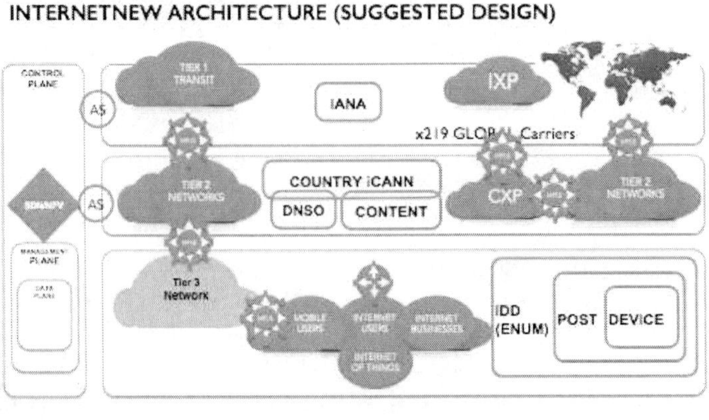

Figure 51 INTERNETNEW

The various elements of the Internet have been built by private companies and as such are also owned by them — little Internet ownership and governance is in the hands of governments. Some argue that the Internet would never have been developed if it had been left to governments. Telco's require government's motivation to raise the necessary capital to invest in new network rollouts. The explosion of the Internet has also produced a range of security issues that, whether we like it or not, has reached a level that goes beyond dominion based developments. A self determined Internet will need adherence to an international charter of rights will need to be signed by each country. At the moment there is no single global authority to govern this, which could mean an expanded role for the UN, ITU, or IEEE to assist in reapplying new rules to the Internet. Obviously emerged countries citizens wish their governments to provide them with all the developed worlds latest trappings and gadgets, (the Internet being a personal identified freedom) but there has to be a rethink here. I have friends dotted around the world who don't want to see this free expression taken away from them but are more scared by the potential data loss of personal information by unknown governments. Self determined dominion Internets achievable as long as everyone signs up to the concept.

A new architecture would re-establish a legacy PSTN-like hierarchy, without distracting from vendors dominance, but adds country and global security and makes net citizens more responsible for their subscriptions. INTERNETNEW is on its way but is being stifled by multiple governance views, some sound and others from leftfield.

10.5 INTERNETNEW - WHAT WOULD IT LOOK LIKE?

INTERNETNEW is being considered by a number of academics three proposals; Rutgers University (The Cognet Protocol Stack), NDN Named Data Networking Convention, and ONOS all being tested. In this section we will review how the Internet got architected and how its roots were embedded in the PSTN of the 20th Century.

In 2014 168 countries spent $307 Billion annually on Internet growth, only to see $761 Billion annually of global business being lost to cyber attacks, (Result Misery[140]) this is now a collective global problem. Besides opening up a countries business to dangerous cohorts of hackers, countries are also wary of global neighbour.

Much of the PSTN was based on Strowger exchanges (Cogs and Wheels) that turned in tandem with the old telephone dial through electro-mechanical signals. Up to the 1970s period these were global, and differed from country to country, using banks of operators to transfer calls across cities and countries. You used to talk to an operator to connect to another telephone, get a wake up call, and get the weather in Washington. Dialling "0" would get your operator to look up telephone numbers and sometimes act as a personal assistant (and even ask them to tell the correct time).

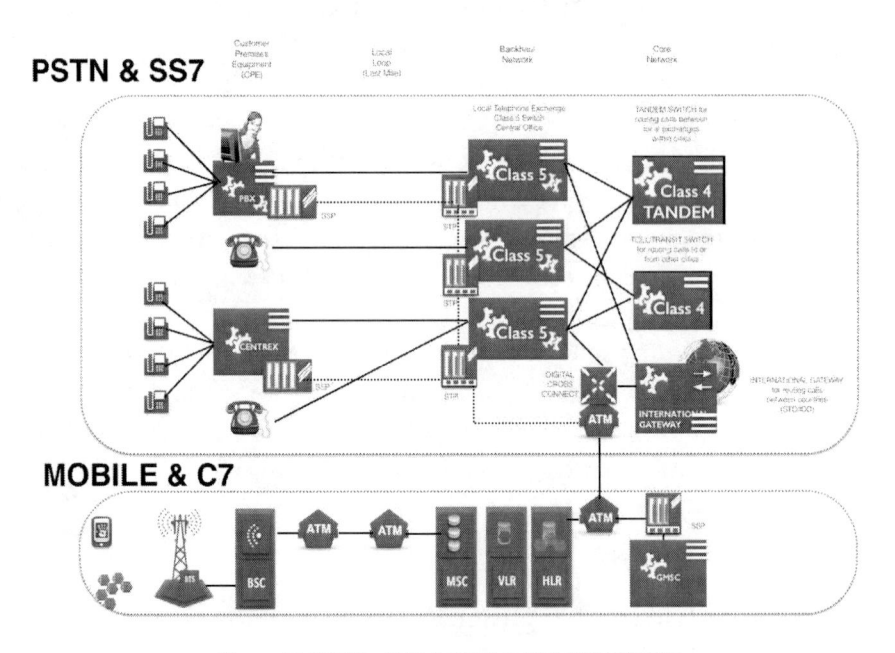

Figure 52 FIXED AND MOBILE CONNECTIONS

When the seventies arrived digital exchanges were deployed. The US based telephone companies started to push automated services and AT&T (who had a million employees at that time) developed SS7 in 1975. Signalling System No.7 became an international standard in 1980. The SS7 overlay network was a set of Unix servers and IP like addressing and not too dissimilar to the Internet today. These attributes helped to establish fast call set up and created a virtual peer –to-peer (number to number) calling to maintain call quality. An intelligent network (IN) on top of a dumb network that allowed for faster set-up and transfer of calls as well as introduce intelligent services and Service Nodes that provided automated services such as Dual Tone Multi Frequency dialling, Direct Dialling Inwards and Direct Dial (eliminating Operator intervention). The architecture was adopted in mobile networks and employed three signalling nodes Service Switching Points (SSPs), Signal Transfer Points (STPs), and Service Control Points (SCPs). A number, a signalling point code, identifies each node on the network. I used to call it the first Internet as it had addressing (a uniform Telephone Book and associated services like Toll Free dialling for services) and the ability to move traffic faster and at better quality.

Mobile networks grew throughout the early 1980's; I was lucky enough to test the first GSM mobile in the UK phoning from Canterbury to BT Mobile in Leeds in 1982. Canterbury had the first GSM mobile mast in the UK and I lived in Canterbury and worked in Leeds. BT gave me a whizzer GSM phone so I called the office at 9am – the words uttered were "One to beam up" not exactly Alexander Graham Bells first call in 1876 " Mr Watson - come here – I want to see you". The SS7 and C7 (Mobile equivalent to SS7) networks provided standard telephone numbers, which still exist today. Linking the PSTN and Mobile worlds using Standard Trunk Dialling (used in the UK since 1958) evolved into International Direct Dialling (IDD) or International Subscriber Dialling (ISD).

Calls are made by dialling the international call prefix for the country one is in, followed by the country calling code for the country one wishes to call, followed by the phone number within that country. When phone numbers are published for use abroad they typically include the country calling code, but replace the international call prefix, a "+" to signify that the caller should use the prefix appropriate for their country. For mobile phones, the plus sign (+) can be used instead of the prefix.[141] The numbering scheme used by IDD allows for caller ID association and this schema is based on Country, City, Exchange, and street (in some cases). This is the E.164 standard.

A Telephone Exchange can typically handle 10,000 homes the discipline of the numbering schema was valuable. With mobile numbering this discipline was lost, a country mobile number range was only designated to a mobile subscriber without geographic pinpointing and provided on a mobile operator basis. This resulted in two diverse numbering schemes (which would then be compounded by the Broadband Network) rollouts and Internet addresses. End user responsibility and accountability became loosely linked and traceable by mobile operators billing systems synchronisation.

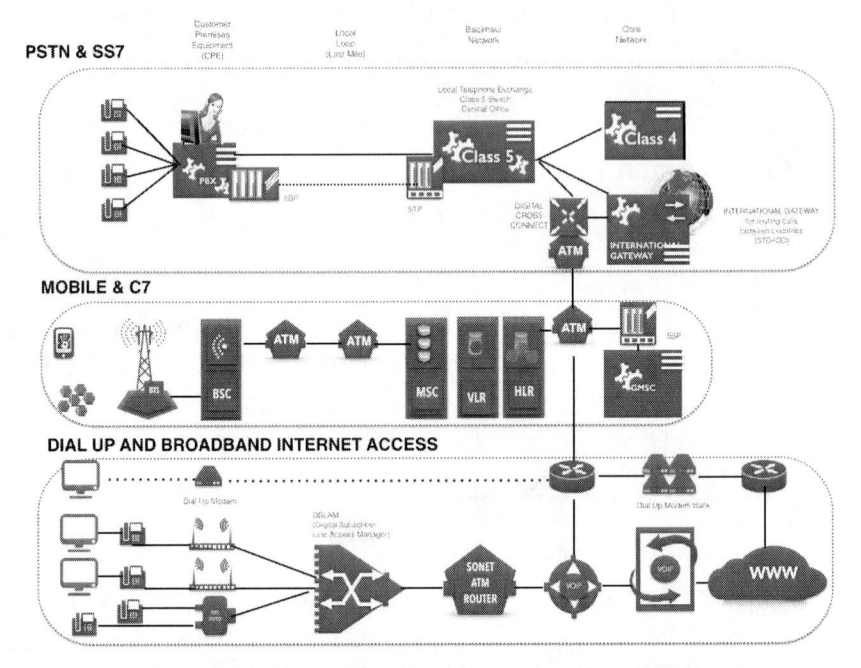

Figure 53 CONNECTING PSTN, MOBILE and INTERNET

In 1989 the world of dial up modems appeared for public access. These hefty sized modems plugged into your home phone socket and after several attempts would connect with Internet Service Providers (ISPs) like Compuserve and America OnLine (AOL). In 2013 2% of the world still use dial up.

10.6 HOTHOUSE

Developing countries ISPs and CSP's now need to start thinking like Telco's and bring back the "Walled Garden " concept on a national basis and for selective services. From hierarchical network deployments and a plethora of proprietary protocols (i.e., SS7) we have moved into an open, IP-based and flat access/core network. The old walled garden is crumbling bringing new players to the game, hackers among others to wander into the garden. In addition, the physical access to key components of the network (e.g.

femtocells) adds new variables to the security equation mobile network operators are requested to solve.[142] In the US and Canada we have witnessed Telco's trying to claw back their investments in infrastructure. Governments therefore need to allow Internet accesses to compete on a global market yet ensure that net citizens are accountable for their actions. For vendors this resurrection would help sell increased technologies in the Dominion Cloud and create a better environment for the predicted $50 billion Internet of Things market.

The revenues though have broken through the old Walled Garden model and ended up in the hands of the mobile and cloud vendors (like App stores, Instant Messaging), mainly US based. This has meant that most devices use data instead of traditional MOU (Minutes of Use) and publicly regulated tariffs. This revenue leakage has meant that Telco's need to transform to Managed Service Providers and regain service revenue through cloud and other services. The problem with this is that these revenues also go to private companies, and this means the governments lose tax receipts. Overseas companies now own smaller Telco's and little is ploughed back into government coffers. National Assets sales such as spectrum is lost in ten year auctions gaps, it would be better to rent these assets out. By controlling Internet, Mobile data and providing cloud services within country boundaries through multiple ISPs, these revenues are re-invested into countries. This should spur local innovation, new companies and spur local employment. This should help turn revenue leakage into positive debt reduction. This could be termed as the New Value Network where value added services stay within the revenue and tax collection of the national providers. By getting the global vendors to invest in this closed loop through partnerships countries can provide a new range of services and create further revenues. It's more of a Hothouse than a walled garden! Regionally we can already see these communities grow like the Bridge Alliance in Singapore that provide Roaming and Cloud interconnections for 39 Mobile Operators.

Content companies like Akamai Technologies (who are the largest) and share globally managed content Delivery Networks. Other providers in the commercial CDN market include Amazon CloudFront, AT&T's Digital Media Solutions, BitTorrent Inc., BitGravity, CDNetworks, Edgecast, GoGrid, Limelight Networks, and PEER 1. A content delivery network (CDN) is a system of servers, interconnected over the Internet, that are placed closer to users across the globe to reduce the distance content travels across long-haul networks, like wide are networks (WANs). These servers contain duplicate content of the originating network. CDNs dynamically provide data to clients by calculating which server is located nearest to the client and delivering content based on those calculations. This eliminates the distance that content travels and reduces the number of hops a data packet must make. The result is less packet loss, optimised bandwidth and faster performance -- improving overall user experience[143]. Cloud and Application Data Centres, and Search Engine Providers revolve around companies like Google and Microsoft's Bing (Bing got its name allegedly termed by internal Microsoft team members as "Because It's Not Google). It has been like this for the last 30 years. It's hierarchal and pyramid like with the roots in the US. The problem is the globes Internet traffic flows freely to these US based companies. In the early days this was acceptable, the Fibre Optic global backbones did not exist, and the Tier 1 Internet peering and DNS resided in 5 major NAPs based in the US.

10.7 INTERNETNEW INITIATIVES FOR SMBS

There are several Works in Progress research projects theorising the future of the Internet all have some element of funding available to the Internet. For those digital focussed SMBs there is help either from Venture Capitalists, Universities, EU through partnership, or, direct government funding to help develop Dominion base technology companies.

10.8 INTERNETNEW SECURITY

Security is a second thought when it comes to the current Internet Architecture. The OSI 7 layer model should have included security as a permanent separate layer; in hindsight it was not that important at the time of concept. Security therefore needs to be built deep into vendors' interoperability offerings today. It should now require encryption, authorisation and authentication protocols as a minimum at each interface. Two proposed models called NEBULA and XIA (Expressive Internet Architecture) propose a security intrinsic model deploying a data plane that establishes policy compliant paths across the Internet. The GENI Spiral 4 proposes multiple virtualised *slices* out of the network substrate for resource sharing and measurement (monitoring is built in). It contains global control and management framework that assembles the building blocks together into a coherent facility These topologies need to break out of the test tube phase and get into the real world.

10.9 IP FIT FOR PURPOSE

The IP protocol has deep operational cracks that still persist even with IPv6 becoming ubiquitous – IPv6 has flaws. So many research projects seek to focus addressing as content led. That means addressing is assigned to the type of content that is accessed by a subscriber, not an address for each subscriber. This paradigm shift is seen as a security layer covering content distribution rather than host-to-host. The NDN (Named Data Networking) project is that the primary usage of the current Internet will evolve from end-to-end packet delivery to a content-centric model. The current Internet, which is a "client-server" model, has experienced multiple security problems.

NDN Named Data Networking Convention

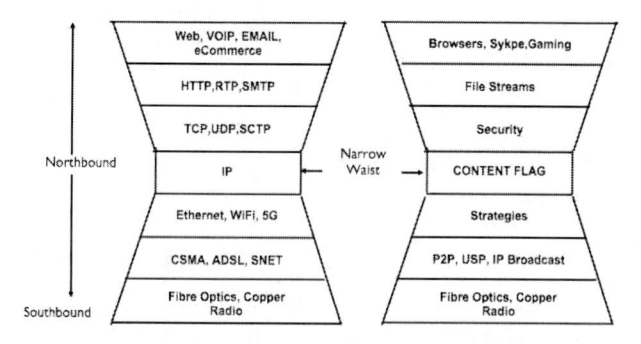

Figure 54 - NDN NAMED DATA NETWORKING

In this NDN model, the network is "transparent" and just forwards all data (it just does not care because its content-unaware). Due to this unawareness, multiple copies of the same data are sent between endpoints on the network again and again without any traffic optimisation on the network's part. The datasets are named instead of their location (IP addresses). Rather than trying to secure the transmission channel using encryption, instead secures the content by naming the data through a security enhanced method. This approach allows separating trust in data, from trust between hosts and servers, which can potentially enable content caching on the network side to optimise traffic.[144] An overlay network may still be needed to provide billing; otherwise revenues would shift to content providers.

10.10 MOBILITY

The world's mobile networks far outstrip those of fixed devices. Researchers therefore look to position mobile content as a more innovative set of applications as opposed to hardware driven networks. In mobile providers the use of VOIP interfaces has demolished most Minute of Use tariffs skewing many traditional Telco and Mobile Operators revenue models. Although most VOIP provider's applications like Skype are not "free" there are a billion users who contribute to the Skype pay as you go model. Again the Mobile SPs have invested heavily in fixed networking and spectrum auctions to provide service. The costs of handsets are also plummeting so retail margins are reducing as the cost of a phone and a data plan hits $10 to $25 a month. So how can a new Internet provide Communications providers with secure revenues? MobilityFirst aims to address the cellular convergence trend providing grid like mobile peer-to-peer (P2P) and DTN (delay-tolerant network) application services which offer robust-ness in case of link/network disconnection. Country based Mobile Operators still need to expand and update their networks and still cope with cannibalisation.

10.11 INTERNETNEW TESTBEDS

The US, EU and ASIA have research organisations that are implementing large scale test beds relating to openness and extensibility, robust system and security tests based on large scale hardware and software designs. IN the US the COGNET, NDN, and GENI projects are showing some real and exciting innovation. In the EU for instance the FIWARE initiative provides open source "cloud friendly" APIs to help develop Smart Cities. Research grants up to EURO15, 000 have been made available to help developers and start-ups assimilate IOT type technologies into smart sensors on a metropolitan scale.

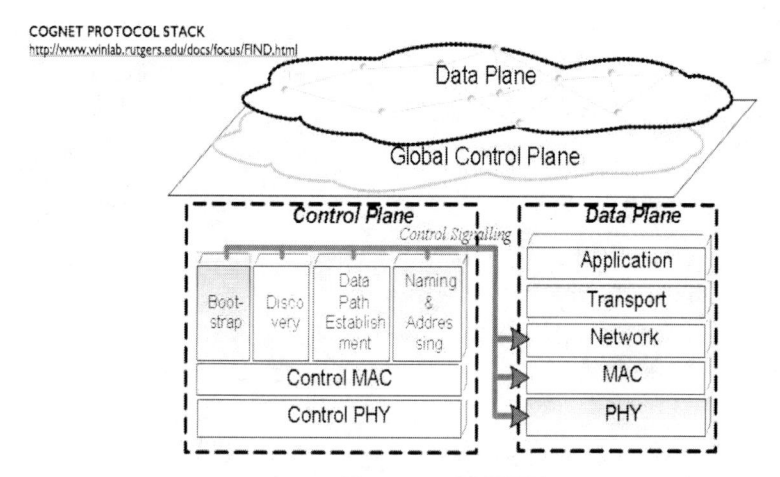

Figure 55 – COGNET

10.12 TELCOS AND MOBILE SERVICE PROVIDERS

The worlds Telco's are facing a dilemma, their traditional model of providing end user broadband voice and data services is being usurped by Over the Top content. Providing monthly data packages where 70% of bandwidth goes to a content provider who does not contribute to network upkeep. In a country context this could prove a significant drain on resources and revenues just to maintain access to global content. The growth of nationally maintained networks is difficult to maintain based on current models unless regulation ring fences country operators. Margins will decrease and if content driven networks take a foothold there is little opportunity to monetise content distribution as a service. Unless a dominion produces home grown content for global distribution. The future of Telco's in an Internet world is not clear, this will mean physical rollouts of network services will become harder to maintain and raise capital for new extensions.

The InternetNew developments described above may be short-circuited by Open Network Operating System. The ONOS model proposes an overlay SDN network that has Northbound and Southbound APIs and East/West path control. Northbound APIs connect to Applications and Southbound APIs connect to network elements (routers switches and servers) and are called White Boxes (a term created under the auspices of the Open Compute Project).

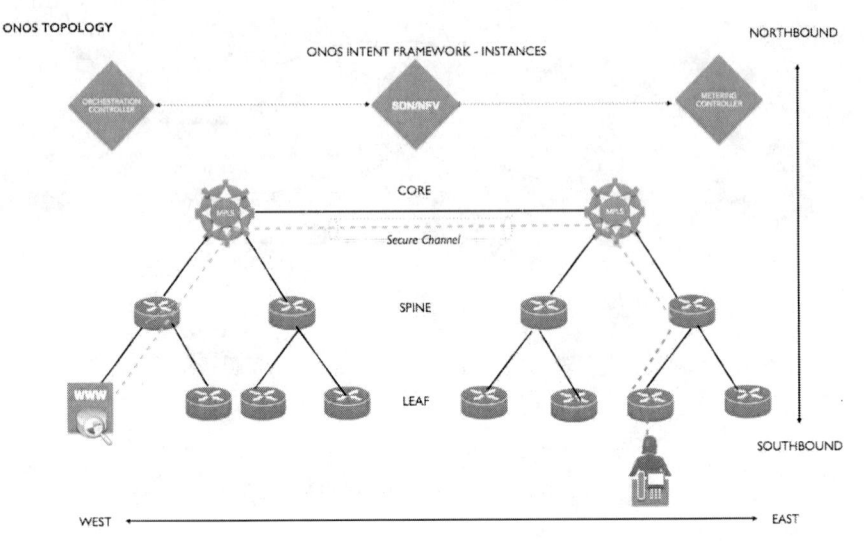

Figure 56 ONOS (OPEN NETWOrK OPERATING SYSTEM)

If, in theory, you combined ONOS with NDN, eNUM and the Open Compute Project to support this merger the promise of an overlay network becomes a reality with very high levels of trust and security. This suggested InternetNew model combines all the elements and mimics SS7 but builds the foundation for countries to act independently in the Internet sphere. This would allow fixed and mobile networks to synchronize rollouts and continued operation

COUNTRY INTERNET

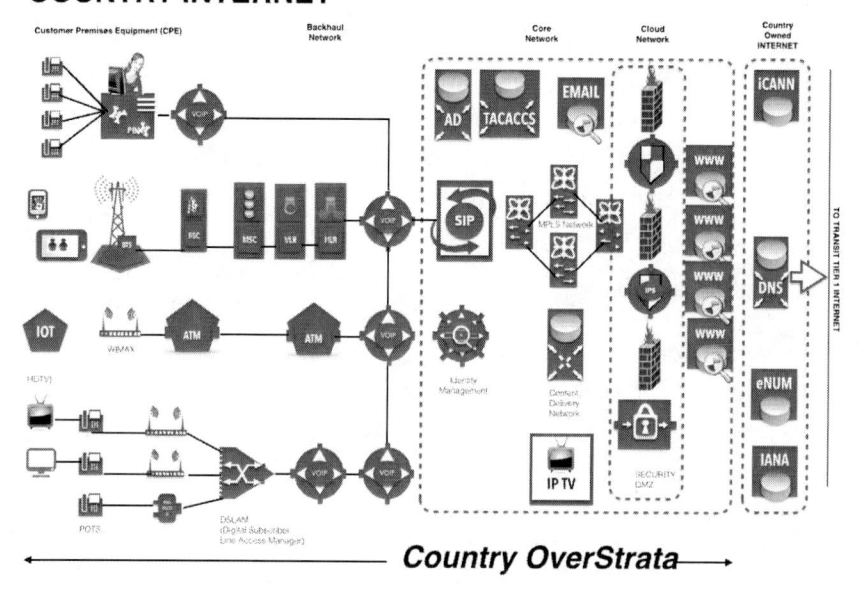

Figure 57 SELF DETERMINED DOMINION INTERNET

10.13 DOMINION INTERNETS

The INTERNETNEW architecture could be heading towards a country based extra Internet. To stymie Cybrid wars the Internet needs to be a global responsibility, a single authority, pushing down to each country, in a disciplined fashion. The next generation Internet could be a secure mesh topology connected globally by over-strata and could mimic the old Public Telephone Subscriber Network and IN capabilities. This PSTN type approach is needed to map the identification requirements of the individuals, organisations and offices. It should also provide access to the international network. Using similar techniques deployed in SS7 networks and relying on ENUM and a revamped DNS platform, the over-strata ensure localised non-repudiation. Responsibility is thrust southbound to users and traceability and accountability. These modes are well known and understood by engineers in every country in the world.

It allows dominion authorities to set their boundaries and enforce their Internet policies inside their territory. It should allow each Nation State to blacklist other countries malicious websites depending on their cultural preferences alliance choice is now a localised decision point. In the UAE for instance it is illegal to access pornographic sites and harmful images are blocked, there is no reason why this should not be extended to countries that wish to maintain religious integrity and cultural identity. It would allow countries to develop their own standards and even help ignite their own technology companies to develop their own technologies, their own Operating Systems, their own components. Nearly every country in the world has enough Computer Scientists to make this work and develop Dominion systems; it only needs the political will to do this. The only overriding standard would be the numbering, which could resemble the Internal Standard Telephone numbering scheme making eNUM an easy decision. It would provide the ability to contact anyone but without being bound by the underlying infrastructure.

It should allow receivers of information, content and data to set policies according to Content type and allow for how and where users receive their information. They should have freedom to select their names, Identities and addresses with as near-to-zero centralised control as possible, but obviously some governments may wish to link these to national identity databases (as many IDs are based on now). In effect it is a return to the National and International Telephone Directory.

Just as an aside to this thrust, back in the 90's the Chinese created an IETF RFC (Internet Engineering Task Force - Request for Comment) proposing 10 Bit addressing, so that IP addresses could be calculated on an abacus. This was obviously rejected at the time because the world was 8 Bit focussed (US driven) and a 10 Bit world would have allowed the Chinese a superior technological advantage. (Note: I have been unable to source to RFC to cite the work). This freedom to address users and devices in country would assist in securing assets from cyber attack as a conversion gateway would be required which would be monitored for illegal traffic.

The case for encapsulating a true point of packet source and origin is however still valid, and until this IP traffic becomes traceable (like a Forensics analysis on an originating electronic signature) defences will remain blindfolded. Due to this cloaking technique the countries servers hosting the attack are implicated and could be legally responsible. This is why I believe network protocols need a complete overhaul generally (especially DNS) and IPv6

The Internet is sufficiently fast to allow Country routers to be inserted into the Internet topology allowing for the BIG FAT PIPE or DUMB PIPE approach. Vendors are now looking at router technologies that will produce zero latency (or reduced to micro seconds), thus providing a real time Internet experience globally. The problem is not all content is needed all the time, so a mechanism is needed to cache data that's appropriate to the country and users. NDN would solve that problem if it can be linked to a billing system. Petabit routers could mimic SS7 – rather that traffic using core based routers at a transit level, distributed edge routers could make routing decisions on a country basis. At this level of granularity tariffs could be applied locally.

Moving the Web Registry (iCANN) to country responsibility level and management and pushing down IANA responsibility to country level allows nationally base Telco's and ISPs to maximise revenues from website creation and value added services to protect SMBs. This new latitude would also allow national encryption keys to be created on a per country basis and avoid remote snooping by hackers. The creation of country based encryption keys would again spur innovation on a country basis.

This would mean that county's would have full control of Internet traffic within their borders and allow for limited censorship. Countries would also be able to make their country Internet availability and resilience (improved uptime by increasing the number of ISPs within a country which would also spur employment) by providing an increased number of border gateways available. This would make the Internet a global mesh network and akin to a peer-to-peer topology but with packet traceability. Akin to the old telephone networks of old there should be an overarching body like the ITU-T to manage and develop emerged markets with capital and expertise.

10.14 COUNTRY OVERSTRATA

It's pretty tricky to remember a 128 bit hexadecimal and alphanumeric address. If you had 100 IOT devices (as predicted) in your home this could create chaos. A universal numbering scheme needs to be put in place so that all the separate networks co-join and each net citizen are assigned a single number that umbrellas a PC, Tablet, Smartphone, IOT, ASOTs and Watch devices. The eNUM standard is the key to this new model. It's a standard that has been around since 1998 and bridges the mobile, PSTN, Internet and potentially the Internet of Things worlds. ENUM uses special Domain Name Server types to translate a telephone number into a Uniform Resource Identifier (URI) or IP address that can be used in Internet communications. Being able to dial telephone numbers the way customers have come to expect is considered crucial for the convergence of classic telephone service (PSTN) and Internet telephony (Voice over IP, VoIP), and for the development of new IP multimedia services. The problem of a single universal personal identifier for multiple communication services can be solved with different approaches. One simple approach is the Electronic Number Mapping System (ENUM), developed by the IETF, using existing E.164 telephone numbers, protocols and infrastructure to indirectly access different services available under a single personal identifier. ENUM also permits connecting the IP world to the telephone system in a seamless manner.

For an ENUM subscriber to be able to activate and use the ENUM service it needs to obtain three elements from a Registrar:

- A personal Uniform Resource Identifier (URI) to be used on the IP part of the network, as explained below.

- One E.164 regular personal telephone number associated with the personal URI, to be used on the PSTN part of the network.

- Authority to write their call forwarding/termination preferences in the NAPTR (a **Name Authority Pointer** (**NAPTR**) is a type of resource record used in the DNS record accessible via the personal URI.

This works as follows: (1) the Country Registrar provides the Subscriber (or Registrant) with a domain name, the URI, that will be used for accessing a DNS server to fetch a NAPTR record, (2) a personal E.164 telephone number (the ENUM number). The URI domain name of (1) is one-to-one mapped to the subscriber E.164 ENUM number of (2). Finally (3) the NAPTR record corresponding to the subscriber URI contains the subscriber call forwarding/termination preferences.

Therefore, if a calling party being at the PSTN network dials a called party ENUM number by touch-typing the E.164 called party number, the number will be translated at the ENUM gateway into the corresponding URI. This URI will be used for looking-up and fetching the NAPTR record obtaining the called party wishes about how the call should be forwarded or terminated (either on IP or on PSTN terminations) – the so-called access information – which the registrant (the called party) has specified by writing his/her choice at the NAPTR record ("Naming Authority Pointer Resource Records" as defined in RFC 3403), such as e-mail addresses, a fax number, a personal website, a VoIP number, mobile telephone numbers, voice mail systems, IP-telephony addresses, web pages, GPS coordinates, call diversions or instant messaging. Alternatively, when the calling party is at the IP side, the User Agent (UA) piece of software of the dialler will allow to dial a E.164 number, but the dialler UA will convert it into a URI, to be used for looking-up at the ENUM gateway DNS and fetch the NAPTR record obtaining the called party wishes about how the call should be forwarded or terminated (again, either on IP addresses, or, on PSTN terminations).

Calling using "verify by name" a new personal E.164 number (the ENUM number) to look-up at a database is therefore an indirect calling support service.[145] This would be a large array of ENUM Registries connected globally. This should solve many of the non-repudiation problems in security and e-commerce. In law, non-repudiation implies one's intention to fulfil their obligations to a contract. It also implies that one party of a transaction cannot deny having received a transaction nor can the other party deny having sent a transaction[146]. A myriad of subscribers and SMB services can be appropriately tailored to subscribers' real requirements without privacy impacts and collections. It would also negate the use of anonymous buying of web servers and creating Botnets.

Cryptographic systems can assist in non-repudiation efforts; the concept is at its core a legal concept transcending technology. It is not, for instance, sufficient to show that the message matches a digital signature signed with the sender's private key, and only the sender could have sent the message and nobody else could have altered it in transit. The alleged sender could in return demonstrate that the digital signature algorithm is vulnerable or flawed, or allege or prove that his signing key has been compromised.

The fault for these violations may or may not lie with the sender himself, and such assertions may or may not relieve the sender of liability, but the assertion would invalidate the claim that the signature necessarily proves authenticity and integrity and would prevent repudiation.[147]

By deploying ENUM on a country basis and enforcing its adoption into country law then many cyber attacks can be traced back to the country of origin, and the originator by name and location, enabling offensive responses. This solves the major problem of determining responsibility for an attack. This enforcement would halt many Nation States attempting remote damage and should halt around 50% of known cyber attack scenarios. By deploying this overlay this should aid the ITU-T to charge a minimal amount to act as global register (a SIP Registrar) or maintainers of the Internet Directory. ENUM is a way to build naturalisation and build in obligations to make Net citizens accountable.

10.15 THE LAST MILE RACE

40% of the world is connected to the Internet; the question is how emerged countries can compete with developed countries infrastructures. US based vendors now seek to partner with developing countries to assist with the spread of the Internet (Google Balloons). The preferred option is via Fibre Optics played to major conurbations, this can be achieved via Automated Train laying,[148] Mechanical roadside laying[149], Blown Fibre [150] and sub terrain drilling systems (Micro Trenching and Mole Ploughing)[151] and traditional civil works. A fibre optic repeater is required every 18 km. Technologies like Microwave Tower to Tower systems, Medium Voltage Power-line system for Backbone Backhaul across jungle or mountainous areas. Obviously Fibre Optic Cable can be run alongside overhead power poles using catenary loops. From the backhaul, last mile technologies range from LTE (4G Mobile), 5G 1(GB mobile networks) and Meshed Tower networks, FTTH (Fibre to the Home), or WIMAX (WLAN). Deployment of macro and micro Cell (Femtocells) infrastructures within campus buildings, and Wi-Fi Points of Presence should accelerate expanded reach.

This entire infrastructure can be funded by VGI (Vendor Government or Public/Private Initiatives) allowing Governments to leverage vendor support and experts, but in particular long term partnership unions perhaps with cash rich technology companies. The ITU could control a slush fund based on country and vendor contributions. Not only will this benefit countries wishing to exploit these financing capabilities but vendors can really assist Governments and ISPs/CSPs reach the next 60% of potential subscribers.

Nation based Telco's can take command of their AS, Addressing and Telco's and ISPs can then build cheap Cloud facilities and associated cloud Services with which to build a profitable revenue base and re-invest in country skills bases and subsequently create an attractive business case for citizens.[152] Content can then be resold to CDNs for additional revenue streams and extends local products for global and traceable sales.

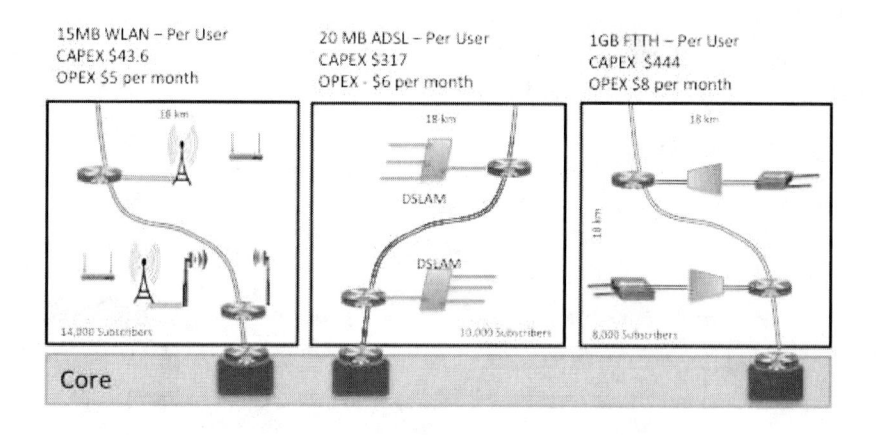

Figure 58 LAST MILE COSTS PER USER PER 324 SQ KM

10.16 INTERNET GOVERNANCE - LEGITIMACY AND SOVEREIGNTY

Internet Governance is based on a multi stakeholder model. Originally it was based on loosely coupled technical authority, which was originally led by the Internet Society (ISOC) principle to keep the Internet "Open and free". Subsequently commercial entities lobbied governments to get involved. An eco system of academic forums (fora) has emerged that have the reverse effect on governance adds confusion and dilutes the progress of reconstructing of the Internet.

The Internet challenges the pillars of the Westphalian model of sovereignty. In the last decade the concept of "Open" has become confused, the US attempting to retain control and drive open discourse, with other nation states wishing to attenuate those principles. The recent surveillance cases and rise in cyber attacks and the Over the Top applications have become the termites in the room that no-one wishes to discuss openly. Many non-western countries are fearful of these issues. China for example has 380,000,000 Internet subscribers more than any other country globally but has no influence on how it is run.

To protect sovereignty eighty-nine countries have adopted updated International Telecommunications Regulations (ITRs). Fifty countries have yet to decide on the way forward (either non technical or no money) and wait for the WSIS plus 10 outcomes in April 2015. In parallel, the ITU attempts to reaffirm its traditional role as the honest global technical policeman. The ITU faces an operating deficit that hinders investing in Least Developed Countries Internet infrastructures and is reliant on contributions to pursue this route.

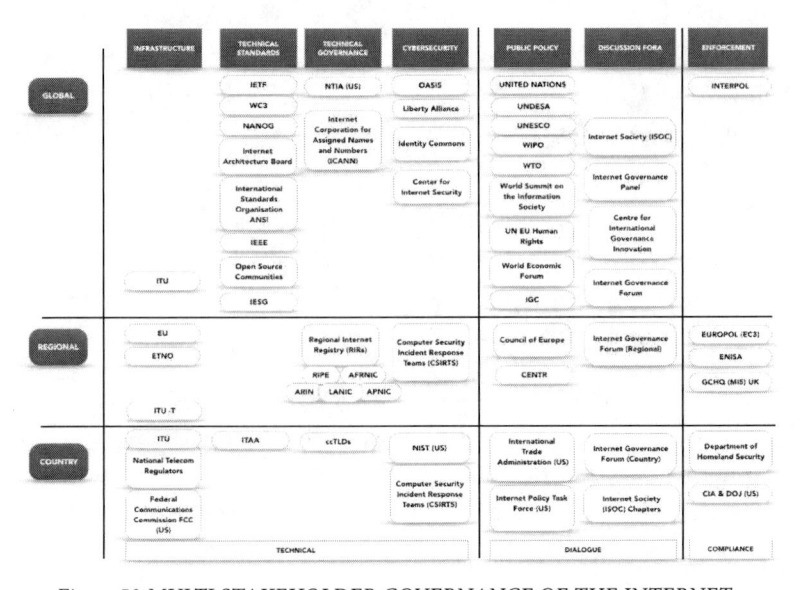

Figure 59 MULTI STAKEHOLDER GOVERNANCE OF THE INTERNET

If you are lucky enough to visit the Trevi Fountain in Rome you will know that when you visit the fountain you throw a coin into the waters (over your left shoulder with your right hand) and make a wish and you will return to Rome another time. The Ancient romans used often to throw coins in fountains; rivers or lakes to make the Gods of water favour their journey and help them go back home safely. An estimated 3,000 Euros are thrown into the fountain each day. The money has been used to subsidise a supermarket for Rome's needy; however, there are regular attempts to steal coins from the fountain. This is like Internet Governance - you have an idea, you throw a coin in, but there's 3,000 conflicting points of view, it's unlikely to be seen or heard of again, and finally the ideas going to get stolen each night. The disparate parties concerns regarding the governance of the Internet has caused deep rifts in who owns what and where. How it would be paid for and how it should be used. It has become a convoluted set of rights that stifle any cohesive agreement. Large countries send cohorts of attendees to maintain the status quo. All this table tennis does not help address users cyber security concerns. There is no single Authority that sits across all of these bodies to help the end user while everyone plays power politics.

The Centre for International Governance Innovation (CIGI) has a view on the inevitability of governance; "The current model for Internet governance lacks an adequate process to obtain the consent that is necessary for legitimacy in that it has neither adequate representation nor the tools of coercion. Non-Western participants could reasonably point out that they did not consent to the existing model, and that being invited later to join is not the same thing as being involved in it's drafting. The greatest challenge to the legitimacy of the existing multi-stakeholder structure is its failure to make the Internet more secure.[153]" Countries want their voices heard and wish to extend their sovereignty into cyberspace governance.

10.17 THE INTERNET AUTHORITY

This section is blue-sky thinking. Internet Governance should be the right of every subscriber. I started thinking about this problem from the bottom up — the subscriber. I considered what voice a subscriber has and the work done by thousands to reach the point we are at now. The Subscriber has no voice. Subscribers cannot vote on key issues relating to the open Internet. There is no single site on the Internet that facilitates questions on rights and enables subscribers to vote. As I have mentioned before there are a myriad of government based Internet ("Do as I say - but don't do as I do") forums and bodies that have expanded a problem many fold without addressing the real problem.

There is not one site on the Internet where a subscriber can go to and vote on Internet policy in a global fashion. This is weird because the Internet was designed to provide an Open Platform where users could voice their opinion.

Where does a subscriber go to alert people of a security blip, or, complain against a vendor? Besides Twitter where can a subscriber go to object to country ruling that is perceived to rob subscribers of freedom of speech? In a democratic and Open Internet how can we measure subscribers views on surveillance? Out of all the bodies where do you start to complain or alert a global user base of security vulnerability? Would vendors react quicker if vulnerabilities were publicly announced? Where do countries get access to collective funds to assist in broadband rollouts? What's needed is a single independent authority that's crowd funded by global subscribers to air their views. (I have called this The Internet Authority for now).

This body would be an uncensored single point of expression for the global Internet community. It would provide a voting platform (accessed by anyone interested) to allow key decisions in an uncensored democratic way, allow subscribers to complain against vendors and report hacking attacks. At the moment no one seems to provide this platform, or facilitate this feedback.

When governments do not get involved with the Telecommunications, Mobile and the Internet; self-determination happens. These infrastructures grow independent of political will. Governments are more concerned with tax collections from these companies and spectrum license sell offs. With the Internet, governments feel left out and see taxes disappear over the Internet to another country. So should we steer the Internet back to its secure single and independent country roots? The 'gear-stick', diagram suggests a simplistic governance model. It attempts to legitimise the technical infrastructure and security bodies best of breed thinking towards a collaborative dominion base. It collates public policy and fora to reduced entities to manage going forward. Joining these disparate entities into a single "The

Internet Authority" should make life simpler for subscribers and SMBs and governance bodies.

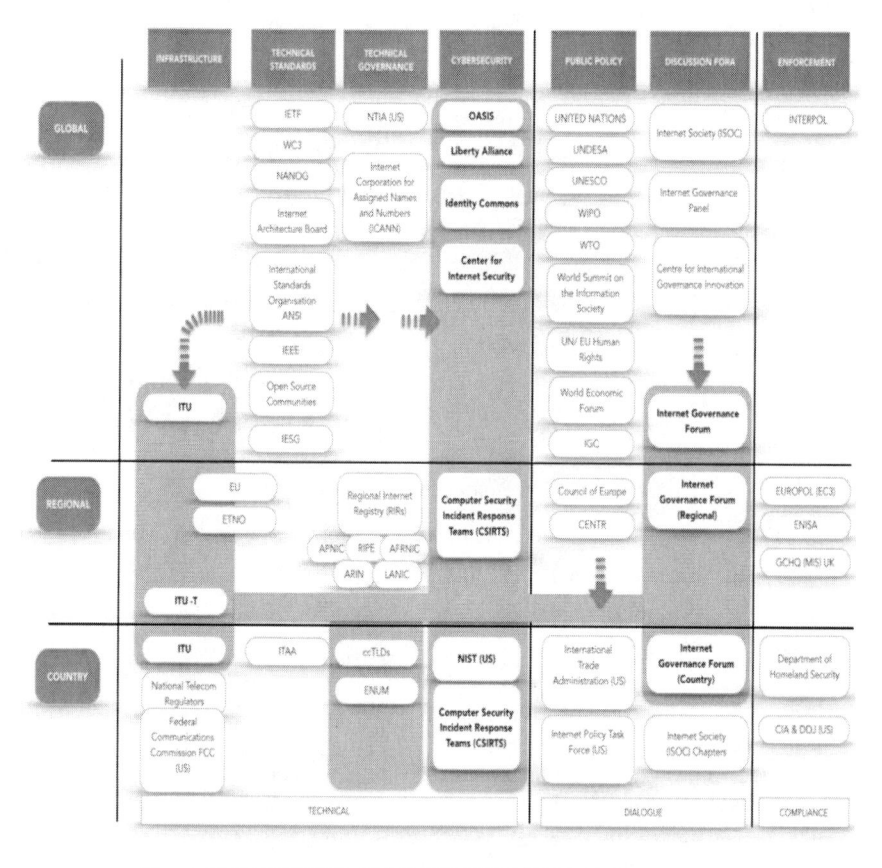

Figure 60 SIMPLIFIED GEAR STICK INTERNET GOVERNANCE

If a country creates a Dominion Cloud then they act as an IXP (Internet Exchange Point) and in theory they do no wrong should they pursue this route. If this was created independently, is this not a dominions' democratic right? In theory as long as they comply with technical controls there is nothing to stop them creating their own fish eye lens view of the InternetNew. This ideal should not stem growing private IXPs within a country. Internet resilience is enhanced when at least three ISPs (or IXPs) are based within a country. This mix not only helps employment but also spurs the development of new services — therefore benefiting citizens. A government could run an IXP explicitly for Government websites (Hospitals, Voting, Social

Security, Tax collections, Import and export duties). Thereafter private IXP entities can focus on Content delivery to mobile or broadband delivery and infrastructure rollouts. The private IXPs can be Telco's and Mobile Operators merging and divesting services?

The Internet Authority should also be a body that helps contribute or allocate funds for emerged cash strapped countries and land locked countries to get citizens on the web. I think this body should coordinate fund raising from vendors and institutions like the IMF, UN Development Board and ITU to assist in the rollout of fibre backbones and local loop broadband. We all know that the Internet needs this fundamental fixed telecommunications infrastructure; sending blimps and drones into the air is not a long term strategy – it seems to be a quick way of getting names and addresses and identities. The idea here is why not invest in the remaining 60% of the global unconnected populace.

Dominion clouds do not cost that much to set up the problem lies in rolling out services to remote areas and providing electrical power. Using the economic model electrical cable can share the same duct work as fiber optic will cost $58 CAPEX per household (based on a 100MW Wind Farm generation per 324 sq km deployment).

10.18 AN ECONOMIC MODEL FOR INTERNETNEW

Minimising the number of diverse groups can help govern the rest of the Internet although I see the arguments that should run it. The Internet is a variable and intangible asset. We know that GDP increases per subscriber per country increases by 15% per annum as country bound self-employment grows which in turn cascades further employment. If the cost to complete 100% coverage of the Internet within a country ranges from .01% to 3% of a country' GDP then you would think that it would be everywhere right? The problem lies with access to capital funding.

The Internet is a utility like electricity and telephony. Electricity is only 137 years old (the Edison Electric Light Company was formed in 1878). In 1877 Alexander Graham Bell formed the Bell Telephone Company. In 1987 (one hundred years later) the first Internet ISPs were formed.

Countries cannot make money out of simple provisioning, and don't have the capital to extend the Internet countrywide. How can a country get that asset value realised? Lets consider a new model for the commercial Internet. Banks hold all the capital. The International Monetary Fund holds even more capital. Countries pay in to become members and release capital as requested. Banks and Countries can raise significant sums to build out communications networks. The payback is relatively quick but revenue would continue for decades.

What if the credit card type model was applied to each country, group of dominions, or, regions wishing to build out real broadband Internet connectivity? The idea is to incentivise the country to extend the number of subscribers and still get paid annually by the number of subscribers maintained. Each country shares the INTERNETNEW model ownership, with a generic company who would be responsible for rolling out overstrata infrastructure. The company would be incentivised to build out and the annual dividend would be paid out to the country based on number of subscribers. To ensure the system works the holding company issues IP-ENUM cost metrics addresses (like a unique credit card) and maintains the security posture necessary to make this work. This has multiple benefits in that the country gets Internet ubiquity within the country, can obviously re-invest in education and government services as well as receive annual income from a trusted Internet source that pays annual income. Banks, Telco's, ISPs, CSPs, and Mobile Operators can share the profits derived from transaction billings.

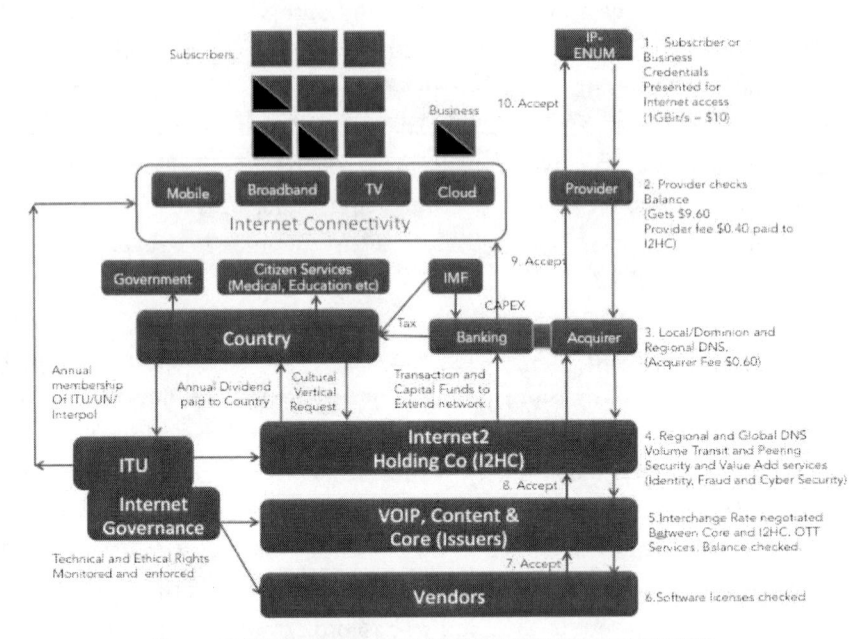

Figure 61 INTERNETNEW POSSIBLE ECONOMIC MODEL

The holding company drives down Internet Transit and Peering costs and allows countries to extend the Internet Service to every citizen whilst also realising service transactions revenues. This would allow banks to provide services to every citizen so extending their capital and customer base. It provides identity transparency that should kill off cyber attacks as traffic is traceable and the end user is responsible. The IP-ENUM is geographic and activity is tied to the user. It also eradicates software piracy as licences will be tied to the IP-ENUM address, the $59 billion saved will be churned back into the INTERNETNEW Holding Company to kick off the INTERNETNEW extensions. In addition because the end user is now responsible for Internet damage replication of identity becomes futile and legally accountable. SPAM servers will need an owner, which will mean SPAM would be eradicated. More importantly than that the annual $731 billion lost to cyber attacks by hackers and countries should cease s activity is recordable and liable to legal and country sanctions.

The model is similar to the VOIP billing model, so little change to existing billing systems or exchanges is required. As the model resembles transaction processing (allowing each level to receive fees) the ability to track duplicate named streams is now possible. This means that an end user as a subscriber, or, as a business user who controls remote servers and perform anonymous Internet activity have a point of origination. Hypothetically an end user or SMB would provide their IP-ENUM to buy a service or a server in another country. This legitimises the transaction and modifies end user behaviours. If the NDN service was deployed then end users could use software or content on a Pay as you Use basis. This would halt the ability to Command and Control DDOS attacks. It can also monitor the types of software used by subscribers ensuring licenses are paid for legitimately and block hacking tools. It resembles a closed loop Pay-per-Use transaction model. Countries benefit in a myriad of ways; Subscribers are linked to Government systems enabling Cradle to Grave welfare services, secures borders, measuring Education and Medical needs and contact voting by the end user. It will allow countries to grow their GDP and assist in extending electrical services to remote locations INUPS (Intelligent Utility Network Pipes). The more users the more annual dividend is returned. The banks are repaid and deficits repaid by the dividends from the Holding company.

This also allows for technology upgrades over the next century. 5G signalling is only 10 years away (1 GB speeds to mobile users). It will require new spectrum to deliver this, the spectrum would be provided by the asset arm of the country to the holding company providing preferential and more lucrative deals from the vendors, which in turn increases country revenues. This system does allow for speedier INTERNETNEW deployment. Banking and other authorities will be able to deploy banking facilities to every subscriber in a country and traceable to out of country activity. If you are in the US and your home base is Vietnam when someone uses your card in Iceland the holing company will be pretty sure you do not originate the transaction. The only drawback I see in the model is that it will eliminate the Prepaid mobile model. However this transitory debt is moved to the IP-ENUM auspices and an extended credit approach would be needed or extended by the mobile providers, however billing is simplified so dramatic operating cost reduction is counterbalanced by legitimate INTERNETNEW transactions.

Now I don't know if this model has be proposed before, if it has then apologies, why it was not implemented is a different question.

10.19 STEPCHECK

- In this chapter we have reviewed the evolution of transmission networks

- This evolution has been built of archaic protocols that are in need of overhaul

- We have seen the US propose a Net Neutrality proposal which could mean a brave new Internet world for the countries around the globe

- We have seen how the PSTN, Mobile and Broadband networks need convergence

- The proposal for a central body is needed to manage the global networks and arbitrate Net Citizens charters to maintain freedom of content access

- Looks at a Country Over Strata to provide country based Tier 1 equivalency and independence from US carriers and associated bad behaviours

- Reviews the Trillion dollar market that will be generated by pursuing this route

- Looks at how country can build their own high tech revenues

- Reviews how global citizens become responsible for their actions.

- Discusses how countries can act locally and trade globally — securely.

- Reviews INTERNETNEW and a revised Governance model.

- Proposes an Economic model to initiate Country and Global Security

11 RIDPOINTS

In this part we will look at security safeguards and components to bolster a cyber security posture. We will look at each RIDPOINT in depth from Physical Security, How to locate and build a Data Centre and what budgets are needed to get a minimum degree of protection through the deployment of security components.

As Churchill so aptly put it "Give us the tools and we will finish the job". The following chapters are the tools and steps needed to follow a Via Ferrata security posture. RIDPOINTS covers the following topics:

Risk Management
Identity Management
Defence in Depth (**Domino**)
Perimeter Defence
Operations Nerve Centre
IT Frameworks and Regulations
Network Monitoring
Training
Security Incident Event Monitoring

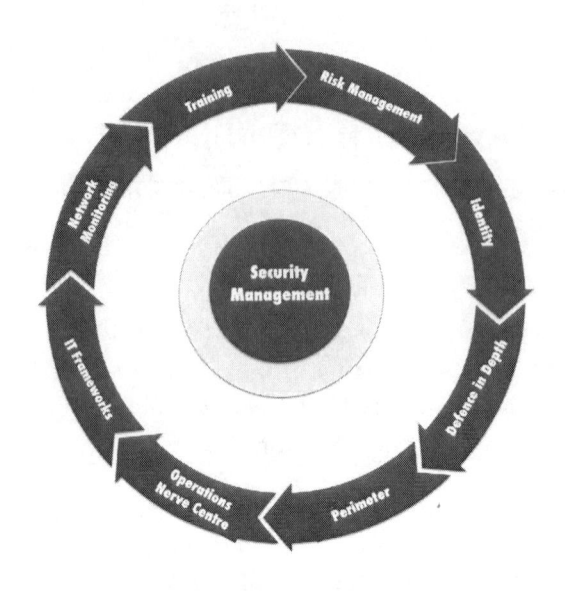

Figure 62 RIDPOINTS

11.1 RIDPOINTS – RISK MANAGEMENT

Adversaries employ new exploits and automation attacks whilst vendors continue to create new exposures. SMBs need an approach to deploy automation to mitigate these attacks and a way to report Risks. Risk communication and planning is necessary to minimise risk. To help SMBs understand the report risk workflow I used the analogy of Via Ferrata (the Iron Road) when I work with customers.

Via Ferrata's were built by armies in the First World War. They originated in the Dolomites and spread across the Alps to smooth the movement of entire armies and equipment. There are 170 in Italy alone but most countries with mountains now use these as tourist attractions.

The VIA FERRATA approach should be an aide memoir and enables any executive or team member get risk averse. Cyber security is like a mountain. An SMB is taking their team members to the summit. The right equipment is needed and doubledouble checked. Each team member is suitably protected and A Via Ferrata is a steel cable from the basecamp to the summit, which runs along the route and is periodically (every 3 to 10 metres) fixed to the rock. Using a lanyard (or two loops), climbers can secure themselves by **looping** to the to the cable, limiting any fall. The cable can also be used as aid to climbing, and additional climbing aids, such as iron rungs (temples), pegs, carved steps and even ladders and bridges are often provided. Team members connect their lanyards to the cable and climb their way to the mountaintop[154]. Therefore, the Via Ferrata allow otherwise dangerous routes to be undertaken without the risks associated with unprotected scrambling and climbing. Each team member is made aware of the risks and their responsibility for safety is self-determined. The control of the loops is within their immediate personal control.

Security is a set of interconnected handoffs not a just a set of products. Products provide some protection, but the only way to effectively do business in an insecure world is to put handoffs in place that recognise the inherent insecurity and risk in the products. The trick here is to reduce your risk of exposure regardless of the products or patches. To reduce risk you need to know what the risks, how they start, and how they progress through a SMBs estate and apply **Omniocular**[155] monitoring and Perpetual Improvement to eliminate those risks. YOU CANNOT OBSERVE THE INVISIBLE, so risk should be visible!

11.2 PROCESS IS DEAD LONG LIVE CRAFTFLOW

In the Artisan age craft flow will eventually replace work. Work is a medieval term from the Old English "perform physical labour" and also "perform sexually". As the Artisan Age is more about "technical labour" and "software" and autogenous creation – the term work appears redundant. I am a craftaholic! A craftsman uses their own tools, they have to communicate closely with other team members to ensure their output is correct. In the last century IT operations box and string processes were indeed needed. After the rigorous checklists operations mantras of the mainframe world, the burgeoning Internet based networks created a high degree of Chaos Thinking and clumsy behaviours. Untrained and inexperienced Operators needed process frameworks and stringent management to get things done. This created vacuum silos and operators sucking on kryptonite lollipops. Discipline was severely lacking and we have all seen "operator error" impacts on business as usual. We have slavishly followed the stress created by processes procrastination compounded by the inability to deliver.

Lets be clear about this. Process is fine, it is a legal term but it's the process interfaces that invariably don't work, interfaces gather dirt and so needs a rethink. Have you ever witnessed lawyers agreeing on a wording - that's why judges were invented! Process is so 20th Century! In the 21st Century process are mitigated by Craftflows. Craftlows are how SMBs will interact with Enterprises. As Enterprises focus on robotica the creative Craftflows will be looped to SMBs. The SMBs become the idea and innovation food that the Enterprises desire. Adversaries don't use processes so why should we? For the last decade in IT that's what we have all followed – process! Dick Brown at Cable and Wireless used to repeat his mantra daily, "It's all about process, process, process". There are a plethora of security frameworks, all process-bound until it has the reverse effect, it sucks up the time to implement and then maintain them. We have created a process framework for every part of IT, but at the front line and in IT Operations it's only 20% of the solution, automated tools and communications account for the other 80%. If all the cyber security frameworks and processes were implemented then there would not be a cyber security problem – right?

One company audited had 3000 IT team members. Few knew the basics of Service or Operational Level Agreements, or the processes that connected them! Once we mapped out these agreements it was clear that 20% of the processes were duplicated and a further 30% of processes were out of date and 30% were not followed, or, ignored (but documented), leaving 100% of FTE effort to make 20% of process work. People using the same tools (mostly illegal), the internal network buckled under the network monitoring traffic alone. Operators turned down alarming levels on the tools so all they would do was wait for the server to go down and reboot. The 12000 servers, some eight years old and only 4% utilised on average only half of these had known passwords. These are familiar stories from large estates. This is why frameworks address only 20% of the problem.

Tools need rules and need documenting. Tools are needed to manage risk. We need to understand the risk before we apply reporting. Making reporting work needs people who all need to know **what** to communicate.

11.3 VIA FERRATA COMMUNICATION

Asides from this harsh and dissonant observation, some fundamental framework practices actually do work. Much of it is common sense. All team members need to learn a loose flow of communication really does help an organisation. This Via Ferrata approach is an escalation from of reporting a method I employ to help owners really understand multifaceted security issues – no need to understand deep box and string processes – but to keep in mind the 5 x C's of PIE. The 5 C's are **Consult, Continuous, Configuration, Change and Check**. The 5 C's should be tattooed on each team member's fingers. The fun of IT is being able to solve hard problems and keep productivity up. For the SO this is a way to make sure the lines of defences within the organisation work. Boards can understand these lines easily.

We need a better approach. The balance here is handoffs 20% and Communications 80%. Without all team members knowing what is going on each day mistakes happen, so **teaming's** replace meetings and **craftflows** and **handoffs** replace process and process interfaces. Closed Loop Processes are replaced by **Loops**. **Stepchecks** replace procedures. You have seen I don't talk about staff, that is replaced with **team members**. Managers replaced by **captains**. QA replaced by **PIE** and **doubledouble**.

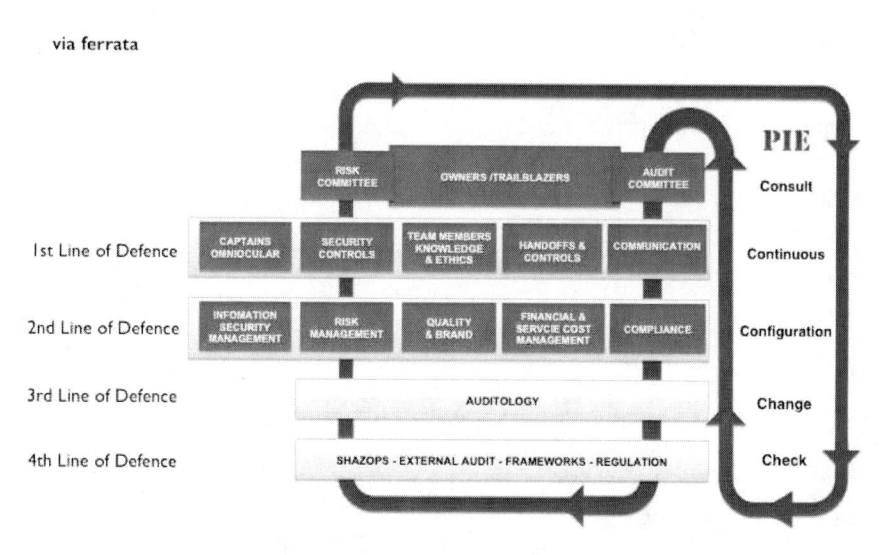

Figure 63 VIA FERRATA REPORTING LOOPS

STP-F2F is my favourite daily mantra here; **S**ee **T**wenty **P**eople **F**ace to (2) **F**ace is the only way to improve communications, increase your personal branding and avoid email dictate. If your team members live and breathe this mantra then the prime principle of Via Ferrata communication is achieved – **go talk about how it should work**. Being a developer or an operator can be a lone wolf occupation and encourages singularity of thought, rumination and procrastination. Lone wolves can get disillusioned fast and need to be part of a pack.

One of my closest friends is a lone wolf programmer; he sits in an office and never integrates with his colleagues. By his own admission he shuns meetings and wiles away the day by reading company documents. This behaviour has led him to snoop on sensitive data. He knows what his colleagues and his bosses earn and foolishly resents their success. He is borderline Insider material and therefore a risk. The challenge here is for SMBs to manage team members with kid gloves. The way I manage team members is to increase their Emotional Quotient Unification and Intelligence Programming (EQUIP). Appealing to knowledge workers intelligence and ensuring they are encouraged to unify their daily activities increases their cognition and eliminates procrastination. It gets developers out of their Shell (*sic*).

Reporting the SMBs security posture through Via Ferrata is a way to engage Owners, Board Members and team members into a cohesive unit. Knowing your defensive posture on any security issue is paramount here. Lets look at some of the outputs that need reporting.

11.4 RISK MANAGEMENT

Once the bastion of the finance sector, Operations Risk Management was a tool required to manage risky business and the capital budget cycle. Today the military, governments, SMBs face risks from all corners of the globe. Risk is a mind-set that should be adopted companywide.

Risk Management is often abused as part of the business vernacular to prove to stakeholders the need to kick off "yet another project" (YAP). YAPs deflect resource are the reason so many projects fail and Project Management reputation plummets. The 'stakeholders' usually not technically au fait enough to actually make decisions, even when the information is complete. This is why Technical Steering Committees and Audit and Risk Committees exist. Stakeholders need constant education until they comprehend anything. Stakeholders in the 21st Century need to have a technical MBA. In fact there should be a Master of Technical Administration post doctorate degree. Van Helsing and Buffy the Vampire Slayer are the only two stakeholders I have ever seen do anything constructive! The compilation of risk is twisted and biased by a few individuals who seek to bend board level decision processes, usually for personal career or financial gain. Over the past decade I have seen risk contrived by senior management teams to underpin a strategy that was decided a year ago on a golf course, usually paid for by a vendor. YAPs skew technical strategies, budgets, handoffs and security stability.

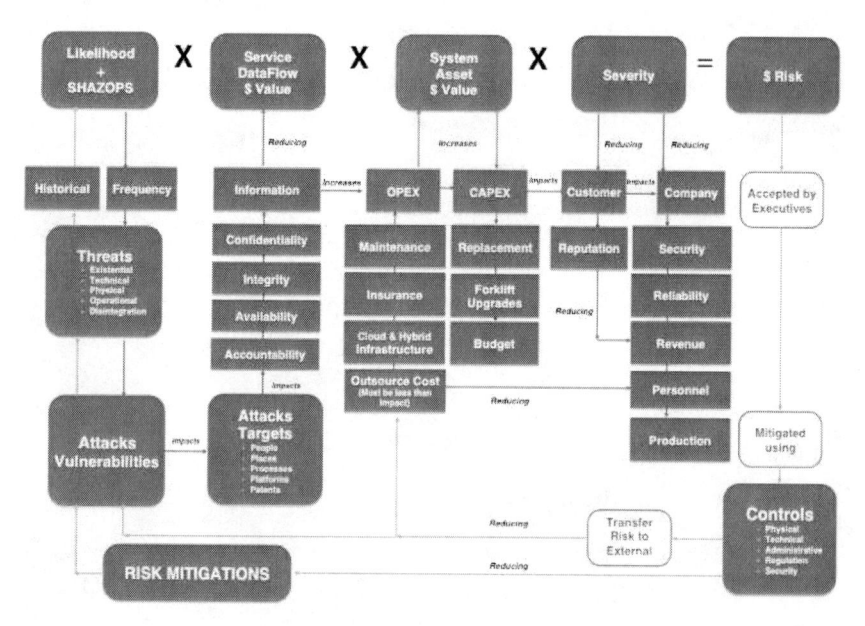

Figure 64 VIA FERRATA RISK FLOW

Risk control begins with the identification and classification of specific risks, vulnerabilities and threats. To measure risk, a must have is a detailed assessment of assets, exposures and losses; once collated a risk can be quantified. I have seen many SO's fail at this task and also fail to clearly communicate the reality to owners and peers. The problem facing risk management is that most practitioners use matrices and quadratic equations that rarely address real cost issues of risk. Most risk managers have tended to think qualitatively and this may do a laudable job, but misses the point. The Risk Matrix is provided as a number from 1 to 5, or as a percentage or worse, in coloured Excel cells as red, amber, and green. Usually these figures do actually represent a clear view of the estate. Risk introduces a dangerous fallacy that structured inadequacy is almost as good as adequacy (Good Enough). The Risk Matrix in isolation does not complete the view or provide Omniocular comprehension. The qualitative risk analysis is a process of assessment of the impact of the identified risk factors. Through this process the priorities are determined to solve the potential risk factors, depending on the impact they could have.

Via Forrenta Reporting- Quantitive Risk Managment Matrix

Company Annual Revenue	5,000,000	Revenue per Hour	571

Tolerance

CATASTROPHIC LOSSES

Historical	Frequency	Likelihood										
Happens several times a year in this company	Minute	7	0	1	1	1	2	3	4	5	6	7
Happens several times a year in this facility	Hour	6	0	0	0	1	2	2	3	4	5	6
Happens several times a year in this facility	Daily	5	0	0	0	0	1	2	2	3	4	5
Expected to occur in this company several times	Monthly	4	0	0	0	0	0	1	1	2	2	3
Expected to occur in this company several times	Annually	3	0	0	0	0	0	0	1	1	1	1
Expected to occur in this company several times	Decade	2	0	0	0	0	0	0	0	0	0	1
Expected to occur in this company in its lifetime	Century	1	0	0	0	0	0	0	0	0	0	1
		Severity Cost	1	2	3	4	5	6	7	8	9	10
		Total Exposure Value	0	71,142	1,595,425	3,120,850	4,646,276	6,171,701	7,477,126	8,782,551	12,698,827	16,615,103
	Service DataFlow Value	(Possible Fine)	0	220,000	440,000	660,000	880,000	1,100,000	1,100,000	1,100,000	1,100,000	1,100,000
		Number of Records		1,000	2,000	3,000	4,000	5,000	5,000	5,000	5,000	5,000
		Avg Cost per Record		220	220	220	220	220	220	220	220	220
	System Asset Value	TOTAL	0	450,000	450,000	450,000	450,000	450,000	450,000	450,000	450,000	450,000
		OPEX	0	200,000	200,000	200,000	200,000	200,000	200,000	200,000	200,000	200,000
		CAPEX	0	250,000	250,000	250,000	250,000	250,000	250,000	250,000	250,000	250,000
	Revenue Loss		0	571	1,303,142	2,606,284	3,909,426	5,212,569	6,515,711	7,818,853	11,728,279	15,637,706
			0	<$100K	< $200K	<$300K	<$400	<$500	<$600	<$700	<$800	<$900
	PE Add		0	600,000	600,000	600,000	600,000	600,000	600,000	600,000	600,000	600,000
	Security Quotient		12%	12%	12%	12%	12%	12%	12%	12%	12%	12%
	Reputation		0	0	0	0	0	0	0	0	0	0
	Reliability	Hourly Loss	0	571	2283	4566	6849	9132	11416	13699	20548	27397
		Downtime Hours	0	1	4	8	12	16	20	24	36	48

Figure 65 VIA FERRATA RISK REPORT

The definite characteristic of the qualitative model is the use of subjective indexes, such as ordinal hierarchy: low-medium- high, vital-critical-important, benchmark etc. On the other hand, quantitative risk analysis obtains numerical results that express the probability of each risk factor and its consequences on the objectives of the company and projects, but also the risk on the entire project programme risk. The process uses techniques such as the Monte Carlo method for:

- Determine the probability of reaching an objective

- Risk quantification on the entire project's level and displaying additional cost

- Identify priority risk factors through the quantification of their contribution to the risk index on the level of the entire project, identifying some realistic changes of cost and applying an activity plan.

The most common formula for evaluating risk exposure is $E = L \times P$, (Think Emerson, Lake and Palmer to remember this) where:

E = risk Exposure

L = Loss

P = risk Probability

When compiling Via Ferrata reporting use real dollars or dominion currency costs of risks. Owners and boards and banks understand these dollar amounts. There is no question on the validity of the exercise and owners can make real decisions on which project should be prioritised.

11.5 RIPS

In the example there is a risk tolerance provided by service data flow and the impact on assets and revenue loss.

The Via Ferrata risk model clearly communicates to senior management and team members the Risk Ignition Points (RIPS). This technique assigns a RIP value that impacts the business value chain. What happens when you show the board this? They focus on just the reds, when in reality it's not prioritising. Risk by its very nature is orthogonal, a 2D image that reflects RAG colours. If you have attended as many risk reviews as I have, you always leave the meeting feeling cold, like everyone conveniently missed the root cause and the RIPS. When you ask a risk manager today what the war situational matrix looks like, they would not be able to give a clear answer – it's not in their sphere. RIPS can help stimulate objective thinking and monetises preparedness as well as showing boards the cost of doing nothing. For example a RIP could be a disaster in a country that ultimately affects the SMB supply chain. Risk should be a living thing that is core to any company's Perpetual Improvement Everywhere programme. Project Risk always needs updating daily. There are two ways to enforce this via the Agile Project Risk reporting and EVM and the Risk Register.

11.6 ALE!

ALE was one of my favourite subject areas, until I found out it related to Annual Loss Expectancy and not beer! The Annualised Loss Expectancy (ALE) is the expected monetary loss that can be expected for an asset due to a risk over a one-year period. It is defined as:

ALE = SLE x ARO

SLE is the Single Loss Expectancy and **ARO** is the Annualised Rate of Occurrence.

The Annualised Loss Expectancy is that it can be used directly in a cost-benefit analysis and plumbed into the Risk Matrix. If a threat or risk has ALE of $10,000, then it might not be worth spending $20,000 per year on a security measure that will mitigate it. One thing to remember when using the ALE value is that, when the Annualised Rate of Occurrence (ARO) is of the order of one loss per year, there may be a variance in the actual loss, or, the probability that a risk will occur in a particular year. How you gauge this is important but should be as a direct output of understanding the Service Data Flow which we will cover in the next sections. Include all sources as a simple omission can have audit implicatios.

For example, if data suggests that a water leak in a Data Centre is likely to occur once in 25 years, then the annualised rate of occurrence is 1/25 = 0.04. For example, lets assume that the ARO is 0.5 and the SLE is $20,000. The Annualised Loss Expectancy is then $10,000. Using the Poisson distribution, we can calculate the probability of a specific number of losses occurring in a given year:[156] The table shows that the probability of a loss of $30,000 is 0.0758, and that the probability of losses being $40,000 or more is approximately 0.0144. Depending upon our tolerance to risk and our organisation's ability to withstand higher value losses, we may consider that a security measure, which costs $30,000 per year to implement, is worthwhile, *even though it is more than the expected losses due to the threat.*

11.7 SECURITY QUOTIENT

Adding a Security Quotient comes from a Top Down analysis of where the company stands on security maturity. Baseline this position against the findings of the last deep audit will help internal teams identify key goals and approaches to governance and compliance. The SO should produce this Quotient league table so that progress can be demonstrated and ensure that funding is made available to address RIPS.

Security Quotient Rating and Multiplier

Company Revenue	5,000,000	
Number of Shares	12,000	
$ Value per Share	417	

	Security Quotient	Variation	Adjusted Share Value	Company P/E Valuation
Company is ISO 27000 Certified	16%	$66.67	483	5,800,000
Company has a CISO/CISSP	15%	$62.50	479	5,750,000
Company has an Incident Response Plan	14%	$58.33	475	5,700,000
Company has Internal Auditor	13%	$54.17	471	5,650,000
Company has Risk Management methodology	12%	$50.00	467	5,600,000
Company has a Security Policy and AU policies	11%	$45.83	463	5,550,000
Company has documented Disaster Plan	10%	$41.67	458	5,500,000
Company has Information Classifications	9%	$37.50	454	5,450,000
Company has custom applications tested	8%	$33.33	450	5,400,000
Company use Encryption for communications	7%	$29.17	446	5,350,000
Company manages SIEM and IPS/IDS	6%	$25.00	442	5,300,000
Company uses Firewalls	5%	$20.83	438	5,250,000
Company manages own infrastructure	4%	$16.67	433	5,200,000
Company has BYOD Policy	3%	$12.50	429	5,150,000
Company has complied with external audit	2%	$8.33	425	5,100,000
Company is regulated by Governance Body	1%	$4.17	421	5,050,000
Zero Influence	-0%	-$0.00	417	5,000,000
Company uses outsource for key Services	-1%	-$4.17	413	4,950,000
Company has no Cyber Insurance	-2%	-$8.33	408	4,900,000
Company uses external application developers	-3%	-$12.50	404	4,850,000
Company has never been audited	-4%	-$16.67	400	4,800,000
Company has unpatched systems	-5%	-$20.83	396	4,750,000
Company has had a security breach in last year	-6%	-$25.00	392	4,700,000
Company has experienced downtime	-7%	-$29.17	388	4,650,000
Company has no endpoint management	-8%	-$33.33	383	4,600,000
Company has no anti virus in place	-9%	-$37.50	379	4,550,000
Company does not encrypt customer databases	-10%	-$41.67	375	4,500,000
Company has unregulated credit card service	-11%	-$45.83	371	4,450,000
Company has no background checks on staff	-12%	-$50.00	367	4,400,000
Company has never had an audit	-13%	-$54.17	363	4,350,000
Company has no Service cost visibility	-14%	-$58.33	358	4,300,000
Company has no end user security training	-15%	-$62.50	354	4,250,000
Company has untested website	-16%	-$66.67	350	4,200,000

FIGURE 66 - *VIA FERRATA COMPANY SECURITY QUOTIENT*

Complementing the Via Ferrata risk assessment it helps boards identify targets that actually benefit the company and stockholder valuation for the company. It's based loosely of Forward P/E (price earnings ration) instead of net income. The better the security posture the better the net earnings are for the company over the next 12 months.

If investors can clearly see a positive and proactive enterprise the more likely the business can raise further funding. Obviously the Security Quotient is at scale and dependent on the company strategy, revenue and service affecting risks. It helps cover some of the essentials for any business to achieve. Adding this as a weekly update addendum to the risk matrix leaves the risk, audit and technical steering committees leaves them in no doubt where they stand. The higher the quotient the better it is for the company and its security policy. Financial analysts seeking to value public companies who have been hit by major data breaches are already adopting this method. Managing Risk is an audited activity. If you have sufficient budget to do this full time then absolutely seek to make this thoroughly inclusive to your general operations. The example row headers in the Security Quotient table are simplistic and not designed to make this a tedious task demanding 100% of a team's time. Once in place it can be automated (there are multiple tools that can do this). It is essential though that driving down risk is on the minds of all the team members so a distributed and multi input approach is favoured here. This could be an agenda item on the security toolbox talk at the start of each teaming.

11.8 RISK STANDARDS

At the time of publishing there are multiple Risk Management and Risk Analysis methods and Tools - pick one. Some are better known than others, but most follow the above example. All have strengths and weaknesses which may be pertinent to company type, location or degree of process engineering required for operational management. I worked on the original CRAMM product a long time back but for SMBs the OCTAVE-S (from CERT.org) is a good choice for SMBs. Risk standards have been developed by standards bodies to address Vertical and Generic camps of thought:

11.9 VERTICAL RISK

- Austrian IT Security Handbook
- Dutch A&K Analysis
- France - EBIOS (Expression des Bosons et Identification des Objectifs de Securitie)
- France - MEHARI (Methode Harmonisee d'Analys de Risques)
- ETSI European Telecommunications Standards Institute - Threat Vulnerability and Risk Analysis (TVRA)
- IT Grundschutz (IT Baseline Protection Manual)
- MAGERIT - (Metodologia de Analysis y Gestation de Riesgos de los Systems de Informacion)
- MICROSOFT Security Risk Management Guide
- MIGRA - (Metodologia Integrate per la Destine del Rischio Aziendale)

11.10 GENERIC RISK

- **CARNEGIE MELLON** Software Engineering Institute - OCATVE-S (For SMBs)
- **CCTA** CCTA Risk Assessment and Management Policy (CRAMM)
- **COBIT** Control Objectives for Information and Related Technologies (COBIT)
- **FAIR** Factor Analysis of Risk Information
- **FIRM** Fundamental Information Risk Management
- **FMEA** Failure Modes and Effects Analysis
- **FRAP** Facilitated Risk Assessment Process
- **ISAMM** Information Security Assessment and Monitoring
- **ISO**
- ISO/IEC 31000:2009 Risk management – Principles and guidelines
- ISO/IEC 30101:2009 Risk management – Risk assessment techniques
- ISO/IEC Guide 73 Risk management – Vocabulary

- **NIST**
    - National Institute of Standards and Technology - NIST SP 800-30 "Risk Management Guide for Information Technology Systems
    - NIST SP 800-39 "Managing Risk from Information Systems - An Organisational Perspective
    - National Institute of Standards and Technology - (Federal Information Processing Standards Publication 200): Minimum Security Requirements for Federal Information and Information Systems, March 2006
    - INFOSEC Assessment Methodology (IAM)
    - INFOSEC Evaluation Methodology (IEM)
- **PTA** Practical Risk Analysis
- **RIPE FRAMEWORK** Designed for ICS facilities to meet the needs to facilities risk management.
- **SHAZOPS** Risk Reduction by Design
- **SOMAP** Security Officers Management and Analysis Project

11.11 APPLYING RISK

About 50% of the companies I have visited across the globe don't have an ERM (Enterprise Risk Management) in place at all. Globally it's believed to be on 22% of companies engage in this activity. That's due to:

- Risk management is an emerging profession
- Diversity in practices is enormous
- Risk disclosures and management are unaudited
- No legal framework is mandated
- Practitioners are often secretive…
- Enabled by technology in a vacuum, methodology and reporting.

- Technology precedes risk management and can shape its standards and practices.

- IT strategy is rarely born out of risk, risk is used as an excuse to achieve a point in time objective

The above list is not an excuse SMBs not to do Risk it will help any organisation **PIE the business** which is the main thrust of the book. Managing out Risk and Risk Reduction by Design (RRAD) are useful tools for your company and assists in Perpetual Improvement.

11.12 SITUATIONAL AWARENESS

The problem with risk engineering is the SO needs to be on constant High Alert. In reality this brings about a high degree of stress until the security officer becomes nearly comatose through juggling constant external threats and compiling business impact assessments. Situational awareness is the process of recognising a threat at an early stage and taking measures to avoid it. Being observant of one's surroundings and identifying potential threats and dangerous situations is more of an attitude or mind-set than it is a hard skill. Because of this, situational awareness is not just a workflow that can be practiced by highly trained government agents or specialised corporate security counter-surveillance teams – it can be adopted and employed by anyone.

Like health and safety in companies and military disciplines, constant hazard awareness can suffer from constant nagging – but gentle reminders makes for a safer environment. Health and safety personnel have had 50 years dealing with these risks and using multi-layered messaging to keep workers guarded and protected when entering a dangerous area. IT is a toddler at this discipline, and communications should be higher on each agenda at every meeting (similar to Health and Safety Toolbox talks).

Two necessities for performing risk measurement and quantification are a quantitative means of expressing potential cost, and a logical expression of frequency of occurrence. Both need to consider low as well as high frequencies of events. It's here that we apply situational awareness, and in Cybrid scenarios a security officer needs to be cognisant of: Access, Natural Disasters,

Environmental Hazards Facilities Construction and Maintenance, Work Environment – Owners/Workers Relationships, Value.

11.13 MAKING RISK PERPETUAL

All companies should have a Risk Committee - usually staffed by a non-executive director, an honest, unbiased and trusted advisor or even a family member. My father for instance is the most risk adverse person and conservative person I know and ideal for maintaining secrecy in the company whilst contributing positively. Age and wisdom is obviously a plus here. The SMB is to decide whether risk reporting to the Risk Committee should be Standards based and therefore a certification such as ISO 27000:2013 supplemented by ISO 31000 is needed. It depends on your budget and contractual obligations, and ISO practitioner availability.

To make Risk part of the Perpetual Improvement Everywhere mantra, the SMB still need the basics put in place to fuel this practice. Quantitive Risk needs true up values, notation and Information. The following techniques help build this;

11.13.1 COST OF SERVICE

Do you really know how much your products cost and how IT is interlocked into that process? 99 times out of a 100 the answer to the question is No! Even in SMBs where pricing is set by an owner some pricing is outlandish, and a prime contributor to a company collapse. Knowing your cost base and the real cost of getting product to market can increase margins and in turn make money. To manage security of a service the true asset value and its contribution to the value chain must be known. Applying the right level of security to a Service Data Flow is also imperative to the Risk Matrix being correct and so avoids revenue leaks. In my experience the following tools are necessary to help manage this.

- Service Management Platform
- CMdB (Configuration Management data Base)
- ITAM and SAM
- Information Taxonomy

- OBASHI Data Flow notation
- SHAZOPS for service integrity
- Software Cost Development

Cost of Service	Cost of Outsource
Direct Costs + Agency Indirect Costs	Total Cost of Annual Contract (incl. Adders)
Infrastructure Cost	Technology and Skills gained
Depreciated Value of Hardware	Tax losses/Write offs
Cost of Software licences	Cost of Software licences
WAN Costs	Encryption Costs
Cabling and Wireless Costs	Maintenance of Contractors Identities
Supplies and Materials	Loss on Assets
Rent/Lease of Office and Production	Management of Contractors Background
Maintenance of Buildings	GeoLocation loss of Privacy
Data Centre Cost	Data Loss Prevention
BCDR	BCDR
Cost of Utilities (Heat Light Power)	Cost of Remote Audit
5% Administration Overhead	5% Administration Overhead
Overhead per User:	Contractor Cost
Salary, Bonus, Commission, Overtime, Benefits	One time commission costs
Security Costs	Information Security lost
Skills retained in house	
Contribution to Security Quotient (plus)	Contribution to Security Quotient (minus)

Figure 69 COST OF SERVICE

11.13.1.1 CMDB

A **configuration management database** (**CMDB**) is a repository that acts as the asset warehouse. Its contents are a collection of IT assets that are commonly referred to as configuration items (CI's), as well as descriptive relationships or handoff linkages between such assets. Some CMdBs display these interlocks and are graphical in nature, speedily helping operators Data Flows and are fundamental to business impact analysis. When populated (properly) the repository becomes a means of understanding how critical assets such as information systems are composed, what their compass points (NEWS) sources or dependencies are. The CMdB is the cornerstone of ITIL (described later) must be updated in real time to be of any real use. Support Information should be held in the database. The CMdB usually comes as part of the Service Management Platform (Help Desk Software) and should also include links to the ITAM (IT Asset Management tool) the SAM (Software Asset Management tool).

For DevOps the Service Catalogue, templates and service costs reside here. Do not place your CMdB up in the Cloud it needs to be able to discover your network and changes to your network in real time. If you do use a Cloud service then ensure the appliance placed on site for device collection is utterly secure. Do ensure the CMdB data that resides in the cloud is encrypted and backed up to your own data centre.

11.13.1.2 ITAM AND SAM

Linking in with the CMdB is IT Asset Management. This is the primary point of accountability for the lifecycle management of information technology assets (mainly Software Applications licences) throughout the organisation. Included in this responsibility are development and maintenance of security policies, standards, processes, systems, documents and measurements that enable the organisation to manage the IT Asset Portfolio with respect to risk, cost, control, IT Governance, compliance and business performance objectives as established by the business.

IT Asset Management is the detailed cost register of anything hardware or software or service ware (such as Outsource Costs), direct and variable cost based. If you have not done this exercise then you don't know what to protect and so applying risk is impossible. This is a physical and logical count of all your assets. This contributes to your annual accounts balance sheet as assets and so improves the value of your company so get it right. You will not believe how many servers I have found in stationary cupboards!

Software Asset Management can save your company by metering licences. In a virtualised environment this essential and saves buying the same thing over and over. If you have ever experienced a Microsoft or Oracle software audit you should do this and save millions. Software will eventually move to a Pay as you Use model. Software vendors are touting this as a way to halt the Software Piracy plague.

11.13.1.3 OBASHI™

The OBASHI™ Methodology was developed to document, map and model how people, process and technology interact, to make a business work and to display the results in a way which both technical and non-technical people can easily understand. It is the best way to map hybrid and public cloud services, and their process relationships. The process is sequential, logical and consists of 6 layers:

- Ownership
- Business Process
- Application
- System
- Hardware
- Infrastructure

OBASHI™ Elements that represent the people, process and technology in a business are placed in these layers. The Ownership and Business Process layers contain information about how the business works; about the people in the business and the business processes. OBASHI provides the common language and platform for the APMG cyber security education schemes. This enables a range of people from various disciplines to understand the impact of Cyber Security & Cyber Resilience on their part of the business or organisation. OBASHI provides a clear contextual picture of your cyber environment and ability to analyse where individual flows of data are vulnerable and at risk.

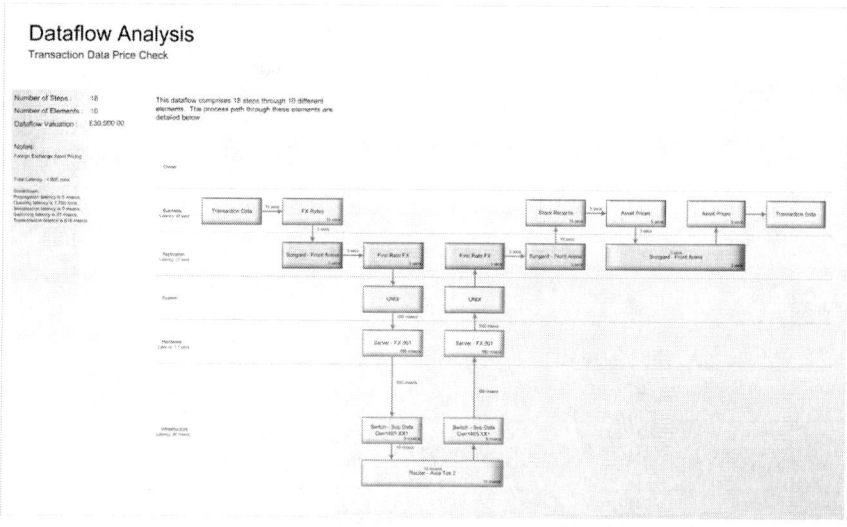

Figure 67 OBASHI DATAFLOW EXAMPLES (courtesy of OBASHI)

OBASHI – Core Principle No.5 states

"A data security model cannot be fully assessed unless the cause and effects of interruptions to a flow of data, or changes to any data contained in that flow of data, have been evaluated in the context of the flow of data in question."

The lower four layers in the OBASHI method contain information about IT assets, A Business and IT diagram provides the framework to store this information usefully, in a way which is easy to understand and communicate across the business.[157] Data Analysis Views (DAVs) can then be developed which detail how data flows between your people, process and technology, effectively connecting silos within your business - allowing you to join the dots. We can turn this data flow into a cost model that feeds into the Risk Matrix. Software to help develop OBASHI diagrams can be found on the www.obashi.co.uk website.

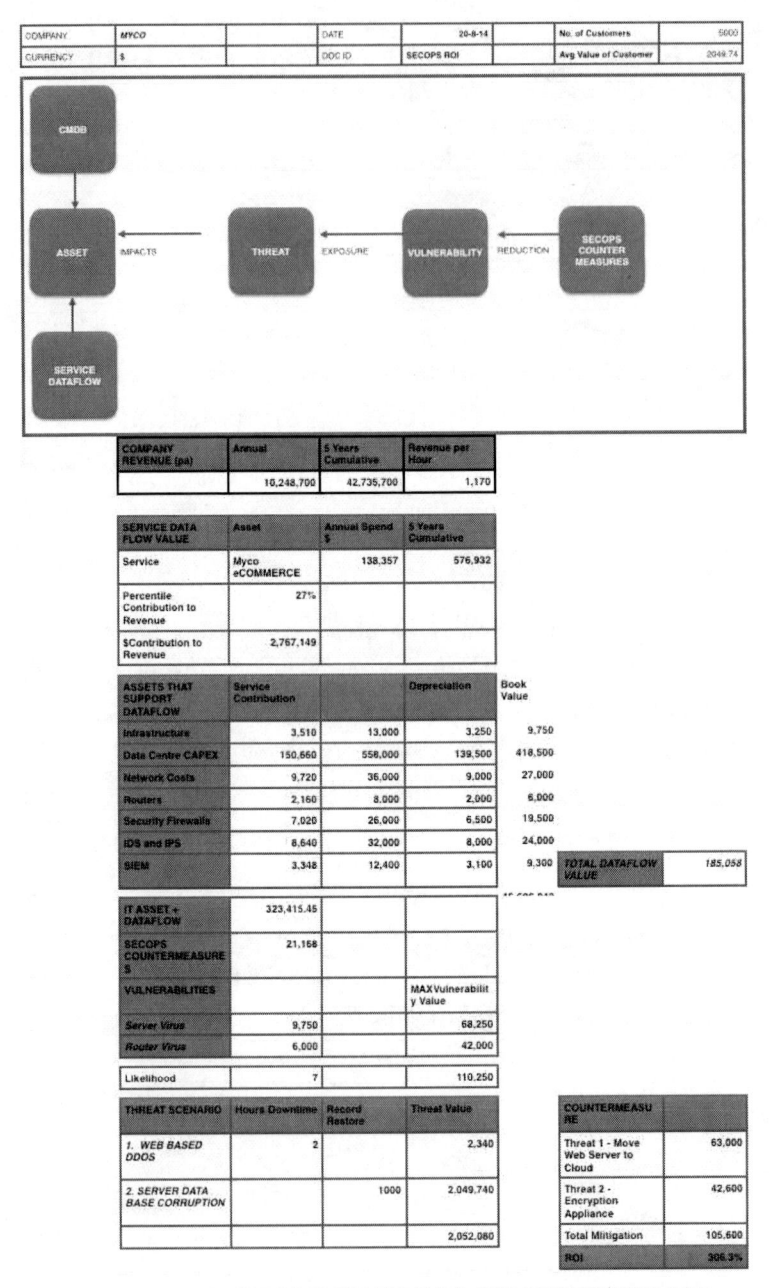

COMPANY	MYCO		DATE	20-8-14	No. of Customers	5000
CURRENCY	$		DOC ID	SECOPS ROI	Avg Value of Customer	2049.74

```
CMDB → ASSET ← IMPACTS → THREAT → EXPOSURE → VULNERABILITY ← REDUCTION ← SECOPS COUNTER MEASURES
          ↑
     SERVICE DATAFLOW
```

COMPANY REVENUE (pa)	Annual	5 Years Cumulative	Revenue per Hour
	10,248,700	42,735,700	1,170

SERVICE DATA FLOW VALUE	Asset	Annual Spend $	5 Years Cumulative		
Service	Myco eCOMMERCE	138,357	576,932		
Percentile Contribution to Revenue	27%				
$Contribution to Revenue	2,767,149				
ASSETS THAT SUPPORT DATAFLOW	Service Contribution		Depreciation	Book Value	
Infrastructure	3,510	13,000	3,250	9,750	
Data Centre CAPEX	150,660	558,000	139,500	418,500	
Network Costs	9,720	36,000	9,000	27,000	
Routers	2,160	8,000	2,000	6,000	
Security Firewalls	7,020	26,000	6,500	19,500	
IDS and IPS	8,640	32,000	8,000	24,000	
SIEM	3,348	12,400	3,100	9,300	TOTAL DATAFLOW VALUE 185,058
IT ASSET + DATAFLOW	323,415.45				
SECOPS COUNTERMEASURES	21,168				
VULNERABILITIES			MAX Vulnerability Value		
Server Virus	9,750		68,250		
Router Virus	6,000		42,000		
Likelihood	7		110,250		

THREAT SCENARIO	Hours Downtime	Record Restore	Threat Value
1. WEB BASED DDOS	2		2,340
2. SERVER DATA BASE CORRUPTION		1000	2,049,740
			2,052,080

COUNTERMEASURE	
Threat 1 - Move Web Server to Cloud	63,000
Threat 2 - Encryption Appliance	42,600
Total Mitigation	105,600
ROI	306.3%

Figure 68 SECOPS ROI VIA FERRATA REPORTING EXAMPLE

The SecOPs Return on Investment example below shows how Asset and Security costs impact an Obashi Dataflow and the ROI investment that contributes to the cost of service. In the case of the ROI example an e-commerce service for Myco Inc.

11.13.1.4 SHAZOPS™

SHAZOPS is used to plan, reduce RIPS, substitute and eliminate Risk before it starts. In 1963 Trevor Kletz developed a study technique to identify and design out hazardous process safety in chemical plants. This technique was adopted by the Oil and Gas and Nuclear industries and is a well-known engineering practice of in-depth fault tree analysis. The Hazard and Operability (HAZOP) study technique was originally developed for the evaluation of systems of interconnected pipes and vessels. The technique requires a panel of subject matter experts to perform a systematic and comprehensive analysis using guidewords and parameters. The guidewords and parameters allow the panel to produce What Ifs, Concept Hazard Analysis, Fault Tree Analysis, Cause Consequence Analysis, FMECA (Failure Modes, Effects and Criticality Analysis) and Maintenance and Operability Studies. Guidewords and parameters can be combined in sequence to redress multiple and complex iterations. The panel selects a process, explains the design intention, selects a variable and applies a guideword. Consequences are then associated with a deviation and then address safeguards to prevent deviation. Then assess acceptability of the risk based on consequences, causes and protection. Finally a suite of action plans are developed and the guidewords are repeated to the new adjusted process.

GUIDE WORD	PARAMETER	DEVIATION
No	+ Flow	NO FLOW
More	+Pressure	HIGH PRESSURE
As well as	One Phase	2 PHASE
Other than	Operation	MAINTENANCE

Table 8 - GUIDEWORD GLOSSARY

The disadvantage of this technique is that it is a singular sequenced study. There is no adjustment to the study findings unless the panel reconvenes. The method has been developed primarily for the process industry (and has been applied in great scale in the oil and gas sector); use of the approach has been applied with success to critical operations (i.e. lifting, drilling, start-up of plants etc.) and for working environment studies. Unfortunately, the spritely Trevor Kletz died in 2013, but his fundamental principles still apply today.

The advantage of this technique is how it can be developed and applied to cyber security, as it is a set of mission critical handoffs and technologies and allows security to shape the defences. In SHAZOPS model the guidewords have been adjusted (and parameters have been changed somewhat) and updated to reflect a development environment. Overlaying the Guidewords, Parameters and Deviations an orthogonal set of variables are added, VESTA:

- Vectors – Client, Network, Cloud, Systems, Virtual, Information
- Elements – CIA RAA
- Scenarios DataFlows, S/Use cases, Misuses, Abuse, Fraud
- Type – User, Accidental, Adversary, Insider, Fraud
- Attacks- Guideword, State, Deviations and Description

The techniques can be used in Readiness Assessments, Continuous Resolution. Audit Trail Forensics, Due Diligence preparedness (Mergers and Acquisitions – linking IT Infrastructures and Security postures, Conflict and Product Releases), and Risk Assessments. These security elements with the final output identify risk mitigations and Bug (Defect) reports. Fault Tree Analysis and FMECA are joined with Threat and Attack trees. The intention here is to make it relevant to a holistic development environment that can be applied to a new system (or platform) and monitored for deviation during development and normal business as usual operations.

The SHAZOPS can be used as part of a development process adhering to Deming's Plan, Do, Check, and Act cycle. The SHAZOPS™ technique supplements the Via Ferrata reporting cycle and Audit functions. SHAZOPS Licenses and Certifications are available through Combat Ready IT.

11.13.1.5 SHAZOPS ™ ATTACK AND THREAT LOOPS

Shazops outputs and stories or Use Cases can be early stage enablers for Agile in existing SMB's. Before an SMB commits to the vast investment in a new or refreshed application, forklift upgrade, or Cloud Migration, running a SHAZOPs study lifts the lid on the trashcan of potential risks. The study can help the TVC and developers craft stories and apply early stage rugged code. It can be also used in a reduced form (SHAZOPS Lite) to manage significant Change Management programs and build Business Impact Analysis files. SHAZOPS™ bases many of the threats and attacks on Attack Patterns, Cloud Patterns Classifications. Scenarios variants are built from DataFlows, CRIT Use Case, and Frexagon attack models. Vector Quotients are scored against Element compilations, Type inputs and correlated against Scenarios. The outputs are costs to eradicate Risk Mitigations and this is chunked in to DevOps, SecOps and Operational criteria. The team moves through 300 compiled threats and attacks, so an engagement takes about a week. Threats can also be sourced from SANs or OWASP (see Appendices).

The trees are pretty self-explanatory and types should be married to the type of project or application being developed. An experienced SHAZOPS Chairman can marry the application to expected risks and threats and subsequently the company. Therefore SHAZOPS is perceived as a bespoke consultation tool. The core concepts allows for deep analysis and preparedness for audits so reducing costs of annual financial and security audit engagements. This technique has been employed by a number of Venture Capitalist and Financial Institutions to assess start-ups operational viability. Dot Coms who rely on a single application as their kick-start can save millions in start-up, acquisition, execution and build costs by adopting recommendations in the SHAZOPS First Pass Seal.

11.14 DISCIPLINED AGILE DEVELOPMENT

Continuing further along the tracks with Via Ferrata reporting and Risk Ignition Points – programme and project status is key. Like all good things, Agile is evolving. Eight years ago my own company was devoted to AGILE practices and consulting. Like all frameworks, it has to evolve a little. There are developments in the DAD (Disciplined Agile Development) that put a lot more process around XP (Extreme Programming, Kanban, Agile Data, Unified Process, Lean and Agile Modelling). I will discuss this in depth later but its useful to get an early grasp on the DAD concept.

Disciplined Agile Delivery Manifesto (Section courtesy of Scott Ambler December 2014)

"We believe that the changes we're suggesting are straightforward:

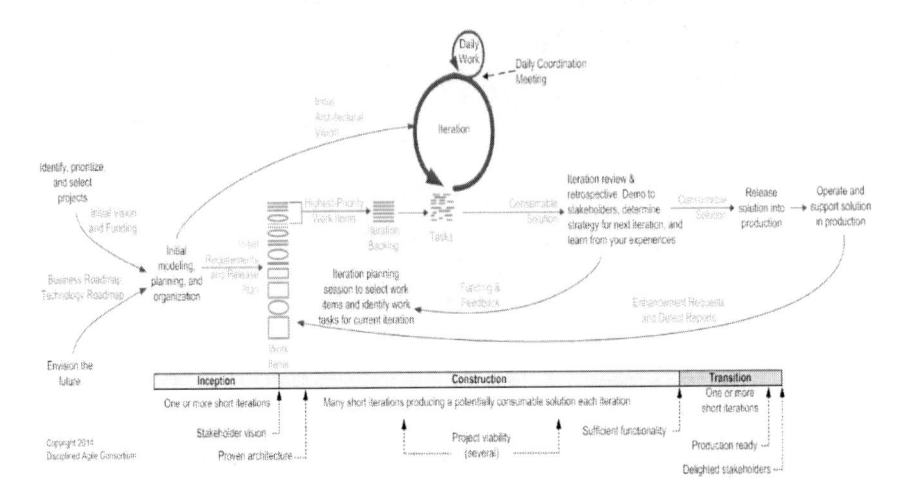

Figure 69 DISCIPLINED AGILE DEVELOPMENT (courtesy Scott Ambler)

1. Where the original manifesto focused on software development, a term which too many people have understood to mean *only* software development, the DAD framework suggests that we should focus on solution delivery.

2. Where the original focused on customers, a word that for too many people appears to imply *only* end users, the DAD framework suggests that it focus on the full range of stakeholders instead.

3. Where the original manifesto focused on development teams, the DAD framework suggests that the overall IT ecosystem and its improvement be explicitly taken into consideration.

4. The original manifesto focused on the understanding of, and observations about, software development at the time. Since then there has been some very interesting work done in the Lean community (and to be fair there was very interesting work done within that community long before the Agile Manifesto was written). This manifesto incorporates Lean principles, in particular when

considering the whole, visualising workflow, and minimising work in progress (WIP)

One of the key philosophies of the Disciplined Agile Delivery (DAD) framework is that it presents software development teams with choices, and guides them through making the right choices given the situation they face. In other words, it helps them to truly own their craftflows. In Scott Amblers excellent blog posting I'll overview below the DAD Exploratory lifecycle, which is based in part on Lean Start-up strategies.

The diagram overviews the DAD lifecycle extends the Scrum Construction Lifecycle and offers structured interfaces towards DevOps. This lifecycle is followed by Agile or Lean teams that find themselves in start-up or research situations where their stakeholders have an idea for a new product but they do not yet understand what is actually needed by their user base. As a result they need to quickly explore what the market wants via a series of quick learning experiments. In effect this lifecycle is a replacement for the Inception phase of other DAD life cycles.

There are six activities to the DAD lifecycle:

1. **Envision**. Your team will explore the idea and identify a potential implementation strategy for implementing it. This could be as simple as getting a few people together in a room to model storm both the business vision and your technical options on whiteboard and paper. You want to do just enough thinking to identify a viable hypothesis for what your customers actually want. This hypothesis needs to be testable, which implies that you need to identify how you are going to measure the effectiveness of the new functionality that you produce.

2. **Build a little**. Your team should invest just enough effort to build a solution that tests the hypothesis. In Lean parlance, you want to build what's known as a Minimally Viable Product (MVP). The amount of effort will vary, from several days to several weeks – your goal is to make something available very quickly so that you can test your hypothesis.

3. **Deploy**. Once your current solution is ready it is deployed into an environment. This deployment maybe a subset of your customers "alpha" or "beta" release, so that you can determine whether the solution is of interest to them.

4. **Observe & measure**. Once the solution is available in production you want to determine what aspects of it, if any are of interest to your user base. To do this you will need to instrument your solution so that it logs data regarding important events within it. For example, you may decide to record when a screen/page is accessed, when a sale occurs, when certain business functions are invoked, and so on. The idea is that you want to understand which functionality end users find useful, which functionality leads to customer retention, which functionality leads to greater sales, … whatever is important to you. Generation of this data enables you to monitor, to observe and measure, how well the new functionality is received by your user base. This in turn allows you to make a fact-based go-forward decision. If the functionality is well received then you may choose to continue with the existing strategy and add more functionality. Or your strategy may be so successful that you decide that your ready to productise the development of the solution If the functionality was not well received your team might choose to pivot and continue in another direction or even give up completely.

5. **Cancel**. Sometimes you discover that the product idea won't work at all. In fact, this is particularly common in research and development (R&D) environments as well as start-ups. The advantage is that if an idea is going to fail, then it is better that you learn that it is a failure quickly so you can devote your energies to other strategies.

6. **Productise**. After several iterations of building a little, deploying, and then observing & measuring that you've identifying a product that will be successful in the marketplace (or in the case of internal application development successful with your user base). Although you may choose to continue following this lifecycle, a common decision is for the team to adopt one of the other DAD life cycles – such as the Scrum-based Agile lifecycle, the Kanban-based Lean lifecycle, or the Continuous Delivery lifecycle - and effectively

treat the time they spent following this lifecycle as their Inception phase.

To summarise, the DAD process framework takes a flexible, non-prescriptive approach to software-based solution delivery. As a result of this philosophy DAD supports several development lifecycles:

- Scrum
- Lean
- Continuous Integration
- Lean Start-up[158]

The DAD approach provides a solid foundation for sharp project delivery. It is core to the combat ready set of beliefs and we will discuss how Earned Value Analysis complements the Via Ferrata reporting structure. Agile risks are daily risks gathered at the daily meetings. These risks should have a $ value assigned and placed in the Risk Register.

11.15 VIA FERRATA RISK REGISTER

The final stop on the Via Ferrata tracks! Keeping tabs on all these Risks and Risk Ignition Points should be kept in a living document, the Risk register manages tasks and projects and costs. There are several software products that automate this process and send timely reminders to managers to solve outstanding issues.

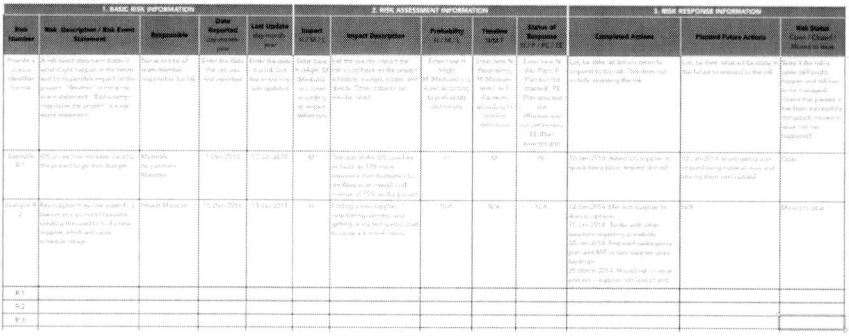

Figure 70 VIA FERRATA RISK REGISTER

The risk register if properly maintained should be reviewed daily. Keeping risk at the forefront of teams minds is critical to designing and managing out risks. Minor risks always grow to major risks so sweating the small stuff here is essential to the mainstream SMBs security posture. The Risk Register can also maintain visibility of Situational Awareness and Rips. It is essential not to ignore this register - the past is another country. Closing the loop on this section, we can combine these StepChecks:

- OBJECTIVES (Company Targets)

- OBASHI DATA FLOWS (Company Information Flows and Infrastructure Interlocks)

- DAD (Project Risks)

- COMBAT READY SECOPS ROI

- COMBAT READY HARM INDEX

- COMBAT READY SECURITY QUOTIENT

- SHAZOPS™ (Company Security Posture Analysis)

- RISK (SMB Management of Risk)

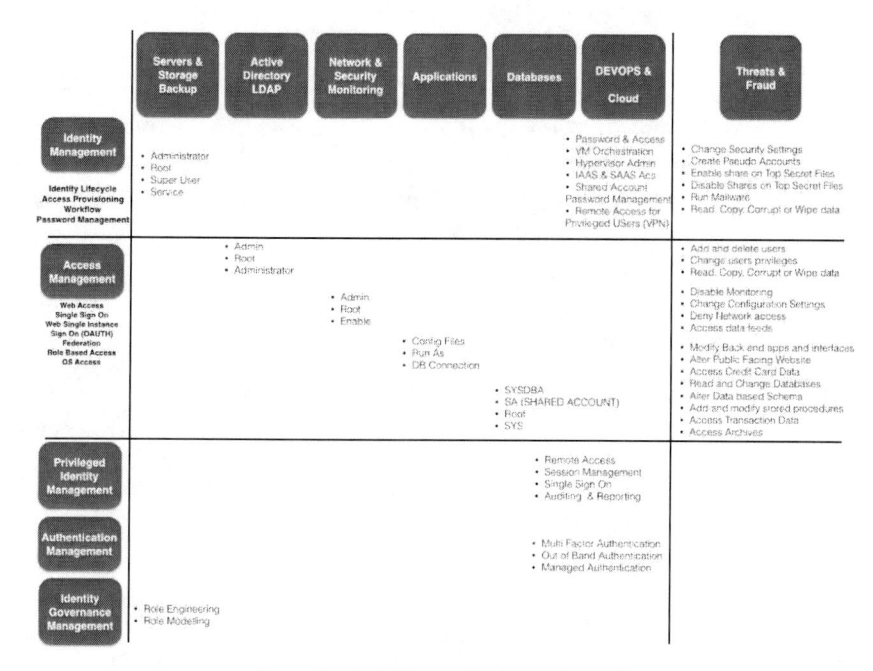

Figure 71 PRIVILEGE MANAGEMENT

11.16 RIDPOINTS - IDENTITY

Would you give the keys to your car to 50 strangers? If you had that many keys to give away and felt like there was nothing to steal but the car itself, you may feel so inclined. Most SMBs don't have time to control access from endpoints (users PCs, Laptops and Smartphones), and servers, Applications and Information. Physically managing PCs, Routers, Storage and Applications Logins and Passwords are usually disjointed within nearly every enterprise and poorly maintained. A synchronised approach is needed from the smallest shop to a global venture to manage Identities and credentials. Each organisation has to assign role and permissions to those who access, use, and those who manage systems. Under the guise of Identity Lifecycle Management (ILM) or Identity Access Management (IAM) these are called privileges (access, rights, authorisations or entitlements) to use systems.[159]

As an entry point to IAM in a company with 10 team members have a possible 600 levels of access are available to any system running within the company. Privileged accounts provide access to a companies data, so are often shared with third parties such as contractors, vendors and even auditors (if trusted). These accounts are ripe for attacks on systems security within (and outside) an organisation. This is a major security gap and once exploited by an adversary becomes a cat and mouse game to eradicate. A TVC cannot keep this under control using manual methods (usually a spread sheet). For instance the Marketing may have to manage Twitter or Salesforce with a single password. If your company decides to develop an application Admin access is required by developers to test the applications. These tests are performed on a number company machines these shared credentials can be exploited by adversaries. Nearly every company PC has LOCAL ADMIN access enabled and as a rule needs to be taken off. Every vendor has a default password and account on each of their devices. These usually look like Logon: "Admin", Password: "Admin". If you have a wireless router at home you can try this out via the web interface. About 15,000 products provided by vendors have these generic credentials

11.16.1.1 IAM INITIATIVES

Single Sign On can enforce a user profile on an individual. Authentication can be via a token, but mostly password-based. IDs can now be stored in a Cloud-based service known as IDAAS. Identity Access Management (IAM) is an administrative area that deals with identifying individuals in a system (such as a country, a network, or an enterprise) and controlling their access to resources within that system by associating user rights and restrictions with the established identity. This service is not yet mature and personally I would worry about putting this information in the cloud. It is similar to DNS (and ENUM) and supported under the OAUTH (Open Authentication Protocol). Some smartphone applications use your Facebook logon and password to sign on (if you had a Facebook account that is, for those who don't it can be confusing). I am never completely satisfied that Single Sign On is good for an SMB or even an Internet Subscriber. Once an adversary has access to the SSO libraries you are not only compromised but you could have encryption keys corrupted and get locked out of your own systems.

Identity management involves defining what users can do on the network with specific devices and under what circumstances, directed by policies or even location. In enterprises, identity management increases security and productivity (sometimes), while decreasing cost and redundant effort, yet it seems to be the most arduous of security management tasks, exacerbated by Bring Your Own Device. Bring Your Own Device is so strategic today, with time-saving features such as automated device on boarding and provisioning, support for a variety of mobile operating systems and automated device status verification becoming common. BYOD is evolving into BYOA Bring Your Own Application. As IDAAS (Identity as a Service) moves more towards the Cloud, BYOI (Bring your own Identity) will become increasingly popular.

An alarm may be triggered when a specific user attempts to access a resource for which they do not have permission. Reporting produces an audit log documenting what specific activities were initiated, so a forensics trail can be kicked off.

There is a scramble to control your Identity. Governments are now outsourcing to third party companies sensitive Identity Management credentials. These companies are unregulated and do not advertise where they store personal data, be it within country or even based in a cloud. Essentially they are trying to standardise on local access cryptographic access methods:

- Iris Scanning
- USB Token Authentication
- Voice Recognition Services
- Fingerprint
- Barcodes

The data they seek to retain in the US and UK covers Biometrics, Credit Rating (Equifax, Experian), Mobile Call Data (Verizon, EE, T-Mobile), Search (Google, Microsoft), PayPal, VeriSign, Passwords (DigiIdentity), Digital Mailbox (Post Office), Mydex, Government Services (Passports, Drivers License, Age Verification, Addresses, Pensions, Medical Care), Banking (Barclays), Email and Cloud Logon and Passwords. The Cabinet Office is testing the Verify system, which is currently testing API, interconnects. This is running into difficulty because of surnames, and data protection. Commercial organisations can only work given a history and a commercial business case advantage.

The ITU pursued a Global Standards Initiative for Identity Management (IdM-GSI), which stopped in 2008. The ITU initiative started IdM to provide assurance of identity information that supported: secure, trusted access control. This IdM concentrated on single-sign-on/single sign-off; user control of personally identifiable information; and the ability of a user to select an Identity Provider (IdP) that can provide verification and delegation functions on their behalf as opposed to providing credential to every service provider. IdM proposed support for a multitude of identity-based services that included: targeted advertising; personalized services based on geo-location and interest; and authenticated services to decrease fraud and identity theft. Effectively a walled garden the mantle for this was taken up by a number of organisations: Open ID, Open Identity Exchange, and Fido Alliance basing their APIs on SAML. The EU has the Prime Life and SWIFT projects, which follow the same lines. The Focafet.org site takes this further with the UETP protocol that logs credentials and economic transactions.

OASIS SAML stands for "Security Assertion Mark-up Language." It's an XML-based standard for communicating identity information between organizations and the cloud that is used for enabling the secure transmittal of authentication tokens and other user attributes across cloud domain. Its uses a three layer approach the Identity Provider, the Service Provider and the User.

11.17 AUTHENTICATE

In computer networks (including the Internet), authentication is commonly done through the use of logon passwords. Knowledge of the password is assumed to guarantee that the user is indeed authentic. You may see the use of CAPTUR pictures and jumbled text in addition to the usual logon and passwords screen on websites. Each user registers initially (or is registered by someone else), using an assigned or self-declared password. On each subsequent use, the user must know and use the previously declared password. The weakness in this system for transactions that are significant (such as the exchange of money) is that passwords can often be stolen, accidentally revealed, forgotten, cracked by an adversary, or forced from the user by threatening violence. Internet business and many other transactions require a more stringent authentication process. The use of digital certificates issued and verified by a Certificate Authority (CA) as part of a public key infrastructure is considered likely to become the standard way to perform authentication on the Internet. Logically, authentication precedes authorisation and can be extended from RFID, Fingerprint, and Smart Cards into Two Factor Authentication.

If you intend to deploy applications to the Cloud then you will need a very strong PAM (Pluggable Authentication Module) solution. A pluggable authentication module (PAM) is a mechanism to integrate multiple low-level authentication schemes into a high-level application-programming interface (API). It allows programs that rely on authentication to be written independently of the underlying authentication scheme. The CSP maintains baseline privileges for Customer Chargeback, Service Catalogues and Blade management. If these accesses are compromised then all hell could break loose. When using DevOps provisioning then Performance Management and Data Protection accesses require close monitoring during changes. Configuration Management here is key - most CSPs don't share their CMdB information as a rule. You are unlikely to know when configurations have been compromised. This is why discipline around accessing DevOps catalogues and templates is necessary. Any change should have multi-factor authentication associated with it to maintain systems assurance. Doing this can prove difficult if you are running an Agile shop as it hinders provisioning and change, so review PAM systems that provide video playback of Privileged Users activities such as Cyber Ark. Another word of warning here, DVR (Digital Video Recorder) type PAM systems that record users activities are monitored by a System Admin. The System Admin has to be watched as even Executive devices can be monitored and played back. If your System Admin is working all night reviewing sessions remove this privilege. Golden Rule: Every program and every user should operate using the least amount of privilege necessary to complete the job.

In a small company creating a super secure spread sheet (*sic*) or a database to manage access may be the only cost viable solution. Costs are variable and based on infrastructure (by router or by VM), or, by privileged user. There are cloud based vendors providing privileged access for $50 a month (Centrify) but in a 1000 team member company that cost may not be feasible. On premise solutions are also expensive and again varies by users/devices (Hitachi, Oracle, Dell, Xceedium, CyberArk, MasterSAM). Some of these can cost upward to $100,000 and take three months to implement. Its

RFP time I am afraid. However, all is not lost there are several Open Source solutions: Forgerock, Asimba, Shibboleth, Shiro

11.18 EMAIL USERNAMES & PASSPHRASES

Email names are traceable and hackable. Passwords are dead easy to crack and Passphrases as I call them now take their place are a tad more difficult. A simple eight-character password can be cracked in seconds (Snow White). Complex passphrases take hours to crack and these attempts and retries are monitored and can set off alarms.

11.18.1.1 EMAILS:

To keep adversaries second-guessing your email address then start to cloak and make it Role Based rather than the fred.bloggs@myco.com. The naming convention started back in the early eighties (RFC 822) to make Active Directory easier (traceable) to populate. Making email role based is easy even in small companies. For example: sales@myco.com, info@myco.com, accs@myco.com, service@myco.com, MVP@myco.com, SPOC@myco.com. Avoid real names as much as possible, adversaries can trace your emails and send phishing emails. Ideally don't use an on premise email system at all, use an email system that is VPN based and unrelated to your business. If you are in a country that likes to snoop on their citizens and unregulated then use a Swiss VPN based email.

11.18.1.2 LOGONS:

Usernames should be kept complex:

385ZASALESDIRSF

User is in Croatia, Zagreb, and a Sales Director using Salesforce.

001IODMREGSALESSF

User is in US, IOWA, Des Moines, Regional Sales using Salesforce.

As Active Directory is a major target for adversaries then its best practice not to make it that straightforward. Therefore don't use real names in emails to populate the AD.

Computer Names should not be named but designed for the CMdB Schema and geographic location. (A CMdB usually has only 32 addressable fields for information to be stored – any higher than this number the database becomes unwieldy). For instance;

A laptop in Zagreb Croatia could look like this; **385ZAHOLYLI2468**

Country (Use STD Code) = +385
CITY = ZA (Zagreb)
SITE = HO (Home Based)
USAGE TYPE = L (Laptop)
Portability = Y
Operating Environment = LI (LINUX)
NUMBER = XXXX (2468)

Golden Rule: Application logons should not be email based; a unique username and password should be created for each company application.

Dumb Passwords:

The most popular passwords of 2015;[160]

1. 123456 (Unchanged)

2. Password (Unchanged)

3. 12345 (Up 17)

4. 12345678 (Down 1)

5. Qwerty (Down 1)

6. 123456789 (Unchanged)

7. 1234 (Up 9)

8. baseball (New)

9. dragon (New)

10. football (New)

11.19 CREATING A PASSPHRASE

How to improve on this sloppy state of affairs? Password cracker application algorithms look for and guess the next logical letter in a password string, foiling this logic step means the attempted crack takes hours of analysis instead of seconds. Making a passphrase starts with a song. Song titles or a line of a lyric that means something to you and is unforgettable helps build a core passphrase.

- Create your core passphrase. This should then have the following letter changes applied;

- Replace all the 'a' with @

- Replace all the 's' with $

- Replace any space with %

- Replace any 'o' with 0

- Replace any 'i' with !

- Replace and 'e' with a 3

- Use date, day, or week numbers add to the mix 2015:03:27:51

- So my core passphrase is 'We are the champions' looks like W3%@r3%th3%ch@mp!0n$

- Now add the website you are logging into for example www.etsy.com (3t$y) …this can be placed at the end or beginning of your core passphrase. 3t$yW3%@r3%th3%ch@mp!0n$

300

- Now add your PIN number. This can be a memorable 4 or 6 digit PIN number like a partners birthday. My partners birthday is 271202 (obviously jumbled up)

- The passphrase should now look like this:
  3t$yW3%@r3%th3%ch@mp!0n$271202

Although this may look tricky it is actually easy to remember after 3 attempts. I used to work in the finance sector and they used a secure Browns Box to access the mainframe via a VPN. It had 13 passwords, all of which had to be unique before it would allow a connection. The 7th and 9th credential fields were date based and were logged to two other separate systems in real time). So memorising your core passphrase is essential! Golden Rule: Don't put it on a piece of paper or stick-it note. An entire French TV station was hacked and brought down when the weatherman was filmed at his computer with the monthly password was displayed in the background (HIVER 2013). Don't enter your passphrase while a colleague or IT support person is nearby. IT Support guys can memorise passwords by watching you type on your keyboard (even upside down!!).

For accessing internal applications you can still use your core passphrase but change your PIN number to a business mobile number or relatives home number.

S@P3RMW3%@r3%th3%ch@mp!0n$00155552555#

I have a colleague whose passphrase are 64 digits long. He has had the same passphrase for 30 years and increments it weekly. It can be done. You will get the hang of it.

Don't let your computer choose a password auto fill for you. It's easy to hack a PC once it's been lost/stolen.

DOMINO DEFENCE IN DEPTH

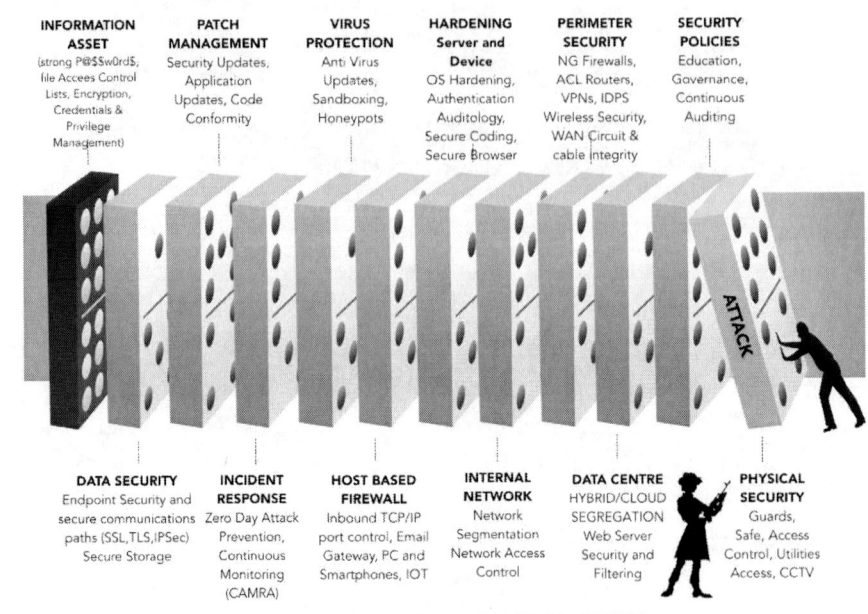

INFORMATION ASSET
(strong P@$$w0rd$, file Access Control Lists, Encryption, Credentials & Privilege Management)

PATCH MANAGEMENT
Security Updates, Application Updates, Code Conformity

VIRUS PROTECTION
Anti Virus Updates, Sandboxing, Honeypots

HARDENING Server and Device
OS Hardening, Authentication Auditology, Secure Coding, Secure Browser

PERIMETER SECURITY
NG Firewalls, ACL Routers, VPNs, IDPS Wireless Security, WAN Circuit & cable integrity

SECURITY POLICIES
Education, Governance, Continuous Auditing

DATA SECURITY
Endpoint Security and secure communications paths (SSL,TLS,IPSec) Secure Storage

INCIDENT RESPONSE
Zero Day Attack Prevention, Continuous Monitoring (CAMRA)

HOST BASED FIREWALL
Inbound TCP/IP port control, Email Gateway, PC and Smartphones, IOT

INTERNAL NETWORK
Network Segmentation Network Access Control

DATA CENTRE
HYBRID/CLOUD SEGREGATION Web Server Security and Filtering

PHYSICAL SECURITY
Guards, Safe, Access Control, Utilities Access, CCTV

Figure 72 DOMINO DEFENCE IN DEPTH

12 RIDPOINTS - DEFENCE IN DEPTH (DOMINO)

Defence in Depth (Also known as the Castle Approach) is an information assurance (IA) concept that comprises multiple layers of security controls (defence planes or zones). These are logically placed to surround an IT system. Its intent is to provide redundancy in the event that a security control fails, or, vulnerability is exploited that can cover aspects of personnel, procedural, technical and physical for the duration of the system's life cycle. It follows the moat, walls, and inner keep architecture employed in medieval castle design. The whole castle concept relies on onion layers of technology loosely coupled with diverse frameworks like ISO, ITIL and COBIT. Adversaries exploit these interfaces as they course their way into the perimeter minefield under the radar. We don't build castles anymore, but we have plenty of domino tiles. The deduction follows that all the technology tiles in the deck need to be physically segmented but uniformly monitored through Omniocular monitoring each domino tile should be regarded diagrammatically as a collection of technologies. Any tile that falls over in any part of the deck will allow an adversary to bypass the technology and successfully infiltrate. The tile analogy follows the same principles described in James Reasons Swiss Cheese model. The Domino Defence In Depth technique fits nicely with the Combat Ready organisational model. Let's look at each domino tile.

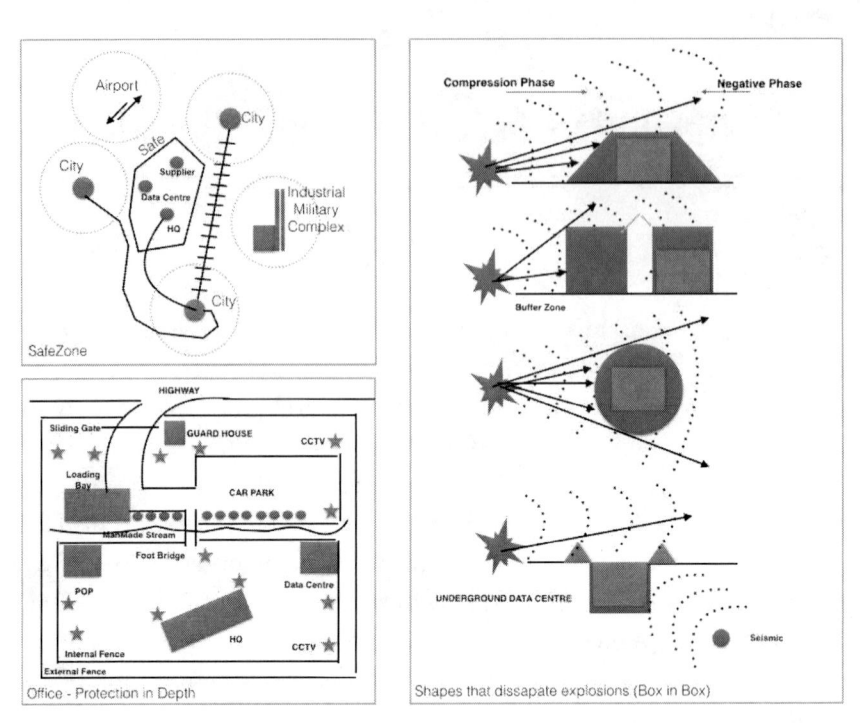

Figure 73 LOCATION LAYOUT AND BUILDING TYPES

12.1 PHYSICAL SECURITY

Does your company need to be city based? Broadband says not. Ideally any company location should be 75 miles from the nearest city centre or urban conurbation, but close enough to major accounts who contribute 80% of your revenue. As long as there are roads and rail links there is really no need to be central anymore. Teleworking can halve your operating costs and double team member's productivity the ubiquity of broadband services and high-speed links means that most companies can exit the commuter grind and attract niche workforces.

Moving a business to a remote location brings increased control over utilities and local partnering. Team members are more willing to move out of cities so a loyal team member workforce can be educated trained and mentored over time. When relocating out of country moves further tax benefits and breaks may make a company move overseas attractive. Consider Soft Robotica for fulfilment workflows, these applications only require a server (somewhere).

Explosives Environment

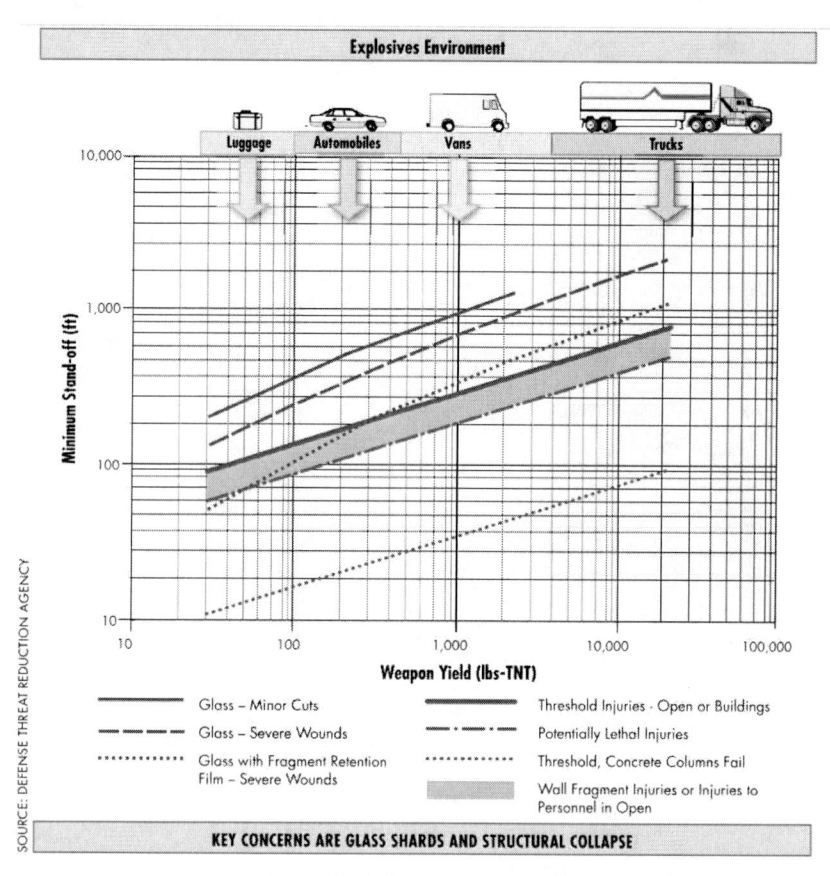

Figure 4-2 Explosives environments - blast range to effects

Figure 74 WEAPON YIELDS

Any location selected should be outside a predicted blast radius. In World War Two the Hiroshima Blast Radius was 1.3 miles. The Little Boy atomic bomb was the equivalent of 15,000 tons of TNT explosive, or 15 Megatons. Most nuclear weapons now carry a minimum of a 250 Megaton payload (hence the 50 mile radius). I would recommend anybody who considers office relocation (or even a home relocation) to use a compass and a map to predict a catastrophic event and identify Safe Zone locations. It is also useful to ensure that your key suppliers are of like mind and within a safe zone.

There are an estimated 30,000 nuclear warheads in the world today. Densely populated areas, military bases and large industrial complexes would be targeted. Locate clear of large storage facilities (Gas, Oil, Propane) within 1000 feet of the property boundary. I was in an office in IOWA once where my desk was 30 feet away from a propane tank!

An office should be at least 1000 feet away from a road. A lorry stacked with a ton of explosive can ignite but not damage the building core where people will work (if you are fortunate to design your own building). Select a building shape that will dissipate the blast wave, and with shatterproof glass. If normal glass was used in the construction of a building then all windows should have a sticky film applied to minimise fragmentation. Never use glass for a data centre - I have been in a facility where someone fired a bullet at the building window - a disgruntled customer.

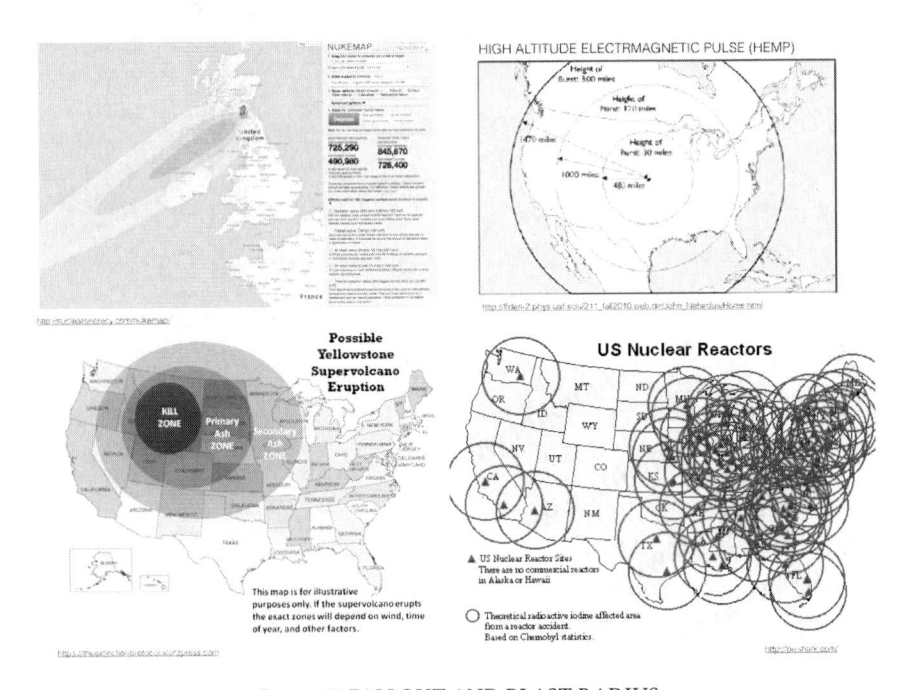

Figure 75 FALLOUT AND BLAST RADIUS

Control Rooms for hazardous facilities should also be remotely located from the main building. Operations Nerve Centres (or Network Operating Centres - NOCs) usually have a wall of screens and essential for viewing unusual activity. The ONC should be separate from Security and TV screens. Ensure that TV screens have dual connections direct from source but routed in diverse ducts. This also goes for security appliances, each one (for example a firewall) these should have three methods of connectivity.

The first is via IP, the second via a KVM switch, and in data centre direct to keyboard and TTY (A/B Switch) secured in a lockable rack. Ensure each rack is video monitored and access activity recorded. An ONC engineer has several duties to ensure the smooth running of the network. They deal with things such as DDoS Attacks, power outages, network failures, and routing black holes. There are of course the basic roles, such as remote hands, support, configuration of hardware, (such as firewalls and routers, purchased by a client). ONC engineers also have to ensure the core network is stable. Configuring hardware in a way that makes the network more secure, but still has optimal performance can do this. ONC engineers are also responsible for monitoring activity, such as network usage, temperatures etc. They would also have to install equipment, such as KVMs, rack installation, IP and PDU setup, running cabling. The majority of ONC engineers are also on call and have a 5-6 day rotation, working different shifts.[161]

Utility services should be double supply. If the office is out of town, seriously consider an off-grid Green approach to electricity generation (windmills, solar panels) as a viable alternative during a National Grid blackout (LEED Leadership in Energy and Environmental Design). The key here is to be as self sufficient as possible. Use hydropower if located to a river (or create your own continuous river around the facility. Investigate Artesian wells and ground heat exchangers by digging boreholes.

To minimise crime and terrorist attacks employ the Security Engineering practices and Crime Prevention through Environmental Design (CPTED) guidelines. The ISO 27000 standard also provides Physical Security standards, which may contribute to certification. I have used SHAZOPS in assisting in the design of a new facility, a beneficial exercise but with the addition of four keywords: Deter, Detect, Delay, Response and Neutralise to predict intrusion timings. In addition, a useful tool is the EASI (Estimate Adversary Sequence Interruption) [162] analysis to predict and lockdown physical attack response timings.

If possible avoid heavily wooded areas to lessen the impact of forest fires. If you are situated in a wood deploy roof based external water sprinklers. Do not build near airports or as I witnessed at the end of an airport runway. Offices and facilities generally should be 200 feet above sea level to avoid floods, catastrophic storms and not built above fault lines. If you are located in a tornado alley then going underground is essential. The office should be securely fenced and the car park should be 300 feet from the car park. The prime reason for this is that a delivery van packed with explosive could detonate and take out windows but little else. If you are building a new facility then a window to floor gap should be built in, this is called a box within a box design where the gap can be filled with white noise (stops eavesdropping) and telescope/zoom lens snooping. Windows should be outwardly reflective to stop external surveillance. As an example of this horizontal cable runs should be enclosed in transparent Perspex conduit revealing the tray work and cables. This will reveal any forced entry into the ductwork to tap the fibre. However, it may not stop mice using the raceways as happened to me when I was showing around a team of top brass around their brand new office.

Security considerations should include regardless of whether the building could be affected by earthquake, if so food and bottled water supplies for at least a week should be maintained for the entire compliment of team members. These metal formed disaster cupboards should be lockable but checked monthly (Don't hide the key)! The water sources should be checked regularly with water quality testing carried out weekly for any contamination traces, or high gas concentrates. A recent report showed that the majority of tap water in the UK has traces of cocaine, (some team members may wish that to continue!) but if you have a drink and drugs policy then (see insiders Frexagon) then stemming this Insider contributor is a good place to start. Most drug free workplaces experience happier team members and less time off anyway. Random checking is a recommended approach and makes for a healthier environment. It doesn't impact on personal freedoms but is a positive impact on team freedoms.

Emergency services such as police, fire and hospitals should be no more than 15 minutes away from the facility. If these are more than 20 minutes away then consider on site fire engines and emergency rooms for medical treatment. Electro Cardio version machines should be on each floor.

If possible keep building markings down to a minimum. Most visitors have a GPS, Tom Tom or Smartphone. Ask Google and Bing maps to fudge the area from aerial view. If the building is too attractive it can attract the wrong sort of visitor. Use Natural Access Control and zoning here. The HQ building should be separated from the surrounding area by a double fence with razor wire the gap monitored by motion sensors. Use guard dogs to roam the gap. The fence should be at least 8 feet high and finger hold unfriendly. Landscaping should be spiny shrubs and raised bushes. Gravel should be used throughout gaps to deter tiptoeing. One company facility I designed had a continuous stream pumped day and night that created a modern day moat. Walkway and footbridges should be the only access available to the HQ building and Data Centre. Although this hampers some deliveries a higher degree of safety is made available to team members. The main gate should have a Level 1 Penetration rating (Class IV restricted access standard) and have Anti Ram capability. (Cars not Sheep)!

12.1.1.1 RECEPTIONS

Reception areas should be inspirational for team members but also act as a smart barrier for visitors. Security guards should check visitor credentials at entry points and all team members and visitors should be X-Ray monitored. Company property should not leave without a large yellow docket and carried out by a security guard. Access to upper floors should be by lifts with biometric scanners to allow access, and biometric access to each floor. If you are in a shared facility and in town do not use outsourced security guards. If you do not know who the security guard is get HR to ensure that even is the guard is temporary an in-depth security background check is provided. Use man trap doors - these are revolving doors that can be locked and only let one person through at a time. It prevents piggybacking. All visitors should be photographed and provided with a badge with a neck halter. The visitors' credentials should also be checked with their passport. All visitors should leave briefcases at reception in a locker (bombproof). Presentations can be sent to the employee prior to the appointment. The neck halter colour should change with the day of the week (Monday, Tuesday etc.). This can be implemented in the smallest of companies. It does take significant time to get visitors into a building.

12.1.1.2 SHARED OFFICES

This is always a problem that requires clear separation both physical and logical. For instance if you are located in a shared office of two or more companies who manages and inspects the external cable ductwork? Who manages the riser and who manages the security? In start up company facilities this can be a nightmare to manage. I once visited a large insurance building in London. A fantastic steel building edifice, decorated with external lifts and escalators on the external facade. The entire facility housed over a thousand small brokerage insurers and underwriters. The main problem here was the data centre was managed by each of the individual brokerages. The data centre was a mess as engineers just threw cables into the floor and the 3-foot void was solid with cables. There were so many cables that the floor tiles did no lay flat and the entire floor was a 50,000 square feet trip hazard. I declined the contract to sort that mess out. Avoid false ceilings and floors; keep industrial pipework exposed ensuring the necessary fire resistance plugging is used. If air-conditioning is used then each vent should be cable of being manually closed by the occupant.

12.1.1.3 URBAN OFFICES

OK your stuck if you cannot yet afford the country pile, but that doesn't mean that you cannot defend yourselves. Following simple controls can make access to your area secure. If other overlooks you buildings then manage seating to face the windows. Windows can still have reflective and sticky film applied with the landlords consent. Create box within box environments - these can be temporary glass offices with glass doors that can be soundproofed and have film applied. Reception can be shared but ask your landlord about fitting card access or even biometric access to your floor. Most offices are multi-tenant so data centre security can become a headache to manage. Usually this can be the basement of the building. Try to avoid this if you have no control over the communications' ingress and egress or riser and horizontal cabling. You can create a centrally based floor data centre but ensure there is an overdose of air conditioning and redundant power available. If these options don't exist then look to build a community cloud data centre with other tenants contributing to the upkeep. We will look at how that can be achieved economically and securely. Avoid the server under the desk approach, reduce open floor positioning to any team member attempting to corrupt the server. Avoid placing the server hanging from the ceiling by two cable ties in the toilet.

12.1.1.4 FOOD AND WATERING HOLES

Avoid the single large canteen. Provide several small canteens so that large numbers of team members cannot congregate and so susceptible to attack. These areas should be monitored closely. Visitors should have a designated single restaurant and separate from team members. Avoid outsourcing catering facilities where food is made off site and served by persons unknown.

12.1.1.5 LIGHTING

Use glare protection lighting to specific areas to deter intruder actions. The whole area should be floodlit to ensure continuous security monitoring. As long as lighting is run off the self-sufficiency grid bills should be kept to a minimum.

12.1.1.6 ELECTRONIC LOCKS

Use Biometric locks throughout and avoid the use of swipe cards. Cards tend to get mislaid and they can wear out in a short period. Only use cards if these are the only way to authenticate laptops. Ensure that Biometric locks have dual power supplies, one leading to an EMP protected non-stop generator. I remember a brand new facility built by DEC in the eighties that locked people in their offices for 3 hours while the server went down. Good job there was not a fire!

12.1.1.7 SAFE WORDS

Employees who may have been kidnapped need a safe word to alert security team members if they are being coerced or acting under external duress. An employee's family may be held hostage while an employee is being monitored and recorded remotely by an adversary. The safe word can also be a facial feature or a cough or sneeze and can be changed monthly. Don't do as one company did and make it a whistle - some people cannot whistle! As long as all employees are aware of this feature then authorities can act accordingly. Setting up this protocol can be tricky but a security guard can act on the strangest of visual indicators.

12.1.1.8 I'VE GOT THE POWER

Power should be an over provisioned mix of Continual Flywheel, 12 hour UPS, and locally generated power (solar/wind). All power should have surge protection to prevent brown out, sag/dip, in rush current and transient fluctuations. ALL power supplies and data centre housings should have lightning and grounding protection and very thing should have Faraday cage protection. To prevent ESD (Anti-electrostatic discharge) maintenance and installation engineers should have wrist strap, flooring, clothing and footwear. Data Centre racks should all be independently grounded. The Data Centre generally should be Faraday cage protected to halt EMP attacks. I know of several Cloud providers and large Manufacturers who do not have this in place. If raised floors are used in data centres then raised floor tiles should have conductive gold leafs to the supporting frame to dissipate ESD.

12.1.1.9 LEGITIMATE SURVEILLANCE

Motion Sensors linked to Continuous Video Surveillance should be deployed in every corridor and office. Even on the roof. Gliders and even toy blimps can be used to carry payloads, or, used for reconnaissance. Make sure all CCTV cameras view and record in High Definition, Colour and provide nigh time monitoring (Infra Red). These can be linked to facial recognition systems in HR to detect friendly faces. CCTV towers should be Wireless and Fixed cabled to provide redundancy. Each camera placed should be able to monitor another CCTV tower. This is to ensure a complete 360-degree 'line of sight' overlapping management of the facility and ensure CCTV towers are not tampered with. CCTV Towers should have their own power source (solar and wind) and linked to the standby generator for continuous transmission. All CCTV surveillance masts should have 30-minute checks.

Bug sweeps should be carried out weekly. Usually cleaning team members leaves bugs or listening devices. Competitors or even visitors can leave pens in offices that contain microphones. This is where a clean desk policy kicks in. This form of espionage is making a significant comeback in recent years. Visitors should leave their smartphones at reception - they are extremely good recorders.

12.1.1.10 SECURE TRASH

All documents that are for disposal should be shredded. One facility I have visited now mushed the shredded papers into paper-Mache blocks that are then burnt in a local furnace that heats the building. Dumpsters should also have padlocks.

12.1.1.11 EXTERNAL DUCTS

Communications companies now provide padlock code concrete plinths for external duct ways. The lock can be unlocked by a code provided by the communication provider remotely. Any work carried out on an external duct must be notified in advance so the company can review and watch the work in progress. (Get all your ducts in a row)? Fibre taps are the most common form of tampering for an adversary that allows them to capture data. In the days of copper cabling I worked with an inventor who could clamp a magnetic strip on the road and be able to record all telephone calls that were made from a building. That's not science fiction, the ability to store 5000 calls a day on a videocassette was fantastic to witness (very Mission Impossible)

12.1.1.12 FIRE

I was in a boardroom when I spied an unusual fire extinguisher. The fire extinguisher was actually a dummy and held recording device. It had been installed two weeks prior by persons unknown! Living overseas most facilities outside the western world don't have fire or smoke detectors. Do get these installed as a matter of safety but do check them physically. Fires can be started deliberately or inadvertently. Laptops and PCs should be turned off each night. There is a You Tube video of a laptop setting itself on fire during broad daylight. Heat dissipation is a major problem caused by CPUs inside computers. In Holland a University uses servers (disguised as a radiator) to heat homes in the surrounding. The server is part of a distributed cloud project used for number crunching and is connected to the University's Data Centre. In control rooms and data centres use FM-200 fire suppression as this does not use water that will destroy most electronic equipment, or kill operatives with a carbon dioxide blanket.

12.1.1.13 POST ROOMS

Post is making a big comeback, as it is a reliable form of secure transmission that exists today - probably safer than the government's own emails? In establishments where Intellectual Property is so highly sensitive and needs protection many companies have reverted back to good old ground post as a way to report, or, guarantee delivery. Post facilities should be housed away from the main HQ and XRAY scanned before opening. Access to the post room should be via a single mantrap. Guard Rooms at the Main Gate and Post rooms should have bulletproof and shatter proof glass.

12.1.1.14 PRODUCTION FACTORY AND DELIVERIES

The main factory space should be surrounded by separate fences and accessible by delivery lorries that are funnelled by ram resistant bollards to a loading bay. Drivers and delivery team members should be photographed at the main gate and verified that a delivery is taking place with the supplier. Pallets that require unpacking should be carried out away from the loading bay. Security guards should inspect what ever is being delivered before acceptance and deployment.

12.2 DOMINO – THE SECURITY POLICY

We will deep dive this subject at a later stage and describe the bare bones of a policy. All the previous physical attributes should be included into the companies overarching security policy. The Security policy will drive the education needs of all team members so is a mission critical piece of company legislation. Although we should now be familiar that words do not stop adversaries this is an auditable document that allows financial backers and your team know you are applying rigour to the subject. This is a piece of evidential work that can be provided to backers. All the features of the company' Defence in Depth systems (going forward from this point) needs to be cited and maintained in the Security Policy. This would also include physical and logical security components Outsource and Cloud facilities, their Security Policies, accompanied by their team member profiles for background checks.

The key message here is managing your assets (no matter how few assets you may have), or, where they may be located should be managed in a unified manner.

12.3 DOMINO – CLOUD SEPARATION

Putting web-facing servers into the cloud is a good thing. Cloud Service Providers can handle most Distributed Denial of Service attacks and can close these down. If your major Telco also runs the cloud service then this is particularly beneficial. If you are developing external public facing information and e-commerce website again this can be advantageous as long as customer records are not held in the cloud. Storage as long as it is encrypted can be useful to place in the cloud and can help Recovery Point Objectives and Recovery Time Objectives. If a Cloud Provider provides your Internet traffic then some Perimeter Defence devices can be placed in the Cloud to monitor traffic, this can be a cumbersome solution.

It is not good to put all the company's data in the cloud - that's borderline thinking! Managing servers is an age-old problem. In the old days we could manage servers in a data centre without IP. A simple serial connected A/B switch meant that secure maintenance of a server could be managed without an IP interface. The minute IP is configured on a server then anyone can access the servers' data. Remote management was done by KVM (Keyboard Video and Mouse). KVM allowed an operator to access a downed server and reboot or re-configure the server OS configuration. Nowadays this is achieved by a direct IP interface. Although KVM can also be IP addressable that means it is also adversary attractive. Any server that is IP addressable can be a valid target - in a cloud that means anyone can manipulate a server virtual or otherwise. This also brings about a dilemma, how do you manage a cloud-based server when the network is down and you are under attack? We seem to have taken away the security pedestal for this in the industry's ambition to have IP ubiquity. In the old days if a mainframe went down (rarely) an operator would need to access the frame via a communications front end and RACF security protocols. IP addresses ranges able to be are scanned and therefore vulnerable. I am waiting for the clever vendor who can provide server blades out of band monitoring via a Smartphone connected to a Browns Box?

12.4 DOMINO – DATA CENTRE

You have probably guessed by now I am still a fan of companies retaining a Data Centre capability. It is solid business sense. When an SMB experiences pivotal growth to have a Data Centre where you can store classified information and trial projects. This is a touchy feely approach to growing systems. Even if you scale out and place everything in the Cloud getting the right data centre and equipment housing and architecture will be a sound investment.

When I discuss data centres with Start Up owners and Pioneers you can hear check books having heart attacks. The thought of parting with cash on bits of tin and cable can send many CFOs into panic and palpitations. Those days are gone no more $60 million to build a data centre to house a mainframe.

Please remember Information is the lifeblood of the organisation and the data centre is the heart. Look after your heart! Don't outsource your heart! Get two hearts like Dr. Who! Your Data Centre may out live your company lifespan. Data centre availability and redundancy is a critical part of the holistic design process, and one that can significantly impact cost. Critical to this is gauging which of the Uptime Institute's tier ratings best suits the business needs.[163]

- **Tier 1**: Non-redundant capacity components with an availability of ~99.671% and 28.8 hours of downtime per year

- **Tier 2:** Tier 1 + redundant capacity components with an availability of ~99.741% and 22 hours of downtime per year

- **Tier 3**: Tier 1 + Tier 2 + dual-powered equipment and multiple uplinks with an availability of ~99.982% and 1.6 hours of downtime per year.

- **Tier 4:** Tier 1 + Tier 2 + Tier 3 + all components fully fault-tolerant including uplinks, storage, Chillers, HVAC systems and servers with everything dual-powered and an availability of ~99.95% with 0.4 hours of downtime per year

Many businesses believe they need 100% uptime, 365 days a year, 24 hours per day -- essentially Tier 4. This may or may not be true for your business; but the initial cost to build a data Center at each tier must be considered. Following are some conservative estimates of cost increases from tier to tier.

- Tier 1 to Tier 2: ~ 30% increase in project CAPEX

- Tier 2 to Tier 3: ~ 50% increase in project CAPEX

- Tier 3 to Tier 4: ~ 22% increase in project CAPEX

To build a Tier 2 capable 30,000 square feet Data Centre a decade ago would have attracted a budget of $15m. Even today you will get vendors who push for similar outlay from a customer.

Big business with enormous data centres often creates multiple data centre "halls" that each meets a specific tier classification for 'right size' availability and redundancy. This tactic can save on construction costs and allows a business to achieve lower operational cost.[164]

When I visit companies you will not believe the hotchpotch of hardware calamities I have seen. I have seen estates built with every flavour of server hardware imagined. Each of these servers had their own version of a standard operating system. Here is the problem when Anti Virus is run on old servers malware is always detected – I can guarantee that the majority of servers and the data sets that sit on them are corrupted. This means your old server can be a massive liability to your security stance. Avoid allowing techies clinging on to past hardware and software – it should be data cleansed then recycled securely. The bugle call is sounding Virtualisation execute it properly. It's Transistor Radio versus Valve Radios. The Cloud Data Centres I design are massive 100,000 square metres, holding 10,000 racks. These are for the likes of Telco's and National governments and Multi National companies. These entities believe Data Centres should be huge and house 500 operators. These behemoths cost up to $100 million to design and build. These temples of technology are a ball and chain for enterprise customers. SMBs and LOBs can easily get a decade worth of capacity (for a 1000-team member's data) in 2 to 3 racks (even a single rack might do it). All the essential security tools, file management and storage can fit inside these racks. This is because

Hyperconvergence is being applied to the Virtualisation world of infrastructure; Server's, Storage and memory can be run from the same chassis or appliance instead of separate controllers and arrays.

12.5 MIGRATION AND PROJECT TRANSITION

You may ask why not throw everything up into the cloud and let them sort it out? Here's the dilemma, in Security terms Cloud technology is still a toddler. Toddlers grow fast, eat lots of food, are uncontrollable, unpredictable and are expensive to run. You need a baby sitter to ensure the toddler doesn't run amok. The baby sitter (if they are part of your family and over voting age) is more likely to be trusted with your offspring. The moral here is use the Cloud for what it is good for but keep your cards closest to your chest. The Cloud has to grow up a little more.

As we are on the subject of Children and Data Centres I will tell you a story. You know when your company has one of those "bring your children to work" days? I took mine in to see my company's Data Centre and the thousand Call Centre agents that relied on it. My son being only 9 at the time pressed the glowing red button on the businesses only AS400. The click of the off switch was followed by a lingering silence in the Data Centre and a nervous sweat started to form on my brow as I realised 1000 people had an enforced coffee break. I grabbed my son to the exit only to find the CEO raging at the doorway. "Must be an electrical fault," I said as I swiftly brushed the CEO aside.

A transition can take an inordinate amount of time (for SMBs this can take at least 6 months), depending on your estate size and complexity.

Migrating to a Hybrid Cloud (private and Public) can be a minimum of a quarter's effort. If you are a start up then this process can be completed within a month. SMBs moving through from on-premises to utilising Cloud technology needs to be a phased approach. Don't try a BIG BANG cutover you will fail! Proceed carefully and do it in little DRIPPS. Preliminary tasks include:

- Help Desk established and ready for all necessary documentation loaded

- Team Members Training Costs (reimbursed if leaving the company within a year of project start)

- Consultant Costs

- Back filling (seconded) team members

Estimate the Man Day effort for the Project Transition: As a rule of thumb it takes 15 Man Days to migrate a server. Fifteen servers migrated in a month will take around 4 Team Members. Attempt to encourage the internal team members to do this. Consultants can be added to supplement the team up to 50%

12.5.1.1 D.R.I.P.P.S. PROJECT TRANSITION TASKS

DISCOVERY PHASE

- First your CMdB, ITAM and SAM, systems must be complete.

- Check Licensing details and contracts and portability of licences from on premises to cloud based infrastructure

- Check your entire network infrastructure is free from rogue taps

- Run a deep scan and inventory the entire estate

- Create As is Service Costs

- Create DataFlows

- Glueprints for predicted Service Costs

- Chargeback mechanisms

- VM and VSAN Sizing

- Capacity and Availability Sizing (Utilisation of 75% per VM, 4 WMs per processor)

- Data Center Sizing and build

- Vendor proposals
- Due Diligence
- Establish Technical Steering Committee and Project Team Members
- Hold a SHAZOPS review on legacy custom applications
- Review Tangible Benefits (15 plus servers to be virtualised, power reduction, maintenance, automatic failover, steady team member numbers)
- Review Intangible Benefits (cost reduction in OPEX, team satisfaction, speed of delivery, and contribution to PIE)
- Review strategic benefits (elastic computing, increased security, success criteria etc.)

RISK PHASE

- Ensure the custom applications developed in the past are tested for backdoors and secure and rugged.
- Apply Shazops output to the Risk Register
- Knowledge Transfer Planning
- Identify users who need tablets and mobiles
- Train the team members.
- Establish Recruitment handoffs
- Analyse craftflows for transfer to soft robotica
- Increase team members salaries

INFORMATION ACQUISITION PHASE

- Identify legal and illegal software and apply hygiene.

- Cleanse the Active Directory

- Cleanse DNS servers

- Inventory and Classify Information

- Clean old Word, Excel and Powerpoint macros are disabled in each document

- Clean PDFs, JPEGS and Images using a metadata cleanser together with an anti virus check

- Ensure archived email data is cleansed

- Run a baseline Security Audit

- Create new profiles and ready Encryption details by Information, Database and user Access

- Run Anti Virus from dual suppliers on any servers and PCs to identify corrupt and malware infected files (before migrating)

- Build Private Cloud

- Build swing space servers

- Use a shuffle to copy data folders from one server to another (don't use USBs)

- Don't restore old Stored data from a SAN onto new servers, or server to server image copies

PROOF PHASE

- Establish the model office on an isolated network

- Encrypt servers

- Enable Private Cloud SAN and Public Cloud SAN
- Apply Configuration Management to all devices
- Build out the new security appliances and deploy on the isolated network
- Modernise Applications
- Ensure new devices tested fulfil user requirements
- Ensure monitoring and dashboards are written and tested before production
- Start the Security Policy
- Apply IPv6 numbering schema.
- Apply Identity and Credential Management
- Consider changing out PC based Operating Systems and test VDI solutions.
- Ensure VOIP works in the Model Office
- Test Snapshot capability
- Check physical Insurance cost reduction and cyber insurance premiums
- Readiness Validation

PROJECT TRANSITION PHASE

- Communication to end Users
- Agree Via Ferrata reporting lines
- Commit Phase
- Encrypt all new end user devices

- Test all applications on hardened devices.
- Ensure all credentials and privileges are locked down
- Run Incident response drills in the model office
- Establish the VMs by hierarchy
- Phase the migration of clean Information by team to the isolated network
- Drill Back Up and restore functions
- Ready self service o Help Desk
- Phase server data ensuring all data is cleansed and working
- Phase users slowly
- Detox, Donate or Destroy old Infrastructure
- Pre Production Test of new organisation
- Audit new environment

STEADY STATE PHASE
- SLA and OLA Management
- Track and Report
- Back Up Drill
- Optimise
- Perpetual Improvement

12.6 DATA CENTRE EVOLUTION

Data Centres are wonderful feats of engineering and planning. They are the temples of IT and over the years the sound of the choirs of Chillers is getting quieter. I spent six months in a data centre chilled to the bone quietly testing

VOIP QOS over MPLS. Stuck in a corner I grew accustomed to the intense cold and slowly lost all sense of time and motivation. My mentor at the time was Dr. Nick Yannacopolous who taught me about the method to understand engineering. He taught me to understand the end-to-end path of an IP packet travelling inside a Data Centre through every physical device, cable type and interface. Data centres have evolved from the simple days of the mainframe to an art form.

The mainframe dominated Data Centre design but because the computing power did not produce heat when processing the mainframes could be kept in relatively uncooled environments. Even the early nineties saw mini computers being put into general office areas. However, there is no need for raised floors, rack can be stood on the screed. The boom years of the turn of the millennium and the following ten years saw Data Centres explode with bigger Cost per Foot and reduced PUE (power used). In the last few years we have witnessed:

1. Virtualisation (100:1 VMs per BLADE Server)
2. Software Defined Networks
3. Reduction in Routing Engines
4. Speed of 10GB/40GB to connect servers
5. Hyperconvergence
6. White Label components
7. Robust Open Source products
8. Hybrid Cloud and Public Cloud models
9. Software Defined Infrastructure

These have all reduced the footprint and computing power into one or two racks.

The big question for SMBs is why invest in a Data Centre? Can we not just put everything in the Cloud? Do I throw my current investment away? How much will it cost? In the course of finding Best of Breed products for this book it became clear that a lightweight model was emerging. No longer were the vast swathes of server racks required. Computing had returned to the footprint density of the mainframe era.

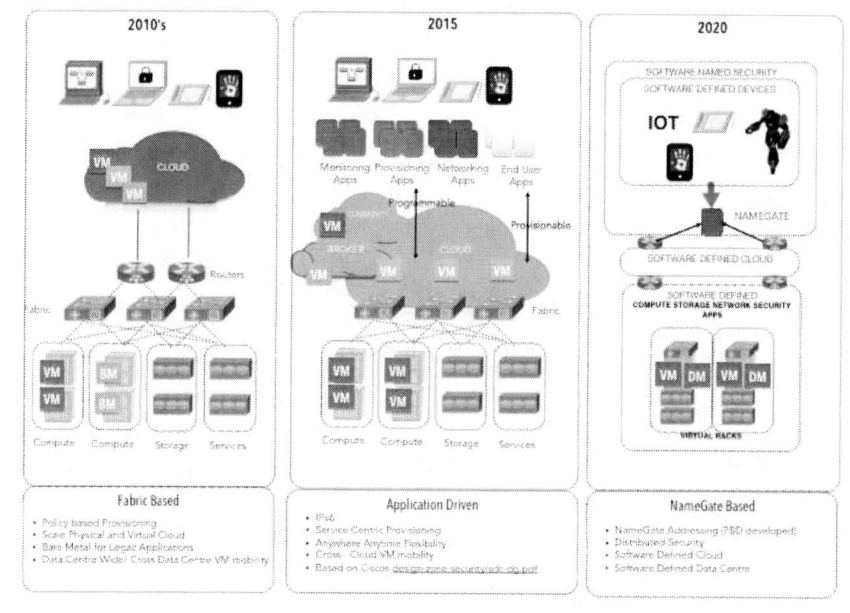

Figure 76 MODERN DATA CENTRES

12.7 COMBAT READY IT DATA CENTRE DESIGNS

To help the reader understand what is achievable and estimate Hybrid Cloud costs it's a useful exercise to architect various scenarios base on 1000 users. The designs estimate the space needed for compute, storage and baseline Defence in Depth appliances.

The baseline designs criteria were as follows:

- Scales from 10 to 1000 users

- Hybrid On Site Compute and Public Cloud operations including automation (moving workloads from on premises to off premises)

- Security Appliances providing Domino Defence In Depth boundaries

- Supports Open Compute and Hyperconvergence
- Linked by dual WAN links to Cloud
- Cloud provided Web Servers and externally facing routers
- 50 VMs and Docker Machines
- 33 VMs for Management
- 32 TB of On Premises Storage
- Capacity to hold 20GB per user per annum
- Chillers and power inbuilt within each cabinet (no external environment controls)

Several designs emerged which demonstrate density and footprint reductions that can be possible. Dual rack Open Compute and Single Rack densities for: Cisco and NetApp (UCS), VMWare SDDC, and SIMPLIVITY.

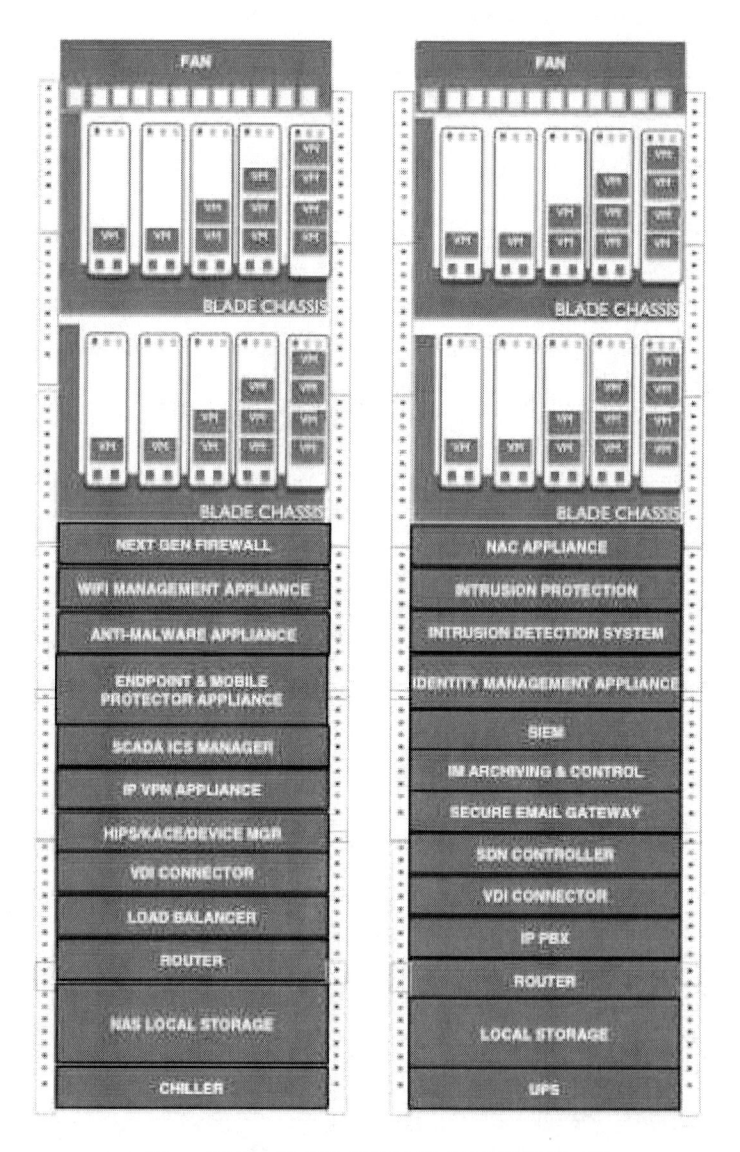

Figure 77 OPEN COMPUTE SMB RACK DESIGN

Remember, these are Hybrid Data Centre designs to be used in coaction with a Public Cloud, the compactness of the designs are the most interesting observation here as they integrations are capable of standalone operation. Component density is obviously reduced if you are starting small this is a bonus. Each design in an independently chilled rack meant that they could be placed within an office environment or in a purpose built Data

Centre Facility (based on a shipping container footprint concept which we will investigate). This demonstrates significant savings in:

- Power

- Reduced maintenance

- Significantly Reduced Infrastructure CAPEX and OPEX

- Portability (you could load your entire company on a forklift)

- 10 Year lifespan without forklift upgrades (not 3 or 5 year)

- Open Compute Design Open Source Software means reduced licence overhead.

The other implications based on this lightweight Computing platform regarding headcount are significant which remain steady, and form of organisation.

What does this mean for the SMB? It means any of the above designs allows a Pioneer from Day 1 to manage the technology budget as part of the 5, or even a 10-year business plan forecast. It also means procure from one supplier you view as strategic and don not deviate from this Glueprint Any of the 3 example baselines will allow a company to scale out by size efficiently. If the company needs to scale up by demand then simply adding Memory, CPU and Storage can be performed on site with real time disaster planning provided by the Public Cloud. All Information can be routinely encrypted at each Information Layer and Boundary. It also allows the compute power necessary to run Robotica and a Virtual Workforce based on the hardware provided. CPU power can be offloaded for Big Data searches whilst still retaining key datasets on site.

12.8 OVERGROUND VS. UNDERGROUND

My grandfather was a Chief Fire Officer for Central London during the Blitz in World War 2. The Blitz killed 32,000 people and injured 87,000. Towards the end of the war V2 rockets (Vengeance 2) were so explosive they created 50 feet deep craters. He attended the Deptford Woolworths V2 attack in 1944, which killed 168 women and children queuing up for tin saucepans.

After that my family spent the remainder of the war underground. The London Underground sheltered 177,000 civilians each night also helped house some important manufacturing. Besides the natural shelters for civilians provided by the London Underground Tube system, numerous factories were constructed underground to protect from aerial bombardment. The Plessey factory that manufactured radio and aircraft components used five miles of underground tunnel between Gants Hill and Leytonstone for 2000 workers throughout the war. There were the Shadow Factory Tunnels beneath Longbridge in Birmingham that manufactured Spitfire engines. I have had the rare pleasure of visiting Corsham Quarries, which was used for armaments storage during the war and later as the UK Government bunker during the Cold War.[165]

12.9 PRODUCTION BUNKERS

Burying manufacturing facilities affords several benefits: the ability to hide the facility from snooping satellites, some measure of protection during bombardment, and protection against EMP.

The recent Industry 4.0 project in the high-tech strategy of the German government promotes the computerization of the manufacturing industry. The goal is the intelligent factory (Smart Factory), which is characterised by adaptability, resource efficiency and ergonomics as well as the integration of customers and business partners in business and value processes. Technological bases are cyber-physical systems and the Internet of Things. Modern information and communication technologies like Cyber-Physical Systems (CPS), Big Data or Cloud Computing will help predict the possibility of increasing productivity, quality and flexibility within the manufacturing industry and thus understanding the advantages within the competition. CPS means combining Robotica and 3D printing capabilities.

Big Data Analytics consists of 6Cs in the integrated Industry 4.0 and Cyber Physical Systems' environment. The 6C system consists of:

- **Connection** (sensor and networks),
- **Cloud** (computing and data on demand)
- **Cyber** (model and memory)
- **Content/Context** (meaning and correlation),

- **Community** (sharing and collaboration)
- **Customisation** (personalisation and value).

In this scenario, and in order to provide useful insight to the factory management and gain correct content, data has to be processed with advanced tools (analytics and algorithms) to generate meaningful information. Considering the presence of visible and invisible issues in an industrial factory, the information generation algorithm has to be capable of detecting and addressing invisible issues such as machine degradation, component wear, etc. on the factory floor.

Industry 4.0 also brings space benefits since most of the production lines can be placed within the confines of a cargo-shipping container. For the military this brings extreme benefits to the supply chain. The factory can be delivered directly to the battle zone and manufacture to order and on site. Of course, operations can be carried out remotely in high hazard or contaminated areas and still produce in the absence of human intervention. For daily production activities a Smartphone can be produced without human intervention in the container sized footprint. This can also apply to food, pharmacy production as well, so a container can be shipped to a conflict site to build emergency supplies.

12.10 DATA BUNKERS

The era of the Data Bunker is already upon us. As customers seek Cloud-based services, the need for mega-secure facilities is an imperative. If your data is stored in an over ground facility then this attracts an existential risk and needs to be moved. There are about 40 such sites in a variety of countries.

Some 80 Swiss Data Centres hold the possessions of rich nations. Recently, an unnamed government negotiated to store all its digital assets in Mount 10 (Moun*ten* – geddit?), at the Data Centre known as 'the Swiss Fort Knox' in Saanen-Gstaad. After the Snowden revelations, data and asset storage has boomed in Switzerland. Data is now regarded as more valuable than gold.

12.11 BRING YOUR OWN BUNKER

When we discuss Clouds, the thing to bear in mind is that it is a very dense computer platform - that's all. I think everyone knows what a rack is? It is a large black metal box with a glass door. They are usually six feet tall and have a square footprint of two feet by two feet. In the old days, you might have been able to get four servers in that space; now it's 400 servers. So in a container you can get eight racks (equates to 1600 to 10,000 virtual servers per container) and a line of Industry 4 Smart Factory robots and 3D fabrication printers. In a conflict the data that will survive will be underground or deep in a mountain.

12.12 DATA CENTRE COSTS

Do SMBs need a Data Centre – when I can save all my data in a cupboard? In a conflict you do need a facility robust enough to guard your essential data. The observation I see is that nowadays you can expand and contract according to market forces and company constraints while keeping RIPS to a minimum.

A proposed Data Centre in a Combat Ready IT world is underground, protected against blast and EMP. Its not energy demanding in terms of power and Chillers and could run off grid. Even if you are a city office based company it's still possible to build your own Data Centre in a rural location and share the capacity (sell) to other companies.

Turn your IT cost centre into a profit centre. It's possible to build a Community (or, even a Dominion) data centre in a simple 8 feet by 22 feet container. A single container can support approximately 10,000 active "business" and 2,000,000 residential users. Using the above rack architectures an Internet deployment can be based on a container per 1,800 sq. kilometres Internet rollout. This model is proven and has been "Googleized". The cost per IT per annum has nosedived[166]:

1960 – $680,000

1970 - $150,000

1980 - $50,000

1990 - $10,000

2000 - $5,000

2010 - $3,000

2015- $75

It is estimated the cost per user per annum will be around $50 per user per annum in 2020.

12.13 CONTAINER BASED DATA CENTRE

A second hand 160 square foot storage container can be secured for around $5,000. Heat and Power will cost $75 per square foot per annum. A Container will hold 8 Racks. @ Racks should be sufficient per 1000 users. Obviously if you chose Docker Containers as your hypervisor choice for virtual machines this would be a container within a container!

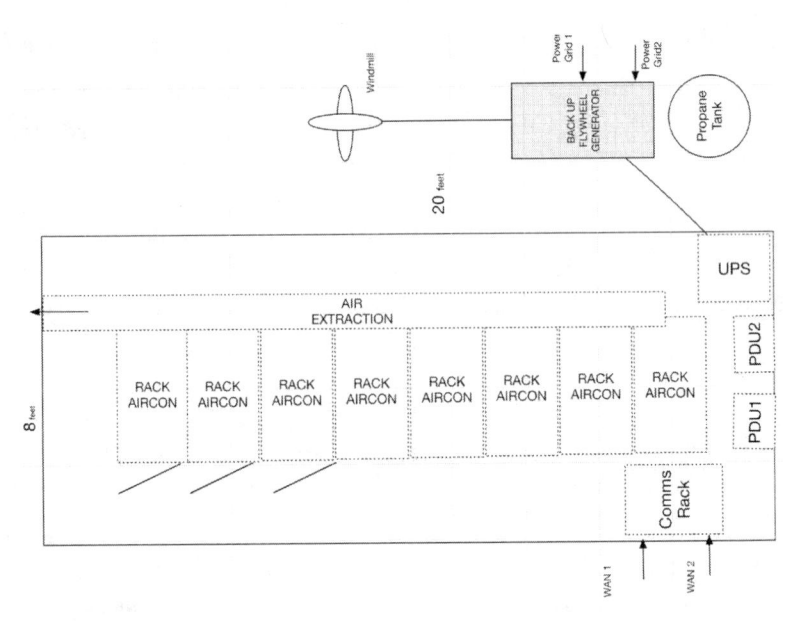

Figure 78 PLAN VIEW OF CONTAINER DATA CENTRE SOLUTION

Using this configuration and the CAPEX Cost would be $1.3m based on RRSP. Expect an 8% annual OPEX charge for maintenance starting Y2 (estimate $104,000) Usually first year maintenance is inclusive and part of the CAPEX outlay. Most of the devices are ready to requiring only an IP address configured to operate. Commissioning costs are low. Dependent on the choice of Open Source Software to Full Pay Licences this would mean a cost per user per annum of $800 to $1,300.

Companies can even prepare Container type cloud data centres prior to delivery, Eltek ASA is one such company that provides this service.

12.14 SPARES

Being ready for a conflict means being prepared for long lead times for maintenance fixes. Any number of obstacles could stop your business receiving the right component to keep your operation live and productive. Typically Data Centres carry 10% spares as a de jure method to maintain uptime and on premises replacements. In a conflict its security and defences that matter first, so ensuring that appliances have been duelled will alleviate this problem somewhat. As backstops ensure your vendors maintenance field engineers also carry a complete working solution as part of your maintenance contract.

12.15 DOMINO – BUDGETARY ESTIMATES

Rack 1 - Blades	106,000
Network Router	8,000
Next Gen Firewall	40,630
WIFI Management Appliance	6,297
WIFI Firewall	1,890
WIFI Access Points	14,310
Anti Malware Appliance	12,390
Endpoint Protection	19,200
Password Manager	5,600
Incident Manager	27,158
Endpoint and Mobile Appliance	43,490
PC Anywhere	8,420
IP VPN APPLIANCE	6,153
DEVICE MANAGER (HIPS KACE)	46,000
VDI CONNECTOR	12,475
LOAD BALANCER	9,980
NAS LOCAL STORAGE	42,400
Enterprise Vault	54,000
Encryption	69,920
File Share Encryption	189,620
Drive Encryption	55,000
Rack 2	-
Network Router	4,000
NAC Appliance	32,000
Intrusion Protection	78,000
Intrusion Detection	83,000
Identity Management Appliance	47,000
SIEM	19,524
IM ARCHIVING & CONTROL	58,000
SECURE EMAIL GATEWAY	54,000
SDN CONTROLLER	8,000
VDI CONNECTOR	38,000
IP PBX	68,000
LOCAL STORAGE	57,000

Table 9 - BUDGETS (APPROXIMATE ESTIMATES) COSTS CAN GO UP OR DOWN

The budget itemises the component devices that are required per rack to provide the Domino Defence in Depth. A complete Greenfield installation will cost around $1.318,000 (a 10% variable should be applied as contingency) as described before but re-use of server hardware will see this reduce.

The SMB should set aside $75,000 for license variables. Costs will vary by location and negotiation.

Note: Budgetary Figures are based on discussions and vendors RRP prices and devices from Cisco, Symantec, Aruba, Dyn, Websense, Veracode and VMWare (2013 to 2015).

Its is interesting to see the VMWare and Cisco UCS solutions that snuggles into a single rack load many of the security appliance functions are software shoe horned into a virtualised environment. There may be uplift in the estimates to accommodate the configuration for these solutions. Security is intrinsic to VMware's design as micro-segmentation is in built into each VM allowing corrupted (or infected) servers to be isolated. This solution is very leading edge but has obvious economic benefits.

OPEX costs used to determine investment in the Public Cloud are variable due to storage and bandwidth costs. Leasing costs would obviously spread initial CAPEX outlay over a 5-year period of the solutions above. In a cloud configuration these costs continue beyond the 3-year breakeven point.

12. 16 DOMINO- PERIMETER SECURITY

Boundary routers are the automated asset watch guards, on duty 24/7. These are networked assets that run Network Asset Controls that monitor and filter traffic based on available rules. Gaps in any of the devices here will create a route in for an adversary. Boundary Management of zones and All Points of the Compass traffic movement (NEWS Northbound, East, West, and Southbound) is essential for a good security posture.

12.17 BORDER AND BOUNDARY ROUTERS

We have looked at the construct of a router earlier in the book. Network routers act as Internet traffic cops, directing data into, out of, and within networks. A border router is a special type of router: the one that stands between your network and an external network. It can be configured as a load sharing configuration, hot standby, and traffic monitoring. Setting up Access Control Lists to deny traffic coming from private RFC 1918 addresses (address Allocation for Private Networks - some undesirable or blacklisted), from bogus addresses, and from your own public addresses (that may be spoofed). A blacklist is the accumulated knowledge provided by vendors of nasty sites not to visit or allow traffic from. This is updated daily by sharp vendors. A whitelist is good if you have the expected behaviour and inputs for a website that your users to visit and input numbers in a text box. You can restrict the text box input to numbers only, so all possible exploits involving letters and symbols are explicitly disallowed, such as logins to external webmail applications.

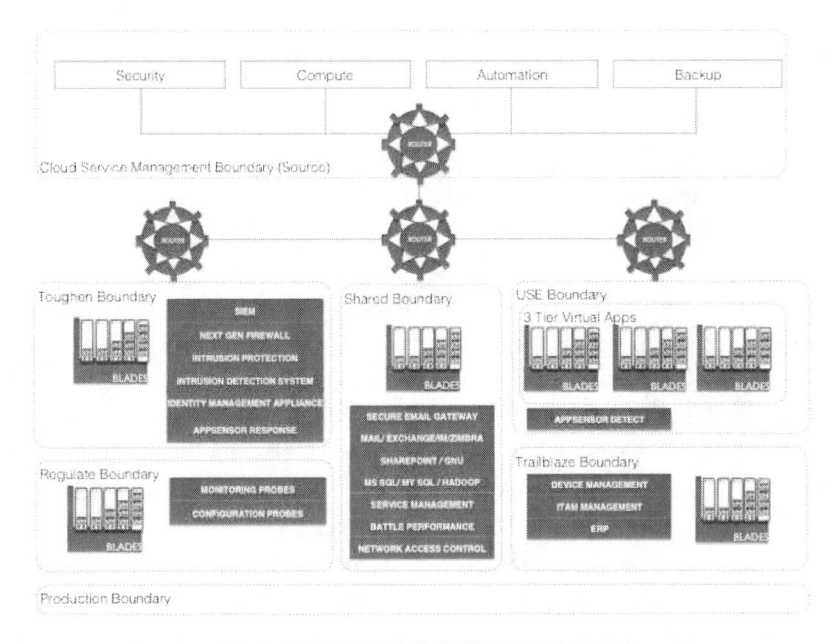

Figure 79 DOMINO TRUST BOUNDARIES

12.18 FIREWALLS

A Firewall does nothing more than filter packets. The Firewall will accept or reject packets. Hardware firewalls are dedicated security appliances on which security software is preinstalled, typical on a proprietary OS. Software firewalls, on the other hand, can usually be installed on any available server that is equipped with a general-purpose network OS such as Windows or Linux or Virtual Machine. Dependent on platform Firewalls cost anything between $70 (per user) up to $12,000 for an appliance.

There are four types of firewall to choose from:

- **Packet-Filtering Firewalls:** With the packet filtering firewall all traffic is carefully scrutinized. Every packet's protocol and address information; content data is not inspected. The advantage of packet-filtering firewalls is simplicity.. Software-only firewalls for home and SMB business are typically of this variety, including the firewalls that are built in to more recent versions of Windows and Apple OSX.

- **Circuit-Level Firewalls:** Does exactly the same as a packet filtering firewall except it doesn't simply accept or reject packets, it also decides whether a connection is valid according to a set of configurable profile rules. These are complex beasts to configure and on-site expertise is needed to install and maintain.

- **Application-Level Firewalls:** An application-level firewall watches traffic based on a specific set of rules. It can be configured to restrict access to specify file types as well as to provide different access levels to authenticated users. The firewall allows some commands to proceed to a server while rejecting others.

- **Stateful Multilevel Firewalls:** A combination of all of the above! Stateful multilevel firewalls perform network-level packet filtering while recognizing and processing application-level data. Usually these are bundled together in an appliance, which include Anti Virus protection, Intrusion Prevention and content filtering.

Always opt for an appliance-based firewall, which is usually harder to hack. Vendors such as Cisco, MacAfee and Barracuda have cost effective solutions in this arena. A firewall's basic job is to permit (or stop) data flowing into or out of a network. For perimeter defence, firewalls are available as software (installed inside a router) as a VM on a dual NIC attached server, or, as stand-alone hardware appliances. Rules can be set to search for malware signatures and drop connections that are deemed Denial of Service. Outbound traffic that may originate from inside the network may be an exfiltration attempt by an adversary to offload collected data. Most firewalls tap into the Active Directory and LDAP (Lightweight Directory Access Protocol) so they can provide traffic analysis on each users network. Operators rarely configure outbound traffic as it can be seen as a business obstacle. Would you not want to know who is sending out customer lists and data? It is a management task to ensure this is configured properly and daily reports should be part of Via Ferrata reporting.

Ensure the configuration is right, limit the use of HTTP over Transport Layer Security (TLS)/Secure Sockets Layer (SSL) Port 38 for web applications. The correct use of TLS/SSL provides integrity of data sent between points A to B. It can also provide a degree of identity assurance and confidentiality. It does not protect web applications at all and as seen in the recent Heartbleed attacks can be piggybacked to access systems. Malicious payloads and activities can be undertaken just as well using TLS! The ramification here is that TLS can shield traffic from an IPDS deep packet inspection while in transit.

Next Generation Firewalls encompass the typical functions of traditional firewalls such as packet filtering, network- and port-address Translation (NAT), stateful inspection, and virtual private network (VPN) support. NGFWs perform deeper inspection compared to stateful inspection performed by the first-generation firewalls. They inspect the payload of packets and match signatures for harmful activities such as known vulnerabilities, exploit attacks, viruses and malware. [167]

Gartner defines an NGFW as "a wire-speed integrated network platform that performs deep inspection of traffic and blocking of attacks." At minimum, Gartner states an NGFW should provide:

- Non-disruptive in-line 'bump-in-the-wire' configuration

- Standard first-generation firewall capabilities, e.g. network-address translation (NAT), stateful protocol inspection (SPI) and virtual private networking (VPN), etc.

- Application awareness, full stack visibility and granular control

- Capability to incorporate information from outside the firewall, e.g. directory-based policy, blacklists, whitelists, etc.

- Upgrade path to include future information feeds and security threats

- SSL decryption to enable identifying undesirable encrypted applications

- Integrated signature based IPS engine

12.18.1.1 SOFTWARE DEFINED FIREWALL

As Software Defined Networks deliver a new array of virtualised capabilities built into virtualised devices. Traditionally security perimeter architecture would be in separate boxes each dealing with a function. As we have seen downtime on any of these devices can lead to a domino effect and subsequently attack vectors created for an adversary. In SDN deployments these bundle all Firewall, Switching, routing and bridging functions into the hypervisor gives a granular approach to defence.

12.18.1.2 BITW (BUMP IN THE WIRE)

Bump in the Wire monitors all outgoing traffic and network users connections to websites and unauthorised server hosts. A BITW scans all ports (no user is able to bypass the Firewall as all ports are monitored). Users who may need to access a website may be stopped by the Firewall as new proxies are needed, in this case a quick shout out to the operations team is required. Many people find this frustrating and feel their freedoms to search the web are being monitored (which is true) but they need to "suck it up" as they say in North America.

12.18.1.3 WEB APPLICATION FIREWALLS (WAFS)

WAFs understand and monitor HTTP traffic and can be an excellent way to screen web applications from generic attacks and can be used for virtual patching. This on the fly technique has application traffic self-learning capabilities; others support custom attack and application logic rule building including support for scripting languages. Web application firewalls have a unique capability using automated static analysis (source code review) and dynamic analysis (run time or penetration testing) and generate "virtual patches" for vulnerabilities discovered. These can be implemented in a web application firewall (WAF) while work is undertaken to remediate the source code if it is available

12.18.1.4 IDS'S (INTRUSION DETECTION SYSTEMS)
An Intrusion Detection System analyses traffic in real time for suspicious activity. If something unusual is detected, the IDS sends alerts to security via direct alerting, or via SIAM. IDS falls into three camps, network-based and host-based, and these can be signature, statistical response, and application types:

12.18.1.5 IDS SIGNATURE BASED
These are simple, fast, and updated easily. Vendors supply signature files - similar to the way anti-virus vendors supply virus signatures. The downside is that they will not identify a new attack unless it has a signature which matches an existing attack therefore updating daily is necessary.

12.18.1.6 IDS STATISTICAL RESPONSE BASED
Employing heuristic algorithms this type of IDS learns what 'good' traffic looks like and alert on anything which isn't normal. This does mean they are much better at spotting new attacks.

With Networked based IDS's these are implemented at the perimeter of an organisation, and they have visibility of all traffic entering (ingress and egress) the organisation. Where traffic has indications that it may be malicious it is logged or flagged to a response system or person.

For any organisation, the volume of different valid traffic types can be high. Traffic types vary over time so on-going configuration and fine tuning of a perimeter network based IDS can be resource intensive. Telecom vendors have better visibility of attacks happening, a scale advantage on tuning and response, and the ability to update signatures for all their clients at once.

In a hybrid environment Host based IDS's are more usually implemented in-house for specific high-value servers. The traffic types and load are much predictable so the resource requirement is usually lower

12.18.1.7 IDS APPLICATION BASED

The OWASP Appsensor Open Source project follows the RASP concept (Runtime Application Self-Protection) where the platform detects activities such as malicious users probing or attacking the application, and to stop them before they can identify and exploit any vulnerability. Deploying tools like Appsensor attract low CAPEX but can be crucial to an agile operation. Building In rather than bolting on this technique can provide a very powerful defence. As it is Open Source it is a highly recommended value added asset to Perimeter Security.

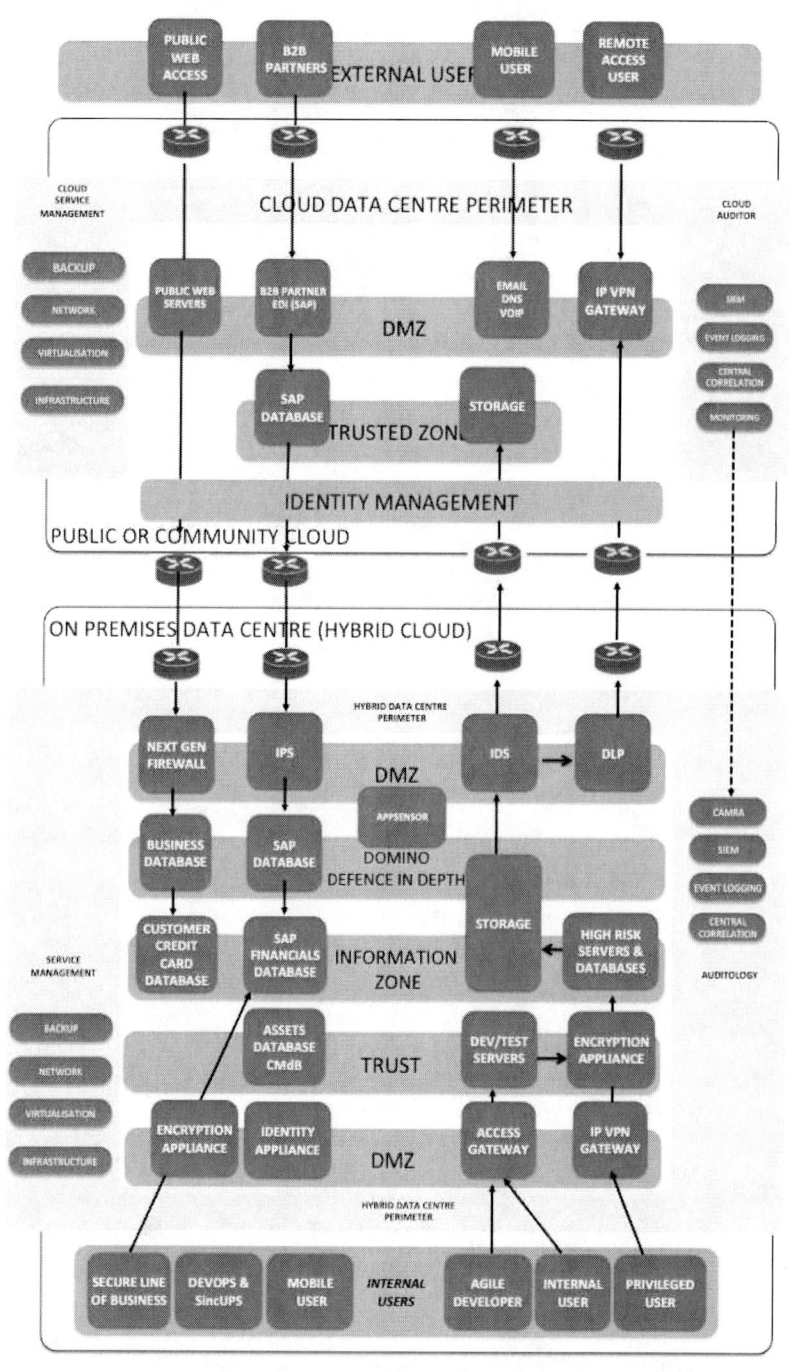

Figure 80 HYBRID/PUBLIC BOUNDARIES AND PERIMETERS

The most common use cases for deploying AppSensor are:

- Identifying attacks (e.g. application or data enumeration, application denial of service, system penetration, fraud)
- Responding to attackers, including prevention
- Monitoring users (e.g. call centre, penetration testing lab)
- Maintaining stability and availability (e.g. application worm propagation prevention)
- Attack intelligence information sharing (e.g. industry verticals, security community).

Application-specific attack detection and response is a comprehensive adaptive approach that can be applied to applications throughout the enterprise. It reduces the risk of unknown vulnerabilities being exploited. The benefits can include:

- Intelligence into whether your applications are under attack, how, and from where
- Certainty due to an extremely high degree of confidence in attack identification
- Fast and fluid responses, using application and user specific contexts
- Protection for software vulnerabilities that you are unaware of
- Defends against future unknown attack methods
- Early detection of both unsuccessful and successful attempts to exploit vulnerabilities
- Insight into users' accidental and malicious misuse

- Information enrichment for conventional network-based intrusion and attack detection systems.

This innovation takes feeds from other perimeter defences, so can enhance real time defences. [168] There are two parts to Appsensor the detection unit and the response unit.

12.18.1.8 IPS (INTRUSION PREVENTION SYSTEM)

An Intrusion Prevention System IPS is similar to an Intrusion Detection System IDS (and requires teaming together), except that the product is designed to take immediate action — such as blocking a specific IP address, or, use. An IPS comprehensively identifies and blocks exploits, and provides real-time and trend intelligence for security policy and reporting. Combing an IPS with a Next Generation Firewall (NGFW) will provide Unified Threat Management; examples of this combination are products from Fortinet, Check Point and Palo Alto.

12.18.1.9 WIRELESS INTRUSION PREVENTION SYSTEMS (WIPS)

WIPS keeps wireless network traffic safe from snooping, data theft and traffic disruption from attacks. They detect and log both successful and attempted attacks, generating notifications for certain attack activity and logging other events for later investigation. WIPS bundle event analysis tools so SMBs can collect WIPS data and integrate those WIPS logs with existing (generally more powerful) analytics tools or correlate these in SIEM. If you cannot afford this then have a whip round.

12.18.1.10 DMZS (DEMILITARISED ZONES)

Usually the logical and physical place for a public-facing Web server but without access back into the internal network it can only forward packets that have already been requested. The technique prevents unrequested and potentially destructive data from entering a company's network. In a hybrid environment Perimeter Security devices can be placed in the DMZ to monitor all northbound and southbound traffic.

12.18.1.11 DATA LOSS PREVENTION

DLP software products use Information Security rules to classify and protect confidential and critical information. This mitigates unauthorised end users cannot accidentally or maliciously share data whose disclosure could put the organisation at risk. For example, if an employee tried to forward a business email outside the corporate domain or upload a corporate file to a consumer cloud storage service like Dropbox, the employee would be denied permission. Makers of DLP platforms are McAfee, RSA, and Symantec. DLP is being driven by insider threats and by privacy laws, many of which have stringent data protection or access components. In addition to being able to monitor and control endpoint activities, some DLP tools can also be used to filter data streams on the corporate network and protect data in motion. Products like DataLock (interguardsoftware.com) can scour PCs for Data at Rest identifying files that have violations attached. These are then sent to the operators for review.

12.18.1.12 WIDE (A) AREA NETWORKS AND CIRCUITS

Monitoring your WAN circuits should not be left to normal SNMP (Simple Network Management Protocol), which is the way, most SMBs and organisations manage their circuits. You need to know if the circuit has been tampered with and it's unlikely your Telco or ISP will tell you. To ensure your network has not been tampered with then use something like T/Mon available from DPS Telecom. This is an appliance that monitors multiple protocols and correlates them to the Telco service provision. Should a discrepancy be identified and correlated with the Telco provisioning and service assurance SLA then you may have a problem.

12.18.1.13 DATA CABLING INTEGRITY

If you are managing a data centre then mange all your power, CCTV, alarms cabling infrastructure as well. An Open Source product for this is openD-CIM, which can also be linked to CMdB. Similar products, are iTRAC, Calient, Vaisalia and Patch Manager.

12.19 DOMINO DEFENCE IN DEPTH – INTERNAL NETWORK

Large networks need to be small networks or micro segmented networks to minimize malware spread. Good network segregation techniques are natural barriers to snooping and communications between these networks should be strictly controlled. In the era of IP ubiquity many networks are designed East to West. This horizontal approach means once an adversary penetrates a perimeter the entire company information is up for grabs. For example in a Credit Card database for customers there is little reason for the entire organisation to have access to this database. Ideally the entire Credit Card database should be encrypted but it should also be on a high-risk server cluster on its own network segment. This controls Northbound and Southbound traffic to a few users, front ended by a router with an Access Control List so NEWS is applied. The ability to control access to the database can be achieved by restricting access to IP Address (or even MAC address), Application two-factor login, Credentials policies and data type movement (see Data Loss Prevention). Logical access to the database can be performed independently of LDAP. Prevent common application and database attacks via SQL injection.

Continuous Scanning of traffic movement is a cheap approach. Create a baseline network traffic model. Use Internet test software such as Sunras cloud software to simulate load and bandwidth utilisation. Test a compromised stream of outbound traffic and use this as a benchmark for normalised traffic analysis. Use the Information Security model to limit traffic access (Top secret or High Risk = No Access). Some NAC systems can integrate with Intrusion detection products such as FireEye and Forescout to isolate systems before adversaries can further access the network.

12.20 NETWORK ACCESS CONTROL (NAC) AND ENDPOINTS

If your believe that managing users from Microsoft's Active Directory is the only way to apply role based access then reconsider. Adversaries speedily attack Windows based DHCP and IPSec links. Network access control tools that used to manage only desktops and laptops are evolving into systems for protecting networks from new security threats brought on by BYOD, ICS and IOT endpoints and employees using their own mobile devices for work.

Before endpoints are let on to the network, the security state of endpoint devices, such as whether they have the most up-to-date anti-virus software installed, has to be verified. Then, users' identities must be authenticated, and checks are made to ensure they have the permissions they need to access network resources. McAfee uses this approach and ideal for call centres that have been outsourced. The endpoint is effectively locked down. Noncompliant devices can be automatically isolated and brought in to line with enterprise security policies, or remediated, before they are allowed to access the network. Cisco, Aruba, Symantec, F5, Mirage, and Infoexpress have proprietary solutions many of which don't interoperate - which is a good thing! Solutions are device, agents or agents, or appliance based (costs start around $20 per endpoint)

12.21 DOMINO DEFENCE IN DEPTH - HARDENING

Most computers offer network security features to limit outside access to the system. Yet, even with these security measures in place, computers are often still vulnerable to outside access. System hardening, also called Operating System hardening, helps minimise these security vulnerabilities.

The purpose of system hardening is to eliminate as many security risks as possible. This is done through removing non-essential applications and utilities from the computer. While these programs may offer useful features to the user, if they provide 'back-door' access to the system, they must be removed during system hardening.

Advanced system hardening may involve reformatting the hard disk and encrypting the whole disk, and only installing the bare bones software that the computer needs to function. File and print sharing are turned off if not necessary and TCP/IP is often the only protocol installed. The guest account is disabled, the administrator account is renamed, and secure passwords are created for all user logins. Auditing is enabled to monitor unauthorised access attempts.

While these steps are often part of operating system hardening, system administrators may choose to perform other tasks that boost system security. While both Macintosh and Windows operating systems can be hardened, system hardening is more often done on Windows machines, since they are more likely to have their security compromised.

Vendors such as Dell are expert at hardening servers and desktop/laptop images. VMWare have extensive guides to hardening virtual machines and environments. These can include; access to machine configurations settings, backups, patches, trusted software and level of cryptographic service validation. Cisco has an excellent treatise on router hardening http://www.cisco.com/c/en/us/support/docs/ip/access-lists/13608-21.html (Cisco Guide to Harden Cisco IOS Devices). SCADA strangelove.org is an ICS focussed community. For general security, device and application hardening visit https://web.nvd.nist.gov/view/ncp/repository; this is the National Vulnerability Database and provides very extensive guides to configuring devices and applications. The Center fro Internet Security has

Hardening should be part of a continuous audit of "anything digital" in the organisations CMdB. Devices should be checked as regularly as you would check the working and maintenance of a fire extinguisher (they do a similar job after all)!

12.22 DOMINO DEFENCE IN DEPTH – ANTI VIRUS

With blended email and web attacks becoming the norm your anti-virus strategy needs to become layered. Relying on a single vendor throughout the organisation may not provide your company with the best armour against malware detection. Besides each device having its own Anti Virus Client PC/Smartphone/Tablet and local disk encryption to provide sandboxing at the endpoint level. Some products also integrate File Transfer Monitoring and Content Filtering at wire speeds. Even if you are feeding traffic from a Cloud fuelled endpoint it should still have to have Anti Virus built into the architecture. The best layering monitors separate traffic fro the Cloud, Public Web (before and after the firewall in the DMZ). There are many new products released lately that act as Boundary Guards. These Boundary Guards monitor SPAM, Web Traffic, and Data Loss Prevention in integrated devices. MacAfee have two great products here their Web Gateway, which fits in well with VM and Hybrid Cloud deployments and their Security Blade products. Kaspersky offer a server based Total Security product, which is economical. Websense Web Security Gateway also offers an urls sandboxing feature. According to threatexpert.com the source of malware originates from the following regions:

- China 32.07%
- Russia 22.29%
- Brazil 6.92%
- US 6.42%
- UK 6.17%
- Canada 0.67%
- Africa 0.17%

Websites and email with inbuilt Viruses built into images are a deep concern, and the most difficult to detect. There are a few devices on the market that can provide a deep scan for reputational intelligence. Images and even downloaded videos can disguise malware. Pornography and other explicit images are coming under tighter workplace laws. These laws make employers subject to law suits with increasingly heavy fines, sexual harassment can cost a 1000 team members size company $6.7 million per year in fines, absenteeism, low productivity and employee turnover. Turning a blind eye to the problem is no longer a valid employer defence. Reputation can be damaged if revelations are made public. In addition, criminal charges against the employer if illegal imagery is found on company email systems. Cisco, Barracuda, and Websense offer pricey solutions but well worth the investment.

12.23 DOMINO DEFENCE IN DEPTH – INCIDENT RESPONSE

So far we have looked at the separate tiles in the Domino deck. The effectiveness of the defence components is only as good as the monitoring software that collates and correlates all the alerts into meaningful and actionable Incidents. We will look at Continuous Monitoring (CAMRA) in depth in the next Part of the book, but human eyes reviewing Incidents is secondary to an effective IP plan. Companies IT therefore need to automate alerts and Omniocular all possible Incidents. In a Black Minute the Incident Speed of Response (iSOR) is crucial. If your end users complain you are too late anyway so team members need to be continuously hunting for signs of intrusion and other anomalies when not focussed on forensics.

	Automatic	Cloud Operations Nerve Centre	Manual
Domino IPS/IDS/Firewall/Unified Threat Management	Yes	Partial	No
Endpoint Host IDS Sys logs	Partial	NA	Yes
Network Based Scanning (Cisco NetFlow)	Yes	Yes	No
Distributed Sniffer (Troubleshoot/Incident in process)	No	Partial	Yes
Manual Log Analysis	No	No	Yes
SIEM (SIAM) Correlation and Analysis	Yes	Yes	No
Encryption and SSL tools at Boundary	Yes	Yes	No
Configuration Management Alerts (Tripwire et al)	Yes	(If Available)	No
Cloud Threat Alerting	No	Yes	Yes
Browser and Screen Capture Tools	No	No	Yes
Sandboxing Forensics	Yes	NA	Yes

Table 10 - OMNIOCULAR CRITERIA

For some strange reason this part of IT is the most underfunded and amateur function in the entire organisation. IR procedures are rarely drilled or practiced. I have only seen one Security Incident Response Plan that is automated and this was also integrated with the Disaster Recovery Plan. I often get from companies that their steam members have never been involved in an IR or DR alarm situation. In Combat Ready mode every person in the organisation is involved and stops production work. Every team member needs to be jumping on the Fire Engine or starting the Spitfires. In recent years companies have created surge teams have been created to manage IRs and then production is halted while a third party is engaged to do the remediation. This can take days to organise dependent on the vicinity of your Blue Team IR external company.

As part of the Security Policy a fixed Incident Response Plan is needed. This should also be linked to the Disaster Recovery and Business Continuity Plans.

12.24 INCIDENT RESPONSE

A Cyber Security Incident Response Team is a service organisation that is responsible for receiving, reviewing, and responding to computer security incident reports and activity. Their services are usually performed for a defined constituency that could be a parent entity such as a corporate, governmental, or educational organisation; a region or country; a research network; or a paid client.

- **Internal CSIRTs** provide incident-handling services to their parent organisation. This could be a CSIRT for a bank, a manufacturing company, a university, or a federal agency.

- **National CSIRTs** provide incident handling services to a country.

- **Coordination Centres** coordinate and facilitate the handling of incidents across various CSIRTs.

- **Analysis Centres** synthesise data from various sources to determine trends and patterns in incident activity. This information can be used to help predict future activity or to provide early warning when the activity matches a set of previously determined characteristics.

- **Vendor Teams** handle reports of vulnerabilities in their software or hardware products. They may work within the organisation to determine if their products are vulnerable and to develop remediation and mitigation strategies. A vendor team may also be the internal CSIRT for a vendor organisation.

The IR plan should also be extended to your Cloud Provider if used. The Incident Response Steps are detailed as follows.

Key Incident Response actions.

1. Two trusted third party remediation vendors should help build your plan

2. At any point in the Domino chain the plan should help remediate the isolation of that domino until the attack is contained, nullified or eliminated

3. The Incident, DR and BC plans need to be drilled with the business every 6 months

4. All alerting should be correlated to one master screen with the rest of the team able to view remediation solutions

5. Legal and HR should be adjusting company policy to help facilitate extraordinary responsibilities during and Incident. Finance should monitor all costs during the Incident and resumption.

The average time to respond to a data breach is 2 to 7 days. That means the business; your network and your employees need to find alternate secure ways of working during the Incident eradication.

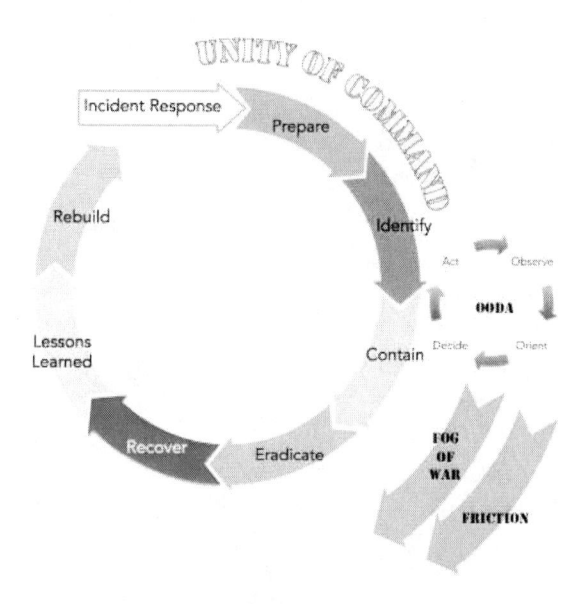

Figure 81 INCIDENT RESPONSE CYCLE

12.24.1.1 SIX STEPS OF INCIDENT RESPONSE
1. Preparation

- NTP – Network Time Protocol – Ideally the NTP on all the business devices and management systems must align with the Cloud Service Provider time signature.

- The key members of the Incident Response team should have elevated credentials during the Incident cycle.

- All emails will halt during the whole process.

- Establish a central logging capability for logs, syslog's and SNARE

- Check the Users identification credentials

- Prepare the War Room – this should comprise several laptops not yet connected to the network

- Checklists of all Assets

- Forensics tools (sniffers etc.,)

- Separate emergency communications – Blue Team needs separate external email accounts.

- Agree the triage process

- Agree the attendees of Blue Team

- List all contacts for every asset

- Agree the network Pull the Plug keyword

- Update the Preparation phase after all major application changes or releases.

Prepare eradication procedures for the following:

- DDOS Attack

- Insider attack procedure

- Worm response procedure

- Virus response procedure

- System failure procedure
- Active intrusion response procedure - Is critical data at risk?
- Inactive Intrusion response procedure
- System abuse procedure
- Property theft response procedure
- Website denial of service response procedure
- Database or file denial of service response procedure
- Spyware response procedure

2. Identification

Start the War Room log timings – Internal Audit as Scribe
Man the War Room

- Internal Audit
- Service desk
- Defence in Depth monitoring personnel
- Security, System, Network, and Database administrator
- A business representative
- A manager
- The security department or a security person.
- External Blue Team (via Skype, video conference)
- Depending on criticality the entire IT team

Collate all alert information on the Criticality Checklist below:

- Are the assets affected, business critical?
- What is the severity of the potential impact?
- Name of system being targeted, along with operating system, IP address, and location.
- IP address and any information about the origin of the attack.
- Is the incident real or perceived?
- Is the incident still in progress?
- What data or property is threatened and how critical is it?
- What is the impact on the business should the attack succeed? Minimal, serious, or critical?
- What system or systems are targeted, where are they located physically and on the network?
- Is the incident inside the trusted network?
- Is the response urgent?
- Can the incident be quickly contained?
- Will the response alert the attacker and do we care?
- What type of incident is this? Ex: virus, worm, intrusion, abuse, damage.

An incident ticket will be created. The incident will be categorized into the highest applicable level of one of the following categories:

- Category one - A Black Minute
- Category two - A threat to sensitive data
- Category three - A threat to computer systems

- Category four - A disruption of services
- Category five – A threat to public safety or life.

Dependent on the Category; contacted members of the response team will meet or discuss the situation over the telephone and determine a response strategy.

3. Contain

The type of Incident will determine the remediation path:

- DDOS – Cut WAN links
- Virus – Isolate servers from LAN
- Remote Break-in – Firewall, net trace, update Access Control List
- Data loss - user activity
- System held hostage - recover from backup, harden and reconfigure
- Website attack – repair and harden
- Insider - alert Auditing and HR

Notify External Governance and Authorities

Take Immediate Action

- Disable pseudo accounts
- Disable compromised accounts
- Change Account passphrases
- Create a Firewall rule to block adversary

- Dependent on Category and application type Freeze all user activity (Pull the Plug)

Start Initial Forensics – traces, logs, timings, memory images, system volatile information

Isolate and segment infected and targeted shutdowns.

Adversary is on a single server – isolate server but do not power down, block outbound and FTP traffic.

4. Eradicate

- Determine the Root Cause
- Determine rootkit potential
- Improve Defences
- Perform Vulnerability Analysis

5. Recovery

- Verify systems, applications and data bases are operating
- Coordinate operations restoration in line with business awareness
- Implement monitoring first

6. Lessons Learned

- Every team member to write up report before the Blue Team leaves site.
- Instigate SHAZOPS™ to ascertain potential systems and business impact.

Further in-depth analysis of the Incident Response can be found in Don Murdoch's excellent book Blue Team Handbook: Incident Response Edition.

[169] This book should be provided to each team member as an Incident Response aide memoir.

12.24.2 PATCH MANAGEMENT

Why do major re-bootable patches always happen the morning of a really busy day? I always get caught by this déjà vu moment. However, it is critical that all machines and devices are patched the day of release. Companies that experience month old patches should change their operators. If the excuse for non real time updates is reliance and effect on major applications then your applications have been poorly written.

12.24.3 DATA SECURITY

Secure communication protocols authenticate clients and servers on the Web a to protect the confidentiality between clients and servers. A variety of secure communication standards that use public key technology have been developed, including Secure Hypertext Transfer Protocol (SHTTP), IP Security (IPSec), PPTP, and L2TP. The leading general-purpose, secure Web communication protocols are SSL 3.0 and the open TLS protocol that is based on SSL. The SSL and TLS protocols are widely used to provide secure channels for confidential TCP/IP communication on the Web.

One disadvantage of SSL and TLS, however, is that the strength of the cryptography that is used for secure channels is subject to government export and import restrictions. For example, the strength of symmetric key encryption that is used by technology that is non-exportable is much higher (128 bits) than the strength of the symmetric key cryptography that is used by technology that is exportable (40 bits or 56 bits). Both servers and clients must use the same cryptographic strength and the same cryptography algorithms when they communicate over a secure channel. At the beginning of SSL and TLS sessions, the server chooses the strongest cryptography that is available to both the server and the client. Maximum security for secure SSL and TLS communication is available only between servers and clients that can both support the higher-strength non-exportable cryptography.

12.24.4 SECURE STORAGE

Should you need to encrypt data for storage then this is perfectly feasible. As a company I store my data in a Swiss Mountain Data Centre. These services are also open to individual users through companies like Tresorit, securesafe.com, Swisscom Storebox. Just don't misplace your passphrase or your encryption keys!

12.24.5 INFORMATION ASSET AND REDO

This is adversaries ultimate target. After negotiating the 10 layers of defences that surround the information what happens when an adversary actually gets to this point. This is where credentials, segregation, file encryption, identity and privilege management kick in. Documentation management is key to business survivability. If you allowed me to choose between an SO and a Technical Author I would opt for the TA! This is a demanding job but worth several security teams. Maintaining information applies generic rigour to the organisation. The taxonomies, ontologies and words need constant crafting, assessing, classifying and manoeuvring. Unfortunately Technical Authors have always been easy targets in redundancies, and so it is seen as a dying profession. As people tell me they would rather put in SharePoint than employ a TA, it needs a TA to manage it! Why you would do that in a cyber security attack is now the question, in fact, returning to good old technical Information Management is the mainstay of any security posture. As described later within the Combat Ready IT model this is revived as an essential element as DocOps. Restore Essential Data Only (REDO) will save on volumes of Tiered storage.

12.24.6 INFORMATION TAXONOMY

If you don't have Taxonomy for your Information you wont know what to do with it! This discipline used to be the remit of the Technical Writing section or the Quality managers' role in organisations. This sector seems to have been wiped out over the last decade but with the need to encrypt essential and confidential data this is now an imperative. We will deep dive this subject later in the Organisation chapter and the increased importance documentation plays in times of conflict, but also how representing well lay documentation saves hours of revision and look-ups.

12.24.7 DATABASES

80% of a company's valuable Intellectual Property languishes in a multiple databases. These databases have grown organically overtime or if a single instance can manage your entire company. When we encrypt databases there are two approaches inside the database and outside. Internal key management removes most of the complexity and management burden by allowing the database to provide key generation and encryption functions without changing application logic or data processing. External key management services offer superior management capabilities, with greater cost and complexity. Internal services include key creation, storage, retrieval, and security; most systems can handle both symmetric and public key encryption. Use of keys can be handled by proxy, as with the transparent encryption options, or through direct API calls to the database package. The keys are stored within the database, usually within a special table that resides in the administrative database or schema. Externally all key operations are performed outside the database in a dedicated key management server.

The servers are dedicated software or hardware appliances (Hardware Security Modules, or HSMs), available through network or local application procedure calls. Both types provide a full range of functions including key creation, storage, and retrieval. The ultimate goal here is to stop data breaches. As we can see from the Domino deck it only takes an external tile to fall and the adversary can access your data, so my best advice here is to keep all encryption internal (unless you are sharing information within the database to external users as part of a service.

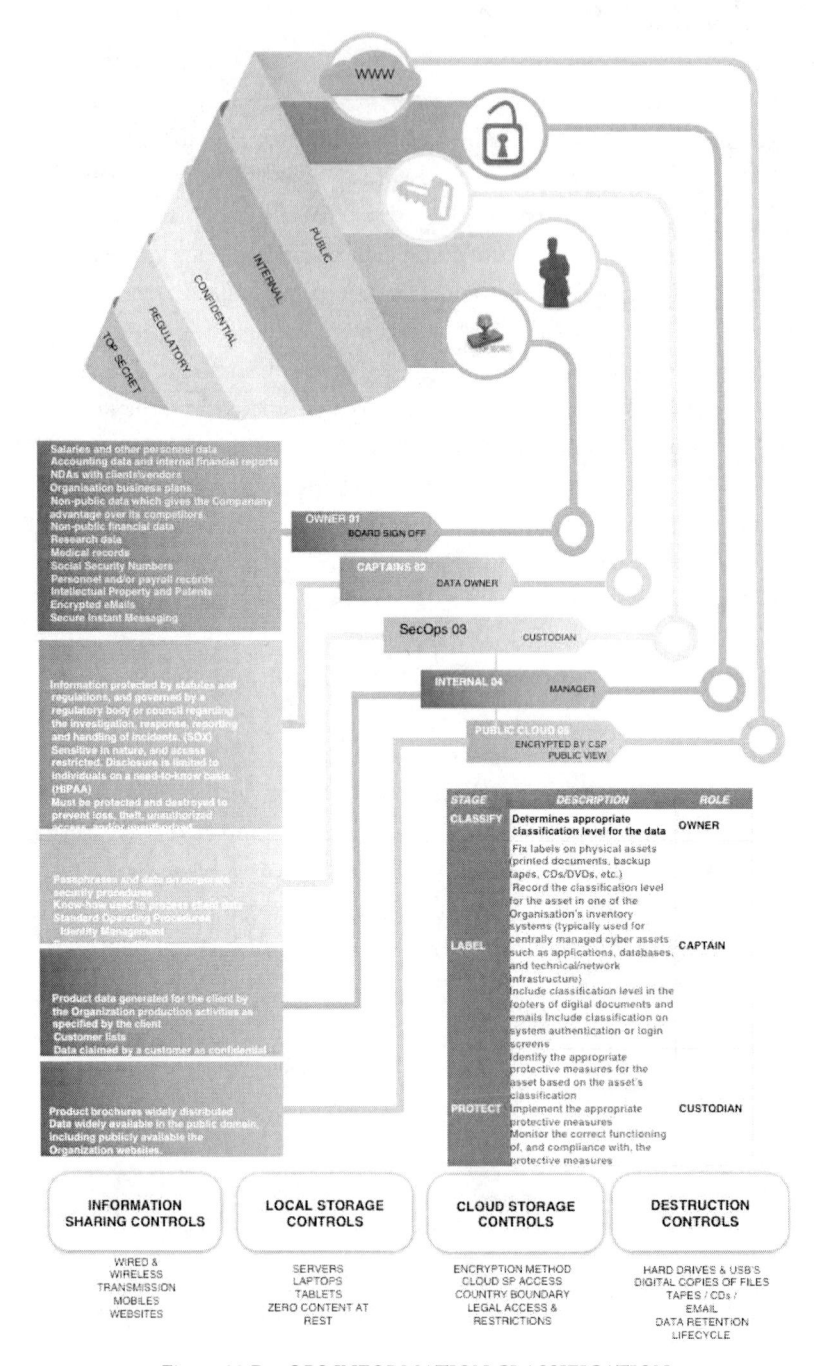

Figure 82 DocOPS INFORMATION CLASSIFICATION

12.25 RIDPOINTS – PERIMETER DEFENCE

Although much of this RIDPOINT is covered in the Defence in Depth section, there are significant variables around how this gets implemented, Perimeter or Endpoint defence is one level of defending your network from attacks, and it works to protect as a firewall from external attacks.

Perimeter defence is just part of the protection suite, so think of it as the peasants' village outside the castle moat. Endpoints run AV independently and then use virtual connections to join the corporate network's border. Put simply, the perimeter is the network's boundary: the frontier where data flows in from (and out to) other networks, including the Internet. Perimeter defence functions like a checkpoint, allowing authorised data to enter unencumbered while blocking suspicious traffic. Cyber attackers now use malicious documents as an attack vector to bypass enterprise perimeter defensive measures and anti-virus solutions.

Macro viruses are making a resurgence comeback. So the latest consensus is to avoid Anti Virus running on an endpoint.

12.25.1.1 ENDPOINTS

Usually means the PC or access device having its own standalone or independent security anti-virus and anti-malware programs. As boundaries of the business are extended via hybrid clouds into public clouds (and vice versa) the endpoint needs more intelligence than it used to (in that it must handle single sign on and increased audit and forensics capability.

There is a school of thought that locks down configuration through software lockdown. As long as the endpoint software configuration remains unchanged then the likelihood that the endpoint is infected is low. Once a malware program has loaded this changes configuration and subsequently the root and core file sizes. When this happens then the desktop administrator is alerted. The endpoint is isolated and wiped and reloaded with a new operating system. All the users data is analysed and restored back once the endpoint is proven clean. Proponents believe this saves the cost of running an AV program the endpoint out of production time is less attractive.

This approach is used daily by Google. They have an endpoint support team of four team members who manage 15,000 Apple Macs with simple open source configurators and applications.

13 THE CLOUD AS THE NEW PERIMETER

This is the era of network-centric computing, software-defined data centre architecture and network-centric content availability. Some 80% of business intend to use the Cloud, but probably are unsure of the ramifications of doing so. The Cloud has some fantastic advantages and some awful drawbacks in terms of security and operations.

To understand the Cloud, we shall review what might be the best service opportunities, and what scope and shape it should take. A Cloud-based data centre uses blade servers. That means a dense packing of the CPU on a card and then in a housing. There are usually eight blade servers on a rack-mounted power and network bus. These eight servers are able to handle up to 100 virtual servers on each blade, making 800 VM Servers in each two feet tall device. Usually you can get four of these devices in a standard rack, which means there is a target of 3,200 servers per rack. In a standard shipping cargo container you can get 10 fully loaded racks, which means a container can have a predicted 32,000 virtual servers for computing power. In terms of architecture that's the equivalent of a mainframe computer in millions of instructions per second (MIPS). There is an excellent video, which details similar components in a Google data centre. In a data centre containers can be stacked and put on the back of a truck, so movement of servers is fast and flexible. As an example of scaling, a single container can handle the computing capacity of a million users for the next five years.

For safety, availability and cost, the Combat Ready Model uses Public Cloud and Hybrid Cloud Infrastructures, and workflow patterns. Ideally when procuring these options it is best to have your Public CSP to match the same toolset as your Hybrid Cloud.

13.1.1 TYPES OF CLOUDS

- **Public Cloud** - the infrastructure is made available to the public or a large industry group and is owned by the organisation selling Cloud services.

- **Private Cloud** - infrastructure operated solely for an organisation. This is completely internal but the architecture and patterns mirror the Public Cloud

- **Community Cloud** - the infrastructure is shared by several organisations and supports a specific community (PetroCloud is an example of this).

- **Hybrid Cloud** - composition of two or more Clouds (public, private, or community) bound by standardised technology that enables data and application portability. This can be migrated from an existing data centre estate. In the Combat Ready model it is assumed that companies retain secret data in the Hybrid Cloud usually on site and in a protected zone, mixed with development VMs and encrypted file and data storage in the Public Cloud. Ideally the choice of cloud provider should match the technology or at least the Management tools for security and automating (Cisco to Cisco, VMWare to VMWare as examples)

13.1.2 CLOUD SECURITY GOTCHAS

The way that VMs behaves sometimes allow kernel vulnerabilities, some vendors have started to shore this fundamental hole up.

In a layered structure, a defence mechanism at some layers can be disabled by malware running at a layer below it. It is feasible to insert a rogue Virtual Machine; a Virtual Machine-Based Rootkit (VMBR) between the physical hardware and an operating system. A rootkit is malware with privileged access to a system. The VMBR can enable a separate malicious OS to run surreptitiously and make this malicious OS invisible to the guest OS, and to the application running under it. Under the protection of the VMBR, the malicious OS could observe the data, the events, or the state of the target system. Most likely, besides stealing actors' photographs, it can run services such as spam relays or distributed denial-of-service attacks, or interfere with the application.

13.1.3 CLOUD SLA

A Service Level Agreement is a negotiated contract between the customer and the Cloud Service Provider (CSP); it can be legally binding or informal. Objectives:

1. Identify and define the organisation's needs and constraints, including the level of resources, security, timing, and QoS.

2. Provide a framework for understanding; a critical aspect of this framework is a clear definition of classes of service and the costs.

3. Simplify complex issues; clarify the boundaries between the responsibilities of clients and CSP in case of failures.

4. Reduce areas of conflict.

5. Encourage dialogue in the event of disputes.

6. Eliminate unrealistic expectations

13.1.4 BULLETPROOF NETWORK

In the UK, during a period called the Big Bang, the Financial Services Authority issued a diktat that all IT systems should have a hot standby system. In their confusion, banks typically reproduced an exact mirror of what they had already. Everything was bought in two's as if this would solve all the disaster recovery and business continuity performance criteria. In reality it was a great time for order-takers and sales commissions, the net effect being lots of licences duplicated for no reason. Banks to resolve the requirement, resulting in many visibly fat bankers by the end of the year, spent $20 billion!

Throwing money at the problem could have helped in some cases, but did not achieve the desired goal. The positive outcome of the futile exercise was that at this time people did start to buy bullet-proof networks, which meant that any given system had to have two points of ingress and egress for each communications link. So if one link went down, the other would theoretically survive. The requirement also drove the need for completely diverse routing so that the links would not share the same ductwork back to an exchange, or geographically diversely routed to two exchanges and repeated beyond the next hop. In a Cloud world, data can be load-balanced and latency responses can be tuned to migrate pooled resources - automatically. This is the nub of network complexity.

There are several ways to manage virtual servers. Microsoft, VMWare, IBM and HP have differing Virtual Machine management platforms. If I describe the VM Ware approach, it may help the reader understand how this computing power can expand or decrease instantly.

13.1.5 VMWARE

VCloud Air and VMNSX are VM Ware's automated management tools. They can provision VMs for clients instantly; it can measure server capacity and utilisation. As a rule of thumb, most VMs rarely exceed 5% utilisation, allowing 95% of memory to be used elsewhere on the site resource pool, or even across geographically dispersed containers. This means an organisation can have a container's worth of servers in-house (a Private Cloud) with a complete mirror offsite in a Public Cloud. VCloud Air can deploy the bubble of spare memory to any other VM in the estate automatically. An operator rarely needs to intervene to manage this. The 95% of memory is dynamically moved to servers requiring additional capacity. This ability to move workloads is the key to cost-effective and highly available computing. Before a VM is moved, a snapshot is taken of the VM and this can be restored on any available server at will. In a Cloud environment with multiple physical data centres data can be replicated across 10 other sites, depending on what you pay for. Alarms are sent to operators either in the relevant Cloud provider or to the SMB monitoring platform.

In traditional data centre environments and using traditional servers it could take weeks for IT Operations to buy, accept delivery, load OS, load applications, configure network, build and test network, deploy the server into production and monitor. It could take up to a month to provision a basic service. With the virtualisation route, a VM is set up within seconds.

So when you buy a Cloud server you are accessing a pooled resource. The proliferation of Cloud Data Centres means that data sovereignty is key here. You may insist that data must reside within a state, a country, or even the same continent, and that backing up that data should stay within dominion boundaries to satisfy data privacy and protection laws. If you were based in the US and didn't want your data subject to legal recovery by the authorities, you might want to put your data in a Swiss data vault for example. In conflict situations the ability to spin up, provision and tear down servers at will across global locations provides risk reduction.

The blades are usually connected to a 40 Gbit/s network the same speed as a backplane on a Blade server (so no traffic IO bottlenecks occur). The network throughput of a Public Cloud container should handle half a million concurrent data streams (or even voice calls using VOIP) per second. Bottlenecks are managed by deploying flexible bandwidth using SDN. Network capacity limits usually top out at 70% utilisation. With an SDN, this network availability can be spread to short-term high-capacity locations on demand. This dynamic allocation of bandwidth saves adding 'another router'. This also defines the network IP routes and associated paths to ensure volume leakage is within countries. Network Functions Virtualisation (NFV) is an initiative driven by the ETSI Industry Specification Group to virtualise network functions previously performed by proprietary dedicated hardware. The goal of the ETSI effort is to reduce the cost of telecom network infrastructure by allowing the appropriate functions to run on a common, commodity platform that hosts the necessary virtualised environments.

Almost any network function can be virtualised. The NFV focus in the market today includes virtualisation of (NASA):

- **N**etwork Services – examples here are Network Management applications such as traffic analysis, network monitoring tools, load balancers and accelerators.

- **A**ppliances – network functions that today require a dedicated box can be replaced with a virtual appliance. Examples include security functions such as firewalls and gateways, Broadband Remote Access Servers (BRAS) and LTE Evolved Packet Core (EPC).

- **S**witching – physical ports are connected to virtual ports on virtual servers with virtual routers using virtualised IPSec and SSL VPN gateways.

- **A**pplications – almost any application you can imagine. For example, there is a great deal of development today for cloud applications, such as virtualised storage and photo imaging services, to support the explosion in tablet and smartphone usage.[170]

This ability to move resources at will to provide continuity of service in a software-driven world means we apply the same principles to routers (because they also have spare CPU and memory) and storage because they have CPU, memory and hard disk volumes that can also be pooled. In addition, thin clients (desktops, tablets and iPhones) can be provided with virtual OS, applications and hard disk space. If you recall all the separate appliances per tile and described in the various Domino Defence in Depth designs, these will be ported to blade servers (eventually). To me this can be likened to a Rolodex. This Rolodex (a box with cards) architecture will facilitate choice at will and allows selection of Hardware and Software services just by flicking through the Rolodex wheel and stopping at the required card (or service).

Storage can be profile-driven on demand. That means a backup of the data is driven by the performance characteristics, redundancy characteristics and retention policies set by the company. With the Cloud you can create data on any OS and deliver this to a VSAN to create a data plane. This data plane allows large quantities of data to be accessed by any device. So in the traditional storage world SANs (Storage Area Networks) were usually LUN attached (this was a Logical Unit Network attached bus that required direct attachment to a physical server), both costly to manage and disastrous when it failed. Network Attached Storage allows geo-distribution, as long as the network bandwidth is sufficient; this type of deployment was reasonable for Telco's who own their network. In a VSAN the storage is not driven by technology (SAN/ NAS), it is driven by policy.

In VMware's VSAN it is capable of storing 4.4 Petabytes of storage at 2 million IOPS (that's 2 million Input Output Operations per Second). This combination of virtual server, network and storage provides the ultimate goal for SMBs, that of meeting capacity, performance and availability management KPIs.

13.1.6 VIRTUAL SAN

The problem with virtual machines and servers was the feature to back up the virtual data on a virtual server that could be in any container, data centre or country? Until recently the only way was to do this physically, i.e., taking a complete backup of the physical server and all the configuration parameters and virtual settings that were bound to the server. This was a time-consuming and required storage appliance to handle the required DRAM and IOPS. The time was also dependent on the hard disk spinning to optimal speed to reduce IOPS bottlenecks and even type of data. The advent of Flash Storage in large data storage arrays has overcome the IOPS problem but exacerbated the cost per terabyte of storage. It's expensive but at least the hard disks are not (yet) compromised by Firmware hacking. Most team members generate around 20GB of storage per year including e-mail. To store and maintain a SAN would cost around $50,000 per one hundred employees per annum. The wage bills around this would also be significant.

VSANS now herald the death of desktops. There now is no need to provide desktops when the storage can be Hybrid Cloud-based, held on virtual servers and VSANs on site. I was advising a company recently who, midway through a vast XP to Windows 7 rollout, basically gave up the project; instead they bought tablets for everyone. The reason, the cost to migrate a PC was $700 when the cost of a tablet was $400. Besides the human ergonomics problems (RSI and a lack of a keyboard) it allowed team members to roam. In the manufacturing setting this is a godsend. Machine and robotics operators were not constantly reverting back to their desktops (which could be located in the separate office facility) to check the sequencing or reprogramming of automated machinery, instead they roamed the factory floor and were able to step-check their machines while standing next to them. In robotics programming this saved months of walking to and fro configuration step-checks between robot and desktop. In addition, the applications could be controlled centrally and data backed up immediately. This meant that data and configurations, were monitored by supervisors and quality control regained a foothold.

13.1.7 TEAM MEMBER RATIOS
In traditional IT, a sys admin would manage the end-to-end provisioning of a server. Typically this ratio would be one operator to 40 servers, one operator to a hundred virtual servers, or in a Cloud environment one operator to a thousand servers. I can see accountants rubbing their hands with glee at Christmas time so they can slash more jobs. For a network team the ratio was 1:1000 team members, and for storage team the ratio was 1:100 team members. In Cloud Service Providers managers espouse the '2 Pizza' rule, no team should exceed this amount of food when working a late shift.

13.2 HYBRID CLOUD
A Hybrid Cloud frees an SMB to build out according to service demands and capacity. By combining a Hybrid and a Public cloud services a company can extend compute power or storage as required. This is termed Elastic Consumption Model or (as one cash strapped CIO used to term it) JAMAICA (Just Action! Make Asks of IT Instantly Chargeable and Available). A common management platform is managed by a DevOps IAAS Administrator on SMB premises who uses templates in a Service Catalogue to build servers on or off premises. Software Defined Networking allows a seamless network provisioning and Authentication can be delivered from the SMB data centre. As control rests with the SMB a common Governance and Security Glueprints can be maintained, ensuring auditability. As DevOps needs to pull together all the custom APIs, end-to-end handoffs and craftflows, Service Catalogue, live sandboxing, custom Service Delivery features and Cloud Automation tasks this is known as Cloud Automation. In addition, the DevOps Administrator uses Cloud Automation can manage multiple public cloud instances within territorial boundaries or across dominions. The DevOps role is pivotal and complex. Using Cloud Orchestration (a subset of Cloud Automation) portal to create a server the DevOps can take a template to bootstrap a server (refers to the process of loading an operating system. The technique is: initialize the hardware, reading a small amount of code into memory, and executing that code. This small bit of code then loads a larger operating system. Once the operating system is loaded, it then creates its entire environment. It only takes about 30 lines of code to build a server and configured with about eight IP addresses from the SMBs IP

Schema. It's estimated (given a hefty chunk of planning) a DevOps can spin up about 20 servers in a day and still have an hours lunch-break.

Policies can segregate endpoints based on different performance drivers. This means that different environments can be attached to various tiers of storage, or, encryption based on Information classification. One virtual data centre can attach to high- performance storage while another virtual data centre can be attached to a more economical standard tier of storage. By leveraging policies, a business can direct applications to the best location for that workload based on cost. The ease of orchestration is therefore relatively easy for an individual. This role does not require an army; division or battalion rather a sniper will suffice.

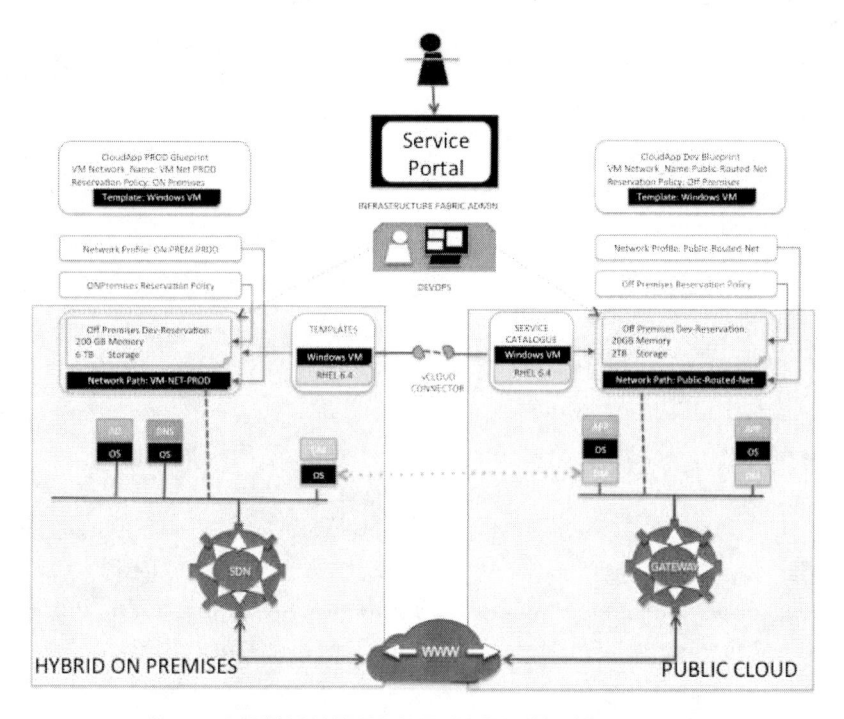

Figure 83 AUTOMATION AND ORCHESTRATION FOR Devops

13.2.1 CLOUDIFYING APPLICATIONS

If your sales team uses Salesforce, this is a Cloud-based service (SAAS). This means your data is stored in a pooled environment ready to be accessed by a browser. SAP is now moving down this distributed architecture route, and hopefully their software will rationalise on a standard set of APIs and templates. Mobiles and tablets can be managed from the Cloud, in terms of virtual extensions of an enterprise application set, or e-mail encryption. The problem with Cloud implementations is that developers and operators can lose sight of logs and content availability, so a high degree of automation is required. The platform for creating future applications seems robust.

The future Internet will be based on High Definition. There are voice codecs that produce High Definition audio calls and High Definition on-demand videos providing 3D and stereo increased frame rates. 3D printing and even virtual product testing can be delivered by sharing the resources of the Cloud. The world of Cloud-based 3D gaming is in its infancy, but will start to become reality in the next few years. In terms of military drills, the ability to train soldiers in a 3D environment created by years of geographic data collection means missions can be trained for in advance. Commando raids can be trained for in virtual environments and timings measured for efficiency. The use of drone soldiers is also being tested in the near future. Robot soldiers can be deployed to operate in highly radioactive post nuclear fields and circumvent dangerous territories, as human soldiers control the robots from a remote location.

13.2.2 HADOOP 2 SPARK

We discussed how VSANS create and reside within a data plane. This bubble of data can be pooled, thrown into a vast array of memory and interrogated using Hadoop, which uses a data query language (SPARK) from Apache. Big Data can be useful to any SMB wishing to uncover niche markets. An example of this is the beer and nappies data mining in the retail sector. Most parents, especially fathers, usually do a rush shop to buy nappies for new-born children, as these are bulk items. As the father rushes into a shop, the next shelf is a beer stall. The male parent is 70% more likely to pick up a six-pack of beer when buying nappies. Big Data allows for these idiosyncrasies to be identified and leveraged for product placing. It can also fuel crowdsourcing, whereby viruses detected on a certain machine or operating system can be quickly highlighted globally and acted on by anti-virus vendors. Customers can set up multiple Hadoop virtual clusters and use each one for a different workload. Companies can then site these virtual clusters in different geographies, for redundancy, load balancing and/or content distribution including data encryption and security. The data can be segregated or, using replication technology, it can be synchronised between sites to create a 'logical data cluster'. This logical data cluster can tag on to other companies' data sets and data sources can be mixed to provide highly targeted products (or people).

13.3 CLOUD SECURITY?

I love the Cloud but like Chicken Little, Cocky Locky, Ducky Lucky, and Goosey Loosey, I don't want the Cloud to fall on my head. The technology and automation systems in the Cloud are reaching a maturity level that's becoming attractive. It does bring its own set of challenges, so how is this to be managed? If you work with CSP security teams any data breach is your fault and your responsibility. Even when Security As A Service is provided it is still your accountability. No CSP would accept a data breach even though they are running your service, which you pay them to secure. They may alert you through tools such as Alertlogic or EM7 but the onus falls at your doorstep.

I have witnessed a Cloud succumbing to a DDOS attack (it's not pretty) and also an entire Cloud data centre going offline for a day. If you are concerned with uptime then best practice is to always keep your own data centre and implement a hybrid Cloud solution to deliver a 100% SLA (Service Level Agreement). In the Combat Ready Model you don't want a great deal of computer power taken away so it cannot be closely managed or audited during conflict. By all means put your public-facing Web servers in the Cloud. Cloud Service providers provide Web services and some hosted customer facing security appliances would not be stymied by a DDOS and affect operation and production time. Service Providers are also adept at halting these attacks at source so not a bad option. Dyn provides this as a service that can alleviate many of these normalised attacks today. If you are in retail, nearly half of all cyber-attacks target the Web servers. This type of service is a critical choice. Obviously take advantage of the data security a Private Cloud can deliver; getting this mix right is the next challenge

14 RIDPOINTS OPERATIONS NERVE CENTRE

Think NASA in Houston (Not Euston), a vast array of big TV screens providing an Omniocular view of the entire estate. These screens sit at the front on a large room manned by worried people fiddling with metal slide rules and books on logarithms. This Omniocular view of end-to-end services is more important than ever as virtualisation increases server farm automation, and networks become outsourced to national or international Telco's. The human eye and brain can correlate and marry multiple attack and alarm patterns faster than most automated systems. I have started to use the term Nerve Centre (and Nerve Response Centre) more than Command and Control, NOC (Networks Operating Centre) or Ops Room as it seems to purvey a speedier type approach to seeing and detecting malware spread of viruses and the concept of quick reactions. Do invest heavily in the ONC, it is a way of seeing the full picture and applying CAMRA to spot a Black Minute unravelling.

14.1 OMNIOCULAR MONITORING

Out-of-Band monitoring started in the early 1980s. It usually meant that every server had a modem attached (or a modem bank) so that administrators could access the Operating System remotely. It was still hackable. Hackers used to find the range of modem telephone numbers associated with an enterprise and dial each one until a modem answered. The terms in-band and out-of-band generally refer to whether the solution sits in the flow of all network traffic, or out of the flow, analysing instead only some of the live data streams. It has always been accepted that being in-band can offer better security and greater functionality than an out-of-band approach, but could represent a performance bottleneck or a potential point-of-failure in a mission critical network. **In-Band** network management requires SNMP (V3) to be on each device. Simple Network Monitoring Protocol versions 1 and 2 are hackable. Check that your devices, servers, routers only support SNMP V3 and not earlier versions.

SNMPv3 provides important security features:

- Confidentiality - Encryption of packets to prevent snooping by adversaries.

- Integrity - Message integrity to ensure that a packet has not been tampered while in transit including an optional packet replay protection mechanism to minimise MITM attacks.

- Authentication - to verify that the message is from a known source.

Other protocols that supply similar functionality such as WMI (Windows Monitoring Interface) are viable and can be used, as a cheap way to collect metadata for a CMdB. Out-of-band requires VLANs. The terms in-band and out-of-band requires stateful firewall policies and continuous malware detection and allows continuous monitoring, and protects vulnerable or infected clients from each other.

14.2 REAL TIME MONITORING

Real Time Monitoring Tools use SNMPv3 and monitors and displays the current system performance across the estate. They sum up the performance for a particular form factor such as heat, CPU performance, memory usage, hard disk volume usage, component failures or configuration changes. These tools rely on system calls that are built into the operating system to extract the performance readings. Because these calls are built into the operating system, they do affect the system performance, sometimes significantly. They are also very difficult to change since the operating system source code is not usually readily available.

14.3 CLOUD MONITORING

I've spent the past few years deploying Remote Monitoring and Management (RMM) software platforms designed for Managed Services Providers (MSPs). When you deploy all your hard-earned data to the Cloud, the MSPs need to be absolutely transparent when it comes to informing you of what's really going on through a shared Omniocular observation screen. There are about 50 such offerings on the market that manage VMs, Applications and Identity. Granular platforms deliver network and security heuristics, like SPLUNK.

14.3.1 FORENSICS

After a Black Minute and as a part of the Incident Response, Cyber forensics describes the investigation and analysis techniques used to gather and preserve evidence from a particular computing device in a way that is suitable for presentation in a court of law. The goal of computer forensics is to perform a structured investigation while maintaining a documented trail of evidence to find out exactly what was changed on a computing device and ultimately who was responsible for it.

Forensic investigators typically follow a standard set of procedures: after physically isolating the device in question to make sure it cannot be accidentally contaminated, investigators make a digital copy of the device's storage media. Once the original media have been copied, it is locked in a safe or other secure facility to maintain its pristine condition. All investigation is done on the digital copy.

Investigators use a variety of techniques and proprietary software forensic applications to examine the copy, searching hidden folders and unallocated disk space for copies of deleted, encrypted, or damaged files. Any evidence found on the digital copy is carefully documented in a 'finding report' and verified with the original in preparation for legal proceedings that involve discovery, depositions, or actual litigation.

14.3.2 VULNERABILITIES

Security management identifies and analyses alarm, security threats and vulnerabilities. The adequacy of the countermeasures provided to mitigate the threats. Vulnerability Assessment is a technique to help the owner/operator make decisions on the need for and value of enhancements. Security enhancements are determined partly by factors such as the degree and scope of the threat, risk level, the degree of vulnerability, the possible consequences of an incident, and the attractiveness of the information asset to adversaries. Usually tests are carried out over network attacking web applications,

Cloud and software development functions. Ideally these should be carried out after a major change or upgrade, but due to cost (about $5,000) these are bi-annual although they should be done monthly by an internal team.

It is a law of application development that the cost of detecting and remediating any defect is dramatically reduced when the flaw is found early in the development lifecycle – the earlier the better. The trial-and-error approach to scanning and remediating code adds a significant amount of time to the development process, which risks delaying the delivery of product upgrades and enhancements—eroding the organisation's competitiveness and threatening revenue.

Application scanning can be implemented after production release and remains a critical tool in ensuring the security of those applications. Unfortunately, because this occurs late in the development lifecycle, security defects aren't discovered until they're very expensive and time-consuming to fix. Even the costs of hardware, software, and personnel required could be staggering: organizations with comparatively modest application portfolios easily spend millions of dollars per year.

Today, Application Security professionals spend hours scanning applications and working with developers to fix simple bugs. The output of these scans—a lengthy report outlining thousands of issues across an entire application—requires hours of prep work by a small team of security personnel before it is ready to hand off to the development team for remediation so this discipline should be embedded early in an agile workflow. With little to no guidance outlining how to fix these vulnerabilities, developers are pushed into another development loop focused on remediating and retesting the application. The expected outcome is a Quantitive determination of risk to provide a sound basis for rank ordering of the security-related risks and thus establishing priorities for the application of countermeasures, which forms part of the Via Ferrata reporting.

These objectives should be highlighted and expanded upon as part of the output of a SHAZOPS study. Appropriate strategies for managing security can vary widely depending on the individual circumstances of the organisation. As a result, SHAZOPS does not prescribe security measures but instead suggests a means of identifying, analysing, and reducing vulnerabilities and ultimately risk elimination. Any deficiency should be addressed on a case-by-case basis using best judgment of applicable practices.

14.3.3 PENETRATION TEST
A Penetration Test is a method of evaluating computer and network security by simulating an attack on a computer system or network from external and internal threats. The same tools, know-how and methodologies are being used, as malicious hackers would employ. The difference from a real attack is the fact that testing is done with the explicit written consent of the client and the purpose is to produce a comprehensive report and to close down security holes before a real attacker can exploit them. About 70% of technical attacks are aimed at the Application Layer. External companies, who attack the Web application from a coding and implementation flaw perspective, but also attempts SQL Injection, and cross-site scripting attacks, MITM and Denial of Service testing usually carry out the Penetration Tests. SMBs should dual trusted penetration testers as a matter of course.

15 RIDPOINTS - IT FRAMEWORKS AND REGULATIONS

ITIL, ISO, TOGAF, CMMI, PMI, ITSM, and many other frameworks are designed to enforce processes across IT. As we will discuss, these can bring necessary disciplines and audit trails to help give visibility to operations.

15.1 SECURITY BEST PRACTICES

These are the core Security Implementation Principles and key Security Objectives:

CIA (44 USC Sec. 3542)

- **Confidentiality** – Preserving authorised restriction on information access and disclosure, including means for protecting personal privacy and proprietary information.

- **Integrity** – Guarding against improper information modification or destruction and includes ensuring information non-repudiation and authenticity.

- **Availability** – Ensuring timely and reliable access and use of information.

- **Need to Know** – Users should only have access to information (or systems) that enable them to perform their assigned job functions

- **Least Privilege** – Users should only have sufficient access privilege that allow them to perform assigned work.

- **Separation of Duties**– No person should be responsible for completing a task involving sensitive, valuable or critical information from the beginning to end.

No single person should be responsible for approving his/her own work.

- **Job Rotation**

  To reduce risk of collusion

  To ensure no single point of failure

- **Mandatory Vacation** - To allow auditors to review records

15.2 ITIL®

ITIL v3 2011® is a framework of best practice guidance in Information Technology Service Management (ITSM). It describes processes, functions and structures that support most areas of IT Service Management, mostly from the viewpoint of the Service Provider, and leans on the Deming Plan, Do, Check, Act cycle (see the centre of the ITIL diagram). One of the many processes it describes is Information Security Management (ISM).

The ITIL® Organisation is ideal for any IT Department over 50 team members strong. The Organisation Chart needs at least this number of people to drive all relevant processes. The adoption of ITIL is dependent on the circumstances of a particular provider, customer or implementation, depending on various factors such as size, culture, existing management systems, organisational structure and the nature of the business. ITIL® is not prescriptive and because of the necessary implementation tuning, there is no rigidity of application that would indicate that tests of compliance are appropriate. It really does help people to understand Incident, Problem Change and Release Management. ITIL is recommended training for anyone in the technology field. This applies especially to apprentices who need to see the deeper workings of technology and the interactions and interfaces required in the service life cycle.

I have been using and teaching ITIL® for over 25 years. ITIL® came about when the UK Government procurement team (the CCTA) in Norwich (Norfolk, UK) and specifically asked for a set of support documents to help government departments maintenance team members support PCs. For years the CCTA (Central Communication and Telecommunications

Agency) had bought Mainframes with dumb terminals. When a terminal died, it was simply replaced by a maintenance engineer. With the advent of PCs and the availability of new applications the CCTA had to give guidance to setting up Help Desks and the support processes. I worked on GITIM (Government Information Technology Infrastructure Management) in 1985 specifically on the Help desk elements. In 2000, the CCTA merged into the OGC; Office for Government Commerce and in the same year Microsoft used ITIL as the basis to develop their proprietary Microsoft Operations Framework (MOF). MOF interlocks with their management platforms to products such as such as SCCM and SCOM (for Data Centre's).

In 2001, version 2 of ITIL® was published. The two streams of Service Support and Service Delivery books were condensed into more concise usable volumes. Over the following few years it became, by far, the most widely used IT service management best practice approach in the world. I have implemented this version in 28 companies around the globe so I know its impacted 6000 IT team members to the positive. In 2005 The BS 15000 (British Standard) that emulated ITIL became ISO20000.

In 2007 ITILv3® was released. This adopted more of a life cycle approach to service management, with greater emphasis on Security and IT business integration. ITIL V3® was upgraded in 2011. It links with PRINCE 2 ® and M_O_R ® (Management of Risk).

One of the key tools ITIL V3 2011 ® describes is the CMdB (Change Management Database). This tool holds all the assets for the IT estate, describes linkages to network and applications and helps drive financial management. This adopted more of a life cycle approach to service management, with greater emphasis on Security and IT business integration. The next version of ITIL is predicted to include more security processes.

15.3 RIDPOINTS - TRAINING

15.3.1.1 TEAM MEMBERS

It's important to perpetually train all team members about security. This applies to everyone include the SMB owner. Apparently this is still not happening. I have seen several Computer Based Training attempts on enterprise intranet portals, but this is usually aimed at new starters.[171] It should also be updated quarterly, (and more frequent if physically possible). The Security Officer should supplement this with daily newsletters and weekly presentations. I find that running CBTs on Ethical Practices, Fraud Detection and Whistleblowing, and managing and handling Company Intellectual Property reinforce self-determination behaviours. The "Stop-Think-Connect" Toolkit from the US Department of Homeland Security has provided educational materials and tips tailored to all segments of the community from school students and older people to small business, government, and more. Do you remember the Suggestions Box? For anyone under the age of 30 you have probably never seen these. If a problem was encountered in any office or production facility team members used to jot their ideas down on a slip of paper and post them in the deployed ballot style boxes. Replicating this in a simple email system address is the modern equivalent. Ideas make team members valued.

15.3.1.2 SECURITY TOOL BOX TALKS

Every meeting agenda (like Health and Safety) should start with a Security toolbox talk. These 3-minute slots are a consistent reminder to reinforce the security culture at the start of every meeting. Topics like passphrases, risks of new malware are a no-brainer, but because there are so many data breaches daily then these can be given as real life use cases to help educate or curtail behaviours.

15.3.1.3 GAMIFICATION OF APPLICATIONS

When did drones suddenly begin to be a key weapon in the fight against terrorism? I cannot remember when this started. How much fun it must be to sit in a warm room with an Xbox controller and shoot missiles at an anonymous enemy 8000 miles away. The word gamification is used to describe companies integrating game mechanics into their non-gaming product or service to drive user engagement. These companies are 'gamifying' their products and services by adding light game mechanics on top of them. The deployment of drones can be a risk as they have been successfully hacked by terrorists. Gamification can be used to eradicate the tedious tasks that IT is prone to.

The average length of tenure on a Service Desk is a measly 11 months. If your goal was to be an IT Guru working on a Service Desk is a good place to start for many. If you don't know how to manage an end user or assist with remediation of a users problem end to end then you will not understand the organisation or be able to sway strategy. I used to employ McDonalds service team members and put them on Help Desks. Their grasp on understanding the real elements of customer service are rammed home, politeness, listening and hygiene are the basic skills all team members should have. Besides moving the Service Desk Support line to every member in IT on a rota basis (no matter what level you are at within the organisation) allows a deeper insight into the business. For long- term employees the Service Desk needs to be rethought. This also applies to Security team members. Day-to- Day routine can be left or ignored. A cloud based Service Desk application[172] has "gamified" the application.

Just as GEN Y/Z live and breathe gaming terminology (Collect Badges, points, prizes, stars etc.) so game mechanics is seeping into applications to maintain high levels of engagement. In the IT Support and Service Desk environment this can be translated into a number of similar potential activities such as; call handling, request processing, incident resolution, customer satisfaction scoring, knowledge base building, and tool logging/updating. There is a school of thought whose eyes roll skywards when I encourage this, believing this is for kids. Actually I am an oldie who loves this. It helps to increase agent performance by 300% and helps team members over achieve. Applying this method to security defences would also benefit companies. The Individuals can be encouraged to use their initiative to define and implement knowledge articles. Intra company white papers are great ways your team members can contribute to internal processes and problem fixes. Some papers can be used as company collateral. Points can be accumulated through publishing and qualifying quality feedback from their peers. [173] Running self-service FAQs and Self Resets of passphrases can alleviate 80% of user calls and email trouble tickets. At SMBs where this is executed this saves not only overhead but increases availability.

15.3.1.4 SECURITY APPRENTISHIPS

There is a dearth of qualified security people globally. So my recommendation is to grow your own. An SO is hard to attract attracted to an SMB environment. Running security apprenticeship programmes for young (or old) smart people may be a better way to create a security culture. I believe that given the right automation tools providing funds for online learning will be an attractive proposition for career-minded professionals. When I have run these programs the apprenticeship runs for three years. This locks in the apprentice during the tenure. If existing IT members wish to move into this arena then apply the cost of training payback to their contract, (should they leave before a 3 year tenure). If you don't do this then people will do the initial year, get a certificate and skedaddle. Also consider real performance bonuses for team members based on metrics. Metrics are traceable and show real results. Maintaining a security environment to a high Combat Ready status means real deliverables must be achieved Incentivise your team members just as you would sales team members. Zero hacks get an award of a holiday for instance.

16 RIDPOINTS - SECURITY MANAGEMENT

So how do SMBs maintain a high-grade perpetual security stance? You need to have the best in breed tool sets and team members motivated to act on their outputs. Investment in deep monitoring and monitoring software is the key message here. Not investing in tool sets in a digital age is like doing a Route 66 road trip on half a tank of gas. It "isn't going to work". So kick off your Security Policy based on the successful implementation of management tools. This means – DO NOT SCRIMP on the budget here, arming your soldiers with weapons that work in any eventuality. The tools you select need to support the Security Policy and Controls you deem necessary for your company.

16.1 CONTROLS

Controls are needed in all organisations. In security they need to be followed to the letter and managed accordingly. There is no way around these directives (believe me I have tried)! They can be entirely process bound. I have included a summary of the Top 20 Security Controls and the OWASP Top 10 in Appendix 3.

The following **ADAPT** bullets describe the controls that apply to any organisation:

- **ADMINISTRATIVE Controls**. Advise team members of expected behaviours during their interfaces with or use of information systems.

- **DETECTIVE Controls**. Detective controls involve the use of practices, handoffs, and tools that identify and possibly react to security incidents.

- **AVAILABILITY Controls.** Once an incident occurs and compromises availability, the implementation of recovery controls is necessary to restore the system or service to a normal operating state.

- **PERPETUAL Controls.** Included in perpetual controls are physical, administrative, and technical measures intended to prevent actions violating policy and minimising Risk Ignition Points

- **TECHNICAL Controls.** Involves perpetual, administrative, and technical measures designed to react to alarms and incidents to reduce or eliminate recurrence.

16.2 SECURITY INFORMATION EVENT MANAGEMENT (SIEM/SIAM)

(*Spleen Vent Moment*)- Personally I cannot stand the term 'event management', it gets up my nose each time it's used by the industry. Apologies in advance but to me "Event Management" refers to conferences or party planning and should be used in that context, is on equal terms with the snobbish parlance use of "Actors". Like most buzzwords in the industry in the last five years, these terms cause confusion, disdain and rhetorical debate. It's a term coined by people who have never run an IT Technical Operations function. To me it feels like it was stolen from a Hotel and Catering College textbook. It should be precisely termed Alarm Management, or SIAM (Security Information Alarm Management). I would not mind 'Attack' either, I am flexible! Unfortunately SIEM has been bounded as the acronym by vendors and regulators and not Wedding Planners, so I will continue to suck it up.

All IP connected devices on a network create logs. Routers, servers, laptops, and appliances generate logs. Logs are key to security to capture and trace alarms and attacks, capture for Incident Response and Forensics. The logs are collated in real time so visualising illegal patterns in traffic to hosts is readily monitored.

- LMS - *Log Management System* This subsystem collects and stores Log Files from multiple hosts and centralised instead of accessing them from each system individually.

- SLM /SEM *Security Log/Event Management* Aimed at security analysts instead of system administrators. SEM highlights log entries as more significant to security than others in the organisation.

- SIM *Security Information Management* An Asset Management system (sometimes an add on extension to a CMdB), but with features to incorporate security information too. Hosts may have vulnerability reports listed in their SNMP Management Information Base (MIB) summaries; Intrusion Detection and Anti-Virus alerts may be displayed in relation to the systems involved.

- SEC - *Security Event Correlation* User access to an application resulting in, three failed login attempts to the same user account from three different clients are just three lines in their log file. To an analyst, this indicates a potential attack, and Correlation (looks for these patterns in log files) and creates an alarm.

- SIEM Security Information and Event Management SIEM (grrr) is 'all of the above', and the above technologies are merged into a single product.

16.3 METRICS

One of the best books on the market right now is *Pragmatic Security Metrics* by W.Krag Brotby and Gary Hinson. I love these guys' sense of humour and recommend it as further reading. What I like about this book is the way they leverage metrics into an effective management protocol. Communication is so fundamental to real-world activities. The ultimate aims include:

- Cutting Losses
- Assurance Increases
- Supporting the Business
- Enabling Rational decisions

In their book they describe the use of Metametrics to reveal reality-based metrics a step ahead of SIEM type dashboards that don't always provide this degree of predictability. Their definition of the "PRAGMATIC" approach is a way to ascribe meaningful pieces of information. Their 9 steps are:

1. Predictive
2. Relevant
3. Actionable
4. Genuine
5. Meaningful
6. Accurate
7. Timely
8. Independent
9. Cheap

What is ingenious about these basic concepts is the way these authors approach the use of Continuous Scoring Scales instead of the usual YES/NO answer criteria, the use of heat maps to describe (in a graphical way) Low, Medium, and High Risks instead of a mean scoring approach. Personally, I have translated their heat maps and overlaid a cash value to these scores.

The heat maps can speedily present the key areas of risk to owners and team members and can be updated daily due to the brevity of the report.

16.4 POLICIES

Most Security Policies and Acceptable Use Policies derive from country-based standards (verticals) and global generic standards those such as the International Standards Organisation set of Security Standards (ISO 27XXX). There are no alternatives to the international standards – they are the international standards! However, there are a number of complementary but different standards and frameworks that set out to achieve many of the same objectives. Examples would be the NERC, FISMA, Information Security Foundation (ISF) Standard of Good Practice (SoGP), and ISACA's wider-focused Control Objectives for IT (CoBIT). The ISO standards relate accordingly:

- **ISO 27000** Introduction with principles, concepts and vocabulary

- **ISO 27001** Originating from the ISO adoption and enhancement of British Standard BS7799-2, 27001 has a long history dating back to the 1990s. It lays out requirements for 'establishing, implementing, operating, monitoring reviewing, maintaining and improving' an Information Security Management System (ISMS). As such it provides a high level framework for the governance of Information Security in an organisation. It provides summary high-level control objectives, but not detailed controls. There are four published Information Security Management standards in the ISO/IEC 27000 family:

    - 27001:2005 Information Security Management Systems (ISMS) Requirements standard
    - 27002:2005 Code of Practice for Information Security Management
    - 27005:2008 Information Security Risk Management

- 27006:2007 Requirements for Bodies Providing Audit and Certification of Information Security Management Systems

- Plus ISO/IEC 27799:2008 Health Informatics Audit and Certification of Information. Using ISO/IEC 27002, which is particularly aimed at one industry sector (HIPAA may also apply).

- **ISO 27002** The origin of this standard pre-date 27001, based on the original BS 27002. This is the standard that sets out actual controls to be addressed through a formal risk assessment process. Whilst 27001 is relatively timeless, 27002, being more specific, can be a victim of changing times – social media, for example. ISO 27002 is of more practical use in establishing information security controls, whilst 27001 provide the overall framework and process. This is why the two standards are often referred to as 'ISO27001/2' – they are complementary and designed to be used together. **For SMBs seeking to attain a certificate this is the preferred standard(s).**

- **ISO 27003** The focus of this newer standard is on implementing 27001, based on the PDCA (Plan, Do, Check, Act) cycle. Its purpose is help and guidance, recognising that 270001 by itself requires an approach to implementation.

- **ISO 27004** This standard recognises that once an ISMS has been implemented, an approach needs to be established for monitoring and measuring the security condition of the organisation. As such, it provides a process for determining and establishing effective, objective and justified measurements and suggests specific metrics aligned to controls in 27002.

- **ISO 27005** This standard provides guidelines for information security risk management supporting ISMS based on 27001. 27005 is process driven, stopping short of requiring a specific methodology.

- **ISO 27006** has a slightly different audience from the other standards in the series, setting out requirements for accrediting organisations that certify against 27001. It's not one for end user organisations to worry about, but worthy of a mention.

- **ISO 27007** Guidance to auditors of Information Security Management Systems, matched against the specification in ISO/IEC 27001.

- **ISO 27008** (Technical report) Guidance for auditors on ISMS controls.

- **ISO 27010** ISM issues in inter-organisational and international communications.

- **ISO 27011** ISMS implementation guide for the telecommunications industry.

- **ISO 27031** ICT readiness for Business Continuity (role of IT and telecoms).

- **ISO 27032** Cyber security. Guidance to ISPs and other Internet users.

- **ISO 27033** Network security. Seven parts currently planned (updates 18028 part 1).

- **ISO 27034** Information security for IT applications. See Application Maturity below.

How are these standards used?
Use 27001 to establish a framework for information security governance, 27002 to design controls and 27004 to determine an approach to monitoring your security condition. 27003 & 5 help deliver implementation.

An example Security Policy based on ISO 27002 can be found in the Appendices and the full version on the combatreadyit.com website

16.5 CMMI APPLICATION MATURITY

Twenty years ago developing code for an application was like building the Eiffel Tower with a Meccano® spanner. With the advent of Cloud APIs (if you chose the right ones) you can build a server in 32 lines of code. Carnegie Mellon University developed a way to improve the quality of software development practices (Paulk et al., 1995). For the last 25 years the Software Engineering Institute is a leading light in Computer Science and at the leading edge of many genius frameworks. These frameworks have real business applications. I have been constantly amazed at the quality of Engineers and Professors that graduate from this institution.

CMM (Capability Maturity Model) sets five levels for software quality attainment. In CMMI models with a staged representation, there are five maturity levels designated by the numbers 1 through to 5[174]:

1. Initial

2. Managed

3. Defined

4. Quantitatively Managed

5. Optimising

16.6 CMMI SECURITY GUIDES

To address user security concerns, two unofficial security guides are available. *Considering the Case for Security Content in CMMI for Services* has one process area, Security Management. *Security by Design with CMMI for Development, Version 1.3* has the following process areas:

1. Establish and maintain organisational processes and process assets for vulnerability handling. Analyse the available processes and activities for handling vulnerabilities.

2. Create repositories to hold history and records of vulnerabilities, incidents, resolutions, etc. When reported, all details regarding the vulnerability are recorded and stored in the dedicated repository.

3. Establish evaluation criteria to determine vulnerability severity

4. Ensure that the process assets for vulnerability handling are appropriate for use across defined life cycle phases of the product. This includes lifecycle phases handled by organisational units other than development (e.g., service organisation). They have working interfaces to and from other development process assets (e.g., to product security risk management, configuration management).

5. Establish an infrastructure that vulnerabilities can be reported to (e.g., email address, hotline, website).

6. Fix vulnerabilities by the organisation in a timely manner to prevent further damage.
   This may be done by coordinating handling across projects or by creating projects to handle the vulnerability.

7. Manage the vulnerability report to closure

16.7 BUSINESS CONTINUITY AND DISASTER RECOVERY (BCDR)

This was called plain good old Tape Back Up and Restore. Tapes were made daily weekly and monthly (Grandfather, Father and Son cycle). Tapes older than a month were dispatched to be stored in a safe or archived somewhere. Old tapes rely on all the necessary operating software to be in place when the tape data is restored. Recovering data off old tapes is cumbersome and 50% of the time did not work at all! Video Cassettes have been used by Mainframe computers that stored the tapes in a floor to ceiling tape silo (like a grain silo) with a robot arm that retrieved data when requested. CD ROMS have been used, but the media started to disintegrate after 5 years and became unrecoverable! People replaced whole server estates with new servers only to find they could not reload archived data. Until the last five years on-site storage was expensive but eliminated the tape, DVD, scenarios. Now we have virtual machines that can be snapshot or sent across the WAN to another site without human intervention. So here is the question – do you need a Business Continuity and Disaster Recovery Plan? Ideally no - each month the business should drill, swapping the BAU environment for the Back Up environment. Business Continuity Plans, Team Members and Contacts are usually out of date the BCDR plan is published. This means that in a real disaster nearly all BCDR plans do not work. Once implemented there should be no test required, but a monthly swap out of production services to a mirror estate should be the actual BCDR plan.

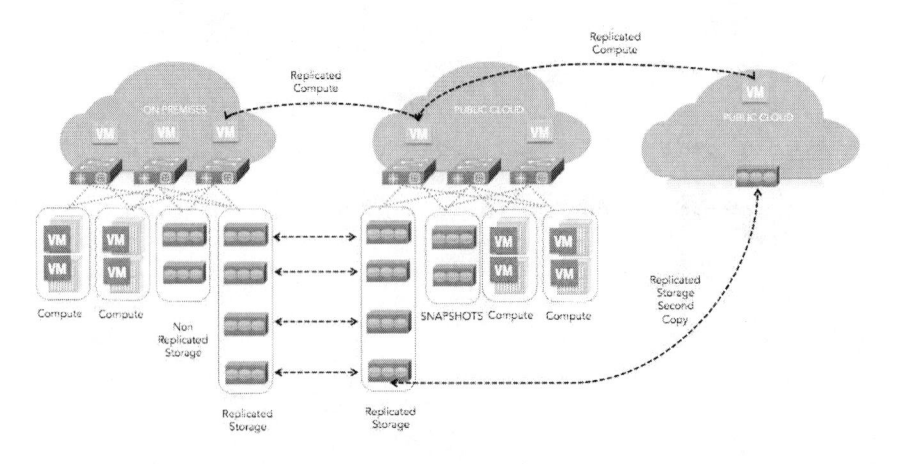

Figure 84 BCDR DATA CENTRES VM SNAPSHOTS[175]

The Technology Value Centre will be called upon to work closely with Business Continuity Program (BCP) team members whose responsibility is to work closely with business owners to determine the criticality of the business applications and their respective Service Level Agreements (SLAs) as they relate to Recovery Point Objectives (RPOs) and Recovery Time Objectives (RTOs). The BCDR team will also determine how those business applications map to business users who use the business applications services during their daily operations. The list of business application services then gets mapped to both physical and virtual systems, along with their appropriate dependencies. This list of systems forms the basis of the BCDR plan that will be implemented in part by the TVC who are responsible for the non-virtualized business applications services.

16.8 THE TAI-CHI OF BCDR

Virtualisation saves a lot of money on BCDR. The management portals are able to Track All Information (TAI) and move this information in a disaster I the estate (manually or automatically) Virtual machines have inherent properties (CHI) that facilitate the planning and implementation of a BCDR strategy:

- **C**ompatibility. Virtual machines are compatible with all standard x86 computers.

- **H**ardware independence. Virtual machines run independently of underlying hardware and encapsulate a complete compute estate.

- **I**solation. Virtual machines are isolated from other each other as if physically separated.

The Combat Ready model uses hybrid on premises compute and directly links to public cloud compute (through a dedicated leased line - not via IP-VPN). This means that snapshots of local VMs can be saved using NFS to a secure storage in the Cloud. These snapshots can be taken incrementally every 20 minutes. This means if you lost your Public Cloud service the last twenty minutes work may disappear. If you lose your on premises Data Centre the public Cloud should have a copy of your complete environment. This is where using the same Management System as your Public Cloud supplier comes into its own. Although BCDR is not a standard per se it's a technical advancement of technology that nullifies many frameworks. The cost savings and contribution to availability can only benefit an SMB.

16.9 SNAPSHOTS

Not all a SMBs data needs to be under a snapshot regime. Your company core and essential data (the documents that maintain commercial survivability) usually accounts for 15 to 20% of your overall Information Assets. You can store increments of this core data on the cloud as long as it is **encrypted**. You can also ask your Cloud provider for complete cloud backups of within country boundaries or transferred to a haven. Snapshots can balloon in size so managing the variations is a full time role for a team member. The key snapshot variants include:

- **Copy-on-write snapshot**
- **Clone/split-mirror snapshot**
- **Continuous data protection (CDP**

As we have covered under the BCDR section - traditional Back Up may not be part of your (anyone's) strategy. I prefer the steel belt and braces approach. Using the right Information Taxonomy will identify what information can be moved and stored on site or off site, or, ideally a combination of both.

16.10 COST OF DOWNTIME

For SMBs the collected cost of downtime in the US alone is $26.5 billion a year[176]. Avaya estimate network downtime at $100k per outage although the data behind this figure seems grey. The average outage experienced in Data Centres is 97 minutes a year according to CA. Emerson estimates the cost to business is approximately $7,900 a minute. These figures seem to be based on Enterprise scale turnover.

For SMBs with an annual turnover of $5 million a day lost would cost around $13.6 thousand. If you are a website based company a 3 day take out would therefore mean a loss of around $40k. Let's include another variable; the average Cyber attack takes 13 days to recover from. This means that

$178,082 would be lost in trading because all the company machines need forensics to discover the malware and clean servers and endpoints. So adding the cost of lost revenue and Business Continuity to the cost of a Black Minute is $2,304,578 for 13 days outage. The Ponemon Data Breach Study 2014 reported the lowest Data Breach cost $1.37 million. Loss of trust, reputation, churn and increased insurance premiums are cost adders.

Even if we took the lowest Data Breach cost, and the downtime cost the sums outweigh the cost of moving to one of the hybrid designs detailed earlier in the book. The designs will bridge the old worlds of tape, CD into the realm of managing continuous data protection. Eliminating the old methods saves significant costs. The management of tapes and CD silos would have set a company with a 50 TB of data over a 10 year period around $95k per year. In addition, specialist DR recovery sites with desks chairs phones etc. would be around 30k per year in reservation fees. In all traditional DR Back Up and Restore would have cost approximately $20 k a month to maintain with the worry that these would not work (or be a viable solution) during a crisis?

We can eliminate the Recovery Time Objective as a viable metric here. RTO's were always calculated in days. In one company I worked in it would have been 132 working days to get back to 100% uptime after a Data Centre Loss. With Continuous Data Protection the RTO is 0. The need to buy new hardware is eliminated and work can continue. In addition, the RPO would need to be as near real time as feasible. However, new wave of technology has created a sea change means a new reliance on a new skill set of team members to ensure this service is efficient.

16.11 CLOUD OPEX

So lets assume we replicate one single rack design from the designs earlier. If we replicated the entire estate in the Cloud and ran CDP the monthly OPEX charge would range from $24k to $29k per month. Network bandwidth and Storage volumes will impact these estimates, these are variables that need weekly microscopic attention, as it could be cheaper to rehouse on premises. That's an OPEX spread over 5 years. This means the Cost Benefit Analysis (payback time) is pretty much instantaneous. I believe Cloud pricing will rise with the FCC ruling but even at these price levels currently it is worth making a clean break with the past. In my view it's always best to make a clean break with the past and start small. You will need to start a data retrieval project and architect a solution around the Combat Ready glueprints to make this happen.

Do remember that VM sprawl will dent your bottom line. I have seen a Cloud operation outweigh the benefits that it is designed to fix. The checks and balance on building new VMs is needed so the whole operation does not get a huge OPEX hit. CSPs are also experiencing churn. Ballooning costs in the Cloud has meant some companies are being more stringent on due diligence. An on premises solution is economically preferable.

Cloud instances must be torn down after application use and not left hanging (cost and security). Old instance create gaps in security hygiene and maintaining old instances leaves backdoors.

16.12 STEPCHECK

- We have reviewed the RIDPOINTS.

- We have delved into the workings of Domino Defence in Depth

- Conceptual views on what and where to store your data

- How to split Information security between Hybrid (On Site) and Cloud (Public) compute

- We have looked at several designs and budgeted a baseline

- The Cloud is viewed as a new part of Perimeter Security

- Use of the Hybrid and Public Cloud that eliminates traditional Recovery techniques Save money on BCDR

- Finally reviewed 2 key contributors to a safety culture ISO 27001/2 and CMMI.

- Save money deploying Hybrid and Hyperconvergence

- Save money on Data Centre builds

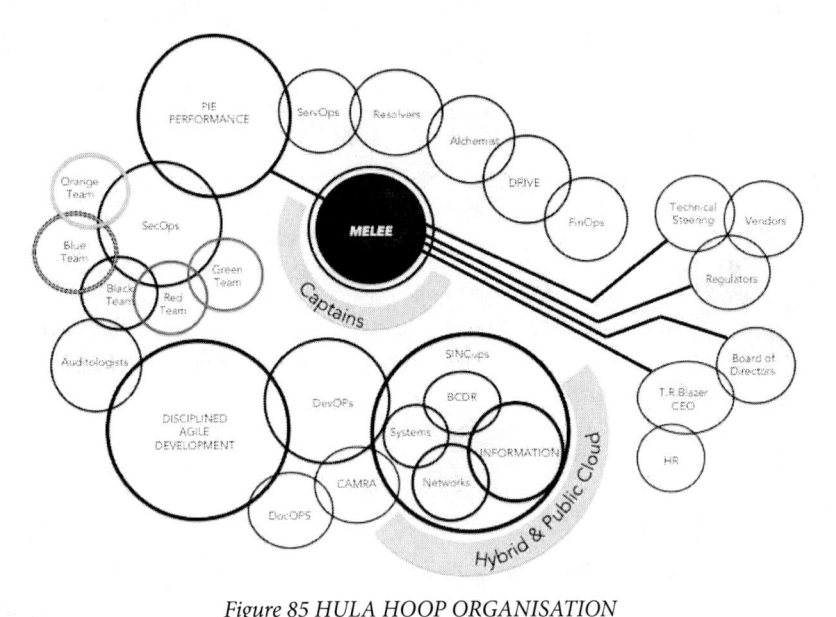

Figure 85 HULA HOOP ORGANISATION

17 SLICES OF PIE

People are the foundations of being Combat Ready. Each team member needs to contribute to the Cyber Security culture. This change is necessary to create a Perpetual Improvement Everywhere culture thinking and behaviour.

17.1 GET PERPETUAL

Most frameworks alone do not make us **Fast, Focussed, Flexible and Friendly**, they conspire to make jobs sequential, boring and disengaged. Loosely coupled handoffs and tight cohesive communications are the key to a **Happy, Healthy, Hygienic and Harmonious** Technology Value Centre.

CIO's can crumple under the weight of multiple projects, a myriad of frameworks and truculent unmotivated team members. Many firms resort to outsourcing to solve these problems but this is a temporary distraction that not hits a company's bottom line but exposes the organisation to a poor security posture. Technology continues to evolve, and instead of desktop PCs, the move to the Cloud, tablets and smartphones has become pervasive. In parallel, Cyber-crime has got worse and many infrastructures (commercial and technical) would most likely collapse in a Cybrid attack. The business owners see IT as a cash cow, although they would not last long without it, but have managed to erode the possibilities of making the IT department proactive rather than reactive. Once the IT department moves to a stance of predicting, it has a better chance of becoming a cash generator. In the cyber security age the way to ensure controls are properly technically managed requires a new approach.

There is a place for heavy ladles of process syrup in large organisations but for SMBs this is a step too far and outside company owners comfort zones. The times have changed and technology has enabled this change. As long as team members understand the accountability map they should be responsible for choosing how they get there. In a conflict there are fewer resources, fewer people, and less time to get things done. In a war footing, the luxury of employees just will not exist and erode production and quality KPI's and metrics. Many companies would not cope with a headcount reduction of 50%. We will see Enterprises moving away from maintaining large headcounts and technology cottage industries will emerge, a model that resembles the Industrial Revolution age. This will be a massive Change Point for commerce globally. For SMBs these are contributory reasons to look closely at the Combat Ready ideals. Investment by the SMB now in the right equipment, tools and people will attract Enterprise work orders. This investment in the right things needs a vision to keeping the cyber security culture Perpetual.

17.2 THE CONSUMERISATION OF IT

The days of the mainframe Ivory Towers have long gone. Jobs were plentiful, well rewarded, heaps of training and a long-term career was possible, from warehouseman to CIO. Nowadays such careers are impossible to find, knowledge workers are not respected and paid shelf stocker rates. That's not the right way to cosset knowledge contributors. We need team members to focus on Java Beans not Baked Beans. Every other work function in an organisation does not get treated in this way.

Here is an expression I have not heard for the last decade "I love my job!" Developers (if they are good) they are developing their own company and writing the Golden Application cash generator on their own time. Enterprise Management expects team members to be multi skilled masters of at least 10 technologies with the accompanying pictures on the wall. These expectations are nonsense. Training has been non- existent, for most people training is self-funded and self-taught. HR departments cannot expect 10 years experience in a software technology that's only been in existence for the last three! No wonder there is a lack of enthusiasm in this sector. What's going wrong here? Has the IT industry cried wolf too many times? Technology is playing its part; most software is Commercial Off The Shelf (COTS) so the business expectation is that it would just work once the disks are received. The opposite is the reality. Infrastructure is old and tired and subject to budget freezes for the last seven years. SMBs are only able to afford OPEX based expansion and that means cloud services, most of which are out of control. Now with cyber security issues this misery is doubled. We need to attract and incentivise team members to add value and innovation. The right architecture, infrastructure and tools are needed to build a well-rounded and happy workforce. A happy workforce seeks to Perpetually Improve itself through self-determination

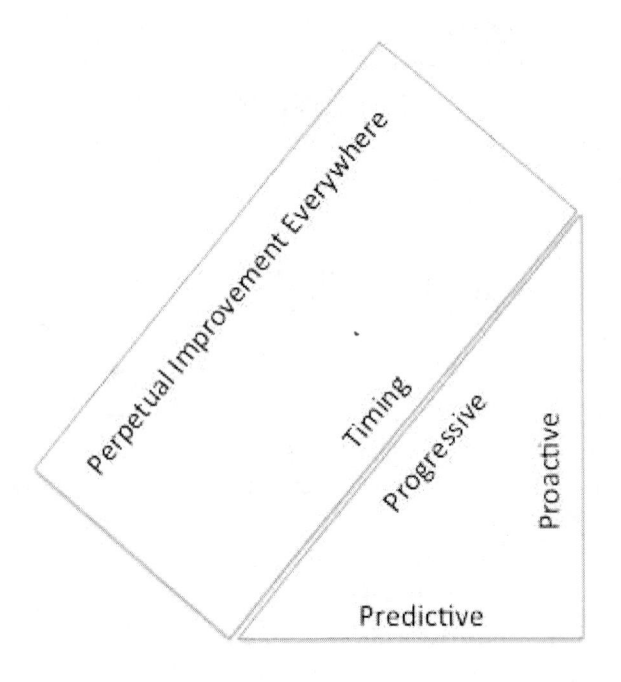

Figure 86 PIE CALCULATION

18 PERPETUAL IMPROVEMENT EVERYWHERE

If you are panicked by the words Combat Ready these words can easily be translated into Change Ready or even Craft Ready! Massive Change will reform the hierarchal commercial model and our traditional notions of organisation, production and sourcing. A Commercial Plane and a Production Plane will sandwich a flatter Knowledge Plane. SMBs will need to manage this transition. This means applying a stance of perpetually improving and applying continuous assurance throughout the IT organisation and business. This can only be achieved by automation, automation and automation not Process, Process, and Process. Automation and Robotica tools are the key to meeting Change and Conflict. Setting up automation means reduced workloads allowing knowledge workers in the TVC to get **Proactive, Predictive and Progressive**. We may even witness the emergence of an IT Luddite movement spurred by dissonance - so timing is an imperative.

I was in an organisation where we spent $1m on a graphical Storage allocation and reporting tool (It wasn't for Dr. Evil). After two years, the tool was not working. The database crashed in the first six weeks and the storage team preferred to ring-fence their jobs by reverting to spread sheet-based data storage statistics. Another company I audited had spent a grand total of $72 million dollars over five years on 600 developers creating an integrated asset database and server warning system. In collusion with the vendor, the 200 operators and sys admins managed to turn this into a 'Euston-type' situation where nobody is accountable. Servers' red alarms were turned up to 100% – so alarms only went off when the server capitulated and died. The whole point of the system was to determine the slow rise of messaging alarms so a sys admin could investigate the root cause and analysis via logs. Never mind the fact that this could have been done for 1% of the total cost of the project the end result was that unless the introduction of automation is managed then rebellion would be a result. In the Hybrid and Public a configuration auto alarms and segregates itself from the network until a remediation check can commence.

These antagonistic practices sill exist today, and this is why attacks are invariably successful. An adversary slowly gaining increasing rights over multiple systems in an organisation causes real damage to any organisation. Without a configuration management tool to highlight core OS and applications changes this acquisition of rights becomes unstoppable. Exfiltration of an attacker is usually seen when a server dies and has to be rebooted. As you can see, monitoring and automation of servers is no good once the server has crashed: an attacker can clear their tracks with ease. Even systems administrators tend to just reboot without checking the permissions and user sets on the server, so an attacker can get even more permissions on a server until the old configuration is repaired. It is easy to understand why data breaches are successful in large Enterprises.

Finding an attacker is a needle in a haystack of our own making? Once an adversary exits an attack and exfiltrates, it is usually with all the pertinent data and information they needed anyway and they have hidden their trail. Many data breaches are carried out this way, and that's why incidents go unreported because most security officers don't even know it's happened. This simple fact means a security office needs to be alerted to any abnormal activity and outliers to prevent the spread early. Early detection means an attacker, once in a complex network of servers, can be directed to a honeypot where information can be studied to bounce the attack back to the attacker. Micro segmentation helps stop the clock on the Black Minute. It retains the configuration parameters of routers and servers and any change to these are immediately escalated to the security office. Employing a Big Data approach can also help. There are now tools that can monitor a stream of data leaving a database server to a remote source and kill the transaction until it's verified. Of course, in a large organisation there are billions of transactions per second, but the tools are scalable and they're to monitor and stem these activities.

18.1 PREDICT THE BLACK MINUTE

It takes one minute to transfer a set of files at 250MB over a 4G network. In one minute an adversary can download 20 CAD drawings that would comprise the plans for the next invisible nuclear bomber, or the attack plans and locations of an army division's geography, or 4 million names and addresses. Actually to download 4 million names and addresses would have taken 13 hours to download. The Government department who was in charge of this data should have had an automatic alarm to shut this outgoing traffic down? Black Minutes usually peak and transpire during lunch hour, people leave their computers on and usually unlocked. The Black Minute problem will linger, as no one seems to be able to pull together a coherent defence strategy. The Combat Ready IT Model is a step forward to establishing the Knowledge Plane mentioned earlier. OK it's the sandwich filler that's holds the Production and Commercial planes together. I would say that wouldn't I! The Knowledge Plane is a flatter mini hierarchy where defences get double double-checked. An army cannot move without IT. Intelligence needs to be fed into the hierarchy to make plans of attack with the correct weaponry and sufficient support systems.

The application of **PIE** is key in this new Knowledge world and hybrid organisation. The Combat Ready IT model needs to be underpinned by the principles of: Progressive, Preventative and Predictive.

Is this possible given the budgetary and team members headcount constraints that IT has succumbed to in the past decade? The answer is yes principles cost nothing. The challenge is getting all team members in the same battle formation so they act as one. It's a move towards a **Software Defined Organisation.** If an organisation's focus is to prevent outages in operations and development, then the team needs to be singing from the same hymn sheet with the right software handoffs. If TVC is fully aware of the plan, then everyone will pull together with the same objective. Similar to the CMMI pillars, the PIE has Slices. Slices are the measured parts that make the whole of the PIE. Like George T. Dorans Goal Setting mnemonic acronym S.M.A.R.T. (Specific, Measureable, Achievable, Relevant and Time Bound) is tasked to measure themselves against them daily. So team members are your coherent defence strategy. Daily teaming's and interactions at all levels encourages smooth handoffs and Craftflows.

18.2 THE SEVEN SLICES

PIE becomes whole when all slices are joined up. To remember the slices use the SPACERS/RACOMED Slices mnemonic acronym:

SECURE	– **Everything we do eliminates**	**R**ISK
PERPETUAL	– Everything we configure is	**A**UTOMATIC
AVAILABLE	– Everything we plan has	**C**APACITY
CENTRAL	– Everything we build is	**O**MNICOCULAR
EFFICIENT	– Everything we do is	**M**EASURED
RESOURCED	– Everyone is	**E**NGAGED
SERVICE	– Everyone	**D**ELIVERS

Figure 87 ELIMINATE RISK AND RISK APPETITE

18.3 GET PROGRESSIVE

Tell your teams to get Progressive. In major projects I always have daily roll call – that's a daily get-go meeting for all team members who get to see and hear issues and risks in a fifteen-minute time slot, so everyone is au fait with the exact status of the project and communications, starting with a Security toolbox talk. Daily teaming interactions between each department and adjacent teams usually around noon enable teams to gauge the deliverables for that day. No meeting is ever longer than **15 minutes** and is a two-way initiative to check on progress and deliverables. Changes to infrastructure are communicated at the midday teaming. If team members are remote, then organise 'screen hugs' according to their time zones, and when possible get local teams to interact. When I worked at large international Search Engine, I helped set up constant uptime video conferencing links. Technical development teams could shout out from Ireland to the US. The entire workforce was visible to the team and able to ping the main team with a query or question at any point in the day. The Progressive goal ensures that everyone knows where the TVC is going daily, and not delayed by updates at the obligatory annual off site conference. How can we change a system or practice that can improve the security stance?

18.4 THINK PREVENTATIVE

In the Combat Ready IT Model, automation, risk aversion, knowledge and situation awareness are the key preventative tools. The engagement of crowdsourcing, effective configuration management and Big Data analysis are essential new age toolsets for solidifying the security posture. **PIE** can only be achieved by monitoring key activities, transactions and events whilst balancing the core systems and processes. Use Battle Performance to shore up and harden the weak links in the chain. Measure **Health, Issues, Possibilities and Success** criteria (HIPS) as part of each face-to-face meeting to ensure that each team member is thinking preventatively. What is the daily health of each server is there an issue that may cause a potential outage, what's the possibility of a system downtime caused by a change, what would the successful outcomes look like when these are solved.

18.5 ACT PREDICTIVE

To get to predictive, the company has to be positioned to predict attacks, levels and flows. Availability Management is key here. One of the least acknowledged tenets of ITIL v3 2011 is Availability Management, which to me is the key to any highly effective operation's success.

The ability to predict demand and pull on resource's means that capacity and continuity models should be reviewed daily. What RIP would impact the business? This is the modus operandi that any good **Ops** manager should demonstrate to owners, however it is the most lacking in every organisation. This discipline may seem retroactive, and not all models can capture the unexpected, but daily snapshots can provide team members with the ability to do something about the problem.

What is needed is real-time access to data and even identity management, the ability to gauge transactions in any human interaction and the ability to predict change in configurations. This means auditors need to get stuck into the Agile (DAD) and DevOps type roles to ensure delivery of solid and rugged code that has had bugs manages out at an early stage. This is a key to reducing the risks in heat maps.

18.6 TEAM CULTURE BUILT ON SELF DETERMINATION

There are new organisational models that follow an Open Organisation structure where departments are self-organising and without defined management positions. In IT generally it is felt that knowledge workers need a flat organisation structure that enhances collaboration. Middle Management thinks flat could mean anarchy; they would say that wouldn't they! Self Determination is a contract with an owner, it means each team member commits (in writing) to make teams, technology, and tools work harmoniously. SMBs need to become progressive in how they deal with knowledge workers and create this harmonious organisation. A high level of management time is spent for consensus to be an effective route to decision making. However, consensus does not scale well beyond a small group of close collaborators who are perfectionists. If an SMB has a " boss less" culture from start up then flat organisational models should be encouraged. There must be a hierarchy for decision making and arbitration but restricted to four layers denoted by salary bands. If the start up has become a toddler then some form of discipline needs to be applied to help guide autonomous teams and team members. When the toddler becomes a teenager then strings of command need to be put in place with strong mentoring and training. Millennial's now actively seeks alternates to the traditional hierarchic, mechanical and growth constraints in 99% of all organisations. They don't want to be zombies.

To attract the right talent SMBs need to become attractive. Don't follow the String and box hierarchal tree typical of most organisations. The balance here is cyber security controls and how to enforce rigour without resorting to ogre like middle management techniques. In SMBs this assumes the leadership resolves conflicts through his or her power, expertise and influence, but from the other point of view this (autocratic) power may destroy creative and innovative potentials of diversity and conflicts. Owners, Pioneers, and divisional heads need to change to adapt to the digital world. Further a manager not necessarily has to be perfect and all knowing like the charismatic leader, but he or she needs to really technically au fait with all aspects of IT to manage Knowledge workers properly. Frankly there are few of these savvy managers around.

18.7 HOLACRACY

In an attempt to stop IT workers disengaging Holacracy avoids consensus building and politics. Holacracy provides a flat management structure that distributes authority into circles that allows team members a greater degree of autonomy. The constitution goal of a Holacracy is to ensure that those responsible for completing work are given the authority to decide how that work should be carried out. According to proponents, Holacracies lead to greater efficiency, agility, transparency, accountability, employee engagement and innovation. To be effective, the roles, responsibilities and expectations for group members in a Holacracy are clearly defined, but flexible. Connecting roles, sometimes called link roles, sit in multiple groups and ensure that those groups are operating in congruence with the organization's overall mission and objectives. Holacracy has a licensing programme for Agents and Providers wishing to facilitate new Holacratic organisations.[177]

18.8 SOCIOCRACY

This type of organisation structure also follows agile principles. Is a method of governance that ensures members are included, accountable, and productive! It involves all members in the organisation in policy decisions. The majority of employees don't feel empowered to contribute to decisions in mechanic organisations. Policy and communication flows southbound. Sociocracy is based on a circle organisation structure. The Sociocracy topology is considered flat and foundational, consent governs decisions. Circles that have double links enforce stronger communication and therefore the Service Level Agreements and Operational Level Agreements between circles are hygienic. A selection of team members engages in open discussion to roles and responsibilities.[178]

18.9 HULA HOOP ORGANISATION

The Hula Hoop organisation is a people centric map of the knowledge plane. It reflects scope and responsibility. Within each hoop sits team members and a hoop for Captains who reinforce culture initiatives and controls. A TVC cannot be managed by; a favourite son, accountant, politician, project manager, secretary, or an office administrator. The days of Madmen office shifts and instant promotions on a whim is over, I am afraid. It's a technical management role for managing technical knowledge people. The Hula Hoop organisation shows which skills are (Venn Type) reliant on other departments for handoffs and interlocks and the realm of their responsibility aligned to commercial goals. You cannot recruit skilled professionals on a secretary's salary anymore. In recessionary periods and tight budgets it is an SMB goal to obtain highly skilled workers at a percentile of normal salaries. Managers without appropriate technical skills create workplace tensions. Staff and workers do not exist – they are team members. Generally SMBs need to get out of the hierarchical mind-set.

Effective Perpetual Improvement Everywhere does rely on a degree of autocratic technical influence, like Holacracy and Sociocracy it relies on SMART team members delivering quality and value. The word Controls is essential to the cyber security culture and therefore a degree of discipline is needed. In the Technology Value Centre the Core team has a steady team member complement of around 30 (in the Combat Ready model). This size of team is usually the equivalent of a troop or platoon. In the army hierarchy Lieutenant commands this size or troop. Usually a Lieutenant has the opportunity to gain specialised skills outside of their unit. Captains are key players in the planning and decision making process, with tactical responsibility for operations on the ground as well as equipment maintenance, logistic support and manpower. Captains have roving roles to technically manage end-to-end of operations. That's really the limit of the command structure. In the Combat Ready model everyone is hands-on and technical and major strategic issues are thrashed out through the Technical Steering Committee. You may ask yourself why two Captains? This is down to eyes on work and face-to-face governance. The Captains need to engage at every level within the platoon to ensure quality and security is fully maintained. The gambit here is the soldiers in the platoon do not need to be told to fire a gun at a suitable target but timing is crucial and needs co-ordination. Two Captains are there for balance and to ensure team members don't start pet projects that are not in the company interest. Support, mentoring and communication are the guidewords here.

The Hula Hoop organisation is a hybrid and reduced traditional chain of command and flat organisation providing orthogonal and multiple management planes.

Team members are self-managing in this new environment. This means team members need to be actively communicating and present and not focussed on single task delivery. Lone Wolves need to be part of the pack. Team members need to plan their time and know where they are going. How many managers know what their teams are doing at any given point in a day? Its rare if you do. Does your team members know how to do time planning? Can your team members write a Project Plan? Being an IT professional is not about being a "techy" any more is being an all rounder. If a team member says that's not my job – it is now. Being able to plan time, execute tasks and readily contribute to the team may take face-to-face time but it does not take more than an hour out of a team member's day. Everyone who has ever worked for me knows how to write a project plan and work to it – that's because I turned all of them into Project Managers. I spent days training them after I revoked their self-coding. Everyone who has ever worked for me understands the responsibility of Security that's because they are trained t to be responsible. Good Captains do this – its de rigueur. So team members need to be engaged and contributing to **PIE** – not just 'Steam Members'

At the beginning of the book I alluded to the fact that no SMB ever lives for a month on back-up systems. This is a drill that should happen monthly. The internal responsibility for these drills should never be externalised to a Managed Service Provider. MSPs have no visibility into your business and can never match your metrics or expectations.

18.9.1.1 5 X 5 X 5

Team members are key to managing out errors. Do you remember suggestion boxes? When was the last time you saw one? Does your establishment have a portal that emulates a suggestion box? I have seen this twice in the last decade. Staff can see operational defects that need addressing. Encourage members to get this written down each week – I get everyone to write their 5x5x5s and time sheets each Thursday evening. The 5 x5x5 helps each team member formulate their time and jot down something that niggles them. It's a weekly 'Think Piece' where you step away from BAU and plan, comment and helps others improve. It's about transparency, being able to jot down a problem may help the entire company fixate on a problem to its successful outcome. What's a 5x5x5? The 5 things you as a team member achieved last week, the 5 things you plan to do next week, the 5 things that need to happen to make these tasks happen next week. This encompasses management support, systems availability, software that needs additional licences and the why.

18.9.1.2 THURSDAYS

All Project updates should be completed by Thursday evening. This means that Project summary roll ups can be completed by Monday morning. This means that if a team member has a task to complete then at least they have a weekend to deliver on a task, without it being detrimental to the overarching project plan.

18.9.1.3 DRESS CODE

Every Board always asks me how IT people should dress. I don't know why this is such a big thing! People should always come to work dressed to avoid embarrassment? Outside of the US IT people are still rolling into work wearing three-piece suits. Technical people should never have to wear suits. Suits were made for 18th Century horse riders and ties were 17th Century cravats, worn before ties were invented. The world has moved on since the 18th Century! Team members should not need to tug forelocks as the boss walks in. As long as team members don't turn up in monkey suits or clowns costumes (I have coulrophobia) a degree of leniency is required here. Techies work really long hours! Personally I like getting suited and booted, but IT people don't need clothes to look clever. Business casual is the order of the day. For men that means a business casual clean shirt every day and a high level of hygiene. In India the dress is chinos and a lumberjack shirt – the heat would kill you if you wore a suit. If you are in a team and you stink then go home and change. Women can wear what they think appropriate and business like. As long as you are comfortable that's the aim. Companies that provide team members with branded polo shirts as long as everyone gets one are fine (and at least 6 off). I liked my teams to be in black (black polo and black jeans). If you are visiting a customer site and they wear suits - mirror their dress code. People are the best advert for a company – dress accordingly.

18.9.1.4 ROTATE AND SEPARATE AND SEGREGATE

Like the WW1 French commander Marshall Phillipe Petain, I am a firm believer that team member rotation is key to a happy, well-rounded task force. Team Members should be moved from any part of the business to another on an enforced rota basis. This can happen monthly or fortnightly, but it helps team members become more cognisant of all aspects of the organisation. Yes, they should attend board meetings, yes, a coder should sit with finance, and owners should sit with the ops team.

Create Green and Yellow teams to help cross-fertilise expertise. These 'green' and 'yellow' teams are pairs comprising an experienced (Yellow) and a youthful (Green) team member. Green and yellow teams are not constrained to just a pair, they can scale to any size depending on the demand required. Mixing teams experience can create friction but usually out of friction comes respect and attitude. (By the way, 'red' teams are usually external or outsourced functions – these are obviously brought back in-house during a conflict event).

This also helps with dissemination of technology knowledge. Back in the days of monolithic PABXs and the emergence of VOIP, I used to sit a PABX stalwart with a VOIP coder to maximise knowledge exchange. This melting pot approach is very useful for personal perspective integration (PPI). Encouraging PPI across the entire organisation is an absolute must for breaking silos. Obviously, there is conflict and distrust and sometimes personality clashes can arise, but it aids Progression and over time older team members are willing to retrain, and younger team members are willing to listen to wisdom. Team members actually feel valued as dialogue is enforced and productivity and job satisfaction shoots through the roof. It leverages this skill mix to become more rounded, which helps prevent issues. Of course, there is a degree of learning. There are free training lessons available on the Web to help team members prepare for their placement. Does this distract from team members' objectives and deadlines? Only in a handful of cases have I witnessed team members complain about this mixology. Are they more productive after this placement? Absolutely - you guessed correctly!

I worked in a Telco that unfortunately went on strike. All the union-based team members walked out, and this left the middle and senior management to manage and fulfil the business as usual support, service provisioning and maintenance roles and become customer facing. The customer satisfaction reviews went through the roof – the company made more money and was more profitable during that period! The managers looked back on the whole experience as being uplifting and pleasurable. Managers were up poles fixing broken transmission wiring, in data centres replacing cards, managing software updates and storage routines. The whole company was loath to go back to its original organisation make-up once the strike was over. Many managers did not want to return to their original roles of managing, preferring to stay at low-level stress-free maintenance tasks. Managers learnt the benefit of segregation and rotation of duties and the true benefit of documentation. In a conflict, imagine an IT decimated by call-ups to fight. Where are the skills needed to maintain the processes and functions and complexity of the systems? In your next drill, swap these roles and document the results – you will be pleasantly surprised by the positive reactions.

18.10 PIOSOPHY AND PIOLOGISTS

The Technology Value Centre is so pi(e)vital to marrying technology with operational manoeuvres that it should be the sounding board for the entire organisation. The companies that don't invest in their organisation by increasing IT budgets and security spending will continually fail. In a conflict situation, those companies that are not in a state of preparedness will quickly fail. **PIE** should be in every team member's mind-set the minute they start work. Owners need to espouse the **Piosophy** of guarding against cyber security. Turn each team member into a **Piologist** so they can help the company Perpetually Improve? What can I contribute to make the place I work that much better? What can I do to improve my skills and how can I contribute positively to the company? It's not a work practice it's the practice of work. Owners should create PIE moments at each meeting just like security and safety talks. What's going to make this SMB a Giant Enterprise (if you want that)! What can we do to help people do to be self- sustaining and self-managing? As you can see PIE is not limited to the TVC. We are teaching team members to self-code. In a software-defined world can we not introduce software defined team members? We are basically re-coding their behaviour to become self-determined. What we expect of each team member is to become embedded code in a team resource. Poor behaviours can be viewed as bugs.

18.11 MEASURING PIE

I don't want to sound like a *"PIEromaniac"* but you cannot manage what you cannot measure! How do you measure **PIE**? For all those who thought

PIE Chart – well nearly there! Measuring Performance is key to a successful Technology Value Centre. How do you know you are adding value when you cannot measure it? Well you can and should create a customer-facing portal on how well the TVC is doing. Battle Performance is essential feedback to Owners and Customers. Using Via Ferrata reporting and feeding this into an on-going dashboard helps the entire company judge your performance. PIE should have several key metrics based on performance improvements but focussed on people. This justifies the investments into getting predictive. The TVC should constantly benchmark performance against KPI's (Key Performance Indicators) against the company profitability, Balanced Scorecards and cost improvements. Above all, value should be expressed in monetary terms. Team Members should contribute directly to the portal to display thought pieces, white papers and demonstrate that IT is not a sinkhole. How can the business as a whole contribute to this? Team members should rotate through the business units as well as intra TVC. This allows team members to help business units make technology choices. Team members should get rewarded for their contributions. It turns technical focus into business focus which can only be of benefit to the other divisions or parts of the business.

18.12 PIE IN THE SKY

Or should it be **PIE** in the Cloud? The question I get asked a lot is: so what does this world look like in really practical terms? Can my company become a **PIE** culture, and how much does it cost? How long does it take!

Answers:

- ✓ **PIE** is everyone's responsibility and goal
- ✓ SMB owners can become **"Pioneers"** overnight
- ✓ It needs to be an acceptable scoring applied to everybody's roles and responsibilities
- ✓ HR and Personnel needs to adopt this as part of a cyber security contract with all team members

- ✓ Any companies can speedily move to this culture, it should dramatically reduce the risks companies face. Double quick time is the order of the day. It can be applied irrespective of the underlying organisation

- ✓ I find team members own this flexible way of working and quickly identify limitations and possibilities

- ✓ Cost relies on the cost of training internally and how this culture is driven down

- ✓ Implementing this **Piosophy** can take less than a month

In the last seven years we have seen Agile and DevOps coming to the forefront. That's great! We have seen people do more with less, but what if we applied that thinking to the rest of the IT organisation? In effect pushing the **PIE** philosophy through every function from the Technology Value Centre outward. Would the agility in the SMB functions not be even more efficient and effective? The problem is in defining and managing the handoffs and workflow touch points. If we can bring all the diverse functions together in a coherent and simplified manner, would this not be a far more positive way to address events like conflicts and Black Minutes. The answer is a BIG FAT YES. When team members are engaged and involved (with the right amounts of self-determination and self-code) they feel a moral right to shore up their defences and guard the backs of their brothers in arms. This can only help everyone.

18.13 STEPCHECK

- How to stop team members turning grey
- Introduction to Perpetual Improvement Everywhere
- Creating an organisation that is **Happy, Healthy, Hygienic and Harmonious**
- Enable team members self-determination and get engaged
- Making your company attractive to knowledge workers
- Slices make up the whole of the PIE
- Drive the Perpetual Improvement Everywhere

- Getting Progressive, Preventative and Predictive

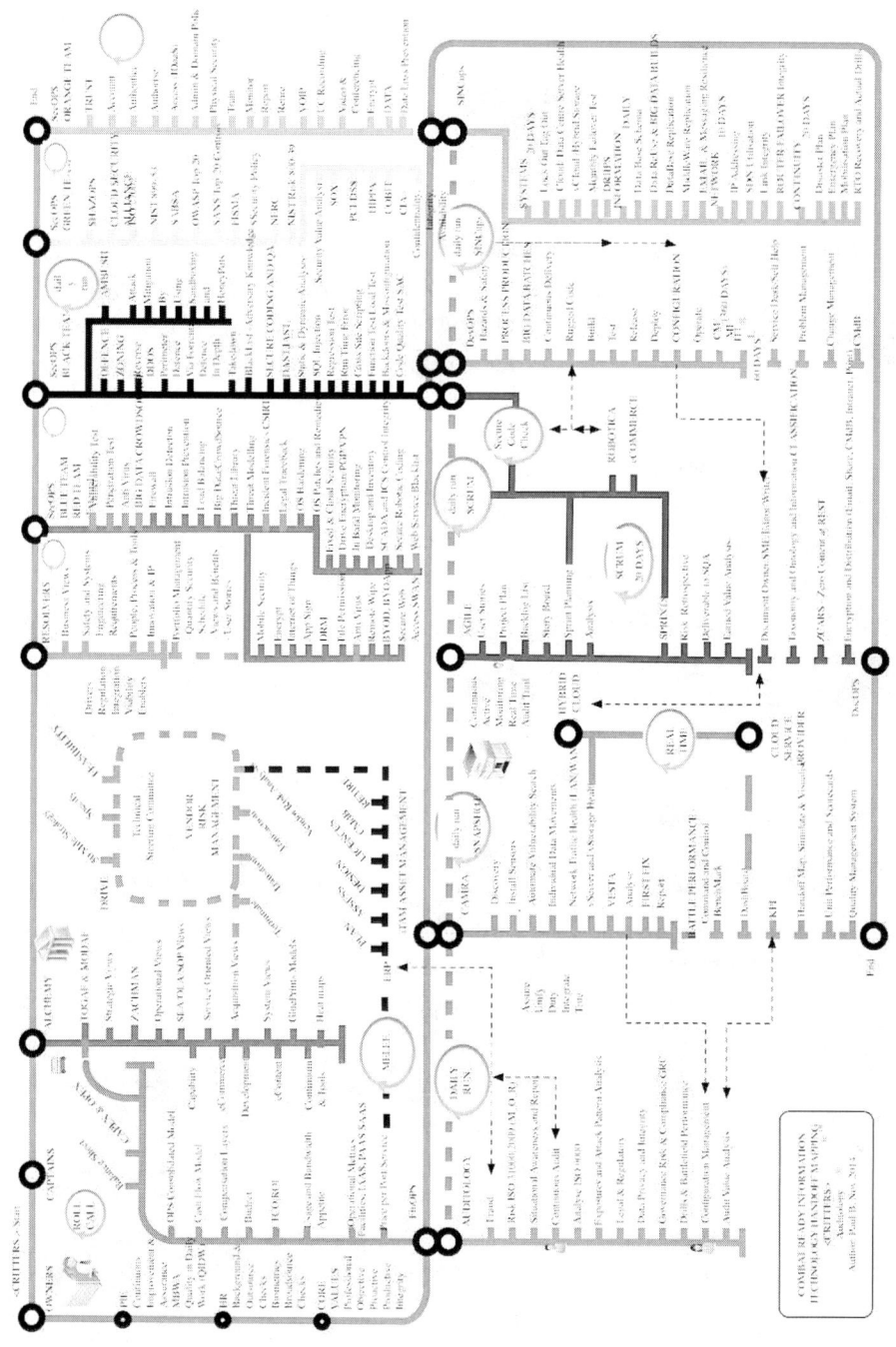

Figure 88 COMBAT READY METRO MAP

19 PULLING IT ALL TOGETHER

In this chapter we pull together the various strands that support the company's security culture. We will review each function handoffs within the Technology Value Centre and the roles and responsibilities of team members.

The easiest way to show the graphical handoffs and meeting points is through the above metro map. Each "branch line" is a set of functions or responsibilities by ownership. Each branch line has handoffs (stations) and communications are enforced through daily melees or teaming's. One of the tenets of the model is to identify the IT activities that are traditionally hidden and passive, and change them to active and transparent activities.

This model is built around technology handoffs and not processes. Many of the tool sets have automation built in; it also assumes automation and that the majority of labour uplift not alien to the teams. This describes how the various areas can be aligned, and should not be viewed as a de jure standard. I realised four years ago that business transformation had to change tack daily. Traditionally based hierarchal IT organisations cannot do this that means, don't burden the teams that actually do the work with team members who act as obstacles. Owners and captains are the support functions that need to guide team members through the acceptance period. The move towards hybrid working requires the ability to rein back some Gung Ho attitudes in team members and encourage them in other areas.

It leverages the known Agile/Scrum model as a basis for day-to-day interconnects with other parts of the business, also relying on rotation of skills, roles and responsibilities. The map extends the Agile manifesto to the remaining functions in the Technology Value Centre.

19.1 LEADERSHIP

During the last decade I was an independent advisor for about 20 CIOs (captains) all from different market sectors. During this time I was a confidant to eight boards (owners) who used me as a sounding board. All bar one executive are still in their roles (he left to open a coffee house on a Caribbean beach), and all the companies have survived the recent double-dip recession. I used to review their strategies and major bids and help guide decision-making criteria. About 90% of my advice was used, and I am confidently heartened by that success. I have saved companies literally billions of dollars, or $s, over the decades. Whether they could survive a triple dip or a war is the key question. In a conflict I would say 50% would disappear due to their focus on global market sectors and where they source their materials and team members. During this period I encouraged companies to retain good team members, shop locally, save money and invest in R&D as well as nurture the culture of their company team members openly and inclusively. I have applied some of this experience to the model. For this part, we will review the financial strategy part of the model.

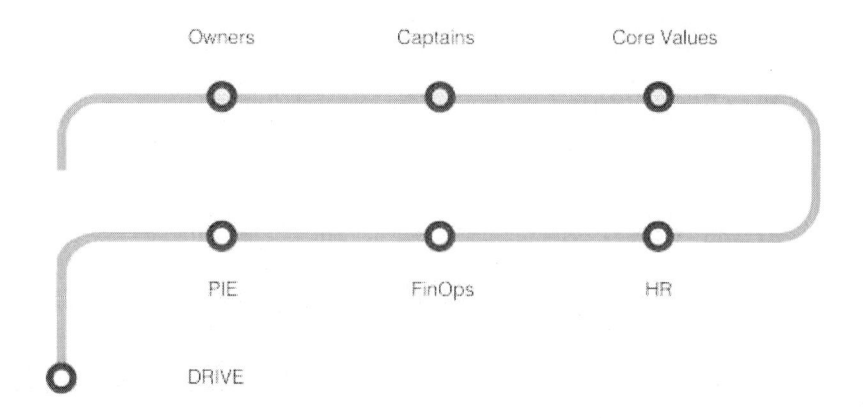

Figure 89 LEADERSHIP HANDOFFS

Good owners and captains should be able to have internal two-way dialogues, one in the head and one in the gut their focus areas should overlap. They should be used in unison because at key decision points it is only you that leads. Your reputation is built on these actions, and without actions people won't remember what you did during your tenure. Owners and captains must have intuitive thinking to re-scope the existing problems of today and get creative about conflict strategies.

Catchphrases live long in the collective team memory, and they can endure over many years. The Deming Plan Do Check Act is the foundation of Total Quality Management, ITIL and security. Even 'Get it Right First Time Every Time' still pervades my daily activity. These phrases emanated from the post-war period, when everything was mechanical and logical, a natural progression of work that slotted in with the philosophy of that era. As technology took hold we became customer-centric and leaders had to take a new approach, making service the king lynchpin. This gave rise to sayings such as 'Fast, Focused, Flexible and Friendly'. When the Web hit us, the technology took over: 'there's an app for that' became more product-focused. IT projects spawned the saying 'Proper Planning Prevents Poor Performance' (the 5 Ps, which can be broadened into 6, 7 and 8 Ps). What can we use nowadays in this Cyber Warfare timeline? When I headed my own IT division teams, my mantra was Optimal Organised Operations and Safe, Secure, Systems (Triple OS) as team aspirational goals.

As an owner, leader of a company, what is the key objective of your existence? Do you sit with your team force and understand all your company hand-offs, craftflows, interlocks and technical complexities and ramifications? As a consultant I ask executives to go and visit the sharp end of normal day-to-day work activities to experience what employees and contractors really go through. The CEO of a 30,000 strong team members Telco I worked at finally sat down for a day to sit in a call centre and listen into calls from new customers, and he experienced the pain the call agent went through as he scoured 14 different applications to provide the new customer with a simple telephone service. These 14 different services were obviously merged into a single provisioning tool in a month, which cut down new customer acquisitions from three days to 15 minutes. This company now insists on all executives spending a minimum of three days on this annual venture. In the UK as an owner you would have been put in the company as an apprentice and encouraged to work your way up the ladder, you would have known the company flaws. The same can be said for military and police career progressions through the ranks until your ready to be a Captain, Colonel or General. Conversely, there are personnel who are just unfit to manage their way out of a paper bag and rarely listen to external consultants. Executives above the level of manager should change roles annually respecting separation of duties. Not only is this good for an organisation but it requires a manager to make good his work in a quality manner. Since the Dotcom boom in the 1990s there has been a noticeable decline in the quality of managers and executives, quality being the key word. The argument is that quality should be part of everyone's professional stance and attitude to work, but unfortunately this is not the case. In the case of the IT department, there has not been a quality management role defined – the last I saw one was in 1998 in a German mobile company and gosh he was good. It was reflected in everybody's work in that department. Knowing that the 100-page report you compiled would be minutely torn apart by a QM meant everybody's game was at peak constantly. The quality of the documentation was astounding and the library was impeccable.

So an owner's responsibility is to know the company and the products, and impose a PIE regime that bears real results.

Owners should revive the MBWA (Managing By Wandering Around) ethos to improve the quality in daily work. There is a common term flying around IT nowadays and its 'Good Enough'. I encountered this phrase in the US, and it's a lethal pairing of words. Undisciplined team members that can never finish projects or see a task to its end usually uses it. To stop that lack of finishing, I tend to go all 'Sergeant Major-ish' and commence a toolbox tirade. If you are not sure what a toolbox talk is, it's usually a start to every safety meeting. It addresses a safety tip or rule or a safety story at the start of a general weekly meeting. It's something I learnt from my wife's profession and applied in daily roll call or melee meetings. I always pull something (or someone) from history and discuss their traits; in the hope some team members may be inspired. We come to work to take pride in our day-to-day activities and be proud of our deliveries, being "Good Enough" is a weak statement that leads to sloppy output.

19.1.1.1 BATTLE HARDENED LEADERSHIP TRAITS

General George S. Patton: The king of self-belief.
Armed with an excellent knowledge of Roman Army strategies and tactics, in particular the campaigns of Julius Caesar. Patton was bullish, direct, and

supremely confident. He was intimidating and aggressive and went headfirst into all situations.

General Douglas MacArthur: Focussed on goal setting and goal getting.
Set a goal and committed to it no matter what the politicians thought.

President Harry S. Truman: Honesty.
Known for a blunt, straightforward communication style which inspired trust and respect.

Julius Caesar: Showed how a soldier could rule an empire.
Understood and fought with his men. Not only did he set the plan of attack, he was not afraid to lead from the front and dive into a melee. Many of his battles were won by speed and a deep appreciation of supply chains.

Alexander the Great: Inspiration
Continually motivated his 10,000 men to conquer most of the known world and reach as far as India.

Marshall Philippe Petain: Flexibility and high emotion quotient.
Realising his soldiers fought best when fresh rotated them every two weeks off the front line for rest and recuperation, unlike the British counterparts who would be revived every two months.

King George V: Managed By Wandering Around.
Visited the trenches in World War 1 to understand the situation and observed actual battles being fought. This motivated his armies and army team members to appreciate the "We are all in this together" attitude.

Churchill: Brevity
A master of organisation and motivation No report was on more than a single side of paper. Like Samuel Pepys, managed war munitions and the supply chain supremely. Bold enough to dictate to the war office and parliament to get things done. He ensured food supplies and the supply chain were paramount to soldiers wellbeing. Able to accept and learn from defeat (Gallipoli in World War 1), he learnt the strength and power of correct articulation and great oratory skills. Had an ability to put across great ideas

in memorable phrases that the public and team members would not forget during the Second World War.

Henry V: (with apologies to Shakespeare) saw off several knighted armies with bows and arrows.
Once more unto the *data* breach, dear friends, once more;
Or close the wall up with our English dead.
In peace there's nothing so becomes a man
As modest stillness and humility;
But when the blast of war blows in our ears, then imitate the action of the tiger …

19.1.1.2 INSPIRE THE WORKPLACE AND PIE WILL FOLLOW

Offices should be informal to allow for free space movement. Those offices with cloth walled cubicles are ghastly for developers to work in; they are the 25 square yard pigpens that leaked from the minds of deluded interior designers in the 1950s. They are distracting, hell to work in and expensive. It is cheaper to have glass partitions and a door rather than pay for these fabric barriers.

The most efficient offices ever were Victorian era office spaces. They are separate offices with no more than four people in each; they are quiet and a place to concentrate. Team members can decorate their areas to suit the team's brand. Also, you don't need to cable everything everywhere. I have witnessed enterprises that have a complete wireless delivery network (secure Wi-Fi is achievable) that is not only cheaper to install and maintain it also provides the freedom to roam. In the 1990s the Management Consulting group Accenture; proposed that meetings should take no longer than 45 minutes and everyone was to stand up during the meeting. Chairs were taken away, and the boardroom desks were raised to standing height. This culture imposed a need for managers to get properly prepared for a meeting and not produce seventy PowerPoint slides to explain what could be said on a single side of A4 paper. This initiative has been adopted in agile meetings, where programmers get to input daily using Kanban as a guideline. Instead of long-winded PowerPoint's, stories and post-it notes are used for meeting facilitation, and everyone knows what is going on at all parts of the project.

To aid workplace transition, implement a Wi-Fi only policy and eliminate the need for cabling. Providing a solution like Aruba or Cisco secure Wi-Fi not only means that getting a signal to a desk costs a tenth of that of a cabled solution, but also there is no planning needed for cable maintenance and checking of cable taps. Wi-Fi solutions can carry end-to-end encryption, so it is equally secure as a cabled solution.

There is always a place for a Chief Happiness Officer. I find that self-deprecating humour in technical and development team members makes a workplace happier and more productive. Operations need the diversion of humour to encourage new ideas. In the face of adversity, humour also bonds workers and soldiers and helps team members get beyond the extra mile. I once visited the strangest company, where the company culture was a sloppy handshake, no one smiled, there was a sense pervading the IT department that lizard-like aliens had invaded key personnel. In a month I heard no-one laugh out loud or encountered any banter during their long tedious meetings. The whole place felt like a funeral parlour. When I presented to the board my findings at the end of the project, it was pretty clear that each of the board members had stepped out of a Dickensian storyline. The dour misery they created pervaded the boardroom and the entire organisation. There's nothing wrong with seriousness and gravitas, and there's always a place for this, but the air of emotional bullying and posturing (much rattling of cuff links) had sunk into every crack of the organisation. That company had got it completely wrong was taken over in 2002 and everybody was sacked in three months.

19.2 HUMAN RESOURCES

Owners should to avoid micro-managing the team member quality. They need to have honest and open dialogues as well as make the tea and run the organisation and mop the brow of the bank manager. The cloning activities of Human Resources can create a grey gloop pool of people being created that contribute zilch to a company's wellbeing. I once worked in a 100 strong employee company; four of the employees were in Human Resources and the boss asked how he could save 5% of salaries. The obvious answer was to eject the HR team members and make managers responsible for on boarding (and with exceptions letting go of team members). Strangely, it worked and for the better; over time the use of profiling was dropped and managers had to rely on a gut feeling about new candidates. It turned out that once the HR department unplugged from the organisation new joiners and were inducted quicker, and the quality of the team members went up along with the diversity and skills. Managers took a long-term punt on people, devoted more mentoring skills and it changed the whole culture of the company with new team members' innovations. Broadsourcing will help identify a much better level of team members that will help lead your business into increased profitability. To help their decision criteria I developed the Doers, Designers, DevOps and Directors matrix to help place current people in the organisation as well as identify replacement roles for potential candidates. This is a step change away from traditional recruitment directives. An eye-to-eye interview can reveal more about a person's true motivations and helps define where they would initially sit in the organisation.

19.3 GET STRAIGHT A'S

I devised the team members' evaluation 8xA's form to assess the right sort of people to thrive in a Combat Ready environment. There is no category for doofus! You don't have to be ultra sharp to be in CRIT, a CRITTER does need attitude to react on the fly. This helps Captains designate individuals and balance teams without psychological profiles. Profiling just on-boards 'forelock tuggers' – which no company needs.

During re-evaluations, existing team members felt involved, and engaged with their real reasons for working also stepped up their game. In the same company there was an individual who questioned everything – and I mean everything – but contributed nothing. He was able to take this stance because he felt protected by the Human Resource's department, which he used as a weapon when everyone requested his silence. When that mainstay disappeared, he turned into a model employee and his demeanour changed dramatically and then people started to really listen to what he had to say. It turned out he was a disgruntled genius, and once he was able to exercise his newfound abilities, he created an application that brought millions into the company. Listening skills are a must have skill here a team member can be experiencing personal or work related problems or may have just invented a Golden Application. We were born with two ears (well most of us) and one mouth and should be used in direct proportion.

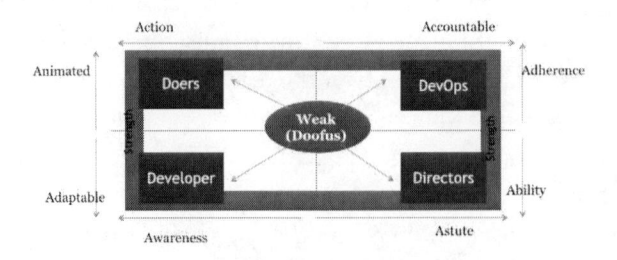

People Profiles	Ability (Expertise)	Astute (Risk and Fiscal)	Accountable (potential Captain)	Adherence (to process)	Animated (Motivation)	Action Proven Task delivery	Adaptable (to Change)	Awareness of new technologies
S/W Developer	H	L	L	L	H	M	H	H
Service Agent	M	L	L	H	L	L	H	L
Network Engineer	H	L	H	H	L	M	H	H
IT Alchemist	H	H	M	L	H	M	H	H
Business Analyst	H	H	M	H	M	M	L	H
Sys Admin	M	H	H	M	M	H	H	H
Captain	M	H	H	M	H	H	H	H

Figure 90 TEAM MEMBERS EVALUATION STRAIGHT A's

Zero to Hero stories won't always happen, and we tend to lean on HR recently to sort out the increasing vagaries of regulatory workload and team members. I do think though that any company that asks for HR to screen resumes (CVs) before they reach a manager should cease that activity. The amusing job descriptions I see need a 23-year-old with a PhD, expert in 12 different areas in IT, with multiple qualifications and willing to work for three months on zero money. These job descriptions are laughable and demeaning to anyone foolish enough to apply for these over-stringent roles because if you have all these skills you are Walter Mitty. Please don't wish for everything when advertising for a role keeps responsibilities to no more than 5 key skills. For the last 30 years there have been annual campaigns to get women into IT. IT is not perceived as a stable career and moving around every three years to a new job or town isn't in some women's desired career path. It's a great pity because the women I have worked with can complete any task with phenomenal diligence and intelligence. You will see women opt for project manager or business analyst type roles, but in coding, networking and compute it's a rare sighting. Companies need to provide a much friendlier environment for women, the Hula Hoop organisation helps women create the communications boundaries and networks that are part of their make up. Behind every successful woman is herself.

HR compounds and increases the likelihood of ageism; in fact in IT it's impossible to get a job if you are over 50. In the UK this is in part because of National Insurance contributions. In an Agile and DevOps world, it is essential to attract and retain grey hair. The grey hair brigade knows tricks and workarounds, and have levels of experience needed to balance out development and operations activities. They are accountable and adhere to rigour and their experience invaluable. They are also healthier and have great attendance levels compared to younger employees. One of the best programmers I worked with was 62. He knew how to write dense code and write one line instead of a hundred. He had spent years writing in Cobol and C in the mainframe world, and was probably the first to use REST 10 years before anyone had considered it as a concept. He is still working in his seventies on ultra-reduced secure code set modules. Did the company retain these skills – nope is the unfortunate answer. He was made redundant by external cost cutters who saw this guy as an easy target on paper.

19.4 ORGANISATION BUDGETS

Over the years I have observed a plethora of IT organisations, from start-ups to huge enterprise monoliths with support teams that needed several AO sized paper to show the IT organisation alone. Now outsource blob shapes appear on the slide org charts, and no one knows what happens there. I have used ITIL to help structure IT organisations, and usually the minimum headcount needed to meet the obligations of an ITIL v3 is around 50 to 60 IT team members.

Before the recession started in 2008 in earnest, the average team members size of an IT organisation was around 8% of the total number of team members in an organisation. So as an example, in an enterprise of around 30,000 people and $10 billion in annual revenues an IT department was some 2,500 people. So the annual IT budget also kept in direct correlation with the budget. Now I know this sort of scale is not representative of all organisations, in the latest depression over 250,000 IT people globally lost their jobs. This effectively knocked down the average IT spend to 5% of a company's team members and budget. IT Budgets were CAPEX frozen for around three years. Although this has loosened this year (2015) the burden of security has meant an uplift of 20% of budget allocation just on security optimisation. This uplift in security costs needs to be budgeted.

In times of conflict, IT will need to be pared down yet again. A useful exercise is to drill this in real time during a three week Christmas break. In my estimation, team members will account for around 4% of overall team member's levels. To achieve this level a huge amount of automation is required to continue to support *any* business. Getting fit for a conflict means reprioritising where and how to spend automation monies. If producing and manufacturing goods and foodstuffs, then CAPEX investment into automated manufacturing systems and robotics is essential. If the predication that 50% of the manual workforce jobs will be replaced by robots in the next decade, so you may as well start now and get ahead of the game. The investment into robotics will in turn create a raft of peasant riots and Luddite rebellions, so don't omit this off the risk register. Investing in robotics means you will need IT to be more robust and software-driven. The focus is on getting IT out onto the production floor, and this in turn means beefing up the IT spend in the next two to three years. This sword of robotic Damocles entails new developers, resilient infrastructure and simple modular rugged code. So where does this leave the new IT?

If we take the metro and hula hoop maps and translate this into a more recognisable organisation chart it will look a like the diagram below:

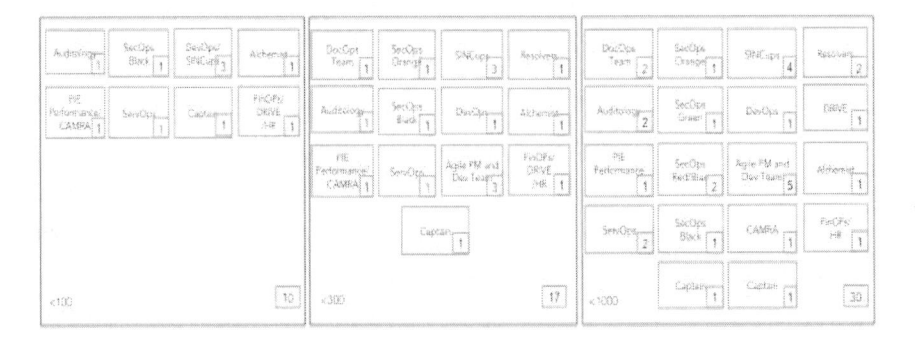

Figure 91 CAREER LAYERS

You will probably sigh when you first look at this: for a start it's upside down and resembles a Macedonian phalanx attacking formation – perhaps this is what we should be achieving. This is a reverse hierarchy, which places the onus on the owner and captains to be in a supporting rather than downward dictation role. You can turn this upside down if you want, but it to be in a supporting rather than downward dictation role. There is obviously an increased responsibility placed at each of the five layers, rather each layer adds increasing accountability to ensure the production service level is 100%. What's interesting to note here are the layers create an instant career path and pay structure based on the five bands. This is to encourage rotation and flexibility across the team. The blocks are regimented because these blocks represent small agile units. The chart can be replicated like a cookie cutter.

19.5 SALARIES

I have been in companies where there were as many salary bands as there were employees, which is ludicrous. There are salary bands, for instance, that range from $20,000 to $2,000,000 within the same department. If you decide to operate on a similar model, then leave a 20k (location dependent) gap between each pay band and bonus all team members decently. Bonuses should be 20% of the salary and paid every in November. Entry-level salary should start around the $80k basic mark. IT salaries across the globe change dramatically and by currency. Countries with cheaper team members seem to be disappearing; most emerging countries now have parity (and a job) akin to their western counterparts. Whether this continues in a conflict remains to be seen. So incentivising local team members is the clever and strategic option and avoid turning to the outsourcing saga. Most western-based IT team members will enjoy this standard logical approach.

19.5.1.1 HULA HOOP SCALE OUT

A CRIT model can be made to work with a team members of 10 team members and increase from there. To reach optimal efficiency 30 team members is needed to make valuable. It's based on a 5% team members level of the total organisation numbers, so would suggest a company size of 100, and this will need to go up as the complexity and direction of the organisation and deliverables increase. So view this as a baseline that will require increasing over time. The whole IT organisation shouldn't need to exceed 30 as long as sufficient automation is in place.

Above 50 you will need to rejig perspectives and rely on ITIL frameworks to align processes against. The whole model is to provide flexibility but the pivot point is the number of developers needed by project - each new in house application needs a Disciplined Agile Team and this ranges from 4 to 8 personnel in size. Increased flexibility and decreased overhead is a direct result of automation tools that I have described later.

The better the automation tools, the fewer people you will need to manage your IT going forward. This doesn't give organisations the right to regard IT team members as shelf-stockers. IT is going the way of supermarkets, and you don't need to have a PhD in Computer Science to stack cans of beans. You do need scientists to code RFID tags and align the cans of beans with pricing structures and then analyse the supply chain so it meets the number of cans required to fulfil customer needs. So beans need minds. Another way this can be gauged is the DevOps Ratio of 100:10:1 (100 developers: 10 operators: 1 captain).

Obviously the Cloud is ideal for growing and emerging companies on a pay-as-you-go service. If you are in this team member's numbers ballpark and don't need to develop your own software solutions, there is always an app than can grow and shrink with your business requirements. I started a company up with four guys (all in different global locations) and we used our own PCs, Instant Messenger, e-mail and Skype as a company PABX. This suited our needs and zero IT budget was allocated. Nowadays word processing, spreadsheet and presentation software is either free or around $20 an app. Most administrative workers don't require a $2000 desktop any more and can make do with a $300 tablet.

All you should ensure is that the data created on these devices is held in at least two locations; this is an absolute Rule of Thumb, secret data on a hybrid cloud and unclassified data on an encrypted public cloud. Do use VPNs and encrypt your internal messages – a must for start-ups where intellectual property can walk out the door in an instant, and the next day someone else has your idea. Remember Insiders are 30% more likely to steal Intellectual Property.

If you are a Service Provider obviously the IT function needs to support Billing, OSS and BSS and fixed and RAN networks.

19.6 AUTOMATISM IS ESSENTIAL
Yes because it allows team members to focus on the Mission Critical Cyber Security threats!

Traditional IT is all about people and processes. The Combat Ready IT model uses handoffs and craftflows. But in IT we are masters of technology and should test and try solutions to make life better. The Cloudifying of IT has brought a myriad of automation possibilities. Finding the appropriate automation tools and solutions that can grow and shrink with your cash flow is essential.

A company had to migrate 6000 endpoints (Windows XP to Windows 7). Alongside 28 internal employees, 17 contractors were hired to migrate each machine –manually at 4 to 6 hours per machine.

Manual Approach
Manpower OPEX Costs – $1,050,000
Management Overhead – $129,600
Expenses – $176,940
Total – $1,356,540
Cost per machine – $226.09
Time to migrate 6000 machines – 9 months

Automated Approach
CAPEX and OPEX – $40,000 including scripting consulting
Management Overhead - $20,000
Expenses -$0
Cost per machine – $10
Time to migrate 6000 machines – 10 days

The price of investing in automation was a clear winner. For 3% of the project cost, keeping customers and CIOs happy, would you consider automation a better route? The real problem arose when the Windows 7 machines had to migrate to Windows 8 after the completion of the first phase. Hit <repeat> button.

Here's another example:

A company has 30,000 Macs and are managed by four operators. The team shows prowess by writing inventory and Ruby on Rails scripts to manage each device. The machines are capable of handling all the various OS (Windows and Linux and others); all logins are monitored minute by minute. Any change to the Macs that do not match the security-hardened configurations, raises an alarm, and are wiped. This ratio of 1: 7500 (operator to devices) is amazing. The best thing about this is the four tools they employ are Open Source and therefore attract little or near to zero CAPEX and OPEX. Cost per machine, an incredible $20 per annum.

In comparison, let's also consider the costs of deploying PCs. An IDC report indicted the *average deployment cost* of a PC was $615 and the five-year annual support cost was $969 ($4845). Assuming a PC costs $1600 and MS Office $365 then a single PC would cost around $7,500. Now that's a significant sum and one likely to plummet soon.

The moral of this is to ask deep questions of your technical team, like "Is there a better way to do this (followed by the 5 x Whys)?" The key takeaway here is automation is good. Always get big internal project double double-checked by an external consultant to see if there is a better map to get to your end goal. Yes, you have to buy the tools (sometimes), and yes you have to ensure each tool is completely resilient and backed up for hot cutover.

19.6.1.1 PREPARE AND SAVE

Owners and team members should workshop a Readiness Challenge introspective. The précis being the company is under attack and in a war. What the first thing that will happen to your company. Are you ready? Would you survive? What would be your plan of action to counter an attack and what would you do differently? Team members' reactions are great to watch in this simulation.

Set aside budget to test remediation of the weak points raised in the Readiness Challenge. When was the last time you saw a company actually save 10% of their annual turnover in a pot for a rainy day? The simple answer is it is a rare as pigs' nail varnish. I have never seen a set of company's published accounts that actually displays this as a sign of good company management. You do see this though in companies that are owned by women.

How many companies go straight to the wall during a 10% drop in the stock market? The answer is thousands. How many companies would go straight to the wall during a global war? Out of a billion global companies, probably 20% of those companies would disappear in the first few weeks. Many companies experienced this during the last two World Wars. In fact, a company that would be able to sustain cash flow and prop up revenues from savings would save millions of companies during a major conflagration and be able to survive most of the recessions we have witnessed recently. We collectively have to change the mind-sets of venture capitalists and banks to make saving a positive management feature. Providing gainful employment and the amount of savings should be a KPI that should be recognised by analysts and not seen as detrimental to stockholders' annual dividends and short-term pay-outs. In the US, banks' refusal to bail out small businesses, while they struggled to find the cash for their annual bonuses wiped the Mom and Pop industries.

The third element is to watch the cash. For years companies have attempted to turn IT facilities into profit-making ventures. This started in the mainframe era when companies had spare capacity to offer to other companies for payroll and the like. It was an early form of outsourcing. EDI (Electronic Data Interchange) was one of the earliest forms of the Internet, where a central company extended their network directly into suppliers' companies, so making the earliest form of supply chain platforms a reality. The cash nowadays seems more to go out of the company, but things may change yet again. A lot of companies have massive processing capacity to spare on existing facilities and data centre infrastructure. In fact, you can create a hybrid Cloud for you and supplying companies. Spare capacity can be sold to Start up companies wishing to share resources. This generates cash.

19.7 ALCHEMY

When you are at a party and someone asks what you do and your reply is an architect, they think buildings. When you say you are an Alchemist they think it's really interesting and leads into a revealing conversation! Alchemists don't walk away when their design is finalised. Isaac Newton's search for the 'alchemical spirit' was his way of identifying an understanding God's action in the world. Still one of the greatest minds in this planet's history, Newton's work in alchemy influenced his scientific thought. Newton sought a unified system of God and nature, and his work in mathematics, optics, motion, matter and alchemy all supported this goal. Unification is the Alchemists prime directive.

When we think about developing systems, and in particular SMB software systems, whatever is produced usually maps directly to the SMB culture. They tend not to follow the rigidity type disciplines needed in military systems, jet fighter targeting systems, fail-safe in oil and gas processes. There are start-ups with college kid coders who scratch their heads when security is mentioned. So with each SMB, a set of code can vary enormously. Once one application is compromised every application is compromised.

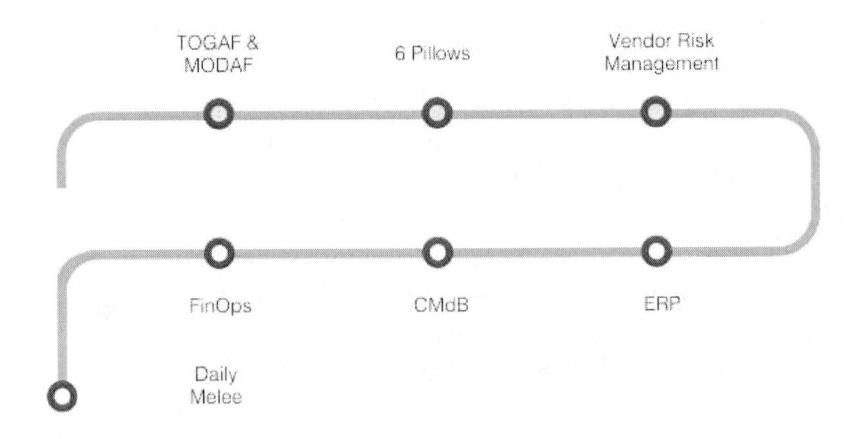

Figure 92 ALCHEMY HANDOFFS

The alchemist's task is to make this tie together and work and ensure that all the necessary costs and components match the desired outcome. They strike a balance by applying discipline to a set of immediate goals required by business. Some of the best alchemists I know are chemical engineers; it's something that is in their psyche to understand the ramifications of what is truly fit for the strategic deployments.

Their task, should they decide to accept it, is to make the strategy work with re-use of existing software and infrastructure and tools and to create the strategy. Now you may have surmised that I cannot stand the word architecture; the reason is that it does not reflect the IT view of the world. Architects build structures that stand for 30 plus years and never get concerned about the soft furnishings

19.7.1.1 GLUEPRINTS AND PATTERNS

This is what happens in the IT world. An 'architect' designs a three-year programme and uses vendors to help drive the enterprise direction and decision-making process these are usually termed Blueprints - but no-one ever sticks to them. As the world '*Cloudifies*', alchemists need to build Glueprints that ensure all the diverse strands of an organisation stick together. I use Cloud Patterns that are available on the www.Cloudpatterns.org website run by Arcitura and the Cloud Controls Matrix v3.0.1 which is available at https://Cloudsecurityalliance.org/research/ccm.

The Cloud Controls Matrix encompasses and complements the following linkages to existing security controls such as OWASP (See Appendices) and the SANS Top 20 Security Controls

It has all the mappings necessary for interconnecting to several major standards:

1. AICPA 2014 Trust Services Criteria
2. Canada PIPEDA (Personal Information Protection Electronic Documents Act)
3. COBIT 5.0
4. COPPA (Children Personal Information Protection)
5. CSA Enterprise Architecture

6. ENISA (European Network Information and Security Agency) Information Assurance Framework

7. European Union Data Protection Directive 95/36/EC

8. FERPA (Family Education and Rights Privacy Act)

9. HIPAA/HITECH act and the Omnibus Rule

10. ISO/IEC 27001:2013

11. ITAR (International Traffic in Arms Regulation)

12. Mexico - Federal Law on Protection of Personal Data Held by Private Parties

13. NIST SP800-53 Rev 3 Appendix J

14. NZISM (New Zealand Information Security Manual)

15. ODCA (Open Data Centre Alliance) Usage Model PAAS Interoperability Rev. 2.0 + PCI DSS v3.

There used to be an expression bandied about ten years ago "You don't get fired for buying IBM" That may have been the case ten years ago, but like all great IT companies their decade in the sun is over, now they are more of a service based consulting company having exited the hardware side of the business. This also goes for most giants of the Internet vendor world. It does not stop them leveraging their legacy positions and their behaviour remains the same, bullish and arrogant.

Alchemists need to rise above this behaviour and avoid the freebies and brown envelopes. Rather, the beauty of this role is to concoct gold out of manure. A great alchemist can be experimental and innovative. The people that do this really well are few and far between.

An alchemist can perform their magic on any given solution. For instance, a colleague of mine was designing a new array of blade servers and the problem was the vast amount of heat generated by compacting the server space. More heat meant more cooling, which meant more electricity and so a higher price point. So he sourced a chip that actually performed better in the heat and did not require cooling. The chip did the same amount of processing but because of its characteristic make-up it actually required more heat to perform better. This sort of lateral thinking is the stuff that makes operations interesting.

The alchemist needs to add Views (as used in MODAF) to the mix whilst juggling with the new world results of Big Data. A Big Data result can change the course of a company, a product set or a deployment overnight. This can also impact on the integrity and security of a company's IP, the organisation, e-commerce and e-content delivery, flexing the infrastructure to meet instantaneous demand, and ensuring campaign availability through development and deployment. This demands daily melees with the Fin Ops, DRIVE and Resolver teams.

Ensuring applications get fully utilised is an increasingly difficult task. In the past decades I have seen IT spend millions on application licenses and deployment costs only to use about one tenth of what an application can really deliver. This modular madness sees departments use a single element of an application and go and buy another nine applications to meet particular business needs (allegedly). Alchemists can stop this nonsense and improve the continuum of readily available tool sets. How many network monitoring tools have you seen being used in the network department? Every network engineer has a favourite. On one network engineer's desktop I found about 50, lots of these downloaded from the Web and full of cross-site scripting.

19.8 FINOPS

This is where I hear most CIOs throw their hands up in the air and say "I don't need to prove, and justify our costs, I just need to go to the board once a year and tell them how much I need". That strategy might have been good twenty years ago, but now IT departments (more than any other department in any business) have to justify every penny cent spent. This does not mean book keeping or controlling. The Financial Department reports to the TVC. Accounting is a function that sits under the IT remit. This does not stop you having a CFO! It does mean Fraud is lowered because the finance team members are continuously audited. Think about this carefully, 98% of finance work resides in spread sheets and ERP systems and not on ledgers anymore.

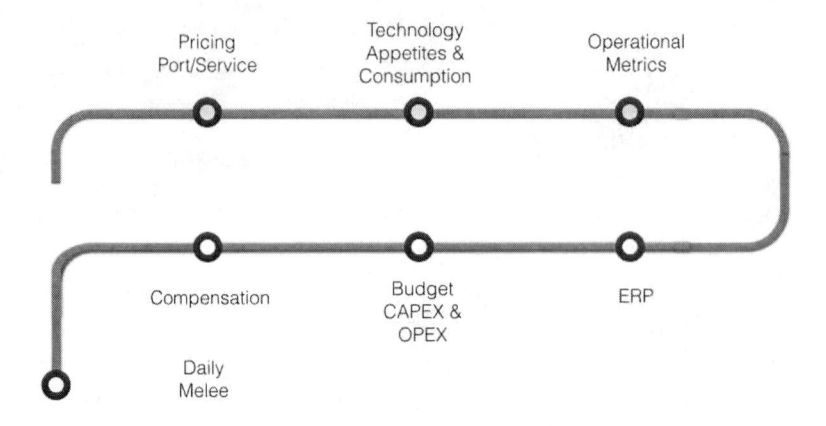

```
Pricing          Technology        Operational
Port/Service     Appetites &       Metrics
                 Consumption
     O────────────────O────────────────O─┐
   ┌─┘                                    │
   │                                      │
   │  O────────────────O────────────────O │
   └──┤                                  └┘
   O  Compensation    Budget             ERP
                      CAPEX &
      Daily           OPEX
      Melee
```

Figure 93 FINOPS HANDOFFS

The value of an IT department is worth a twenty times its budget as a business revenue contributor. In the last twenty years the ability to drive significant profits each year is tenuous. The normal IT budget for a company is around 5% to 8% per annum, but the profit it generates by direct correlation has a value of twenty times that sum. Without IT, a company dies. There are massive drains on a company, like HR and Accounting where the value contribution falls into the negative zone. Without IT SMBs would die..

This is where Green and Yellow Teams sit with the Finance teams to build Cost per Port and Cost per Service models. This mixing helps technical team members learn the full ramifications of budgets, and the TCO/ ROI of their actions and help SMBs cut costs. The baselines created can be directly fed to product managers and marketing teams to help construct new revenue streams. It is also critical to manage bandwidth and utilisation costs – there is more reliance on mobile data costs in a cloudified world. Ensuring Hybrid/ Public cloud variable costs sits firmly with FinOps and Drive. Demand Management monitoring contributes to this exercise. Demand from sales and production is a closed loop that usually gets discussed monthly. As FinOps are now in the team viewing HIT to PURCHASE ratios the capability of production to gear up in predictive time forces quality up dramatically.

19.9 DRIVE

Does your Procurement always take the back seat? 'Just order it and do it quick' - is what I hear from procurement teams. No matter what procurement does, it is always the last to know what's going on. In the CRIT model it is critical and tracks directly from the demand handoffs. It's rare to see technically au fait procurement team members, but to enforce the PIE culture the DRIVE team need to in the know daily. This is the area where the Technical Steering Committee (TSC) is held weekly. The TSC is responsible for bringing together business representatives (who usually moan about the cost of IT) and make them or their representatives ask for what they really need. This could be mobiles, tablets, storage retention, new servers et al. The TSC makes this happen and publishes minutes to the Intranet. Transparency is the key here. Too often the business espouses the view that IT hide projects, the need for projects, and the rationale for cancelling projects.

DRIVE was designed to baseline the need for applications or technology devices and ensures that the supply chain will work in a conflict.

Liaison with the alchemists to ensure the consistency of Glueprint acquisition views is paramount here, and don't renew licences until DevOps gives the team the nod. Keeping track of software licences and usage has become exponentially harder due to the proliferation of versions, inconsistent naming and tracking mechanisms, and increasingly complex licence structures. This often leads to internal divisions of thought processes. I have seen companies renew Microsoft Enterprise Agreements six months before they procured Office 365 (Cloud licence). Ensure that projects don't double-count licences for a new production system. I have seen large database providers claim a double count for SAP licences as well as a Web version (double the revenue for the salesman).

Alchemists

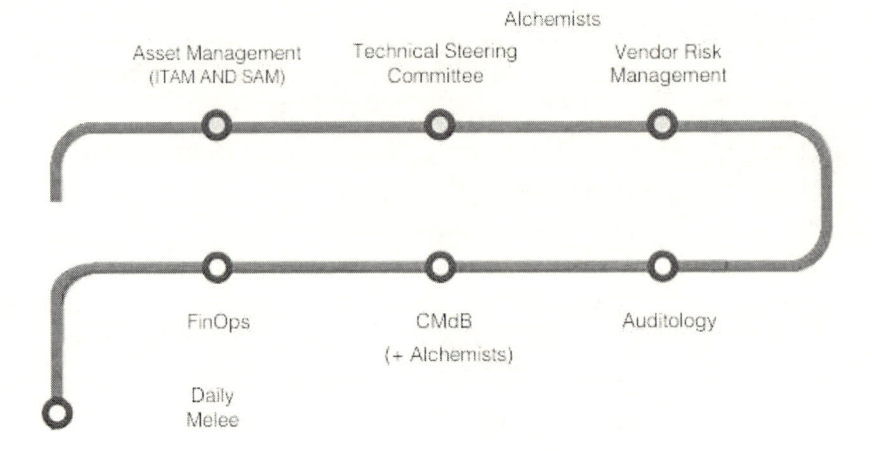

Asset Management (ITAM AND SAM) — Technical Steering Committee — Vendor Risk Management

FinOps — CMdB (+ Alchemists) — Auditology

Daily Melee

Figure 94 DRIVE HANDOFFS

1. **Drivers** – Invites the Procurement team to input into the risk management process. It also assigns responsibility to monitor pricing from vendors. Each Vendor Risk Assessment score to be re-balanced on product releases. Use companies like Evantix to help here. In a Cloud-based technology organisation, the key measurement is the variable OPEX. Cloud services are pay-monthly (Pay As You Go) services that require tight control. I have seen developers in agile teams whip up 50 Virtual Server instances in a day. These costs mount up and costs can escalate depending on the time of the month (beginning, mid and end). It's like outsourcing after the first year of service amendments (changes to services) are added up on a monthly basis. Most outsource first year bills usually exceed the cost savings that were originally seen as positive in the business case.

2. **Regulation** - Actually Procurement teams have more legal parlance than most lawyers. Their world is to create and manipulate contracts' wording towards the benefit of the company. The best clauses I have seen are that the licence issued is valid for a lifetime, and the current cost includes all future upgrade costs to new versions, and should the product be discontinued then a full reimbursement of the complete integration cost shall be credited

to the company. When you plough through a Microsoft Enterprise License renewal you realise that that operations teams are loath to challenge their livelihood. Rather than biting the hand that feeds them many operations teams persuade their boards to continue with the same old. IBM mainframes died because they became stubborn about licence a fee – which is why you should keep lawyers away from technology. In a Virtual world licences can be on a Pay as you Use basis. Only automated tools (Flexera for example) can manage this usage cost effectively.   With enterprise infrastructure moving to the Cloud, it is important to ensure all licensing is Cloud-transferable (from fixed geographic site to dynamic geographical site). Also be wary of per application usage if an application uses per client and per server core licences you get double charged. It's also the role of Procurement to do a fit-for-purpose check against regulatory checklists, so don't buy a product unless it specifically details that the correct standard is fully supported.

3. **Integration** - Vendors are always willing to do integrations for you – this should be encouraged. Do not let your teams tear software to pieces - or just use one module from a complete software package. Engineers love to look under the hood and kick the tyres but this invalidates warranties and can lead to unsuccessful legal cases. It also creates a security risk. Do get any software tested for vulnerabilities before you deploy on the hybrid or public clouds. I have often witnessed internal operators rip perfectly good ready-made software to pieces until it was unrecognisable. I have seen developers add pretty front ends to make very expensive software completely unusable.

4. **Visibility** - There is a stunning Vendor Risk Assessment checklist available from a company called Evantix. They have already completed around 1000 vendor evaluations, and I recommend that your vendors should volunteer their information into this format. It's also useful to write to all your suppliers to ascertain their conflict disaster plan and what they would do in a conflict (very revealing this). Remember to get over provision spares for vendor equipment available on site. A hybrid cloud requires a minimum

risk allocation of 10% spares, in a conflict this should be doubled. Liaise with Availability Management on how to gauge the number of spares based on a four-year conflict. If none are available, then the support function should be within 50 miles of the main production facility (i.e., vendor product developers, access to source code, physical access in case of communications links outages)?

5. **Enablers** - procuring the infrastructure for team members to support the infrastructure! This is the most overlooked part of procurement today with new environments being software driven this comes to the forefront. Most sales people are able to throw in training and consulting services to secure an order. If the ITAM licence count exceeds the cost of change, get credit in tangible items such as training man-days, call-down consulting (draw down man days).

Automate the ITAM process as much as possible: there are adequate tools that can help ease migrations from traditional server-based worlds to virtualisation. There is an ITAM ISO standard to help create a Software Asset Management program, ISO/IEC 19770-1:2012. Most organisations cannot say with a high level of confidence that they have a clear view of everything accessing their network, and that lack of visibility leaves them vulnerable to security attacks, so this tool is key to preventative activities.

Vendors such as Flexera, Dell Kace and Aspera are particularly good tools for such a job. There are Cloud-based services as well. The key feature to look for is automated push of data into the company's CMdB and Service Desk platform. Some Cloud implementations are not that effective at this, but writing a script can populate the Cloud CMdB and Service desks with current snapshots. At a cost of around $20 to $30, a device and monitoring of licence bubbles (where licences are not used and can be redeployed or credited during a 'true up' of the company inventory). Automated tools used for this should also link into the CAMRA practice: the Hybrid Cloud needs constant monitoring and new devices need to be updated in the CAMRA discovery tool set.

IT infrastructure needs constant monitoring and new governance between procurement and finance and the alchemists. Here also is the input into the

Auditology practice. Most organisations have an ERP daily run which needs constant monitoring to fight fraud. The Green and Yellow teams in FinOps, DRIVE and ITAM need to sync daily to tag activities. This should enforce a live view of the audit trail.

19.9.1.1 TELL VENDORS HOW TO PERFORM

You will see through the description of the CRITTERS model how to deal with software applications developed in-house (or in conjunction with a contractor). The model loops until the application is released and the application configuration is audited. But how do we know the COTS and ISV third-party software and even vendors' operating systems are safe? The authors who developed BSIMM[179] got this simple list of questions together that definitely put 80% of vendors on the back foot.

What is your threat model for this application?
What types of security testing are you doing?
Who is doing security testing? Is it independent?
How do you remediate security problems?
What kind of timeline is involved in remediation and what kind of enforcement is in place?
How do you know that security defects are fixed?
How often do you perform security testing?
What kinds of metrics do you have on your software security
effort over time?
Do attackers want to break this particular application or do they want to take down the acquirer's brand?
Can we get involved directly in the RFPs and other acquisition processes? (This includes service selection, vendor assurance, on boarding
and deployment.)
What is our view of risk? (Is this classified government stuff?
Whose name and brand are on the application?)
If we ask the vendor for evidence of security, how much integrity do the measurements we are asking for have? Are they repeatable?

Awareness of and/or participation in the BSIMM or vBSIMM programme?

19.9.2 CMDB

Choosing a CMdB is a ghastly task! It is the cornerstone of all the team's unification efforts to manage configurations. Without a CMdB you will break the fundamental Critical Security Laws. Now most vendors say they have a CMdB, but in practice this is flannel. There are CMdBs from ITIL v3-based Service Management offerings, but from experience the Cloud-based ones just don't meet the brochure ware expectations. The CMdB is best kept on-premise, as multiple systems will need to correlate data and alarming to a central point.

Although you can write scripts from Puppet and Chef-type applications there are CMdBs that have been around for at least a decade. Extracting the data can be painful. You could employ a middleware type solution that can move data around the organisation, but that would take deep pockets to achieve. The best solution I have found to date is the Seamless Data Pump from Avnet.

- **Automatism of the ITIL configuration management process**; populate a CMDB with real-time data, CIs, relationships and attributes from Master Data Repositories (MDRs) in a secure and proven way

- **Enable ITIL process automation views** for Incident, Service Impact Management, DevOps, Change Drift Management, SLA and Configuration Management

- **Remove 99% of the internal maintenance and support of data** to CMDB integrations and federations with commercial support

- **Perpetually synchronise** or federate on-premise data with Cloud based CMDBs for secure, real- time performance

Cloud Procurement Checklist

Before entering into a contract with a Cloud Service Provider, make sure you are satisfied with the minimum of legal and technical guidelines of your organisation:

1. Data to be stored within country boundaries (e.g. no health records for a sovereign nation being stored in a backyard in a different country)

2. Latencies for all participating data centres providing the server to be provided (should be sub 10ms; this is essential for some database applications and IPTV OTT type services

3. Potential loss of control & ownership of data. What happens when a CSP's data centre goes down in a major outage? Minimum 3 months' notice of CSP entering into liquidation or Chapter 11 protection if US located

4. Privacy enforcement and data encryption

5. Multi-tenant data isolation

6. Hypervisor security

7. Audit data and logs integrity protection and accessibility

8. Verified subscriber policies through provider controls

9. Security logs and trails to be provided to the customer

10. Recompense and credits for non-availability of service

19.10 RESOLVERS

Personally I believe the term business analyst is a throwback to the mainframe days – this term is usually given to team members without portfolio in large organisations, usually tasked to document and catalogue process disasters. Dr. Richard Bandler who teaches Neuro Linguistic Programming (NLP) thinks words, or, the constructs of the words themselves have dual meanings. The titles are perceived to influence behaviours and like a self-fulfilling prophecy the words become how a person thinks and adjusts their persona accordingly. For example: the word Director is made up of Dire (has Dire consequences, or sounds like Diabolical). The word Analyst when split becomes Anal (detailed or derriere) and lyst (sounds like cyst)

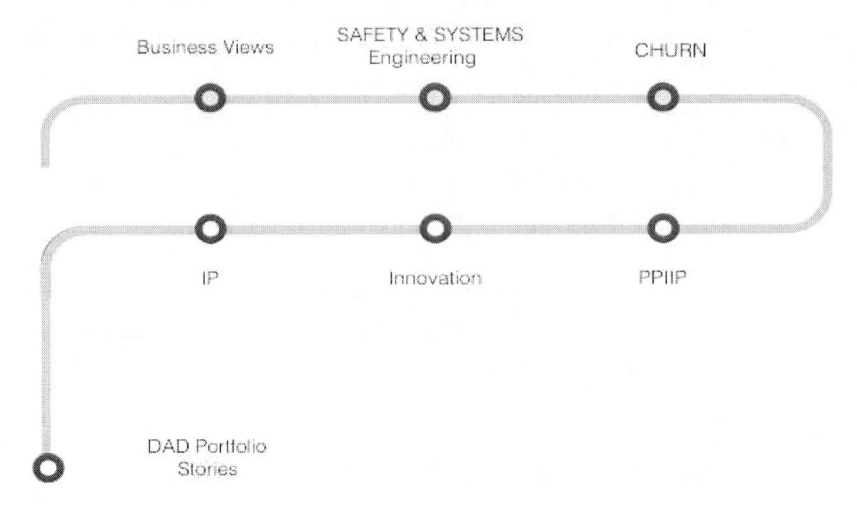

Figure 95 RESOLVERS HANDOFFS

In consulting and accounting companies they are the young graduates with PowerPoint and Excel skills. For years their role has been to be given a problem and draft huge investigative reports and collect and collate data. As a job, acting as a PowerPoint or Excel jockey is not a long-term career target. These are intelligent people (Knowledge Crafters) that need to deliver short-term tasks. Most often these reports are reviewed months after a BA has presented a review to the echelon or managing consultant and rarely do they see an endpoint outcome to their workload (no visibility means no responsibility). Their actions need to be measured, and they need a validation of their work, as this is a waste of their analytical skill-set. How much more satisfying is it to get a business view and translate that into a project? This role needs to be extended into more hands on and active engagement. How can a resolver contribute to PIE when their day ends saving the last versions of excel?

In addition, this is stationed between the alchemists and SecOps, but also has a close affinity link to DRIVE and the Technical Steering Committee. Their role is to identify better ways and investigate alternative tool sets to help oil the handoffs and realise cost efficiencies. Their responsibilities are to diagnose and resolve organisational issues and codify projects; this means identifying process deficits and sizing projects to substantiate the proof of systemisation. So their real-time role is to be a resolver and not just an analyst no task should extend beyond 30 days. They need to attend the multiple daily run meetings to ensure gaps are not created; rather they should fill the gaps as they progress. Applying Obashi, Lean and Kanban type tools is a resolver's tool set. The crux here is they resolve existing problems to a successful resolution portfolio.

As resolvers should know the end-to-end capabilities of the organisation, they are best placed to know what project and workflows and tools would be the best focus for project prioritisation. For these reasons, the resolvers' tasks include the management of the Portfolio Management function. Now most project managers and program managers will start writing to me to question my mental health here. But its purpose is to integrate this role and apply some analytical science to the scope, so the resolvers can see a measurable and reportable target. At the end of this, the resolvers kick off the agile process with the agile teams.

In traditional program management the job is to report back to the Owners on a wide array of simultaneous risk reduction and horizon projects. In practice this is a tardy waste of time and time consuming. Most program managers can add bottlenecks to progress and add to an increasingly slow delivery. Marrying up multiple real time projects is not effective and the necessity of a program manager in the traditional sense can slow down progress. If you are a Program Manager you have too many projects. Analytical resolution is all about ensuring that business views meet safety and systems engineering requirements and translating the alchemist glueprints for security standards, whilst maintaining the project portfolio. In this mode the resolver's team are better placed to shoulder this task and manage multiple parallel projects more efficiently. This is pivotal to destroying rafts of red tape and reducing program management meetings that takes procrastination time out of team members' daily productivity. How many times have you heard that projects have been kicked off that meet a spurious need when an analyst speaks up and says there was a better way to solve the problem with less money? Team members should always log this in their 5x5x5.

It is unlikely that traditional PMs sit well in this environment. In the last twenty years we have seen and read of massively over-manned and over-priced gargantuan IT projects fail. About 60% of all IT projects fail. Resolvers are better placed to create and maintain the linkages between people, process and tools and the constant reviewing of innovative tools can translate into tangible cost savings across a myriad of projects. I have only been able to achieve this set-up once in an organisation, but with four resolvers we were able to deliver a Cloud service in days rather than the three months stipulated by a PM, so I know it works.

And at the end of the day, do you want to be just an analyst for analysis sake, or, be a resolver and getting the job done?

19.11 SECOPS

When you get ask the question "how secure is my organisation?" usually the response is that it is, SOs' are culpable in this myth continuation. Now in the light of all the breaches we know that that is usually just before the Black Minute. We have seen that all the vulnerability and penetration tests only go part way to securing everything. Getting certificates and stamps of approval does not mean 'secure'; an organisation may meet basic safety governance, but that does not mean it is secure.

The problem here is that usually one person manages security in an SMB. If this person disappears from the security stance, your organisation can be kaput. So the model segregates processes and duties into five distinct teams. Yes, this means you need more than one-person managing security.

This belief that one SO can do the job is delusional and applies to 50% of the organisations globally, so no wonder we are in a mess. In an attempt to pull this together, the model provides for five teams.

19.11.1.1 SECOPS GREEN TEAM

This team is responsible for setting the policies needed to manage the business. As you can see from the diagram the key thrust here is managing standards' governance (of which there are many).

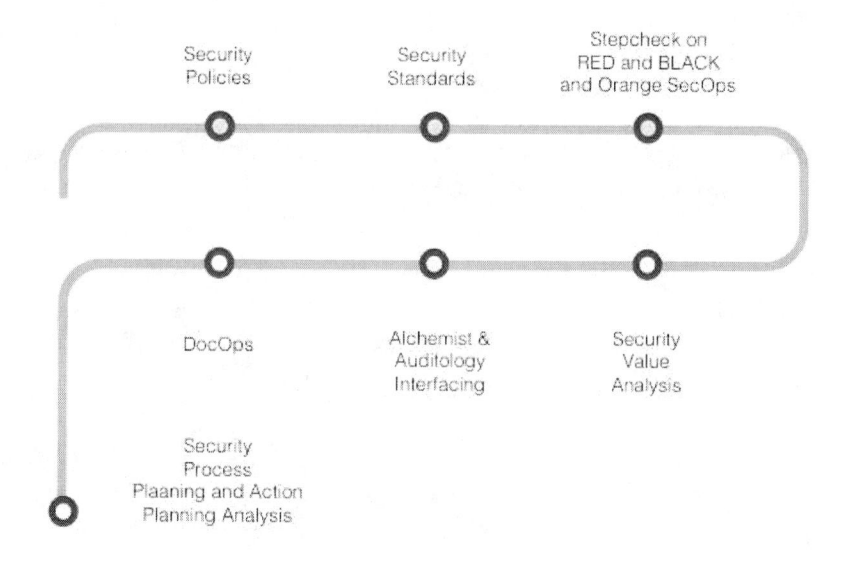

Figure 96 SECOPS GREEN TEAM HANDOFFS

These standards are bespoke to many organisations, and specific to sectors (NERC for example was designed for North American Electrical Utilities). Many overlap, and the security officer would usually be based in this team to ensure the pertinent standards apply to the organisation's functions. Most are irritatingly spread sheet-based, which makes it difficult to distribute tasks to the organisation. This is seen as a strategic role and a tight fit with Alchemy is essential. To manage this you will need some automation, a SIAM based tool. (Note: for my own sanity I will be using SIAM instead of SIEM from this point in the book)! Security and Information and Alarm Management help to get logging and event data from distributed points A, B and C to a centralised point C, stores it, monitors it, reports on it via a dashboard, deletes and purges it when the time comes, and ultimately provides the situational awareness necessary to manage VIA FERRATA operational risk.

Choosing the right SIAM product is entirely based on the use cases an organisation is trying to fulfil (call the consultants!). If you're an SMB without a dedicated team of security gurus, your needs and cost sensitivity will vary greatly from that of a large multi-national firm. You will most likely require a healthy amount of out-of-the-box functionality, while heavy customisation is probably not on the agenda.

Likewise, if your primary reason for deploying an SIAM tool is so you can click the 'yes sir I have reviewed my logs' audit checkbox, and you aren't looking at spending a lot of time on ticketing, workflow and advanced correlation logic, your needs aren't going to match that of a full-featured Operations Nerve Centre or CAMRA. All organisations must have a fluid trouble ticketing and workflow system, to cut and paste event data into an incident 'package', where others might simply need reports that show a set of metrics and pretty graphs. Perhaps the day will come when ubiquitous user interfaces, monitoring, alarm reduction, ticketing, visualisation and reporting mechanisms are all relatively comprehensive, but today the products remain heavily varied in coverage for those features.

Basic log parsing and alerting have existed for decades, and what many consider the first commercial SIAM platforms from companies such as Novell, NetForensics and Trustwave came to market in the late 1990s. There are now vendors that offer an SOC (Security Operations Centre) in a Box.

SIAM Sizing and agent-based or agent less licensing, and appliance deployment costs, depend on the environment (nodes vs. users vs. Alarms per Second **(APS)** vs. Alarms per Day **(APD)**), it also depends on how long you wish to store your data for, so data retention may be an issue in larger sites:

Small Environment

Up to 200 monitored nodes
up to 250 enterprise users
1200 APS sustained / 1500 peak APS • 1 SIAM user
Daily event volume: up to 100M events per day (APD)

Medium-Sized Environment
up to 500 monitored nodes

500 users
5000 APS sustained / 6000 APS peak • 3 SIAM SecOps team members
Daily event volume: up to 400M APD
Daily event volume: up to 4 billion EPD

Typically in a microenvironment there are available solutions that start at $4,000 and for an SMB environment start at $18,000. Remember to clarify with vendors their capacity costs as these vary dramatically. An enterprise can collect at least 10 Terabytes of data of plain text logs in a month. Also, bear in mind that about 80% of providers now offer additional services such as Continuous Threat Intelligence Monitoring and reputation services. The Hybrid Cloud solution can also take advantage of a Managed Service Provider's existing Cloud-based SIAM licensing structure. There is an Open Source solution called OSSIM that seems to have some good reviews.

19.12 SECOPS RED TEAM

In Security parlance the Red Team is usually an external, independent and intrinsically safe (sometimes) company that provides annual Penetration and Vulnerability testing. These teams also assist in forensic and legal data collection. Red Team Testing services provide cyber-attack simulations using real-world tactics, techniques and procedures. Red Team Testing employs blended threat scenarios to test the effectiveness of the IT security defences, policies, and team members.

Unlike traditional testing, Red Team Testing takes an integrated approach to assessing information security defences by combining multiple testing strategies into a comprehensive offensive engagement, with the sole objective of gaining access to customer assets. Cloud-based software also needs testing.

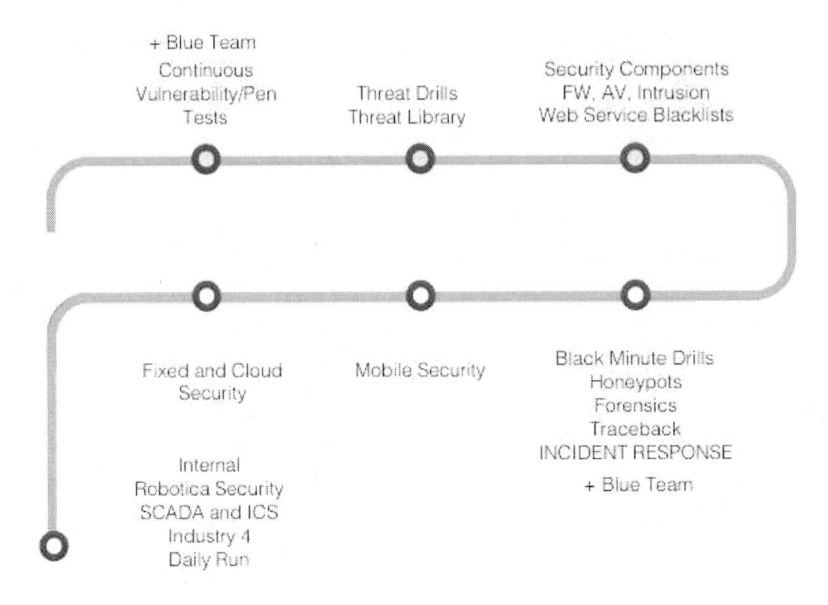

```
+ Blue Team
Continuous                                    Security Components
Vulnerability/Pen        Threat Drills        FW, AV, Intrusion
Tests                    Threat Library       Web Service Blacklists


                                              Black Minute Drills
Fixed and Cloud          Mobile Security      Honeypots
Security                                      Forensics
                                              Traceback
Internal                                      INCIDENT RESPONSE
Robotica Security                             + Blue Team
SCADA and ICS
Industry 4
Daily Run
```

Figure 97 SECOPS RED TEAM HANDOFFS

Vulnerabilities that may exist across your systems and applications can create an easy path for cyber-attackers to gain access to and exploit your environment. With dozens and even hundreds of applications and systems across your environment with access to the Internet, maintaining and updating system operating systems and applications to eliminate vulnerabilities is paramount – especially when those applications and systems are tied to sensitive customer, patient or card-holder information.

Penetration (Tests) can cost $3000 a month to perform (similar to alimony). A complete Vulnerability test can cost around $8000 a month. These prices are indicative and usually up for negotiation. Avoid a yearly set of tests as the Black Minute might have happened eleven months ago. Do a re-test after a new Web service or branch office or application launch happens. Even minute changes to a network routing infrastructure can cause havoc.

When engaging a Red Team make sure of the following:

- The security engineers must be citizens of the country you are carrying out the test in.

- Ask for proof that certifications such as GWAPT, GPEN, CEH, have been passed.

- All engineers must have passed a multi-level police and resume based background investigation.

For internal continuous auditing, then consider using a product like Nessus Vulnerability Appliance that for $5,000 can provide an on-site scanning appliance for Vulnerabilities, Configuration and Compliance assessments. For Continuous Penetration Testing, Open Source Metaspoilt can help audit many loopholes. Another vulnerability scanner is NMap; auditors should also use Wireshark and kismet wireless in their toolkit.

19.12.1.1 BLUE TEAM

This team's responsibilities lie in the core to edge devices, which require continuous testing by the Red Team, it seems to save time merging these two functions. Blue Team is primarily responsible for INCIDENT RESPONSE, therefore, can be dual sourced from two external security integrators. They can also be entrusted with Vulnerability and Penetration testing. This role requires a technical deep dive on all the product sets that provide IP transport from a server to a client.

If the Blue team is available there are daily runs with the SecOps and CAMRA teams and configuration changes are reported to the Auditology team. Blue Team interactions with SINCups Intrusion Detection and Continuous (In Band) monitoring.

19.13 SECOPS ORANGE TEAM

This team monitors all internal logins, access to systems and monitoring of voice and data activity. All identities are managed at this point, even when a new starter begins on boarding, the Orange Team liaise with the DevOps to ensure permissions and policies are correctly applied. It is also responsible for live surveillance of team member's activities.

SecOps Orange Handoffs

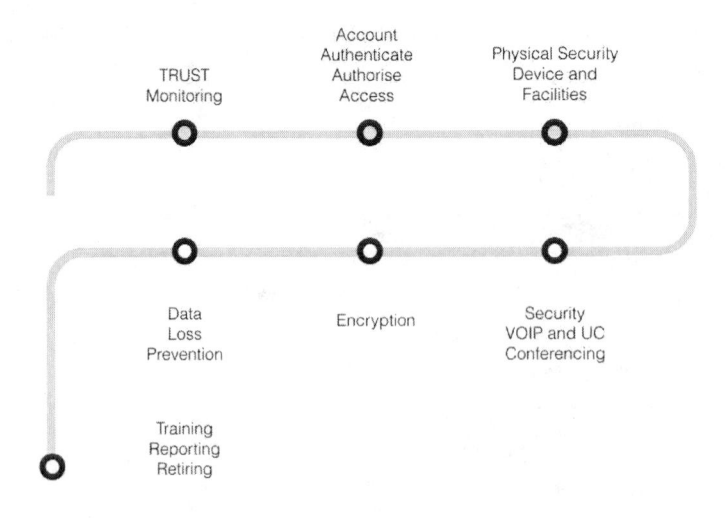

- TRUST Monitoring
- Account Authenticate Authorise Access
- Physical Security Device and Facilities
- Data Loss Prevention
- Encryption
- Security VOIP and UC Conferencing
- Training Reporting Retiring

Figure 98 SECOPS ORANGE TEAM HANDOFFS

There are several live monitoring tools such as Keylogger, MyTeamMonitor, Activtrak that track Website activity and record screenshots, ObserveIT can video user sessions and record remote access sessions, even CITRIX user sessions, Centrify can record and report on historical user activity, pinpoint suspicious activity through real-time monitoring, and troubleshoot system failures by replaying actions for root-cause analysis. The DevOps admin and the Auditologists to monitor user sessions can use these sessions. SecOps teams are usually monitored (who's watching who) and videos can be stored and even searched by keyword. Similar apps are available for the mobile world, like UXRecorder.

19.14 SECOPS BLACK TEAM

As this team's title suggests, their main role is to stop the Black Minute. They are responsible for three tenets:

1. Secure and Rugged Code checks in incremental release

2. Discovering real time attacks and directing the attacker to a honeypot or to manually sandbox infected code.

3. Begin offensive attacks on the adversary (Reverse DDOS, Legal Traceback etc.)

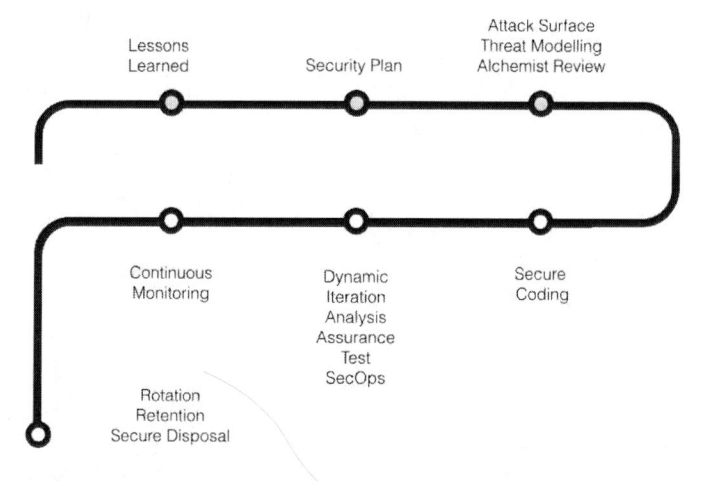

Figure 99 SECOPS BLACK TEAM HANDOFFS

SECURE CODE (SLICES OF PIE)

Code that is secure has security built in at the start and should not be bolted on, Secure Code aligns with PIE slices of:

- Predictive – How would an adversary attack? Through an initial audit finding, application vulnerability analysis, or a SHAZOPS output these should be detailed assessments. By reducing the application attack and threat trees and predicating how safeguards and code will react and which countermeasures can be taken.

- Proactive – Craft code that's scalable and modular with an eye on the horizon. Lockdown Information and Data buckets through privileged access.

- Progressive – Apply PIE and develop automation around small linkable craftflows.

Automatism - What existing tools in the estate can be extended to provide the necessary support functionality?

- Business Views and User Stories to identify the end goal - build the functionality skeleton first and then secure the function

- DocOps should have documented previously used modules, patterns, reusable APIs. Have these been Vulnerability tested? Build in the audit trail from the start - Fraud constraints and alarm triggers

- Stepcheck the release the through Agile, Auditology and DevOps teams with SecOps to ensure a collective agreement

- Stepcheck with Auditology (and legal) on releases success criteria

- Security should be built first and then customer features bolted on.

Transition (SecOps to daily check the incremental builds)

- Does the incremental build or release meet or exceed the Security Policy?

- What governance needs to be built around the build - does it meet external and internal standards?

- SecOps will test against OWASP, SANS, BSIMM and Cloud Assurance Controls

- Account Access - Unique users, passwords and permissions

- Build in segregation Safety and Hazard[180] controls - does this meet safe and secure barriers to the threat profiles?

- Test against all browsers and dumb devices

- Ensure Privacy and Legal Controls are built in

- Test accounts to be deleted before production

- Performance against storage and data retention

- How is data cleansed?

- Test on premises infrastructure first and then port to the Public Cloud

- Ensure all components and APIs can be performance measured and monitored

19.14.1.1 SECOPS TOOLKITS

There are thousands of automated scripts to detect security anomalies, but most of the time they are meaningless and not documented. Would it not be good to capture intrusions and have it fully documented? A forensics bash can take days to decipher and that is where we tend to go wrong; this forensics process needs automation. The Black Minute stable door is worth shutting after the horse has bolted. Is there a more intelligent way to do this?

19.14.1.2 SECURITY CONTROLS

In 2008, the National Security Agency (NSA) asked the same question, and began assessing which controls have the greatest impact in improving risk posture against real-world threats. In concert with a global consortium of agencies and experts from private industry, the SANS Institute created a list of 20 actionable controls with high payoff. These controls were derived from the most common attack patterns and vetted across a broad international community of governments and industries, with very strong consensus on cyber defence.

The resulting set of controls, are the basis for immediate high-value action. They provide your organisation with a framework or checklist, which must be part of your Security Policy

19.15 DISCIPLINED AGILE DELIVERY

Agile has been around since 2001. Usually IT projects are waterfall-based and tasks require finishing before the next one can start: a sequential approach. People used to call this the 'time box approach', or the traditional phase-gate approach to managing progress. The schedule remains fixed, and the work to be performed is the variable.

This type of project was based on infrastructure projects. For example, you cannot configure a router until the WAN (Wide Area Network) link is ready and the LAN (Local Area Network) cabling is ready, and you cannot configure a server until the LAN is IP ready, which means you need a router in place. With software building, code was based on a set of user requirements. These user requirements were needed to ensure the customer satisfaction was met by loading all the features needed into a pre-production model. As most IT PMs know, this can take months before a customer actually gets to see a software product, and then 80% of the time it didn't actually meet their needs. So the project gets to start all over again. When it comes to infrastructure getting a global network circuit ordered and installed can take up to a year depending on what part of the world you want the WAN circuit to terminate. In the 1990s and early decades of the 21st Century, IT projects were famous for failing. In addition, developers were held up by lack of infrastructure; getting a new server delivered could take six weeks out of a software development programme.

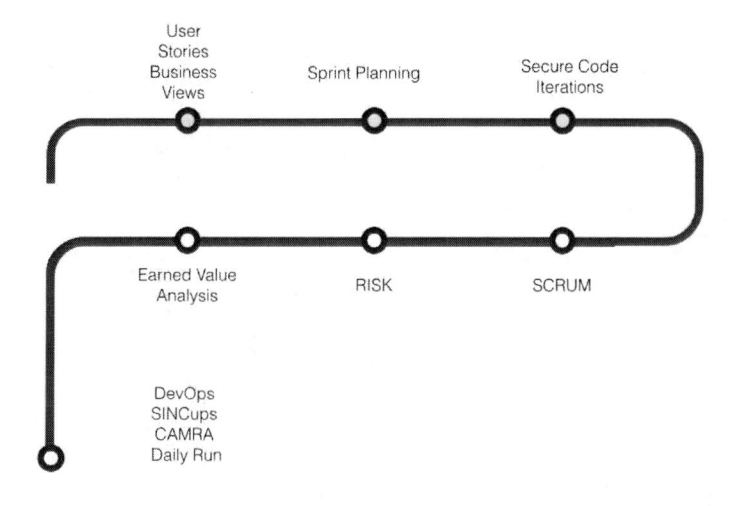

Figure 100 DAD HANDOFFS

19.16 MEASURING AGILE

Agile Measurements have been developed (http://www.sei.cmu.edu Technical Note CMU/SEI-2013-TH-029):

- Velocity: a measure of how much working software is delivered in each sprint (the time-boxed period of work)

- Sprint Burn-Down: a graphical depiction of the development team's progress in completing their workload (shown day-by-day, for each sprint as it happens)
Release Burn-Up: a graphical depiction of the accumulation of finished work (shown sprint- by-sprint)

The Agile team consists of a project manager, a facilitator, a domain expert, an independent tester, an integrator and a team of developers (usually paired and usually an experienced and a newbie). The PM usually takes an initial set of customer requirements (termed stories or views) and speedily implements the most visible of features so that users can quickly see them as prototypes. These stories can be gleaned from the owners and captains, alchemists, resolvers. The PM and the team agree daily their workload and the next feature set to be developed, so the most important capabilities of the software can be produced first to meet urgent needs, then implement the capabilities that represent the infrastructure needed to support the entire software capabilities when placed into production.

What's missing here is how the speed of development can be tested unless the infrastructure has been made available. This is why DevOps becomes important.

- Continuous Integration (CI) is the task of regularly integrating and testing the solution to incorporate changes made to its definition. Changes include updating the source code, changing a database schema, or updating a configuration file. Ideally when one or more changes are checked into your configuration management system, the solution is rebuilt (re-compiled), retested, and any code or schema analysis performed on it. Failing that, you should strive to do so at least once if not several times a day. Tools that are employed for this function include Cucumber (see www.cukes.info and specification)

- Continuous deployment (CD) complements CI by automatically deploying successful builds. For example, when the build is successful on a developer's workstation, he or she may automatically deploy changes to the project integration environment, which would invoke the CI system. A successful integration in that environment could trigger an automatic deployment into another environment and so on. In the Combat Ready IT Model, there is a step check to ensure code is securely built and goes to the SecOps Black Team for review before returning on the loop into the agile cycle. The CD and CI become co-join and become solid in DevOps.

On a developers' workstation the integration job could run at specific times, perhaps once an hour, or even better every time that he or she checks in something that is part of the build. This whole process of continuously integrating a developers code with the rest of the teams code and then running automated QA continues and maintains the cycle.

19.17 AGILE METRICS

19.17.1.1 TECHNICAL DEBT

Measures the Number of deficiencies in lines of code. Code needs a mechanism to test compiler errors and warnings. If the warnings are ignored, code becomes messy and unmaintainable. If code has security holes in it code becomes messy and the organisation becomes unmaintainable. The objective of Agile Ruggedized Code is to maintain a secure controllable codebase.

There's a term that was coined, 'Technical Debt', by Ward Cunningham in 1992. It's analogous to financial debt:

Financial Debt = Borrow Money against a future date
Technical Debt = Borrow Time against a future date.

In real terms this means that to adjust development time and costs to fix errors in the traditional way costs far less in an agile way. The Technical Debt is caused by legacy code and the expectations and manpower needed to make it work again. Fixing old code is painful and leads to massive outages. The ability to pay back debt depends on writing code that is clean enough to be able to re-factor as you come to understand your problem. Creating a controllable and audible code base reduces the need for extremely costly specialised programmers and a more flexible product set.

19.17.1.2 EARNED VALUE MANAGEMENT

It was a bit of a surprise when I started using EV as a measure that someone would turn this into a standard. Earned Value Management (EVM) has proven itself to be one of the most effective performance measurement and feedback tools for managing projects. Timely and targeted feedback can enable project managers to identify problems early and make adjustments that can keep a project on time and on budget. It enables managers to close the loop in the classic business formula, 'Plan, Do, Check, Act'. EVM uses the fundamental principle that patterns and trends in the past can be good predictors of the future.

EVM provides organisations with the methodology needed to integrate the management of project scope, schedule, and cost. It can play a crucial role in answering management questions that are critical to the success of every project, such as:

> Are we ahead of or behind schedule?
> How efficiently are we using our time?
> When is the project likely to be completed?
> Are we under or over our budget?
> What is the remaining work likely to cost?
> What is the entire project likely to cost?
> How much will we be under or over budget?

The project manager can use the EVM methodology to help identify:

> Where problems are occurring
> Whether the problems are critical or not
> What it will take to get the project back on track

- Calculate Planned Value. The planned value of the project must be known when calculating EVM. To calculate PV, multiply the average hourly rate by the total hours scheduled for the work. The planned hours are also called the budgeted cost of work scheduled (BCWS).

- Determine Actual Cost. The actual cost of the work performed (ACWP) is calculated by multiplying the average hourly rate by the actual total hours worked on the project. Calculating EVM is done whenever a company chooses to do so. Companies can calculate EVM at many times during the process.

- Calculate Earned Value. The earned value of the work is the total cost of the work as of the date reporting. EV is calculated by multiplying the BCWS by the percentage of actual work completed.

- Calculate the performance ratio. These previous three elements help a company determine the EVM of the work in progress. A performance ratio takes these elements a step further, allowing further insight into the company regarding the progress. This is calculated by taking the PV by the percentage of work completed. This amount is divided by the ACWP. If the answer is less than one, the company is underachieving. If the value is greater than one, the company is ahead of schedule.

- Determine cost variance. Another aspect in analysing EVM is calculated cost variances. The cost variance is calculated by subtracting EV minus AC, or BCWP minus ACWP. This variance tells whether the project is under or over budget

19.18 DEVOPS

What is DevOps? DevOps is an extension of agile methods that requires all the knowledge and skills necessary to take a project from inception through sustainment and contain project owners within a dedicated team. Surrounding TradOps teams are layers of middle and senior managers who prescribe processes to make things work. The more processes, the more people you need to create new processes, secure practices, Lean practitioners and so on. To help the process external consultants are needed, external auditors to tell management why they keep consistently going wrong. Some of these people you need, but most of them you do not. TradOps surround themselves with heavyweight monitoring products that just add problems, so a vicious cycle is created and everything is slow. DevOps cuts to the chase.

DevOps is viewed as the merging of Development and Operations, but it is a wee bit more than that. It really should be called Agilest because the two are so inter-related and co-dependent. For DAD to work it's necessary to have access to elastic compute and infrastructure, for DevOps to work containerised portable code needs to work in a simple and automated fashion.

TRADITIONAL OPS	DEVOPS
Slow MTTR (Mean Time To Repair)	Speed Of Delivery
Security Reworking	Secure Code At Start
Project Work Seen As Painful	More Time To Fix Craftflows
Slow To Deploy	Backlog Of Work Reduced
40% Fire fighting	20% Communicating
Rejects Change	Easy To Diagnose Big Faults
Poor Root Cause Analysis	Shorter Release
Endless Patches	Fewer Troublesome Installs
Excuse Glossary	Self-Determination
Reactive	PIE
Frustrated Clients	Happy Customers

The ability to spin up and tear down servers, memory and disk storage on demand for testing new software products is of supreme benefit. That's really how the Cloud became a hit so quickly. The main thrust of DevOps was a developer who had some expertise to create Cloud-based servers. From that grew a second set of applications and the ability to orchestrate and provision using standard scripts that could be replicated over and over again. That led to the belief that normal operations guys were not needed and DevOps as a discipline burst onto the scene.

The chasm of trust between DevOps and TradOps teams is still massive. DevOps are seen as reckless, engineers who don't document a single thing and ignore security. Because DevOps is embedded in the developer world, they manage to get problems solved quicker. Conversely, TradOps are slow to provision anything, networks, databases, servers and storage but have a raft of rigorous standards and processes to follow. However if you put developers in the TradOps world problems get solved quicker and are also documented.

When VOIP was integrating with mainstream PSTN (Cogs and Wheels Strowger support teams) I used to sit each VOIP team member with a PSTN counterpart alternately so that the best of both worlds would cross-train each other. Now for me I prefer having the programmers sitting amongst the operations teams anyway. The room is a lot quieter for a start. Ops teams tend to shout to get things done and the banter can be amusing but for development work when you are deep in code and patterns this can be the wrong sort of distraction.

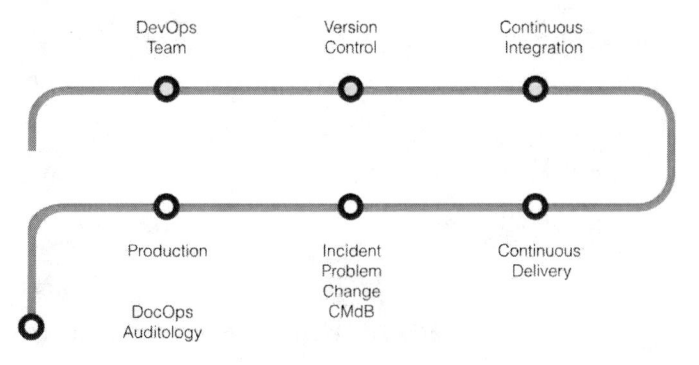

Figure 101 DEVOPS HANDOFFS

19.18.1.1 CAMS

- **'CAMS'** [181], an acronym describing the core values of the DevOps Movement: Culture, Automation, Measurement, and Sharing. Damon Edwards and John Willis at DevOpsDays Mountain View 2010 first espoused the values:

- **Culture** DevOps breaks down barriers between teams. An enormous amount of time is wasted with tickets sitting in queues, or individuals writing handoff documentation for the person sitting right next to them. In pathological organizations it is unsafe to ask other people questions or to look for help outside of official channels. In healthy organizations, such behaviour is rewarded and supported with inquiry into why existing processes fail. Fostering a safe environment for innovation and productivity is a key challenge for leadership and directly opposes our tribal managerial instincts.

- **Automation** Is the most visible aspect of DevOps. Many people focus on the productivity gains (output per worker per hour) as the main reason to adopt DevOps. But automation is used not just to save time, but also prevent defects, create consistency, and enable self-service.

- **Measurement** How can you have Perpetual Improvement without the ability to measure improvement? How do you know if an automation task is worthwhile? Basing decisions on data, rather than instinct, leads to an objective, blameless path of improvement. Data should be transparent, accessible to all, meaningful, and able to be visualized in an ad hoc manner.

- **Sharing** Key the success of DevOps at any organization is sharing the tools, discoveries, and lessons. By finding people with similar needs across the organization, new opportunities to collaborate can be discovered, duplicate work can be eliminated, and a powerful sense of engagement can be created among the team members. Outside the organization, sharing tools and code with people in the community helps get new features implemented in open source software quickly. Conference participation leaves team members feeling energized and informed about new ways to innovate.

DevOps effectively takes developer skill-sets (those who write scripts and programs) and allow them to do operational tasks such as deploying servers, creating and running user accounts and configuring databases and effectively takes over the system admin areas of infrastructure control. The culture around DevOps tries to emulate doing these tasks in a repeatable and automated way. Now there's nothing wrong with this approach, because for years the system admin tasks and roles have been driven by the plethora and complexity of server builds, monitoring and maintenance.

In the 90s we saw the emergence of LAN-based servers, or servers you could stuff in a cupboard and run a 100 man company on a single appliance. This helped spread the Novell's of this world, which enabled these LANs to be connected and create campus-type networks. As time went on we needed a server for every single task: one for mail, one for database, one for applications, that servers proliferated and then this demanded a new breed of operations teams to maintain these. Usually the ratio was 1 to 10 servers (1 ops guy to manage ten servers). In the year 2000 I worked in a facility with 12,000 servers and 600 operational people and 2000 software developers. In fact the ops guys were a waste of space, as they never really maintained these servers properly. In fact, they waited for the server or service to stop and simply rebooted the server until something worked again, and all they did was moan about how boring their job was. You make your bed and lie in it!

19.18.1.2 CONTINUOUS INTEGRATION AND DELIVERY

Continuous Integration (CI) is now a central process of most agile development efforts because it's been waiting for the right tool sets to be delivered. CI started out as a way of minimising code integration deficits. It purports frequent code integrations rather than punt big code changes into production. These small chunks of code are deployed by DevOps (after code and security checks) into pre-production servers and compiled. Automation was the big selling point for CI. Tasks that would previously have been manual, error-prone and time-consuming could now be done automatically. These automated tools cannot only deploy builds, but also check performance on deployments to multiple environments (different OS etc.). This eliminates human error, and software can be made more secure and more rugged.

Years ago Microsoft used a 'Solid Code' mantra to ensure their GUI behaved and third party applications writers followed basic rules of thumb. In the Agile and DevOps worlds there are similar tenets. "Building solutions to handle adversity will cause unintended, positive benefits that will provide value that would have been unrealised otherwise."(James Wickett).[182]

People want security but probably guess they can never get it, which begs the question "Why Not"? Is it because most coders are lazy, put in mimic code, or resort to cut-and-paste programming to get that business function needed so badly, and generally don't devote more than 5% of their time ensuring security. That's probably why the cycle of backdoors still pervades today's code. Rugged Software is an approach to try and solve these basic issues. The Rugged Code approach uses the 6 'Rs:

19.18.2 THE 6 X RS OF RUGGED DEVOPS

- Repeatable - No Manual Steps, CI

- Reliable - No DOS here

- Reviewable - Auditology, Infrastructure as Code

- Rapid - Fast to build, deploy, restore

- Resilient - Automated Reconfiguration

- Reduced-Limited attack surface

The adoption of Rugged gives the following security benefits:

1. Absence of events through verification of quality
2. Lower cost
3. Positive
4. Reduced FUD through known values
5. Reduced toxicity
6. Improved configuration management

In the Combat Ready IT Model it goes two steps further, a Black Team security check and post-production an audit check.

The Black Team Security Check should use the OWASP (Open Web Application Security Project) Top 10 that continually provides not only the Top 10 threats listed below, but also deep guides on AppSec and modular security.

19.18.3 DEVOPS ASSURING CODE

We have to make security testing, intrusion detection, prevention and response, and run time protection a part of every application. To do this and not hamper the Agile and DevOps worlds, we need to get their code releases security-hardened before they go to Release Management. The SecOps Black Team should also apply BSIMM.

Any code that gets to production needs to have satisfied all the OWASP Top Ten and SAFE code mitigations and a plethora of lethal security issues hidden in custom code and libraries. Tools are starting to emerge which automate this process, such as Contrast Security and Veracode. This service can be run in the Cloud or on premises.

19.19 CONTINUOUS DELIVERY

DevOps starts out as writing simple scripts to help you out of immediate operational problems, for instance a database on a particular server has created abnormal numbers of temporary files and these need to be flushed from the system daily to avoid corruption. Another example is applying consistent role-based authorities for a user across several applications. In the Windows world the problems with DNS and DHCP are always badly managed by system admins. In one company I consulted at, the entire system had not been changed for six years, which led to a year's project to clean the names out. Most companies experience a churn of around 20 to 30% annually, this means bar the core 10% that keep a company going most people stay for a three-year tenure. If these accounts are not retired properly then all sorts of historic accesses can leave a company open to ex-employees.

19.20 DEVOPS TOOLS

No matter what we believe of DevOps, this initiative now has a lot of 'cheap' tools to help in the release management, provisioning, orchestration and delivery.

- MaestroDev
- Puppet
- Chef
- Unusable
- SaltStack
- RANCID
- Ubuntu Juju

These tools are real value for money compared with the monolithic provisioning tools that exist today. Besides costing millions to deploy, these legacy products need highly specialised teams to run them. In the Windows world there are Microsoft's SCCM and SCOM – products designed to spin up servers and desktop images and then distribute them. The infrastructure needed to support such tools is significant. They are not bad solutions once they get going, and great as a first step into automation.

Finally DevOps would be the Tier 1 for most trouble tickets. The service help desk team that still sits in the ITIL-bound world will send tickets directly to the DevOps and SINCups teams for validation and resolution: the two teams are also representative of the Problem and Change Management processes. Also, alarms created by SecOps and sensors deployed in the CAMRA world will kick off automated tickets during alarming situations. In addition, for change to happen, it needs to be documented.

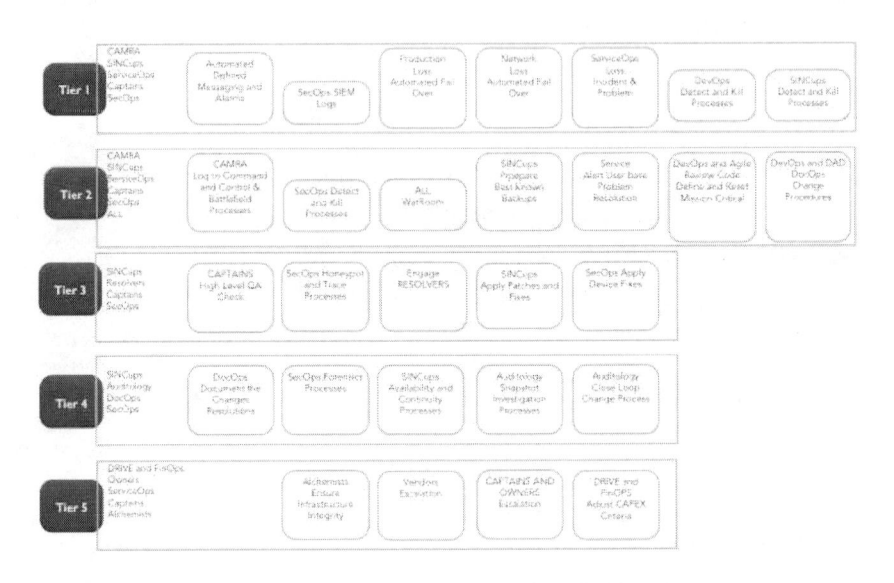

Figure 102 - 5 x TIERS RESOLUTION WORKFLOW

19.21 DOCOPS

There are Intranets, Documentum, GITHUB, and SharePoint products that provide effective document-sharing capabilities throughout an organisation. The main problem with these is not making everything shareable. In addition, they are usually stuffed to the brim with voluminous reports that take hours or days to check out and download, read and even print. For front-line operators such as ServOps teams this can be a nightmare to wade through 60 page reports during an emergency.

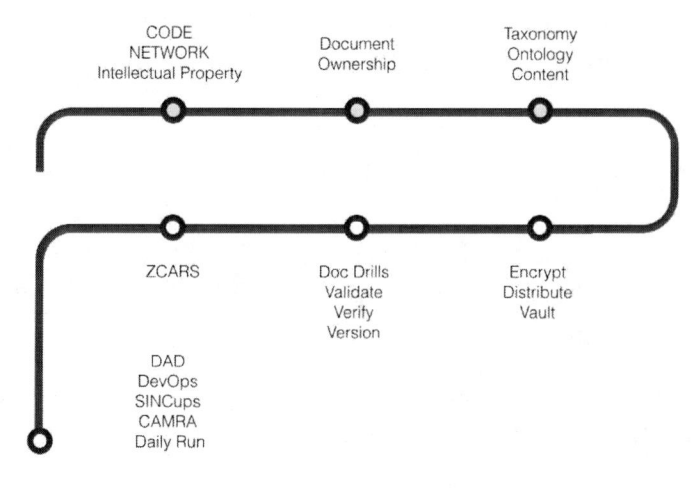

```
        CODE                                  Taxonomy
       NETWORK          Document              Ontology
   Intellectual Property  Ownership           Content


        ZCARS           Doc Drills            Encrypt
                        Validate              Distribute
                        Verify                Vault
                        Version
         DAD
        DevOps
        SINCups
        CAMRA
       Daily Run
```

Figure 103 DOCOPS HANDOFFS

Before we go any further on this subject you will hear a concerted moan from every part of the organisation, like truculent teenagers who have been grounded. **Yes, everything needs to be documented, yes, it needs an audit trail, no, and it does not have to be a mini novel.** Most stories, code bytes, network configurations can be reduced to a page. Most policies, (SOPs) Stepchecks or Craftflows can be put on a single page. It just needs a bit of mental juggling to squeeze down the bulk of words to the relevant information. There is a company that helps in this process (Information Mapping) but it doesn't really go far enough. Why stick to this single page mantra? Think of an iPDA type device with a set of Craftflows and stepchecks. In an emergency, would I want to go through 60 pages for the solution to troubleshoot and reset a certain device? How much time and data storage does one need to devote to this? Why do we need paper at all I hear? Well, you need paper because in times of conflict you need start-up instructions for systems in an emergency.

As I've mentioned, Churchill used to say "If you cannot express it on one page then it's not necessary". Let's put a myth to bed right now: documentation is essential. In a communication's melee the only recourse to an IT

Guide is that which is on paper. Technical authors are rare beasts nowadays; most were scalped out of the IT departments globally after the 1992 recession. But documentation has to be done – it's how you do it that matters.

Reports do not need to be 60 pages long. Brevity is King.

- The indexing and filing process can take more time than in a paper based process
- Typical systems limit the customer to only a few indexing criteria
- Documents do not have a hierarchy of signatures and are not owned by Senior Management - anything can be read by the entire company if not controlled

Summary: do systems limit the customer to only 'paperless' because the processes are too labour-intensive and there are no time and cost savings? Typical DMS systems have the only advantage that documents can be retrieved quicker, not more readable.

Even better, once you have identified the taxonomy and ontology of a document management system and its three superiors who are responsible for sign off, change, and archiving of the document, life gets easy. In organisations where ZCARS is needed (Zero Content at Rest) is a term I employed in a financial house to stop printing of secure documents and is the same as the TV police show in the 1960s – you won't remember that obviously). Each document is also managed in a single vault. The best place (and tool) for managing this is your CMdB. The document becomes a CMdB item (or child) and has a CMdB configuration number. No need for massive document-sharing products and becomes completely secure. It also shows the document is checked out and new versions are assigned a new CMdB number, so a history and audit trail is available for audits – simple. All CMdBs are capable of handling docs as Configuration Items (CIs). This availability and management of documentation allows all configurations to be managed and updated. A CI is logically linked to another or multiple other CIs.

Network diagrams are best kept on a single page. Routers can be displayed in an upstream and downstream link together with the key code attributes. This means that a hacker will need all the pages and CIs necessary to complete a fully loaded CI. IP addresses are kept within the organisation and locked down in the CMdB. This allows Service to retrieve essential data and service a trouble ticket. Also when an alarm is set off in the monitoring system and an IP address is alarmed, the CI can be forwarded to all team members with the configuration documentation attached, thus saving bucket-loads of time trying to find what's on a particular server (including applications, data etc.).

In our Hybrid Cloud and Public Cloud secure network we would classify all secret classification documents to be encrypted and password locked. All other documents can be stored in the Public storage and encrypted.

19.22 SINCUPS

SINC stands for:

- Servers
- Information
- Network
- Continuity

Simply put, this is the synchronisation handoffs between the physical Hybrid infrastructure, Information and Data base management, development and DevOps.

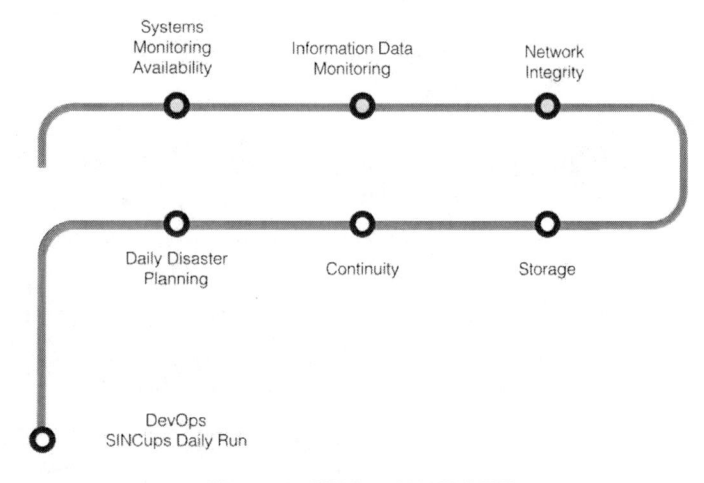

Figure 104 SINCups HANDOFFS

Why on earth would you want these guys in place? This team is responsible for the on going monitoring of key systems and data and Tier 2/3 resolutions of trouble tickets. The argument here is that it is a step check and validation on DevOps activities (rather a maintenance of duties and not segregation). The beauty of DevOps is thousands of systems can be set up and built by a single DevOps engineer. In auditing, this is lethal and open to abuse. Secondly, in a Hybrid and Public Cloud scenario you need to segregate some duties to ensure that steady secure practices are in place. Thirdly, this is an olive branch to the experienced TradOps world. We are talking individuals here and not teams. This is a hands-on management role that requires deep technical expertise. Servers need closely managing and documenting. Configurations in a virtualised world may need manual intervention; most times a DevOps explorer cannot do justice on this. The role traces the configuration changes and can make configuration changes based on availability and utilisation – this ability to Lock Out and Tag Out on highly secure servers meets most of the requirements that are must-haves for PCI, military and HIPAA standards.

Information SINCups is the replacement for the DBAs and other data explorers like Business Intelligence. The need to manage batches and Big Data queries is not a task that can be taken lightly. Setting up queries can take hours and monitoring progress even longer. The Information SINCups explorer can manage community and middleware batches and queries. This is the role that manages the CMdB and e-mail using automation tools as it are envisaged that these applications will be mostly based on-premise. Restoration of Essential Data Only (REDO) is the key role for Information SINCups.

The Network SINCups ensures bandwidth costs and utilisation. The internal and external network still needs this function. Do not outsource your network to large global Telco's and make them responsible for the uptime SLA. In a conflict scenario you may need to re-route traffic on a dime spin so this function is needed to maintain all IP transmissions including VOIP and Mobile Continuity. If you don't have a disaster plan and you have not tested it you are a disaster waiting to happen. In conflict you will be invariably done up like a kipper. The two main thrusts of Continuity are RPO and RTO, Recovery Point Objective and Recovery Time Objective. These are both prescribed in ISO 17799.

The Maximum Tolerable Period of Disruption is the maximum amount of time a company can go before its reputation or overall relevancy will be seriously questioned. MTPODs vary greatly based on industry. For a Telco, the MTPOD cannot be more than a few days before subscribers start to leave. The Blackberry outages are an example of this customer churn, but for a manufacturing plant the MTPOD can be as long as there is still inventory in a warehouse. Additionally, if there is a great deal of publicity focused on your company post incident, investors will become wary of your company's ability to recover. There are a plethora of consultants available to help you here.

In a cloudified world, Recovery is seen as snapshots and cross-Cloud backups. If you run a Hybrid and Public Cloud, the ability to store essential data once and then replicate many times is viewed as an ideal scenario as long as data is not sent outside of legal jurisdiction. Snapshots of a server and its Essential Data configuration on virtual machines can be run say once every 20 minutes. This allows an operator to move the server to another blade or even to another data centre. So Restoring Essential Data Only (REDO) in a Virtual Storage Cloud service can mean your organisation surviving most catastrophic events. As long as the data plane remains intact, there is no reason why other Clouds cannot restore this data on another set of Cloud servers. The interoperability between

Clouds have still to be ratified but with the CSP world there should be geographic locations that could be viable sites. With the vStorage feature a set of viable products now available, the ability to cut over and failover to back up systems from a production service should be tested and drilled at least once a month. There is no excuse for this to be overlooked any more. The mix of Hybrid and Public Cloud interworking gives a high degree of availability and fault tolerance at a reasonable cost. Drills on mission critical systems and accompanying Essential Data to hot standby servers should nullify the need for RPO and RTO metrics. Metrics reporting drill timings and successful MTTR (Mean Time To Repair), restoration of service, code and deployment quality should be fed directly into the Command and Control dashboard. Downtime should actually finish off with a Customer Recommencement of Work metric. This should be available daily rather than a monthly exercise that is presented to the owner. The ability to see a high level view of what's occurring on your goal system or network is imperative to correct and timely decisions being made by owners and captains.

19.23
CAMRA - OMNIOCULAR SNAPSHOTS

The Continuous Active Monitoring Real Time Audit (CAMRA) concept is a must for all organisations. The ability for an operation's department to see what's really happening on the entire estate (Omniocular) can help prevent Black Minutes and blank screens and create a forensics trail so real time traffic monitoring is acted on immediately. Alarming as it may sound, it's helpful for displays to show the red services and help operators commence a drill down even before a trouble ticket starts. This does not mean a super array of TV screens in a Network Operating Centre: the NASA (and Euston) type wall of screens has long gone. The days of swivel chair management have gone, leaving us with the single pane of glass approach. It should be the single pain! Due to the nature of the Cloud, combined with global networking, an azimuthal view of the estate is more appropriate. Active in-band and out-of-band monitoring can get IT in predictive mode - this is the nub of Combat Ready IT.

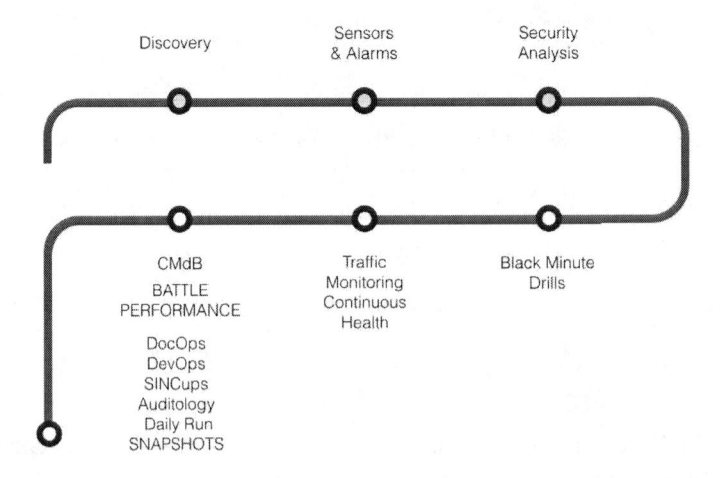

Figure 105 CAMRA HANDOFFS

The concept of *continuous monitoring* has been gaining momentum, driven by both compliance mandates (notably PCI-DSS) and the US Federal Governments guidance on Continuous Diagnostics and Mitigation.[183] As a way and means to move beyond periodic assessment. This makes sense, given the speed that attacks can proliferate within your company environment instantaneously. Although this is a great initiative, it still rings of 1997. Before you intend to go down this route, there is a new wave of equally robust Open Source solutions available. The purpose though for CAMRA is to monitor Cloud activity as well as on-premise events. There are numerous Open Source products available and very robust tools to manage and snapshot activities across both platforms. Supplementing security tools and correlating suspicious activity can strengthen the organisation's security position. Configuration changes sent from DevOps are first placed in the DocOps queue and then forwarded to be analysed and approved by Auditology completes the cycle.

AUDITOLOGY

Here is where Auditology kicks in. Auditology is the appliance of Multi-Dimensional Attack Scenarios, Handoff Mining Continuity, Predictive Auditing, Visualisation and Sandbox Analytics. Annual auditing is good and should still be maintained (but at a reduced outlay) the focus should be on daily tasks to eliminate the Black Minute.

The problem with annual audits is they give everyone a false sense of security that everything is hunky dory; the action plans that are left behind soon get committed of the year long tasks in the risk register and people wonder what the annual month of audit pain is about when nothing gets done until the next audit comes around. I seem to remember a major financial bank collapsed two weeks after a signed-off business and IT audit.

The final piece in this closed loop process. It usually has two teams Green teams constantly review Configuration Management and dovetails this with the DevOps and DAD and SINCups teams on a daily step check, and a Yellow team responsible for the Continuous Audit. Both teams ensure continuity of linkage the investigation of change and financial impacts to the business. Checking SAP and ERP changes for spurious activities.

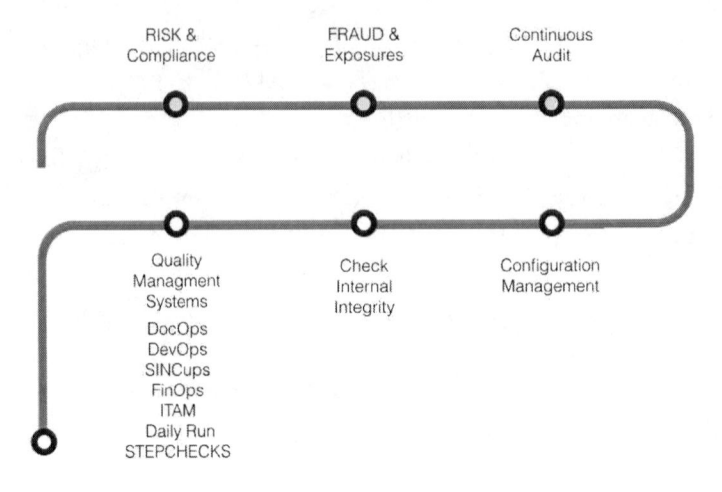

Figure 106 AUDITOLOGY HANDOFFS

Their prime objective is to eradicate Insider activity that accounts for 30% of cyber attacks.

Why would any size organisation require constant auditing? Well here's the nub of the problem: events like Black Minutes can happen 525,600 times until your next annual audit.

It got me thinking that all this great expertise was being brought into an organisation a year after it really mattered. Then it also made me contemplate that the reason organisations are open and waiting to be hacked is the "Plan Do" is being done, but not the "Check Act" elements of Deming's cycle. Organisations plan, build processes and get down to the delivery level, then it all falls to mush, as we never check it's been done so we can Act on it effectively. This then got me thinking the reasons behind the lack of quality that exists in every IT organisation that is evident everywhere.

From the previous chapters a picture should have emerged that Cybrid attack techniques are real-time incidents. That is, companies' and governments' IT systems are in reactive mode against potential attacks. The traditional approach to risk management and auditing has been an annual visit from an external or internal auditor to check compliance and recommend remedial actions. This is sufficient where an infrastructure does not change from year to year, or expect insider threats to occur. Obviously this is futile, where the average trouble ticketing system that records changes in an organisation says the entire IT infrastructure changes 80% on an annual basis. So churn on a single server in a year could demonstrate at least 292 changes (recorded or not) annually. It's OK to satisfy and justify a process audit, but deep down we all know that IT changes every three weeks and any application in an enterprise-wide environment will experience a 20% sea change annually. It also assumes that risk management has correctly assessed the quantitative and qualitative approaches. To be honest, I have worked in companies with large internal audit departments and even larger security departments undertake a full-blown audit on a 12-month cycle. The intention of risk is to identify the BIG projects and put them in a quarterly validated risk register in collaboration with an IT department SMB (Subject Matter Expert). The risk register is presented to the CIO and the board annually, to build out essential budget benchmarks and then include them in the Program Management life cycle.

In real time, Risk Ignition Points, and probability may change in a nanosecond. In finance, transactions risk and operations can be prone to errors. So under 'Auditology' we need a different mechanism to gauge the level of risk, to aid decision fixes at a DevOps level or program level whilst satisfying existing IT frameworks and certificated ISO standards for IT And Security compliance. The mechanism to input to the risk register needs to be, in business-speak, demonstrable. Most security officers build probability as if it were a hazard in terms of safety. But even if we apply design theories, business leaders, owners and lenders make qualitative decisions. Let's be honest here! The house built on sand needs electricity. If the utility has been broken by a high tide, breaking the feed, a quadratic equation isn't going to help you here. In your mind you know you will be without the feed and will probably get a bill for $5000 to contribute to emergency restoration of service. So what is more important over time is to predict the monetary reserves necessary to maintain service continuity.

Now Continuous Auditing has been around for decades, but it is viewed as a tool and not a working function. The intent is to provide reasonable assurance that the control structure surrounding the operational environment is: Suitably designed, Established and Operating as intended.

Years ago I came up with a model to help find the unit price of downtime by service, a simplistic show-and-tell to management that displayed revenue leakage and bottom line impact. Ops guys and marketers could quickly ascertain the cost of service, downtime and remediation and customer satisfaction. This TIMPY model is created for each product and:

- Risk

- Brand exposure

- Customers impacted

- Customer trust

- Revenue loss

- Ops unit cost

Team x **I**nfrastructure x **M**aintenance x **P**roduct price x **Y**ellow team cost to fix (TIMPY).

19.23 AUDITOLOGY ROLES AND RESPONSIBILITIES

The role of Auditologists is to perpetually monitor service and costs and gauge the operational cost balance in line with FinOps expectations. Tom Nolle, the president of CIMI Corp.wrote[184]:

Internal auditors are endlessly frustrated because every time they nail down compliance and governance methods for an application, changes render their model obsolete. The Cloud can be a special source of frustration with governance because it changes the most fundamental of all assumptions in IT: My stuff is running here, under my control. Ensuring that governance methods survive a Cloud transition means following three steps:

- Assessing how much you depend on physical security and access

- Evaluating your governance methodologies for Cloud's weaknesses

- Making sure your governance changes are final

Many companies rely on control of their physical facilities to frame the critical security and compliance strategies that form the foundation of internal governance. No application-level protection mechanism or encryption strategy will defeat a simple theft of a backup tape or direct meddling with software versions. However, nearly all-major Cloud providers have very specific certifications for security and compliance -- including ISO and specific ones for financial and health care.

"Cloudifying" your governance practices means finding out what your proposed provider and other viable competitors offer. It's critical to know whether you have governance practices that are "fragile," or might fall short of regulations in case you switch providers. There are companies that specialise in tracking global compliance requirements, which are a good resource for companies considering all areas in which they may be at risk.

In the Combat Ready IT Model the Auditology team provides the WWW (Who's Watching Who) element to close many of the loops and teams' endpoint deliveries. This team manages the fraud and risk elements of the enterprise and monitors the SecOps Teams. But it's not team members with grey hair men in grey suits wandering in with questionnaires once a year (it may be, but they have to be visible and contribute daily). The Auditology team acts on stories and views and ensures the drills and Performance Metrics are actually managed each day. This team should act as the font of all quality processes and procedures, but does not exonerate them from automation. Using tools like Black Duck, the team can:

- Receive a more thorough and accurate analysis than possible through manual annual audits

- Identify encryption technologies that can impact and restrict the legal export of acquired software

- Make modifications and quickly remediate any potential issues

- Identify security vulnerabilities that can impact software asset value

- Monitor legal ramifications of encryption techniques

The team is the Data and Privacy Office and should provide the SPOC (Single Point of Contact) for all public security fears and questions. This is a major shift departure from even large vendors do not have an addressable place for customers concerns on their websites (have you ever tried to send a security alert message to a vendor - no site has a public facing repository to send this to) and should be remedied!

19.24 SERVOPS

The heart of Combat Ready IT is vastly superior level of service. Step timings between levels are dramatically reduced. Remember the whole model pivots around the Black Minute threat. That does not mean each team should sign up to an Internal Operational Level Agreement and an Organisation-facing Service Level Agreement. These should detail all the various service and product timings so all the teams can meet their targets, be measurable and get their bonuses.

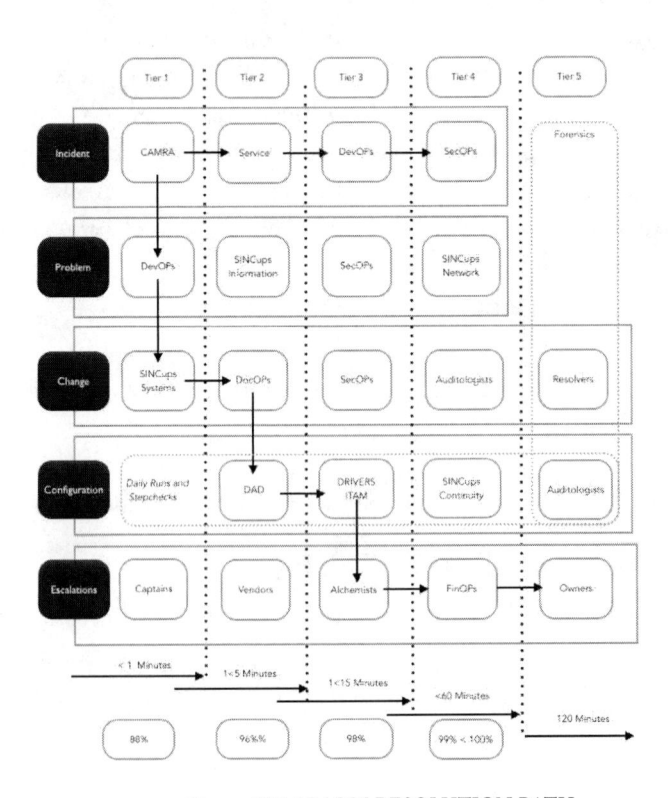

Figure 107 ALARM RESOLUTION PATH

19.24.1.1 INCIDENTS AND ALARMS

80% to 90% of trouble tickets can be cured through providing a self-service front end to the Help Desk. IT Service and Support Management Tools that align with ITIL v3 processes (BMC MyIT, Rocket Aldon, LANDesk are my top three, followed by BMC Remedy, Service Now and others like Axios Systems, CA Technologies, Cherwell Software, EasyVista, FrontRange Solutions, Hornbill, HP, IBM, LANDesk also provide this feature). Your help desk team invariably doesn't need a small army of agents to man the help desk 24/7. Avoid bloated ITSM implementations – I have seen some that take 45 minutes to log a trouble ticket via e-mail.

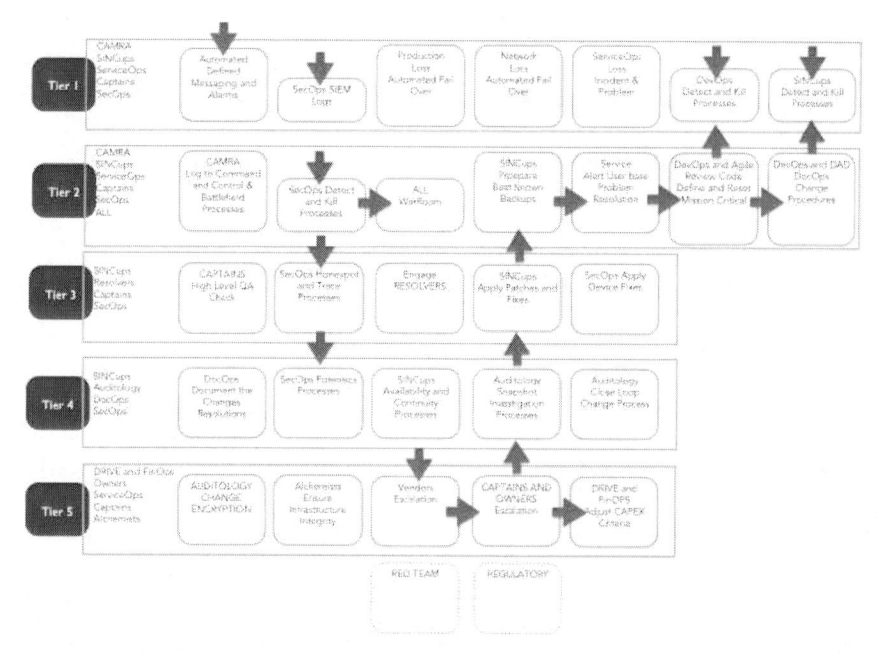

Figure 108 DEVOPS RESOLUTION PATH

With CAMRA and SecOps and Configuration working in sync, picking up spurious traffic and network maladies is instantaneous. It's the level of alarms and arm alerting criteria that need careful management here. I have seen TradOps just turn these alarms off, so nothing happens until everything is red!

19.25 OPEN SOURCE SAUCE

I have been waiting 30 years for Hewlett Packard to produce a product called Sauce. 20 years ago HP Openview was an amazing product and still reigns for the products' diversity. In the meantime, I believed Open Source software to be clunky and nightmarish to deploy and maintain. The companies that now use Open Source as a flagship development platform and then build commercial offerings around it are becoming really interesting. Products look solid, rugged and cohesive. When I started to devise Combat Ready IT, I discovered mature worthy alternatives to many legacy products and seemed to suit SMB requirements. To support the Combat Ready IT model I reviewed as many products as humanly possible to see how they would underpin the technology driven model. The result was very interesting.

Typically in organisations and mainly in enterprises, when you think of buying a software product, the starting point is a million (in whatever currency). 80% of the tools suggested here are way below that plucked-from-the-air figure and are free, with commercial versions really worth investing in! This is a task for the resolvers and the alchemists to sift through and create the base business case as you apply the mode

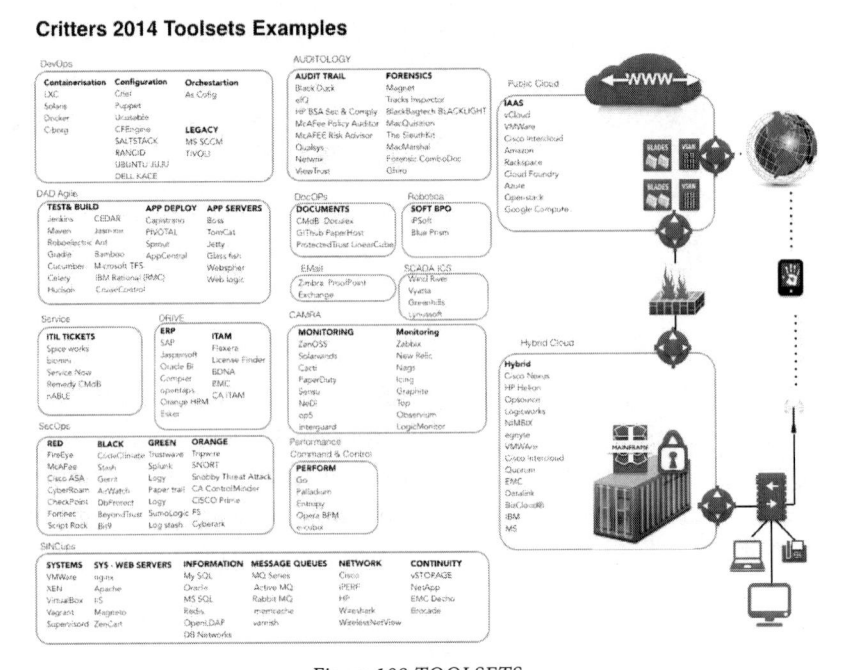

Figure 109 TOOLSETS

19.26 IMPLEMENT COMBAT READY IT
JFDI!

I recently visited a 2,000 strong global company. They said to me that they lost $10,000 a *second* in revenue when a single server went down. When I recommended the Combat Ready IT approach they sucked air through their teeth and said, "It's too cheap"!

Obviously all three statements are a nonsense and laughable. Then I piped up with "Well, your architecture is wrong because you let the server go down in the first place, you can do more with less people and not the 3000 outsourced IT team members that made the server go down, and if you don't consider this then your strategy, like your old strategies, is skewed."

Implementing large frameworks is expensive that's well known. Growing a predictive IT service is an easier route. You just need to take a deep breath and get everyone concerned around the table and just go for it. If your company is under 1000 people then this structure can make a lot of sense to you and it also scales to the large enterprises.

Start with DevOps and some supporting tools like Puppet or Chef, and try it out on a Public Cloud or virtualise your old estate. You will soon see the benefits of this approach and how ultimately the payback is in weeks not months.

19.27 ROLES AND RESPONSIBILITIES

ROLES	RESPONSIBILITIES
OWNER	Responsible for all Team Members HR PIE Governance Security Policy SHAZOPS
CAPTAIN 1	Prime Focus for Team Members Facilitates Teamings Hybrid/Public Virtualisation Proponent Handoffs KPIs Change Management
CAPTAIN 2	Secondary Focus for Team Members Facilitates Teamings Business/Line of Business Relationship Demand Management Craftflows Segregation of Duties
AGILE PROJECT MANAGER	Disciplined Agile Development Scrums EVM and Technical Debt Risk Facilitates Teamings Robotica Business Views/Subscriber Stories
AGILE DEVELOPER	Secure Code Development QA Release and Test Prototyping and UED
ALCHEMIST	Strategic Views Operational Views Glueprints and Patterns Perpetual Improvement Initiatives CMdB ERP
AUDITOLOGIST	VIA FERRATA Risk FREXAGON Management Continuous Audit Configuration Management PIE Quality Management Systems
CAMRA	Management of Omniocular estate Security Analysis Discovery CMdB Battle Performance PIE KPIs
DocOPs	Information Classification Document Owner Management Zero Content at Rest (ZCARS) Encryption Taxonomy Ontology of Document Management System

DevOps	Orchestration and Continuous Delivery
	Continuous Integration
	Change Management
	Shell Scripts and Programme Automatism
	Automation Modelling Patterns
	Maintenance
DRIVE	Vendor Risk Management
	IT Asset and Software Asset Management
	Technical Steering Committee
	Regulation
	Contract Management
FinOPs	Price per Port/Service
	Cloud Volume and Bandwidth Variable Costs
	Budget
	Compensation, Bonus
	CAPEX and OPEX expenditure
	Balance Sheet
RESOLVERS	Cloud Performance Management
	Safety and Security Engineering
	Service Desk Catalogue
	Innovation
	Product and Portfolio Management
SecOps RED	Continuous Vulnerability Test
	Continuous Penetration Test
	Blue Team – INCIDENT RESPONSE
	Mobile Security
	Domino DID
SecOps BLACK	Security Plan
	Secure Coding
	Continuous Monitoring
	Domino DID
	Assurance Test
SecOPs GREEN	Security Policy and Governance
	VIA FERRATA Risk Reporting
	Framework
	Regulation
	Authorise Architecture
SecOPs ORANGE	Subscriber Management
	Identity Management
	Encryption
	Communications Security
	Data Loss Prevention
ServOps	Subscriber Management
	Service KPIs
	Service Desk
	SLAs and OLAs
	Services Portfolio
SINCups CONTINUITY	End to End Service
	Monthly Back Up
	Drills
	BCDR
	Capacity and Availability
	Existential Risk

SINCups INFORMATION	End to End Service DBMS STORAGE Storage Virtualisation
SINCups NETWORKS	End to End Service IP addressing Schema SDN Capacity and Availability Incident Problem Change Physical Checks
SINCups SYSTEMS	End to End Service DRIIPS TRANSITION Incident Problem Change CMdB Capacity and Availability

20 PARTHIAN SHOT

Combat Ready IT and PIE 2015 is a base camp – it provides the starting blocks for a predictive environment. This book will be reissued for Combat Ready IT 2016, so please send your feedback and comments to me. At info@combatreadyit.com

20.1.1 WHAT HAVE YOU LEARNT?

I hope you have learned at least one good thing from this book?

There will be a conflict, and it will start to escalate through the coming summer. The Cold War II has started, and the eastern powers are converging. As these powerhouses merge, the need to provide the populace with food and fridges means high demand for fuels and new energies. New energy sources mean new territories. In the west, our infrastructure is being attacked every minute by a source we cannot even see or legally tie down. However organisations try to measure this risk, the problem lies in the fact that the western powers give away the crown jewels to the east to manufacture and maintain, be that hard goods or intellectual goods. This is the basis for disaster, and the next Cybrid War and the crisis have already begun.

The sources of the software that vendors have been peddling are inherently insecure, and this is the root cause for the majority of attacks. As yet, the vendors have ignored the fact that key data from organisations and personal data from individuals are in the hands of adversaries already.

20.1.2 KEY TAKEAWAYS FOR SMBS

Prepare for conflict. Learn from the past; understand the cycles of Boom and Bust and how inevitably war follows. Create strategies, policies and solutions to protect assets and reduce the likelihood of losses from operational risks.

Drill scenarios and create crisis and resilience plans to minimise the impact of an event to acceptable levels and safeguard reputations in times of crisis – the key here is to assume 50% of your team members are unavailable for work. Get the right people. Review, audit, and benchmark all the existing arrangements to identify gaps or misaligned resources.

Build the right sized IT team and automate production via 'robotica' and deploy AI in repetitive tasks.

Move data underground.

Make the network bulletproof and secure.

Drill for the Black Minute and get the forensics process in place.

Automate Everything.

Perpetual Improvement Everywhere not only transforms the TVC - it will transform your business!

20.1.3 IT TO TVC?

The recession has hit IT team members hard, and the disciplines and frameworks that are relied on to bring some semblance of sanity are falling to pieces. Consider thinking differently about Innovation and Value Creation:

1. Build the right defences to manage out Malware.

2. Make the organisation Progressive, Preventative and Predictive.

3. Make sure your RISK knowledge protects the business.

4. Build a Hybrid infrastructure and be selective in the Cloud.

5. Dump the desktop and move to tablets.

6. Dump cabling and move to Wi Fi.

7. Continuous Auditing, Continuous Configuration and Continuous Service. Perpetually Improve Everywhere

8. Motivate your team members and make IT attractive again.

9. Smart Documentation.

10. Automate Everything.

11. PIE

12. Save Money and Make Money but do it Securely

20.2 FIN

The Combat Ready IT model helps you meet and exceed the majority of IT Security Governance frameworks.

Governments Telco's, CSPs and ISPs: the Internet must change to meet the demands of global subscribers and end cyber insecurity – change it before it gets changed for you by someone else!

Finally, the Golden Wave of the SMB is starting so now is a very good time to get your Innovation house in order. The Artisan Age and Roboshoring can only be a positive time for SMBs. Build your Knowledge, your team member's security culture now.

----------- Bonne chance profiter de votre métier---------

21 FREQUENTLY ASKED QUESTIONS

Will the number of Cybrid instances increase?
Conflicts are increasing - Yes, and as IT teams become less able to cope, more data breaches will occur.

Is this scaremongering?
I was afraid you would ask that! The world seems to be hitting a prolonged depression. After all depressions comes a traditional war; it's in our nature to follow the zombie cycle. When I started to research this book I believed the topic would remain just technical and focus on IT Operational models, then as the number of cyber-attacks rose after the Russian incursion into the Ukraine, the Greek crisis emerged to herald a triple dip. New infrastructure solutions were released I changed the slant of the book. When I saw how bad cyber-warfare had got, I decided that drastic re-organisation was necessary.

Why does the Combat Ready IT Model have only 30 IT team members?
In reality that's all you need. This number of team members relies on Hybrid Cloud technologies and automation tools and the number of devices that need supporting. In reality, this number of team members depends on what the organisation wants to achieve. The organisation chart does not need to change, and unless you are implementing ITIL, the number in the Combat Ready IT Model does not really need to change beyond the baseline.

Is Cloud infrastructure cheap?
Buyers beware! Get on top of usage-based pricing. A heavy server can cost over $20k per annum plus bandwidth usage and storage volume increases. You need to be very aware of bandwidth utilisation, as some Cloud Service Providers use this as extras. That's why I recommend building a Hybrid and interworking with a Public Cloud. Essential Data needs to be close to the IT department (sometimes for legal reasons).

What is REDO?
Not all data is necessary. Restoration of Essential Data Only is a way of saving data storage costs in the Cloud, and it also relies on data retention policies. By Essential Data I mean the code for running manufacturing or robots or any process mechanisms. This is ED (Financial and Intellectual Property). The stuff you don't need is probably 80% of e-mail data.

We have a lot of legacy tools and spent millions deploying them. Why should we change tack all of a sudden?
I have seen $100 million spent on one Network Monitoring tool over a period of 8 years. It took 12 programmers to change an alarm, and the licence's annual renewal made your wallet cry. Most of the tools are ZERO CAPEX or need a monthly subscription. 80% are Open Source and free, and can be superior in many ways to legacy systems.

Why have four teams in SecOps?
Most companies hire a single security officer if you can find one. I would rather have 4 keen team members than a SPOF. Securities first, then build out the infrastructure. The four teams are segregated and transparent, and also watched by Auditology.

Can this be really run by so few team members?
A single DevOps engineer can provision 24 systems a day: that's a lot of servers a year. In 5 years, you could build an infrastructure that would support 5 million Internet users.

Is there CRIT training available? Can people get certified?
Yes. To satisfy auditors that Combat Ready IT CRITTERS are competent, a certification is available. Further info can be obtained by e-mail: info@combatreadyit.com or visiting www.combatreadyIT.com website.

COMBAT READY CRITTER A universal accreditation for all Team Members. It is assumed team members have read the book and bought into the concept. The certificate is based on 10 questions and costs $100. For unemployed IT workers and students it's only $25.

PIOSOPHER Details on www.pie.institute

SHAZOPS FACILITATOR A Master, Trainer, and Country Operators are under licence. For more details contact us.

Is there a Forum for Combat Ready IT?
Yes. Actually the intent is to keep the model lightweight and developed by CRITTERS. It's a technology-based model that scales as much as the technology.

APPENDIX 2 - VIRUS EVOLUTION

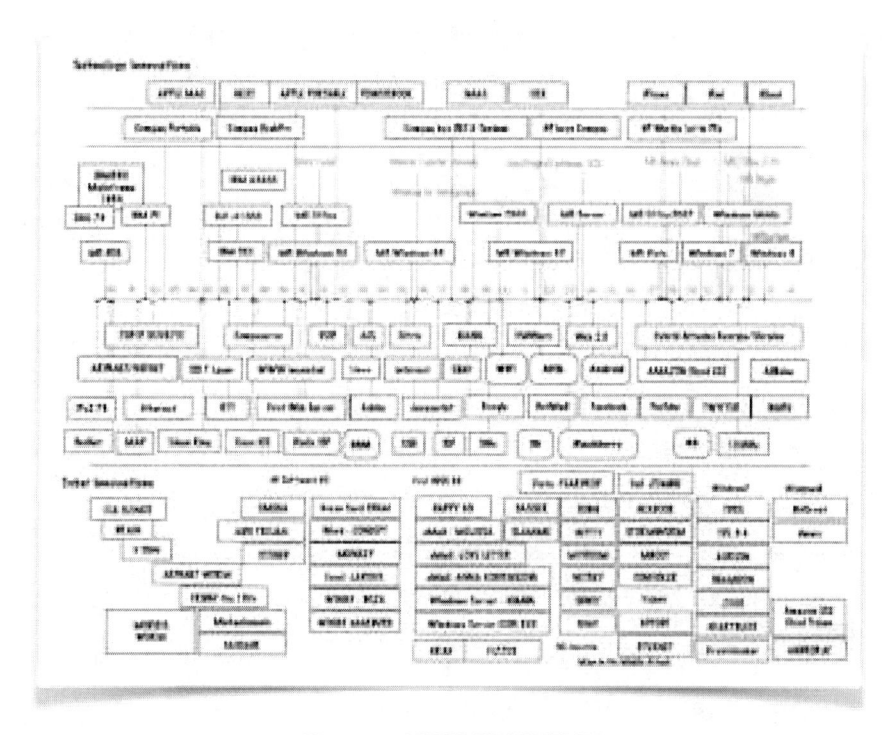

Figure 110 VIRUS EVOLUTION

21.1 A BRIEF HISTORY OF EXPOSURES (LOOK BACK IN ANGST)

To help build a basis for the mental scenarios facing a security defence and understand the cyclical malware attack process, it is necessary to understand the enemy, and the re-use of seemingly old technologies to breach defences. A key problem facing Combat Ready IT is that there's a world of complex networks and associated risks; the new defence is predicated on predicting the adversary's next move. This approach, as you see in Part 2, is how to make this the guiding principle in security.

I have often been asked to build a book devoted to this but I think my head would explode with the mountain of data needed to be collected and diluted, however, it's useful to review how this branch of evolution has impacted the twenty-first century. The objective is to relate the complexity of attacks over time; it isn't an in-depth technical overview and would only address 0.0001% of the malware in cyber-space today. It's useful though, to look back 30-odd years to see how we arrived at the mess that we are all in nowadays. "What a tangled Web we weave" [1] is very appropriate. The Internet, in an attempt to be all things to all men, has deceived us through complication and trying to cover its ass at every twist and turn.

The first known virus was on the ARPANET (the precursor to the Internet) in the early 70s. It was a test virus called Creeper, which was self-replicating and infected DEC PDP-10 terminals.

In the early days of the PC it was relatively easy to trace viruses down and eradicate them. There were few nasty viruses, and anti-virus companies were small and able to handle new viruses on a monthly basis.

1982

This was really the year of IBM. The IBM PC XT had a 20MB Hard Disk and ran emulation programs that mimicked a mainframe terminal. This emulation was called 3270 and could connect to a mainframe over 4 MBit/s Token Ring. The cost of the machine was about $5000 and it fell off the shelves. Application software written for it included WordPerfect and Lotus 123, retailing at about $300 each.

BITNET the 'Because It's Time Network'. The original acronym stood for 'Their' instead of 'Time', in reference to the free NJE protocols provided with the IBM systems. The network provided electronic mail and listserv servers to distribute information, as well as file transfers.

The first virus to affect Apple computers wasn't written for the Macintosh (that iconic computer wasn't set to appear until 1984). A 15-year-old student, Rich Skrenta, (who is now a CEO of Blekko, a proposed Google replacement) wrote the Elk Cloner virus, capable of infecting the boot sector of Apple II computers.

On every 50th boot, the Elk Cloner virus would display a short poem:

Elk Cloner: The program with a personality

It will get on all your disks
It will infiltrate your chips
Yes, it's Cloner!

It will stick to you like glue
It will modify RAM too
Send in the Cloner!

After learning that the Soviet Union planned to steal software from a Canadian company to control its Trans-Siberian Pipeline, the CIA altered the software to cause the pipeline to explode. It is considered the first cyberattack.

1983

This year saw the emergence of PC start-ups Compaq and Gateway. The industry was full of self-build fanatics, and integrating these machines became a headache. Fred Cohen of the University of Southern California, while working on his dissertation, formally defined a computer virus, as e machines became a headache. Fred Cohen of the University of Southern California such a way as to include a (possibly evolved) copy of itself."

1984

Backdoors were created in modified C compiler through inserting code at the login command.

In his novel, *Neuromancer*, author William Gibson popularises the term 'cyberspace', a word he used to describe the network of computers through which characters in his futuristic novels travel.

DNS (the Domain Name System) is introduced.

1985

This was the year of the Apple Mac. The first Friday the 13th virus was seen in its first iteration. The Cascade virus is a prominent computer virus that was a resident written in assembly, and it was widespread in the 1980s and early 1990s. It infected .com files and had the effect of making text on the screen fall down and form a heap in the bottom of the screen. It was notable for using an encryption algorithm to avoid being detected. However, one could see that infected files had their size increased with 1701 or 1704 bytes.

Dr. Yik San Kwoh invented the robot-software interface used in the first robot-aided surgery, a stereotactic procedure. The surgery involves a small probe that travels into the skull. A CT scanner is used to give a three-dimensional image of the brain, so that the robot can plot the best path to the tumour.

1986

PC viruses started to appear. One of the first, emerging from Pakistan, is known as the Brain and is a 'boot sector' virus (floppy disk) created in 1986 by the Farooq Alvi Brothers in Lahore, Pakistan, reportedly to deter piracy of the software they had written. These two still run BrainTelecom, which is a telecoms company in Lahore. Mikko H. Hypponen (a veteran of F-Secure) has an amusing YouTube where he visits the two brothers and asks them their motivation. Mikko, along with Eugene Kaspersky, are the voices in the wilderness when it comes to expelling the huge risks around malware. In this year, I met the brilliant Dr. Alan Solomon, who was a PC security expert who gave a talk on how to hack into a network. He described how he sat in a customer's boardroom and tapped directly into a spare data wall socket and began to monitor the network server file system. Besides being one of the best speakers I had ever had the chance to encounter, he also produced an anti-virus toolkit, which was eventually bought by McAfee in the late 90s. What Dr Solomon gave me was an insight into how easy it was to hack a network, and how I approach operations from that point onward.

Over the course of 10 months, beginning in August, Clifford Stoll, a physics researcher at the University of California at Berkeley, tracked down a hacker who had broken into computers at the Lawrence Berkeley National Laboratory, a US Department of Energy facility, and other military computers in the US. He traced the hacker to Germany. It was the first such investigation. [1]

The IETF (Internet Engineering Task Force) is established to manage RFCs (Request for Comments) allowing academia and vendors to drive and develop Internet technical innovation.

1987

'File' viruses began to appear (largely affecting the essential system) in those days the only way to transfer data was via a 5 $^{1/4}$ inch floppy drive, which was passed from machine to machine and even posted to other countries. To see viruses spread globally to 100 countries was always fascinating to track. Appearance of the Vienna virus, which was subsequently neutralised, was the first time this had happened on the IBM platform.

Boot sector viruses such as Yale from USA, Stoned from New Zealand, Ping Pong from Italy. The Jerusalem virus is a derivative of the Suriv family. The virus destroyed all executable files on infected machines upon every occurrence of Friday the 13th. Jerusalem caused a worldwide SCA virus; a boot sector virus for Amigas appears, immediately creating a pandemic virus-writer storm. SCA also released another, considerably more destructive virus, the Byte Bandit. Christmas Tree EXEC was the first widely disruptive replicating network program, which paralysed several international computer networks in December 1987. Yeah, thanks for that. That was a great Christmas for me as it took three weeks to clean 1000 machines. Viruses like Yankee Doodle, Form and Dark Avenger were cartoon-based, so you had a clear indication that your PC was actually infected many were in colour, unless you had the Compaq Portable that had a green or orange screen.

DR-DOS: Digital Research developed DR-DOS, a 32-bit operating system, in 1987 as a fully compatible alternative to MS-DOS for 80286- and 80386-based PCs. It succeeded creator Gary Kildall's Control Program for Microcomputers (CP/M). The most popular legend told is that Kildall, the CEO of Intergalactic Digital Research (later shortened to Digital Research), was piloting his plane the day IBM approached the company about licensing CP/M for its first microcomputer – instead, IBM signed Microsoft's MS-DOS.

In 1991, Novell acquired Digital Research, DR-DOS and CP/M, with plans to compete against MS-DOS in the DOS market. When Novell CEO Ray Noorda failed to capitalise on the plan to take over the DOS market, Novell sold DR-DOS to Caldera in 1996. Caldera, which Sparks founded with Noorda's assistance, then sued Microsoft for lost sales and unfair competition and settled out of court for an unspecified amount.

DR-DOS was a wonderful solution for running a simple 4-node network over RS232 or Ethernet cabling. It gets a mention here as it has been revived by a start-up in 2002 for embedding into single machines.

1988

This seems to be a really quiet year for malware. Perhaps everyone was on holiday? The ARPANET worm, written by Robert Morris, disabled approximately 6,000 computers on the network.rm, written virus, thought to be the first encrypted virus, was discovered.

IBM had a very large Customer Conference Centre in Belgium called Lehulpe. It was a gorgeous state-of-the-art building with concrete windows (in case of nuclear attack) and set in a large expanse of woods. I believe it windows (in case of nuclear attack). I was invited to speak at an IBM technology innovation meeting on my pet subject, which was IBM Token Ring (a cabling product for supporting Local Area Networks). It had University-style furnishings with orange duvets and orange plastic chairs, which must have been the same supplier as the Brussels Airport at the time. It also had an amazing bar with Belgian beer on tap. I had a shiny new laptop at the time, an Amstrad PPC 640 that had dual 720k 3.5 inch Floppy Drives (man - was I cool or what!). I went to the Amstrad factory and thought it bleeding edge technology. It weighed 22lbs – like carrying around 10 MacBook Airs – and it really hurt your knees after using it for 10 minutes, giving bleeding edge a new meaning! I digress. IBM was doling out floppy disks with the presentations (including mine) to the 1000 odd customers. Unfortunately all these disks were infected with Cascade. One of these disks I took back with me to the UK, and after seeing letters drop down the screen like the Matrix I knew I would be in trouble with the office, so I 'accidentally' dropped the laptop under a London bus so I could get a new replacement. I don't feel that guilty about it, just something I had to get off my chest!

The biggest problem at this time was that vendors would not acknowledge there were such things as security problems. Users used a site called '8lgm', which was a bulletin board (Eight Legged Groove Machine) to allow system operators to log bugs and security vulnerabilities. This probably was the earliest form of crowdsourcing, in an attempt to inform everyone that there was a problem. It also started to address the full disclosure of vendors' affected software and reported this to vendors and the public in an attempt to speed up patch delivery. The problem kicked off several rounds of vendors' lawyers either attacking the site legally, or the user reporting the vulnerability. One of these disks I took back after the vendors had written and released the patch. Vendors started to acknowledge they had a major problem on their hands, and the decade of massive Terms and Conditions began to surface from vendors' legal departments. To this day it's not unusual for a 100-page Terms and Conditions of Use to be seen in licensing installation routines and websites that deny that any damage caused by the vendor software actually existed, and claims everything is the user's fault. This state of affairs continued to 2011, when Vendor Security Mailing Lists were compromised and vendors moved to Bug Bounties.

Internet Relay Chat (IRC) developed by Jarkko Oikarinen.

1989

The number of connected machines to the Internet exceeded 100,000 and the AIDS Trojan appeared, reflecting the author's lack of imagination. It was unique at the time because it demanded payment for removal. The Dark Avenger (a Sofia-based virus writer) release a malware kit called Mte that allowed viruses to become polymorphic, that is the ability to transform itself. A BBC news reporter called Sarah Gordon actually interviewed the Dark Avenger, but the transcript has disappeared.

This year saw for the very first time the authorities get involved. The DataCrime virus (written by Fred Vogel in Holland) came to the notice of the Dutch police, probably because it mentioned 'crime' in the title. This was a FAT table cruncher that just displayed the DataCrime on the monitor. However, the virus didn't actually spread – it was research analysts that made a mountain out of a molehill and stirred the press up. In America it was blamed on Norwegian terrorists. Anyway, the Dutch Police commissioned a virus detector and sold it to the general public for a buck. It actually created false positives and a second program was released, and apparently long lines were seen outside Dutch Police Stations with confused users huddling their PCs in the rain.

British computer scientist Sir Timothy John Berners-Lee, while working at CERN, proposed a computer-based, global hypertext project, which would allow people and organisations to more easily work together and share information. His concept becomes known as the World Wide Web. In December 1990, the Web becomes available within CERN, and by the summer of 1991 becomes available on the Internet.

1990

Anti-virus software began to appear. Mark Washburn, working on an analysis of the Vienna and Cascade viruses with Ralf Burger, developed the first family of polymorphic virus: the Chameleon family. The Chameleon series debuted with the release of the 1260 Chameleon virus.

1991

Worldwide Web (WWW) released by CERN; Tim Berners-Lee developer First Web server has address (URL) nxoc01.cern.ch. This is Tim Berners Lee's machine and was refurbished last year and continues to work, launched in Nov 1990 and later renamed info.cern.ch. This server was a NEXT machine. NEXT was the brainchild of Steve Jobs. It was a Unix machine with a graphical front end.

PGP (Pretty Good Privacy) released by Philip Zimmerman.

This was the first year of the commercial Internet, as we know it.

Norton Anti-Virus software released by Symantec. World Wide, the Dutch Police morphic virus, Tequila, is released. Omega was another form of cartoon-based virus, which would display the Omega symbol. Michelangelo was one of the first destructive viruses; it would overwrite the first 100 blocks in the FAT and so your PC would self-destruct.

1992

Well over 1,000 viruses are now thought to exist, which I think reflected verdant experimentation with the workings of PCs. Other graphical viruses include V-Sign, Tequila, Walker, Q2, CHAD, Alex, Cosmos G, Frodo, Crash Coffeeshop, Ambulance, Flame, Flip. Game-based viruses that actually played games with you like Happy Birthday. Joshi, (which asked you to type Happy Birthday one day per year). The VCL (VIRUS CREATION LABOR) virus kit was also spotted this year, which was a Graphical User Interface for trainee virus writers to change the coding of viruses and added encryption.

1993

There seems a dip in activity during the year; probably due to a massive team members culling of IT team members globally. In that year over 100,000 IT team members were laid off during a mini recession in the UK alone, which, if you think about the impact of laying technical team members off, would have coincided with lack of virus authors.

XTREE, who were a company who wrote an excellent program that allowed IT team members to merge two PCs file systems, announced that they were quitting the anti-virus business.

A new virus creation group appeared called Trident. The Netherlands-based Trident author, Masouf Khafir, wrote a polymorphic engine called Trident Polymorphic Engine (TPE), and released a virus named GIRAFE. The TPE was more difficult to detect than its forebear the MtE (see 1989). A variation on this was the Cruncher virus, a data compression virus that automatically added itself to files to auto-install on as many computers as possible. John Tardy joined the group and wrote a fully polymorphic virus in 444 bytes.

First TV virus? Tremor rocketed to stardom when it was included in a TV broadcast of software (received via a decoder). It hit one national cable channel on its first day of broadcasting.

The first webcam was put on the Web and called the Trojan Room Coffee Pot. Internet Underground Music Archive created by students at the University of California, Santa Cruz to help promote unsigned musical artists. Music was shared using the MP2 format, presaging the later extreme popularity of MP3 sharing and online music stores.

April 30th – Officials at CERN issue a formal statement declaring that the World Wide Web software developed by Sir Timothy John Berners-Lee is in the public domain. To become an indispensable tool of the Internet, and accelerates growth of the contemporary global information infrastructure.

By the end of 1993, there were 623 websites, according to MIT Researcher Matthew Gray.

1994

During 1994, PC's shipped by IBM and Compaq with 10MB or 20MB drives. These drives were pretty unreliable but somewhat faster than the floppy drives. The emergence of 3 $^{1/2}$ inch drives made an appearance; in fact Windows 95 had 10 floppy drives shipped in a box with the OS on them. I also seem to recall the Windows NT Server having over 30 disks, which was a complete nightmare. First virus hoax; known as "Good Times" surfaces. The Casino virus was also a game-playing virus where you had five attempts to retrieve your FAT. The virus copied your FAT and then put it into memory and then you had five attempts to get three $ signs in a row, or you would lose all your files completely. If you won, then it rewrote your FAT back to the drive, and you kept all your files.

Computers at the Rome Air Development Centre at Griffiths Air Force Base in New York were attacked 150 times by anonymous hackers, who used a sniffer program to steal login credentials and sensitive information from the lab, which conducts research on artificial intelligence systems, radar guidance systems, and target detection and tracking systems. The hackers then used the login information to access the computers of other military and government facilities, including NASA's Goddard Space Flight Centre and the Wright-Patterson Air Force Base. [1]

By the end of 1994 there were almost 10,000 Websites. Yahoo and Lycos became popular alternatives to the America Online public portals. Usenet newsgroups became the leading community based websites and attracted Internet pornography image sharing. Before this point the only way to share pornography was FTP/Gopher into a known server, the most popular being "tudelft", which was a server in a university in Holland. The only way to access this was via an IP and a dial up modem.

Two search engines emerged, World Wide Web Worm and WebCrawler.

First Virtual became the first cyber-bank. Security First Network Bank (that opened in October 1995) is cited as being the original virtual bank. This is untrue. Security First may have been the first banking operation to refer to themselves a virtual bank– but they weren't the first to offer banking services without branches. Manulife Bank, located in Waterloo, Canada, has been offering banking services without brick and mortar branches for almost 15 years. Manulife Bank shed their retail outlets in 1993 (sold them to Laurentian Bank) and transformed themselves into a bank that provided banking services through advisors, banking consultants, call centre personnel, interactive voice response and, in the mid 1990s, Web banking.

Not only was Manulife Bank an innovator when it came to virtual banking, they also created the first product of its kind in North America (the Manulife One product). Manulife One is a loan product suitable for more sophisticated consumers who are not highly leveraged.

ING DIRECT was another early virtual banking success for Canada. ING DIRECT opened their virtual banking doors in Canada by 1997, years before they opened for business in Spain, Australia, the United States, France, Germany, UK, and Austria.

1995

The first major 'Word' virus emerges, known as Concept, a virus that infects documents using VBA scripting language.

Accidental adversaries – thousands in Minneapolis-St. Paul (USA) lose Net access after transients start a bonfire under a bridge at the University of MN, causing fibre optic cables to melt (30th July).

The Browser War commences as Microsoft adopted an Internet browser and bundled it into the Windows Operating System. This caused a furore with its rival Netscape, who cried foul, and legal battles commenced. Even the European Union insisted that Microsoft 'unbundle' the browser. At this time Netscape had 80% of the market and were going places.

The birth of JavaScript created by Brendan Eich, while he worked at Netscape and was deployed in Netscape 2.0. The beauty of JavaScript was it was object-based, allowing small modules of code to run as a thin client. This Thin Client approach meant small applications could be run anywhere on a dial-up line (effectively a 64k link PSTN line), and remote applications could be run anywhere. This ability to run Word and Office applications that did not rely on a desktop's local hard drive is probably the first Cloud-like application. The intent was to write mobile code for Internet phones.

The first official Internet wiretap was successful in helping the Secret Service and Drug Enforcement Agency (DEA) apprehend three individuals who were illegally manufacturing and selling cell phone cloning equipment and electronic devices

Operation Home Front connects, for the first time; soldiers in the field with their families back home via the Internet.

Richard White becomes the first person to be declared a 'munition', under the USA's arms export control laws, because of an RSA file security encryption program tattooed on his arm.

1996

Not wishing to be left out of the history books, Australian hackers from the virus-writing crew Boza created the VLAD virus, which was the first known virus to target Windows 95. More e-mails were sent than posted mails. Laroux was an Excel spreadsheet virus that ran random numbers that incremented the numbers in the spreadsheet by 0.0025% so the user would not notice the number changes. However over time this would corrupt the backups and the original, so nothing made sense in the accounting department for at least a year. Military hacks included US Dept. of Justice (17th Aug), CIA (19th Sep), Air Force (29th Dec), NASA DDCSOL - USAFE - US Air Force (30th Dec)

Microsoft adopts JavaScript to appease its critics and to stave off the ability of the Netscape pretender to provide thin client applications. I was an early beta tester for Microsoft s IE. Open Source Office-like applications began to emerge.

1997

Encrypted, memory-resident stealth virus Win32.Cabanas was released – the first known virus that targeted Windows NT (it was also able to infect Windows 3.0 and Windows 95 hosts).

The NSA conducts a test, known as Eligible Receiver, to assess the vulnerability of government and military computers to a cyber-attack. The exercise reveals that systems throughout the country could be hacked and disrupted with relative ease, using commercial computers and software.

1998

The Marburg virus was probably one of the last cartoon viruses; it just infected the desktop under Windows. CIH, whose unique feature was to be able to erase flash ROM BIOS code was also known as the Chernobyl virus. Happy 99 was the very first e-mail worm. It would wish you a Happy New Year and display a picture of fireworks; whilst this was being displayed it would copy your e-mail contacts in Outlook and then send that to everyone in the list.

February

Analysts with the Air Force Computer Emergency Response Team in San Antonio, Texas, notice intrusions into their computer networks from several academic institutions, including Harvard. The hackers, who turned out to be three teenagers, exploited a weakness in the network's operating system. The event is a wake-up call to the government and prompted President Bill Clinton to develop a cyber-security plan.

December

The Department of Defence establishes the Joint Task Force on Computer Network Defence to defend the department's networks and systems "from intruders and other attacks" [1]

This year saw the release of the UK Data Protection Act (1998), and then three years later the USA PATRIOT, that stands for **U**niting and **S**trengthening **A**merica by **P**roviding **A**ppropriate **T**ools **R**equired to **inter**-**c**ept and **O**bstruct **T**errorism Act of 2001 (Wikipedia).

E-Commerce and the notion of e-auctions developed (The Amazon and eBay concepts).

1999

The Melissa virus, written by David L. Smith, infects countless thousands of PCs (estimated damage = $80 million). It replicates by sending copies of itself to addresses in the Microsoft Outlook address book, together with a word macro virus, and leaks confidential information. The author is subsequently jailed for 20 months.

WIN32/PrettyPark is the first known IRC mass-mailing worm.

Now at this time, the whole world was in deep panic because of the Y2K date change. PC Operating Systems and Networks (routers', bridges', modems' and Telco's core infrastructure) would suddenly stop working. Coders had hard-coded systems dates, and when the 1999 turned into 2000 it caused all sorts of problems. This was seen at the time as a doomsday scenario, because it impacted on SCADA systems and nuclear power plants. In the eighteen months prior to this, every Telco, brand and enterprise had to test and upgrade all the software residing on every device. All devices were checked, tested and put back into production. On New Year's Eve each country would report the country status in terms of whether electricity grids, telephones and television networks were still working. As it turned out, only a few networks were impacted and only two nuclear power stations went into emergency shutdown. Anyway, lots of IT team members earned big bonuses for keeping the world alive and avoiding the Y2K meltdown. At the time viruses were seen as dangerous, but also small fry in the eyes of the governments.

2000

The " I Love You" virus written by a Filipino student, infected 45,000,000 PCs. Probably the single largest virus in terms of number of infections, but nowadays e-mail filters catch these on the Internet backbone. I was deeply hurt and an emotional wreck when this was disinfected, but as luck would have it, a derivative called NewLove followed suit. It is similar to Melissa but sent passwords back over the network

The Honda Motor Company introduced its ASIMO humanoid robot. ASIMO is actually the eleventh in a series of walking robots created by Honda engineers in a focused development effort (starting in 1986) to create a two-legged (bipedal) humanoid robot that can walk and perform useful functions in human society alongside people.

IPv6 was deployed on JANET (Joint Academic Network) in May.

Microsoft's Internet Explorer held an 80% market share.

HTML v4 was released by the W3C.

The ASP (Application Service Providers) emerged with around 300 companies providing outsourced application services. These included AT&T, UUNET, Aristasoft, Metratech and Telecomputing. These providers used Citrix and Windows Terminal Services to provide data centre services to network computers or Thin Clients running browsers. This was the ground rock for the Cloud.

2001

The BitTorrent protocol was devised. This fulfilled a need on the Web to transfer large files over peer-to-peer networks. The ability to transfer large files in chunks allowed Torrent users to download movies, songs and software. Today it is estimated there are a quarter of a billion users.

The Anna Kournikova virus was a mail-based virus. It had an attachment .Jpeg picture of said Anna inviting the recipient to click on the picture. Of course, all red-blooded males clicked on the image immediately (and I probably still would today). The .Jpeg had a further extension, which was .vbs. This was Visual Basic Script (as used in the Laroux virus). After that, Anna didn't write or call. (See also Emma Watson in 2012)

In July, the Code Red worm infected thousands of Windows NT/2000 servers, running Web IIS server's, it actually sought out other Windows Web servers on the Web using an IP address scanner and cross-infected them causing $2 billion in damages (estimated).

60,000 types of Malware recorded.

This year also saw the first Network Share replicating virus called Nimda, a week after the 9/11 incident. Nimda infected in two ways, Local and Network;

File infection - By locating EXE files from the local machine and infected them by putting the file inside its body as a resource, thus 'assimilating' that file (think BORG of Star Trek fame). These files then spread when people exchanged programs such as games.

LAN propagation - By infecting file shares in the local network, either from file servers or from end user machines. Once a share was established, it dropped a hidden file called RICHED20.DLL. When users tried to open DOC or EML files from these directories, Word, WordPad or Outlook executed the RICHED20.DLL, causing an infection of the PC.

Mass mailer - By inspecting e-mail addresses via MAPI from the Windows e-mail client as well as searching local HTML files for additional addresses and sending an infected mail to these addresses with a README.EXE attachment.

Webworm - Nimda started to scan IP Address ranges on the Internet, specifically seeking out www servers. In 2001 there were not many of these, and a complete Web search took around half an hour to sniff the Internet. The worm then infected it by using several known security vulnerabilities. Once successful it modified Web pages, surfers would get infected by deploying ADMIN.DLL.

Code Red spawned copycats Slapper and Sasser that would remotely crash a PC in 60 seconds. Code Red also knocked out the servers in the White House. [1]

Agile Model first hyped.

2002

Klez accounted for 62% of virus infections this year, first detected on October 26th, 2001. Never before in the history of 'virology', has a malicious program been able to hold onto the highest position among the Top 10 for such an extended period. Throughout the year only two of the 10 various forms of the Klez worm were able to rise up to mass levels – Klez.H (detected April 17th, 2002,) and Klez.E (detected January 11th, 2002). It is worth noting the macro viruses Thus, TheSecond, Marker and Flop. These macro viruses targeted Microsoft Word and had been in existence less than one year.

This year saw the rise of network worms that infected LAN/P2P, and IRC channels were traditionally predominated by e-mail worms (most notably Lentin) that utilised e-mail as a main means of transport. It should be noted that more and more e-mail worms use a direct method of connection with SMTP servers.

2003

Floppy disks are declared officially dead (thank the stars!). Slammer worm (son of Code Red) spreads at the fastest rate thus far, and infects hundreds of thousands of PCs. Ramen worm discovered on Red Hat Linux systems. Swen is the first phishing virus; it purported to be sent from the Microsoft

Support Team pretending to be a security update and included a .exe patch (the virus). This virus went around for years. Code Red derivatives still had high circulation, as most companies did not have firewalls. The sheer amount of network traffic caused by the viruses severely impacted critical infrastructure, ATMs and nuclear power stations, SCADA networks, hospitals, and more worryingly the impact on air traffic control was potentially damaging. This also impacted on credit cards; in a large New York-based wholesaler over a 100,000 numbers were stolen. Sasser had actually infected the main servers, as they didn't have a firewall. I actually called the Head of Networks at the time as I was doing the forensics on the case. When I asked for a network diagram, he faxed me a hand-drawn piece of A4 with six servers (and included their IP addresses) and the routers. When I asked where the DMZ was he replied, "what's one of them?"

Windows Service Pack 2 released by Microsoft. Fizzer was the first money motivated virus that sent spam that infected PCs and created a DNS Proxy from them which then was used to mass mail.

Anonymous, the group of hackers who refer to themselves as 'Internet activists' and attack government, corporate, and religious websites, is organised. While the group avoids adhering to a strict philosophy, its members seem united in their opposition to censorship.

February
President George Bush announces the creation of a new office under the Department of Homeland Security, the National Cyber Security Division, and lays out a National Strategy to Secure Cyberspace to protect the nation's computer and information systems from a cyber-attack.

November
Hackers, believed by US officials to be backed by the Chinese military, search to find vulnerable computers in the military's computer network and steal sensitive information. The attacks continued for about three years and were given the name Titan Rain by US officials.

2004

Bagle is a mass-mailing worm affecting all versions of Microsoft Windows. There were 2 variants of the Bagle worm. Evolving from the Ramen worm, the L10n worm ('Lion') was a Linux worm that spread by exploiting a buffer overflow in the BIND DNS server. The MyDoom worm LINK "https://en.wikipedia.org/wiki/MyDoomNetsky worm spreads by e-mail and by copying itself to folders on the local hard drive as well as on mapped network drives. Witty worm exploited holes in Windows Internet Security Systems (ISS), the first worm to carry a destructive payload and it spread rapidly using a pre-populated list of ground-zero hosts. The Sasser worm famous for exploiting a vulnerability in the Microsoft Windows LSASS service and causes problems in networks, while removing MyDoom and Bagle variants, even interrupting business. The Caribe worm infected mobile phones that run Symbian OS Bluetooth. Nuclear RAT (short for Nuclear Remote Administration Tool) is a backdoor Trojan that infects Windows NT family systems (Windows 2000, Windows XP, Windows 2003). The Vundo Trojan caused pop-ups and advertising for rogue anti-spyware programs, and included performance degradation and denial of service with some Websites including Google and Facebook. Bifrost – a backdoor Trojan that can infect Windows 95 through Vista. Bifrost uses the typical server, server builder, and client backdoor program configuration to allow a remote attack. Santy, the first known 'Webworm' is launched. It exploited PHP and used Google in order to find new targets. It infected around 40000 sites. SDBot emerged as the first Open Source virus (versions of this are still found today), actually licensed under GNU.

An attack on Akamai caused a domain name outage and a major blackout that affected Google, Yahoo and other sites.

The first mobile virus appeared on Symbian. A Trojan variation, itSMS used the contact directory of the phone to spread adware. Soon followed by Skuller, which overwrote the systems files. Mosquito was also found on SymbOS.

2005

Zlob mimicked a video codec MP4 in the form of the Microsoft Windows ActiveX component. The Sony BMG virus was written as a hit back by virus writers as an anti DRM licensing protest. For years Sony had put a root kit onto the CDs they manufactured, which was OK if you put the CD into a CD player, but if you loaded this into a PC it would then surreptitiously install an installer, which was then hijacked by virus writers. However, the root kit exposure led to a raft of new viruses that were used to hide binaries, dlls, and .exe under legitimate OS naming conventions. A Mac root kit was also built for Sony. Bandook Rat (Bandook Remote Administration Tool) is a backdoor Trojan horse that infects Windows variants. It uses a server creator, a client and a server to take control over the remote computer. It uses process hijacking/kernel patching to bypass the firewall, and let the server component hijack processes and gain rights for accessing the Internet.

More mobile viruses on the Symbian platform; Commwarrior-A was spread via Bluetooth to nearby phones. It did not spread too far due to the Bluetooth limitations.

Pakistan suffers a near complete Internet outage as a submarine cable becomes defective. India has a single 155 MBit/s link feeding the entire country.

2006

The Nyxem worm was discovered. It spread by mass mailing. Its payload, which activates on the third of every month, starting on February 3, attempts to disable security-related and file-sharing software, and destroy files of certain types, such as Microsoft Office files. Mac OS X, a low-threat Trojan horse known as OSX/Leap-A, or, OSX/Oompa-A, is announced. Bkronto was a mass e-mail worm and the origin for the worm was from Indonesia. Warezov worm first discovered.

Zimbabwe loses most of its Internet access after satellite connectivity, and, services cut by the provider for non-payment.

A gang led by Albert Gonzalez attacked an unsecured Wi Fi network in a mall and stole the credit card data of 46 million customers and the social security and addresses of 450,000 customers. Eleven people were charged and one committed suicide.

2007

Storm Worm identified as a fast-spreading e-mail spamming threat to Microsoft Outlook and Exchange. Compromised 10 million computers by September. Thought to have originated from Russia, it disguises itself as a news e-mail containing a film. The public began to call the virus Storm Worm because of the e-mail title "230 dead as storm batters Europe." Antivirus companies came up with other names for the worm; Symantec dubbed it Peacomm while McAfee refers to it as Nuwar. These name variations came about to differentiate between a 2001 virus W32.Storm.Worm. The Storm Worm was a Trojan horse program, which installs a malicious program. Some versions of the Storm Worm turned computers into zombies or bots. Others create a botnet and use it send Spam mail across the Internet

Most versions of the Storm Worm coax people into downloading the application through fake e-mail links. Adversaries used the virus change the e-mail subject title to reflect current stories, clicking the links to the stories then downloads the worm and infects the computer.

Several news reports and blogs have called Storm Worm the worst attack in years. According to the security company Postini, more than 200 million e-mails carrying links to Storm Worm were detected during a three-day attack, fortunately not every email led to the downloading of the worm.

Zeus targets Microsoft Windows to steal banking information by keystroke logging.

In the mobile world, Symbian saw SymbOS Multidropper appear. A SMS which sent a money request then also installed SymbOS Besolo, a MMS worm that sent messages every two minutes to every contact in the phone's address book. Then it also spread Symbos/ComWar.C which propagated by Bluetooth and ensured it was not erased from the phone.

CIPAV is an Android app that is an agency-written spyware app that allowed law enforcement agencies to track all your movements. The app is pushed to the Android phone without request from the Google Play Store. By the end of 2007 there were about 350 known malware for mobile signatures. The large anti-virus companies F-Secure, McAfee, Symantec and Trend started to produce protective software for Smartphones.

April-May
Estonia's government websites are hacked by distributed-denial-of-service-attacks and are compromised for 22 days. The hackers appear to be backed by the Russian government. Targets include the president's office, Parliament, law enforcement officials, and Estonia's two biggest banks. [1]

June
The e-mail account of US Secretary of Defence Robert Gates is hacked. Officials blame China's People's Liberation Army. [1]

September
British government officials announce that hackers have breached the computers of the Foreign Office and other government agencies. The hackers are believed to be members of China's People's Liberation Army. [1]

First Cloud Hack: Google We Service vulnerability leaked database usernames and passwords. Hackers stole credentials of Salesforce.com's customers via simple phishing attacks.

2008
Mocmex Trojan, which was found in a digital photo frame. The virus was traced back to a group in China. Torpig, also known as Sinowal and Mebroot, is a Trojan horse that affects Windows, turning off anti-virus applications. It's the basis for the deadly malware we see today. It allows others to access the computer, modifies data, steals confidential information (such as user passwords and other sensitive data) and installs more malware on the victim's computer. Rustock.C, a hitherto-rumoured spambot-type malware with advanced root-kit capabilities, was detected on Microsoft systems and analysed, having been in the wild and undetected since 2007. Bohmini.A is a configurable remote access tool or Trojan that exploits security flaws in Adobe Flash. The Monica Bellucci website gets a mention here as the first Website that was used for a 'Drive by Download'. So if you accessed the Monica Bellucci website you would get instantly infected. This is the Number 1 method used today to spread malware; it uses Java to enter your browser and run infectious code, which in turn corrupted Flash and Quicktime. This could also be found in some YouTube videos; it also corrupted the boot

sector of the hard drive that would trash your PC. Koobface computer worm targets users of Facebook and MySpace.

Cisco started to combat network-based viruses with the IOS product set. Their IDS started to filter out virus signatures, specifically Code Red (of 2003 fame) and Nimda (of 2001 fame) in 2008.

NASA successfully tests the first deep space communications network modelled on the Internet, using the Disruption-Tolerant Networking (DTN) software to transmit images to/from a science spacecraft – 20 million miles above Earth.

Google's crawler search engine reaches 1 trillion pages. For comparison, Google's original index had 26 million pages in 1998, and reached 1 billion in 2000

The Middle East, India, and other parts of Africa and Asia see a major degradation in Internet service, including outages, after several undersea cables carrying Internet traffic to the region are cut within 1 week. (Jan-Feb)

July
In the weeks before the war between Russia and Georgia, Georgia is hit by distributed-denial-of-service-attacks and many of the government's computer networks are disabled, including that of President Mikheil Saakashvili. Media and transportation companies are also affected. Georgian officials accused Russia of launching the attack.

October
Pentagon officials discover that a flash drive containing a covert program was inserted into a laptop at a base in the Middle East. The program collected data from a classified Department of Defence computer network and transferred it to computers overseas. Government officials say the hack was carried out by a foreign intelligence agency and called the intrusion, "the most significant breach of US military computers ever." [1]

The IT industry shrank along with most other industries in the 2008 recession, with large layoffs at companies such as Motorola and Seagate and declining revenues at Intel and other companies. Adobe Systems laid off 680 employees, Microsoft laid off 5,800, Sprint Nextel announced plans to lay off 2,500 and Sun Microsystems announced it would lay off 3,000 people. Smaller IT companies were also affected.

2009

First 'state-on-state' cyber-attacks, Reciprocal Dozer attacks on the United States and South Korea. Conficker infects anywhere from 9 to 15 million Microsoft server systems running everything from Windows 2000 to the Windows 7 Beta infects French Navy, UK Royal Navy warships and submarines and the MOD administrative PCs.

Daprosy Worm. Said Trojan worm is intended to steal online game passwords in Internet cafes. Intercepted all keystrokes and sent them to its author.

Malte Spity, a German politician requested from Deutsche Telecom the last six months of his phone data. Besides recording calls Minutes of Use, SMS and total Internet connections, it also recorded his geo-location data (all his movements).

January

Israel's government Internet sites are attacked during the conflict with Hamas in the Gaza Strip. Government computers are barraged with as many as 15 million junk e-mails per second, and the computers are temporarily paralysed. Israel suspects Hamas financed the hack.

The US Congress recognises Data Privacy Day every year on January 28th.

March

Canadian researchers at the Munk Centre for International Studies at the University of Toronto announce that hackers based in China had penetrated almost 1,300 computers in 103 countries, including those belonging to embassies, government offices, and the Dalai Lama, and stole documents and other information.

June
Twitter is asked by the US Government to delay planned maintenance of its service on 15 June as a result of heavy use by Iranian users during unrest in that country.

December
News reports say that Iraqi insurgents had hacked into live feeds being sent by US drones to military officials on the ground. [1]

Thousands of customers lost their data in the Cloud due to the Sidekick disaster of Microsoft/T-Mobile. The Botnet incident at Amazon EC2 infected customers' computers and compromised their privacy.

Google was the target of a distributed denial of service attack that took down Google News and Gmail for a week.

The recession starts to bite at multiple global countries and companies. IT departments are decimated and the events herald a slowdown in innovation. Thousands of start-ups, unable to maintain loan repayments, disappear.

2010
A Botnet called Waledac sent spam e-mails. Microsoft[185] announced that a BSoD (Blue Screen of Death) problem on some Windows machines was triggered by Patch Tuesday updates were caused by the Alureon Trojan. Stuxnet, a Windows Trojan, was finally detected. It is the first worm to attack SCADA systems (Supervisory Control and Data Acquisition)[186], in particular the Siemens Step7 PLC automation controller. It targeted the Iranian nuclear facilities and caused centrifuges to speed out of control. It caused the production to stop for at least 6 months until the malware was disinfected. It uses a valid certificate from Realtek (Realtek are a Taiwanese Integrated Chip manufacturer that produces chips and semiconductors for Gigabit LAN Cards, LCDs, routers, and gateways. ADSL, et al). Now several experts have pointed out the only source this would have originated from as a based agency. Now the Siemens Step7 uses a cut down version of Windows XP or 32 Bit Linux for fault tolerance. To upgrade any of the PLCs costs hundreds of thousands and usually the logic is bespoke to the manufacturing facility, which means you have to know what the PLC is being used for and for

which process control(s) it manages. This information is held either by the facility or a contractor.

The virus, called "here you have" [187] or VBMania, is a simple Trojan horse that arrives in the inbox with the odd but suggestive subject line 'here you have'. The body reads "This is The Document I told you about, you can find it Here". The virus called Kenzero is a virus that spreads online from peer-to-peer sites taking browsing history.

January
Google announces on 22nd January that along with 20+ other US companies, it had been the target of a cyber-attack originating in China, and on 22nd March stops censoring its services in China.

Astronaut T.J.Creamer inaugurates the new International Space Station direct link to the Internet (aka Crew Support LAN) with a tweet (22 Jan) – "Hello Twitterverse! We r now LIVE tweeting from the International Space Station – the 1st live tweet from Space! :) More soon, send your ?s".

March
Chinese root DNS server is taken offline after disrupting some services in Chile and US.

April
University of Toronto researchers report that hackers broke into India's Defence Ministry and stole classified information about the country's national security system. The report, which points the finger at China, also says that the computers of embassies throughout the world had been compromised.

June
Security experts discover Stuxnet, the world's first military-grade cyber weapon that can destroy pipelines and cause explosions at power plants and factories, as well as manipulate machinery. It is the first worm that corrupts industrial equipment and is also the first worm to include a PCL (programmable logic controller), software designed to hide its existence and progress.

In August, security Software Company Symantec states that 60% of the computers infected with Stuxnet are in Iran.

August

Kaspersky Labs reported on Trojan - SMS.AndroidOS.Fakeplayer.a.' The first malicious Trojan sent SMS to Premium rate numbers.

Gingermaster: An Android Trojan that propagated by installing applications that incorporate a hidden malware for installation in the background. It created a service that steals information from infected terminals (user ID, number SIM, phone number, IMEI, IMSI, screen resolution and local time) by sending it to a remote server through the Web.

DroidKungFu: Another Android Trojan obtained root privileges and installed the file com.google.search.apk, which contained a backdoor that allowed files to be removed, open home pages to be supplied, and 'open Web and download and install' application packages. This virus collected and sent phone data to a remote server through the Internet.

A Chinese root DNS server is taken offline after disrupting some services in Chile and US.

The Pentagon declares cyberspace the "new domain of warfare."

November

Iranian president Mahmoud Ahmadinejad acknowledges that the Stuxnet worm destroyed about 1,000 of the country's 6,0000 centrifuges at its nuclear facility in Natanz. Israel and the US are believed to be behind the attack in an attempt to slow Iran's progress toward obtaining nuclear weapons.

US Senate authorises the US Department of Homeland Security to seize domains of sites suspected of piracy.

Myanmar is temporarily taken offline by a denial of service attack.

December

Anonymous attacks several businesses (MasterCard, Visa, PayPal, and Every DNS) seen as 'enemies' of WikiLeaks. The action was in response to the arrest of WikiLeaks founder, Julian Assange. This also included the Swiss PostFinance Company that froze Assange's account. In 2010, WikiLeaks provided several news organisations with hundreds of thousands of secret government and military documents about the wars in Iraq and Afghanistan, as well as cables that gave a behind-the-scenes look at American diplomacy from the perspective of high-level officials.[188]

Thousands of Hotmail accounts were hacked due to technical flaws in Microsoft's software.

2011

SpyEye and Zeus merged code is seen. New variants attack mobile phone banking [189]information. Anti-Spyware 2011was a Trojan horse that attacked; Windows 9x, 2000, XP, Vista, and Windows 7, posing as an anti-spyware program. It actually disables security-related process of anti-virus programs, while also blocking access to the Internet, which prevents updates. The Morto worm attempts to propagate itself to additional computers via the Microsoft Windows Remote Desktop Protocol (RDP). Morto spreads by forcing infected systems to scan for Windows servers allowing RDP login. Once Morto finds an RDP-accessible system, it attempts to log into a domain or local system account named 'Administrator' using a number of common passwords. ZeroAccess root-kit (also known as Sirefef or max++) was discovered. Duqu is a worm related to the Stuxnet [190]worm. Blackhole RAT hits Windows and Mac devices.

March

EMCs' RSA Security (the worlds most popular company providing random number authentication) got hacked. Cyber attackers stole data and the random number generator algorithm relating to SecurID tokens, rendering them insecure. These tokens were designed to authenticate remote access into companies via VPNs (Virtual Private Networks).[191]

The US seeing the sharp rise in Cyber related attacks decide to strengthen the US Agencies surveillance powers. On May 26th 2011, President Barack Obama 192 signed the PATRIOT Sunsets Extension Act of 2011, a four-year extension of three key provisions in the USA PATRIOT Act: roving wiretaps, searches of business records (the 193"library records provision"), and conducting surveillance of 'lone wolves' (individuals suspected of terrorist-related activities not linked to terrorist groups). FISA (Foreign Intelligence Surveillance Act) was amended by section 214 (Pen register and trap and trace authority under FISA) to clarify that pen register and trap and trace (means Phone Taps) surveillance can be authorised to allow government agencies to gather foreign intelligence information. Where the law only allowed them to gather surveillance if there was evidence of international terrorism, it now gives the courts the power to grant trap and traces against:

- Non - U.S. citizens.

- Those suspected of being involved with international terrorism, those undertaking clandestine intelligence activities

By the first quarter in 2011 Android viruses started to spawn. BD.AndoidDream.O (and U and V) took advantage of two exposures to root and silently installed a package called com.android.providers.downloadsmanager in the background. It stole all users' data and sent them to a remote server. DroidDream[194] variants had 50,000 downloads a day and seemed to stem from one author who had multiple apps including:

The offending apps from publisher Myournet:

- Falling Down
- Super Guitar Solo
- Super History Eraser
- Editor
- Super Ringtone Maker
- Super Sex Positions
- Hot Sexy Videos
- Chess
- 下坠滚球_Falldown
- Hilton Sex Sound
- Screaming Sexy Japanese Girls

Over 30 more were found by Lookout:

I have no idea what the oriental writing stands for and I dare not put it into Google Translate in case I spark an international incident with 'those who watch everything'. During this year Cisco reported that the most popular search term on the Internet was Japanese School Girls.

The femme fatale, Anna Kournikova rears her head again. Fans who searched for her by name on the Internet was Japanese School Girls.am/" exposures to root and silently installed a package "mednd busted" were at risk of running into online threats designed to steal personal information. Clicking on these sites and downloading files like pictures and videos exposed surfers to the risk of downloading viruses and malware. McAfee research found that searching for the latest Emma Watson pictures and downloads yields more than a 12.6% chance of landing on a Website that has tested positive for online threats, such as spyware, adware, spam, phishing, viruses and other malware. McAfee research also lists other female celebrities with a similar modus operandi including Selena Gomez, Shakira, Halle Berry and Megan Fox.

The Zeus Trojan Virus that activated when users were doing mobile banking hit blackberry. It blocked calls, registered a new administrator so company administrators could not re-image the phone, stole private data and sent it to the hacker. Blackberry and IOS phones were hacked at the CanSecWest Security Conference.

In this year, Symantec's Virus Definition File had identified 17,702,868 separate malware signatures.

June
Officials at the International Monetary Fund report that in the previous months it had been hit by "a very major breach" of its computer systems. The FBI announced evidence linking the Chinese government to the attack.

December
Malware, named Mahdi after the Messiah in Islam, infiltrates about 800 computers of government officials, embassy employees, and other business people in Iran, Israel, Afghanistan, the United Arab Emirates, and South Africa. The malware was embedded in e-mail attachments and users who opened the documents were susceptible to having their e-mails and instant messages read by hackers.

Vendors began to offer Bug Bounties as vendors realised this research was valuable. Google offer up to $20,000 for a reported vulnerability to be reported, and others like PayPal don't put a limit on the reward offered.

Global Browser Market Share
The Browser share remains in Microsoft's stronghold. With 56% market share of the Desktop computers the bundled browser still reflects vulnerabilities. 52% of Botnet 'zombie PCs' exploit several bugs still.

- Microsoft IE - 52%
- Mozilla Firefox - 22%
- Google Chrome - 13%
- Apple Safari - 7%
- Opera Software - 3%

2012

Flame, [195] also known as Flamer, sKyWIper, (Skywiper), attacked Microsoft Windows. The program is being used for targeted cyber-espionage in Middle Eastern countries. CrySyS stated in their report that the "sKyWIper" is certainly the most sophisticated malware we encountered during our practice; arguably, it is the most complex malware ever found". Shamoon [196] is a computer virus designed to target computers running Microsoft Windows in the utilities sector. NGRBot is a worm that uses the IRC network for file transfer, sending and receiving commands between zombie network machines and the attacker's IRC server, and monitoring and controlling network connectivity and intercept. It employs a user-mode root-kit technique to hide and steal its victim's information. This family of Bots is also designed to infect HTML pages with iframes, causing redirections, blocking victims from getting updates from security/anti-malware products, and killing those services. The Bot is designed to connect via a predefined IRC channel and communicate with a remote Botnet. In February two prolific spam Botnets were shut down.

Smishing was discovered, a sort of premium rate SMS chat method. An Android iRC Bot also showed up in an application called Madden NFL-12 (this was a re-emergence of the Gingerbread Trojan).

Lightning caused a prolonged down time at Amazon affecting EC2 Cloud services.

McAfee showed a rise in attacks on mobile devices rose from 792 in 2011 to 36,699 in 2012 (97% of these attributable to Android).

March
Canadian Political Party Elections were subject to a DDOS attack that delayed voting and reduced turnout.[197]

Apple released a brand-affecting news alert that the Flashback Trojan outbreak had affected 600,000 owners. Spread by malicious websites, it pretended to be an Adobe Flash upgrade and exposed Java vulnerability and stole users' passwords.

An IBM mainframe was compromised by vulnerability in an attached Linux server. Of the 2700 mainframes in the world this is the first known exposure and was personally very upsetting to me.

April
UK and US Government sites subject to a Massive DDOS attack by Anonymous (Group of Hackers)

May
Flame, malware that attacks computers using Microsoft Windows, is discovered. Its development is believed to have been state-sponsored. A report, released by Budapest University's CrySyS Lab, states that: "arguably, it is the most complex malware ever found." Flame is capable of recording Skype conversations, audio, keyboard activity, network traffic and screenshots. It is spread over a local network or USB stick. Flame also has a kill command, wiping out all traces of it from the computer.

The US Department of Homeland Security announces that spear fishers have penetrated the computer systems of US gas pipeline systems.

August
Hackers, who say they are Islamic and call themselves the Cutting Sword of Justice, infiltrate the computer networks of Saudi Aramco, a Saudi Arabian oil company, and wipe out the hard drives of about 30,000 computers. Hackers left their calling card on each affected computer, displaying an image of an American flag on fire.

September
Nine banks in the US, including the Bank of America, Wells Fargo, and JP Morgan Chase, were hit by a distributed-denial-of-service attack that denied customers access to the banks' websites for several days. The Islamic Hacktivist group Izz ad-Din Al-Qassam Cyber Fighters (also called the Al-Qassam Brigades) takes responsibility for the attack. The group is linked to the military wing of Hamas.

October

US Secretary of Defence Leon Panetta warns that the US must protect itself against a "cyber Pearl Harbour." He also warned the Senate Armed Services Committee that "a cyber attack that cripples Americas electrical grid and its security and financial systems" could be confronted.[198]

2013

This was a comparatively quiet year for Malware activity. I believe this is because of the number of new Operating Systems releases from Microsoft. The Microsoft Server 2012, Windows 7 variants and Windows 8 OS's were announced and Microsoft's own push into the tablet market was started. I am sure that hackers needed to dissect the new elements and components of these systems, so, were probably distracted.

January

Two computer hackers were jailed for a series of cyber-attacks by the hacking group Anonymous that cost the US online payments giant PayPal millions of dollars. Prosecutors said the attack had cost the company £3.5 million ($5.5 million, 4.1 million euros) in loss of trading as well as software and hardware updates to fend off similar attacks.

Anonymous attack. Targeted websites were directed to a page reading: "You've tried to bite the Anonymous hand. You angered the hive and now you are being stung." In a campaign codenamed "Operation Payback", Anonymous also targeted companies in the music industry and opponents of music piracy including the Ministry of Sound nightclub and record label, the trial had heard.[199]

CryptoLocker [200]Trojan horse is discovered. Crypto-locker encrypts the files on a user's hard drive, and then prompts them to pay a ransom to the developer in order to receive the decryption key, making it the first true Ransomware.[201] The Game Over Zeus Trojan is discovered; this type of virus steals all of your login details on popular websites that involve money. It works by detecting a login page, then proceeds to inject a malicious code into the page, keystroke logging [202]your details.

Apparently the best seller game Angry Birds iPhone App tracks your username and password, your contacts list, your location, your Phone ID and then this is used by third party analytic companies (result: Angry Customers). 47 smartphone applications send your location to one or more parties and 56 transit unique device IDs including SMS messages.

June
RT.com the Russian TV News broadcaster was temporarily disabled Monday for just under five hours by a DDoS attack. It coincided with RT's reporting on the trial of Bradley Manning and massive anti-government protests in Turkey, with coverage continuing uninterrupted on Twitter. The attack, claimed by anti-WikiLeaks hacker group 'AntiLeaks'.[203]

Fortinet reported over 250,000 malicious Android samples.

Samsung TV's web browser hacked, providing a backdoor into Broadband Home networks.

First IOT Hack? A baby monitor (a Wi Fi Webcam) belonging to a family in Houston was hacked by a British verdant. The camera did not have encryption and the default login is admin and blank password.

The world's first Bitcoin ATM set up in a coffee shop in Vancouver.

2014

January
Another major landmark was an IOT Thingbots attack. Proofpoint, Inc., a leading security-as-a-service provider, has uncovered what may be the first proven Internet of Things (IoT) - based cyberattack involving conventional household 'smart' appliances. The global attack campaign involved more than 750,000 malicious e-mail communications coming from more than 100,000 everyday consumer gadgets such as home-networking routers, connected multi-media centres, televisions and at least one refrigerator that had been compromised and used as a platform to launch attacks. As the number of such connected devices is expected to grow to more than four times the number of connected computers in the next few years, proof of

an IoT-based attack has significant security implications for device owners and enterprise targets. It featured waves of malicious e-mail, typically sent in bursts of 100,000, three times per day, targeting enterprises and individuals worldwide

The malware variants **TDSS/TDL3 /TDL4** (was known as Alureon) are still around, manually downloading and installing Trojan software usually infect PCs, and Alureon has been seen bundled with the rogue security software Security Essentials 2010 in the past. When the dropper is executed, it first hijacks the print spooler service (spoolsv.exe) to write a file system boot sector at the end of the disk and change the boot sector at the end of the disk and installs the Trojan software. When the dropper is executed the Windows Registry to block access to Windows Task Manager and the desktop, blocks access to Windows Update and attempts to disable some anti-virus products.

GPCode Trojan infects your PC and waits for it to idle and then encrypts your hard drive. Then it changes your Windows wallpaper and tells you your files have been encrypted. It points you to a file on how to decrypt your disk, which basically is a demand for money. They ask for $125 you have to send them, and then they will then un-encrypt your disk (which they always do). This has now spread to organisations local area network shares, which for IT Operations must be a logistical nightmare. Firstly the IT guys would need to explain how this happened and then find someone with a corporate credit card to pay the $125, obviously this is as rare as hen's teeth.

Win32/fakesysdef could be a logistical IT nightmare. Firstly the IT guys when repairing a PC or Laptop hard drive would need to execute a Hard Disk Drive Defragmenter, hence the name FakeSysdef or Fake System Defragmenter originates, running the fake program spreads the virus. Win32/FakeSysdef manifested itself as an array of programs that scanned the device for 'hardware failures' in system memory, hard drives, and general performance. After finding false faults, they scan the computer, show false hardware issues, and present a remedy to defragment the hard drives and fine-tune the system performance. They then request, from the user, a payment in order to download the repair update and to activate the program in order to repair these contrived hardware issues.

Zero-access was a root-kit responsible for Botnet spread throughout millions of Microsoft Windows operating systems since 2009. It is used to download other malware on an infected machine and to form a Botnet spread throughout millions of Microsoft Windows operating systems since 2009.

The Mask was an advanced threat that had been involved in cyber-espionage operations since at least 2007. What makes the Mask special is the complexity of the toolset used by the attackers. This was an extremely sophisticated piece of 'no stone left unturned' malware, a root-kit, Mac OS X and Linux versions and versions for Android and iPAD/iPhone (iOS). The Mask relied on spear-phishing e-mails with the usual links to a malicious website. Upon successful infection, the malicious website redirected the user to a benign website referenced in the e-mail, such as a YouTube movie. The malware then collected a large list of documents from the infected system, including encryption keys, VPN configurations, SSH keys and RDP files. This appears to be part of a Cybrid government campaign.

Epic Turla: this infection targeted several hundred computers in 45 countries, including government institutions, embassies, military, education, and research and pharmaceutical companies. Turla, also known as snake or Uroboros, is one of the most sophisticated on-going cyber-espionage campaigns, according to researchers at Kaspersky Lab. It did not appear to be a widespread public type attack. The attacks used at least two zero-day exploits: privilege escalation vulnerability in Windows XP and Windows 2003, and, arbitrary code-execution vulnerability in Adobe Reader.

It exploited against older (patched) exposures and vulnerabilities in pre-Windows 7 machines using social engineering and watering hole strategies. The primary backdoor used in the Epic attacks is also known as WorldCupSec, TadjMakhal, Wipbot or Tavdig. Victims were infected via a sophisticated multi-stage attack, which begins with the Epic Turla. In time, as the malware cocoons, this is emerged to more sophisticated backdoors run in tandem, and used to 'rescue' each other if communications are lost with one of the backdoors. Once the attackers obtain the necessary victim's credentials they deployed the root-kit.

Since 2011 there seems to be a resurgence of old code and malware being reused, refreshed and used in campaigns. Epic Turla is one example of these campaigns. The coding appears to be beyond expert and deep expert knowledge is needed to hook into kernel level and dynamic link libraries. The campaigns are also focussed on military targets and are so sophisticated that they have established a 'digital beachhead' as one general puts it. However, it is highly focussed which could mean (at a stretch) that by reducing the publicity the attack can be used again in other domains.

March

Very Large Botnet Attack: In March this year over a period of a few hours 162,000 WordPress sites performed the Mother of All DDOS attacks. The size of the attack exploited a WordPress vulnerability to attack a popular WordPress site. As much of this was internal to the Cloud where the WordPress site was located it didn't cause much of a problem. The worry was that a controller could have accumulated such a large collective of Botnets.

April

In 2014 the mobile malware took firm hold. The world is mobile, and criminals are now prioritising their scams to target smartphone and tablet users. There are now more mobiles in the world than toilets! McAfee identified 3.73 million total pieces of mobile malware in 2013, and an astounding 197% increase of total samples from the end of the previous year. Mobile malware in advertisements was the main conduit for malicious content. What makes these 'malvertisements' so dangerous is the fact that they are often delivered through legitimate ad networks and may not appear outright spammy, but can contain [204]Trojans or lead to malicious websites when clicked on. An innocuous banner ad promoting vitamin supplements may seem harmless, but it could be luring you into unsuspectingly downloading malware onto your mobile device.

Malicious mobile ads behave just like others setting a well-cloaked trap that tricks users into putting their devices and personal data in danger. While Android is still the most targeted by dangerous mobile ads, iOS devices are also susceptible to infection. It also became clear that Samsung was switching out the Android based operating system and replacing the calendar, e-mail client, contacts, notification centre, music and video player, voice control (anyone take a stab at why this would be?).

May
The US Justice Department unsealed an indictment of five members of Unit 61398 of the Chinese People's Liberation Army, charging them with hacking into the computer networks of Westinghouse Electric, US Steel Corp., and other companies. Shanghai-based Unit 61398 is the cyber division of China's national army. The move is considered largely symbolic since there is little chance the men will surrender.

July
American officials announced that Chinese hackers had breached the computer network of the Office of Personnel Management in March. They said they believe the hackers were targeting employees applying for top security clearances.

As I write, I received three phishing e-mails from an adversary from Germany. Not only did I get an SMS from said author(s) to follow up this exposure but he also claimed he was Microsoft. Now I only have a single e-mail address for Microsoft so it's pretty easy to trace how he got this information. Overall the quality of these e-mails is getting very good.

One of the oldest active malware families, Pushdo, is again making its way onto the Internet and has recently infected more than 11,000 computers in just 24 hours. Pushdo, a multipurpose Trojan, is primarily known for delivering financial malware such as ZeuS and SpyEye onto infected computers or to deliver spam campaigns through a commonly associated components called Cutwail that are frequently installed on compromised PCs. Pushdo was first seen over 7 years ago and was a very prolific virus in 2007. According to researchers at Bitdefender, about 6,000 compromised systems in the 1.5 million-strong botnet now host this new PushDo variant.[205]

Now, a new variant of the malware is being updated to leverage a new domain-generation algorithm (DGA) as a fall-back mechanism to its normal command-and-control (C&C) communication methods. DGAs are used to dynamically generating a list of domain names based on an algorithm and only making one live at a time, blocking on 'seen' Command & Control domain names becomes nearly impossible. With the help of a DGA, cyber criminals could have a series of advantages like overcoming domain black-listing, resisting domain takedowns by simply registering another domain generated by the same DGA, avoiding dynamic analysis and extraction of C&C domain names.

Brian Dye, a Symantec senior VP, has stated "anti-virus is dead", and as evidence, he explained that their product stopped less than half of attacks. To be accurate, he said that modern anti-virus software only stops around 45 per cent of attacks on computer systems and lets the rest through. It seems one of the global players in this space just cannot keep up with the volume of external attacks. I am not surprised – I noted from the signature databases that updates are not increasing in size, just time and date with marginal volume size shifts. I suspect that finding the company who is ahead of the curve will be the 'one trick pony' as anti-virus companies merge in this sector.

October

White House hacked the unclassified network. A breach had occurred but no damage or data was exfiltrated. Threat detection vendor FireEye Inc. released a report [206] detailing the activities of a suspected Russia-based hacking group dubbed APT28, which the company linked to attacks dating as far back as 2007 against Georgia, who was in conflict with Russia at the time, and other Eastern European governments.

Threat intelligence vendor iSIGHT Partners recently unearthed evidence that a Russia-based hacking team had targeted the NATO alliance, Ukrainian government and others with a Windows zero-day vulnerability, which was patched by Microsoft.

Russia-based hackers like APT28 stand apart from those backed by China, according to FireEye, because they are seemingly not interested in the theft of intellectual property. Research suggests the group is unlikely to be an independent hacking group because it does not focus on financial theft, only targets that would be of interest in nation-state-sponsored operations.

Hundreds of phone numbers, names, IP addresses and email addresses from Chinese government websites have been leaked online by the Hacktivist collective Anonymous in support of pro-democracy protests in Hong Kong.[207]

November

Symantec uncovered Regin malware, part of a long-term nation-state-sponsored cyber espionage campaign, similar to Stuxnet [208] and Flame[209]. The first version of Regin had been seen in 2008. As a modular malware platform, It contains a number of components that rely on each other to function. This design makes analysis difficult; all of the components must be available. It is geared toward collecting a variety of non-specific data and monitoring individuals or organisations for long periods. It is likely that its development took months, if not years, to complete and its authors have gone to great lengths to cover its tracks.

Regin infections have struck organisations in Russia and Saudi Arabia, and European countries. It may have been used by western intelligence agencies as far as back as 2010. It stands out not just for its sophisticated feature set, but also for remaining previously undetected for at least half a decade. Just how was the malware able to stay under the radars of security vendors and vulnerability professionals, some of whom are specifically tasked with finding and analysing such threats?

December

The eBay owned popular digital payment and money transfer service, PayPal has been found to be vulnerable to a critical web application vulnerability that could allow an attacker to take control over users' PayPal account with just a click, affecting more than 156 millions PayPal users.[210] An Egyptian security researcher, Yasser H. Ali has discovered three critical vulnerabilities in PayPal website including Cross Site Request Forgery, Authentication token bypass and Resetting the security question, which could be used by cybercriminals in the targeted attacks.[211]

Wiper Malware was used in a recent attack against Sony Pictures Entertainment, which resulted in the leak of several unreleased motion pictures as well as financial information, e-mails and casting details for movies still in production.

One of the leaked films, *The Interview*, was released and featured a plot to assassinate Kim-Jong Un, the supreme leader of the Democratic People's Republic of Korea, leading to speculation that hackers from North Korea may have been responsible for the incident and new team of hackers called "Guardians of Peace" claimed responsibility. An FBI alert noted that the malware is capable of overriding all data on computers' hard drives, including the master boot record, which contains information on how a drive is portioned and the boot code needed to run an operating system.

2015 + Super Cast

January
VTask a 12-year-old attack tool still operating.

February
Data theft malicious apps found in Apple IOS games: XAgent and Madcap.

HAAS (Hacking As A Service) found in East Asia. Customers are able to buy exploits and employ third party adversaries to execute the attack.

March
Ross Ulbricht (also known as Dread Pirate Roberts) gets a 20-year conviction for his part in the Silk Road marketplace.

RawsPOS a Pont of Sale Malware known to infect 90 vendors' proprietary Point of Sale software offerings.

Rocket Kitten Spear Phishing sends excel attachment that links to Microsoft's One Drive hosted Cloud platform where a malicious Woolerg Keylogger is downloaded.

Word, Excel and Powerpoint Macro viruses return. *TSPY_DRIDEX.WW and W2KM_BARTALEX.SM* is part of this downloader attack aimed at small businesses.

April
The Russian Federal Security Service (FSB uses Carbanak a targeted attack campaign to attack financial organizations. It employs spear phishing email and exploits, commonly seen in targeted attacks. Accordingly, attackers did intelligence gathering about their target networks in order to infiltrate it.

May
Home routers can be used to steal user credentials, and most people just don't know it yet. Bad guys have found ways to use Domain Name System (DNS) changer malware to turn the most inconspicuous network router into a vital tool for their schemes. Routers sometimes ship with malicious DNS server settings. In this scenario, the malware is used to tamper with the router and its DNS settings. In the event that users try to visit legitimate banking websites or other pages defined by the bad guys, the malware would redirect users to malicious versions of the said pages. This would allow cybercriminals to steal users' account credentials, PIN numbers, passwords, etc.

Two Nigerian cybercriminals — identified through aliases Uche and Okiki — who attacked small businesses from developing countries to steal information and intercept transactions with their targets' partners. All this was done through HawkEye, a simple backdoor that costs around $35 but exfiltrates with an average of $50,000 per attack.

The US government announced that all websites maintained by federal agencies must have been using HTTPS by the end of 2016. Second, the Wikimedia Foundation (best known for Wikipedia) announced that they, too, were rolling out mandatory HTTPS for their own sites as well, with full completion expected "within a couple of weeks

June
The Office of Personnel Management (OPM) suffered a cyber attack that affects four millions of government workers.

Microsoft's Anti-Surveillance site hacked.

98% of tested web applications were found to be vulnerable.

Poland's national airline, LOT, suffered an "IT attack" on Sunday that caused several flights to be grounded. The attack targeted the ground computer systems at Warsaw's Okecie Airport that are used to manage flight plans, forcing ten flights to be cancelled and a further 12 to be delayed, affecting more than 1,400 passengers

Adobe Zero Day Vulnerability has the same root cause as older flaws! Adobe has just released an update to address a vulnerability found in its Flash Player browser plug-in. In its security advisory (APSB15-14), Adobe notes that this vulnerability "is being actively exploited in the wild via limited, targeted attacks. Systems running Internet Explorer for Windows 7 and below, as well as Firefox on Windows XP are known targets.

Payments processor Worldpay reveals that nearly nine out of ten known UK credit and debit card breaches in 2014 affected small businesses. The report describes a credit card breach as "the suspected or confirmed loss/theft of any material or records containing account/transactional information".

Small businesses, which the PCI DSS defines as businesses processing fewer than 20,000 transactions per year, per card scheme, were responsible for 85.7% of breaches. Large businesses, which process over six million transactions, and mid-tier businesses, ranging from 20,000 to one million transactions per year, per scheme, were accountable for the rest of the card data breaches. Making up 18.6% of data breaches, the clothing and footwear industry was the most breached sector in 2014, followed by retail (13.9%), and hobbies and specialties. According to the Worldpay report, costs can vary considerably between seemingly similar businesses. They depend on the payment channel under investigation, the number of servers and how interconnected those servers are. The need to employ a forensic investigator may make a huge difference to the time it takes to investigate a breach and the cost of that breach. Businesses can pay £25,000-£50,000 for a PCI level 2 investigation and £100,000 for a level 1 investigation.

Intangible costs such as reputation damage, and loss of customers and other stakeholders also need to be taken into account (11.6%)

Trustwave's 2015 Global Security Report found that a staggering 98% of tested web applications were vulnerable to attack

The Department of Business, Innovation & Skills' 2015 Information Security Breaches Survey was published at the beginning of June and was stuffed full of disturbing statistics. The report highlights how cyber attacks affect nearly every organisation, with 90% of large and 74% of small organisations suffering a breach in 2014

Research undertaken by PwC for their 2015 Global State of Information Security Survey found that only 25% of directors are actively involved in reviewing security and privacy risks.[212]

Of the 380 major data breaches so far this year 117,381,357 records were lost in the US alone.

APPENDIX 3 - SECURITY CONTROLS

According to SANs - 90% of attacks succeed on organisations where the Top 20 Controls are not implemented. Alongside ISO 27000 covered earlier in the book there is also OWASP. These controls are reproduced under the open license and change frequently, its suggested that any serious attempt to implement these should do with up to the minute information. OWASP, SANS and ISO sell these services to help companies cyber defences. I recommend that all companies buy these standards and discuss at daily step check meetings.

In 2008, the NSA had been participating in a public-private partnership involving the Center for Internet Security (CIS) and the SANS Institute for more than a decade. When approached by John Gilligan of CIS and Alan Paller of SANS, NSA agreed to participate in a public-private consortium to share its attack information to provide the same type of control-prioritisation knowledge for civilian government agencies and critical infrastructure. NSA reasoned that the military could not protect the nation if the critical communications, power and financial sectors were not also protected.

The clear consensus of the consortium was that there were only 20 Critical Controls that addressed the most prevalent attacks found in government and industry. This then became the focus for an initial draft document. The draft of the 20 Critical Controls was circulated in early 2009 to several hundred IT and security organisations for further review and comment. Over 50 organisations commented on the draft. They overwhelmingly endorsed the concept of a focused set of controls and the selection of the 20 Critical Controls. These commenters also provided valuable "fine tuning" to the control descriptions.

The consortium reconnected with current and additional members every 6 to 12 months to ensure new attack information was reflected fully, and that new techniques (for mitigating old) attacks were included. Other improvements to the 20 Critical Controls over time include measures by which organisations could know how well they had implemented the controls and a list of automated tools that have been validated (by thorough reference checks) to be effective in implementing the controls.

OWASP[213]

OWASP

TOP 10 CONTROLS

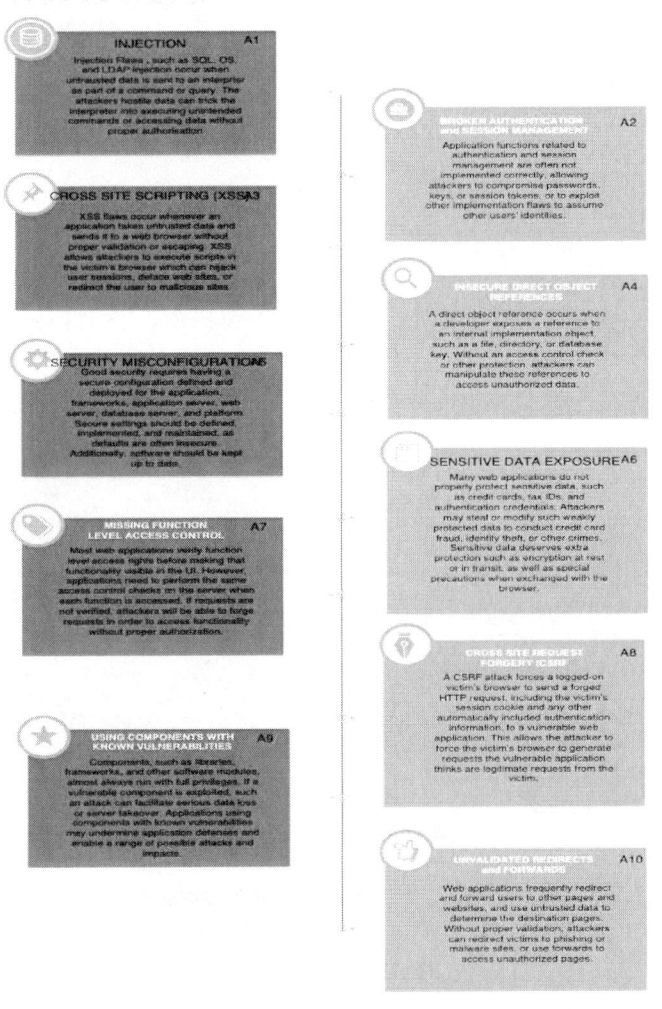

INJECTION A1
Injection Flaws, such as SQL, OS, and LDAP injection occur when untrusted data is sent to an interpreter as part of a command or query. The attacker's hostile data can trick the interpreter into executing unintended commands or accessing data without proper authorisation.

BROKEN AUTHENTICATION AND SESSION MANAGEMENT A2
Application functions related to authentication and session management are often not implemented correctly, allowing attackers to compromise passwords, keys, or session tokens, or to exploit other implementation flaws to assume other users' identities.

CROSS SITE SCRIPTING (XSS) A3
XSS flaws occur whenever an application takes untrusted data and sends it to a web browser without proper validation or escaping. XSS allows attackers to execute scripts in the victim's browser which can hijack user sessions, deface web sites, or redirect the user to malicious sites.

INSECURE DIRECT OBJECT REFERENCES A4
A direct object reference occurs when a developer exposes a reference to an internal implementation object, such as a file, directory, or database key. Without an access control check or other protection, attackers can manipulate these references to access unauthorized data.

SECURITY MISCONFIGURATIONS A5
Good security requires having a secure configuration defined and deployed for the application, frameworks, application server, web server, database server, and platform. Secure settings should be defined, implemented, and maintained, as defaults are often insecure. Additionally, software should be kept up to date.

SENSITIVE DATA EXPOSURE A6
Many web applications do not properly protect sensitive data, such as credit cards, tax IDs, and authentication credentials. Attackers may steal or modify such weakly protected data to conduct credit card fraud, identity theft, or other crimes. Sensitive data deserves extra protection such as encryption at rest or in transit, as well as special precautions when exchanged with the browser.

MISSING FUNCTION LEVEL ACCESS CONTROL A7
Most web applications verify function level access rights before making that functionality visible in the UI. However, applications need to perform the same access control checks on the server when each function is accessed. If requests are not verified, attackers will be able to forge requests in order to access functionality without proper authorization.

CROSS SITE REQUEST FORGERY (CSRF) A8
A CSRF attack forces a logged-on victim's browser to send a forged HTTP request, including the victim's session cookie and any other automatically included authentication information, to a vulnerable web application. This allows the attacker to force the victim's browser to generate requests the vulnerable application thinks are legitimate requests from the victim.

USING COMPONENTS WITH KNOWN VULNERABILITIES A9
Components, such as libraries, frameworks, and other software modules, almost always run with full privileges. If a vulnerable component is exploited, such an attack can facilitate serious data loss or server takeover. Applications using components with known vulnerabilities may undermine application defenses and enable a range of possible attacks and impacts.

UNVALIDATED REDIRECTS and FORWARDS A10
Web applications frequently redirect and forward users to other pages and websites, and use untrusted data to determine the destination pages. Without proper validation, attackers can redirect victims to phishing or malware sites, or use forwards to access unauthorized pages.

Figure 111 OWASP TOP 10

CRITICAL 3		VERY HIGH
Secure Configurations for Hardware and Software on Mobile Devices, Laptops, Workstations, and Servers		RACI: SecOps Blue CAMRA AUDITOLOGY DEVOPS SINCups

DESCRIPTION:

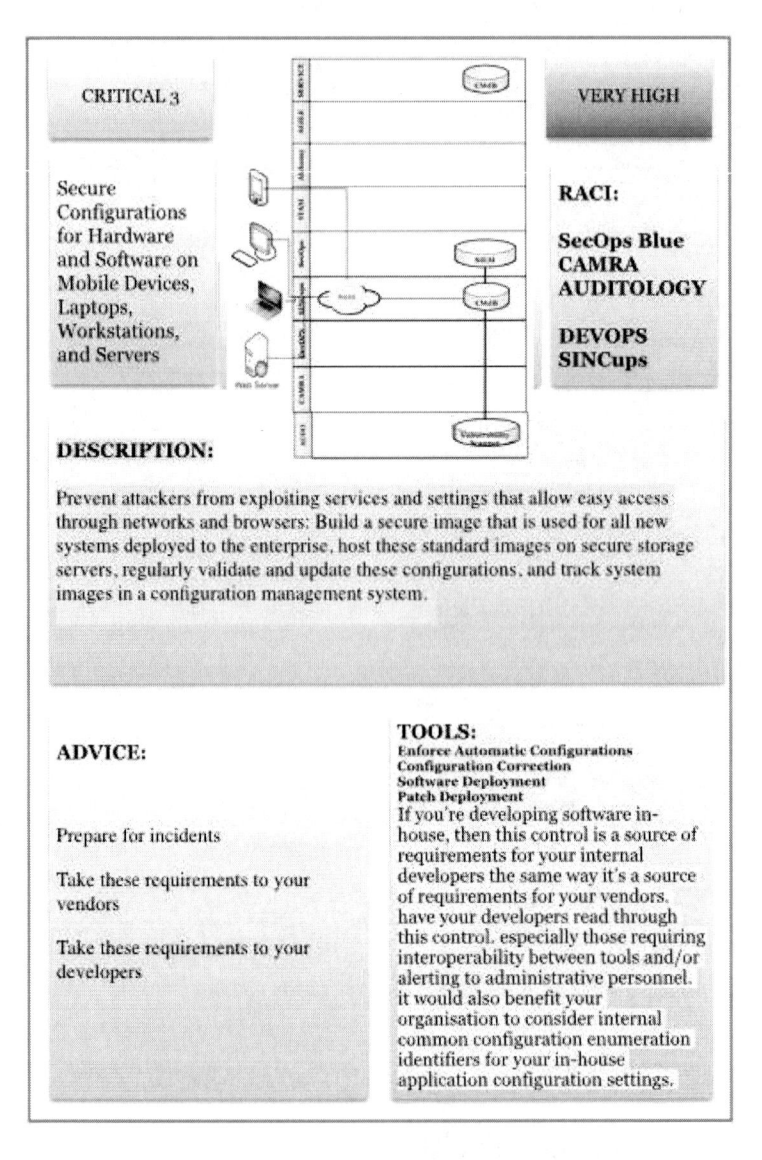

Prevent attackers from exploiting services and settings that allow easy access through networks and browsers: Build a secure image that is used for all new systems deployed to the enterprise, host these standard images on secure storage servers, regularly validate and update these configurations, and track system images in a configuration management system.

ADVICE:

Prepare for incidents

Take these requirements to your vendors

Take these requirements to your developers

TOOLS:
Enforce Automatic Configurations
Configuration Correction
Software Deployment
Patch Deployment

If you're developing software in-house, then this control is a source of requirements for your internal developers the same way it's a source of requirements for your vendors. have your developers read through this control, especially those requiring interoperability between tools and/or alerting to administrative personnel. it would also benefit your organisation to consider internal common configuration enumeration identifiers for your in-house application configuration settings.

Figure 112 SANS CONTROL

The full SANs Controls are available on the www.combat readyit.com website

APPENDIX 3 – CRIT SECURITY POLICY

Figure 113 GRAPHICAL SECURITY POLICY

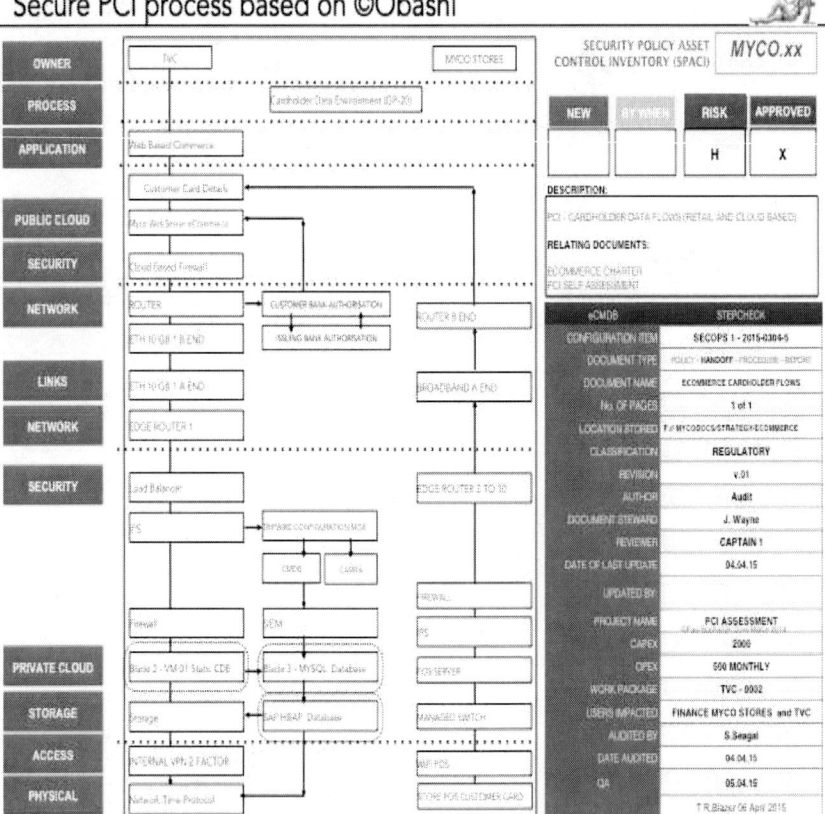

Figure 114 PCI PROCESS BASED ON OBASHI

ENDNOTES

1 http://www.gartner.com/it-glossary/smbs-small-and-midsize-businesses/

2 _http://www.wto.org/english/tratop_e/devel_e/wkshop_apr13_e/salcedo_openentry_e.pdf

3 Chief Internet Evangelist at Google

4 Trolls, Twittertwats, etc,.

5 Black Minute Calculation 40MB file (5000 records) over a 10MB link

6 Andrew France, chief executive at cyber security firm Darktrace (ex GCHQ)

7 UK National Security Strategy

8 http://www.express.co.uk/news/uk/551352/UK-wants-US-as-an-ally-against-cyber-attackers

9 www.searchquotes.com

10 www.doj.com US Department of Justice website July 24th, 2014)

11 https://www.hidemyass.com/legal/privacy

12 www.fcw.com 6 August 2014

13 http://www.telegraph.co.uk/technology/internet-security/10886640/Cyber-crime-costs-global-economy-445-bn-annually.html

14 http://techrights.org/2015/01/03/windows-not-designed-to-be-secure/

15 http://www.computerweekly.com/news/2240047368/Microsoft-Our-products-arent-engineered-for-security

16 http://wolfstreet.com/2013/08/22/leaked-german-government-warns-key-entities-not-to-use-windows-8-links-the-nsa/

17 http://www.net-security.org/malware_news.php?id=2760

18 http://www.darkreading.com/attacks-breaches/report-more-than-560000-websites-infected-in-q4/d/d-id/1132838

19 http://www.isightpartners.com/2014/10/cve-2014-4114/

20 _http://www.itgovernance.co.uk/blog/microsoft-warns-all-windows-users-of-new-zero-day-attack/

21 Sources: McAfee, Symantec and Sophos malware reports 2014

22 _http://www.itgovernanceusa.com/blog/348-million-us-records-compromised-in-worst-year-of-data-breaches/?utm_source=Email&utm_medium=Macro&utm_campaign=S01&utm_content=2015-01-07

23 www.foxnews.com/tech/2014/01/17/atms-running-windows-xp-and-wildly-out-date/

24 www.Informationisbeautiful.net

25 Dell Secureworks Report on Underground Hacker Markets http://www.secureworks.com/assets/pdf-store/white-papers/wp-underground-hacking-report.pdf - Includes Market Pricing for Counterfeit Social Security Cards, Drivers Licenses,New Identities and supporting Utility Bills ranging from $100 to $500 and other product inflations.

26	http://www.cnet.com/news/microsoft-patches-19-year-old-windows-bug/#!
27	www.fcw.com 6 August 2014
28	http://www.isightpartners.com/2014/10/cve-2014-4114/
29	www.kaspersky.com
30	https://www.europol.europa.eu/content/megamenu/european-cybercrime-centre-ec3-1837
31	http://www.dailymail.co.uk/news/article-2323067
32	http://www.dailymail.co.uk/news/article-2331949/More-dozen-U-S-weapons-systems-compromised-Chinese-hackers.html
33	http://www.dailymail.co.uk/news/article-2632719/US-Official-China-cited-cyber-espionage-case.html
34	http://www.scientificamerican.com/article/a-new-cyber-concern-hack/
35	http://www.nbcnews.com/news/us-news/anthem-major-health-insurer-suffers-hack-attack-n300511
36	http://www2.trustwave.com/rs/trustwave/images/2014_Trustwave_Global_Security_Report.pdf?aliId=37609203
37	http://ireport.cnn.com/docs/DOC-756840
38	https://www.duosecurity.com/blog/bypassing-googles-two-factor-authentication
39	USA Today on the 20th October 2014 report
40	http://www.bankinfosecurity.com/hacking-atms-no-malware-required-a-7460

41	http://www.securityweek.com/ddos-attacks-cost-40000-hour-incapsula
42	http://www.fbi.gov/news/testimony/taking-down-botnets
43	http://www.bbc.com/news/technology-21026667
44	http://securityaffairs.co/wordpress/28642/cyber-crime/spike-botnet-runs-ddos.html
45	http://securelist.com/analysis/kaspersky-security-bulletin/58265/kaspersky-security-bulletin-2013-overall-statistics-for-2013/#08
46	http://blog.avira.com/shortcut-express-infected-phishing-websites/
47	Ponemon Institute
48	http://midsizeinsider.com/en-us/article/cloud-attacks-are-on-the-rise
49	http://www.infoworld.com/article/2614579/internet/web-suffered-9-000-service-outages-in-last-five-months.html
50	http://www.forbes.com/sites/tomcoughlin/2013/05/10/2013-hard-disk-drive-projections/
51	http://en.wikipedia.org/wiki/Tor_(anonymity_network)
52	https://scadahacker.com/library/Documents/Threat_Intelligence/FireEye%20-%20Definitive%20G
53	www.kapersky.com
54	http://www.cnet.com/news/darkhotel-hack-targets-executives-using-hotel-internet/#!
55	https://www.freedomonlinecoalition.com/how-we-work/working-groups/working-group-1/debating-cybersecurity/

56	World Economic Forum Insight Report - Global Risks 2015 (10th Edition)
57	http://www.nttcomsecurity.com/en/news-and-events/press-releases/nid-00421/complacent-senior-executives-value-personal-data-above-work-data/
58	Prolexic Q1 2014 Global Attack Report
59	www.Forrester.com
60	http://thehackernews.com/2014/10/reflection-ddos-attacks-using-millions_16.html
61	USSS/CERT Coordination Center research
62	Drmola, Jakub. "Systémová dynamika jako nástroj pro výzkum bezpečnosti." *Obrana a strategie* 1 (2014): 15-28.
63	http://www.fbi.gov/about-us/investigate/counterintelligence/the-insider-threat
64	Rand & https://www.ncjrs.gov/pdffiles1/Digitization/147423NCJRS.pdf
65	http://www.jbonneau.com/doc/DBCBW14-NDSS-tangled_web.pdf
66	The Parrot Matrix
67	Symantec
68	The rising strategic risks of cyberattacks Research by McKinsey and the World Economic Forum points to a widening range of technology vulnerabilities and potentially huge losses in value tied to innovation. **May 2014**	byTucker Bailey, Andrea Del Miglio, and Wolf Richter

69	ISSA Journal January 2015 Randy V. Sabett JD, CISSP at Cooley LLP
70	http://csattorneys.com/target-corporation-data-breach-litigation-has-the-pendulum-swung-in-data-breach-consumer-cases/
71	National Association of Corporate Directors. Cyber Risk Oversight 2014
72	http://www.nttcomsecurity.com/en/resources/whitepaper-downloads/
73	http://www.businessinsider.com.au/sonys-hacking-scandal-could-cost-the-company-100-million-2014-12
74	http://www.justice.gov/sites/default/files/opcl/docs/breach-procedures.pdf
75	http://www.experian.com/assets/data-breach/brochures/response-guide.pdf
76	Ponemon Institute
77	http://www.fraudresourcenet.com/images/newsletter_pdfs/wccf%2003-04-final.pdf (www.cifac.org.uk)
78	http://quttera.com/website-scanner-statistics-last-week
79	http://www.statisticbrain.com/identity-theft-fraud-statistics/
80	http://www.nearfieldcommunication.org
81	Wikipedia
82	http://www.zerodayinitiative.com/about/benefits/
83	https://www.nsslabs.com/sites/default/files/public-report/files/The%20Known%20Unknowns_1.pdf

84	http://www.finextra.com/news/fullstory.aspx?newsitemid=26724
85	http://www.justice.gov/opa/pr/google-forfeits-500-million-generated-online-ads-prescription-drug-sales-canadian-online
86	http://www.finextra.com/news/fullstory.aspx?newsitemid=26877&topic=security
87	http://www.auditanalytics.com/blog/analysis-of-audit-fees-by-industry-sector/
88	http://blogs.wsj.com/cfo/2014/01/24/one-in-three-audits-fail-pcaob-chief-auditor-says/
89	www.aicpa.org Evolution of Auditing:From the Traditional Approach to the Future Audit. From the AICPA Assurance Services Executive Committee (ASEC) Emerging Assurance Technologies Task Force, 2012 Byrnes, Al-Awadhi,Gullvist, Brown-Liburd, Teeter, Warren Js, Vasarhelyi, Pawlicki, McQuilken
90	www.aicpa.org Evolution of Auditing:From the Traditional Approach to the Future Audit. From the AICPA Assurance Services Executive Committee (ASEC) Emerging Assurance Technologies Task Force, 2012 Byrnes, Al-Awadhi,Gullvist, Brown-Liburd, Teeter, Warren Js, Vasarhelyi, Pawlicki, McQuilken
91	"Inside Cyber Warfare" Jeffrey Carr's O'Reilly 2012 Second Edition
92	Computer Weekly November 19th, 2014
93	http://uptime.is/advanced?sla=99.875
94	http://csrc.nist.gov/publications/nistpubs/800-30-rev1/sp800_30_r1.pdf
95	http://www.goodreads.com/quotes/tag/privacy
96	http://www.goodreads.com/quotes/tag/privacy

97	http://malektips.com/computer_memory_definitions_0003.html
98	http://www.cisco.com/c/en/us/solutions/collateral/service-provider/ip-ngn-ip-next-generation-network/white_paper_c11-481360.html
99	Vimana Aircraft of Ancient India & Atlantis (1991) David Hatcher Childress and Adventures Unlimited Press auphq@frontiernet.net www.adventuresunlimitedpress.com
100	The Long Waves in Economic Life(1923) and The World Economy and Economic Fluctuations in the War and Post War Period (1922) Nikolai D. Kondratieff www.kwaves.com
101	https://en.wikipedia.org/wiki/Smihula_waves
102	Thou preparest a table before me in the presence of mine enemies: thou anointest my head with oil; my cup runneth over *Psalms 23:5*
103	The Virtual Battlefield: Perspectives on Cyber Warfare 143 C. Czosseck and K. Geers
104	http://www.theguardian.com/technology/2014/may/01/eugene-kaspersky-major-cyberterrorist-attack-uk
105	Infosec Institute Emanuele De Lucia December 13th, 2013 General Security
106	http://www.statisticbrain.com/student-loan-debt-statistics/
107	https://www.youtube.com/watch?v=zRwPSFpLX8I
108	http://searchstorage.techtarget.com/answer/What-is-a-LUN-and-why-do-we-need-one
109	http://searchstorage.techtarget.com/definition/storage-encryption
110	http://www.comptechdoc.org/docs/craig/sanzoning/

111	http://packetlife.net/blog/2013/may/2/what-hell-sdn/
112	http://searchsdn.techtarget.com/definition/software-defined-networking-SDN
113	Reshaping the Future with NFV and SDN (Arthur D.Little and Bell Labs)
114	http://www.idquantique.com/quantum-safe-crypto/technology/qkd.html?id=129
115	http://www.idquantique.com/random-number-generators/resources/quantis-resource-center.html
116	http://www.blackbox.com/resource/genPDF/BuyersGuides/Black_Box_Cabling_Guide.pdf).
117	IDC Tipping Point
118	PROCESS CONTROL AND SCADA SECURITY GUIDE 2. IMPLEMENT SECURE ARCHITECTURE CENTER FOR THE PROTECTION OF NATIONAL INFRASTRUCTURE
119	Holman, D., Batt, R., & Holtgrewe, U. (2007). The global call center report: International perspectives on management and employment (Executive summary) [Electronic version]. Ithaca, NY: Authors.
120	www.ipsoft.com and www.blueprism.com
121	ISO 8373:1994 (*Manipulating industrial robots— Vocabulary*
122	http://geoiptool.com/en/ip_info
123	IPv6 Calculation from Jacob Cotton (11.02.11) www.sitepronews.com
124	Zero Brain Cell Response

125 www.thephonebook.bt.com

126 www.IPv6.com The Next Generation Internet by Kaushik Das

127 www.http://iot6.eu/about_iot6 (accessed 16.10.14)

128 www.iot.eu

129 http://www.globaltelecomsbusiness.com/pdf/GTB-CFO-2013-05-BackChannel-Barnett.pdf

130 http://www.binarytranslator.com

131 Author Analysis

132 https://net.educause.edu/ir/library/pdf/EST1001.pdf

133 http://www.bgp4.as

134 http://wp.internetsociety.org/routingmanifesto/wp-content/uploads/sites/14/2014/09/MANRS-PDF.pdf

135 http://blog.streamingmedia.com/2014/02/transit-works-costs-important.html

136 http://www.itu.int/en/ITU-D/Statistics/Documents/publications/mis2014/MIS2014_without_Annex_4.pdf

137 GTB-CFO-2013-05-BackChannel-Barnett.pdf

138 http://www.deloitte.com/assets/Dcom-Global/Local%20Content/Articles/TMT/TMT%20Predictions%202012/16470A%20Smartphone%20lb1.pdf

139 http://www.slate.com/articles/technology/future_tense/2013/10/internet_balkanization_may_be_a_side_effect_of_the_snowden_surveillance.html

140 Charles Dickens David Copperfield 1849

141	https://en.wikipedia.org/wiki/Subscriber_trunk_dialling
142	https://lteconference.wordpress.com/2014/05/14/telecoms-walled-gardens-are-falling-apart/
143	http://searchenterprisewan.techtarget.com/Content-delivery-networks-A-primer-of-CDN-providers-and-technology
144	futureinternetarchitecture-130101024138-phpapp02.pdf
145	http://dictionary.sensagent.com/telephone%20number%20mapping/en-en/
146	https://en.wikipedia.org/wiki/Non-repudiation
147	https://en.wikipedia.org/wiki/Information_security
148	http://www.sits-france.com/en/en.html
149	http://www.atpcableplough.com/cable-plough.php
150	http://www.emtelle.com/?id=119
151	http://www.beyondbroadband.coop/kb/installing-fibre-optic-cables-underground
152	http://www.trevifountain.net/curiosities2.htm
153	Internet Governance: Inevitable Transitions James A. Lewis (https://www.cigionline.org/sites/default/files/no4.pdf)
154	https://en.wikipedia.org/wiki/Via_ferrata#Safety_and_equipment
155	From the Latin. omni (all) and the adj. ocular (to see) – See All the Steps on the Path
156	http://www.riskythinking.com/glossary/annualized_loss_expectancy.php

157 http://www.obashi.co.uk/methodology/methodology.asp

158 Thanks to Scott Ambler for his valuable input here.

159 RFC 4949, *Internet Security Glossary, Version 2*, August 2007 (http://tools.ietf.org/html/rfc4949):

Privilege: computer platform / an authorization to perform a security-relevant function in the context of a computer's operating system.

Privileged user: A user that has access to system control, monitoring, or administration functions. … Privileged users include the following types:

- Users with near or complete control of a system, who are authorised to set up and administer user accounts, identifiers, and authentication information, or are authorised to assign or change other users' access to system resources.

- Users that are authorised to change control parameters (network addresses, routing tables, processing priorities) on routers, multiplexers, and other important equipment.

- Users that are authorised to monitor or perform troubleshooting for a system's security functions, typically using special tools and features that are not available to ordinary users.

160 www.gizmodo.com

161 https://en.wikipedia.org/wiki/Network_operations_center

162 http://prod.sandia.gov/techlib/access-control.cgi/2005/057177.pdf Sandia National Laboratories Report Comparison of Two Methods to qualify Cyber and Physical Security Effectiveness Kristl A.Gordon and Gregory D. Wyss

163 www.uptimeinstitute.com

164	www.cablinginstall.com
165	http://www.crystalinks.com/undergroundbases.html
166	Sources: Forrester, Gartner, Arthur D.Little, McKinsey, Roland Berger, Boston Consulting Group, CRIT
167	www.gartner.com
168	https://www.owasp.org/images/1/15/Appsensor-ciso-briefing.pdf
169	A Condensed Field Guide for the Cyber Security Incident Responder ISBN 9781500734756
170	http://www.6wind.com/blog/whats-the-difference-between-sdn-and-nfv/
171	www.treesolutions.ch
172	www.freshservice.com
173	www.barclayrae.com
174	The Model can be viewed at http://www.scs.cmu.edu/link/setting-standards
175	VMWare VMBook - A Practical Guide to Business Continuity and Disaster Recovery
176	CA Technologies study 2011
177	www.holacracy.org
178	Sociocracy by Qaiser Mazhar (Tech Lead-Team Odin) www.slideshare.com
179	www.cigital.com
180	Hazardology © S. Buchanan

181	www.devopsdictionary.com
182	The Phoenix project James Wickett (blog.wickett.me)
183	http://www.gsa.gov/portal/mediaId/189495/fileName/CMaaS_Ordering_Guide_V40_Mar2014_v2.action)
184	http://blog.cimicorp.com
185	www.microsoft.com
186	https://en.wikipedia.org/wiki/SCADA
187	https://en.wikipedia.org/wiki/here_you_have
188	http://www.computerworld.com/article/2511801/security0/hacker-group-defends-attacks-on-wikileaks-foes.html
189	https://en.wikipedia.org/wiki/mobile_banking
190	https://en.wikipedia.org/wiki/stuxnet
191	https://scadahacker.com/library/Documents/Threat_Intelligence/FireEye%20-%20Definitive%20Guide%20to%20Next-Generation%20Threat%20Protection.pdf
192	https://en.wikipedia.org/wiki/barack_obama
193	https://en.wikipedia.org/wiki/roving_wiretap
194	www.androidpolice.com
195	https://en.wikipedia.org/wiki/flame_(malware)
196	https://en.wikipedia.org/wiki/shamoon
197	ARBOR Networks
198	ARBOR Networks

199 http://phys.org/news/2013-01-anonymous-members-card-company.html

200 https://en.wikipedia.org/wiki/cryptolocker

201 https://en.wikipedia.org/wiki/ransomware_(malware)

202 https://en.wikipedia.org/wiki/keystroke_logging

203 http://rt.com/news/ddos-attack-rt-antileaks-178/

204 home.mcafee.com/advicecenter/default.aspx?id=rs_na_su10article3&culture=en-us&affid=0

205 http://thehackernews.com/2014/07/Pushdo-Malware-Computer-hacking-Trojan.html

206 https://www2.fireeye.com/apt28.html

207 http://www.ibtimes.co.uk/hong-kong-protests-anonymous-leaks-chinese-government-data-1469747

208 searchsecurity.techtarget.com/tip/surviving-cyberwar-preparing-for-apts-stuxnet-malware-style-attacks

209 searchsecurity.techtarget.com/tip/flame-malware-analysis-how-to-defend-against-fraudulent-certificates

210 http://thehackernews.com/2014/12/hacking-paypal-account.html

211 http://thehackernews.com/2014/07/Pushdo-Malware-Computer-hacking-Trojan.html

212 Sources:www.blog.trendmicro and www.itgovernance.co.uk

213 OWASP Top 10 - 2010, Release Candidate, The Open Web Application Security Project (OWASP), November 2009. (http://www.owasp.org/index.php/Category:OWASP_Top_Ten_Project)